GW01606831

Quimper Pottery:
A French Folk Art Faïence

(Revised Edition)

by
Sandra V. Bondhus

Color Photography by
Didier Dorot

Catalogs Photographed by
Mitchell Z. Bistany

Editor
Bernard M. Wolpert

Dedication
For Our Lady of Loc Maria

First Printing—1981
Second Printing—1988
Third Printing—1995
ISBN# 09640855OX

Printed in the United States of America

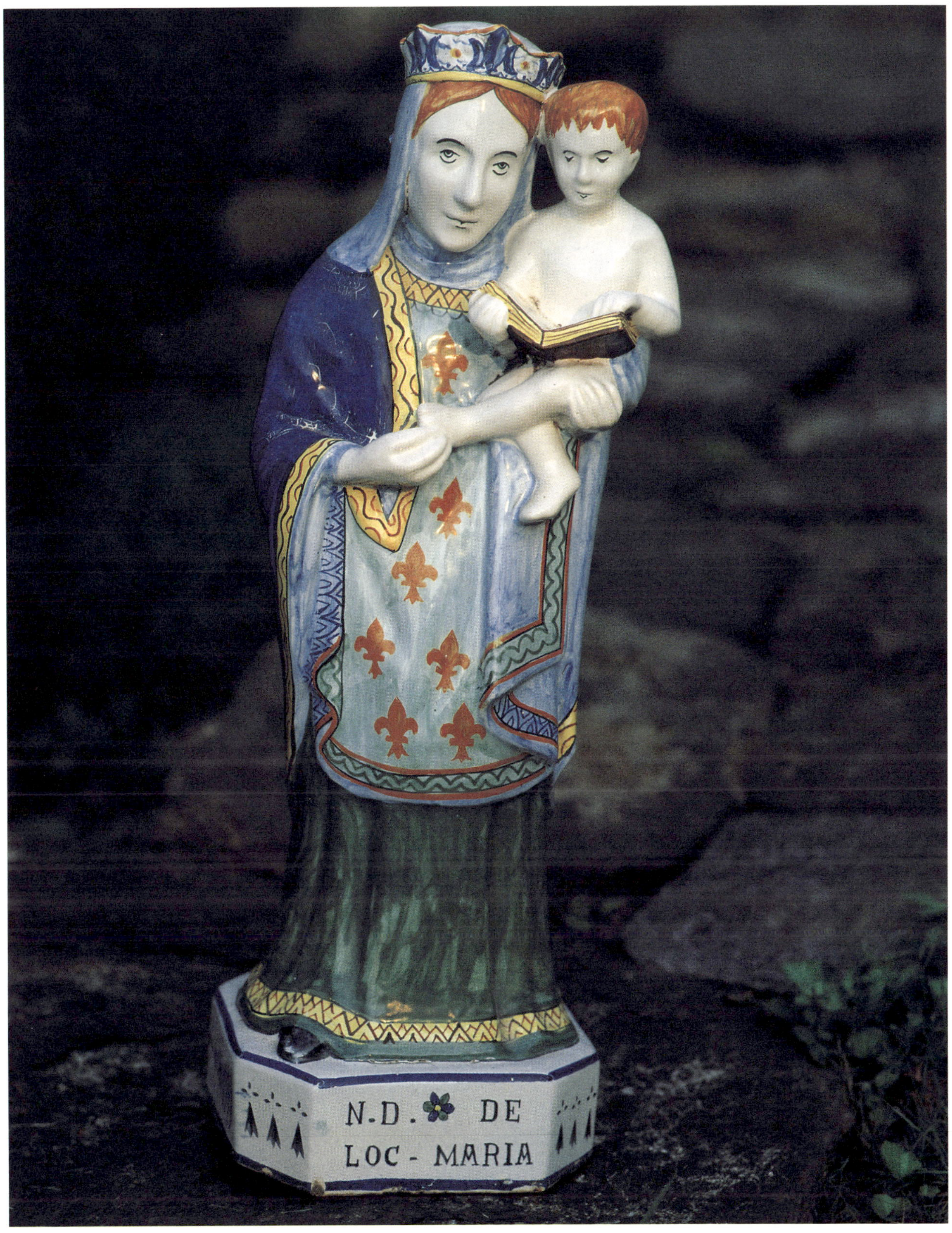

Notre Dame de Loc Maria: This 23.5" tall HenRiot mold is a faithful copy of a 15th century polychrome wood carving. The original remains in Pierre Caussy's Medieval parish church, Notre Dame, which is adjacent to the Faiënceries de Quimper in Loc Maria.

Loc Maria is a suburb of Quimper and derives its name from the Breton word "Loc' (holy place) and "Maria" (Mary). It was here on the outskirts of the city that Jean-Bapiste Bousquet built the first Quimper factory in 1690.

The original statue was broken during the French Revolution and its fragments were strewn onto a woodpile. As Notre Dame de Loc Maria is the patroness of the Quimper potteries, the pieces were rescued by Mme. Caussy and several workman from the HB factory. The bits were lovingly preserved and the statue was restored in the early 19th century and returned to the church. *(Private Collection)*

Table of Contents

Acknowledgments

One of the most satisfying aspects of writing ***Quimper Pottery: A French Folk Art Faïence*** has been knowing the people who have so generously given of their time and talents to make this book possible.

Monsieur Jean Rouillard, Director of the Faïenceries HB-Henriot, whose kindness in allowing me access to the factory archives, made accurate information available. His warm and delightful sense of humor permeated our visits to Quimper and lightened the many long hours which we spent in research together.

Mitchell Z. Bistany, my technical photographer and the photographer for some of the color plates, whose assistance was of inestimable value in reassembling the work for this revised, expanded edition. I could not have produced this book without him. His great kindness and selfless dedication were a true inspiration.

Didier Dorot, my color photographer "extraordinaire", who brought not only his artistic talents to the task, but who also lent many of his own Breton antiques as a background to showcase the faïence to best advantage. He is a consummate professional and an imaginative artist. Working with him was a delight. He understood the artistic vision of the book and was able to capture it on film.

Bernard M. Wolpert, my editor and friend, who set my footsteps on a concrete, literary path. His suggestions and critiques were always made with the utmost kindness and with a vision of the best possible text.

Monsieur Louis Leonus, Technical Director of the Faïenceries HB-Henriot, whose enthusiastic assistance, especially during the final photography session at the Musée des Faïences de Quimper, bubbled over with champagne effervescence into a concern that all would progress well.

Miss Betty Rivera, my literary "guardian angel" and dear friend, whose kindness, faith and encouragement have sustained my efforts throughout the arduous months of work.

Valerie Howard who graciously sent chromes for inclusion in the color plate section. Her kind words of encouragement were deeply appreciated.

The *Rev. Thomas P. Quinn*, pastor of St. Patrick's Church in Farmington, Connecticut, who allowed us to use the church grounds to photograph Our Lady of Loc Maria for the dedication page.

Charlene, my sister, who shared many memorable Breton adventures with me, while on one of our research excursions to Quimper.

My father, who read the manuscript and gave his sound advice. His quiet strength, belief in my endeavor and financial assistance, all contributed to making ***Quimper Pottery*** a reality.

My mother, whose inherent sense of artistic beauty has been a lasting influence on my life. Her joy in collecting with perspective has been a sustaining motivation.

Nelson, my husband, and *Christian* and *Charlie*, our sons, who each in his own way has contributed immensely to the revision of this book. Nelson did all of the photography work in France. He was a constant source of strength and support. ***Quimper Pottery: A French Folk Art Faïence*** (Revised Edition) would not have been possible without him.

Preface

Art is a mirror reflection of its society. No matter what form the artistic expression may take, no matter what the medium may be, this basic tenet seems to remain constant.

Quimper faïence is a folk art form. Reduced to its most elementary level, it is a "faïence populaire" i.e. a pottery manufactured in a provincial location, which appeals to a local populace. Yet, something in the intrinsic nature of Quimper pottery has made it transcend its Breton boundaries. The basis for this growing, universal popularity can be found in the ware's folk heritage.

Peasant life in Brittany was "dûre" i.e. extremely difficult. Each sunrise brought a weary, meager existence. Yet in spite of great physical hardship, the Breton folk maintained a deep sense of pride, faith and personal dignity. Their cultural heritage is rich in folklore: a colorful tapistry celebrating the simple joys of life. This culture which embraces its own language, Cornouaille, is fiercely independant of French influence. It has survived many oppressions and has continued to blossom because it maintains a profound belief in the value of the individual.

Perhaps in its own small way, Quimper pottery captures the essence of this philosophy. At the very least, it reflects the beauty and simplicity of the Breton life style and the great charm of Brittany's traditions.

Ten years ago, when I first began to collect Quimper faïence, there was little general interest in it and even less information available about it. This book appears after six years of research. It comes at a time when the universal appeal of Quimper pottery is reaching new heights of desirability in the antiques and collectibles marketplace. It is my sincere hope that ***Quimper Pottery: A French Folk Art Faïence*** will serve as a reliable source of information and reference for collectors and dealers alike.

Sandra V. Bondhus

Forward

In the fourteen years which have ensued since the first edition of ***Quimper Pottery: A French Folk Art Faïence*** was published, a great many changes have taken place.

Perhaps the most gratifying has been a renaissance in the appreciation of this Breton folk art form.

1990 saw the celebration of the 300th Anniversary of the founding of Quimper faïence. A stunning exhibition mounted at the Musée de Beaux Arts in Quimper with a corollary exhibition at the Château of Kerazan in Loctudy was the culmination of a blossoming awareness of the inherent beauty of the pottery in all of its splendid diversity.

When I first began to research for this book twenty-five years ago, Quimper pottery was considered to be the "poor country cousin" in the distinguished family of French faïence. Today, she has come of age. She is admired in ever expanding circles. The colorful richness of her legacy, which is a reflection of the vibrant vitality of her culture, shines forth with artistic and enduring brilliance.

Vive la Faïence de Quimper!

Chapter 1

Quimper: City of Art and Good Taste

The always colorful and sometimes mystical history of Brittany is closely allied with the development of the town of Quimper. During the 6th century B.C., the Gauls invaded the Breton peninsula and gave the area the name "Armor" (Country of the Sea). A mysterious people had preceded their arrival. This nameless race left behind traces of its Stone Age culture, the megoliths. The huge, primitive, stone monuments still stand throughout the Breton countryside. They remain a curious architectural puzzle of this lost civilization.

In 56 B.C. Caesar invaded Brittany. After a decisive sea battle off the southeast coast, the Romans emerged victorious. Four centuries of Roman rule followed. These conquerors were the first to develop the natural clay deposits of the region. After the decline of the Roman Empire and the subsequent barbarian invasions, Armor returned to a primitive state.

The year 460 A.D. brought the Angles' and Saxons' advance against the Celts in Britain. The routed Celtic tribes fled across the English Channel and settled in Armor, changing the name of their new home to "Little Britain" (Brittany). It was during this period that Quimper was established.

The town lies nestled at the tip of the Breton peninsula in Finistère (Earth's End). Known by its motto, "Ville d'Art et de Bon Goût" (City of Art and Good Taste), Quimper takes its name from the Breton word "kemper", meaning confluence. In this case it is the merging of the Steir and Odet Rivers which gave rise to the settlement of the town.

Founded by the legendary Grandlon, a 5th century British monarch, Quimper is the ancient capital of Cornouaille. The fiefdom was united to Brittany in 1066 by the marriage of Hoël, Count of Cornouaille, to the sister and heiress of Conan, Duke of Brittany. In similar fashion the Duchy of Brittany was later united to France by the marriage of the Duchess Anne of Brittany. Anne first married Charles VIII in 1491 and then, after his death, she married his successor, Louis XII, in 1498.

Under the patronage of a saintly Breton hermit, Corentin, the town was known as Kemper-Corentin until the French Revolution.

Quimper soon became known as the "Sourire de la Bretagne" (the Smile of Brittany). In addition to its famous potteries and celebrated Gothic cathedral, St. Corentin, it was the birthplace of several noteworthy men. Two of its most illustrious sons are Laennec (1781–1826), the inventor of the stethoscope and Jean Fréron (1719–1776), a bitter opponent of the French Philosophers. Voltaire, a leader of the Philosopher's Movement, preserved their fierce antagonism with the following terse verse:

L'autre jour, au fond d'un vallon,
Un serpent mordit Jean Fréron:
Que pensez-vous qu'il arriva?
Ce fut le serpent qui creval.

(The other day, in a dale,
A snake bit Fréron's hide.
You won't believe what happened . . .
It was the snake that died.)

Today above all else, the town of Quimper is internationally known for its pottery. Historically the surrounding region was richly endowed with natural resources which contributed to the birth of the faïence industry. A short distance away at Anse de Toulven was a natural clay deposit. As previously stated, this resource had been explored and utilized since the 4th century during the Roman occupation of Gaul. Many tiles, bricks, pipes, vases, porringers, funeral urns and shards have been unearthed during excavation work in the town and surrounding area. Several examples which date from this period are on display in the Musée de Faïences de Quimper.

In addition to the indigenous clay deposits, surrounding forests provided plentiful and inexpensive fuel to stoke the furnaces for the drying process. Local labor was readily available and wages were low. The Odet River, which connects the area to the sea eleven miles away, proved to be an excellent means to transport the finished wares to market.

All of these factors favorably influenced the successful establishment of the first faïence workshop in Loc Maria, Quimper.

Chapter 2

Origins

What precisely is "faïence"? The word "faïence" signifies a porous pottery. The earthenware is painted and then covered with an opaque stanniferous glaze. It is the tiny particles of tin oxide suspended in the glaze which gives it its characteristic white, opaque nature.

First discovered by the Persians, the technique was passed on to the Arabs. They, in turn, introduced the process into Spain. Eventually the secret of faïence production found its way into Italy. By the 16th century, Italian potters had migrated throughout Europe and had influenced the establishment of several factories. These included the potteries at Nevers and Rouen in France. Because many of these Italian itinerants came from Florence (Faenza), the pottery which they brought with them came to be known as "faïence".

Traditionally, only gold or silver-plated vessels were considered to be acceptable tableware by European nobility. In the early 18th century the wars of Louis XIV left the French treasury nearly bankrupt. By mid-century, the Seven Years War had further added to the financial crisis. These perilous economic predicaments resulted in two royal edicts in 1709 and 1759. The monarchy decreed that all precious metals be confiscated and melted down to refill the state coffers. As a result, the nobility were forced to surrender their tableware. In an effort to find a suitable replacement, they increasingly turned to the use of hand-painted pottery. Thus, the wars and financial ruin of 18th century France, directly contributed to the flowering of faïence.

Three of the major 17th and 18th century centers of French faïence production heavily influenced the early stages of Quimper pottery. These were the factories at Moustiers, Nevers and Rouen.

Jean-Baptiste Bousquet, the late 17th century founder of the Grande Maison, used Moustiers-inspired patterns at Loc Maria, Quimper. The major attributes derived from Moustiers were:

1). a Chinese influence in pattern designs and forms
2). the occassional use of "grotesques" (i.e. people with highly-exaggerated characteristics such as a protruding nose)
3). the Berrain style which resembles lacy draped curtains whose swags are gathered by tasseled cords.

The Moustiers line continued to influence several Quimper patterns through the 19th century.

Pierre Bellevaux brought the Nevers style with him to Quimper in the early 18th century. The major characteristics adapted from Nevers include:

1). a Chinese style employing Oriental subjects
2). the use of the distinctly Chinese color sceme: blue and white
3). a richly-intertwining border pattern of leaves and flowers
4). the use of the "coq" (rooster) as a suitable central theme.

By mid-18th century, Pierre Caussy had introduced the Rouen period at Quimper. When he travelled from his father's pottery workshop in a suburb of Rouen, he carried many tracing patterns with him. Perhaps Rouen exerted the strongest influence.

1). the "décor rayonnant", a richly-intricate pattern of stylized leaves and florals which garnishes the outer border and then cascades in swags around a central flower burst. This pattern was adapted from delicate lace and intricately-scrolled ironwork of the period.
2). the mid 18th century Rococo patterns . . .
    a. the "décor à la corne" (cornucopia) which depicts a cornucopia overflowing with fruits, flowers and leaves; often one or more dragonflies dot the perimeter
    b. the "décor au carquois" (quiver and torch) which shows a delicately-detailed torch intertwined with a floral-filled quiver; the border is highly decorative with criss-cross latticing and stylized greenery.
3). the polychrome Chinoiserie style which embraces Oriental subjects and occasionally features parrots or other exotic birds.

Quimper pottery has never been considered to be of comparable quality to the wares produced at Moustiers, Nevers and Rouen. Serious collectors of faïence have always looked askance at the Breton pottery. Quimper was categorized as a minor factory of little importance. Its wares were grouped under the term "faïence populaire" i.e. a provincial earthenware of limited appeal. It is therefore ironic that the prestigious French faïence houses are no longer in existence, while Quimper remains.

Perhaps in large part the success of Quimper has been because of its appeal to the common folk. Throughout three centuries its factories have incorporated what is finest in other potteries, while improvising, adapting and adding to the genre until it reflected a unique vitality of spirit. Its very nature is so deeply embedded in the cultural roots of Brittany, that the pottery has almost spontaneously evolved from the hearts and hands of the local artisans. No one knows who first introduced the peasant motif at Quimper or the geometric patterns or the floral designs. For this reason, Quimper faïence is a true folk art form. For this reason also, it has survived the centuries as a living, viable artistic expression.

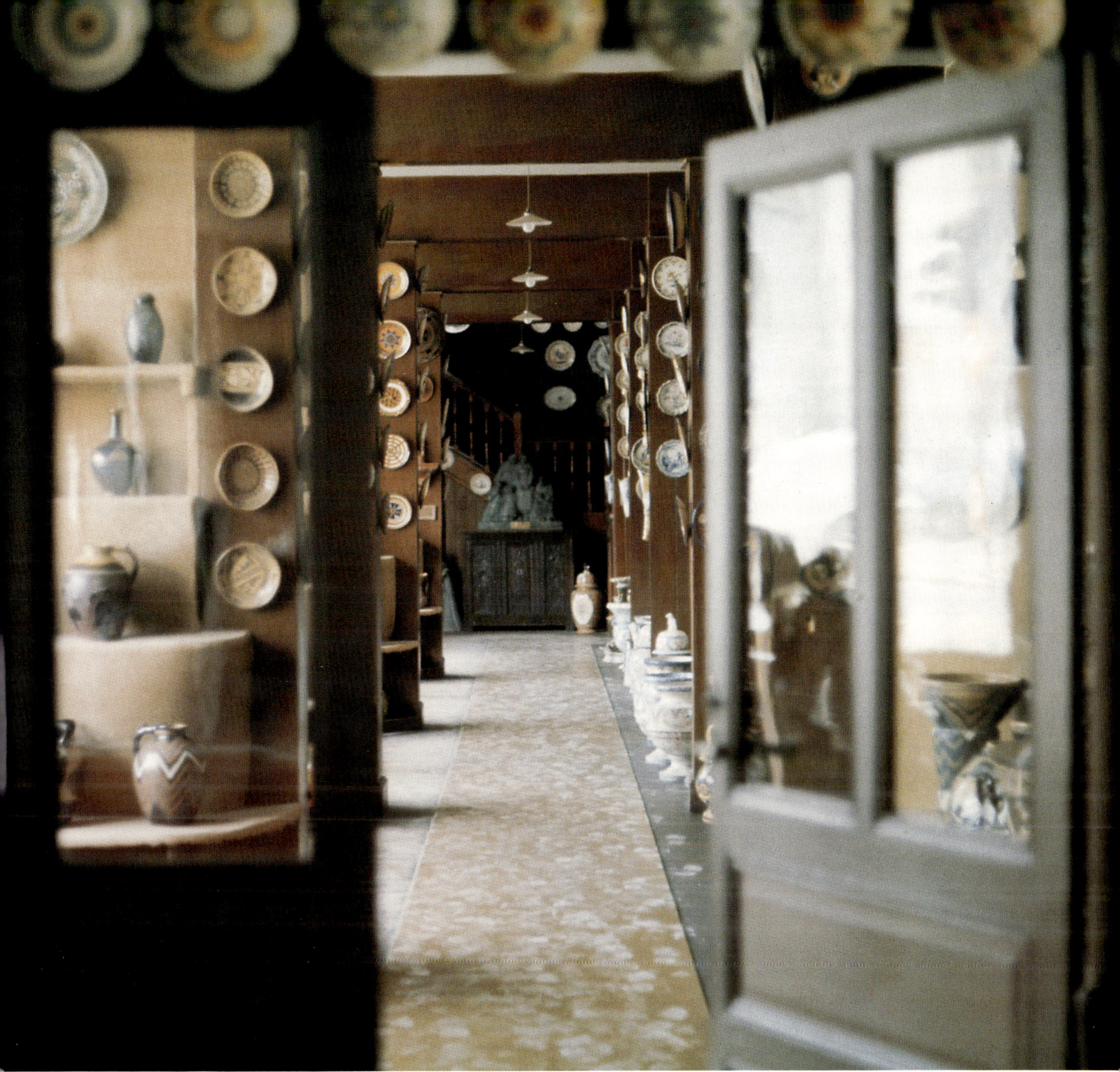

The open doorway of the old Musée de Quimper beckons invitingly. Closed for renovations and later when the factory was sold in 1984, it has re-opened as the new Musée de la faïence Jules Verlingue. The photo serves as a reminder of an earlier, more genteel era in the annals of Quimper faïence.

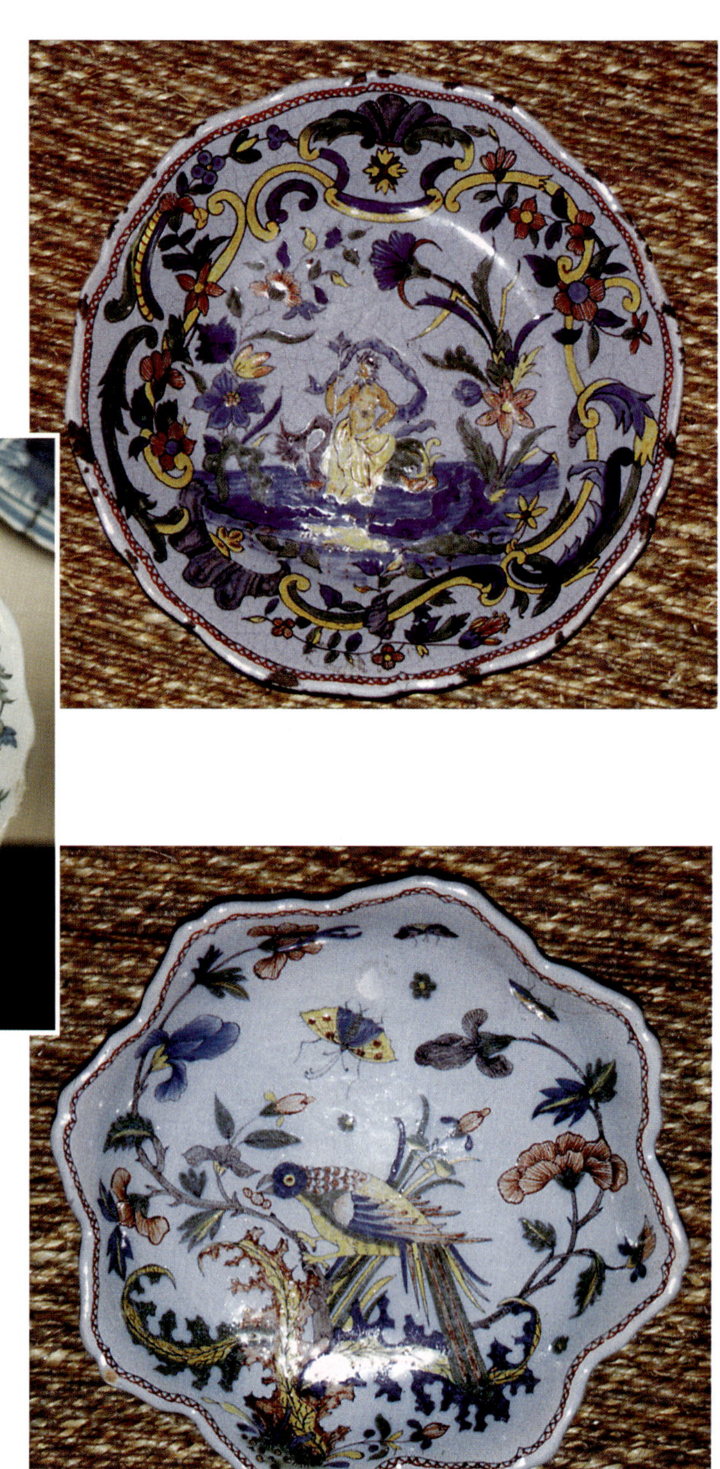

Photo 1: "Neptune" seated on a dolphin, the 9.5" diameter plate has a Rouenesque influence. Early Porquier dating from the Second Half of the 19th century. *(Courtesy Valerie Howard, London)*

Photo 2: "Les jouers de cartes" (The Card Players) is an amusing example with a Lillelois influence. Dating from the early 19th century, it documents the developmental stages of the human form as an acceptable Quimper motif.
(Courtesy Musée de la faïence Jules Verlingue)

Photo 3: A 9.5" diameter plate in the "Aux Perruches" (Parrot) manner of Rouen and Sincerny of the 18th century. Registered HB mark of 1882. Circa last quarter 19th century. *(Courtesy Valerie Howard, London)*

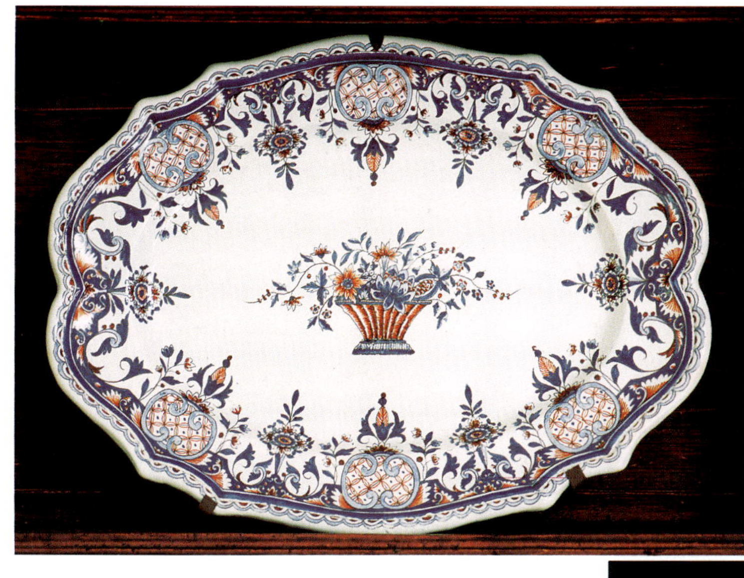

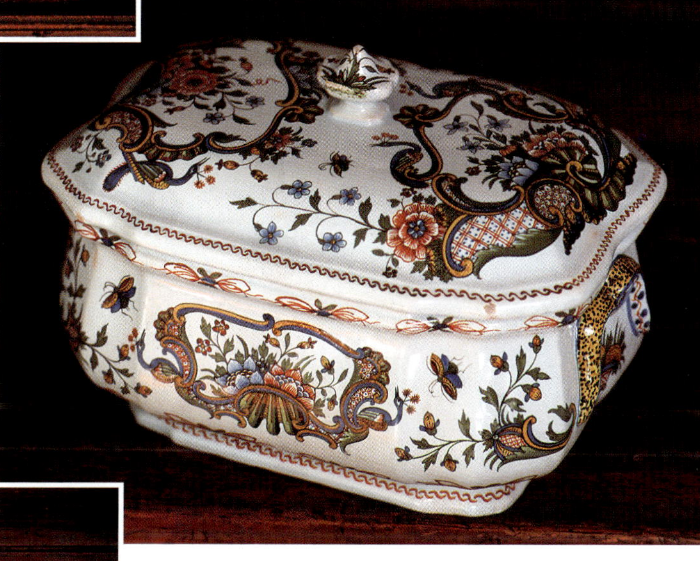

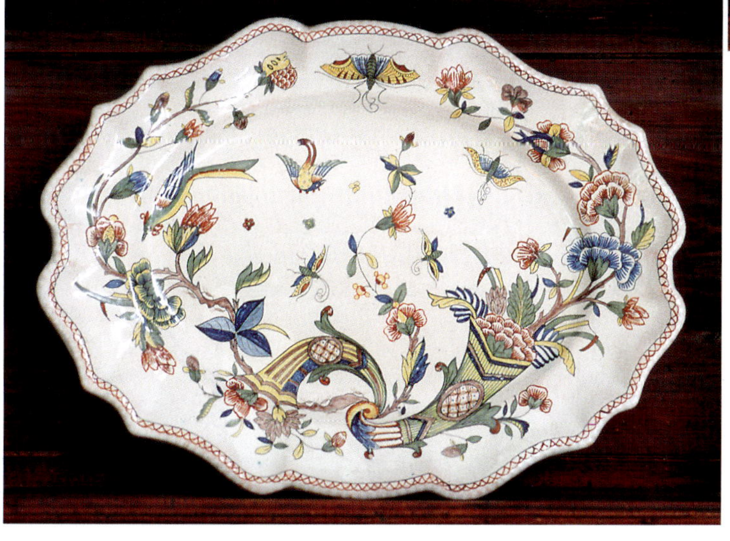

Photo 1: A 17.5" oval platter ornamented in blue and red of the Rouen "Panier Fleuri" (Flower Basket) pattern. Having worked for a time in Rouen, Pierre-Paul Caussy brought patterns with him to Loc Maria. These were also utilized at the factory by his son, Pierre-Clément Caussy. This example bears the first registered trademark of 1882: HB *(Private Collection)*

Photo 2: Copiously festooned with flowers, baskets, butterflies, peacocks and lattices in the Rouen manner, this superb soup tureen carries the HB registered trademark of 1882. *(Private Collection)*

Photo 3: A 19th century 16.5" platter in the Rouen "A la corne d'abondance" (Cornucopia) pattern. It carries an unusual double mark: The HB mark of 1883 and the rarer impressed triangular mark of de la Hubaudière. *(Private Collection)*

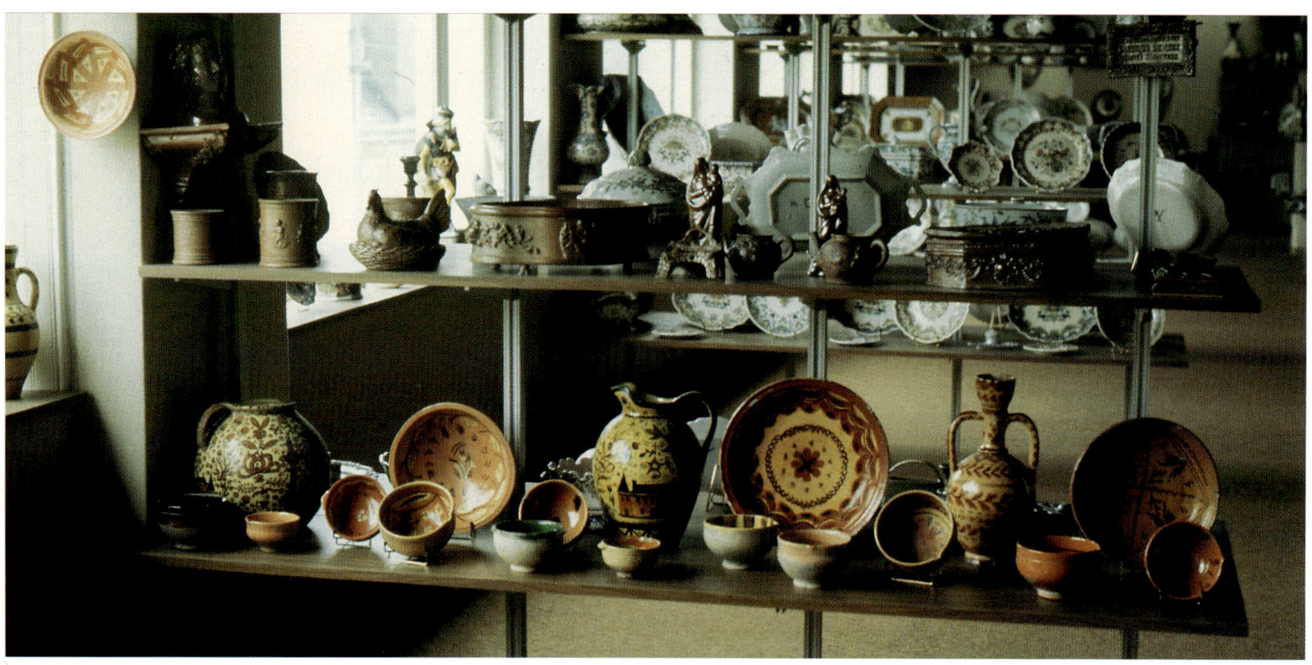

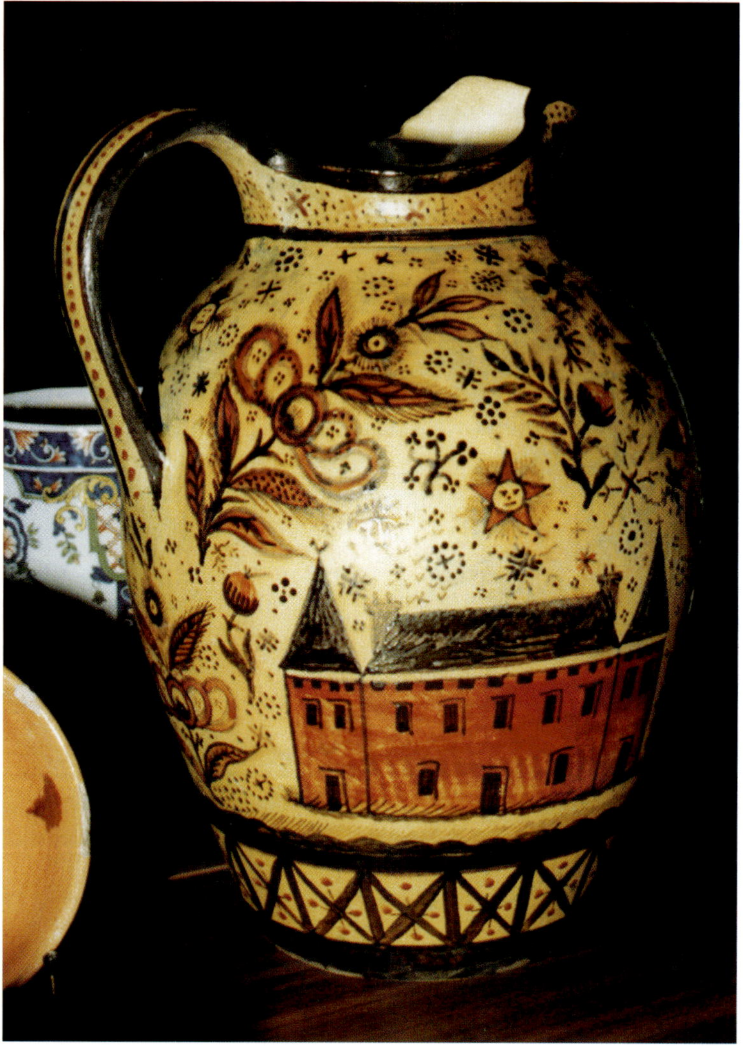

A great deal of 18th and 19th century production was given over to "Poteries vernissées" which were more practical, simply decorated and used daily by the local populace. These examples were made of the heavier grès (a type of stoneware), which insured a greater durability.

PHOTO 1:
The top shelf shows a parade of the monochromatic "grès" glazed in dark brown. The lower shelf demonstrates the more ornamental "poteries vernissées".

PHOTO 2:
The close-up of the large pitcher is executed in the "Manoir" (Country Home) pattern and dates from the first half of the 19th century. (Courtesy Musée de la faïence Jules Verlingue)

Facing page: "Cul Noir" (black back) plate in the "panier aux fleurs" (flower basket) pattern. During this period white stanniferous (lead tin) enamel was very costly. Hence a large amount of "faïence populaire" produced before the second half of the 19th century was bi-colored. The white glaze was reserved to adorn the front, while the back was coated with a less expensive dark brown enamel made from manganese.
If the brown glaze was applied too thickly, it would drip onto the examples which were stacked beneath it in the firing oven. The resultant splotches came to be known as "larmes du potier" (potter's tears). *(Private Collection)*

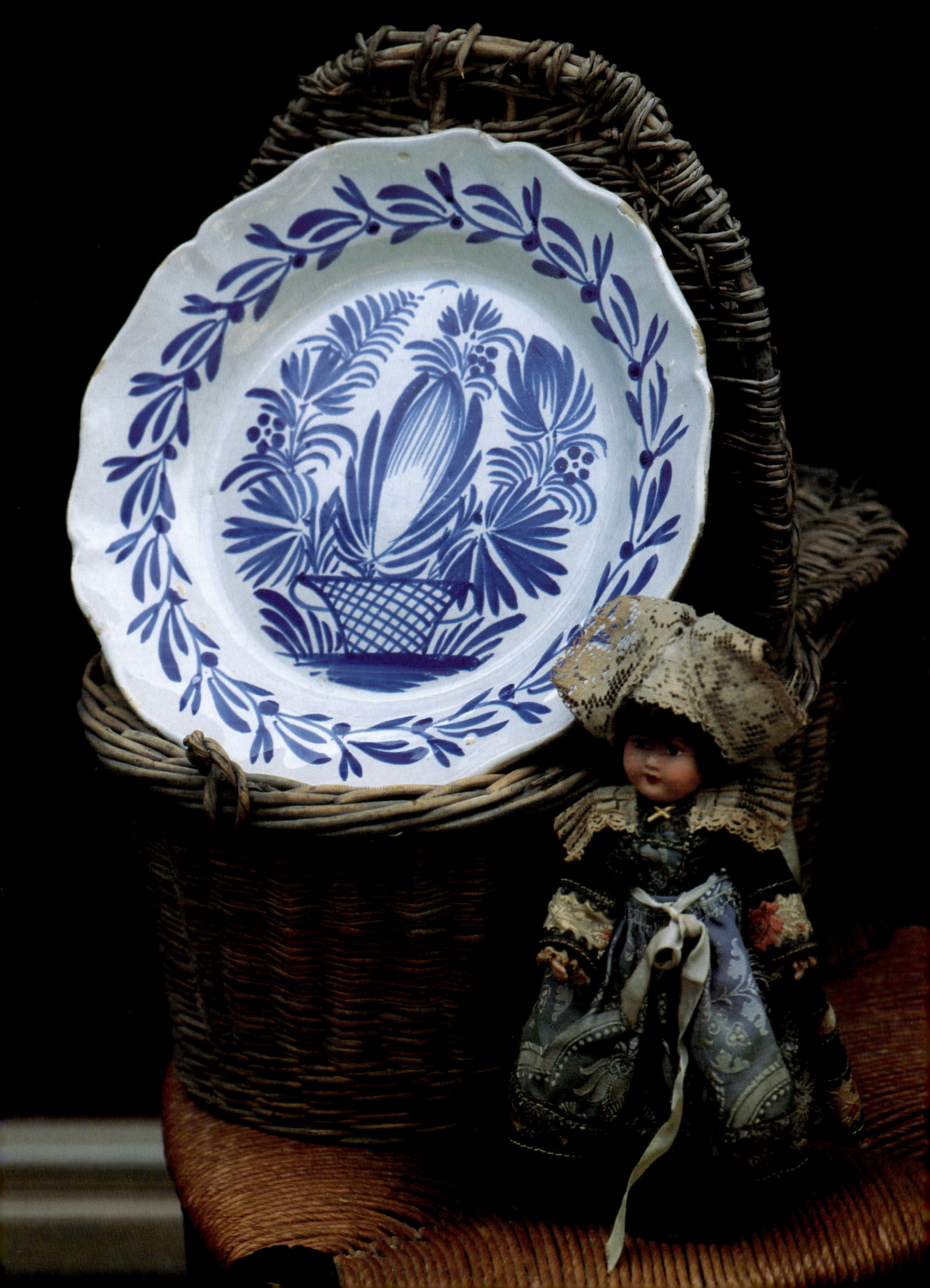

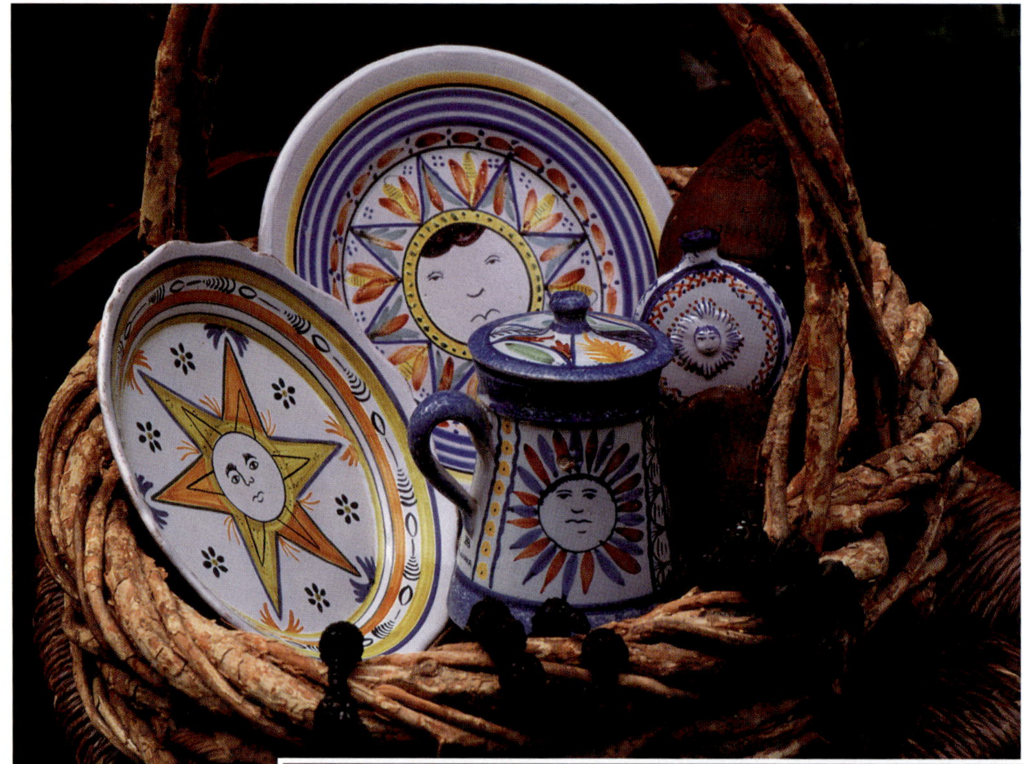

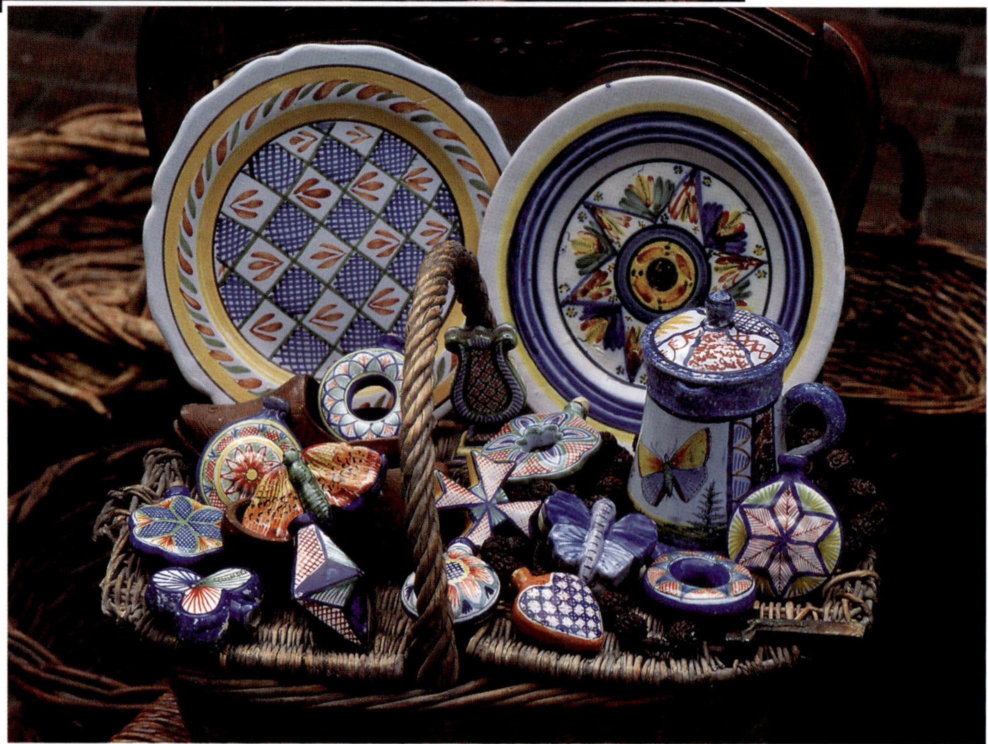

Photo 1: One of the more whimsical "faïence populaire" patterns uses the face of the sun as the focal point. Pictured here are examples dating from the 19th century to the early 20th century. The 19th c. HB plate in the foreground is a re-issue of an 18th c. example. The later plate in the background is marked HR Quimper. *(Private Collection)*

Photo 2: Geometric patterned snuffs display a wonderful variety of form and freshness of color. These "secouettes" were frequently offered as tokens of love or friendship. The two butterflies are especially noteworthy: the blue from HR and the red attributable to AP.

Two geometric plates and a tankard further exemplify the rich palette and diversity of "faïence populaire" production. *(Private Collection)*

Facing page: A panoply of 19th Century "faïence populaire" delights the eye. The pitcher in the foreground is a rare representation of a man in oriental clothing exemplifying the "chinoiserie" (Chinese) influence. The earliest example in the grouping is the adjacent plate, which dates from the first half of the 19th c. The covered vegetable typifies the "bluets" (forget-me-nots) pattern. Random geometric patterns, a pansy and two primitive ladies round out the array. Note that not one of the examples pictured carries a mark. *(Private Collection)*

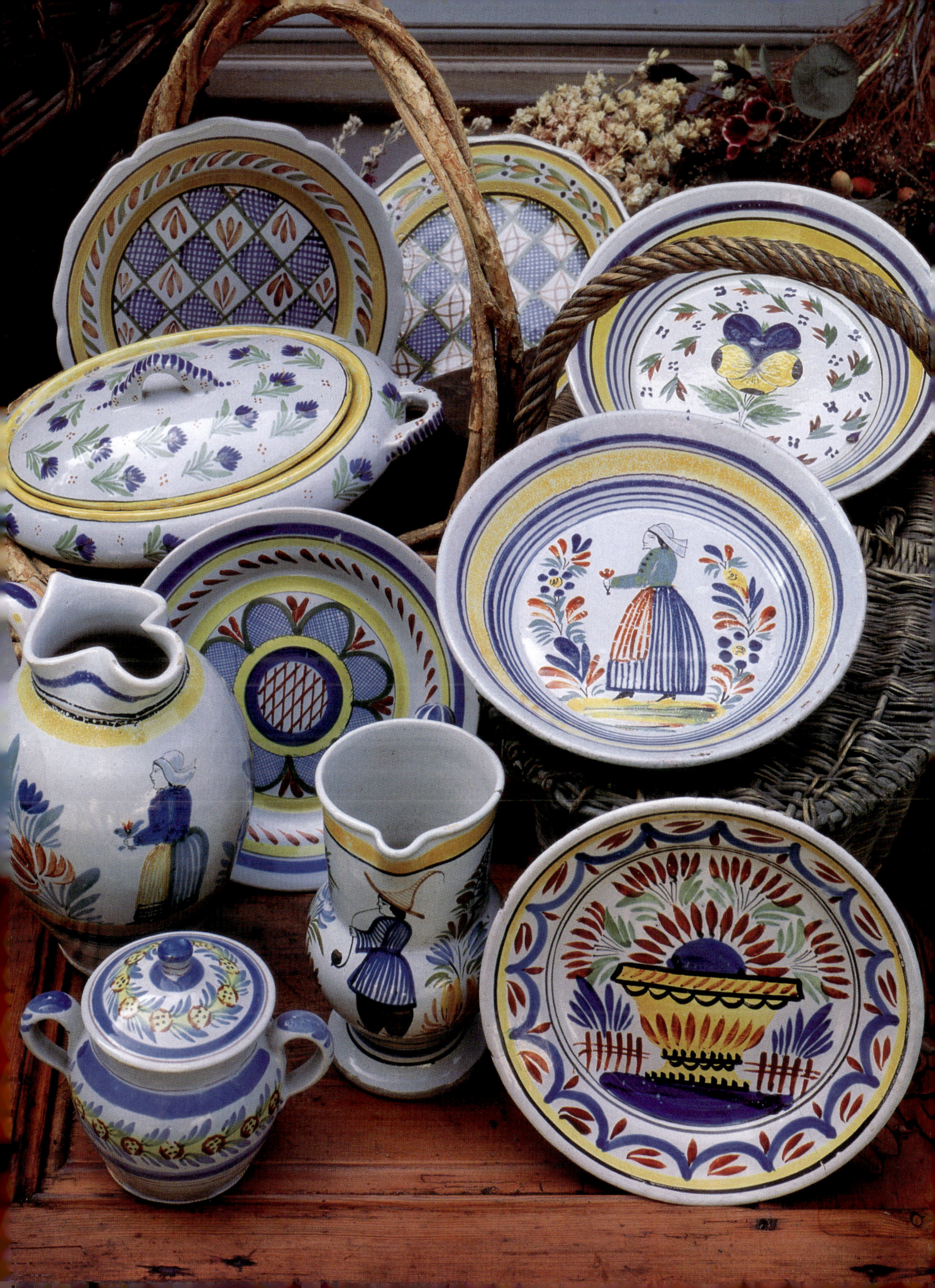

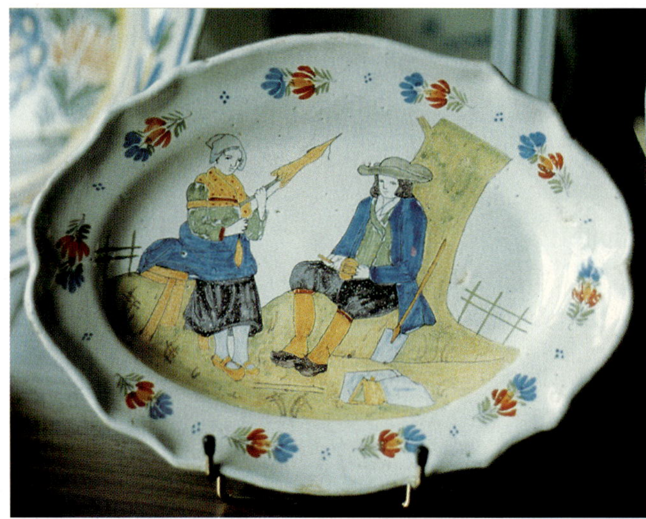

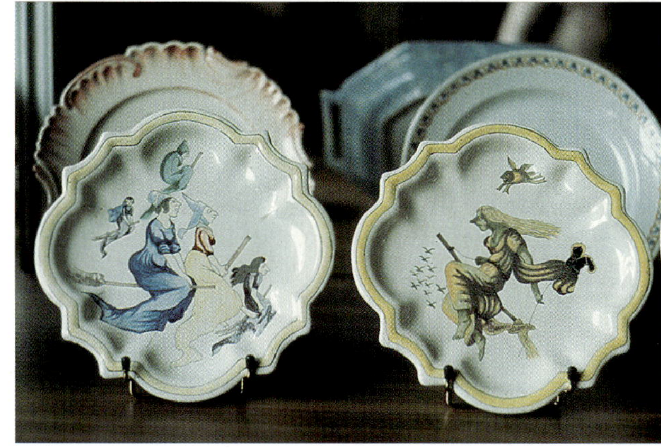

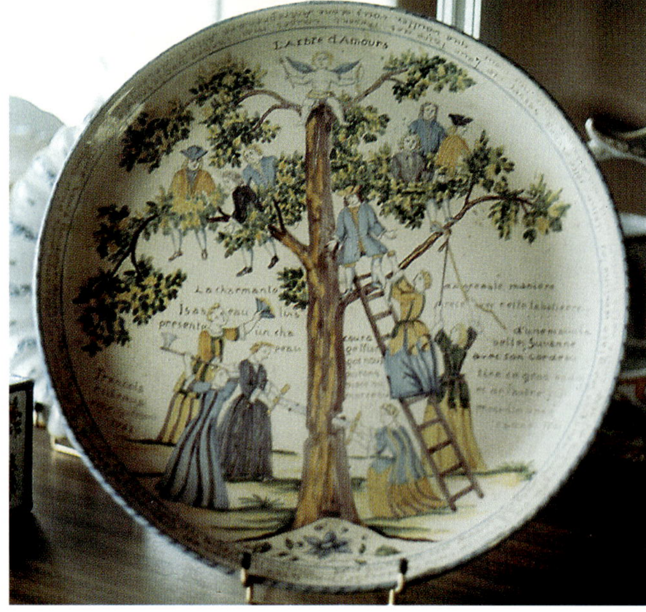

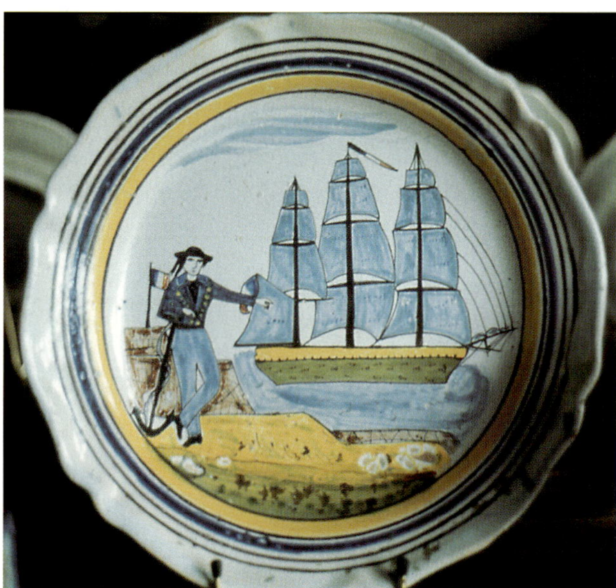

Five 19th century examples which define the diversity of the human form as a subject of study. The two "sorcières" (witches) i.e. the bad witch and the good witch, and the "L'arbre d'amour" (Tree of Love) add a humorous touch. The seated couple and sailor with his ship portray a more traditional pose. *(Courtesy Musée de la faience Jules Verlingue)*

Facing page: Ever faithful to their Catholic Christian heritage, the production of religious statues was and continues to be an integral part of the tradition of Quimper pottery. Displayed here are five molds of the Sainte Vierge. Top left to right: Mère de Dieu, HR Quimper; unsigned Notre Dame dating from the First Empire Period; Notre Dame de Pitié, unsigned, HR attribution; bottom: Ste. Marie, AP; Notre Dame des Agonisants, HR Quimper and Ste. Marie, unsigned HB. *(Private Collection)*

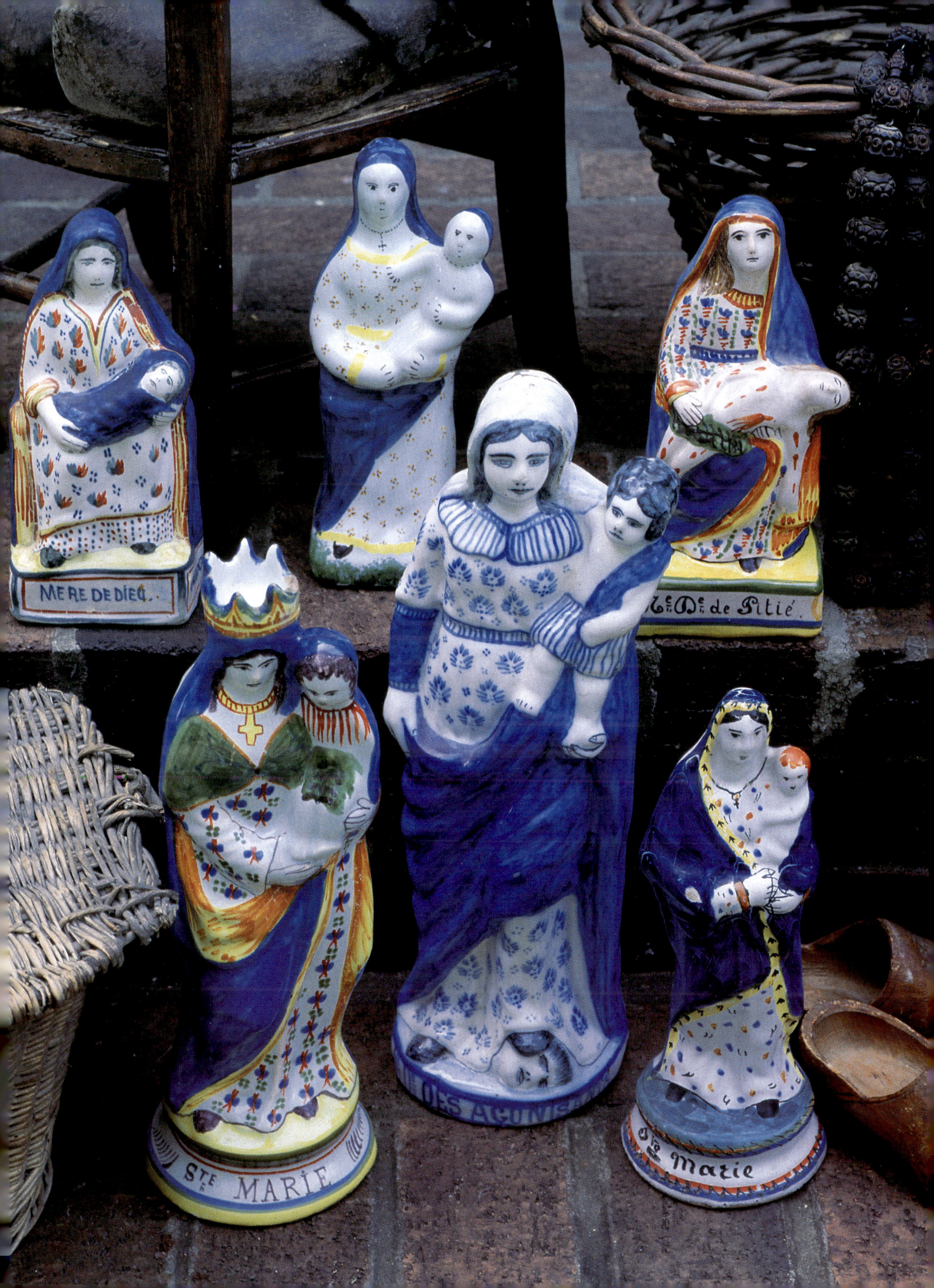
MERE DE DIEU
de Pitié
STE MARIE
Marie

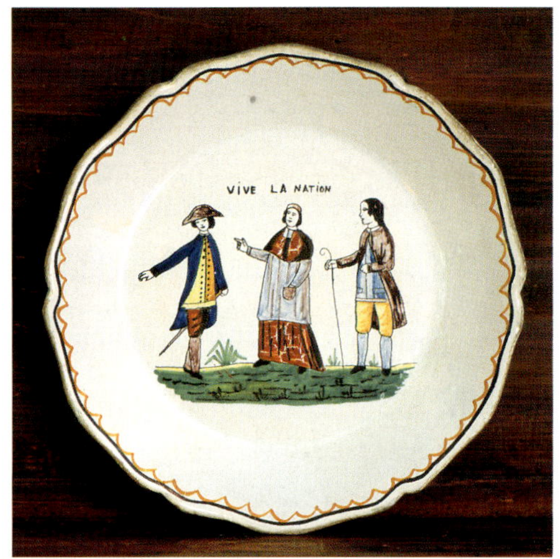

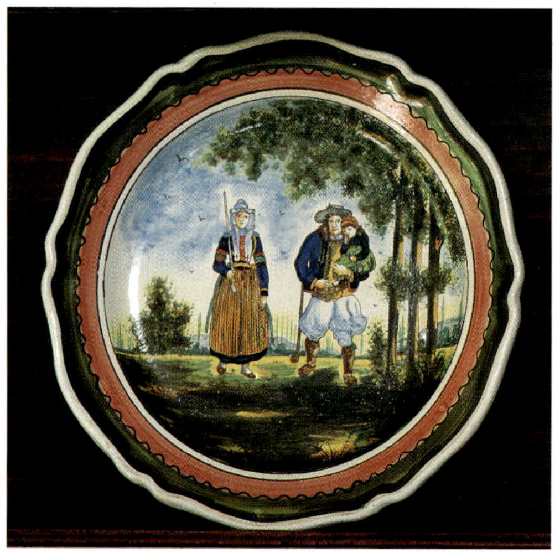

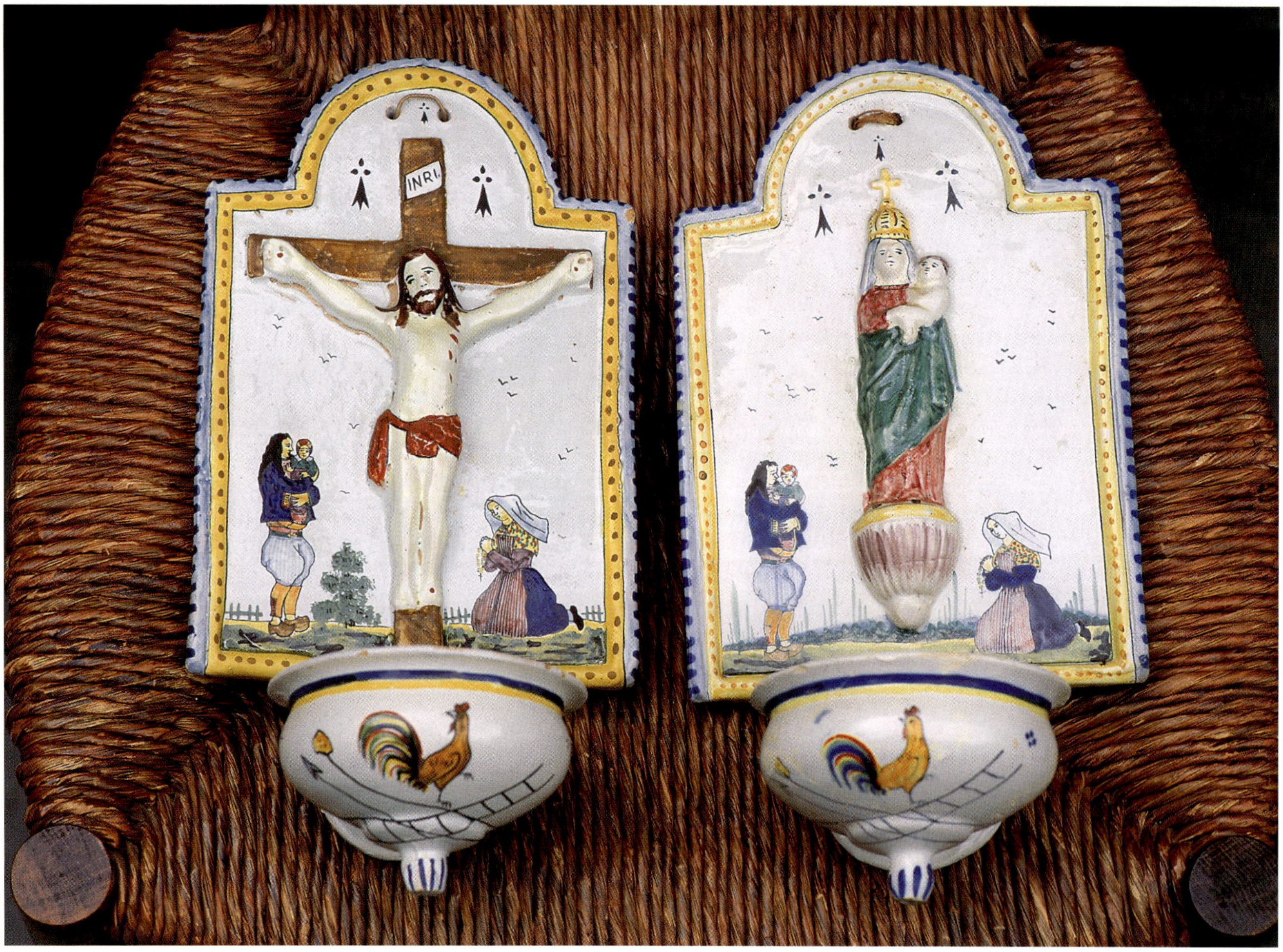

Photo 1: "Vive la Nation" (Long live the Nation) a 19th c. Revolutionary plate depicting the three pillars of French society: the gentry, the military and the clergy. It was customary for the oldest son to inherit the land, for the second son to join the military and for the third son to be ordained into the priesthood. In this manner all the needs of society were fulfilled. Impressed triangle HB mark. *(Private Collection)*

Photo 2: The family was the cherished focal point of Breton culture and the foundation of society. Here depicted on a charger is a portrait of a young family. Note the rich detail and the highly unusual pink and green border treatment of this 19th century de la Hubaudière example. *(Private Collection)*

Photo 3: The rugged, peasant life-style could best be described as "dûr" (hard). Faith was their source of strength and consolation. Shown here are two 13" "bénitiers" (holy water fonts). Smaller molds were customarily given as Baptismal gifts. These were hung next to the doorways and were filled with blessed water to be used when entering or leaving home.

The above examples are rich in symbolism: on the bowl portion, the coq represents Peter's betrayal, while the ladder, lance and sponge commemorate the implements present at Jesus' death. Grand Maison HB mark of 1883. *(Collections of Didier and Susan Dorot and of the author)*

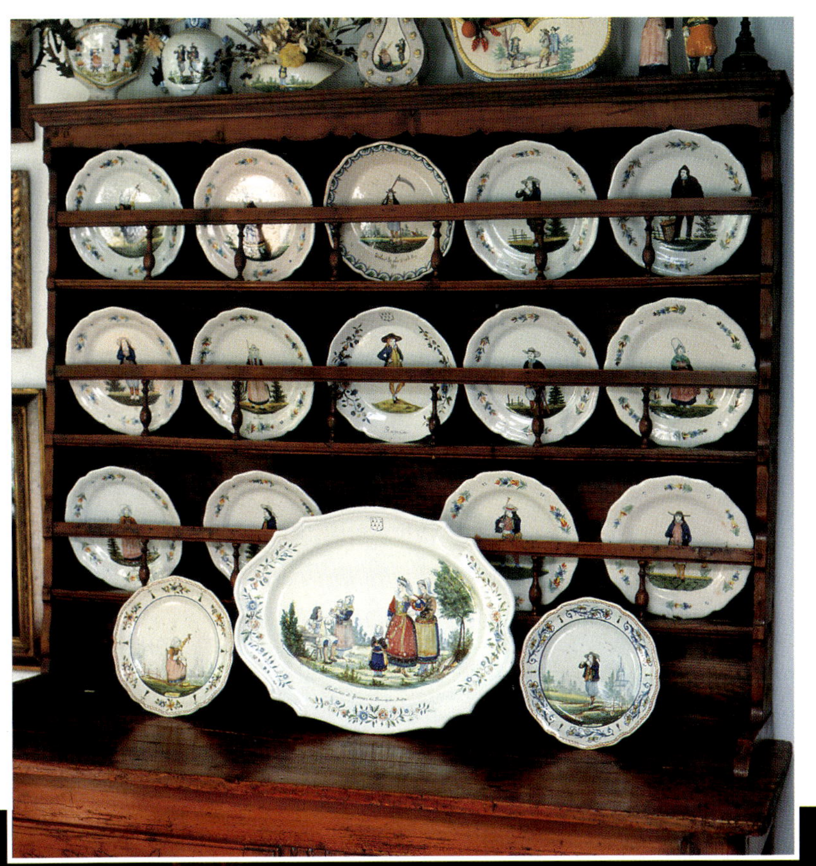

A country French cupboard displays a collection of late 19th century de la Hubaudière wares. Especially noteworthy: the platter in the foreground and the two unusual border variant plates on either side. Directly above the platter is a man from "Rosporden" and above him, a Revolutionary plate with the impressed triangle mark. *(Private Collection)*

Detail of platter: "Paludier et femmes du Bourg-de-Batz" (Salt worker and women from Bourg-de-Batz). The area of Bourg-de-Batz was a salt collection center. Using a process of natural evaporation, salt crystals were collected from the salt marshes of the region by "paludiers" (salt workers).

Note the uneven pitting in the glaze on the pink apron of the center lady. These irregularities are typical of 19th c. production where oven temperatures were difficult to control and soot particles frequently adhered to the glaze.

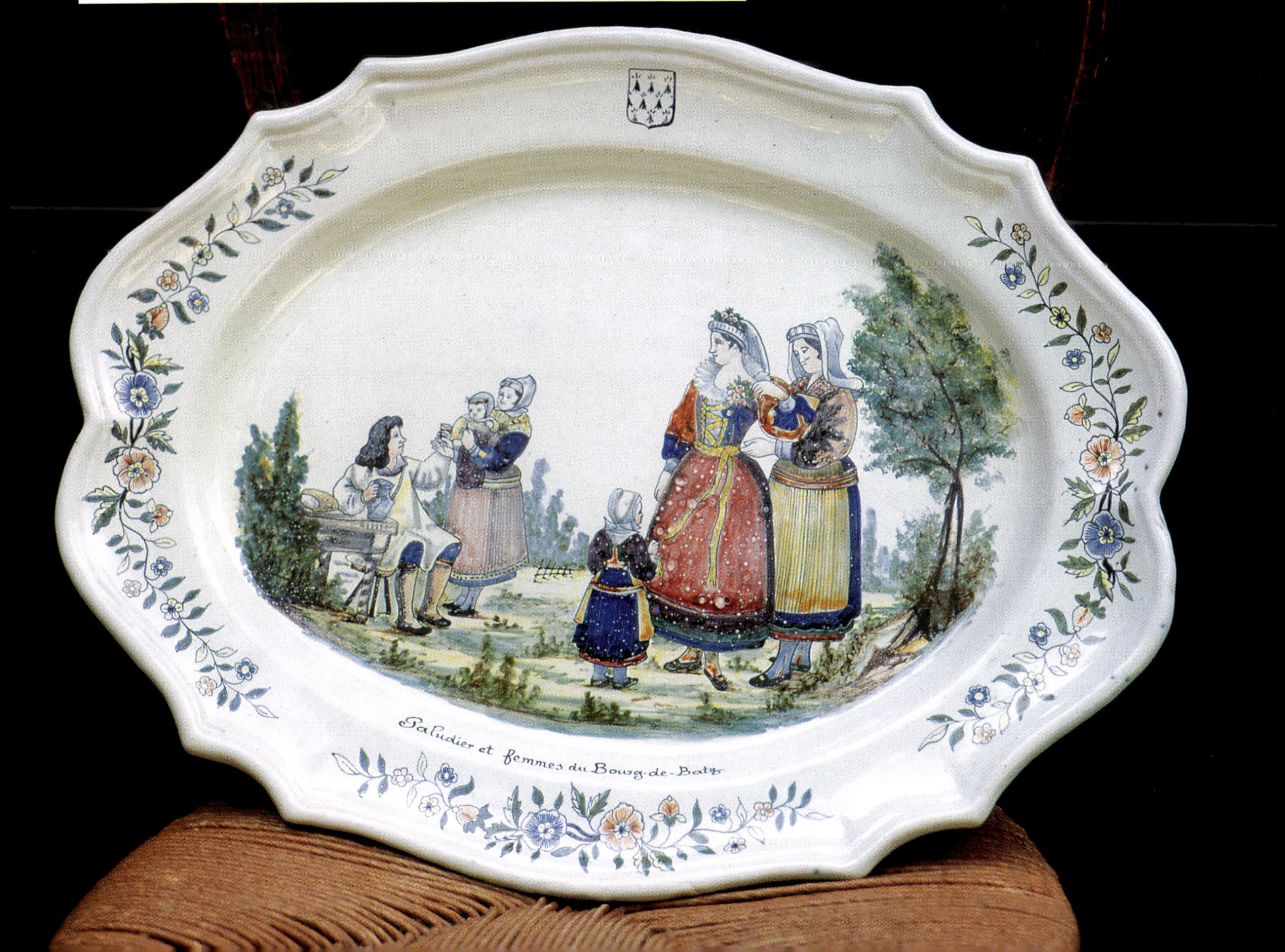

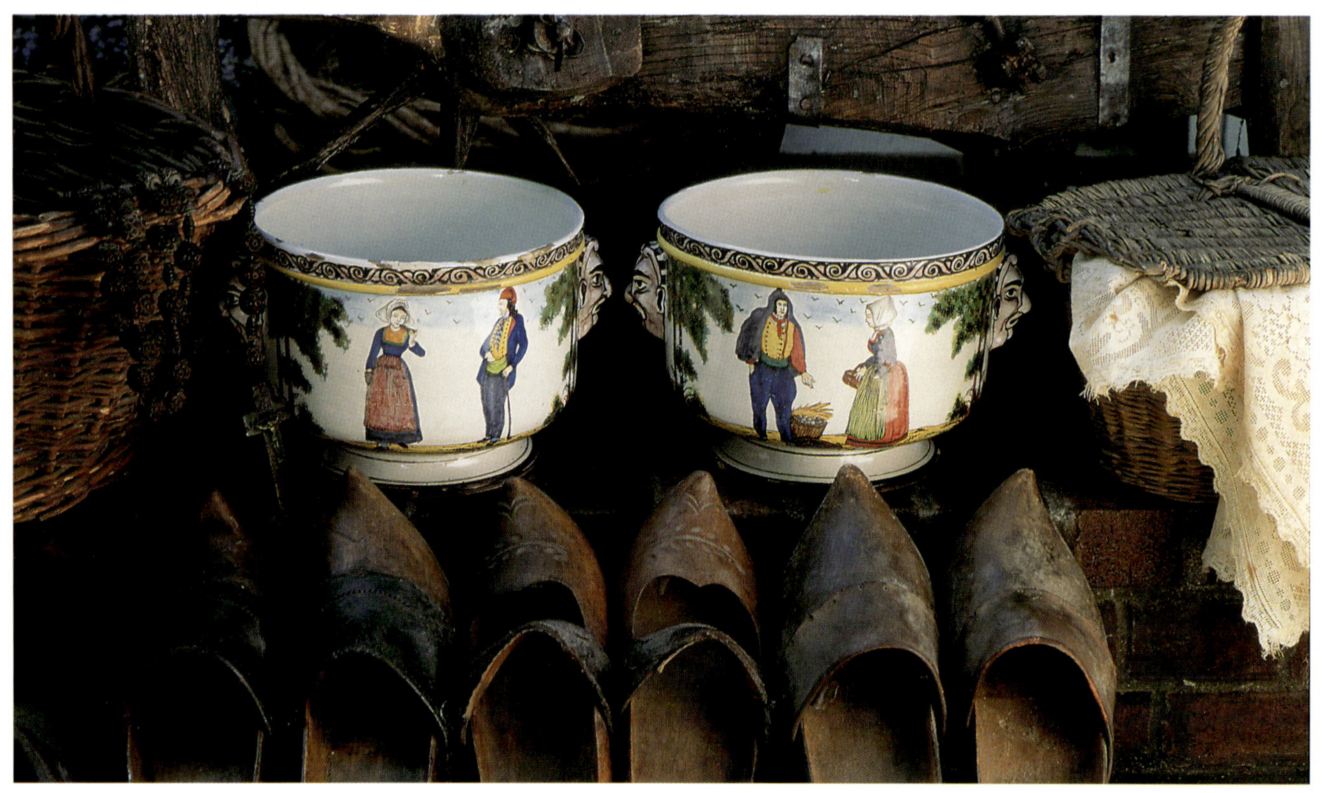

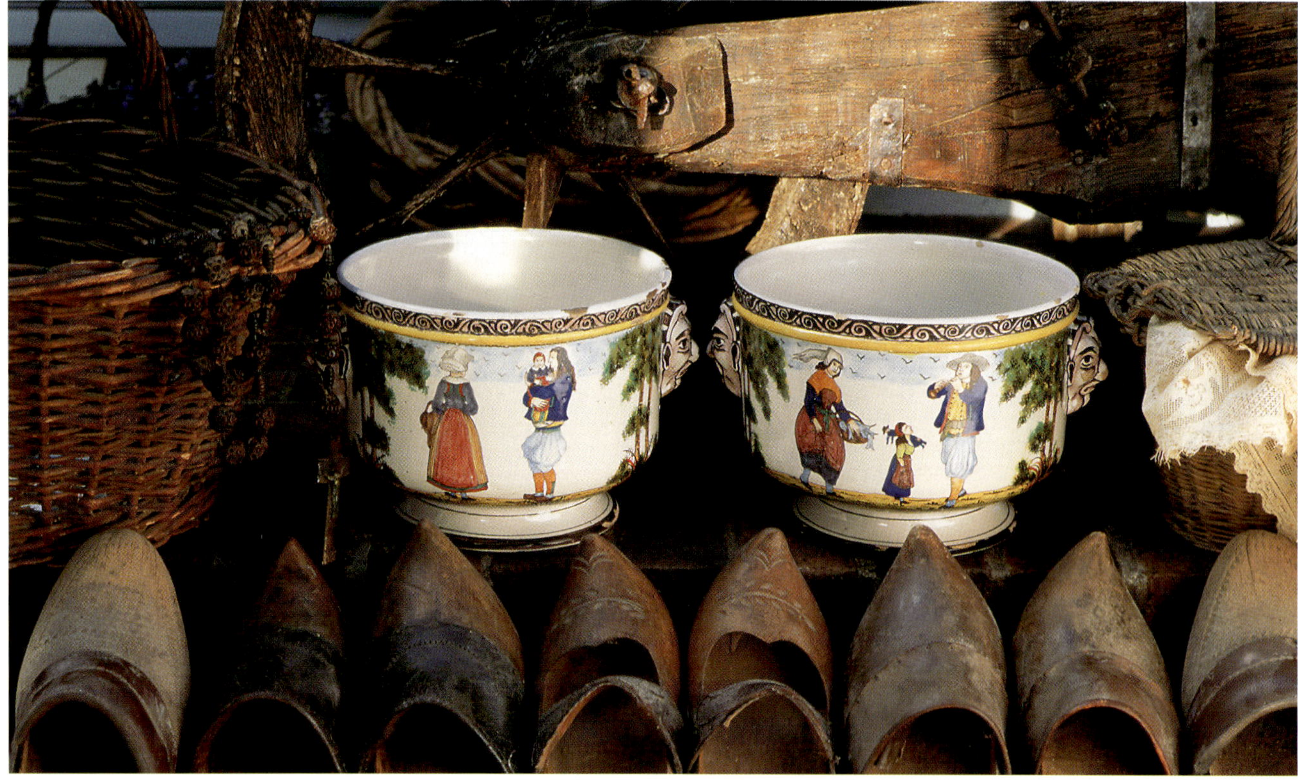

A superb matched pair of large cache pots dating from the last quarter of the 19th century and signed HB. The scene with the little girl holding the priest doll (lower right) is an anti-clerical political statement rooted in the anti-religious sentiments of the French Revolution. *(Private Collection)*

Chapter 3

The Grande Maison HB

During the 17th century, any faïence worker would be familiar with all of the steps involved in the production of the pottery. Jean-Baptiste Bousquet was such a man. Having worked as a master craftsman at the Moustiers factory in the South of France, he was well prepared to take over the management of his own workshop. Born in 1649 at Saint-Zacherie (Var), he and his family moved to Marseilles. In 1685 Bousquet and his eldest son, Pierre, took over the management of a small pottery in the suburbs of Loc Maria, Quimper. Bousquet chose the location because, in all of Brittany, there was only one other existing faïencerie, in Rennes.

His original workshop prospered and in 1690 he built the first large drying ovens in Quimper. Expanding his modest establishment further, he annexed two neighboring properties shortly thereafter. In order to assist his father's growing business, Bousquet's younger son, Charles, left Marseilles to join the family in Loc Maria.

When Jean-Baptiste Bousquet died in 1708, he left a solvent business. Very few pieces, however, are attributable to the factory during his management. As was the custom of the period, nothing was signed and no original patterns were executed. It is probable that Moustiers motifs greatly influenced his work.

Pierre, Bousquet's eldest son, inherited his father's factory. He continued its expansion by acquiring a small island on the Odet River. Building continued from 1708 until 1746. An important addition in 1740 was a large building purchased for use as a warehouse. Under Pierre Bousquet's direction, the factory grew from a small family establishment into a large industry.

A large part of the wares made during this period were simple vessels destined for use in the local farm houses. Clay pipes also comprised a large part of the inventory. The monotoned pipes had very long stems. As the bit wore down, the smoker would break off the tip and thus the pipe could be repeatedly used until a mere nub remained. The tobacco bowl and tiny stem stub would then be discarded. For this reason none of the pipes from this era remain in existence. Tobacco jars and snuff bottles were made as companion pieces to the pipes.

During the factory's expansion, two tragedies struck the Bousquet family. First, Pierre's only son died at the age of fourteen. Then in 1722, his younger brother Charles died. These deaths wrought havoc within the family, since there were now no existing heirs to insure the continuity of the business. Therefore, Bousquet sent for his brother-in-law, Pierre Bellevaux, at Nevers.

Pierre Bellevaux had married Pierre Bousquet's sister, Marie-Jeanne. Historically, his family had been involved in pottery production for generations. The secrets of faïence were passed down from father to son as a part of their inheritance. Bellevaux was therefore recognized as a full partner in 1731. His particular contribution to the development of Quimper pottery was the introduction of the Nevers style.

No sooner was Bousquet's mind at ease over the arrival of an heir apparent, then tragedy struck again. The premature deaths of both Bellevaux and his wife again left Bousquet alone to manage the business. At the ripe age of seventy-two, he resumed control of the shop.

Feeling death approaching and still wishing to insure his family's interest in the faïencerie, Bousquet successfully sought the marriage of his grand-daughter, Marie-Jeanne Bellevaux, age fifteen, to Pierre Clément Caussy. With the family's inheritance assured, Bousquet died later that year in 1749. Like his father, Pierre Bousquet did not sign any of his wares. He is considered to be one of the most prominent and accomplished of the 18th century French potters. So firmly did he establish the Loc Maria factory, that in spite of the fact that the house produced only copies of other wares, he laid the ground work upon which the pottery's Breton characteristics would later be developed.

Bousquet's choice of Caussy as a successor was a wise one. Caussy had come from Rouen to work at Quimper. Once he succeeded to the directorship and for the following thirty-three years, he managed the factory with care, devotion and an astounding expertise. This period proved to be one of the most illustrious of all in the history of the factory.

Pierre Clément Caussy was descended from a long line of faïence craftsmen. His grandfather, Paul Caussy, owned a workshop on the outskirts of Rouen. In addition, he had invented a revolutionary method employing a vaulted-ceiling oven which facilitated the drying process of the wet pottery. Paul Caussy's son, Pierre Paul Caussy, was also a consummate faïence technician. In 1747 he had written a book entitled *Traité de la Faïence* (A Faïence Treatise). This lengthy work precisely detailed all of the secrets and patterns involved in the production of faïence at Rouen. The original manuscript of this potter's bible was passed down from generation to generation. It went with Pierre Clément Caussy to Quimper. The entire original remained in the archives of the Musée des Faïences de Quimper until World War I. Today, only fragments remain and there is speculation that the major body of the work is somewhere in the United States, given by one of the descendants of the de la Hubaudière family to an American friend for safe keeping. It has never been found.

After Paul Caussy died, his son Pierre Paul Caussy inherited the Rouen workshop. The business continued to prosper until 1744. In that year the French government restricted the amount of fire wood allowed to be burned for the drying process and also limited the number of colors that could be used in faïence production. As a result, many of the factories in Rouen began to experience financial difficulties. Pierre Paul Caussy sent his son, Pierre Clément Caussy, to work at Loc Maria. Bousquet and the elder Caussy were friendly acquaintances. Bousquet needed help at Quimper and Caussy's son could provide it. At the same time, the Quimper factory would offer a fresh opportunity to the next Caussy generation. Bousquet's business would not be

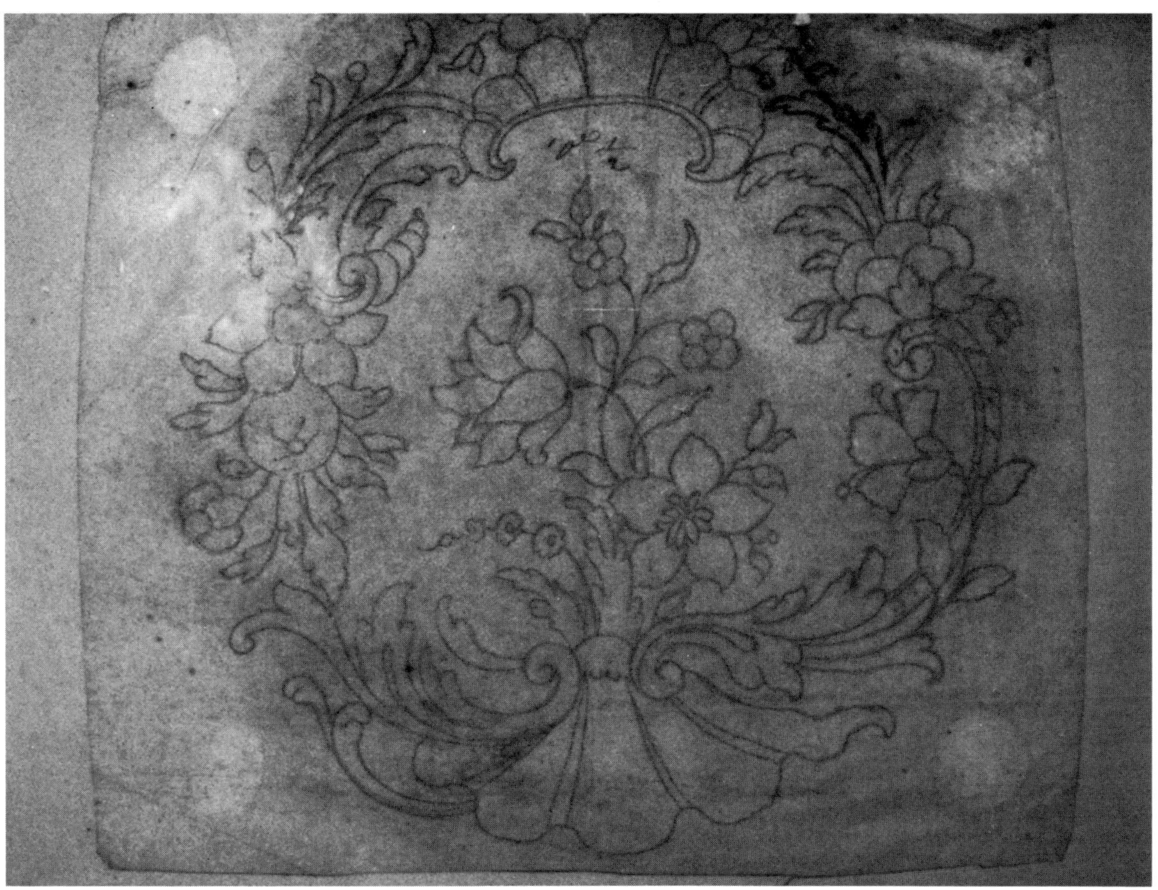

ROUEN "PONCIF" This fragile tracing pattern was brought from Rouen to Quimper by Pierre-Clément Caussy in the 18th century. In 1872 it was rediscovered in the Grande Maison HB archives by Monsieur Fougeray. Today it is on exhibit in the Musée de la Faïence Jules Verlingue

affected by the restrictive governmental measures. Because Quimper was in Brittany, it was directly under the jurisdiction of the Breton Parliament. This governing body maintained a fiercely-guarded independence from the King in as many matters as possible

As a result of the government's policies, most of the potteries in Rouen were forced to close. Many of the workers departed to find employment in the factories of other regions. Several arrived in Quimper. They brought with them a finer caliber of workmanship than Loc Maria had ever known.

With such an extensive family history involved in faïence, Pierre Clément Caussy was well suited for his managerial succession at Quimper. In 1749 he constructed additional drying ovens. An inventory dated ten years later indicates that he employed sixty skilled workers and an equal number of unskilled laborers. Four drying ovens were in constant use to produce the copies of Rouen and Nevers faïences, fine potteries and pipes. Caussy also introduced a different type of ware. This was called "grès". Grès is not considered to be traditional faïence. It is a heavy stoneware which is well-suited for items destined for everyday use. The ware is sturdy and practical. Some of the utilitarian forms which the grès took were: bottles, jugs, pots and tobacco jars. The glaze color of these examples is usually an unadorned medium to dark brown. *(See page 8 & 79 Tobacco Jar)*

Approximately thirty-five vendors sold the wares of Loc Maria. With business growing at a rapid rate, Caussy received permission in 1768 to sell his pottery seven days a week instead of only on market or festival days, as in the past. He offered merchandise in four categories:

1). *la marchandise bonne et loyale,* i.e. the best quality; perfect examples
2). *le second choix,* i.e. items with slight imperfections such as smudges or uneven glaze
3). *le troisième choix,* i.e. items with slight damage
4). *le beau rébut,* i.e. damaged goods too lovely to discard

In spite of Caussy's talented control of the factory, the business legally remained in his wife's name and his brother-in-law's name. Upon her death in 1759 a crisis arose. Pierre-Jean-Marie Bellevaux, Caussy's brother-in-law, inherited one half of the factory. Caussy's two surviving daughters inherited one quarter, while Caussy inherited the final quarter. After many legal technicalities were resolved, the factory was offered for sale at public auction. Aside from Caussy, no serious buyer appeared and he was therefore able to buy back the business. He agreed to pay his brother-in-law a yearly sum, who then relinquished all of his rights to the inheritance.

During this period Caussy was greatly indebted to his workers for their support. He always insisted upon joining them in their family celebrations. His name can be found on the church registry at Loc Maria attesting to his presence at many of his workers' marriages or at the baptisms of their children. Frequently his employees would become ill. The fine dust in the factory's air contributed to many pulmonary problems. The toxins inherent in the lead-based glaze added further to health hazards. Caussy would often lend small sums to the families of recuperating workers in order to help them through the difficult financial period. This practice was hazardous to his purse: more often than not the diseases of the potters proved fatal.

In writing about his employees, Caussy categorized them into three major groups:

1). The master craftsman who did the finest, detailed painting. This was usually the work in the center of a plate or platter. These men also designed and made the molds.
2). The apprenticed craftsmen who painted the lesser details of border and trim work. These men also worked on the molding and unmolding of pieces.
3). The unskilled laborers who stoked the fires, stacked the wares and performed other custodial tasks around the factory.

Apprenticeships lasted four years. No food or salary was included as payment. At first, only the sons of the craftsmen or vendors were allowed to be apprenticed. In time, however, local youths from other backgrounds were accepted. Each craftsman instructed only three students to limit the possibility of saturating the area with skilled technicians who might leave to work at a distant, rival house.

In 1766 the King published an edict which favored the factory at Sèvres. Madame de Pompadour, the King's favorite, was the direct cause. She preferred the wares made at Sèvres above all others and persuaded the King to give it alone royal patronage. All other establishments were to restrict the production of their wares to one color or to a white background decorated with one color. In addition, only Sèvres was permitted to manufacture porcelain.

Caussy, out in the distant province of Brittany, did not restrict the colors used at Quimper. There are two plates in the Musée des Faïences de Quimper dated 1767 and 1773 respectively, both of which are multicolored.

Another unfavorable circumstance arose in 1786. All legal restraints against imports were lifted by the insertion of a clause in the commercial treaty between France and England. Inexpensive British "creamware" subsequently flooded the French market. The French were not able to compete with the English because of their lower production costs. One of the main factors in keeping British manufacturing expenses low was the use of child labor.

In order to compete with the British wares, Caussy decided to open another factory adjacent to the existing one to manufacture "faïence fine", i.e. copies of Leed's cream-coloured ware. Royal authorization however was denied him, and the second factory was never built.

The importation laws were not the only factor which began to restrict Caussy's work. François Eloury, one of his employees, left in 1776 to open a rival faïencerie nearby. Then, in 1778, another factory was begun at Quimper by a Normand, Guillaume Dumaine. By the close of the 18th century, there were three pottery houses in existence in Loc Maria. The products flowing from these three establishments generally carry no marks from this period. All of the examples are true European Delftware. It is practically impossible to distinguish one manufacturer from the others. There are, however, a very few pieces bearing a Caussy mark. The signatures include a P. C. or a CO or a C impressed directly into the clay. These are extremely rare marks. There are no examples of them even in the Musée des Faïences de Quimper.

The exact date of Pierre Caussy's death is not known. By 1782 his name had disappeared from the official files of the factory and had been replaced by that of Antoine de la Hubaudière. De la Hubaudière had married Caussy's eldest daughter, Marie-Elizabeth, in 1771, and the ownership of the business had passed to him.

Born in 1744 at Rennes, De la Hubaudière was a road and bridge engineer. Not wishing to break with family tradition, he joined his father-in-law in the faïence business upon his marriage. He was not destined to direct the factory for long. Soon the tides of the French Revolution were sweeping over France and the patrician potter's family was not to be left unscathed.

De la Hubaudière was firmly committed to the Revolution. Tired of Royal edicts and restrictions which hampered commercial success, he welcomed the freedom to expand and develop his business unimpeded.

Throughout France, two factions were struggling to seize power. In Paris the Jacobins stated that they best represented the interests of the people. In the provinces support was stronger for the Girondins who claimed the same honor. A major conflict arose between the two.

As were most of the people in Brittany, De la Hubaudière was an avid supporter of the Girondins. Under the influence of Marat, the Jacobin's revolutionary leader, the Girondins' government fell and its deputies in Paris were arrested. Several of them managed to escape. Among those who took flight were a group from Finistère (Brittany). Disguising themselves, the deputies travelled towards Quimper in the hope of being welcomed there by friends and supporters. One dark night they were met on the road by Clément de la Hubaudière, the oldest son of Antoine de la Hubaudière and Marie-Elizabeth Caussy. With his parent's knowledge and consent, he brought them to the factory. There they were given refuge until they could clandestinely be moved to a family-owned house across the street from it. From there the plan was to smuggle a few of them at a time aboard Antoine de la Hubaudière's boat, "La Diligente", to be taken as far as Bordeaux. Now the Girondins' intention was to break all ties with France and form an independant Republic comprised of Brittany, the Loire region and neighboring areas.

Tragically, the plot was exposed. The remaining men who were still in hiding were found and executed, and Antoine and Clément de la Hubaudière were forced to flee into the interior of Brittany where their family had relatives. Antoine de la Hubaudière was captured and massacred at Beaucé with his brother, the Abbot André de la Hubaudière, by a band of Breton Royalist insurgents. Clément de la Hubaudière escaped detection and eventually was pardoned.

As a result of its Girondins' sympathies, Brittany was severly punished. The use of the Breton language was forbidden. Quimper's name was changed to Montagne-sur-l'Odet. All of the churches were desecrated, including the Medieval parish church of Loc Maria. This tiny church housed the highly-venerated statue of Notre Dame de Loc Maria (Our Lady of Loc Maria), the patroness of the faïencerie. Even the statue felt the Jacobin's wrath. It was torn from the church, broken, and thrown on a wood pile. Marie-Elizabeth Caussy, now Citizen Caussy, set out together with a small band of men from the factory to rescue their beloved patroness. She found the broken remains of the statue and carefully preserved them. (The statue was restored at the beginning of the 19th century and now stands in its original place in the parish church of Loc Maria, adjacent to the faïencerie.)

Citizen Caussy took over the management of the factory. The beautifully-decorated examples of Rouen and Nevers patterns were abandoned in favor of the production of grès. The house survived by making stoneware cooking pots, bottles and utilitarian vessels. It also made a large quantity of the double-handled porringers which had been used locally since before the Roman occupation of Gaul and which were still greatly preferred over the use of plates. One interesting fact is that no plates with Revolutionary slogans were made at Quimper at this time. It wasn't until just before World War I that the Grande Maison issued a series of commemorative Revolutionary plates.

Despite the upheaval stemming from the Revolution, the faïencerie prospered in its production of grès. There is on record a petition bearing Citizen Caussy's signature which requests permission to add another firing oven to the plant.

Towards the beginning of the 19th century, the first true mark was placed upon the De la Hubaudière pottery. It is a joined HB with a curve extending from the base of the "B". It is a very rare mark. Another 19th century mark is a tiny triangle with the letters HB (Hubaudière-Bousquet) in the center and a fleur de lis (the symbol of France) directly above it in the top corner. Two ermine tails (the symbol of Brittany) appear in the two bottom corners. This mark was often directly impressed into the wet clay of a piece. The size of the stamp used to make the impression was so small, that the finer details of the mark were frequently obscured. Consequently, the mark usually appears to be a tiny, incised triangle. It too is a rare mark, as most of the examples dating from this period still bore no signature. After the mid-19th century, this mark was simplified to the use of only the "HB" initials. Many times the lone "HB" was placed on the front of a piece.

It is interesting to note that the factory got its name from its location. First situated on the Rue Haute (High Road) which overlooked the route to Benodet, it obviously must have been an imposing structure to those traveling along the road. Hence people began to refer to the De la Hubaudière factory as the Grande Maison (Big House).

In the beginning of the 19th century faïence production in France had nearly ceased. Not a single pottery workshop remained in Rouen or Nevers after the first decade. The tumultuous churnings of the French Revolution coupled with the continuing influx of British wares had taken their toll. Traditional faïence was dead.

Yet somehow Quimper's potteries persisted. Many factors influenced their survival. First, Brittany's location segregated it from the mainstream of France's evolving life style. It was isolated from many of the industrial changes that were taking place after the Revolution. Second, traditions remained firmly embedded in the habits and tastes of the local folk. Bretons still used the double-handled porringers, milk pitchers and plates on their farms. Lastly, Brittany continued to harbor a deep devotion to Catholicism. The people purchased statues of saints to venerate in their homes and also held the "pardons" (religious festivals) during which they would buy a holy water font as a souvenir gift.

Consequently, as the production of faïence failed in the rest of France, the true Breton characteristics of Quimper pottery were gradually beginning to emerge. The predominent use of the primary colors (blue, yellow and red) to decorate the ware, the concentric-banded yellow and blue line border trims, and the increased use of "décor à la touche" (the utilization of a single paint brush stroke to create a flower petal or leaf) were beginning to evolve. These simple provincial traits, which have endeared the pottery to its many devotees, began to make their appearance.

Félix de la Hubaudière became the director of the Grande Maison in 1853. During this period, the factory settled into a routine. Madame de Béru, the widow of Félix de la Hubaudière, was the first to hire outside help to manage the factory. In 1872 she introduced Monsieur Fougeray as the new director.

Concurrent with Fougeray's arrival was an interesting discovery. All of the 18th century tracing patterns which had been in use during Pierre Clément Caussy's time, were re-discovered in the factory. Madame de Béru and Monsieur Fougeray decided to reissue adaptations of the early Rouen patterns. The pieces were marked with an "HB", so as to distinguish them from the true antique pieces, which were for the most part, unsigned. So good were the copies that many of them were reputedly sold as authentic early wares by disreputable antiques dealers. It is important to keep in mind that these "copies" are now more than one hundred years old.

The last quarter of the 19th century was an extremely fertile period for Breton commerce. The idea of spending one's vacation on the picturesque coast of Brittany had much appeal to the infant tourist trade. The growing use of the railroads enabled increasing numbers of people to visit the area. It became common practice to bring

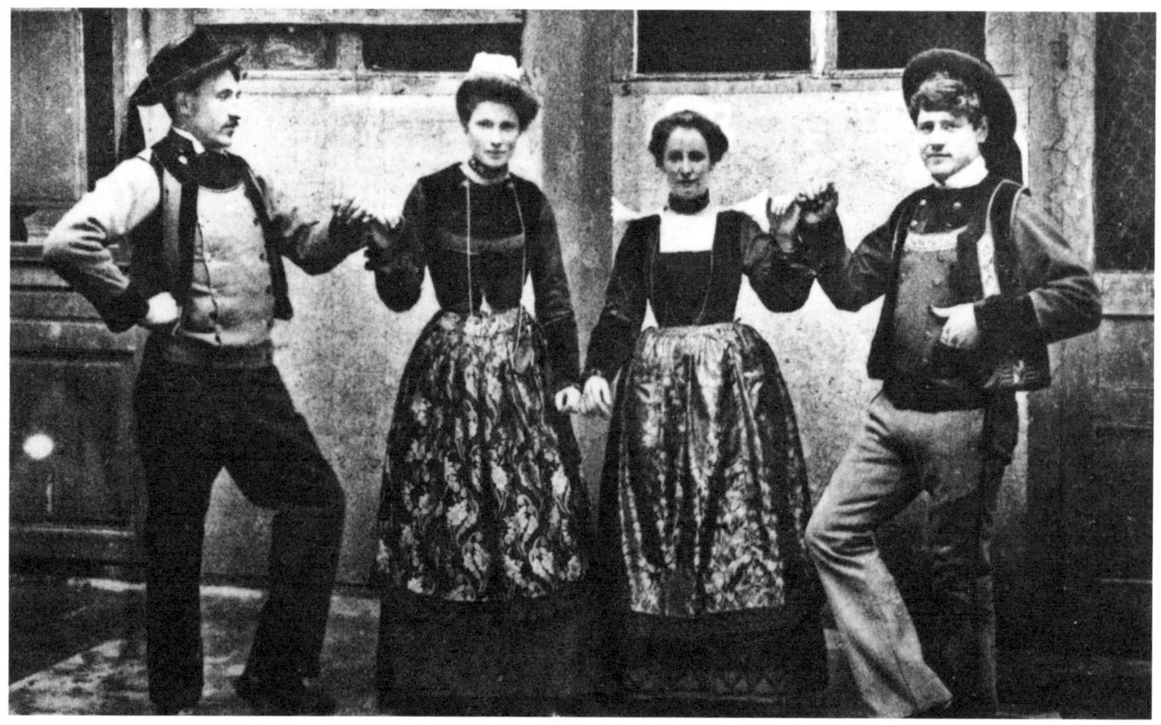

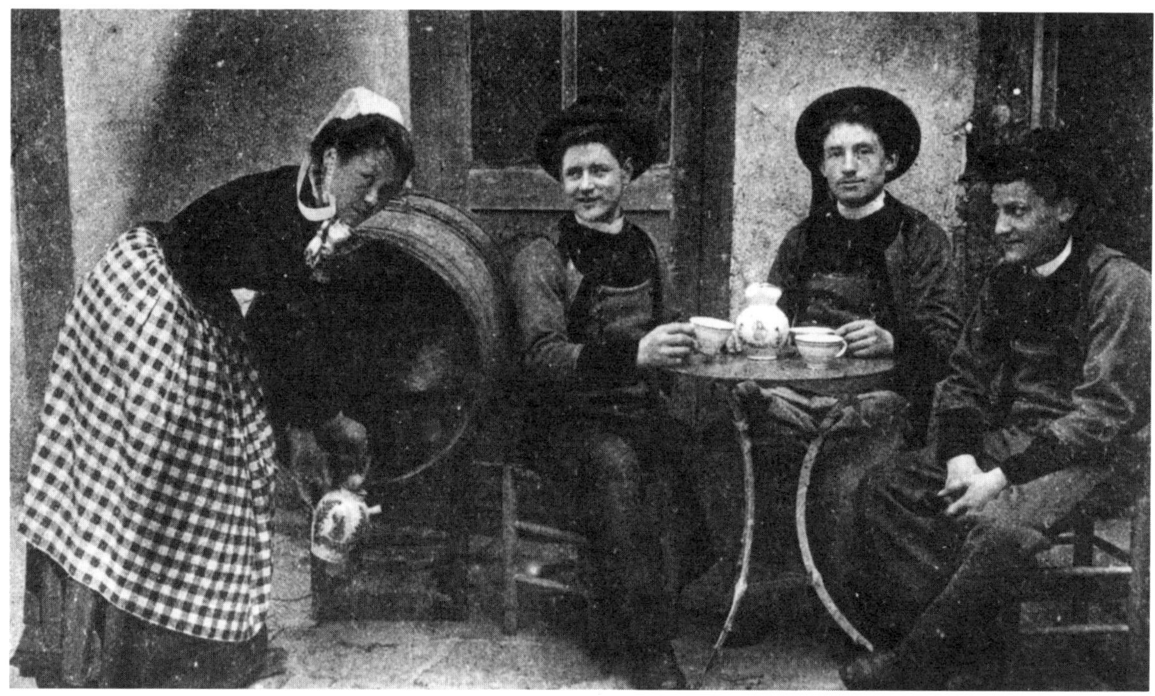

"CARTES POSTALES" A series of postcards were issued for Quimper's growing tourist trade. They portrayed local activities such as the "Danse de Gavotte" (Gavotte Folk Danse) and "Le bon cidre de Fouesnant" (Fouesnant's delicious cider). Also included in this series of postcards were photographs of the various stages of pottery production at the local faïenceries. Note the use of Quimper pottery pitchers and cups in the bottom card. *(Private Collection)*

home a souvenir of the region. Increasingly, it was the gaily-colored country pottery of Quimper which was tucked into valises and brought home. The charming peasant faïence insured treasured memories of the pleasant Breton sojurn and thus gained wide spread popularity.

Due to the growing public awareness of the faïence, the Archeological Society of Finistère decided to mount an exhibit of 17th, 18th and 19th century Quimper pottery. Appeals went out to the populace to search attics and cupboards in an effort to uncover long-lost, early, rare examples.

The Exposition, which opened in 1876, awakened a new interest in Quimper faïence. It allowed a close scrutiny of the influences which Moustiers, Nevers and Rouen had had upon the initial patterns, and equally as important, it provided a showcase for the evolving Breton style.

By the end of the 19th century a new "popular" style was firmly ensconced. This pattern consisted of scenes taken from the everyday life of the Breton peasant folk. Occasionally, an 18th or 19th century example would be decorated with the likeness of a human figure. "Les Jouers de Cartes" *(The Card Players, page 6)* is one of two 18th century plates in the Musée des Faïences de Quimper collections which depicts people as the central theme. Mid-19th century examples decorated with a naively-painted peasant figure are more common. However, the use of the peasant man or lady did not reach general usage until about one hundred years ago. The change was due in large part to the creativity of one man, Alfred Beau. His invaluable contribution to the development of Quimper pottery will be discussed in the following chapter.

Shortly after the turn of the century, the De la Hubaudière family decided to put the factory up for public auction. Huge posters proclaimed the sale throughout the region. Jules Henriot, the owner of the rival faïence house, left the auction on October 17, 1906 convinced that he was the new owner of the Grande Maison HB. A curious incident followed. One of the members of the De la Hubaudière family did not want to see the business pass out of the family's control. Quietly, Joseph de la Hubaudière slipped into the notary public's office after the closing hour. There he pleaded with the notary to invalidate the sale of the factory to Jules Henriot. At the final hour, he had managed to raise enough capital to buy the house himself. Tradition and custom being strong in France, the notary did not hesitate to grant his plea. The following morning news quickly spread throughout the city of what had transpired. Henriot was furious and sued. The court decided in Joseph de la Hubaudière's favor—for the factory had been in his family's control since 1690. The two rival faïenceries were to remain separate for a little while longer.

The last descendant from the line of Jean-Baptiste Bousquet to manage the business was Guy de la Hubaudière, who was killed in battle during World War I in 1915. After his death, the house was purchased by Messieurs Verlingue, Bollari et Cie.

Monsieur Jules Verlingue began a series of modernizations at the Quimper factory. In 1920 he hired a noted Breton sculptor, René Quillivic, who brought a fresh and revolutionary design to the faïence. Large and small figurines of peasant folk appeared. Patterns were up-dated and many took on an Art Deco appearance. The soft, pale colors of the older pieces were superseded by brighter, deeper and more varied hues.

Under Quillivic's guidance, additional artists were hired and designed molds to which they added their signatures. Among those working for the Grande Maison HB were: M. L. Bar, F. Bazin, Bouvier, Georges Brisson, François Caujan (who signed his work "Fanch"), A. Chanteau, Louis Garin, Marius Giot, Georges Renaud, Georges Robin, Berthe Savigny, Marcharit Houël, Marthe La Barrère, Adolphe-Jean Lachaud, Constant Lamothe, J.-C. Bozec, Jacques Nam and A. Porson.

Although these artists were bringing a fresh artistic approach to the pottery, the earlier patterns and forms were being produced simultaneously.

In 1968, the Grande Maison HB and the Maison Henriot merged. Although now housed together under one roof on the HB site, each retains its own patterns, molds and mark.

The owner of the factory during this period was Jean-Yves Verlingue, the son of Jules Verlingue. It was during this period that Jean Rouillard became the director general and Louis Leonus, the technical director.

Under their auspices the factory was modernized and the historical documents, which had been neglected for decades in the archives, were re-evaluated.

The early 1980's brought difficult financial hardships. Once again the company was in danger of closing its' doors. On March 12, 1984 the ailing and nearly bankrupt company was purchased by an American group of investors headed by Paul and Sarah Janssens.

The new company, the Société Nouvelle des Faïences de Quimper, saw the beginning of an innovative technical era in Quimper production. A renovation of equipment and a fuel conservation program were instituted. At the same time a commitment was made to keep to the standard of a consistently fine quality product which would still be painted entirely by hand.

Paul Janssens' astute marketing acumen has promulgated a new renaissance for the ware. He has opened successful retail shops in Paris and Locronan and in Alexandra, Virginia.

Chapter 4

The Eloury-Porquier-Beau Factory

At the end of the 18th century, two potteries in competition with the HB factory were established at Quimper. One of these was headed by Francois Eloury, a former employee of Caussy. In an effort to block the opening of this faïence workshop, Caussy had unsuccessfully argued that firewood, which was needed for the drying process, was becoming scarce. The ruling magistrate felt that increased competition would benefit the faïence industry and therefore he granted Eloury permission to open his establishment.

By the end of the French Revolution, Eloury's plant was manufacturing grès and faïence in Loc Maria. Seven years after opening his factory, Eloury's son, Guillaume, became the manager.

Guillaume Eloury had three children: Hélène Thérese, Nicolas and Sophie. Hélène Thérese married Charles Porquier in 1809. Porquier was accepted as a full partner and the business changed its name to Eloury-Porquier. Under Porquier's direction, the first mark of the house was introduced. The lone "P", an extremely rare signature, was used prior to mid-19th century.

After the deaths of Hélène Thérese and Charles Porquier, the business was inherited by Nicolas Eloury. He had no interest in the factory and promptly sold it to his nephew, Guillaume Auguste Porquier. This young man, who was known as Auguste Porquier, became the head of the workshop at age twenty-six. He greatly expanded the business between 1838 and 1869. Towards the end of this period, his son, Adolphe Porquier, worked with him. An inventory taken in 1869 lists some of the wares made at the Eloury-Porquier factory. They include: lavabos, inkwells, religious statues of the "Ste. Vierge" in different sizes, holy water fonts, tobacco jars, barbers' bowls, apothecary jars and an equally diverse list of practical grès wares.

Adolphe Porquier randomly used an "AP" mark to sign pieces from the factory. The mark, however, did not become a legally registered trademark until 1897, when it was used again by his son, Arthur Porquier.

In 1872, Adolphe Porquier's widow, Augustine Carof, became associated with Alfred Beau. The partnership, although eventually not a financial success, produced some of the most exquisite Quimper pottery of all times.

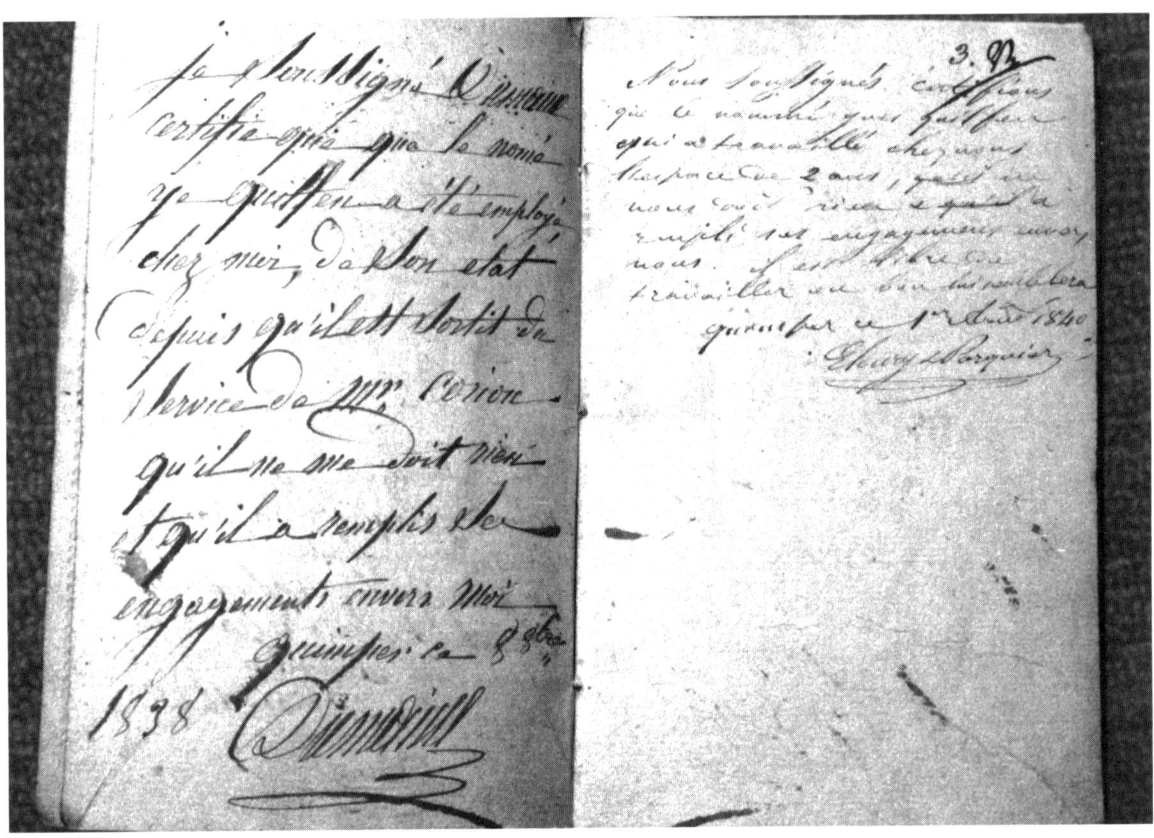

ARCHIVE DOCUMENT A 19th century diary dated 1838 and 1840 bears the signature of Dumaine and his rivals, Eloury and Porquier. *(Courtesy Musée des Faïenceries de Quimper)*

Born at Morlaix, Beau was the curator of the regional Quimper Museum. He was also an artist, photographer and innovator par excellent. Beau's artistic imagination was fired by Emile Souvestre, his father-in-law, who had written a book entitled *The Last Bretons.* With the intention of immortalizing the Breton people, Beau decided to give his pottery a distinctive Breton character. In accord with the Romanticism sweeping Europe, Beau sought to depict the scenes from everyday life which he found around him. He took inspiration from the simple existence of the peasant folk and colored it with a touch of humorous characterization. He began to sketch the provincial comings and goings, depicting the local peasantry in their sundry, homely activities. He borrowed further ideas from the engravings of the "Galerie Amoricain", where in fine detail he found men pictured in their "bragoubraz" (pantaloons), accompanied by their delicately coiffed womanfolk. Bagpipes and flutes, large-brimmed, buckled hats, lacy beribboned coifs, long pipes and walking sticks were all in abundant evidence. Beau's sketchbook overflowed with magnificent folk art detail.

He also collected early postcards of peasants in their local costumes. Here and there his artist hand was evident as he penciled over the prints and changed bits of garb to give the people a more Breton "flavor". In the factory archives today, over two hundred scenes of local lifestyles survive as a legacy of love to his dream of perpetuating the regional folk life through his pottery.

For his efforts, Beau received a silver medal at the Paris Exposition of 1878 for the award-winning piece entitled: "Mendiants Bretons Demandant L'Aumône" (Breton Beggars Receiving Charity).

It was Beau's genius which to a large extent made Quimper faïence recognized and cherished internationally. Few people could resist the charming country scenes he depicted: marriages and baptisms; children at play; dancers twirling to the folk dance "gavotte"; pipers piping and flutists playing; grandparents spinning tall yarns, as their grandchildren sit spellbound; sailors; lovers; all celebrating the joy of life. Each of these provincial activities decorated his pottery in an elaborately detailed, fine, loving manner.

The resulting "Scènes bretonnes" are among the most successful patterns ever executed at Quimper. They are also among the most highly cherished and sought after examples by collectors.

Alfred Beau also issued three-dimensional figurines and bas reliefs of peasant folk. Up until that time, generally, only religious statues had been produced at Quimper. In sharp contrast to his highly detailed painted "Scènes bretonnes" these figural pieces are very naively executed. This obvious difference of style is readily apparent. The figural pieces lack the exquisite workmanship of the painted examples. They are plain, simple and somewhat primitive. Artistically, they are considered to be less successful.

This comparison can be carried over from Beau's peasant themes to his architectural subjects. The Porquier-Beau factory also made a series of wall plaques depicting various towns in Brittany. Those examples with a detailed, painted view of the town are considered far superior to those where the town is shown in bas relief.

In addition to his peasant patterns, Beau drew upon the wild flowers and plants, the birds, fishes and insects, which were indigenous to Brittany, for inspiration of his work. A series of tableware entitled "Botanique" was the result. These pieces depict a spray of plant life coupled with a bird, fish or insect. Each combination is different and distinct. So irresistably lovely and successful were these flora/fauna decorated wares that a plate from this pattern is on display in the faïence section of the Victoria and Albert Museum in London, the only example of Quimper pottery to be so honored. So artistically timeless and appealing are they, that during this writer's last visit to the factory, representatives from Tiffany and Company in New York, were ordering reissues of "Botanique" to offer to their customers. *(See page 35, 36, 37 & 80)*

Beau also designed a series of plates depicting the "Légendes Bretonnes". These commemorate the local legends and folklore tales of the region. Porquier-Beau made excellent copies of Rouen, Nevers and Delft wares as well.

With few exceptions, Beau's creative talents produced exceptionally lovely faïence. A great deal of the appeal of his wares can be found in the colors, as well as in the patterns of the examples. The colors used during Beau's association with Madame Carof are distinctly beautiful. Soft, delicate and mellow, they capture the gentlest differentiations between hues. The Porquier-Beau glaze always seems to bear the tenderest hint of pale blue. Borders are intricately scrolled floral patterns which intertwine to create a visual fluidity. The color variations of the border work usually include an overall blue on blue or green on green predominance. Frequently, a regional Crest or Coat of Arms will be included as a part of the border design. For the "Botanique" and "Légendes Bretonnes" patterns, the outer rim of the example is outlined by a simple yellow or blue linear stroke.

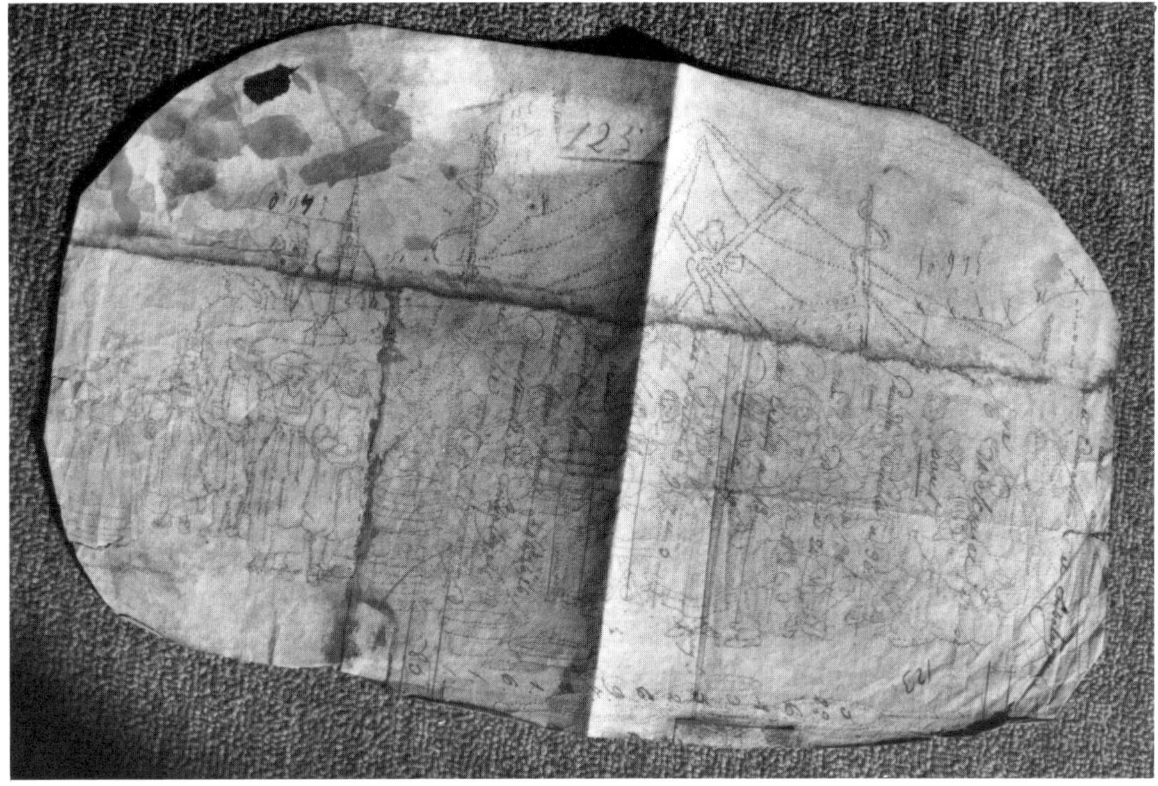

"PONCIF" Tracing patterns were painstakingly pin pricked on the most unlikely scraps of paper. Here, an old letter is transformed into a 19th century Porquier-Beau pattern. *(Courtesy Archives of the Faïenceries de Quimper)*

In contrast to the painted pieces, the figural and bas relief examples have a distinctive coloration. While the shades employed are again soft and muted, a different glaze gives a warm beige-tone cast to their appearance. Border designs are geometrically oriented; the predominant trim colors used include terra cotta, off-white and black. Breton Crests and Coats of Arms are also often employed as a part of the border design. *(See page 44)*

Alfred Beau hired several talented artists to work with him in creating his "Scènes bretonnes". Madame Majatta Taburet in her book, *La Faience de Quimper,* states that Beau used several of the people associated with the factory to pose as models for his sketches. The patterns evolved in the following way. First, an idea for a new pattern was sketched in pencil. It was then executed as an "aquarelle" (watercolor). Next the drawing was transferred to a tissue-like paper or to a scrap of paper such as an old letter. The entire outline of each figure and detail would then be painstakingly pinpricked. The "poncif" (completed pattern), or portions of it, would be placed on a blank piece of pottery. A fine, black charcoal dust would be delicately brushed over it. As the pattern was carefully lifted, a faint outline of the sketch would remain on the piece in charcoal dust. The "peinteuses" (young women hired to do the painting) would then complete the piece.

Many times only a portion of a pattern would be used. Different scenes therefore show the same person appearing in various capacities. For example, one might find a flutest as the sole figure decorating a vase. The same man might appear as one of many members celebrating a wedding procession on another example.

In her book, Marjatta Taburet describes how eighteen women were personally selected by Beau to reproduce his patterns. Four "peinteuses" were needed to complete one example. The first young woman transferred the pattern to the object; the second painted half of the colors; the third added the remaining colors; the fourth, called the "finisseuse", outlined all of the forms and completed any necessary retouches.

On rare occasions, for special presentation pieces, Alfred Beau would do the painting himself freehand. These examples resemble true canvas paintings and are always signed with the artist's name.

The other pattern-produced pieces were signed with the Porquier-Beau mark: an intersecting "PB". The "P" stands vertically and is intersected at mid-point by a horizontal "B". One might see several words such as "Retour de Pardon" or "Environs de Quimper", etc., written along with the Porquier-Beau mark. These are descriptive titles which apply to the scene which is shown on the example. They also refer to the name of the pattern used.

Quimper pottery was very much in vogue during the last quarter of the 19th century. As a result, the three potteries of Loc Maria found themselves at the center of a controversy. Suddenly, their wares were being copied by other manufacturers in France, Germany and Japan. In order to differentiate their products from the spurious pottery, the Grande Maison HB and the Maison Henriot added the word "Quimper" to their mark at this time.

The Porquier-Beau factory had an especially trying experience with counterfeit wares. A potter named Pouplard began to reproduce Beau's "Scènes bretonnes", along with other typical Quimper patterns. These excellent copies were made at his factory in Malicorne in the Sarthe region to the west of Paris. To further add to the confusion surrounding his wares, Pouplard used the "P" from his own name and the "B" from his wife's maiden name, Béatrix, to form a "PB" mark of his own. The "P"

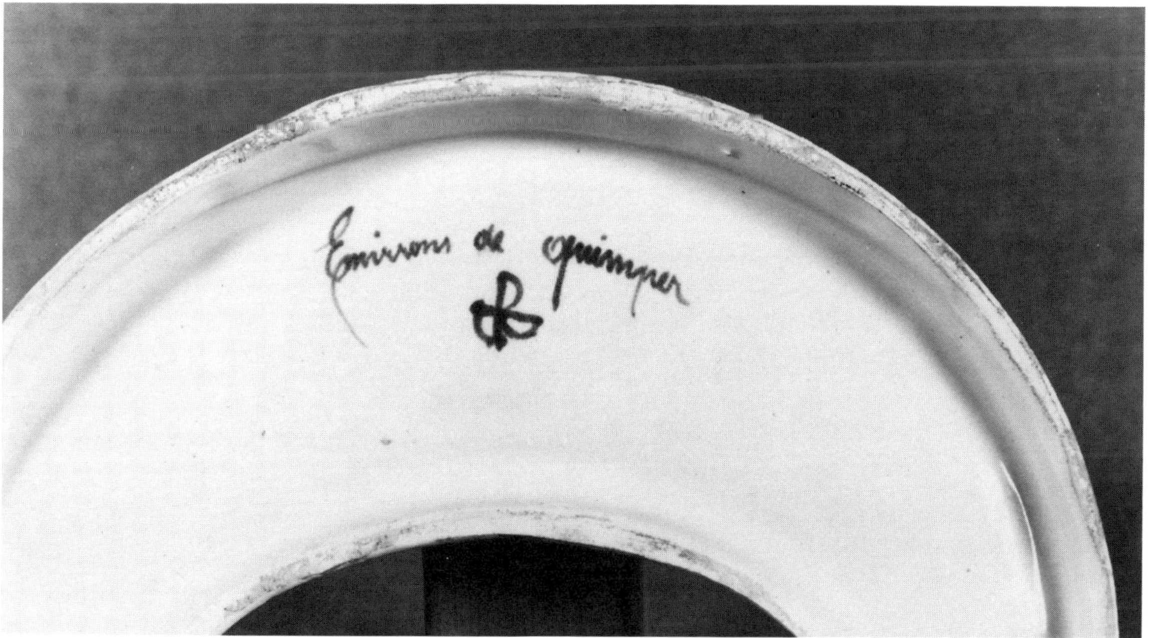

The Porquier-Beau Mark shown here is preceded by the title, "Environs de Quimper". This refers to the name of the scene which adorns the crescent inkwell on page 35.

and "B" are separate initials and are followed by a small "x". Occasionally, the "P" is also written backwards. Porquier-Beau brought a legal suit against Pouplard and the case was decided in 1897. Malicorne was ordered to cease production and to destroy all of its remaining stock and molds.

By 1890, Porquier-Beau was experiencing financial difficulties in spite of the tremendous success of its pottery products. Beau decided to leave Quimper and Arthur Porquier resumed sole control of the factory. In 1897 he registered his father's "AP" mark and began to use it once again as his trademark.

In 1904, the Porquier factory closed. Jules Henriot, who was the proprietor of the third faïencerie in Quimper, bought all of Beau's sketches, patterns, molds and the "PB" trademark in 1913. From 1918 to about 1930, Henriot reissued many of the highly acclaimed Porquier-Beau examples. To differentiate them from the original pieces made during Beau's tenure, Henriot marked the wares "PB Quimper". To the experienced collector, the differences between an authentic Porquier-Beau and a reissued example under Henriot are obvious. The colors lack a certain delicacy and fragility. The attention to detail and to the fineness of the drawing is notably absent in the newer pottery. *(See page 64)* The glaze also appears heavier and lacks the pale blue cast.

After 1930 all of the pieces reissued by Henriot from the Porquier-Beau factory carried the Henriot mark.

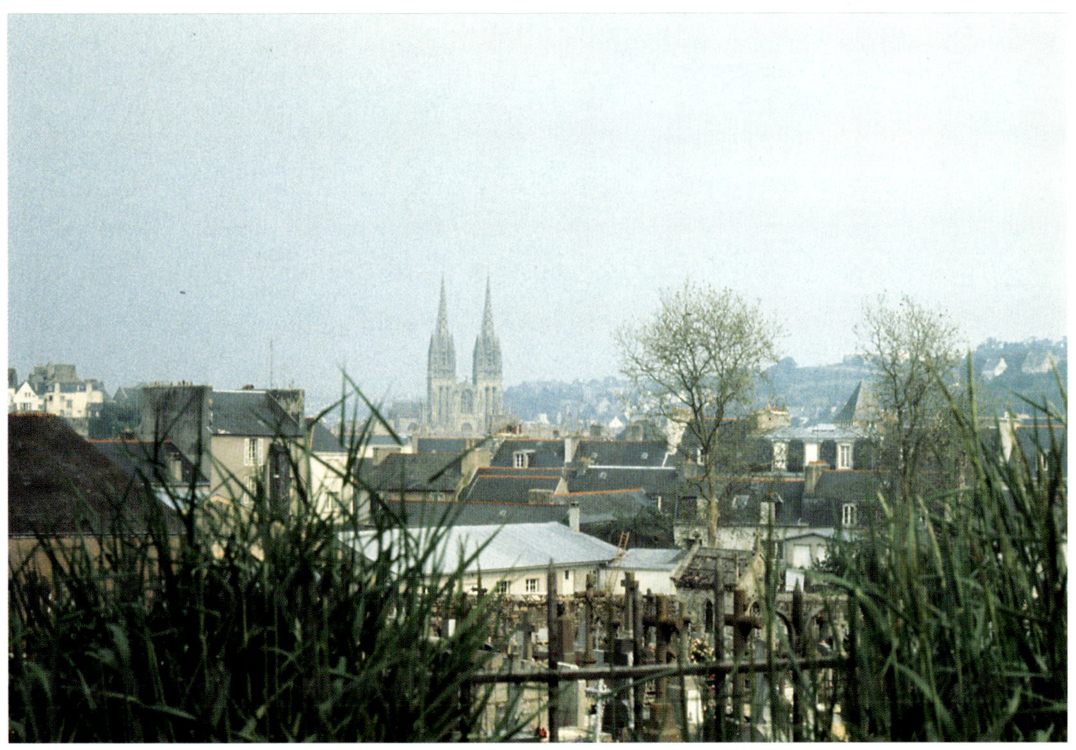

Photo 1: Shrouded in an early morning gauze of mist, the twin spires of Quimper's St. Corentin Cathedral rise above the town.

Photo 2: The wooden figure of a "Petite Breton" stands above a shop in the town square. Coiffed with the distinctive cap of the town, she welcomes all to "Cornouaille", which is the ancient name for this corner of Brittany.

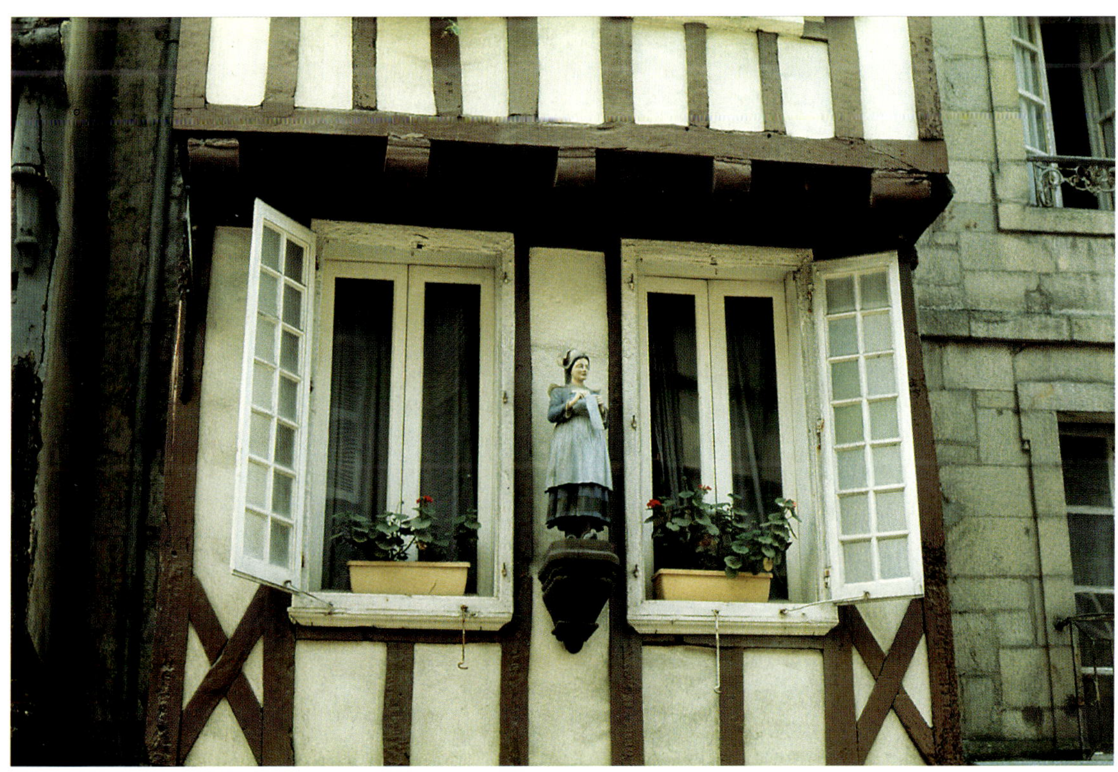

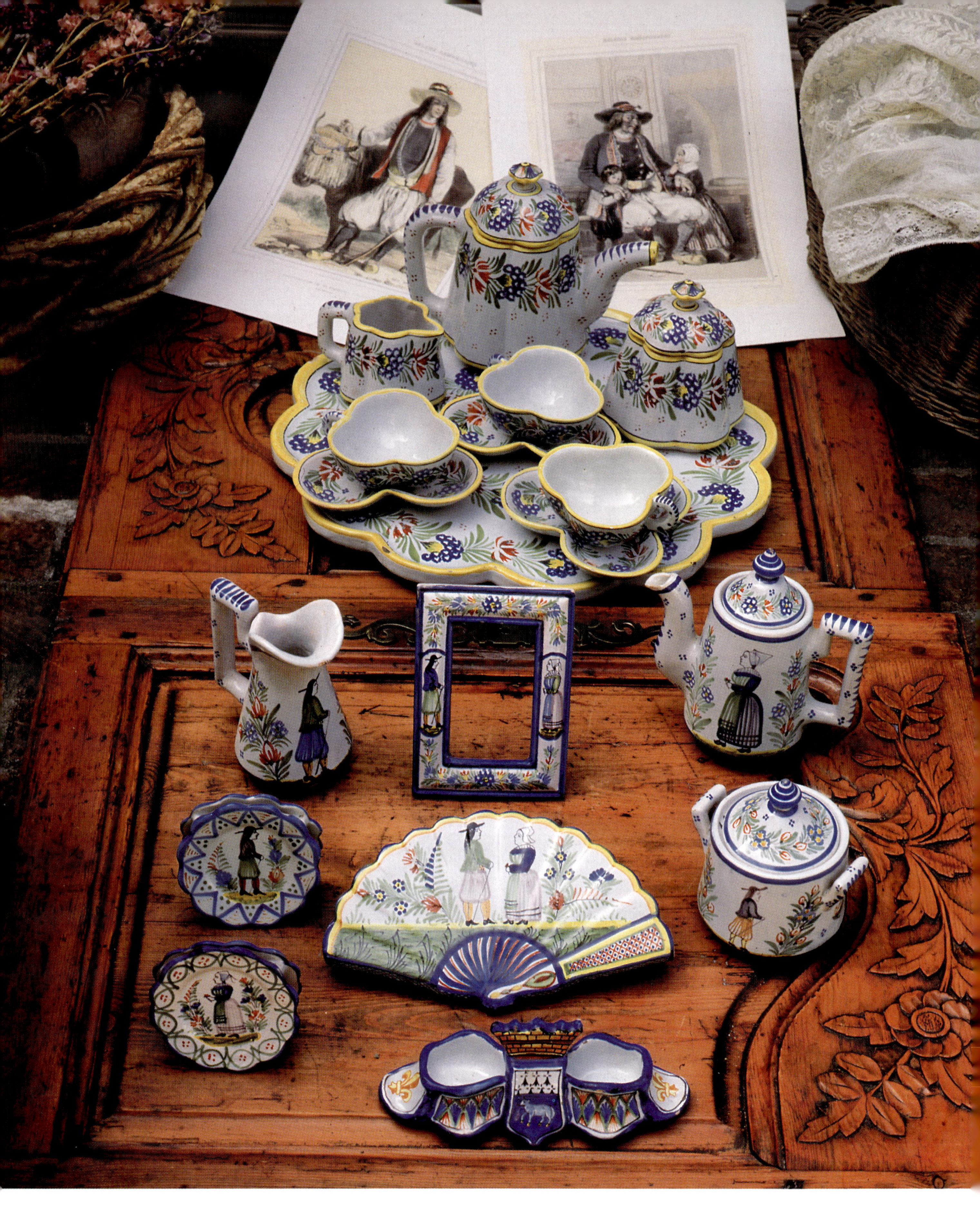

Examples of 19th century Adolphe Porquier production are just as likely to be unsigned, as signed. Their vibrant, fresh glaze colors and distinctive treatment of the peasant figures help to authenticate the attribution. The double salt, picture frame, sugar and creamer with small coffee pot are marked AP. The teaset on tray and fan vase are not. One of the placecard holders is signed, the other is not. *(Private Collection)*

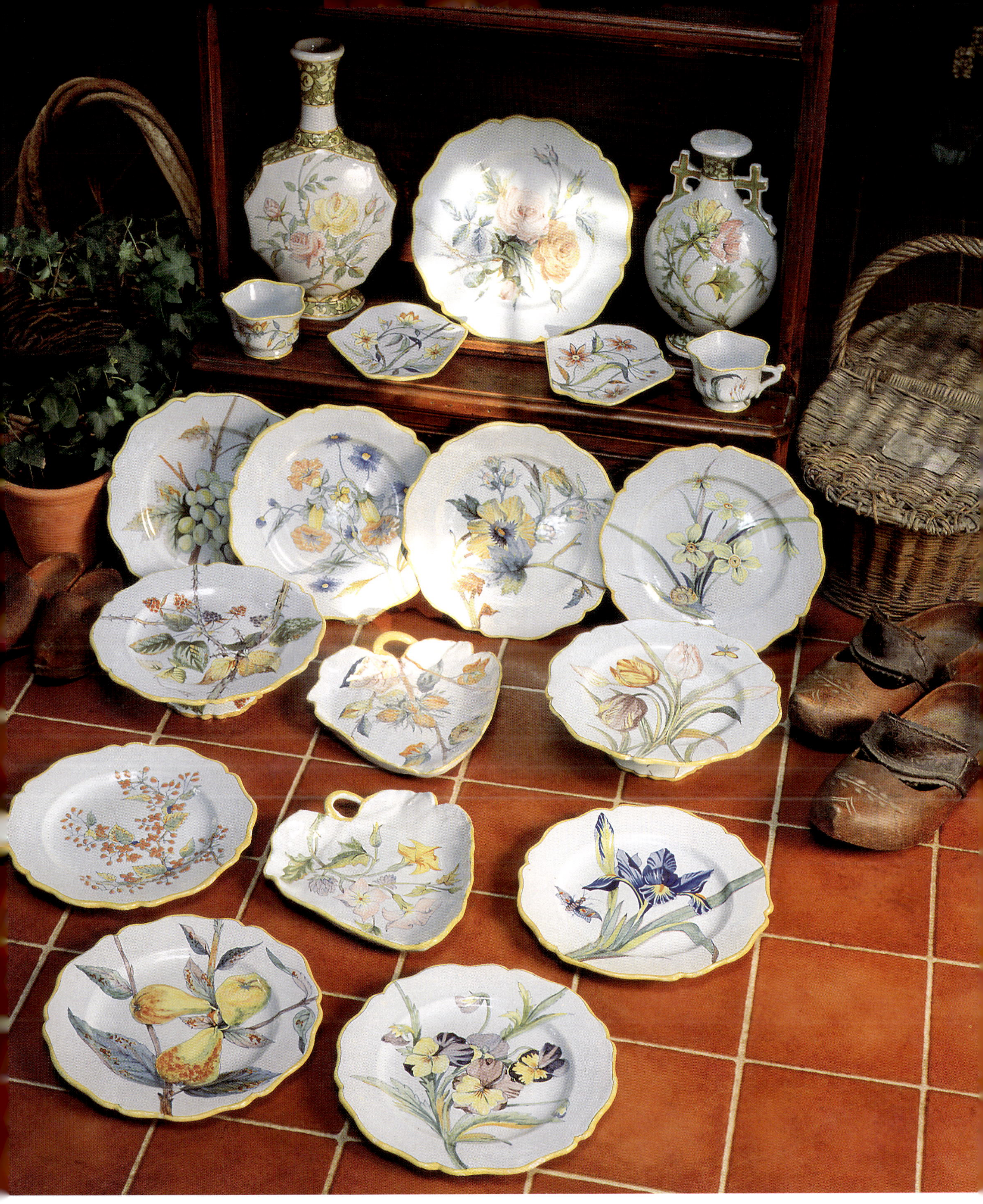

Based on a British Chelseaware pattern, "Botanique" (Botanical) continues to be a favorite among collectors. The yellow linear border perfectly compliments the central theme. On hollow examples one frequently finds a Botanical pattern on the reverse side of a "Scène Bretonne". Last quarter 19th century Porquier-Beau. *(Private Collection)*

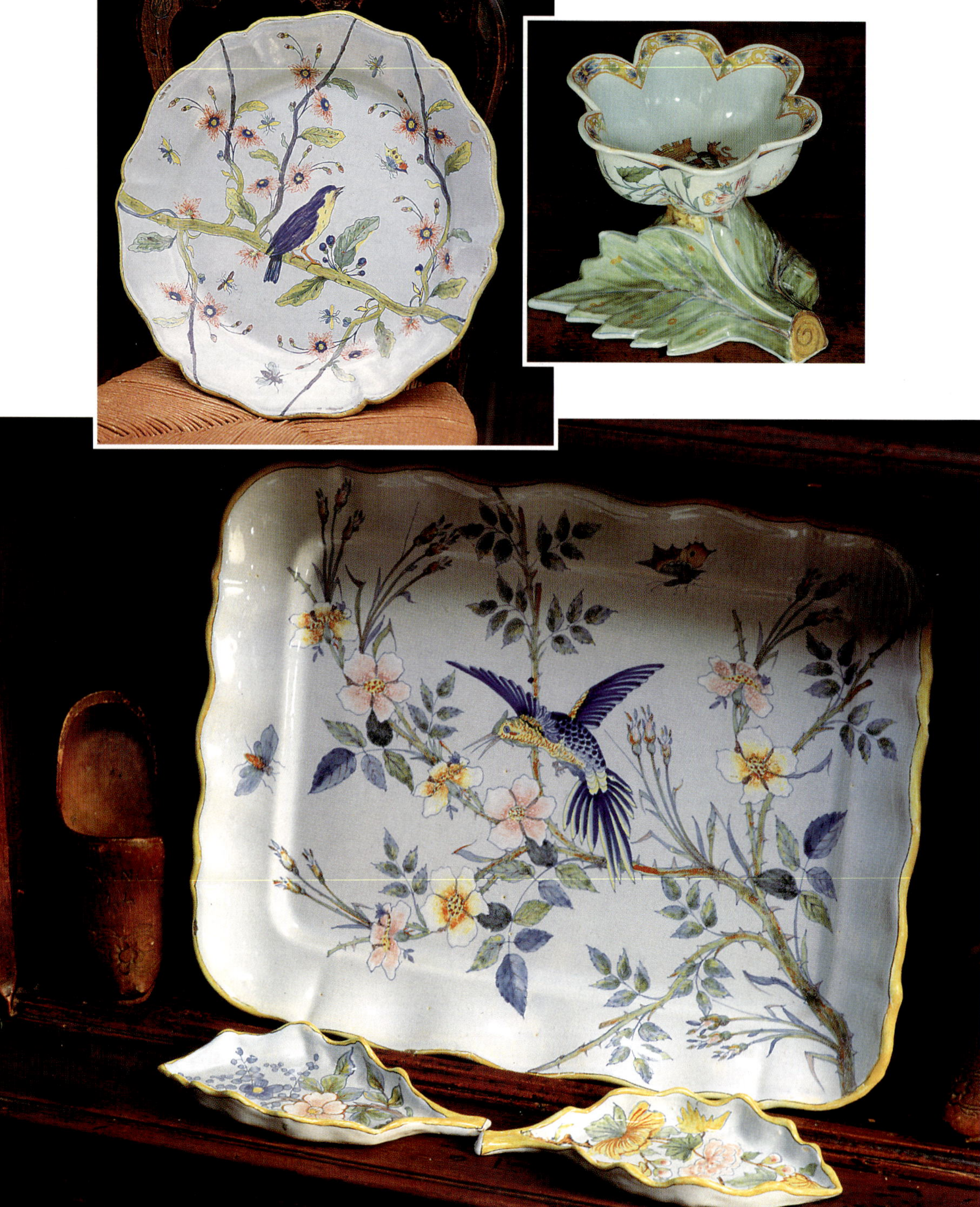

Photo 1: A 16.5" diameter "Botanique" charger with a yellow breasted bluebird perching on a blossoming branch. Insects flutter among the buds. Note the pronounced glaze skips along the rim which frequently occur in 19th century production.
(Private Collection)

Photo 2: Especially elegant this "chou-fleur" (cauliflower) compote is decorated with a delicate floral exterior and the Crest of St, Malo on the interior. First Period Porquier-Beau mark. *(Private Collection)*

Photo 3: The 15.25" rectangular platter displays a hummingbird feeding among wild roses. The molded leaf plates were little serving pieces. First Period Porquier-Beau. *(Private Collection)*

Following page: Nestled among an 18th c. Breton wheelbarrow, baskets and "sabots" (wooden clogs) a grouping of 19th c. Porquier-Beau examples demonstrates the diversity of the Botanical pattern. The series included flowers, fauna, fruit, fowl, fish and insects. *(Private Collection)*

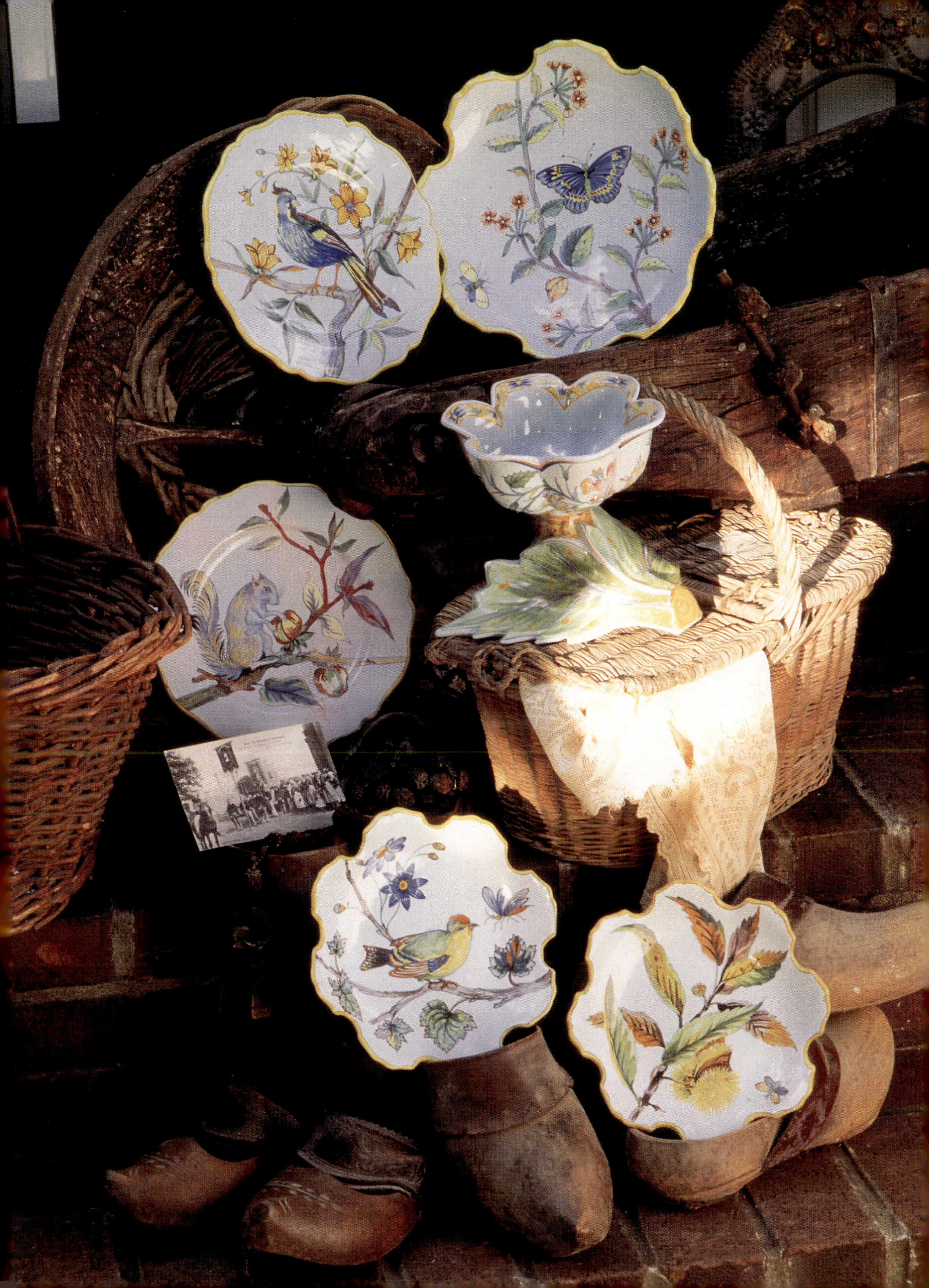

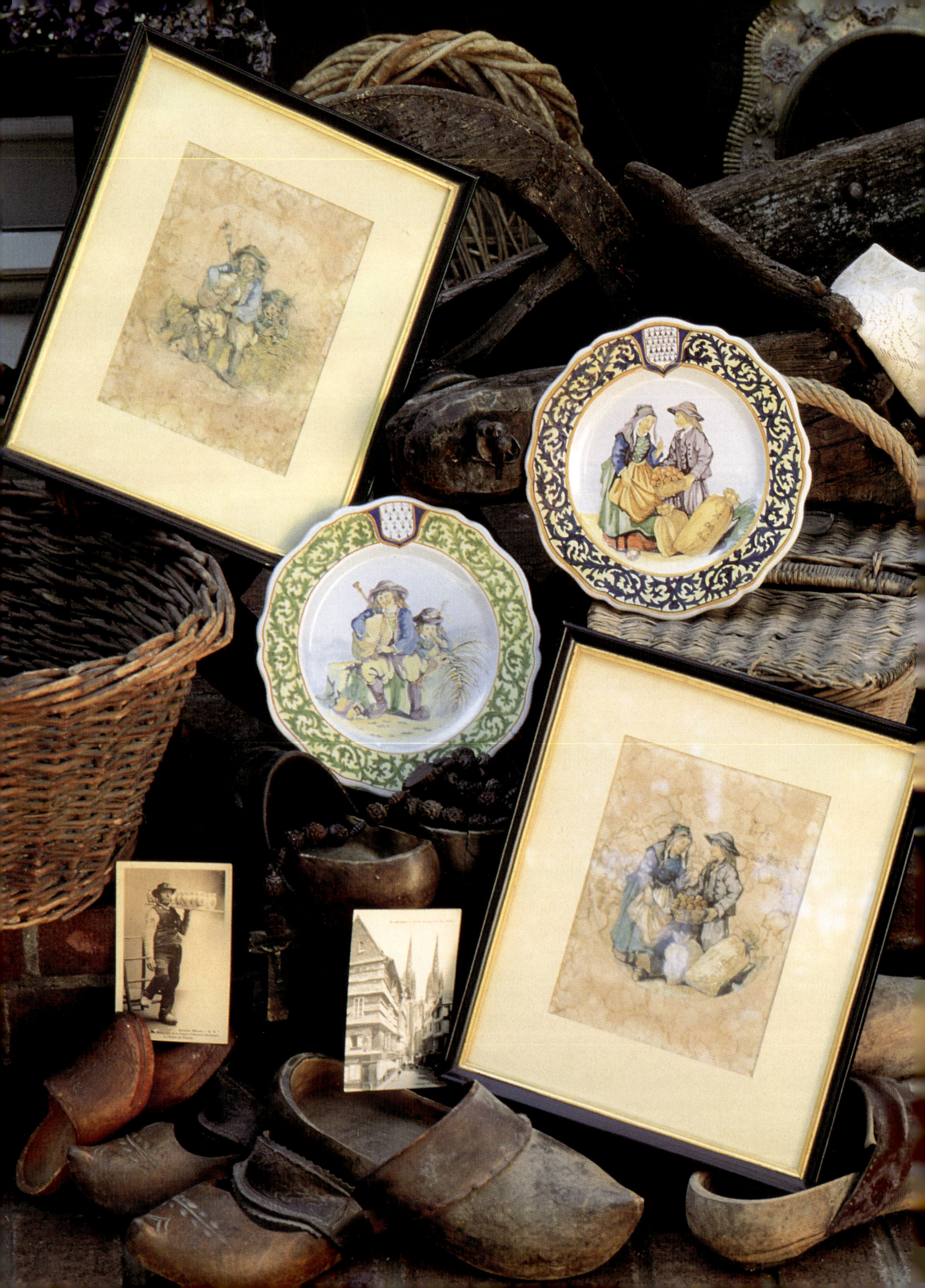

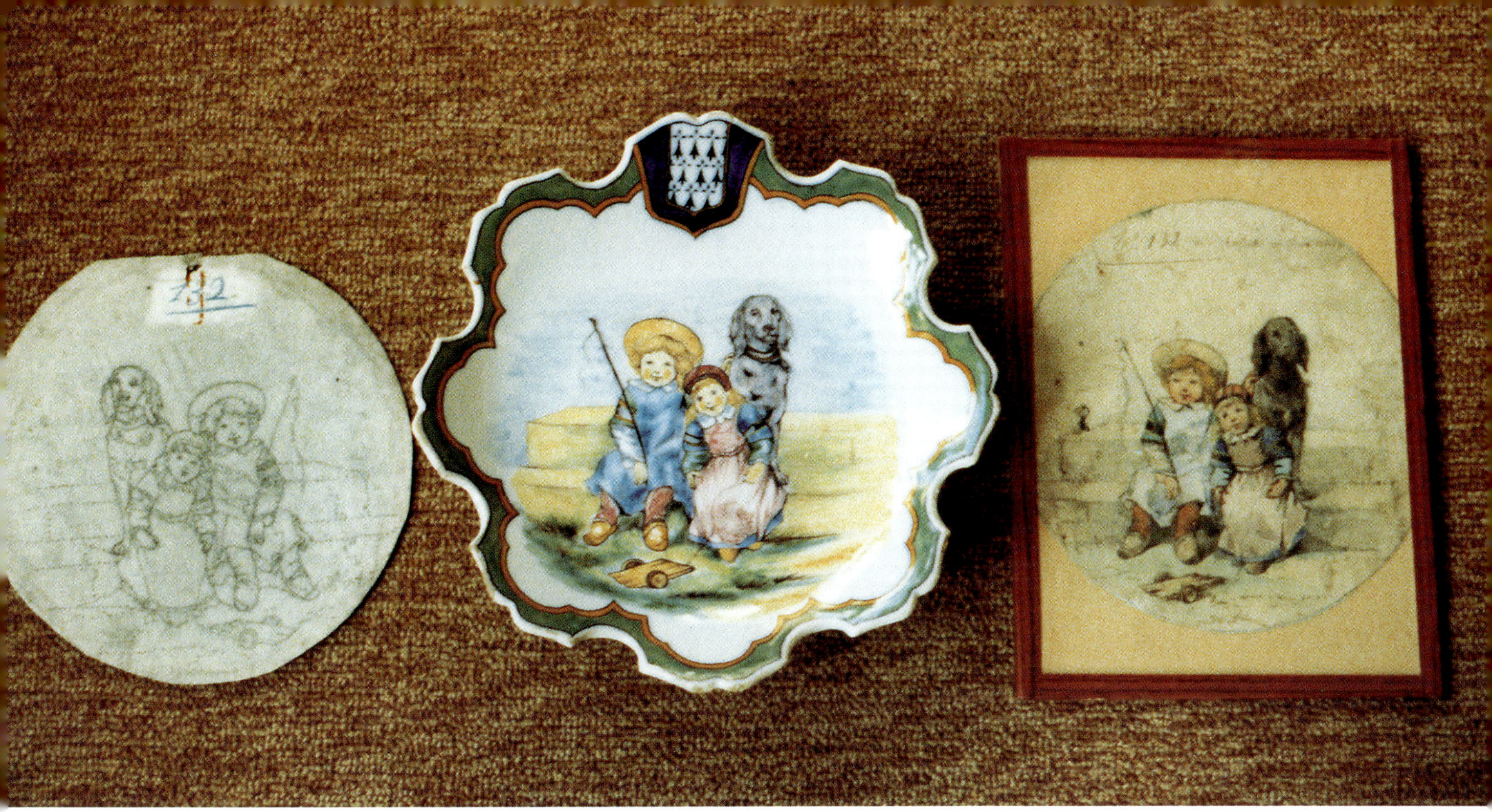

"ENFANTS au CHIEN NOIR" (Children with a Black Dog) The final product, a plate with the "Scène bretonne" entitled "Enfants au Chien noir", is seen in the center. To the left is the "poncif"; to the right is the original "aquarelle". Note that the "poncif" is reversed. Porquier-Beau. Circa late 19th century. *(Courtesy Musée des Faïenceries de Quimper)*

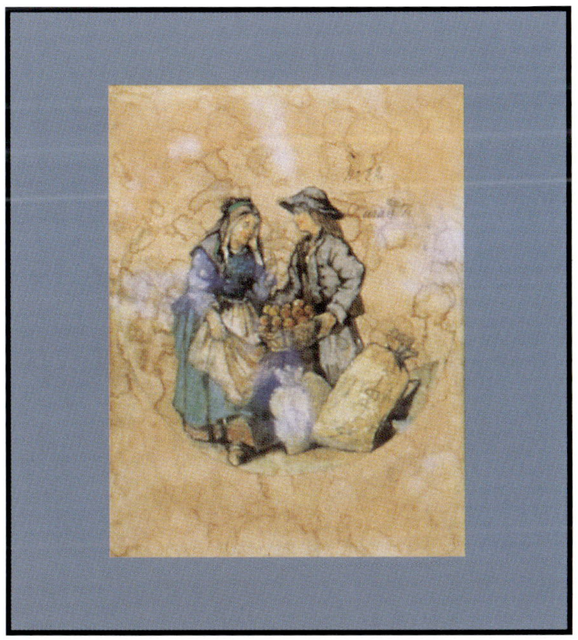

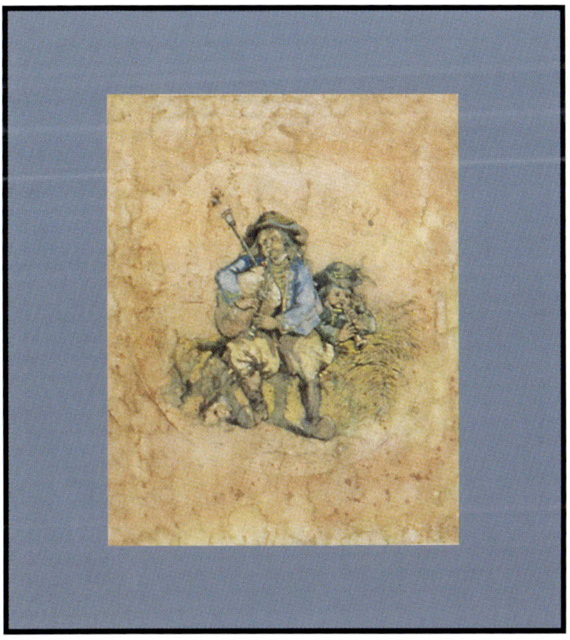

Preceding Page: Two framed "aquarelles", entitled "Gourin" and "Carantée", are re-echoed by their faïence counterparts. First Period Porquier-Beau. *(Collections of Didier and Susan Dorot and of the author)*

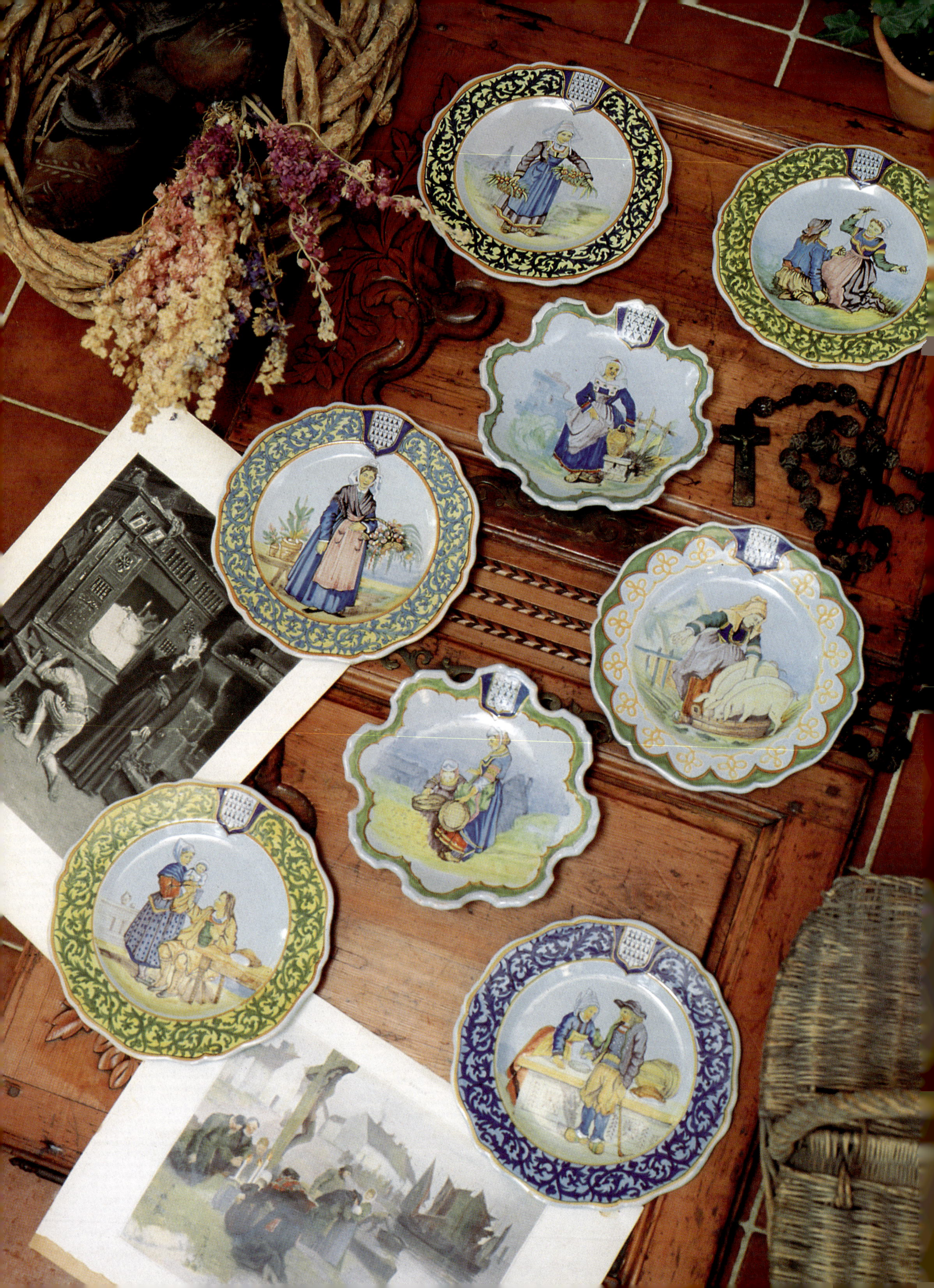

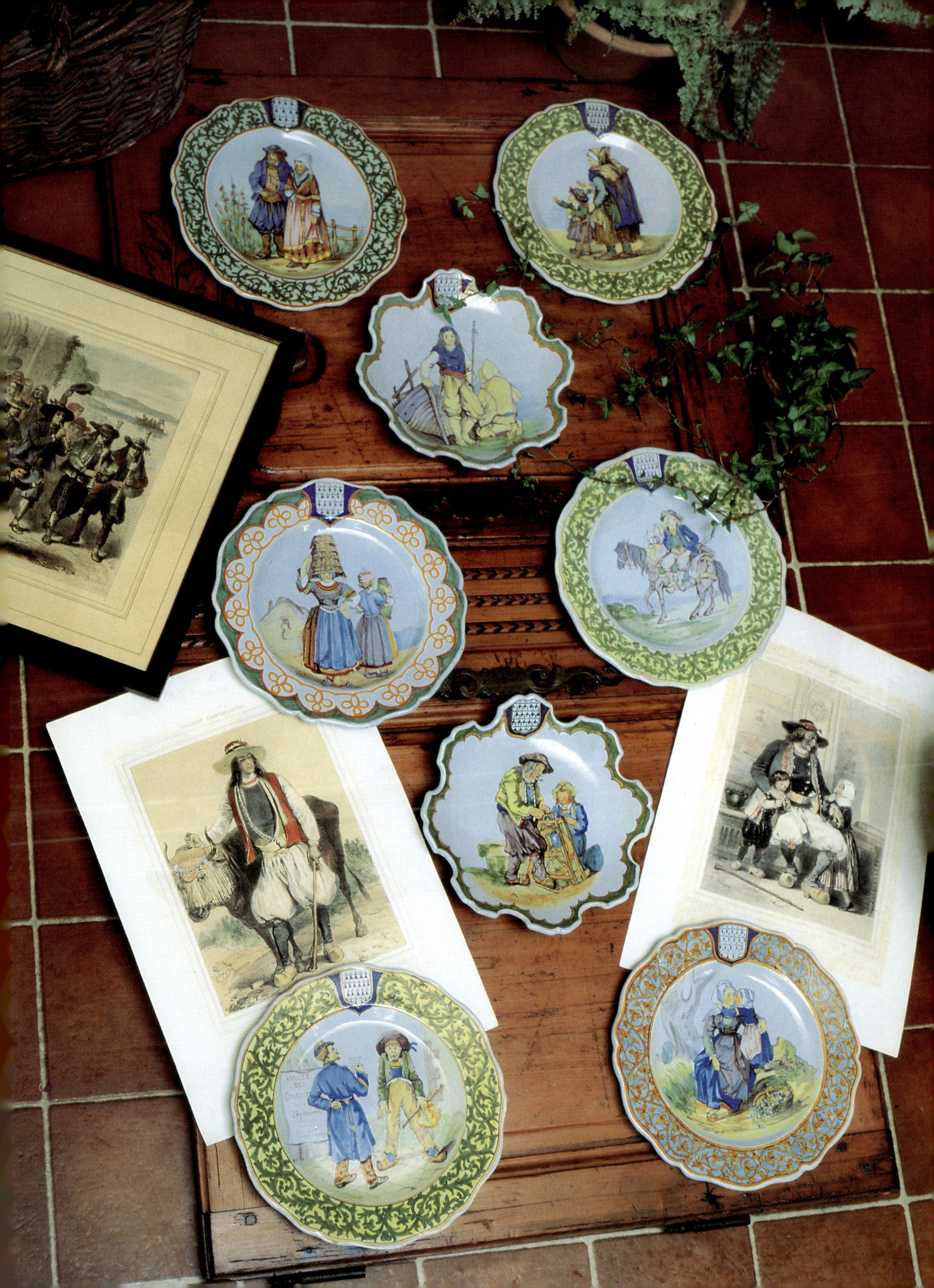

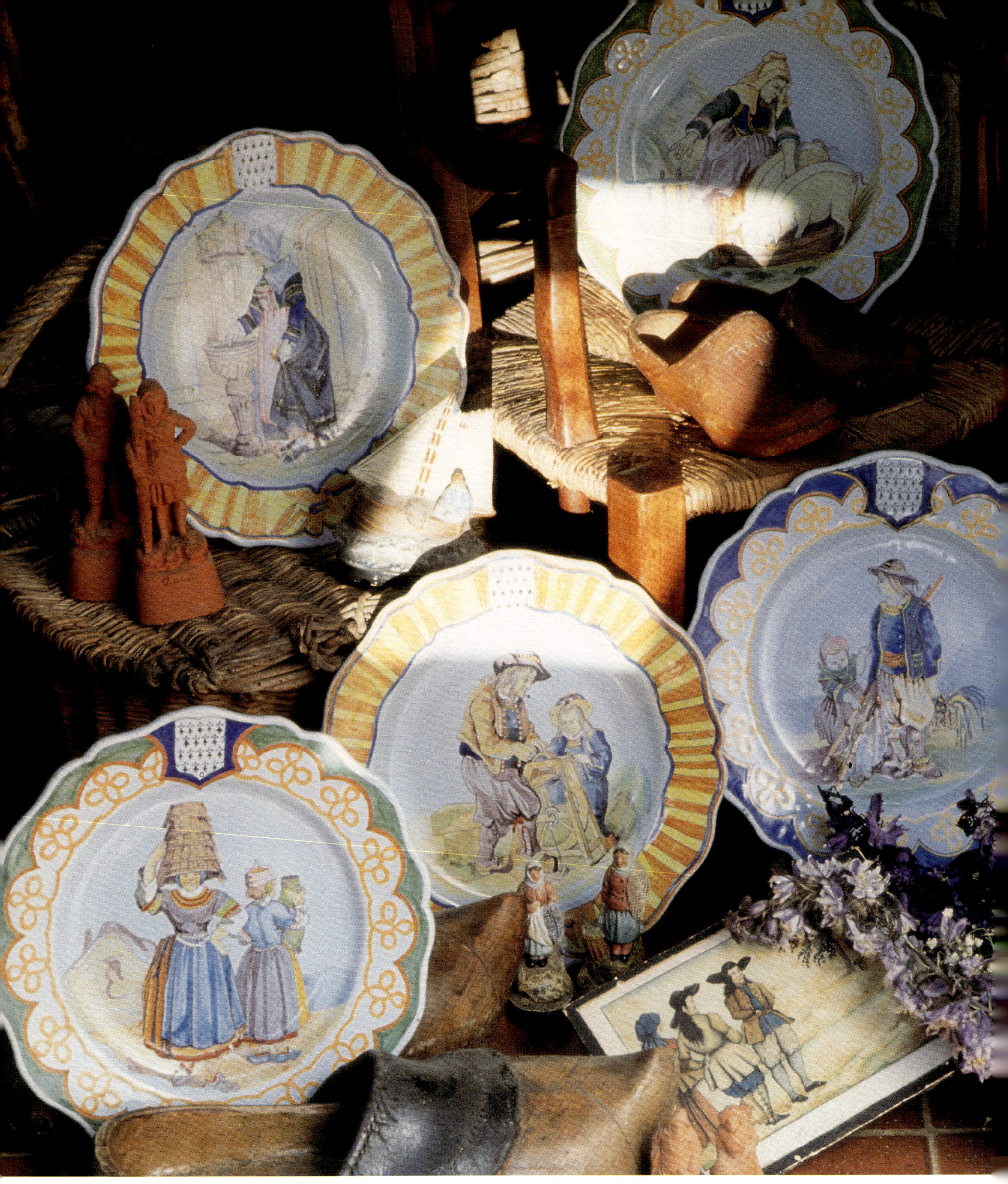

Above: Border variations on First Period Porquier-Beau plates are generally either a yellow ribbon trim or in a green and yellow "italianté" style. The blue trim on the plate to the right is much more uncommon. *(Collections of Didier and Susan Dorot and of the author)*

Preceding pages: A collection of First Period 19th c. Porquier-Beau plates and coupes in the "scène bretonne" pattern. Intricate details and a soft glaze palette make these examples among the most highly prized by collectors. Note the color variations in the acanthus borders.

The plate in the foreground is unusual: it depicts the conscription of a Breton youth into the military. *(Private Collection)*

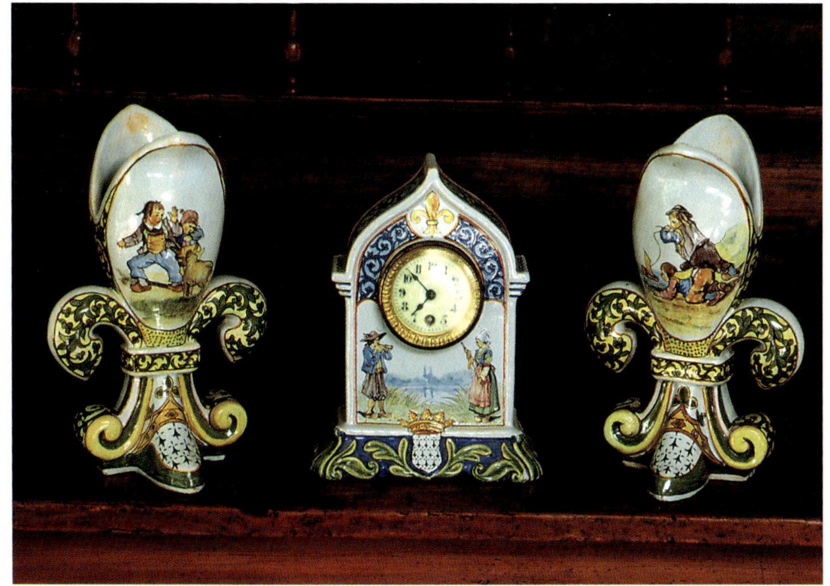

Photo 1: A matched pair of fleur de lys vases with the "Banalec" scene compliment a rare Porquier-Beau clock. Circa last quarter of the 19th c. *(Private Collection)*

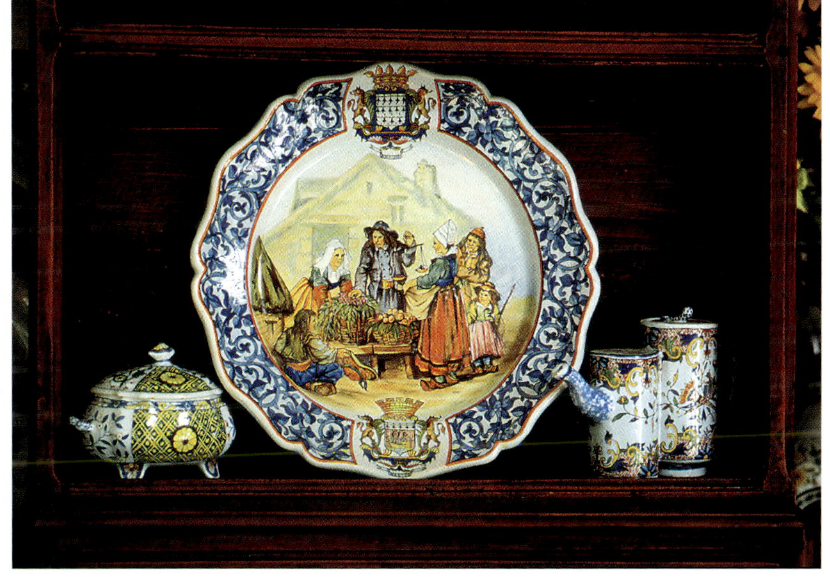

Photo 2: A 13.5" diameter charger with a Breton market scene entitled "Ploneis" which also incorporates the Crests of Brittany and Nantes in the design. To the left, a diminutive covered tureen in a rare "chinoiserie" pattern. To the right, a double chambered teapot in the "au carquois" (quiver and torch) Rouen pattern. First Period Porquier-Beau. *(Private Collection)*

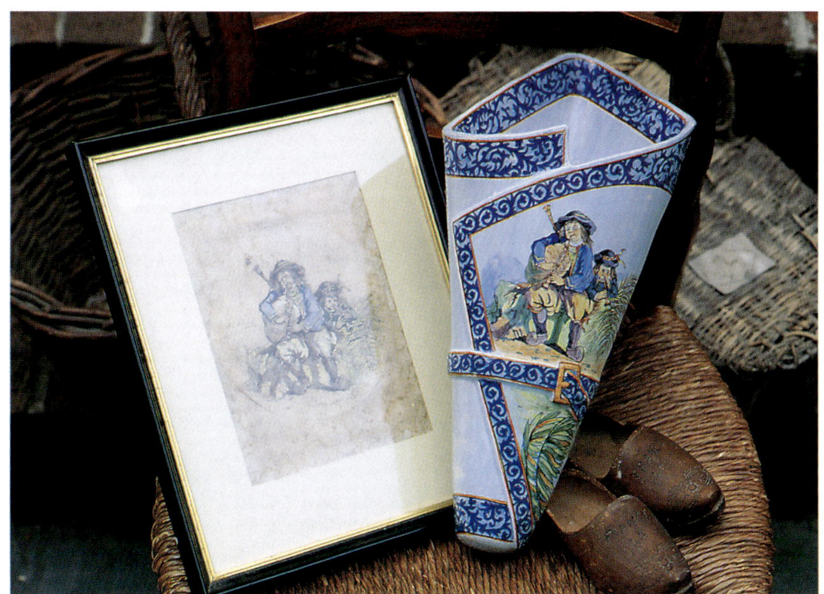

Photo 3: Entitled "Gourin" this 16.5" wall pocket is complemented by its mirror image in the original aquarelle beside it. First Period Porquier-Beau. *(Private Collection)*

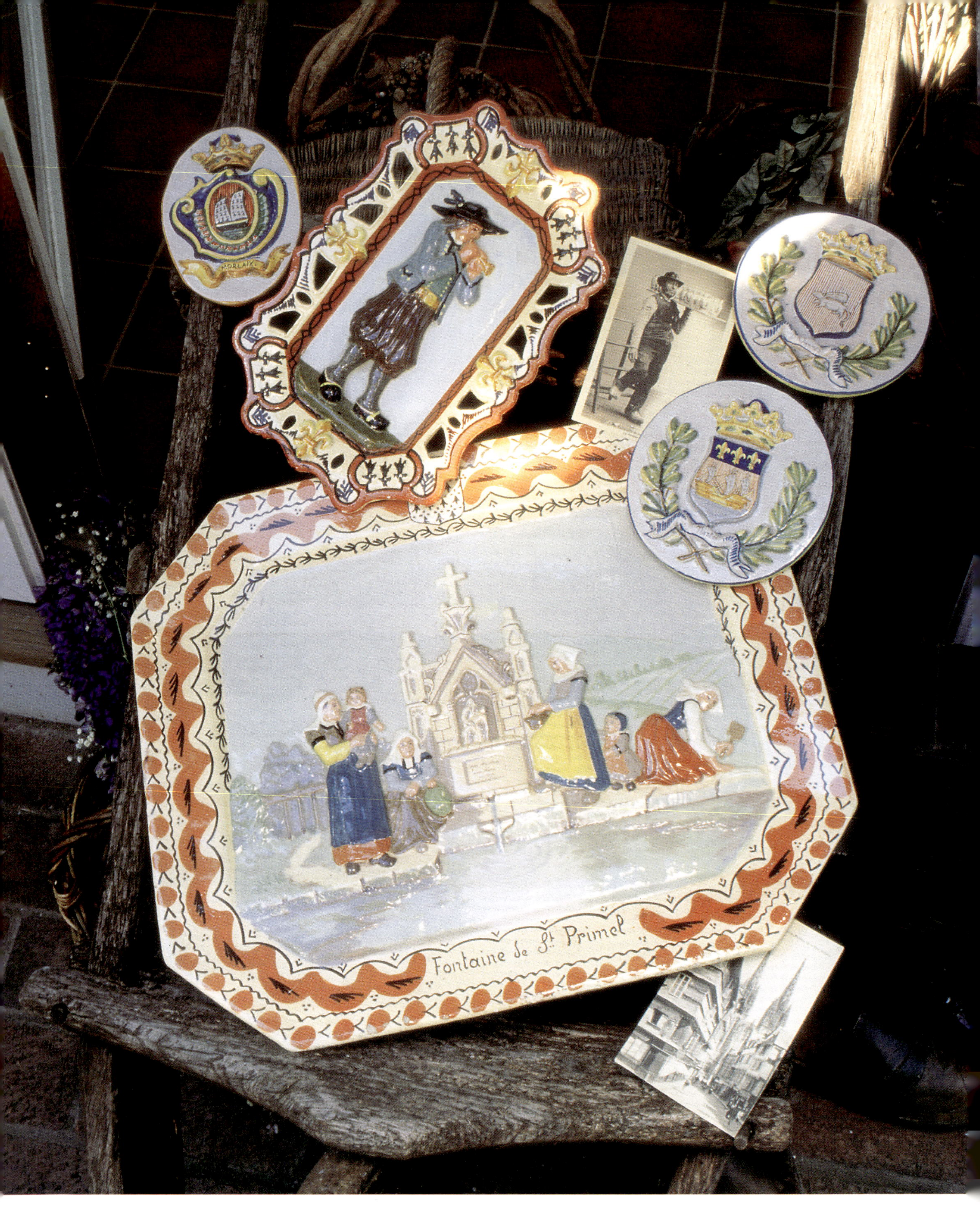

Examples done in base relief: Crest of Morlaix (AP), Crest of Vannes and Nantes (HB). The large plaque is entitled, "Fontaine de Ste. Primel" and together with the flutist example gives a good representation of this genre under Porquier-Beau. Beau's figurines and plaques were stylistically different from his tableware. Usually simple in detail, the colors employed were muted and tended to browns, beiges, greys and terra cottas. Circa last quarter 19th Century. *(Private Collection)*

Chapter 5

The Dumaine-Tanquerey-Henriot Factory

The third factory at Quimper was established in 1778. The founder, Guillaume Dumaine, emigrated to Loc Maria from Ger. When Dumaine left Normandy to establish his workshop, his family had been practicing the art of grès production for over two centuries. Because of the tradition which grès played in his family history, the stoneware formed the main bulk of the new factory's inventory. The wares were designed for practical use. Their shapes were strictly utilitarian: jugs, bottles, salt cellars, etc. The pieces were for the most part a solid brown color. Some were sparingly decorated with primitive floral sprigs, checks or daubs. Marjatta Taburet states that the naive patterns of this period were usually applied without the use of a paintbrush. The artisan would simply dip his bare finger into the color and proceed to apply the design.

Dumaine left the factory to his son, who was also named Guillaume, in 1821. The new director was soon stricken with a severe case of lead poisoning, which he had contracted over the years by working at the factory. He was forced to sell the business to his brother-in-law, Jean-Baptiste Tanquerey. Tanquerey had married Marie-Rénee Dumaine in 1821. He assumed the directorship about 1858 and continued to produce grès, while at the same time, diversifying the stock to include more faïence. His faïence pieces were decorated with simple Breton designs: geometrical motifs, large flowers, roosters or paint brush daubs and sponging. None of the wares dating from this period bear any distinguishing mark. They greatly resemble the pottery which the other two existing Quimper faïenceries were also making at this time.

After Tanquerey's death, his children inherited the business. One of his daughters married Pierre-Jules Henriot in 1864. It was his son, Jules Henriot, who took over the factory's management in 1884.

Jules Henriot devoted his entire lifetime to his faïencerie. He assumed the directorship when he was only eighteen years old. For over sixty years he guided, expanded and molded the Maison Henriot to his specifications. An astute businessman, Henriot envisioned the merger of the three existing Quimper factories into one corporation. The purchase of the Grande Maison HB eluded him in 1906, but the acquisition of the Porquier-Beau factory in 1913 was a step towards achieving this goal.

In order to distinguish his wares from those of his competitors, Jules Henriot began to use an HR mark about 1886. It did not become the legally registered trademark of the factory until 1904.

As stated in a previous chapter, the end of the 19th century was a renaissance period for Quimper pottery. The Breton style had crystalized. The tourists, who flocked to the beaches of Brittany in increasing numbers, found the ware to be an appealing souvenir. Its popularity grew, resulting in copies of the pottery being made in other parts of France, Italy, Germany and Japan. In order to protect the unique Breton style of Quimperware, Jules Henriot wrote "De la Protection des Faïences Bretonnes ou Faïences Quimper" (Protecting Breton or Quimper Pottery). This fiery sixteen page pamphlet, published in 1908, denounced the forgeries and called for a strict law to insure that the Breton style would remain the exclusive property of the Quimper manufacturers.

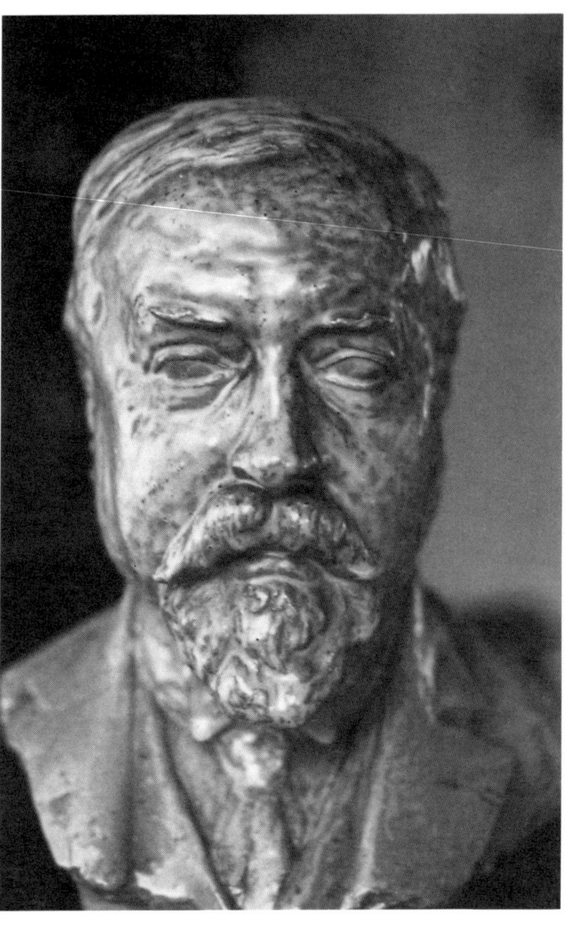

BUST OF JULES HENRIOT A legendary businessman, Jules Henriot assumed his factory's directorship in 1886. He added the Eloury-Porquier-Beau House in 1913 and envisioned the eventual incorporation of the Grande Maison HB. The dream of a single Quimper factory eluded him, as it was not until 1968 that the merger of HB and Henriot finally took place. *(Courtesy Musée des Faïenceries de Quimper)*

During the first quarter of the 20th century, several events affected the development of the Maison Henriot.

First, Henriot introduced an additional step in the glazing process. As always, the pattern was directly painted onto the opaque, white glaze. But now, there was the addition of an over-glaze which melted during the firing and gave a "flow" affect to the painted details. The soft, "watery" colors which resulted are considered to be the most artistically pleasing attribute of Quimper pottery of this period.

The acquisition of the Porquier-Beau factory in 1913 enriched the Maison Henriot by giving it access to all of Alfred Beau's sketches, patterns and molds.

A short time later, in 1922, Jules Henriot encountered a legal suit. The Grande Maison HB sued the Maison Henriot. It claimed that the "HR" Henriot mark was too similar to that of its own "HB" Grande Maison mark. The court decision was in favor of the Grande Maison. It retained the "HB" trademark, while Henriot was forced to change his "HR" mark to "Henriot" as his new trademark. Therefore, from 1922 to the present, all pieces from the Maison Henriot have been signed "HenRiot Quimper" in lieu of "HR Quimper". It is of interest to note that for several years after the litigation, both the "H" and the "R" in the new Henriot mark remained capitalized to connote the original "HR" mark.

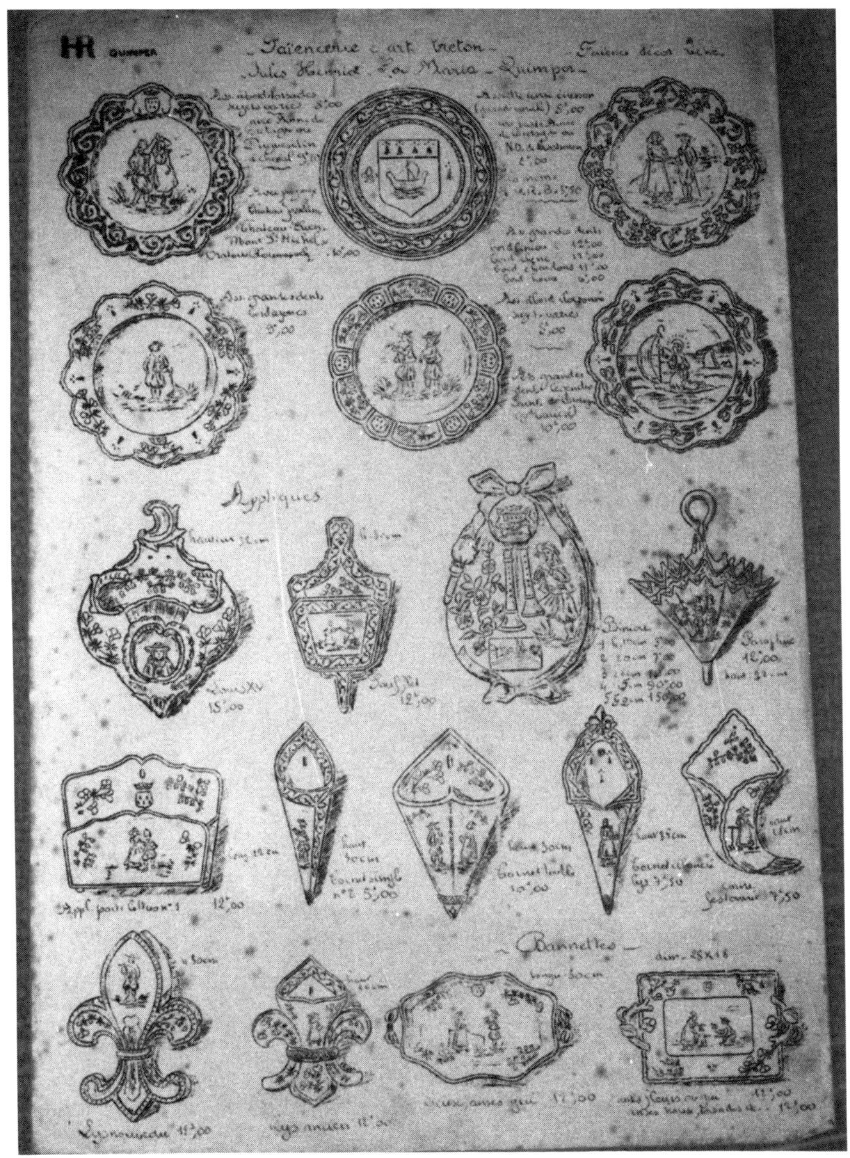

19th CENTURY CATALOGUE PAGE This reprint represents a page from a late 19th century, HR catalogue. *(Courtesy Archives of the Faïenceries de Quimper)*

In 1925, a disastrous fire swept through the Henriot factory. All that remained of the establishment were charred, gutted walls. The pottery was rebuilt on a new site. It was enlarged and modernized. A modernization of the pottery's style followed under the auspices of Mathurin Méheut. This noted Breton marine artist was hired by the factory to introduce the current trends in artistic pottery designs. During this period, the palette of colors employed by the Henriot factory became more varied and many of the patterns reflected an Art Deco or Art Nouveau quality.

Among the other 20th century artists who worked for the Maison Henriot are: J. Sevellec, Y. and S. Creston, Georges Fourrier, Galland, J. Bachelet, Armel Beaufils, Floch, Lenoir, C. Maillard, R. Micheau, L. H. Nicot, Blandin, Chevalier-Kervern, J. Haffen and Anie Mouroux.

The Maisons HB and Henriot merged in 1968 and were completely consolidated in 1984 under the auspices of the Société Nouvelle des Faïenceries de Quimper.

Chapter 6

Twentieth Century Artists Before World War II

The 20th century artists of both Quimper factories introduced a refreshing new style of faïence. Their modern insights contributed to the continuing evolution of the Breton character of Quimper pottery.

One group of sustaining influence was the "Ar Seiz Breur" (Seven Brothers). Founded in 1923 by Jeanne Malivel and René-Yves Creston, the association was passionately devoted to the preservation of Breton culture. Intensely interested in promoting Brittany's language, history, religious and folklore traditions, the original members were supported in their efforts by both the HB and Henriot Maisons.

Those associated with the Maison Henriot included: R.Y. and Suzanne Creston, Jeanne Malival, Mathurin Méheut and Robert Micheau-Vernez.

Those employed by the Grande Maison included: James Bouille, René Quillivic, Xavier de Langlais, Jules-Charles Le Bozec, Georges Robin and Pierre Abadie-Landel.

Artists of the Grande Maison HB

M.L. Bar: Madame Bar studied at the École de Beaux-Arts in Paris. A member of the Salons d'Automne and Nationale, she was the 1929 winner of the Prix Lecreuse. Madame Bar is best known for her figurines of marine birds.
(Examples pages 109 & 110)

François Bazin: Monsieur Bazin was born in Paris on October 31, 1897. His sculpture won the Second Grand Prix de Rome in 1925. In 1929, his monument "Aux Bigoudens" won both the Médaille d'Or au Salon and the Prix National des Beaux-Arts of French artists. Many of his examples are sculpted in terra cotta.

Bouvier: Monsieur Bouvier was born in Paris on July 15, 1881. A talented sculptor, the artist won a gold medal at the Exposition des Arts Décoratifs in 1925 and was a medalist of the Salon des Artists Français.
(Examples pages 108, 112, 125 & 126)

A. Porson: Madame Porson was born in Nantes. She studied in her native city with Chanteron and Fougerat. Later, in Paris, she completed her painting apprenticeship with Laurent and her sculpting studies with Gaucher. She was a recognized member of the Sociétaire des Artistes Français. While at Quimper, Madame Porson worked as a sculptress. The statue of "Sainte Anne des Bretons", her most popular example, continued to be reissued until recently.
(Examples pages 108, 110, 113, 125, 126 & 132)

René Quillivic: Born in Plouhinec in Brittany on May 13, 1879, Quillivic was a fisherman until the age of eighteen. After he nearly lost his life in a marine tempest, he took up the woodworking profession. The fine wood carvings which he produced to adorn furniture lead him to study art. He obtained a scholarship to the École des Beaux-Arts in Paris. Many of his molds for the Grande Maison were issued in limited, numbered editions. Quillivic was a major motivating force of the 20th century Modern Movement. He is recognized as a outstanding sculptor.
(Examples pages 106—108, 131, 150, 152, 153, 186 & 188)

Paul Fouillen: Monsieur Fouillen graduated from the École des Beaux-Arts in Nantes. He worked as an artist for the Grande Maison as a contributor to their grès line. He was later promoted to a managerial position. In 1928, he left the employment of the factory to establish his own faïencerie in Loc Maria. (Chapter 10)
(Examples pages 115, 116, 118 & 123)

Jos Kervella: Jos Kervella was born in Quimper. He studied at the École des Beaux-Arts in Paris and began work at the HB factory in 1938. Kervella sculpted large figurines which usually depict peasant folk dressed in their colorful costumes and engaged in a local tradition i.e. dancing the "gavotte" or returning from celebrating a "pardon". His style is simple except for the attention which is paid to the embroidery work which embellishes the costumes. He was also a decorator/designer of vases and tableware. These examples depict portrait busts of full length peasants portrayed in an Art Deco manner. *(Examples page 52)*

Georges Brisson: Born in Nantes on March 15, 1902, Monsieur Brisson was a talented colorist. While studying at the École des Beaux-Arts, he captured every first prize in competition. His talent as a colorist is exemplified in the grèsware which he produced for the Grande Maison's Odetta line. Many of Brisson's vases depict bold geometric patterns.
(Examples pages 110, 111, 114 & 116)

François Caujan (Fanch): Monsieur Caujan was born in Landerneau on July 22, 1902. As a young sculptor he was admitted to the Salons d'Autome, Tuilèries and Nationale. In 1925, the artist was a medalist at the Exposition des Arts Décoratifs in Paris. His special talent is his ability to meld the traditional themes of Breton Art with the modern style. He is perhaps best known for his groups of small figurines which depict traditional Breton activities: a religious "pardon" procession or the return of the fishermen from the sea. Examples of his work, which are signed "Fanch", are fairly accessible to collectors.
(Examples pages 112, 124—126 & 128)

Alphonse Chanteau: Monsieur Chanteau was born on May 18, 1874 in Nantes. He studied at the Concours Généraux de la Ville de Paris and thereafter entered the École Bernard-Palissy. In 1910, the artist was named painter of the Ministère de la Marine. In 1925, he was honored for his renderings of marine flora and fauna at the Exposition des Arts Décoratifs. Chanteau was also a fine engraver. He contributed to the Odetta line at Quimper, producing grèswares which bear the mark of his engraver's talent: decorative lines which are etched into the wares.
(Examples pages 114 & 115)

Louis Garin: Monsieur Garin was born in Rennes on June 23, 1888. His love of his native Brittany is expressed by both his paintings and by his architectural adornments of hotels and villas which dot the countryside. Garin illustrated various literary editions.

His grèsware for the Odetta line at Quimper usually depicts peasant folk in a simplified, stylized fashion.

(Examples pages 110, 114, 115, 117, 118 & 123)

Marius Giot: Monsieur Giot was born in Étoges on April 21,1897. He was a diversified artist who designed commemorative World War I monuments and was a member of the Sociétaire des Artistes Français. There his work was recognized by a bronze medal in 1925 and by a silver medal in 1929. Later that year, Giot received a gold medal at the International Exposition in Nice. His figurines frequently employ the use of animals as a statement of whimsical humor.

(Examples pages 110, 111 & 113)

Georges Renaud: Monsieur Renaud was born on August 20, 1901 in Paris. He was awarded the gold medal at the Exposition Coloniale for his ceramic patterns. He designed both figurines and grèsware for the Odetta line. His grès objects bear bold, geometric patterns. The figures of the Quimper man and lady, which stand on either side of the entry doors to the Faïencerie HB-Henriot, are examples of his work.

(Examples pages 70, 123, 125 & 131)

Georges (Jorj) Robin: Born in Nantes on July 12, 1904, Robin first learned the art of sculpting from his grandfather, who was a sculptor of religious subjects. He attended the École des Beaux-Art in Nantes and later studied under Dantel and Boucher in Paris. In 1925, he became a member of the "Ar Seiz Breur" movement in Quimper.

His sculptures, especially those of women, are said to express the interior Breton "soul". More often than not, his works inherently portray the poetic and mystical nature of the Breton culture.

Sadly his brilliant career ended abruptly with his untimely death on August 14, 1928. He was 24 years old. *(Examples pages 107 & 109)*

Berthe Savigny: Madame Savigny was a native of Quimper. Her talented sculpting ability was widely recognized by the Breton people. Her finest artistic contributions at Quimper are her baby figurines. These irresistible "bébés" with their soft, round, pudgy faces, express the sweet innocence of childhood. Their poses are natural and in many cases, touchingly tender.

(Examples pages 108, 109, 111-113 & 125)

Jean Lachaud: Monsieur Lachaud was born in Paris on December 27, 1898. A student at the École des Beaux-Arts, he travelled to Brittany as a young man and later became the Curator of the Museum and School of Fine Arts in Brest.

His first attempts at the Grande Maison appeared in 1923. This was a table setting utilizing the traditional themes of flowers and garlands, but boldly characterized by wide sponged borders of orange, blue or green. These works usuaily carry the fish mark i.e. a fish cut in half above the word Quimper.

His work also includes tableware created to celebrate "Armor", the land of the sea; "Argoat", the land of the forests; the Hunt, Fish, Fishing Boats, Sailors' Songs, Fishing Gear, Costumes of the French Provinces and the Flowers and Fruits of Provence.

Many of his dinner sets were made in grès. The colors were restrained i.e. usually only two or three shades of brown were employed. His decorations are simple and direct and are also reflective of the techniques which he employed in his wood carvings.

Jean Lachaud died in 1952 leaving a legacy which combined the art of realism with the Modern Movement spirit. *(Examples pages 52, 110 & 127)*

Jules-Charles LeBozec: Born in Saint Mayeux in 1898, Jules-Charles LeBozec attended the École des Beaux-Arts in Rennes. Later, he studied in Paris under Jean Boucher and Jean Dampt.

In 1930 he joined the staff of the Grande Maison and became the Vice President of the "Ar Seiz Breur" group in 1935.

His work was profoundly influenced by his Christian faith and by his Breton cultural heritage. His whole life was totally dedicated to his work as an artist.

A member of the Sociétaire des Artistes Français, Le Bozec was the recipient of several awards. "Méditation", the portrait bust of his wife, is perhaps his best known mold. He died in 1973. *(Examples pages 113, 125 & 126)*

Jacques Nam: Monsieur Nam was born in 1881. He was a Chevalier of the Legion of Honor, a member of the Conté de la Société des Dessinateurs Humoristes and of the Salon de Artists Décorateurs. Celebrated for his animal studies, he has a particular affinity for sculpting cats. His work is usually monochromatic grèsware.
(Example pages 79, 108, 110 & 111)

Brion: Monsieur Brion worked at the Grande Maison as a sculptor of large figurines. One of his most popular works, "Les Deux Vieux" (The Old Ones), has been produced for years and was recently issued again.
(Example pages 109 & 111)

Beauclair: Monsieur Beauclair was a prolific contributor to the Odetta stoneware line. He worked in imaginative, abstract geometric patterns.
(Example page 118)

Additional Artists: No biographical data is presently available for the following minor artists. Examples of their work can be found on the pages listed in parenthesis after their names.

Hagemans: (Example page 107)
Quinquand: (Example page 125)
Girault: (Example page 131)
Pascal: (Example page 133)
Marcharait Houël: (Examples page 110)
Nassivet: (Example page 132)
Le Floch: (Example page 131)
Rol: (Examples pages 111, 117 & 118)

Artists of the Maison Henriot

Bachelet: Monsieur Bachelet was a prolific Henriot sculptor whose work possess an angular quality. He executed several large and medium-sized examples of peasant folk. His figurines are usually marked with his initials "J B" and a small arrow. Although artist's work from this period rarely bears a date, the example found on page 65 shows a Bachelet piece with the date 1924 incised into the clay.
(Examples page 140)

Pierre-René and Suzanne Creston: Monsieur Creston was born in Saint-Nazaire. His two great passions in life were his love of the sea and the regional costumes of Brittany. Both of these were reflected in his designs for the Maison Henriot. His wife, Suzanne, introduced a blue and black on white ground tableware pattern. This was influenced by her fascination with local embroideries. Pierre-René Creston is considered to be a major artist. He was known by the Breton name 'Yannick".
(Examples page 141)

C. Maillard: Monsieur Maillard was probably one of the most prolific artists to work at the Maison Henriot. The style of his designs are singular in that they combine figural forms with utilitarian practicality. One example is a figurine of a young girl hugging a donkey–the donkey's open saddle bags accommodate salt and pepper. In another of his

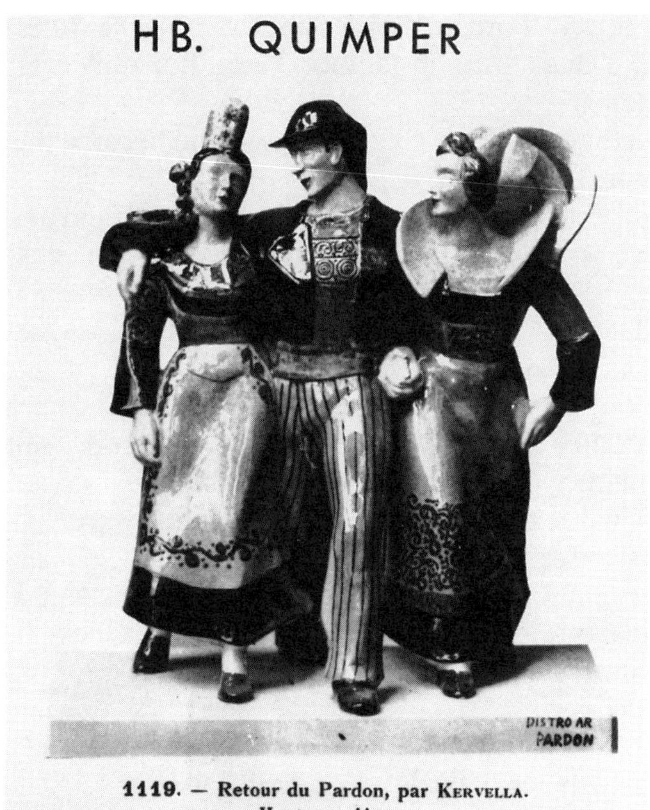

A large mold figurine by the HB artist Jos Kervella illustrates his appreciation of Breton embroidery. Note the care with which he embellishes the costumes.

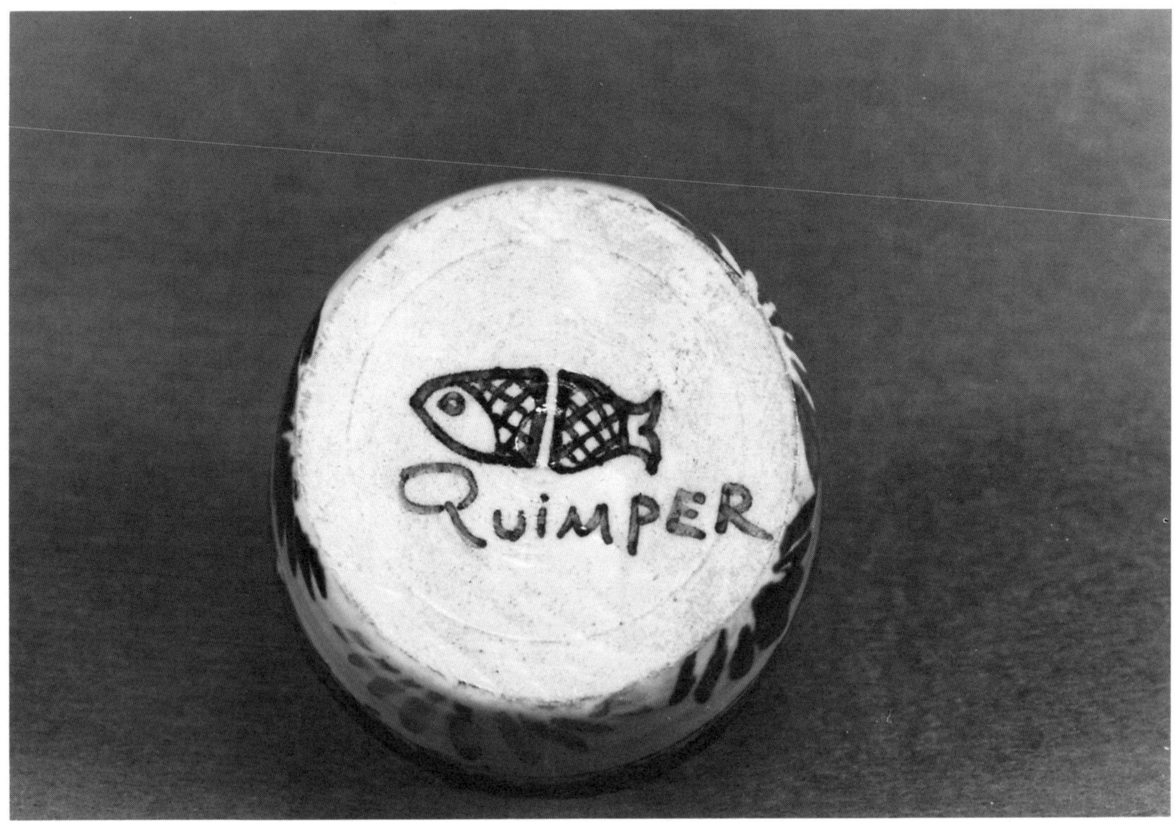

Several artists of the Modern Movement designed their own distinctive marks which were affixed to their designs. The half fish with the word "Quimper" is the trademark of Adolphe-Jean Lachaud.

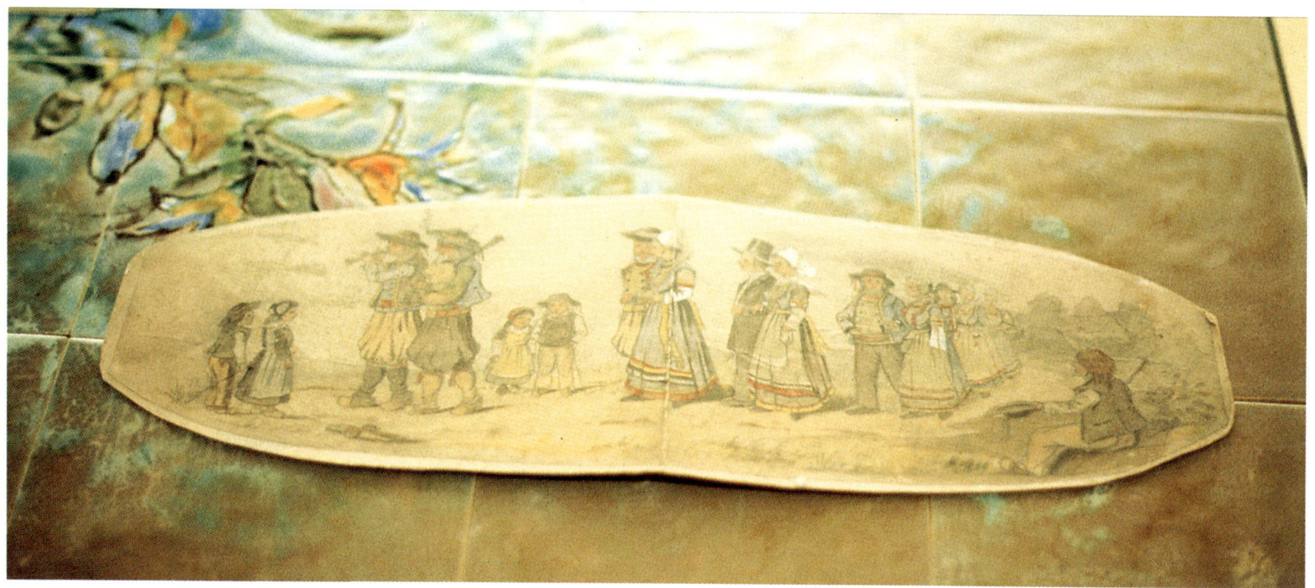

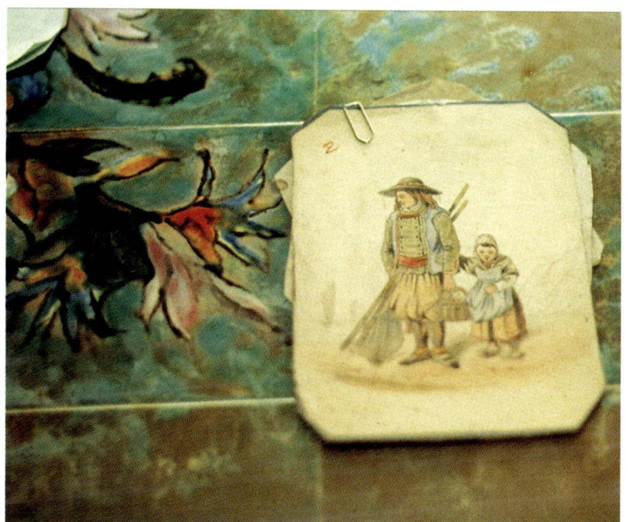

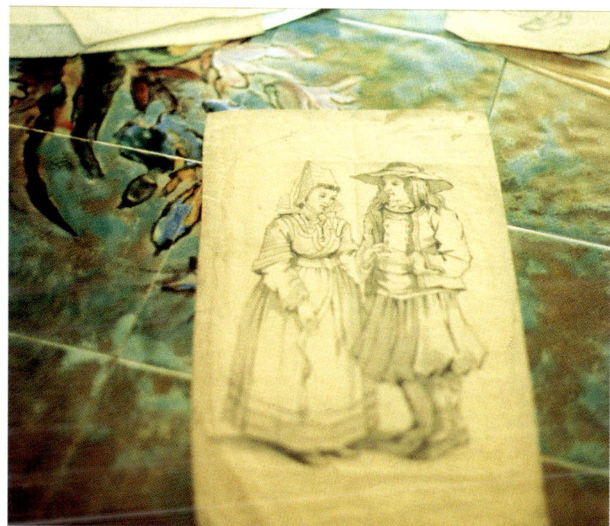

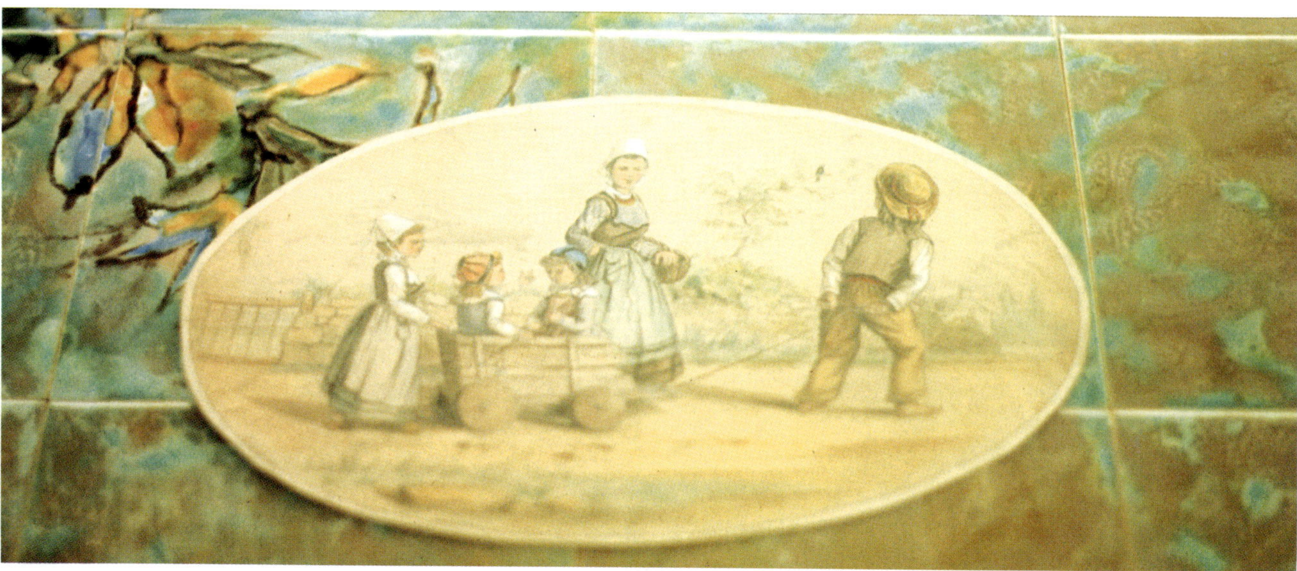

Treasures from the archives: a black and white pencil sketch and three aquarelles from the Porquier-Beau period. Emile Souvestre's book, "The Last Bretons" and the "Galerie Amoricaine" both serve as an inspiration for Alfred Beau's "Scènes Bretonnes". *(Courtesy Archives of the Musée de Quimper)*

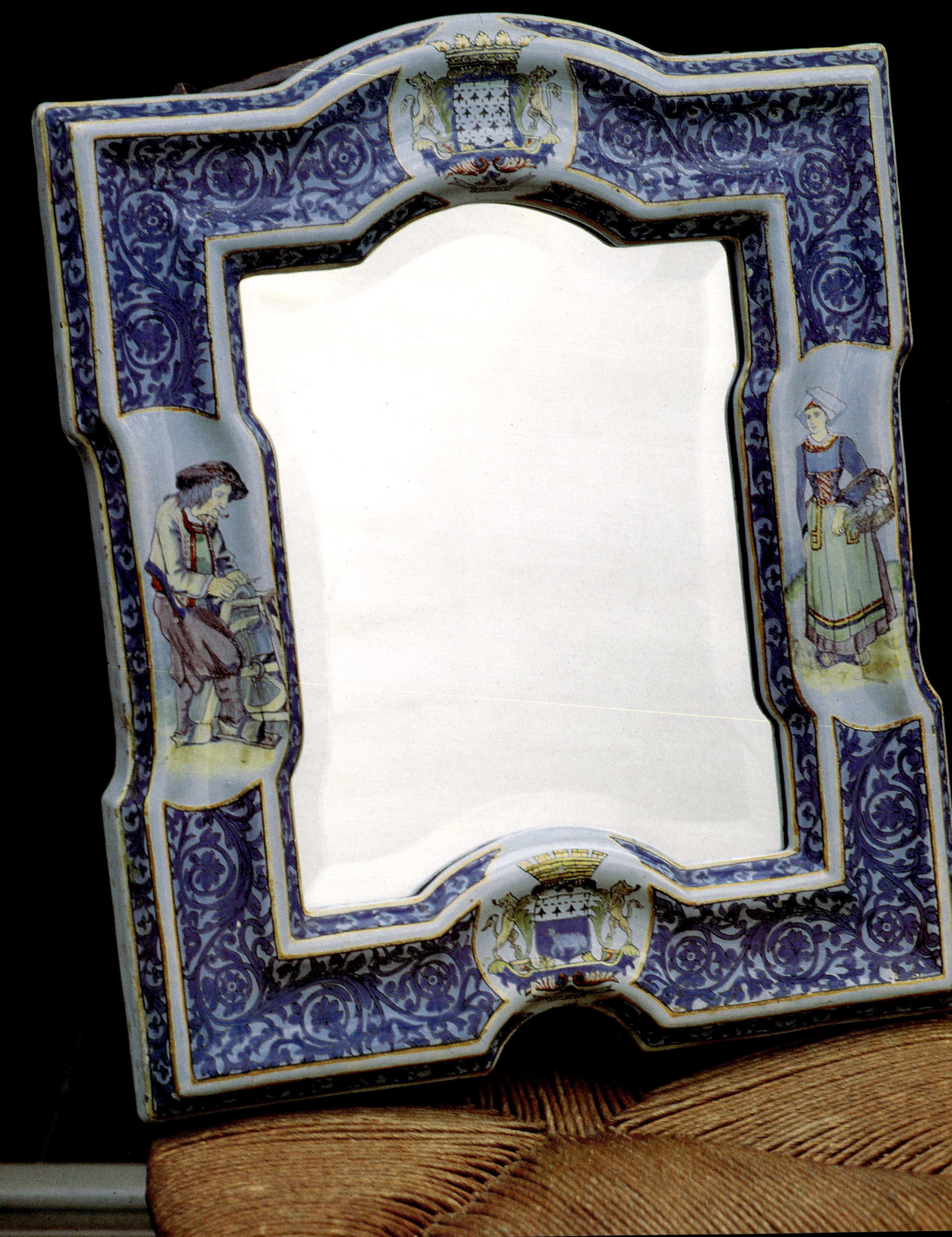

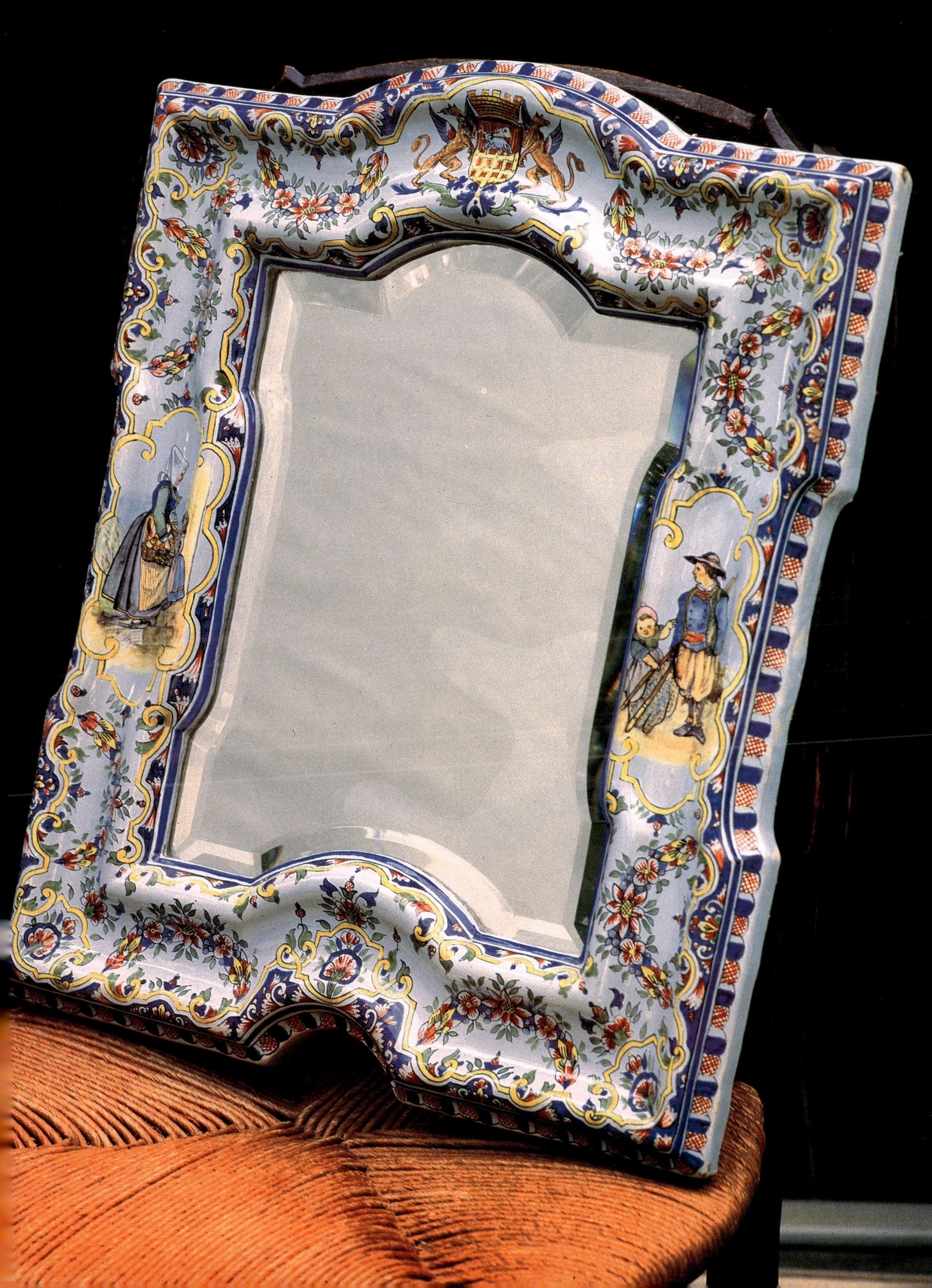

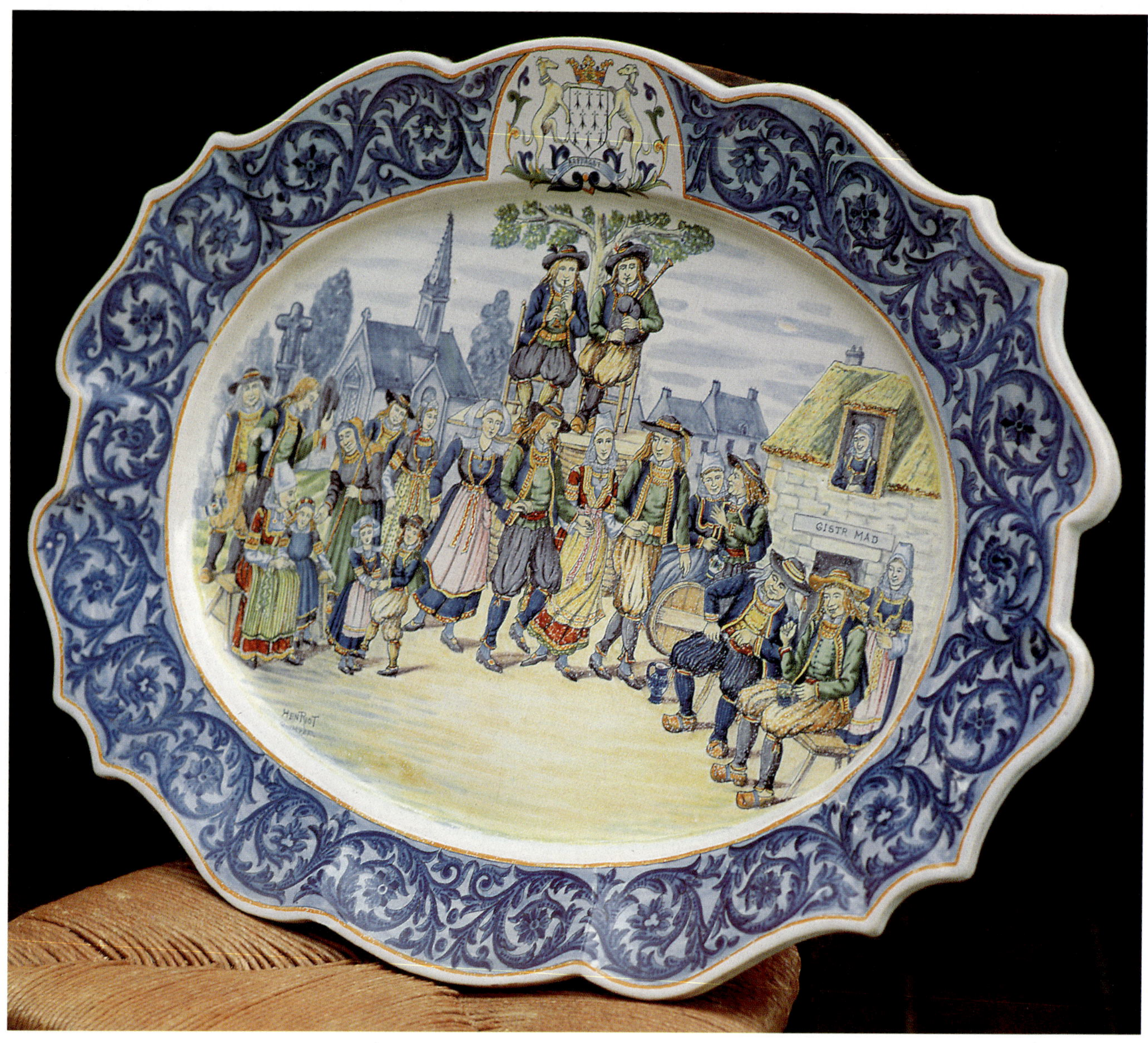

The 23.5" platter celebrates a "Fest Noz" (Night Feast), which is a communal gala commemorating the completion of major farm work i.e. planting or harvesting. Abundant details abound in this scene. Note the miniature Quimper pitchers and mugs which some of the folk are holding. Maison Jules Henriot; signed HenRiot Quimper. Circa 1920's-1930's.
(Private collection)

Previous pages: Twin mirrors from the Maison Porquier-Beau. The left example is decorated in the typical "Scène bretonne" manner with a blue on blue acanthus design encircling the cartouches. The right page exhibits a more atypical border with a Rouenesque interpretation festooning the frame. Last quarter 19th Century. *(Private collection)*

Following page: The "décor riche" pattern takes its name from the rich painting which copiously covers these examples. The charger (background) is entitled "La Danse des Puits" (Dance at the Wall) and is copied from an original art work by Théophile Deyrolle.

Frequently the same scene was repeated on various molds. Note the couple dancing the "gavotte" on three different pieces: the large vase, the umbrella wall pocket and the butterfly-rimmed plate.

HR or HenRiot Quimper marks save for the oval platter which is signed HB Quimper. Circa 1910-1940's.
(Private collection)

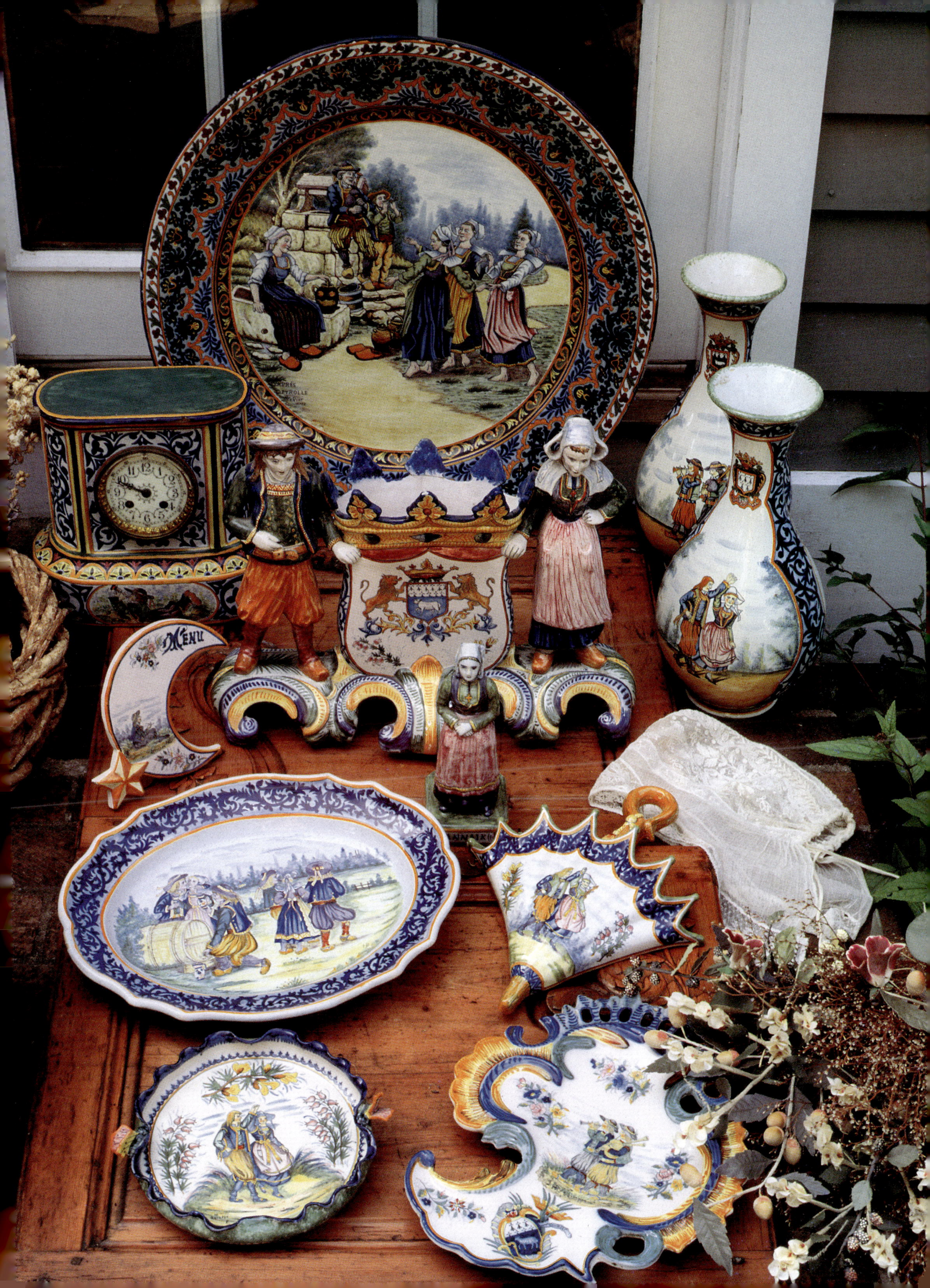
MENU

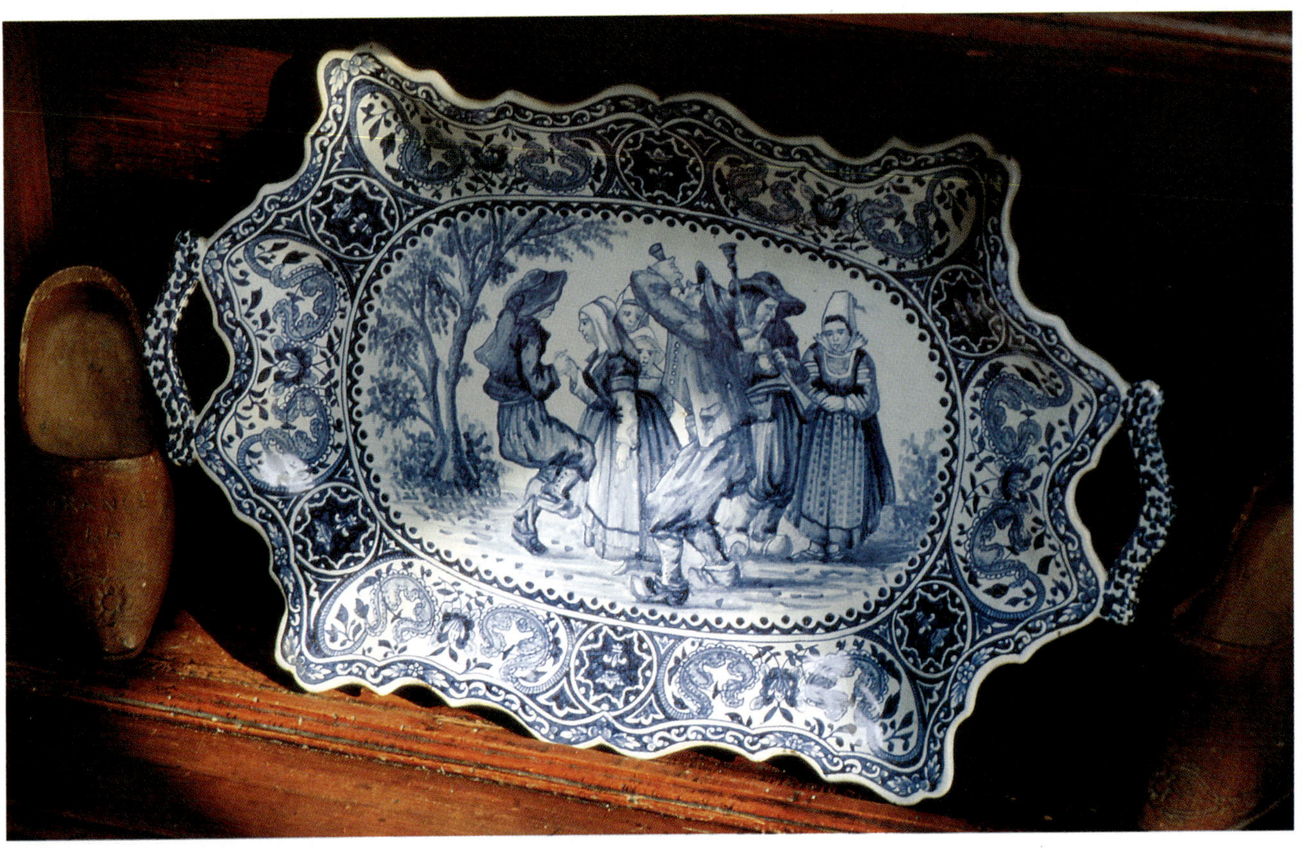

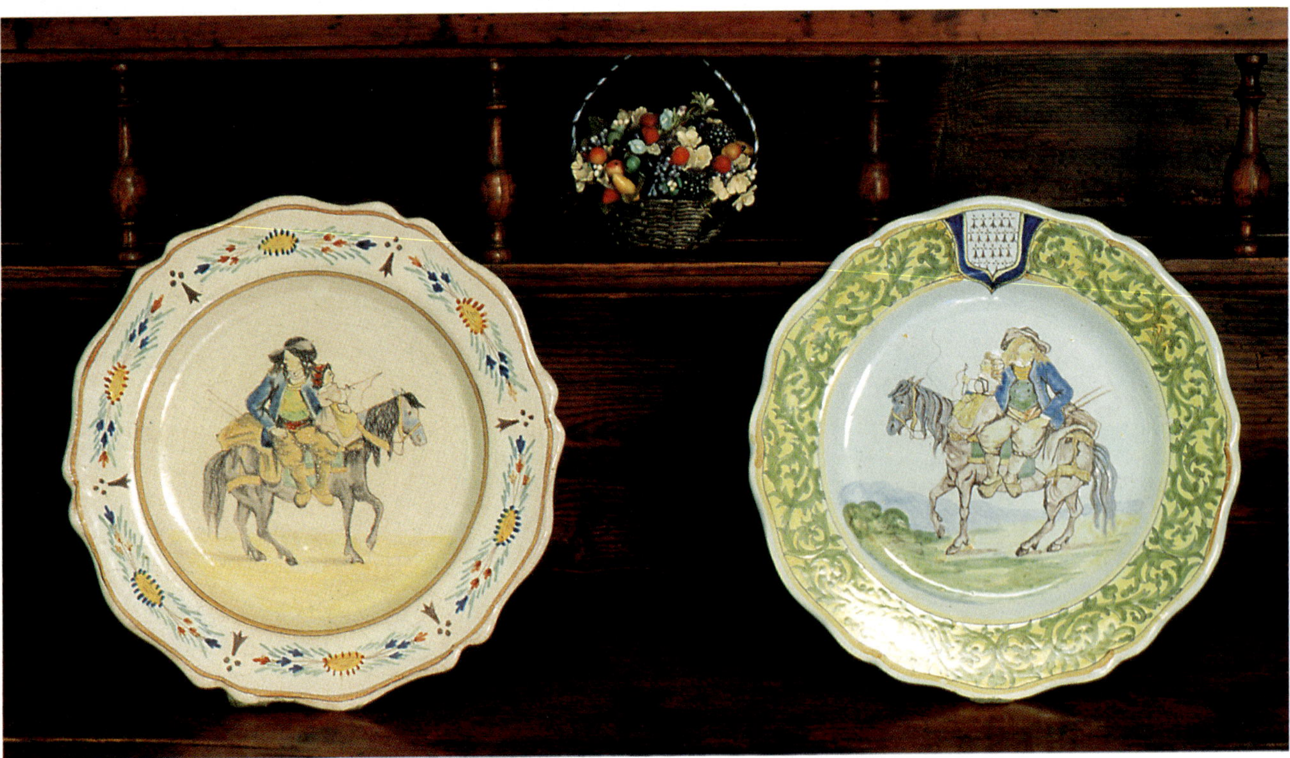

Photo 1: The use of blue and white in Quimper production probably reflects a dual influence: that of Chinese porcelain and that of Delftware. Here the typical polychrome palette of Porquier-Beau is set aside in favor of blue and white. Bannette circa last quarter 19th century. *(Private Collection)*

Photo 2: The famous dispute which arose between the faïencers of Quimper and Malicorne erupted because of Pouplard's blatant copies of Quimper's patterns. Seen side by side are the Malicorne (left) and Quimper (right) interpretations of the same scene. The ensuing lawsuit forced Malicorne to cease production of the Quimper patterns and to destroy all existing spurious stock. *(Private Collection)*

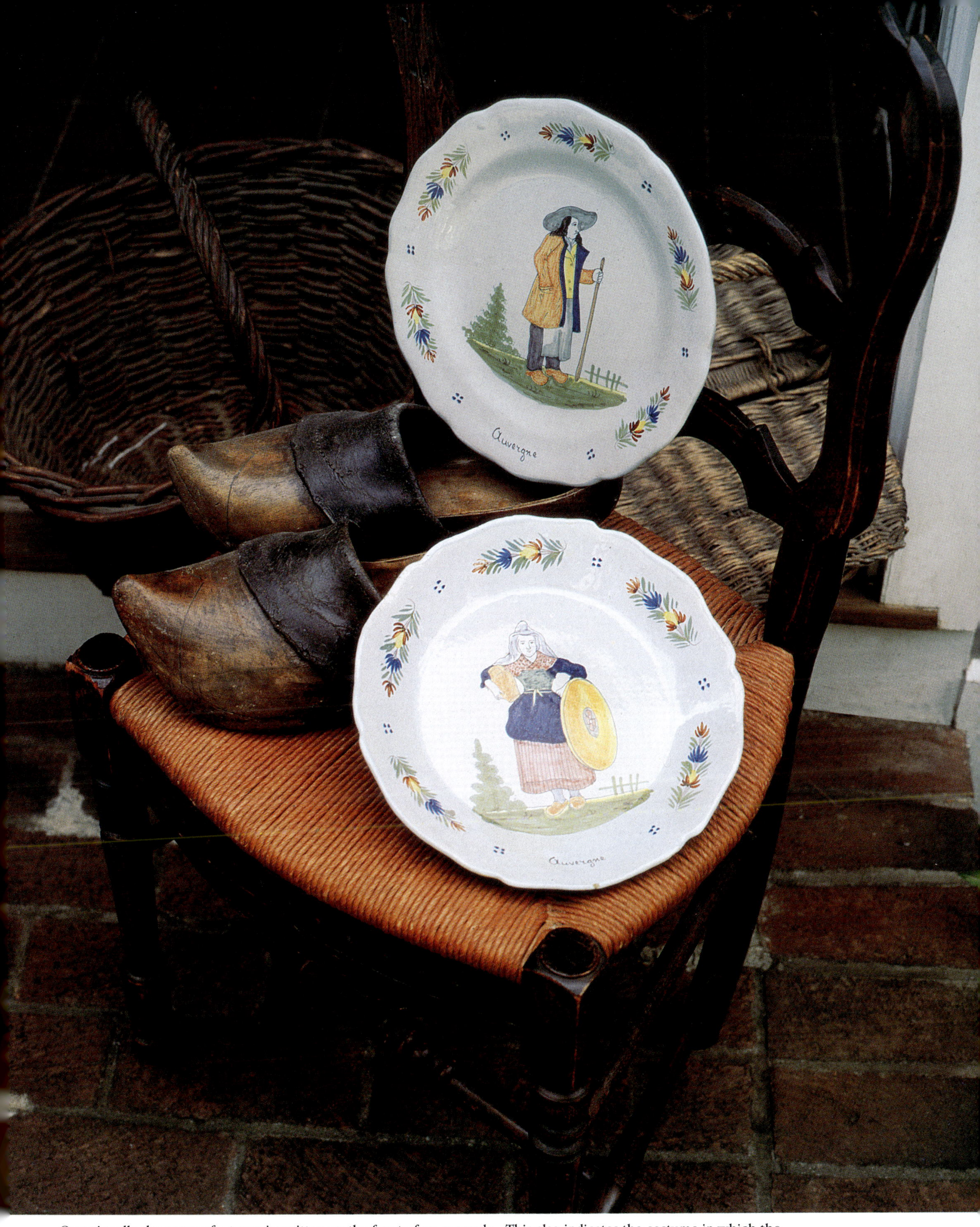

Occasionally the name of a town is written on the front of an example. This also indicates the costume in which the town's folk are garbed. Each village had a distinctive way of dressing, which was especially reflected in the women's coiffes and in the predominant color of the men's costume.

Pictured here are a couple from "Auvergne". Note that they are both wearing "sabots", the wooden shoes of the region. Maison HB last quarter of the 19th Century. *(Private Collection)*

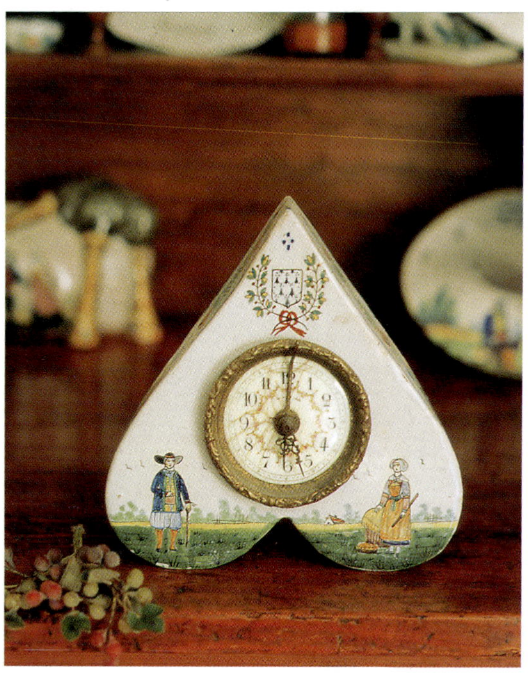

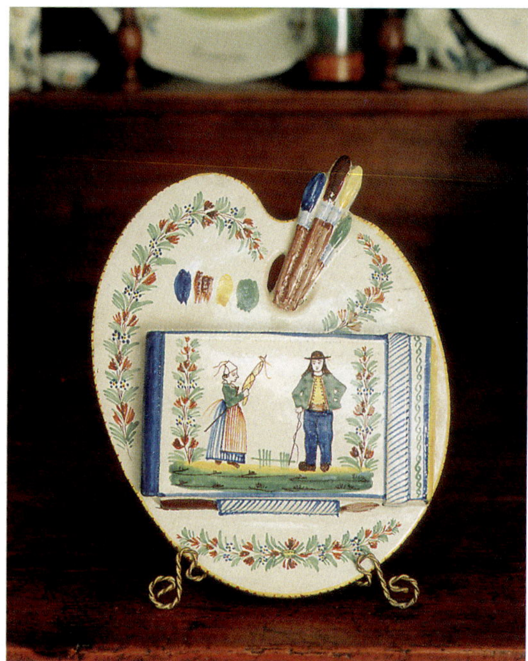

Top photos: An inverted heart-shaped clock from the Maison HB. The figurines are executed in the naive, detailed manner; HB déposé mark of 1883.
An artist's palette wall pocket dating from the same period, but signed HR. Note the distinct differences in detailing between HB and HR. *(Private Collection)*

Bottom photos: A rare grouping of asparagus plates with a highly unusual matching platter from the Maison HB.
A grouping of HR examples which are contemporary with the HB service. Although similar in feeling, the execution of the two factories differs in brush stroke, palette and composition. Last quarter 19th Century. *(Private Collection)*

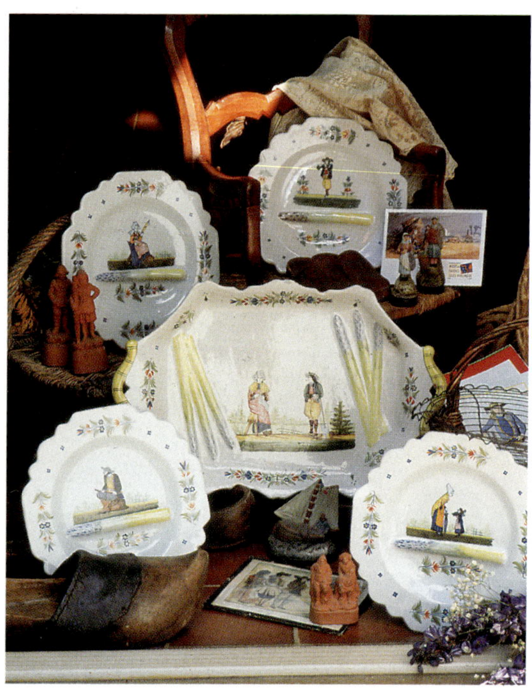

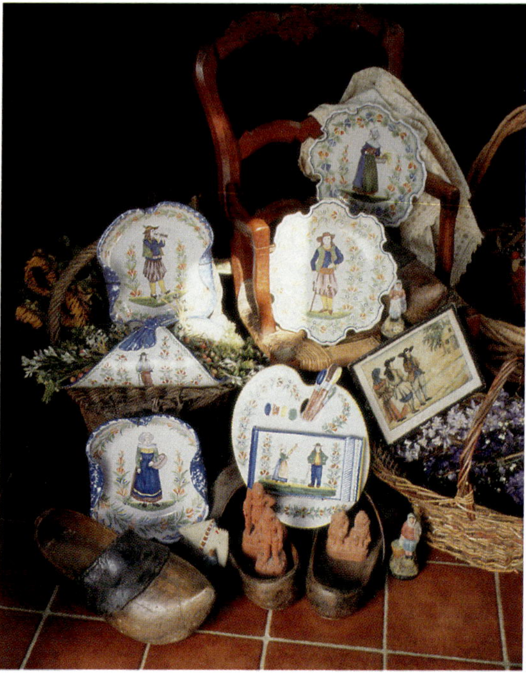

Following page: From the 19th Century through the present, Quimper faïence continues to delight the eye. Here a mélange of two centuries of production blends together in a completely complementary fashion. A Porquier-Beau cache pot rests besides an HB fish platter while a popular pair of HR candlestick people looks on. A variety of figural salts, an HR grandfather's clock and two HB plates form the background for a row of "secouettes" (snuffs). Tiny 3" tall figurines process in a line to either side of a Ste. Vierge. On the top right, a 19th Century HB fleur de lys inkwell rests beside a 1950's "service poupée" (doll's teaset). *(Private collection)*

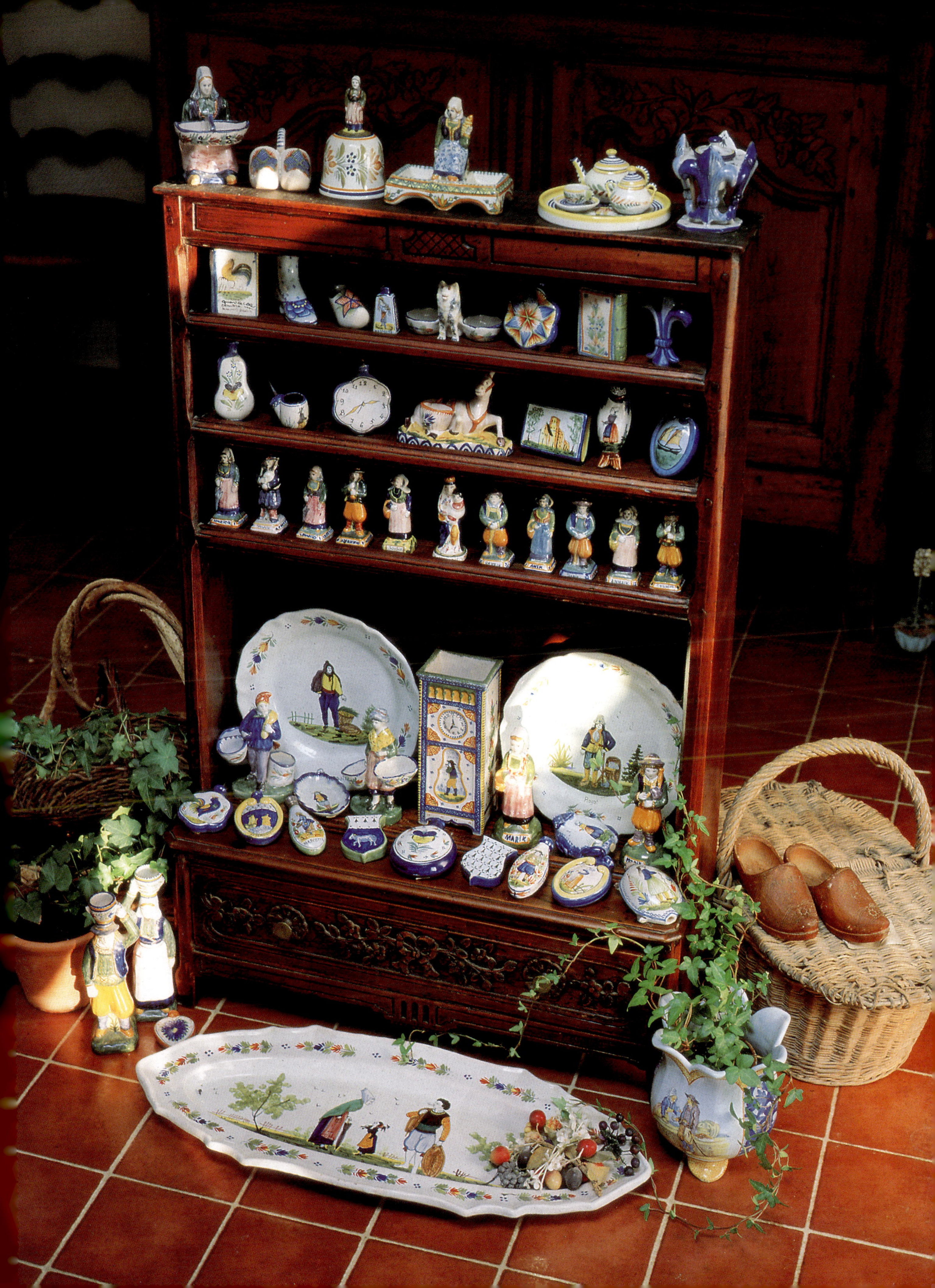

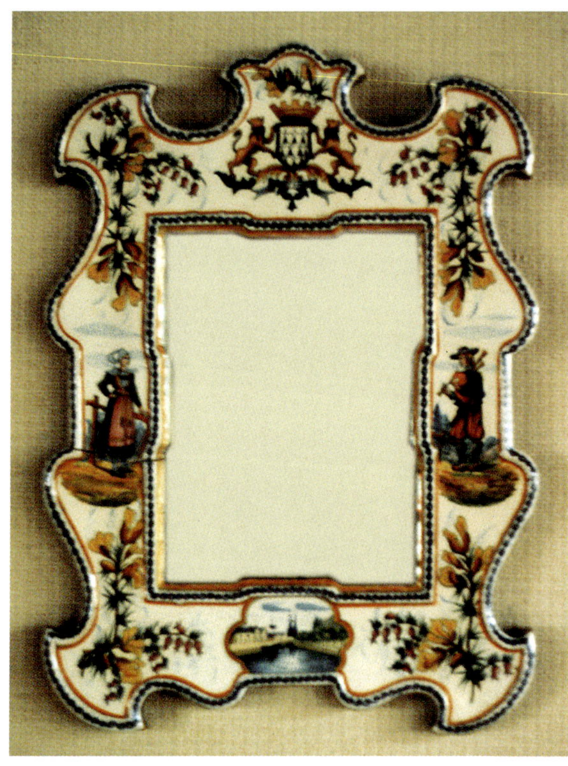

Photo 1: Here "ajonc" blossoms adorn a looking glass manufactured by the Maison Jules HenRiot. Circa first quarter of the 20th century. *(Courtesy Musée de la faience Jules Verlingue)*

Photo 2: Wild "ajonc" (gorse) blooms in profusion throughout the Breton countryside. Quimper patterns habitually draw upon the indigenous flora and fauna for inspiration, thus giving the pottery its' distinctive Breton character.

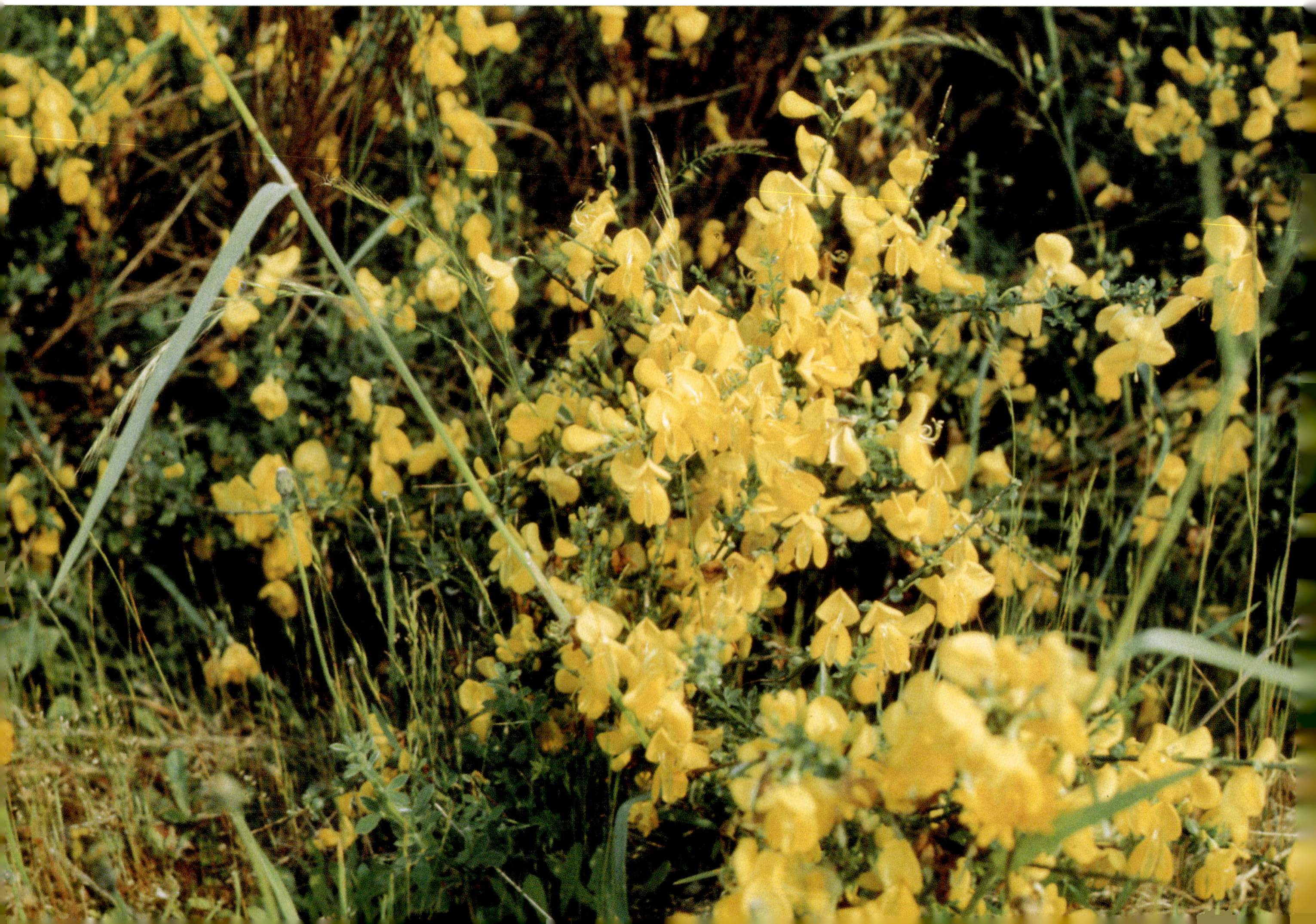

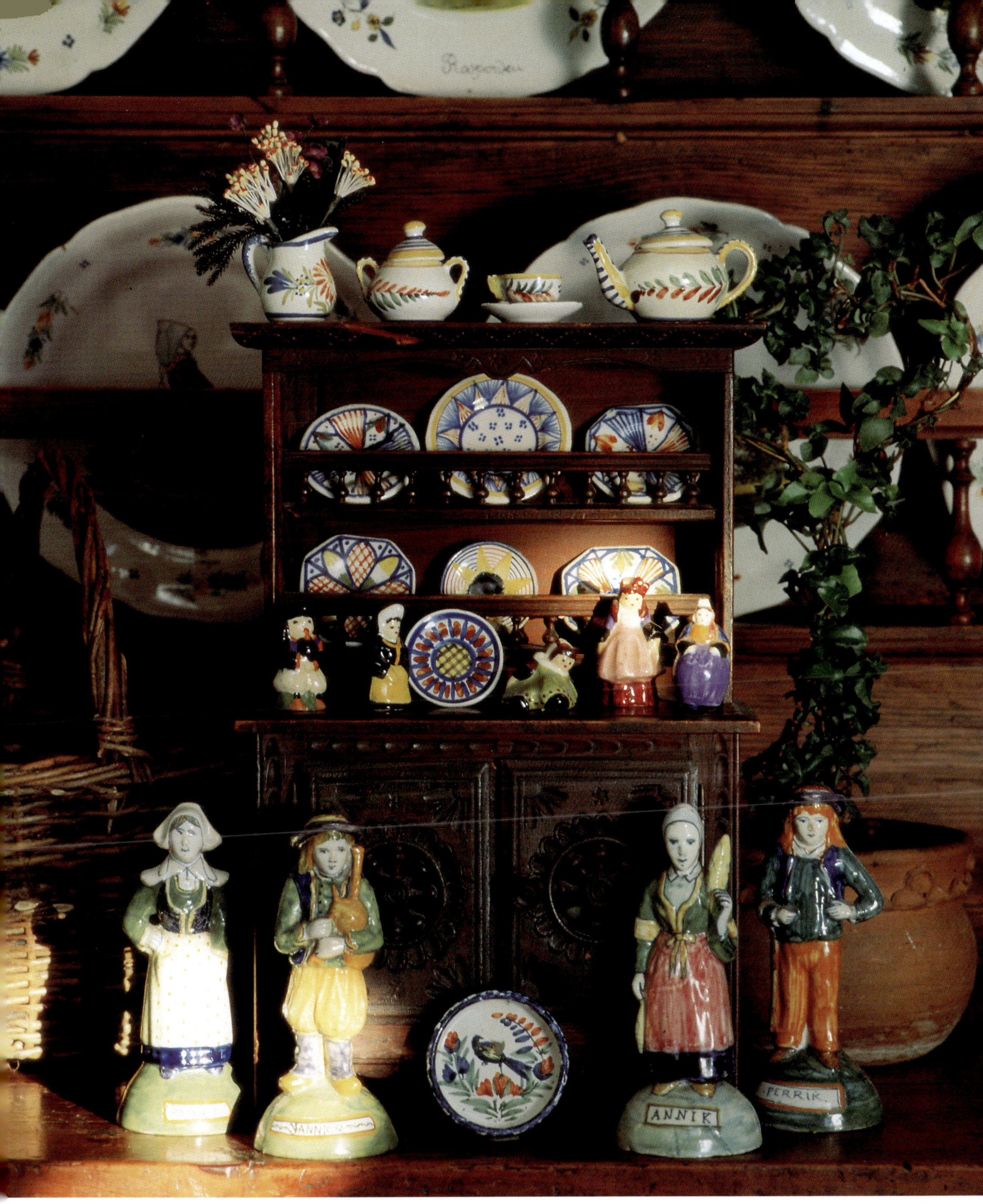

A diminutive Breton "vaisselier" holds a cache of 20th century miniatures. A group of 7" tall Maison Henriot figurines stand sentinel to either side.

Pieces made for children's play were a part of both HB and HenRiot production. Figurines were also very popular because of their charming three dimensional quality. The small copies of Breton furniture originated in Plozevet and beautifully compliment the Quimper miniatures. *(Private Collection)*

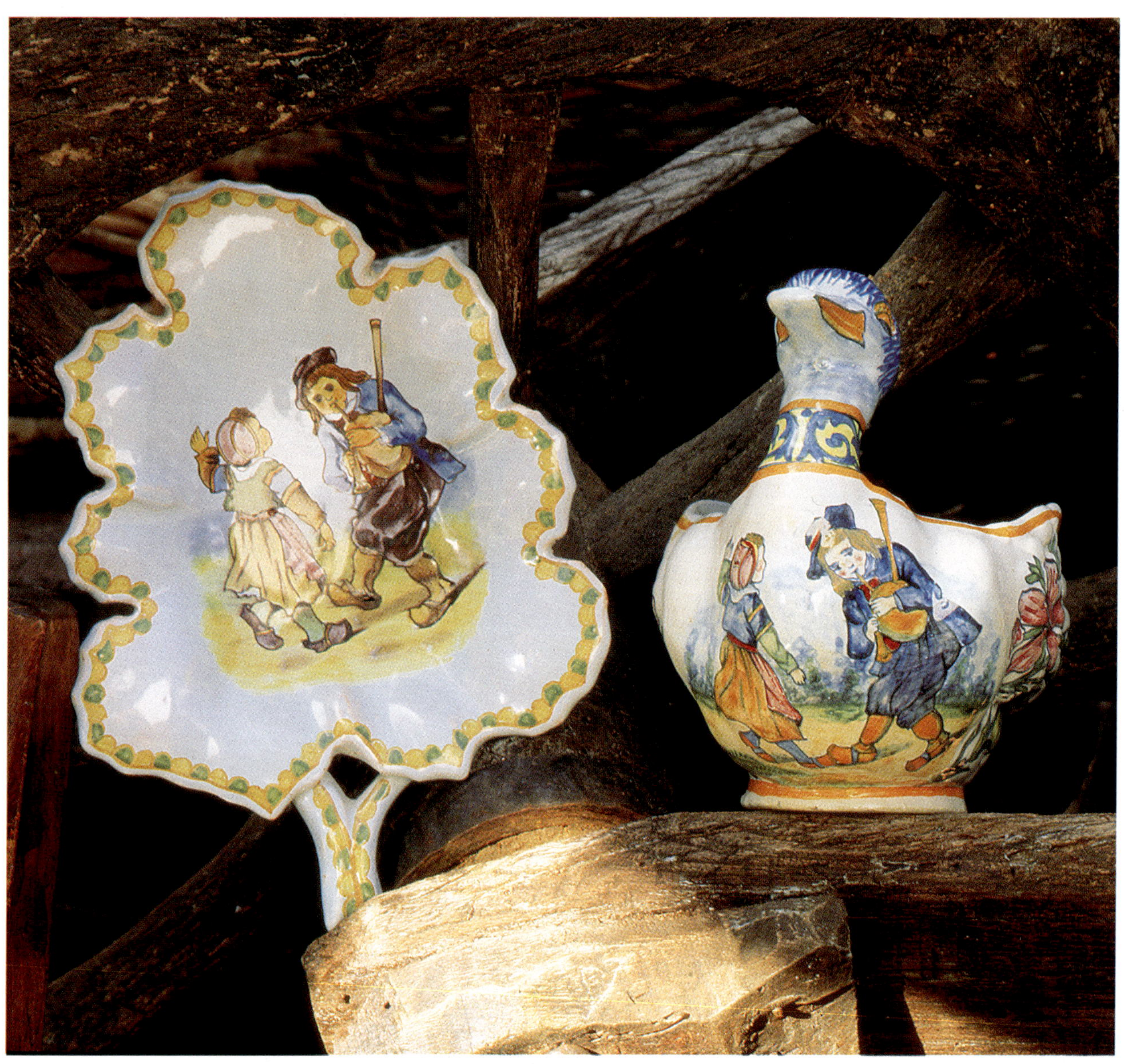

A frequently asked question is how to differentiate between First and Second Period Porquier-Beau. Illustrated here are a First Period leaf dish and a Second Period duck each with the scene of "Banalec". First Period examples have a soft, pale blue tint to their glaze, a fragility of color and very fine detailing. Second Period pieces were re-issues under Jules HenRiot. In contrast their glaze is white, the color palette stronger and the details are not refined. Lastly, the Second Period pieces usually have the word "Quimper" added to the intersecting PB mark. *(Private Collection)*

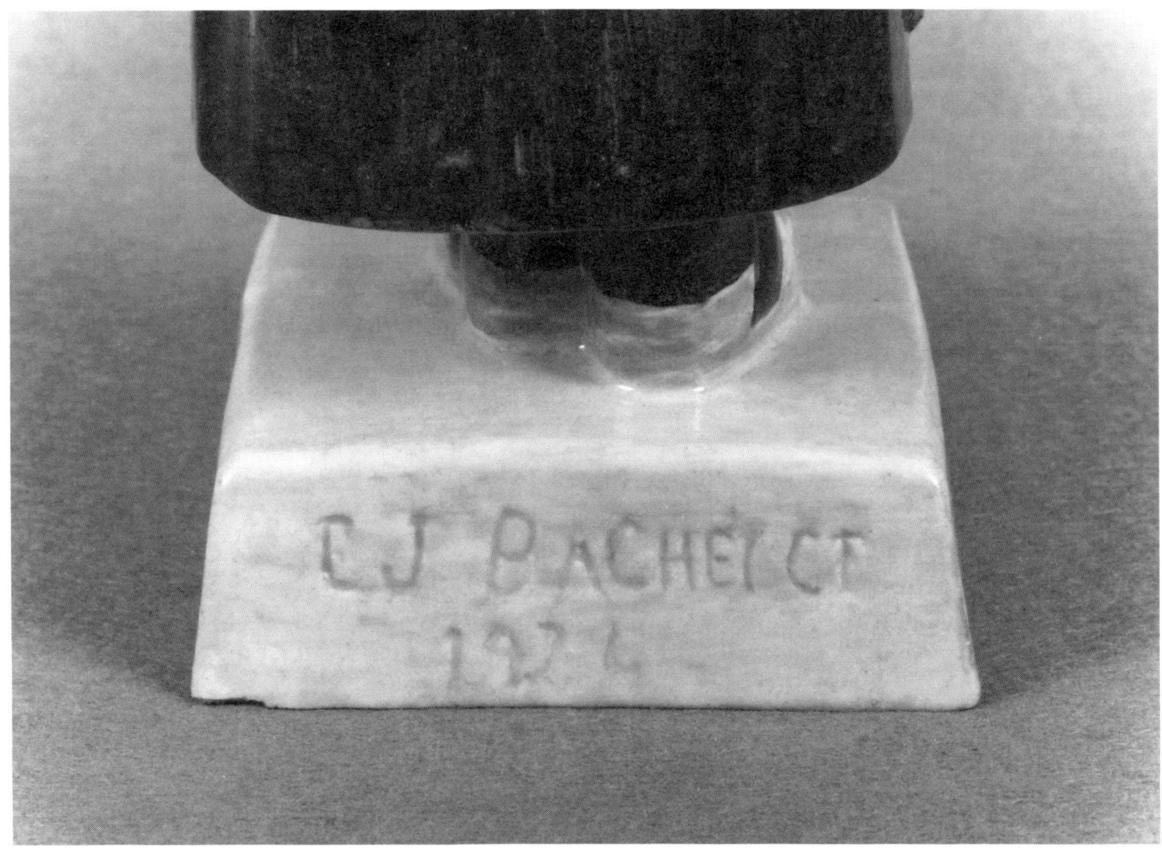

This figure, which carries the artist Bachelet's name, is especially unusual because of the incised date "1924".

examples, a pitcher takes the shape of a coiffed woman's head–the pointed tip of her hat forms the spout, while the bonnet's ribbons make a graceful handle. In Maillard's imagination, even a reclining peasant lady or an out-stretched peasant man could become suitable knife rests. Maillard's work continued to be issued through the 1950's. The recent vintage of many of these examples make them readily available to collectors. Occasionally his pieces are marked with his connected initials "CM" in lieu of a full signature.

Mathurin Méheut: Monsieur Méheut was born in Lamballe in 1882. He began his association with the Maison Henriot in 1919. An eminent marine painter, he was one of the most respected and talented artists who worked at Quimper. He sculpted unique, one of a kind pieces such as his "Pardon de Notre Dame de la Joie". This glazed terra cotta procession of the faithful is on display in the Musée des Faïences de Quimper. In addition to his original pieces, he designed a table service entitled "La Mer". These examples have seashells or crustacians as a central theme with a finely striped green border. His molded examples include a tiny Breton village. Entitled "Mon Village", the quaint scene includes cottages, villagers, fishing boats and even a Breton Calvary i.e. a granite monument representing the life of Christ (these were erected throughout Brittany to ward off the plague in 1598 or as a thanksgiving after the plague had ended).

Méheut also painted all of the frescos for the French ocean liner "Normandie". The artistic beauty of this great ship is legendary.

Monsieur Méheut continued to work at the Maison Henriot well into the twilight years of his life. He died in 1958.

(Examples pages 76, 84 & 140)

Micheau-Vernez: Born in 1907, Robert Micheau joined the "Ar Seiz Breur" group in 1931. He worked as a painter, book illustrator, decorator and poster designer before joining the artists at the Maison Henriot.

A true devotee of Breton culture, Micheau is perhaps best known for his series of dancers and musicians. Executed singly or in groups of two, three or four, each represents a costume from a different region.

In 1932 he married and added the maiden name of his wife to his own, thereby creating his artistic signature of R. Micheau-Vernez.

The last of the "Ar Seiz Breur" group to create figurines, he died in 1988.

R. Micheau was a true Breton patriot. Several of his figurines are marked on the bases in bold black letters with captions in the Breton language. He also designed a cake set.
(Examples pages 77, 142 & 218)

Louis-Marie Nicot: Monsieur Nicot was born near Quimper in the town of Kerfeunteun on January 12, 1878. His sculptures of elderly Quimperoises capture the dignity of old age. Nicot's most celebrated cast is entitled "Les Trois Commères" (The Three Godmothers). The gossiping old women depicted in this mold share a wonderful sense of sorority; their whispers are almost audible. The mold is recorded in two sizes. It is so popular that it continues to be reissued from time to time.
(Examples pages 74, 77 & 137)

Pol: Pol was mainly a decorator/designer of tableware. His most popular pattern is "Mouchoir" (Handkerchief). This is an orange, brown and black checked pattern on a yellow field. It resembles the design that one would find on a man's old-fashioned handkerchief.
(Examples page 141)

Jim Sevellec: Sevellec was born in Cameret in January 1897. From his earliest days he loved to sketch. His family always encouraged his artistic bent.

In 1916 World War I found him serving on the front lines. Fluent in English, he served as a liason to the British troops under Pershing. Twice wounded, he returned to Brest at the end of the war and continued his art career.

An artist of many talents, he painted, sculpted and illustrated. He also worked as an architect, stage director and even window dresser.

The faience which he created for the Henriot factory includes his most ambitious accomplishment: the Village Breton. The series includes scaled to size buildings of a cottage, bank, wine shop, hotel and church. The village is inhabited by over one hundred tiny villagers who bustle about in a whirlwind of activity. A "pardon" (a traditional religious celebration) processes from the church with villagers carrying banners of saints, statues and boats. Musicians, a bride and groom, a priest and a bishop are also included in the retinue. Many more clusters of people watch, dance, stroll or sit and enjoy the festivities. The entire "Village Breton" reflects the vitality of the good Breton people, which Sevellec strove to capture with sensitivity.

In addition to his "Village Breton", Sevellec designed several table services: the Service of the Sea, a tribute to fishermen; the Service of the Earth, a tribute to the farmer; a service entitled "Coiffes", which celebrates the headdresses of the region.

He also designed several charming statuettes of children which were inspired by his little daughter, Annaik.

Jim Sevellec died in 1971 leaving a marvelous artistic legacy of love for the Breton culture. *(Examples pages 74-76, 138 & 139)*

Chapter 7

The Fabrication of Quimper Faïence

A book about Quimper pottery would not be complete without an explanation of how the faïence was produced initially and presently. The following chapter is devoted to the subject. It is subdivided into two sections: the historical and the modern fabrications of Quimper faïence.

Historical Fabrication

In the 18th century the fabrication of faïence was a tedious task. At the site where it originated, the clay was dug by hand, spread out to dry in trenches and pulverized into a powder form. The clay was crated and shipped to the factory by cart or boat. When it arrived, workmen sifted it through a horsehair sieve, mixed it with water and kneaded it into balls of clay called "barbotine". These lumps were submerged into trenches filled with water. There they would soak until enough water had permeated the clay to make it pliable. The barbotine was removed from the water and beaten on wooden planks by hand or by wooden clubs. It was then ready for molding or for the potter's wheel.

The molds were made from terra cotta in the 18th century. Plaster of Paris was used after the mid-19th century. Most of the pieces were shaped on molded forms. Large, hollow examples were formed by using the potter's wheel.

After being molded, the pieces were ready for their first trip to the drying ovens. The kilns had to be maintained at a constant temperature throughout two firings. If the temperature was too hot, the pieces would crack. If the temperature during the second firing was too low, the glaze would be granular instead of smooth. To maintain this perfect balance of temperature was an especially trying task because the ovens were wood-stoked by hand. After the mid-19th century, coal replaced wood and the regulation of the firing process subsequently simplified.

Because the ware was subjected to such a primitive firing process, the pieces had to be protected from the flames and from smoke damage. Therefore, the examples were stacked inside of earthenware cylinders before being placed in the ovens.

When the first firing was completed, the wares were individually inspected for damage. Unbroken pieces were next sent to be glazed and decorated.

All of the glazes and colors used to decorate the pottery were made on the premises of the Quimper factories until the 20th century. Initially a pair of blind horses turned the mill wheel to grind the glaze and colors into powder form. The horses were replaced by a waterwheel in the mid-18th century.

In manufacturing the glaze, lead and tin were mixed to form a paste. This paste was then added to sand, salt and an extract from the glasswort plant to form the glazing compound. The mixture was heated at a high temperature and cooled in vats of cold water. The resulting large chunks of hardened glaze were ground on the mill wheel to a fine, powdery texture. The powder was mixed with water and the pottery was dipped into the liquified glaze. The pieces were then ready to be decorated.

Colors used in the painting of patterns were derived from the following substances: copper (green), antimony (yellow), cobalt (blue), maganese (purple) and iron (red). They were also ground on the mill wheel.

The master craftsmen painted the central theme. The borders and minor details were added by the apprentices. By the end of the 19th century this system was no longer practical. Women called "peinteuses" were employed to paint the decorations. The patterns which they reproduced were copies of existing styles. In order to insure that artistic spontaneity and pride of workmanship would not be lost, no assembly line techniques were used. Each painter was responsible for the painting of one example.

Once the pieces had been painted, they were ready for the second firing. Up until the 20th century, pieces were propped up on three sticks to insure even heating and glazing. Three stick marks may be found particularly on the backs of plates which underwent this process.

After the second firing, each piece was reexamined once again. They were sorted according to quality into the four categories explained in Chapter 3: la marchandise bonne et loyal, le second choix, le troisième choix, and le beau rébut.

The better quality examples were packed in hay or straw for shipment to cities like Nantes, or they were sold by the factory during markets, festivals and fairs. Most of the "rébut" wares were sold to peddlers who traded the pottery at local farms in exchange for old clothing, rags, etc.

Modern Fabrication

At the present time, clay for Quimper pottery is formed from the sand which originates at the Seine and Marne Rivers. Silica from the north of France and dolomite from the tributaries of the Rhône River are added. These three elements are then sprayed with water and thoroughly mixed until they become a soft, liquid slush. The excess water is filtered out until only about 20% water remains. The resulting semi-solid material is then kneaded until it becomes pliable.

Two different processes are followed for shaping the pieces. The clay may be set in molds by hand or by machine and then removed from the mold after it sets. This method is used in making flat objects such as plates, platters, saucers, etc. The second method is to re-liquify the clay to a pourable consistency. It is then poured into molds from which, after several hours, it is extracted. This method is used for making three-dimensional objects, such as figurines, vases, pitchers, etc. Many times these objects are composed of two sections which are joined together after the unmolding.

Items such as handles are also made separately and glued to the main portion of a piece with a substance which melds the two together in the firing oven. Seams left by mold joints are sanded off at this point.

All wares are then dried in the kilns. This first baking turns the clay into a "biscuit" or hard pottery. In 1960, new electric ovens were installed at the Grande Maison HB. Today the pottery makes four trips through the oven at 1020°F: two for the initial baking, and two for the final baking after painting and glazing. The faïence bakes the first time for an average of ten hours.

Once the first baking is completed, the pieces are decorated. Just as in the days of antiquity, cobalt is used to produce blue, antimony for yellow, copper for green, iron for red and manganese for purple. A high oven temperature yields a dark color, while a lower temperature produces a paler, more delicate shade. Artists use both patterns and freehand skills in decorating the pieces. Patterns are used when the decoration requires a great deal of detail, as in the "décor riche" designs. The simple "ordinaire" style is painted freehand.

There are two different methods of decoration. In one, the glaze is applied first and the design is painted on top of it. This technique is the more difficult and requires three months of apprenticeship for the artisan to master. Older examples of the pottery were usually decorated in this manner. By running one's finger over the pattern, one can many times feel the raised effect of the over-painting. The second method consists of painting the details of the pattern first and then applying the glaze. Glaze application is crucial, since a speck of dust or a stray fingerprint can ruin the desirability of an example. Generally, the faïences made today are produced by employing the second method of decoration.

After an item is painted and glazed, it returns to the oven for a second firing at 920°F. It is then inspected, sorted according to quality and packed for distribution.

An additional factory brochure appears in the appendix section. Entitled "Operation Portes Ouvertes dans une Faïencerie" (Operation Open Doors in a Faïencerie), it is a pictoral essay demonstrating the methods used to produce the pottery in 1973.

My special thanks and deep appreciation are extended to Messieurs Jean Rouillard and Louis Leonus for sharing this documentation. It is most important to be able to preserve this record for historical purposes.

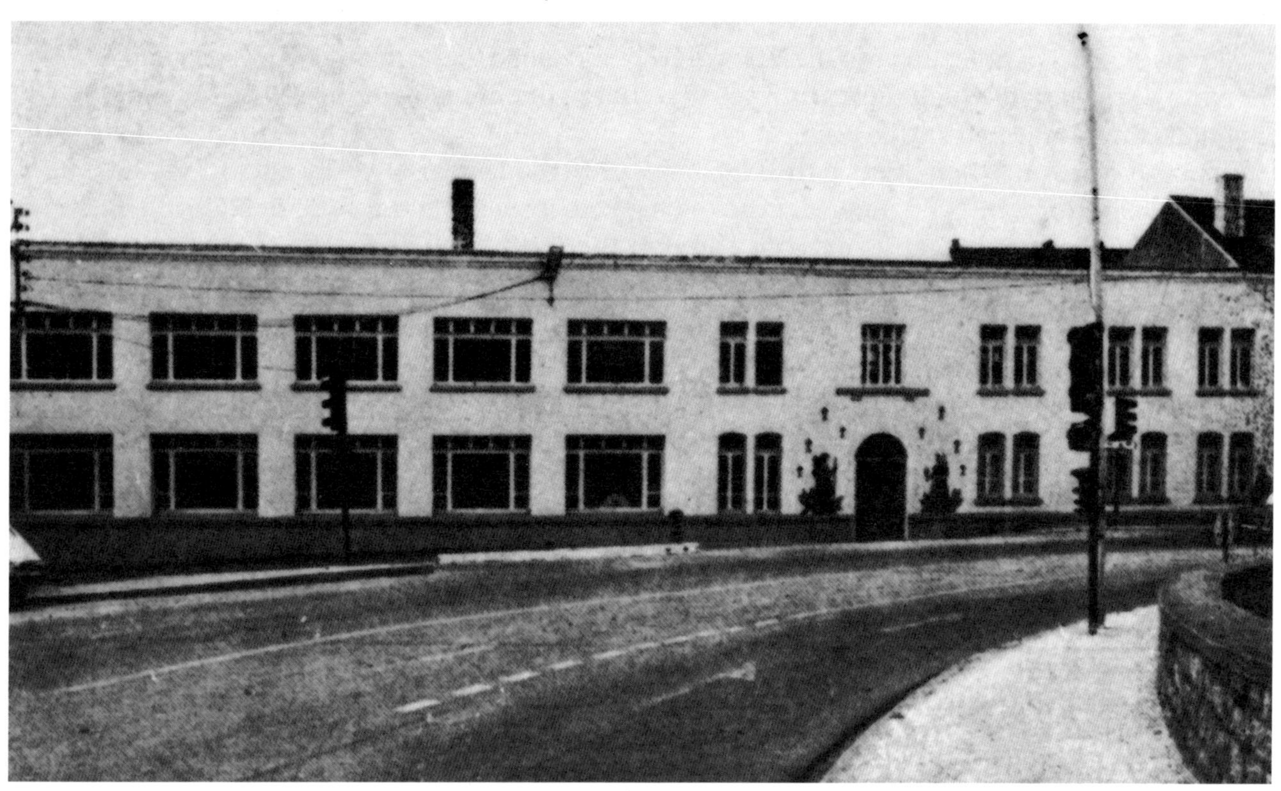

Photo 1: A view of the HB–HenRiot factory in the early 1970's. *(Courtesy "Operation Portes Ouvertes dans une Faïencerie")*

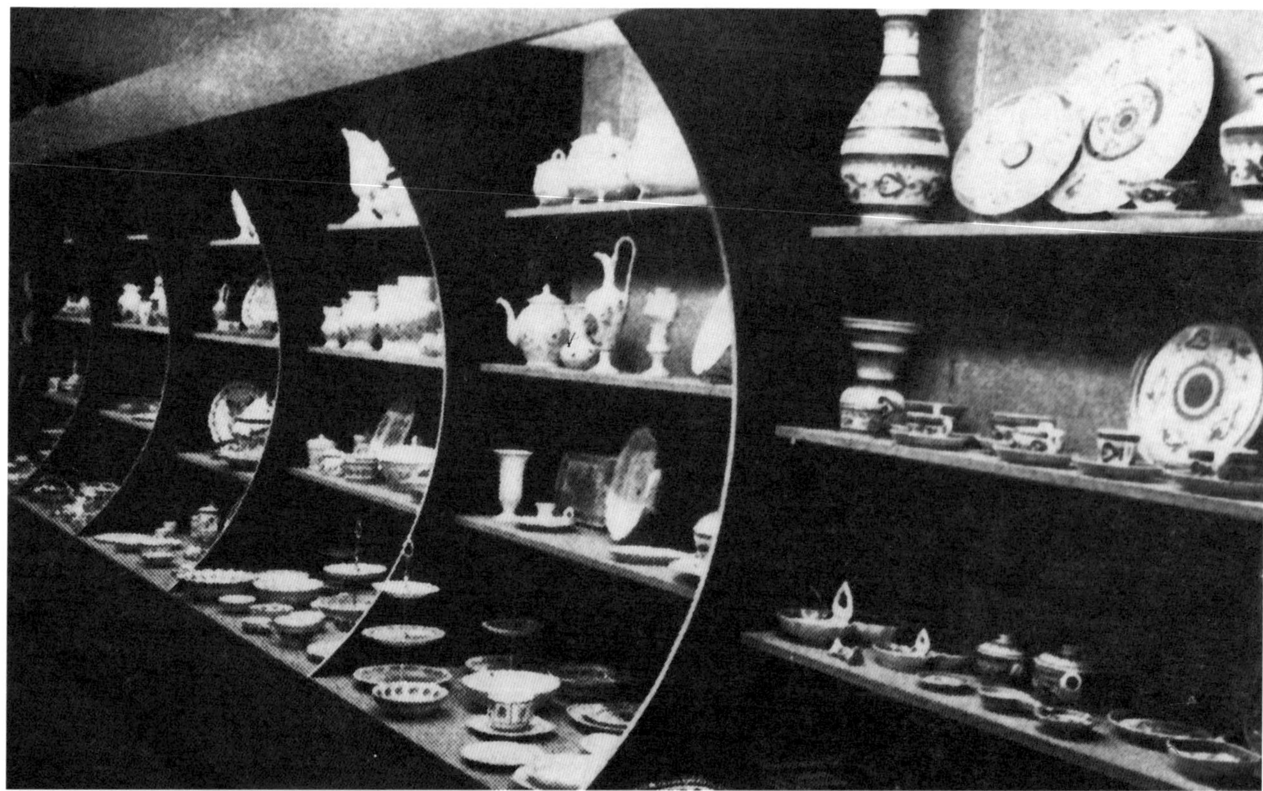

Photo 2: A section of the showroom, as it appeared in the early 1970's, shows a sample of the diversity of production at that time. *(Courtesy "Operation Portes Ouvertes dans une Faïencerie")*

Chapter 8

Numerous Patterns . . . Myriad Forms

The choice of Quimper patterns is infinite. The classification of these diverse styles can be arbitrarily divided into three sections of time and taste:

1). 17th and 18th century—copies of Moustiers, Nevers, Rouen and Delft
2). 19th century—the birth and blossoming of the true Breton style
3). 20th century—the Modern Movement which was influenced by individual artists and the Art Deco period.

In many instances, patterns from previous time periods were reissued simultaneously with contemporary designs. As examples, one can cite the excellent copies of 18th century Rouen made in the late 19th century by Porquier-Beau; the Maison Henriot's early 20th century reissues of the late 19th century "Scènes bretonnes" from Porquier-Beau; and today's modern reproductions of the popular 19th century Breton patterns which are exhibited in the factory Museum.

So numerous are Quimper patterns, that this chapter will discuss only the most commonly found examples from the 19th century up to World War II. A description of the 17th and 18th century styles can be found in Chapter 2.

The Breton patterns of the 19th century drew upon the local folk art traditions of the region. Some of the subjects were chosen because they appeared for centuries as a part of Breton furniture design. Others, such as indigenous flora and fauna, French and Breton symbols and native costumes, further contributed to the evolving folk art style.

Reputed to be the oldest of the Breton-inspired patterns, *"Rose Window"* takes its inspiration from the stained glass windows found in Brittany's Medieval cathedrals. The pattern has a central design which resembles a great stained glass rose window. The effect is reproduced by using the "décor à la touche" (paintbrush daub) technique. The central, stylized rose design may be encircled by a simple line or floral band. This decoration is repeated for the border trim.

The *floral* patterns usually show one or two large blossoms in full bloom as the central design. Green leaves and small buds complete the pattern. The flower petals and greenery are formed by the "décor à la touche" method. Frequently, concentric yellow and blue bands adorn the border.

The *bird* patterns utilize all different types of fowl as the central theme. Crowing roosters, prancing peacocks, swans, pheasants and doves are among the most commonly found examples. As with the flower patterns, florals and leaves executed by the "décor à la touche" technique, appear to either side, and concentric yellow and blue banded borders complete the pattern.

Fleur de lis are historically the symbol of France. A two-tone blue fleur de lis, together with the black ermine tail symbol of Brittany, comprise the elements for the *Lys* pattern. The style is elegant in its simplicity. Occasionally, the fleur de lis will be colored yellow and red instead of the two shades of blue.

The *geometric* patterns are perhaps the most imaginative and diverse. Abstract designs are formed using lines, dots, floral sprigs, criss-cross latticing and floral chains. The combinations of these geometrical patterns vary a great deal in each example. They provide a visual banquet for the collector. *(See pages 10 & 11)*

The *basket* pattern shows a double-handled, open basket with a criss-cross lattice design overflowing with a profusion of flowers and leaves. The floral branches are painted in the "décor à la touche" manner. *(See page 9)*

The *"bleuets"* pattern consists of a simple blue floral sprig design which is randomly sprinkled over the surface of the pottery. *(See page 11)*

The most famous of all of the styles of Quimper pottery is also delightfully diverse: the *peasant* pattern. Many different variations of the peasant motif have developed through the years. They range from the most simple, naive line drawings to the complex and intricately-detailed "Scènes bretonnes". A discussion of the most popular of these styles follows:

The *"ordinaire"* pattern: This pattern depicts a naively-painted, profiled peasant figure with florals to either side. The woman holds a flower; the man carries either a walking stick or long-stemmed pipe. The border has concentric yellow and blue bands. This is the most easily produced and the most commonly found Quimper pattern. While no one is positive about who first introduced this type of figure, isolated, unsigned examples did appear about mid-19th century. *(See page 11)*

The *"festonné"* pattern: This motif used the naive, profiled peasant figure of the "ordinaire" pattern for the central theme. The border is decorated with alternating floral sprigs and the four blue dot design.

The *"couronnes"* pattern: As with the "ordinaire" and the "festonné" patterns, the primitive, profiled peasant figure is the main theme. The border of this pattern is a floral garland.

The *"demi-riche"* pattern: This style bears a more highly-detailed peasant figure. Usually the man carries a flute or bagpipe; the woman holds a distaff or basket of eggs. The pose can be profiled, three-quarter or full facing. The border is decorated with a floral garland. The name of this pattern was changed to "demi-fantasie" after World War II.

The *"croisillé"* pattern: The peasant figures are painted in the same manner as for the "demi-riche" style. The border is more decorative in that it alternates a criss-cross lattice work panel with floral work. *(See page 83 Teaset)*

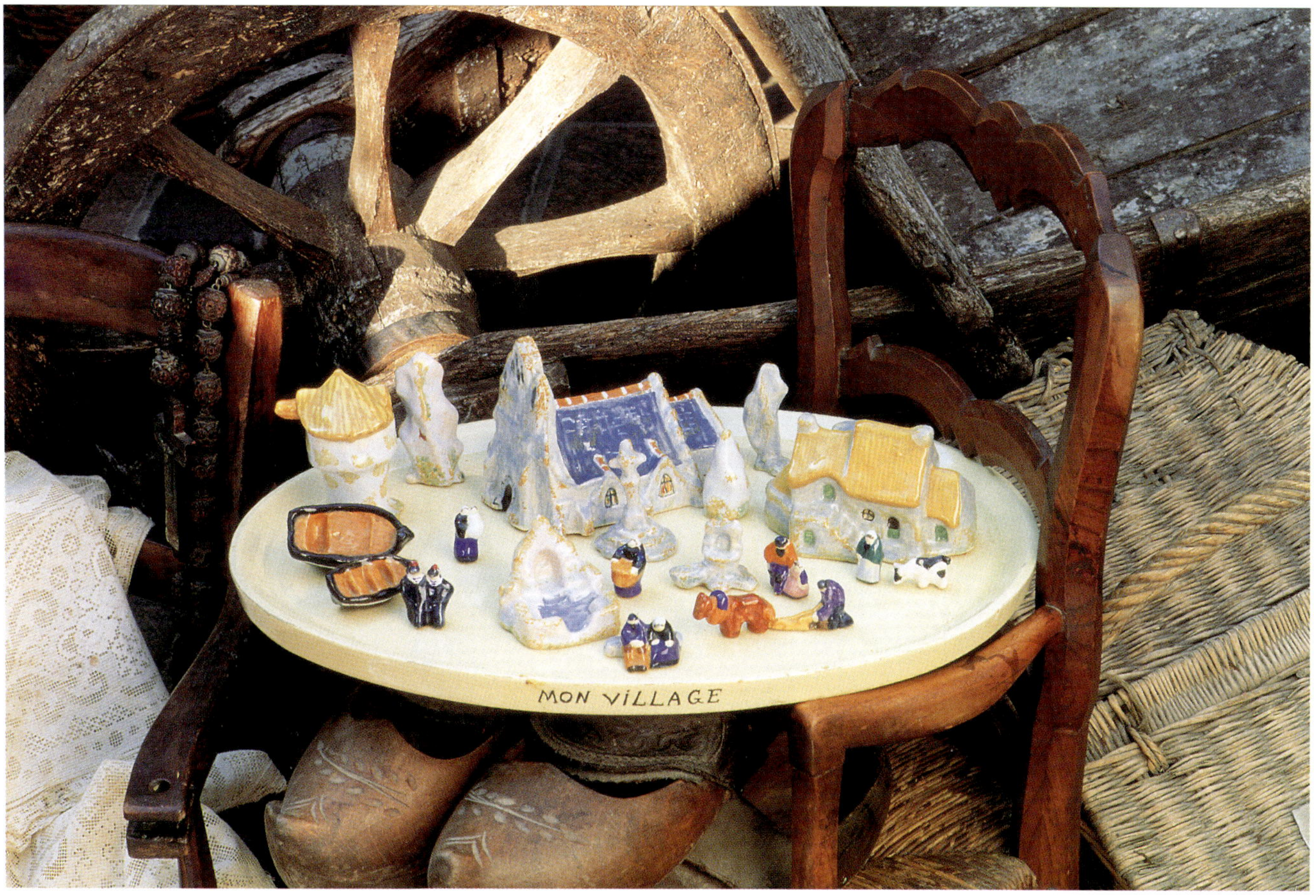

Mathurin Méheut's "Mon Village" draws with an irresistable appeal. Figures barely measuring 1" tall gather among the town's buildings. Church and "calvaire", farm house and silo, boats and "dolmens", well and "fountaine" all reflect the rich tapistry of Brittany's cultural heritage. Maison Henriot; Modern Movement Period of the 20th century. *(Private Collection)*

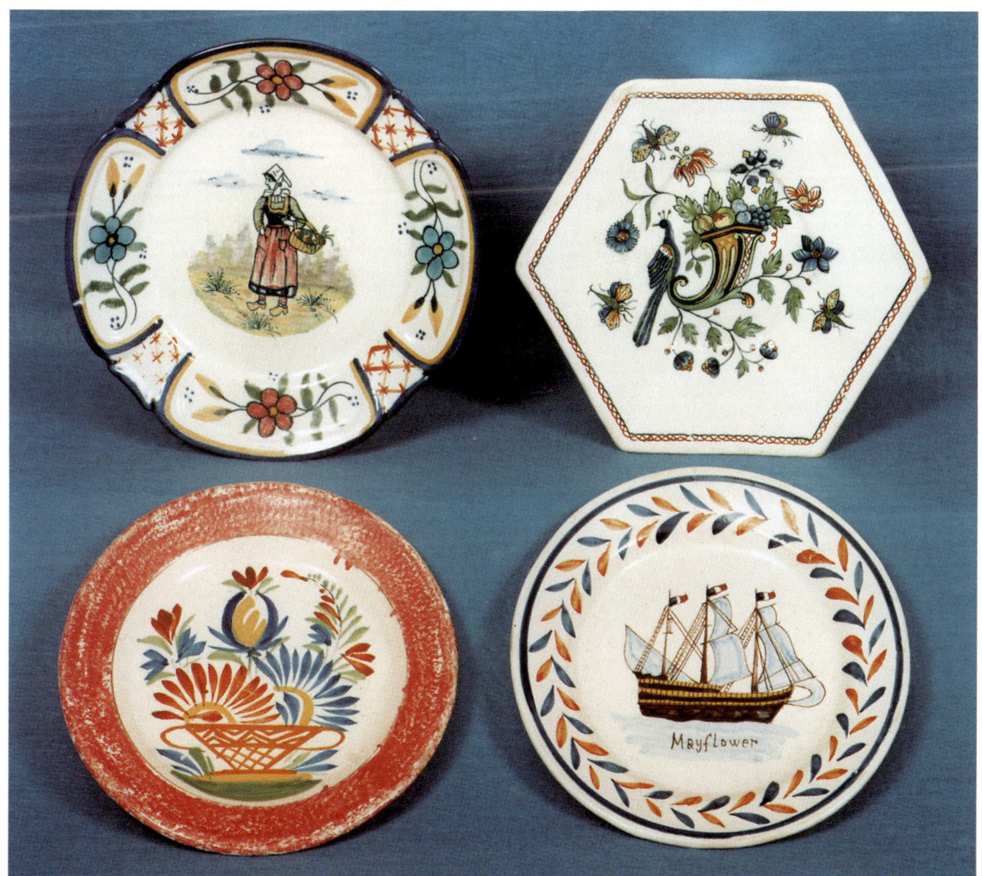

While Modern Movement styles influenced 20th century production, traditional patterns continued to flourish together with new variations of old themes.

Pictured here are four plates. The first is an HB modification of the traditional peasant figure. The second is a modern re-issue of the Rouen cornucopia. The third is an HenRiot rendition of the "panier aux fleurs" (flower basket) pattern. The last is an HenRiot plate which commemorates the "Mayflower". (It is especially amusing to note that the Mayflower is flying French flags from her three masts.) (Photograph by Mitchell Z. Bistany)

Following pages: Jim Sevellec's fantastic"Village Breton" is a bustling beehive of activity. A complete scale model of a religious "pardon" and all of its' auxiliary festivities is captured with great vitality of form and vibrancy of color. In the opinion of many this is Sevellec's apex of artistic expression for the Maison HenRiot. Modern Movement Period 20th Century. *(Private collection)*

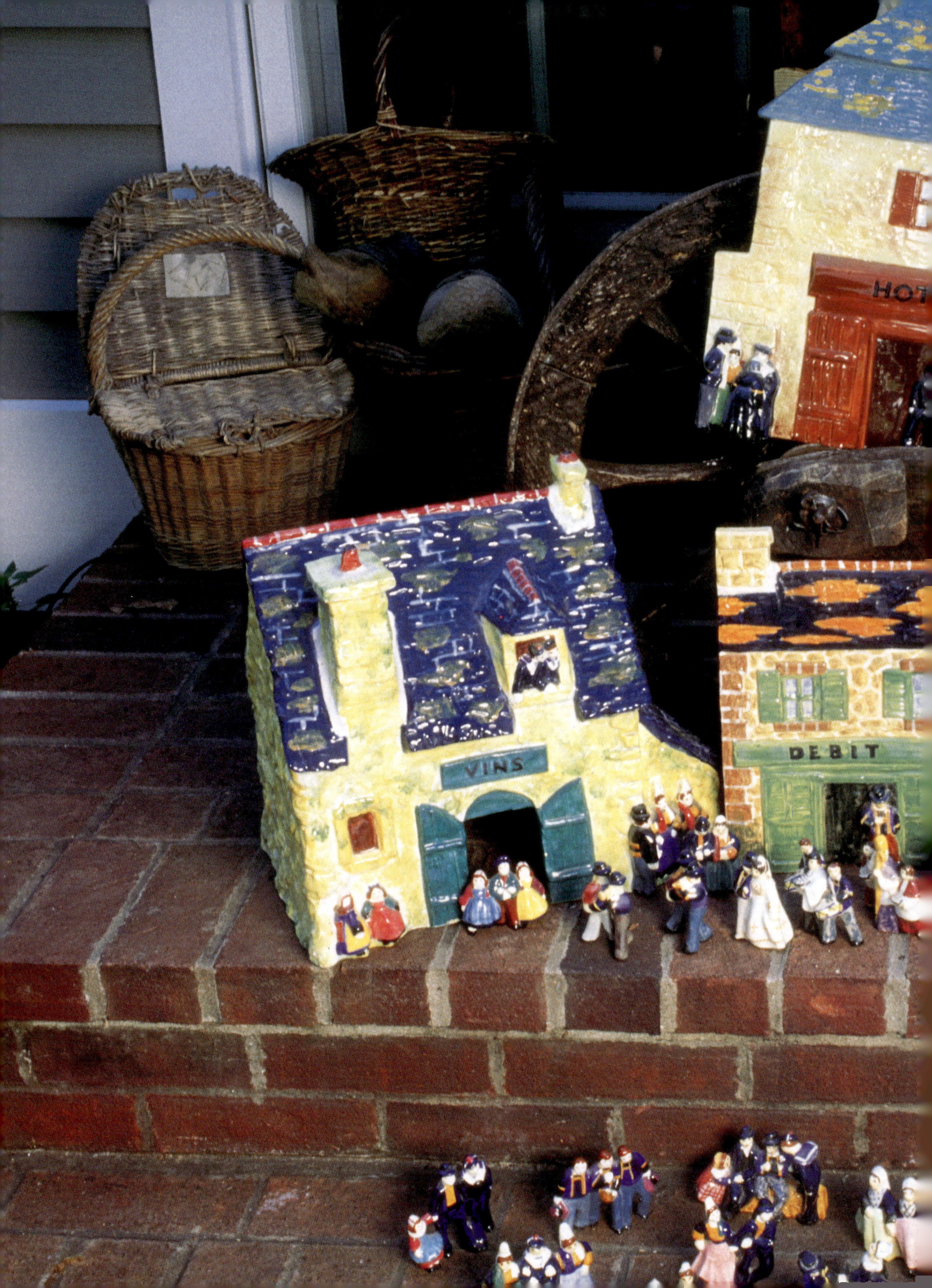
VINS
DEBIT

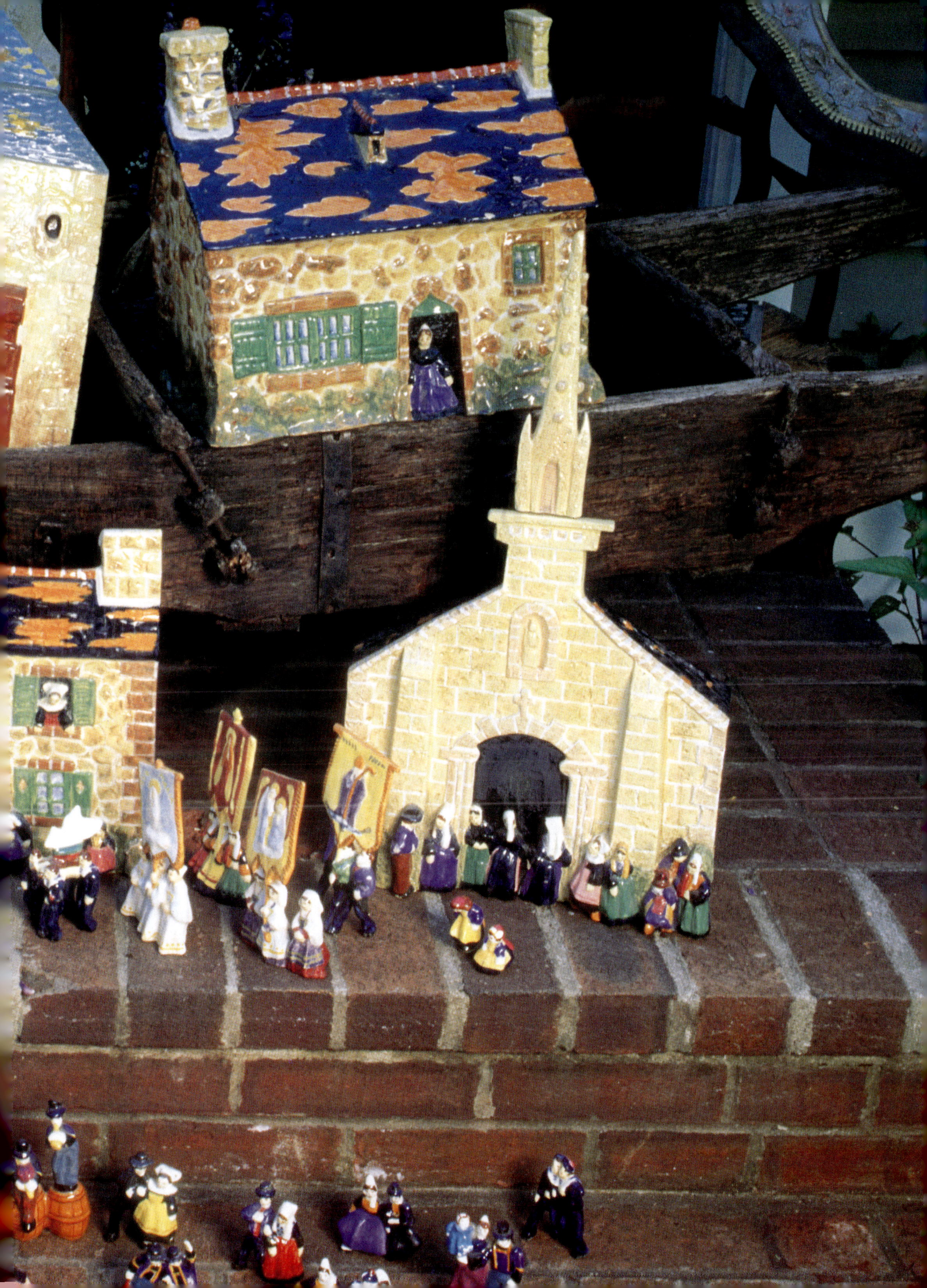

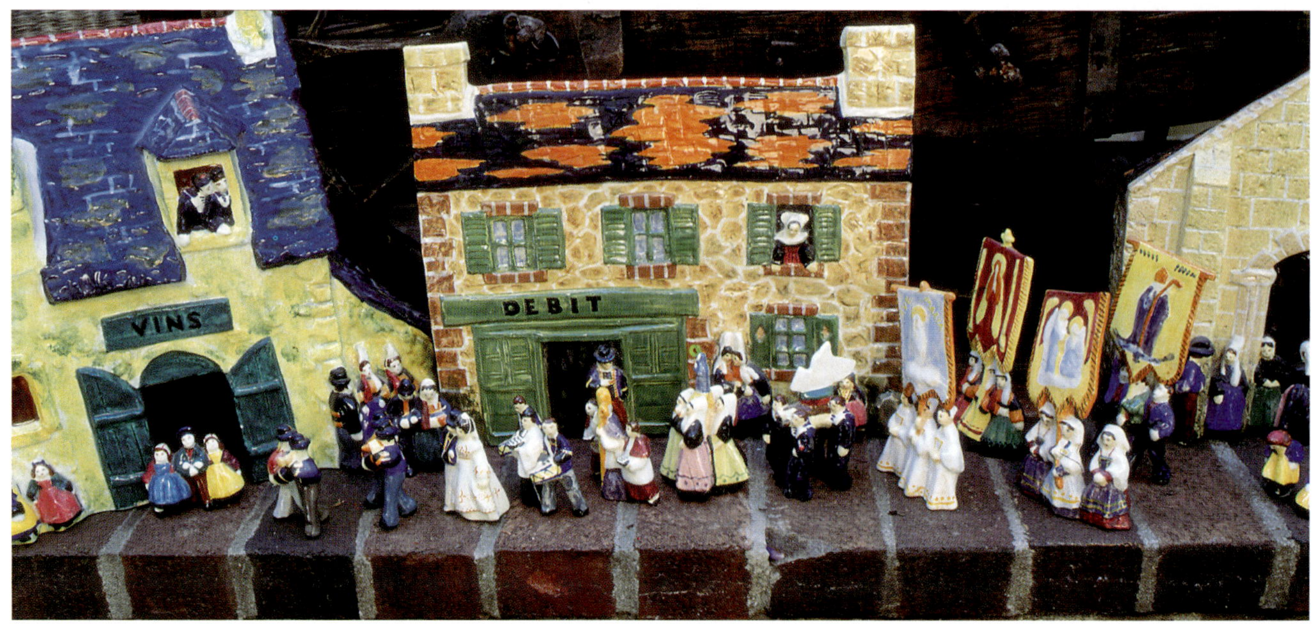

Top: Detail of Jim Sevellec's "Village Breton".

Bottom: "Procession de Notre Dame de la Joie à Penmarc'h" (Procession of Our Lady of Joy to Penmarc'h). Seen in the foreground, the procession is a unique "one of a kind" example which was executed by Mathurin Méheut.

Many collectors fail to realize that the mass produced pieces of the Modern Movement Period were painted by the artisans and not by the artists themselves. Some of the artists were however very particular about which "peinteuse" would decorate their production pieces. (Courtesy of the Musée de la Faience Jules Verlingue)

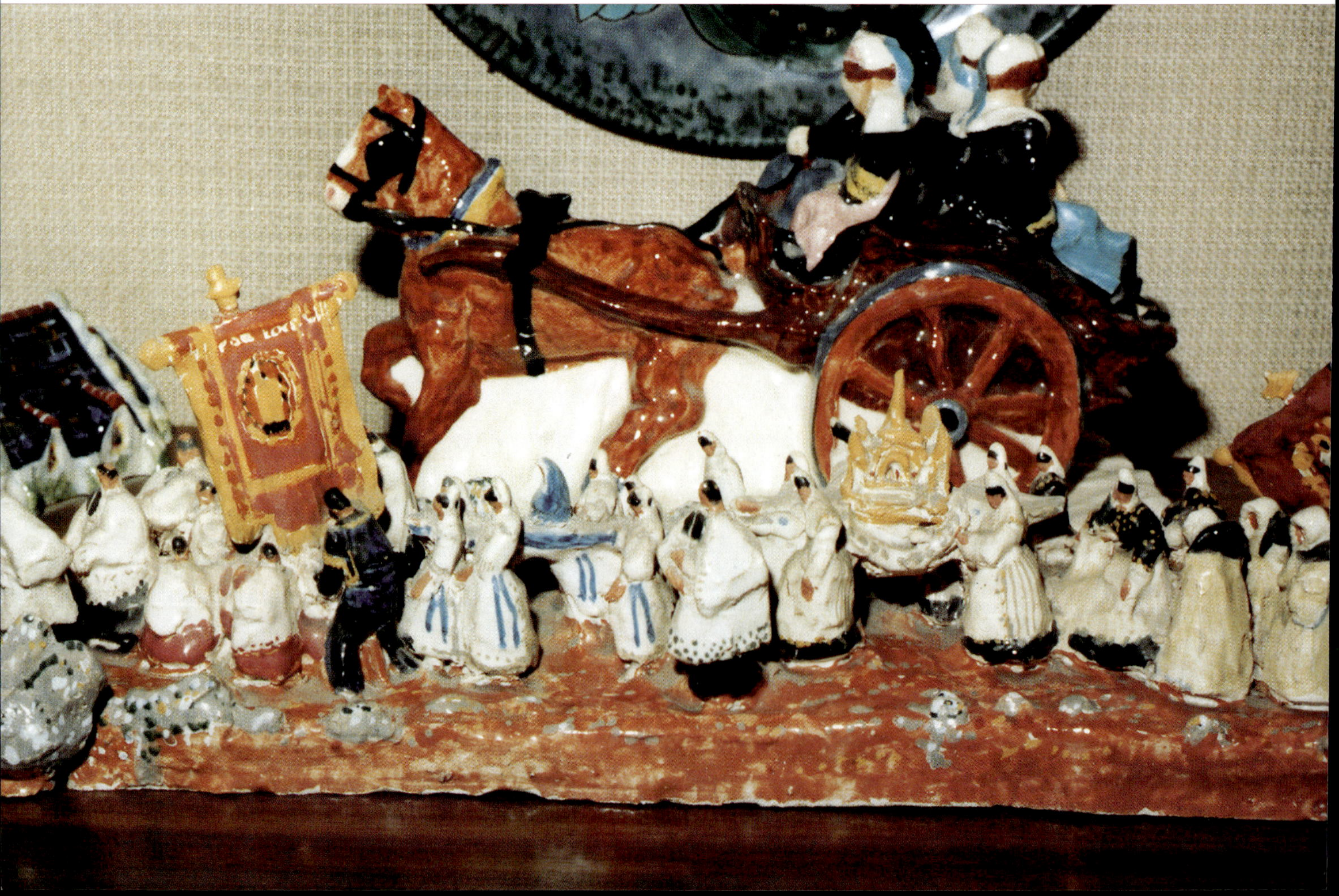

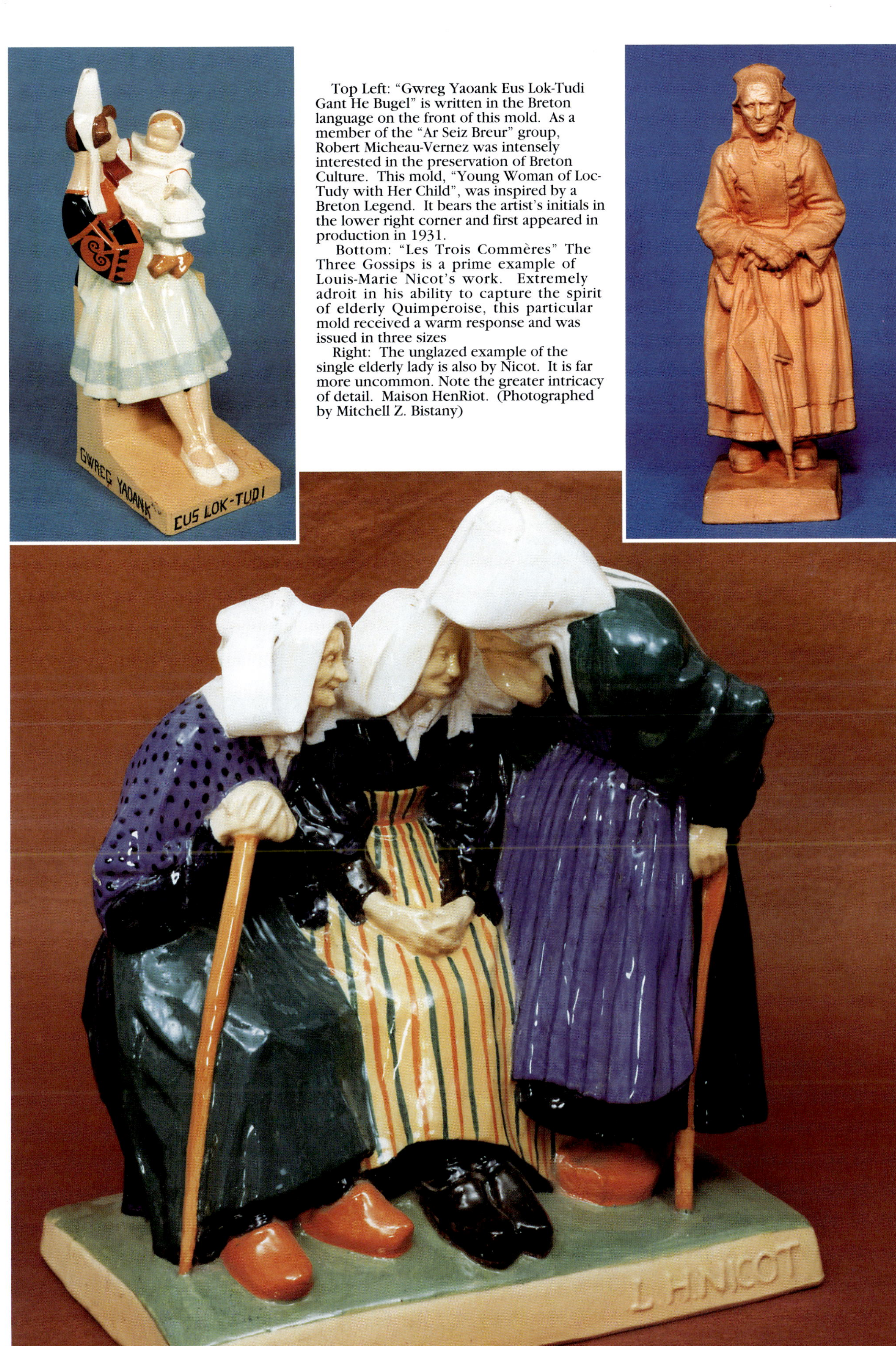

Top Left: "Gwreg Yaoank Eus Lok-Tudi Gant He Bugel" is written in the Breton language on the front of this mold. As a member of the "Ar Seiz Breur" group, Robert Micheau-Vernez was intensely interested in the preservation of Breton Culture. This mold, "Young Woman of Loc-Tudy with Her Child", was inspired by a Breton Legend. It bears the artist's initials in the lower right corner and first appeared in production in 1931.

Bottom: "Les Trois Commères" The Three Gossips is a prime example of Louis-Marie Nicot's work. Extremely adroit in his ability to capture the spirit of elderly Quimperoise, this particular mold received a warm response and was issued in three sizes

Right: The unglazed example of the single elderly lady is also by Nicot. It is far more uncommon. Note the greater intricacy of detail. Maison HenRiot. (Photographed by Mitchell Z. Bistany)

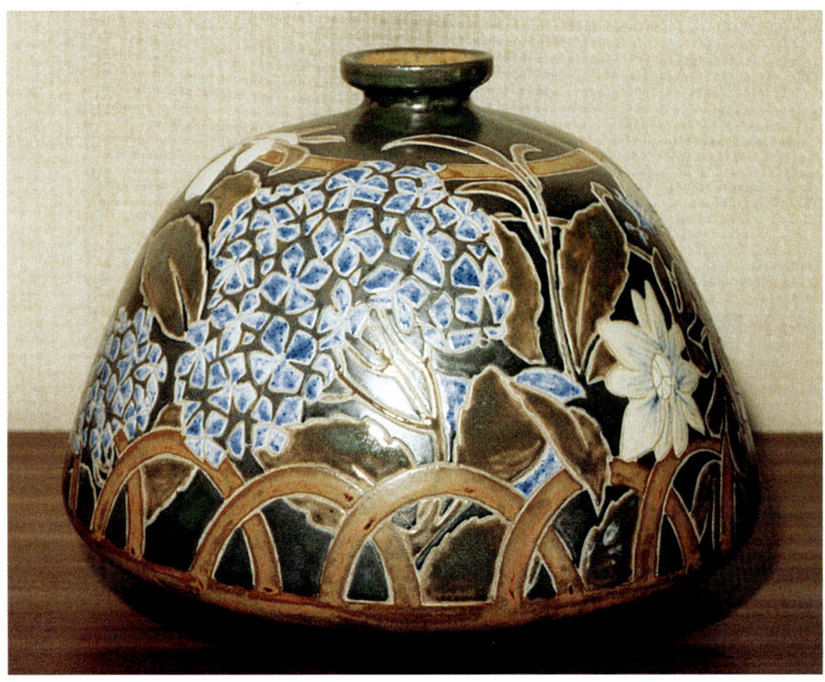

Pictured is an unusual vase by the artist, Alphonse Chanteau. Instead of the typical Art Deco influence usually seen on Odetta pieces, here the strong influence of Art Nouveau is reflected. Grande Maison HB. (Courtesy of the Musée de la Faience Jules Verlingue)

One of the aims of the "Ar Seiz Breur" group was the promulgation of "l'art national breton modern". Odetta was the distinctive fruit born of this desire.

A heavy stoneware, sturdy and dense, it required a higher firing temperature (2400°F). Composed of a mixture of clay with kaolin from Lorient, sand from Nevers containing feldspar and ground porcelain chips, the resulting paste was then poured into molds. Metal oxides were used to color the enamel, which was formed by combining kaolin, calcium, feldspar and titanium.

A new technique of glaze application saw the enamel applied by drops, in lieu of brush stroke. During firing, the thickly applied droplets would melt and run. Thus the exact pattern was never duplicated twice.

The palette of Odetta is virile: a spectrum of browns, a rich black, a glossy gray, a deep blue and a stark white.

The new art form was a success and won accolades at the Exposition des Arts Décoratifs in Paris in 1925.

Odetta was only in production until 1942. Due to war time conditions, fuel needed to produce the ware became unavailable.

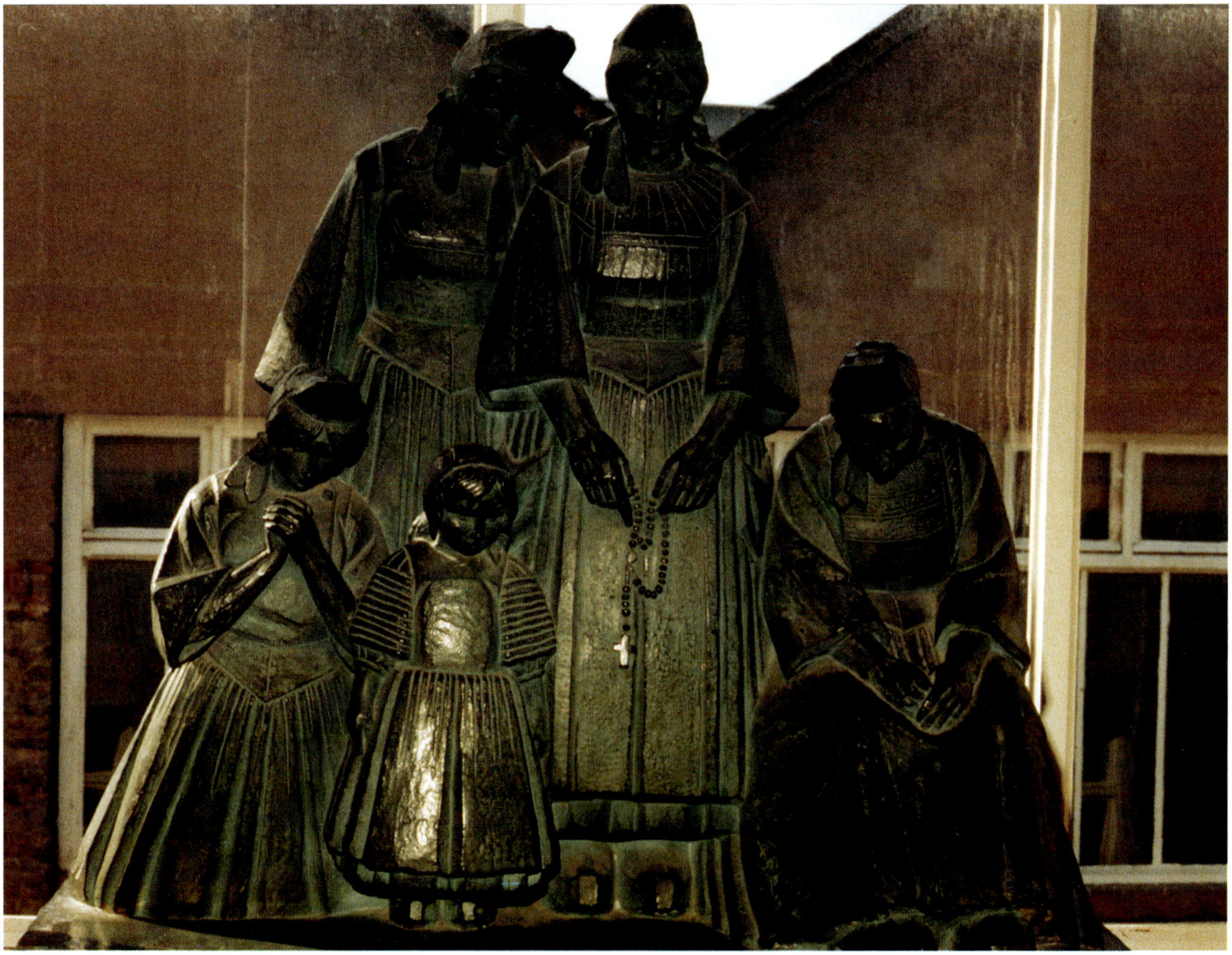

"Monument aux morts de Pont-l' Abbé" by the Grande Maison artist, François Bazin. (Circa 1929). The mold melds the somber mood of mourning with the solid spirituality of the Breton people. These dual elements are beautifully encapsulated by and reflected in the monochromatic glaze and molded linear details of the Modern Movement Period. (Courtsey Musée de la Faïence Jules Verlingue)

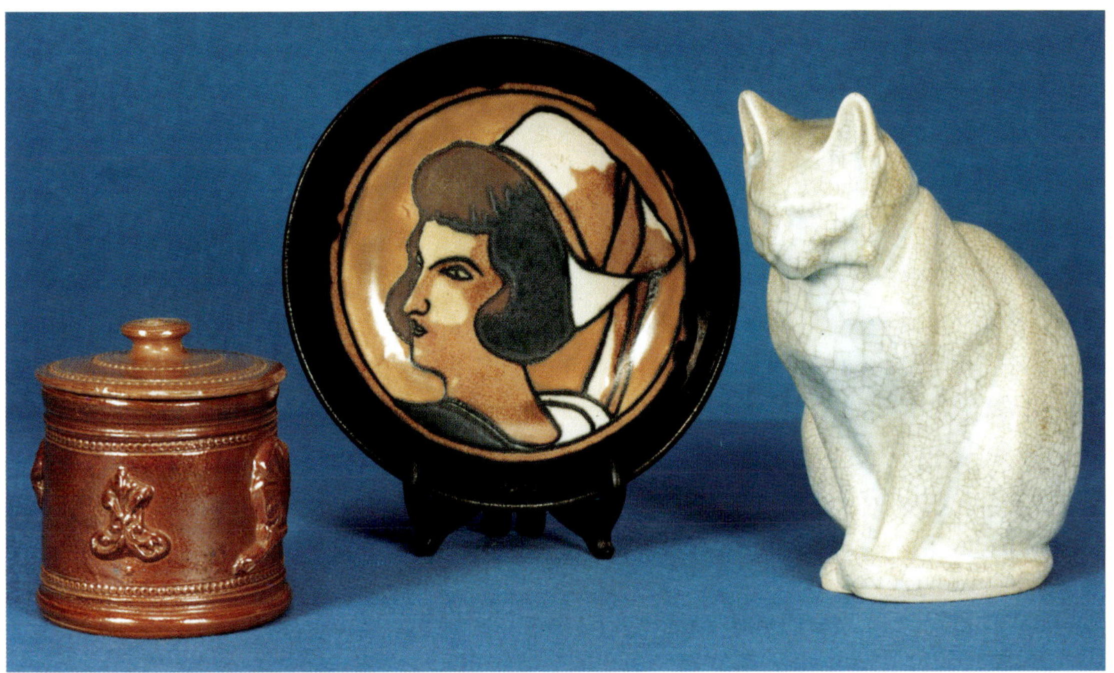

"Grès" These three examples typify the diversity of grès stoneware. The unmarked tobacco jar, probably de la Hubaudière, dates from the 19th century. The uniform brown glaze is a typical salt glaze finish of the period. The Grande Maison HB plate is an example of the Odetta Line.
The cat is by the artist, Jacques Nam. The simple, white, crackled glaze has a strong chinese influence. Circa 1920's - 1930's. Grande Maison HB. *(Private Collections)*

A postcard dating from the 1970's shows the partial diversity of patterns in modern production. Certain patterns have been repeatedly produced over extended periods of time, while simultaneously new designs are being created and introduced.

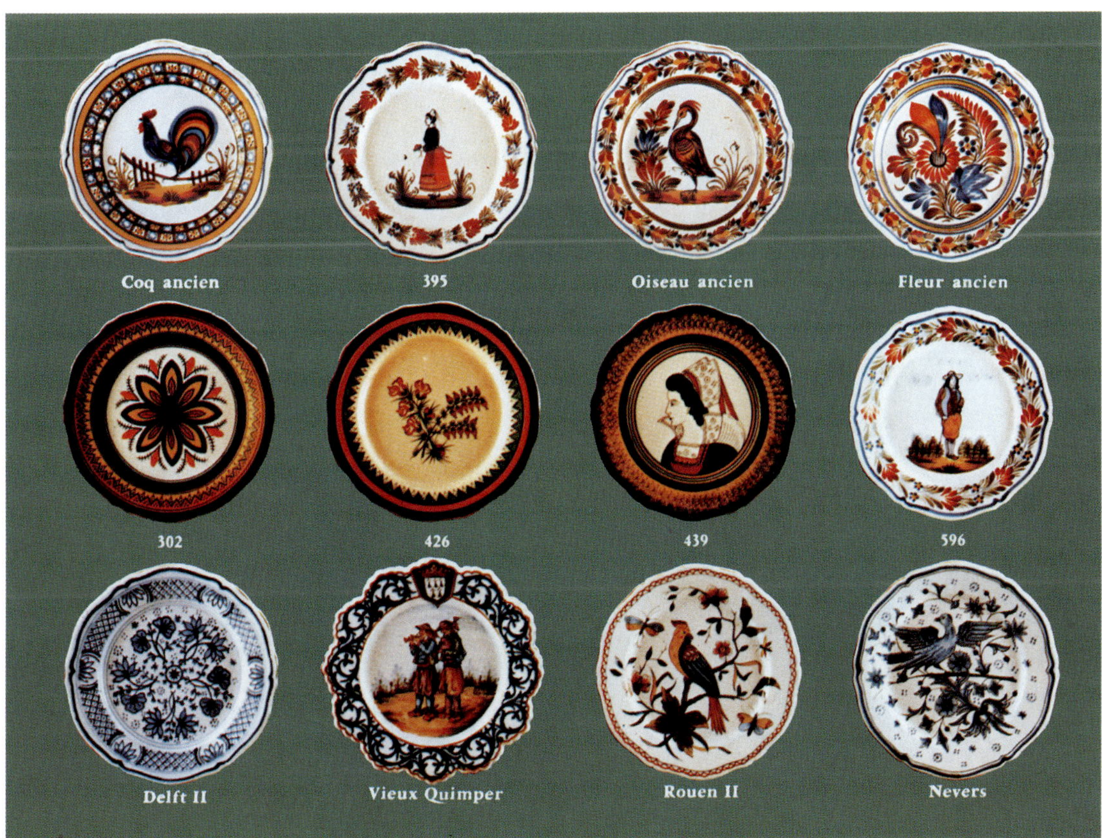

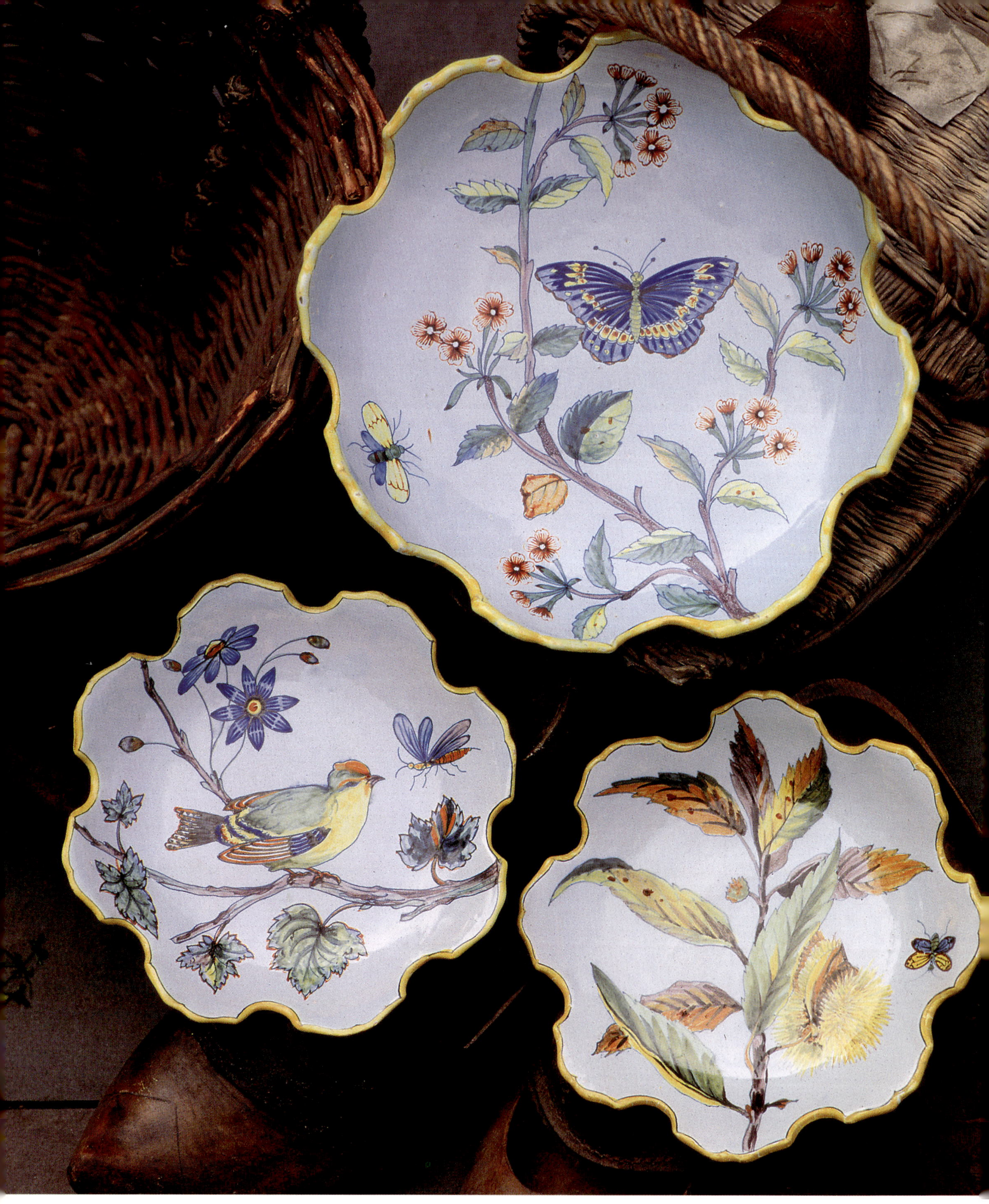

The talents of artists reflect Your splendor,
-may their work give the world hope and joy. (from "*The Liturgy of the Hours*")

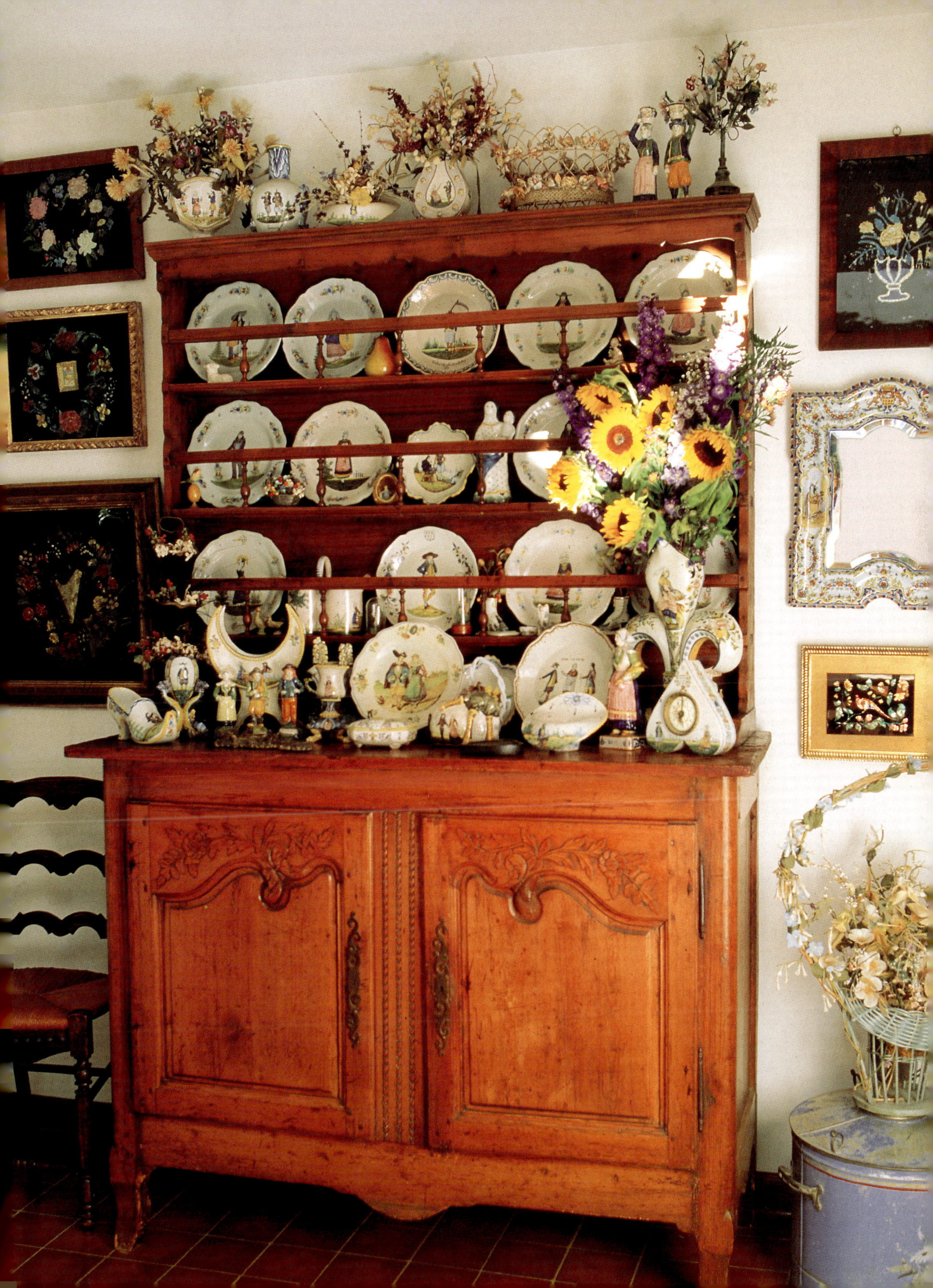

FAÏENCERIE BRETONNE DE LA GRANDE MAISON QUIMPER

HB QUIMPER HB QUIMPER

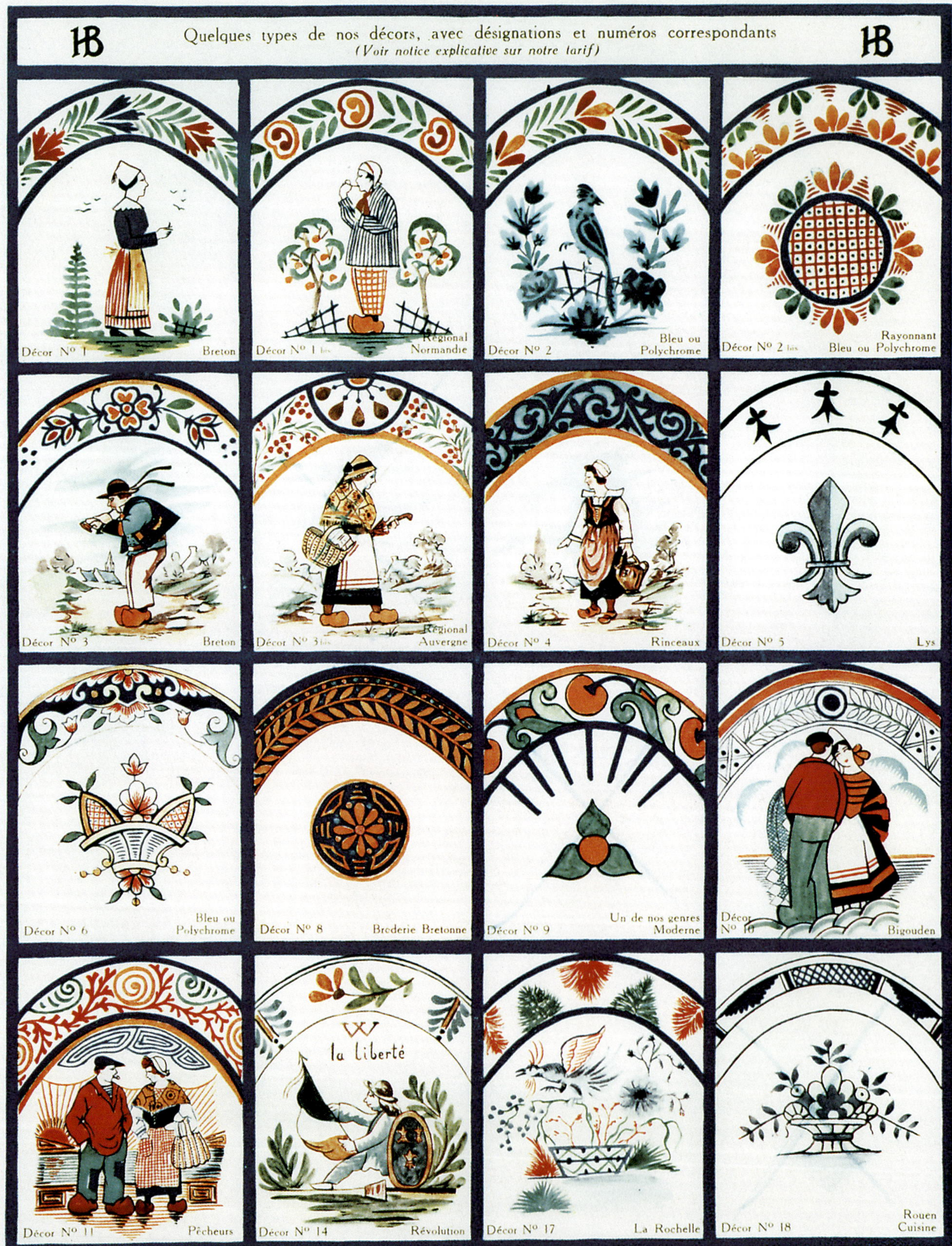

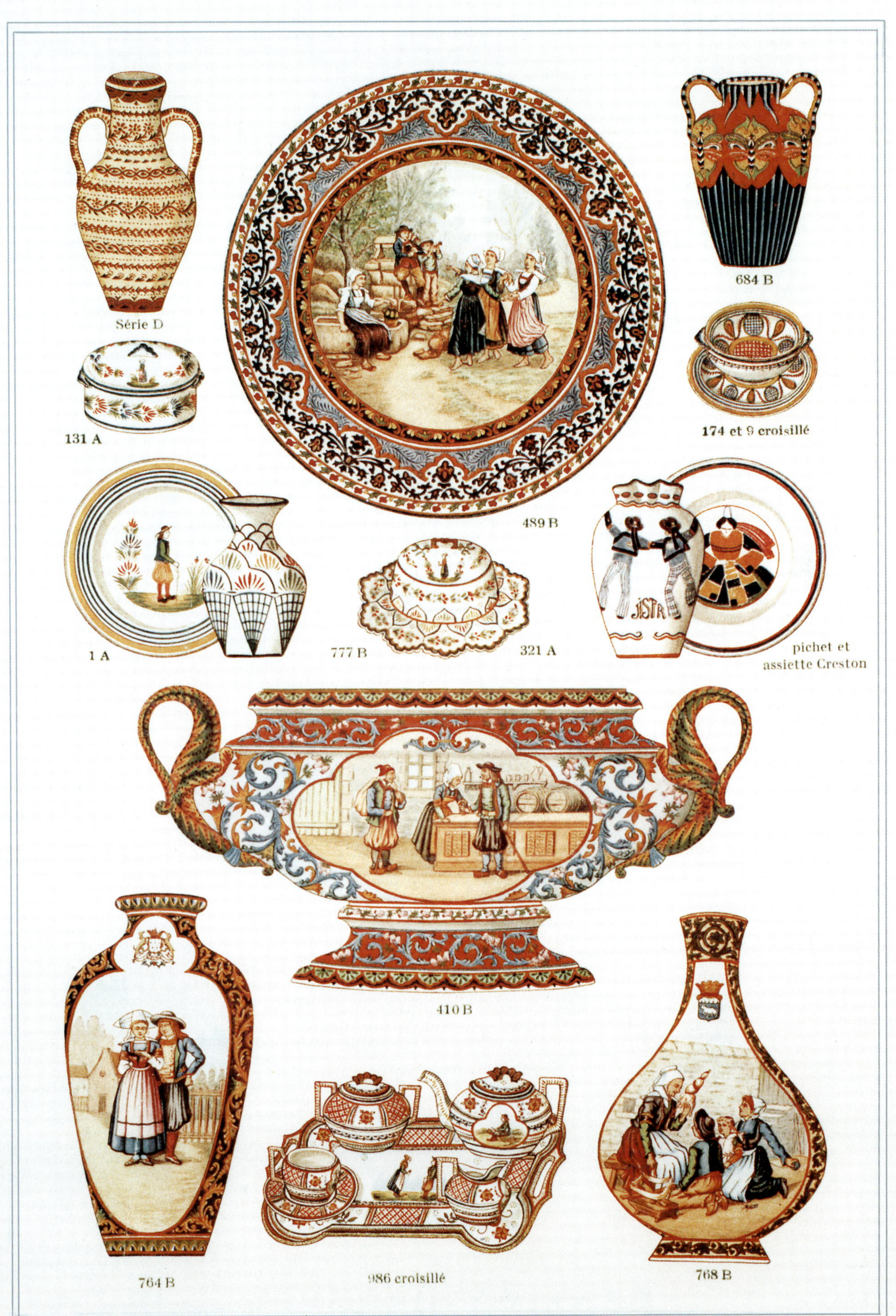

HENRIOT-QUIMPER

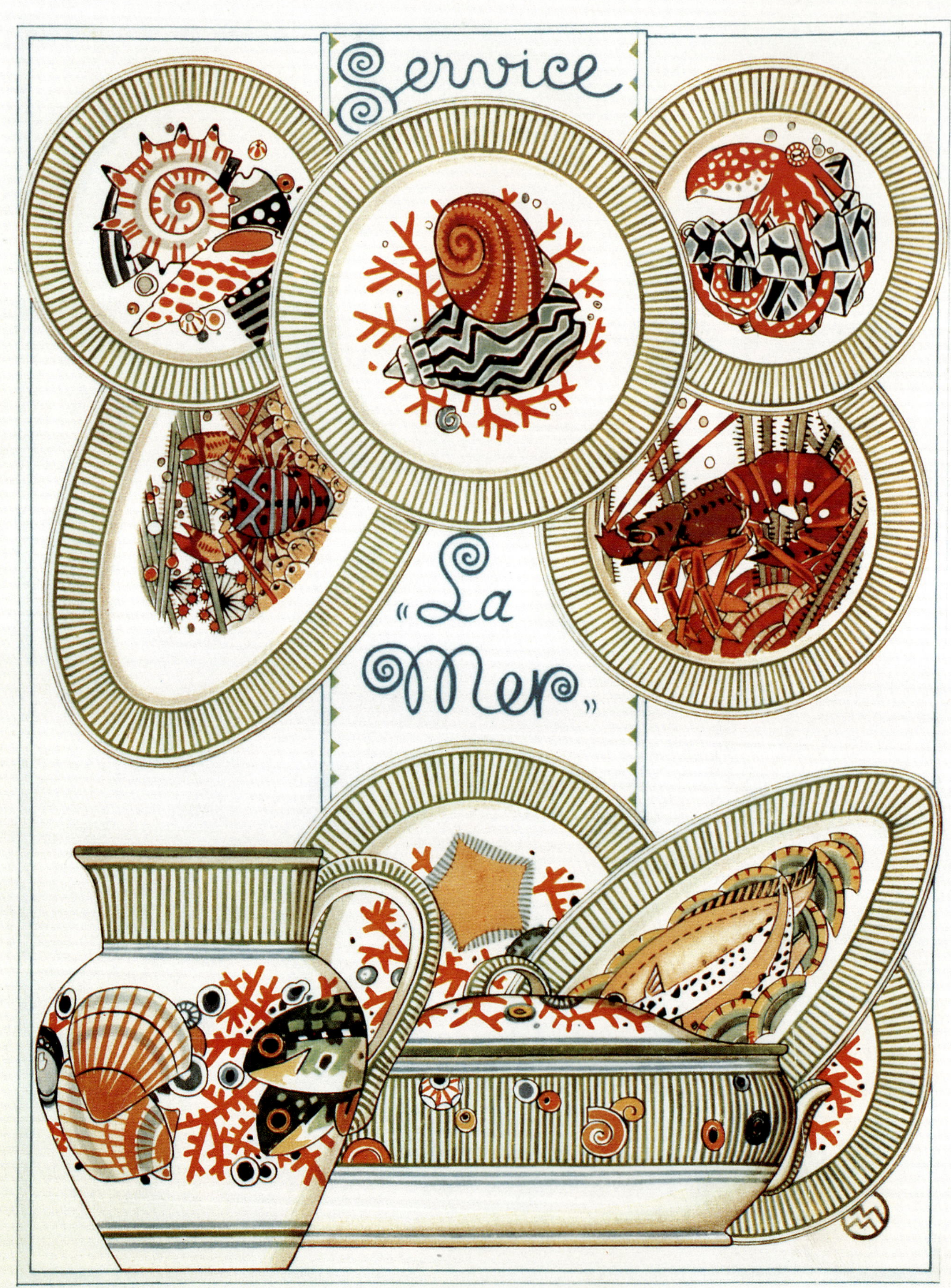

HENRIOT - QUIMPER

The *"décor riche"* pattern: This style is in the true tradition of the Alfred Beau "Scènes bretonnes". Finely detailed peasant figures decorate the pattern usually in groups of two or more. The workmanship is very fine; it resembles a painting. The border is elaborately worked with intertwining acanthus-type leaves. *(See pages 56 & 57)*

There is another variation of the peasant theme which originated at the Grande Maison HB and is only found on examples dating from the last quarter of the 19th century. The peasant figures are painted with delicately fine details. Generally the borders are simply decorated with varying designs. The workmanship on these examples is naive and exquisite. *(See pages 12, 14, 15, 16, & 59)*

The following patterns were introduced during the Modern Movement after World War I.

"La Mer" by Mathurin Méheut. This pattern has a seashell or marine animal as the central theme. A radiating, green stripe border completes the design. *(See pages 84)*

"Pecheurs" (Fishermen): This peasant figure pattern, painted in a modified Art Deco style, shows a fisherman in his cap, smoking a pipe. His companion carries a basket over her arm and wears a checkered apron. Both of them wear slightly exaggerated "sabots" (wooden shoes). *(See Décor #11, page 82)*

"Broderie Bretonne: The stylized flower and leaf motif of this design is based upon a traditional Breton embroidery pattern. The predominent colors are navy blue and orange on a cream background. The work is raised to the touch, as in the case of true embroidery. *(See Décor #8, page 82)*

One other commonly found peasant figure pattern was introduced after World War II. *Ivoire Corbeille* consists of a portrait bust of a man or lady encircled by a ring of blue sponged circles with deep rose-colored centers. The same rose color is used in the "décor à la touche" manner to form the petals of half a stylized sunflower blossom, which completes the pattern. The glaze is cream colored. *(See Décor #339, page 219)*

During the second quarter of the 20th century, different colored glazes were first introduced by both factories. The most common variant is yellow. It comes in two shades: one is soft and pale with a slight greenish cast: the other is more vibrant with an orange tinge. The Grande Maison experimented with a tan glaze. Henriot branched out into other colors. There exists two shades of green: one with a yellow tint and one with a blue cast; a true pink; a medium blue; a peach and a black.

Myriad Forms

The shapes of Quimper pottery can be graceful, interesting, curious, amusing, and in certain cases, even unappealing, depending on personal taste.

The oldest forms of the ware were generally practical kitchen or tableware pieces: plates, platters and the double-handled bowls which had been used in Brittany before the 4th century Roman occupation. Religious statues of the Ste. Vierge were made in the 18th century.

By the mid-19th century, the stock had diversified to include: cisterns, inkwells, barber bowls, holy water fonts and different sized statues of the Ste. Vierge. Three decades later, the inventories show an even greater change in the decorative style: snuff bottles in a variety of shapes *(See pages 10 and 61)*, lavabos, musical instruments, hanging wall pockets and sleigh or cradle-shaped vases, etc.

By the turn of the century, the Art Nouveau period influenced the addition of even more diversified forms. Picture frames, pipe racks, clocks, swan-shaped planters, bagpipe-shaped holloware, etc., all became part of the inventory. Increasingly, the pieces became more decorative in shape and form. In some cases the grotesque contours of the pottery vied with the folk art patterns which adorned them.

Yet, many of the newer forms arose from a solid basis in the traditions of the region. One of the more interesting developments in this area is the production of statues of "saints" who are venerated in Brittany. Some of these are recognized, canonized saints of Christianity. Others are "local saints" who command a deep honor and respect in the folklore tradition. Many are a combination of both.

Ste. Vierge: The greatest number of religious Quimper statues are undoubtedly those representing Mary. Examples of her were made since the 18th century. Some, with deep crowns on their heads, were designed to be used as night lights in sick rooms. A lighted candle fits into the opening of the crown. *(See page 13)*

The mold of Notre Dame de Loc Maria *(See page V)*, is a replica of the 15th century carved wooden statue which stands in the parish church of Loc Maria. She is the patroness of the factory. The fragments of the original statue were saved from destruction during the French Revolution by Citizen Caussy, the widow of Antoine de la Hubaudière.

Ste. Anne: Supposedly Ste. Anne was a Breton woman of noble birth. Folklore states that she left Brittany for Nazareth, but that angels carried her home to Brittany to die. The tale continues by reputing that her grandson, Jesus, visited her before her death. While in Brittany, the Divine Child called forth a miraculous sacred spring called St.-Anne-la-Palud.

Most Quimper statues of Ste. Anne show her with her daughter, Mary: some are entitled Ste.-Anne-la-Palud. *(See pages 112, 113, 126, 148, 184, 212, 235 & 236)*

St. Yves: St. Yves is perhaps the most well known of the Breton saints. Born in 1253 at Tréguier, Yves Hélori studied law in Paris. He returned to Brittany where he was ordained a priest. He practiced law as both a counsel and a judge thereafter. A precursor of free legal aid, St. Yves always took the cases of the poor. He is considered to be the "righter of all wrongs" and the "comfort of the poor". He built a hospital with whatever legal fees he received. Canonized in 1347, St. Yves is the patron saint of lawyers. His statues show him dressed in his legal robes; frequently he is holding a law book and a purse of coins. *(See pages 184, 212 & 235)*

St. Corentin: Corentin was a 6th century Breton hermit. According to local legend, he sustained himself on the flesh of a single fish. Each morning a fish would appear at the river's edge. Corentin would cut it in half and throw the remaining piece back into the water. The fish would rejuvenate itself overnight and offer itself to him anew the next morning. Corentin was later named the first bishop of Quimper. The magnificent Quimper cathedral is named in his honor.

Statues of St. Corentin show him dressed in his bishop's robes and mitre. A fish is usually shown at his feet. *(See pages 184, 212 & 236)*

Ste. Barbe: St. Barbara was a young Breton woman who converted to Christianity. When her father learned of her conversion, he shut her up in a tower and later murdered her with his own hand. Her father was struck by lightening and killed. She is the patron saint of corporations, particularly those who manufacture explosives.

Figurines of St. Barbara show her carrying a miniature tower to commemorate her imprisonment. *(See page 235)*

St. Meen: St. Meen was a Welsh monk who travelled to Brittany during the 6th century. He settled there and converted many of the people to Christianity.

St. Mamert and St. Livertin: These two colorful folklore saints are known respectively as the Breton saint who cures colic and the Breton saint who cures headaches.

The Quimper statue of St. Mamert shows a man holding his exposed entrails. The figure of St. Livertin shows a man clutching either side of his head. *(See page 236)*

The Quimper factories also made religious statues of Christ, St. Joseph, St. Peter, St. Michael the Archangel, etc.

After World War I, the Modern Movement under the auspices of individual artists changed the Quimper forms once again. The shapes were updated, simplified and angularized. Sometimes the pottery was used in conjunction with wooden companion pieces. *(See pages 132 & 133)*

One of the most interesting developments which occurred during this period was the renaissance of grèsware. The stoneware had always been an historically important part of the Quimper production line. The artists during the Modern Movement rediscovered the ware as an appealing artistic medium. Grès was no longer considered to be suitable only for utilitarian purposes. The solid, unadorned, brown glazed earthenware suddenly flowered under the artists' creative touch. The Grande Maison HB produced an entire line of this Art Pottery stoneware. It was called the Odetta line and marked accordingly. The shapes and forms, the stylized patterns and the dark color tones of Odetta ware are usually heavily influenced by the Art Nouveau and Art Deco movements. *(See page 78 & 79)*

Although the shapes of Quimper pottery followed an evolutionary pattern, the molds were not strictly issued in accordance with specific time periods. As in the case of patterns, certain shapes and molds which proved successful were reissued for long periods of time.

In order to provide the reader with a true sampling of the variety of Quimper patterns and molds, an appendix has been provided. Five catalogs dating from the 1880's through the 1950's have been reproduced. The four most recent, which date from the 1920's onward, are photographic. It is hoped that their inclusion will provide the reader with a perspective for study and comparison.

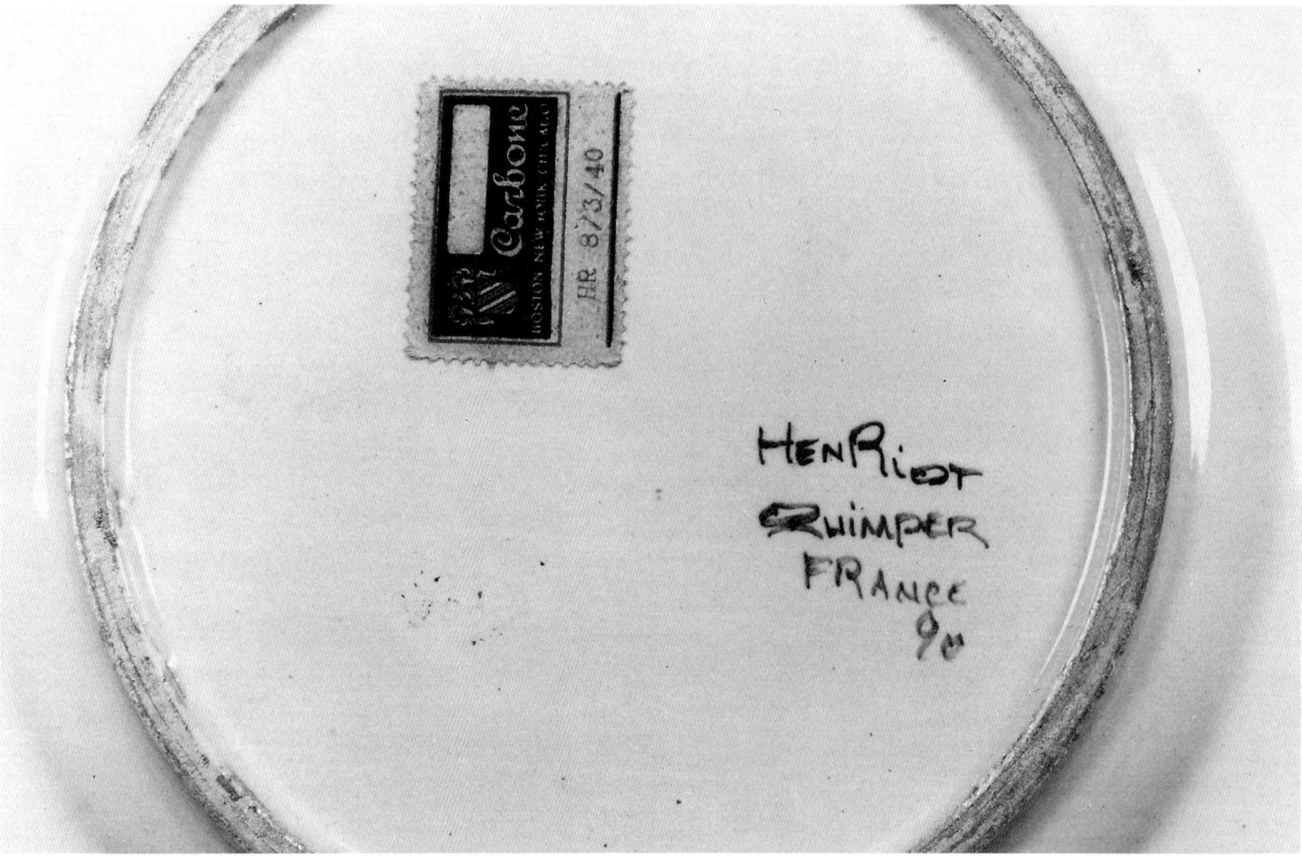

Photo 1: An affixed paper label verifies a commissioned example made for Carbone, a Boston - New York - Chicago department store. It also verifies the date of importation: 8/3/40.

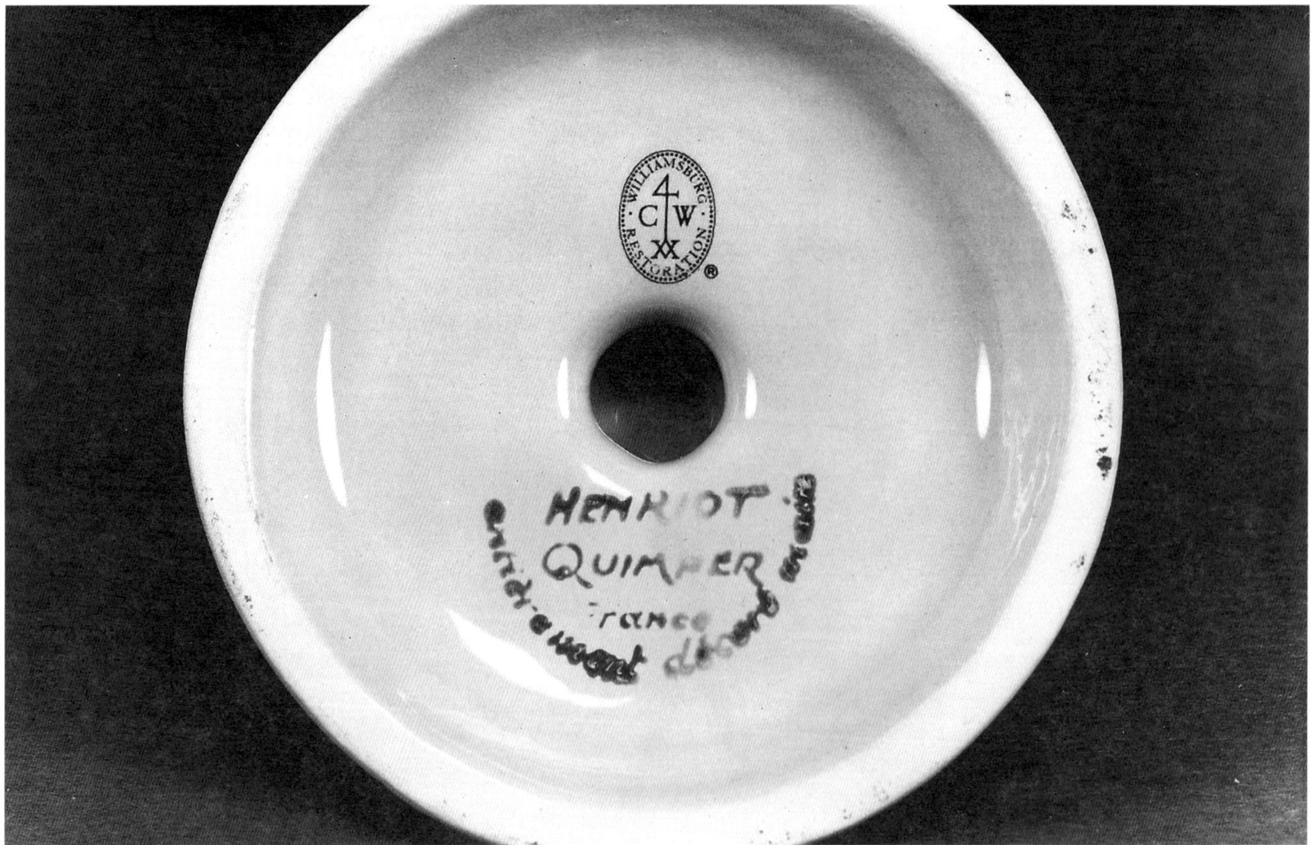

Photo 2: A modern commissioned example dating from the 1960's bears the stamped marks of HenRiot and Colonial Williamsburg.

Chapter 9

Marks and Dates

A list of marks are printed according to each factory at the end of this chapter. A few, brief words of explanation should preface them.

One of the most frequently asked questions regarding Quimper pottery is, "How old is this piece?" The person requesting the information usually expects a definitive date as the answer. This type of precise dating is simply not possible. Certain periods have recognizable traits and marks, and pieces can be fitted into appropriate time frames. Monsieur Rouillard, the Director of the Faïenceries de Quimper, perhaps expressed it best when he suggested that examples be dated according to half or quarter century periods. By using this method, an approximate date can be affixed to a piece, and a true Quimper devotee should be pleased with the result.

The marks and their corresponding historical period, which are listed, should not be interpreted in a strict, dogmatic fashion. Marks cannot be considered solely by themselves in an isolated context. Examples of this danger are discussed below.

The earliest marked examples are extremely rare. Most of the wares dating from the 17th through the mid-19th century are not marked. The chances of finding an authentic example from this period are incredibly remote. Recent, unmarked examples do occasionally appear in the market place. These 20th century wares have simply slipped past the marking procedure at the factory due to human error.

The word "Quimper" was added to the "HB" and "HR" marks during the third quarter of the 19th century. Frequently, the "HB Quimper" or "HR Quimper" signature was placed on the front of a piece, rather than on the base bottom. "Quimper" was added to the mark to differentiate authentic Quimper pottery from the many copies of it which were being made elsewhere at the time. In her book, ***La Faïence de Quimper,*** Madame Taburet states that in several instances, the copies soon followed suit and also added the word "Quimper" to their marks.

The word "France" was not added to the Quimper signature as a result of the McKinley Tariff Act in 1891. Items destined for export to America were identified by a paper sticker declaring "Made in France". Most of these have been worn or washed off. *(See page 90)* "France" was added to the mark about 1920, but only for those examples which were destined for exportation. Many pieces made for the domestic market have found their way into other lands. Tourists or immigrants often brought the examples along with them. Consequently, these pieces do not have the word "France" included as a part of the mark.

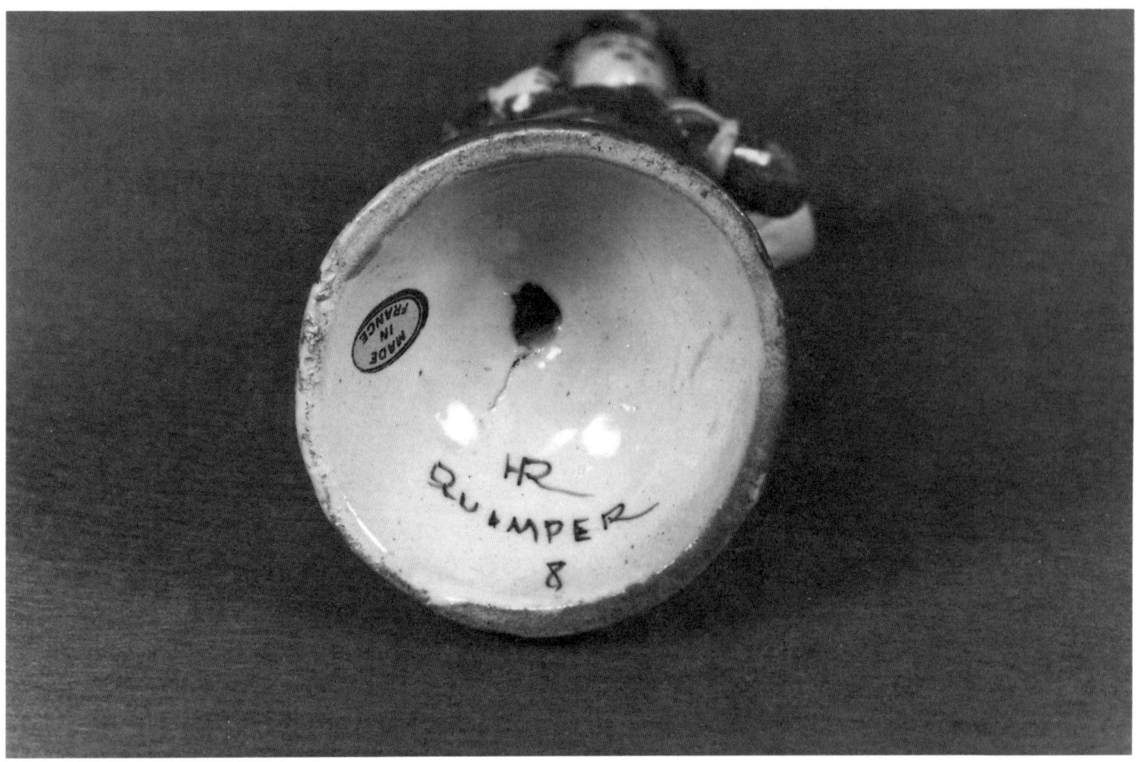

An example of a Maison Henriot piece which was made for export prior to 1922. The original paper label states the country of origin.

Examples manufactured during the 20th century have additional demarcation. At the Grande Maison a series of dots, dashes, x's and circles were added to the mark to specify the individual artisan who had decorated the example. In her book, "La Faïence de Quimper Le Guide du Collectionneur", Marjatta Taburet lists the following artists and their symbols which appeared on pieces before 1942: Mlle Autret o--; Mlle Bozec +..; M. Chapalain___. ; M. Cojan ... ; Mme Le Corre _ _.; Mme Le Meur _ _ ; M. Levenez___..; Mlle Péron ... + ; Mme Simone Roussel + + .

In similar manner the Maison Henriot added a series of numerals to the mark. These also corresponded to their individual artisans. Majatta Taburet lists the following artists and their corresponding numbers which appeared after 1942: Bernadette Guyader 127; Henri Le Phuez 136; Renée Le Phuez 132; Michèle Palud 142; Raymonde Ronarc'h 104 and 68 (after 1962).

All pieces made at the Faïenceries de Quimper after the 1968 merger were marked by hand with numbers preceded by the letters "f" and "d". The "f" stands for the "forme" or mold ; the "d" connotes the "décor" or pattern. In addition the examples were usually stamped in blue with the historically appropriate factory name. Those pieces which traditionally were manufactured by the Maison Henriot were stamped "HenRiot Quimper"; those from the Grande Maison were stamped "HB Quimper". The words "Entièrement décoré à la main" (entirely hand decorated) were usually included in the stamped mark.

Since the consolidation of both factories in 1984 under the new ownership, the Société Nouvelle des Faïenceries de Quimper, the HB and Henriot marks both appear together on all examples.

Three very important exceptions to this present marking system exist.

The first difference can be found on the small or figural examples. In many cases, the shapes cannot accommodate the stamped mark. They are therefore hand signed.

The second and third exceptions deal with reproduction wares.

Many of the impressive, large mold examples which are decorated in the "décor riche" fashion are being reissued. A few of them have indented lines running across the front to simulate an imperfection in the old molding process. A tell-tale indication that these are recent vintage pieces are the "f" and "d", each followed by numerals usually written somewhere on the piece.

The reproduction of 18th and 19th century Quimper pieces by the factory is an even more widespread problem. These copies duplicate the old Museum wares. Plates, platters, candlesticks, barber's bowls, apothecary jars and impressive covered urns are only some of the reproduced molds. The patterns are faithful in feeling to the originals. The examples are fired at low temperatures to achieve the soft, pale shades of the early wares. They have an exaggerated crackled glaze and an "overwipe" of a soft, brown colored substance which gives them an antique appearance. The pieces even have glaze irregularities such as small bare patches of clay and the three touch marks on the reverse side of the flat examples. The pieces are signed usually on the front with either "HB Quimper" or "Henriot Quimper" in a terra cotta color. There is no "France" and generally no numeral as a part of the mark. A paper sticker proclaims them to be a "Ré-édition d'un décor de notre musée, entièrement réalisé à la main" (a copy of a museum piece, completely hand made). These stickers are easily washed off. Readers should be aware of the fact that these reproductions are filtering into the marketplace and are being sold as authentic, old examples by either unsuspecting or disreputable antiques dealers.

The Quimper factories also did commission work. This practice began in Victorian times when neighboring towns needed souvenirs for their growing tourist trade. Quimper pieces marked only with the names of these towns are not uncommon: Mont St. Michel, Pornic, St. Malo, etc. Department stores followed in the 20th century with Ogilvy's, Sterns, Macy's, Bloomingdale's, Altman's, Tiffany's, etc., carrying a line of commissioned Quimper wares. Colonial Williamsburg's gift shop also carries several reproductions made for them by the Quimper factory.

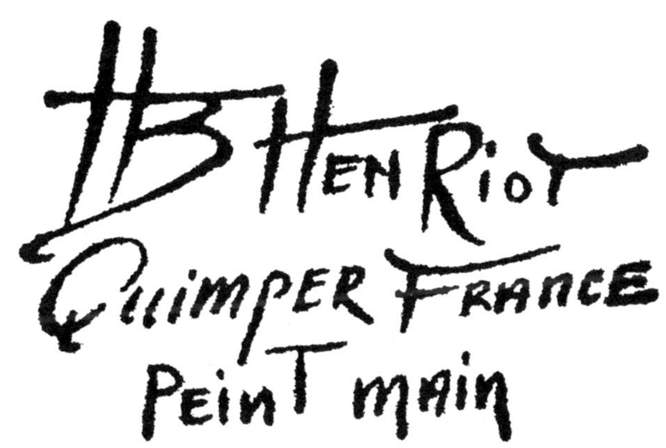

The new mark of the Société Nouvelle des Faïenceries de Quimper 1984 to present.

Marks of the Grande Maison HB

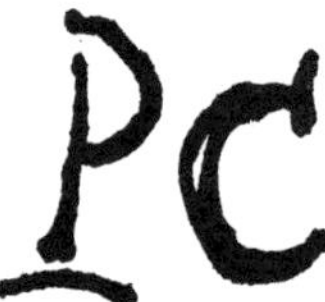

Pierre-Clément Caussy; end of the 18th century

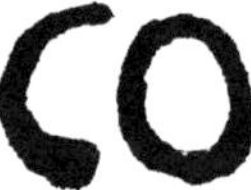

Pierre-Clément Caussy; end of the 18th century

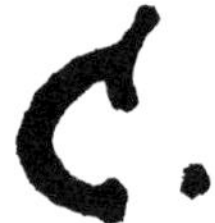

Pierre-Clément Caussy; end of the 18th century

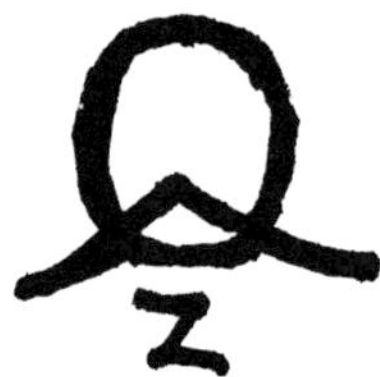

de la Hubaudière; early 19th century; about 1810

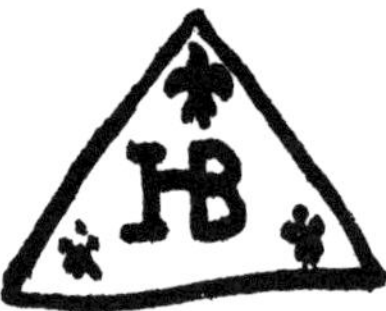

de la Hubaudière; impressed mark; registered in 1898, but previously in use

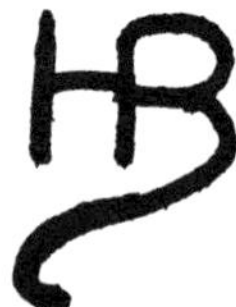

de la Hubaudière; registered in 1882

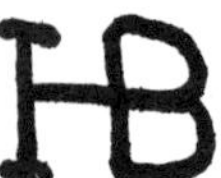

Madame de la Hubaudière; registered in 1883

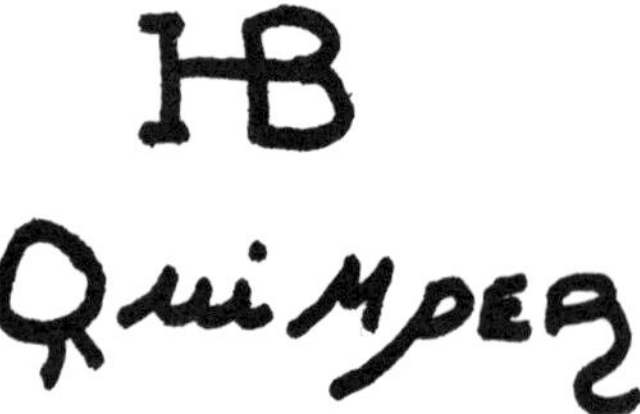

de la Hubaudière; the addition of the word "Quimper" was intended to protect the pottery from spurious imitations; 1883 to about 1910

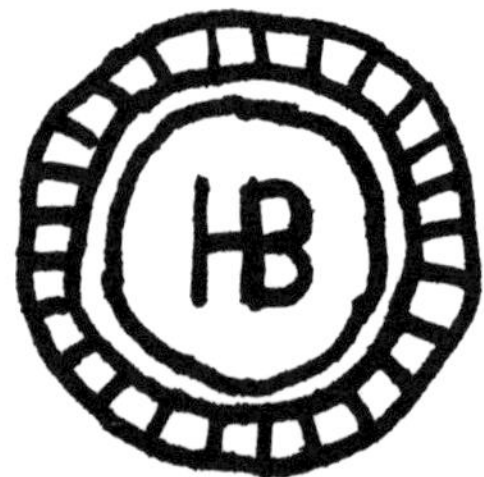

Faïencerie de la Grande Maison HB; 1920

Faïencerie de la Grande Maison HB; the artist, René Quillivic's mark; 1920

HB
ODETTA
LOCMARIA QUIMPER

Faïencerie de la Grande Maison HB; mark used on "grès"; registered in 1922

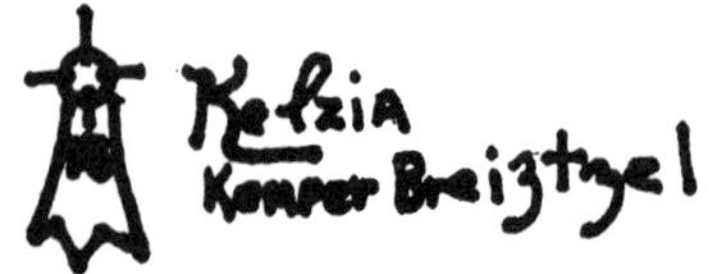

Faïencerie de la Grande Maison HB; 1922.

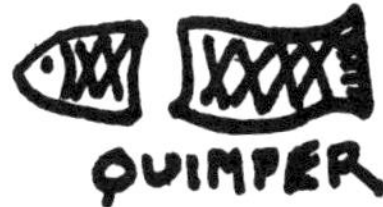

Faïencerie de la Grande Maison HB; mark placed on examples designed by the artist René Quillivic; registered in 1925

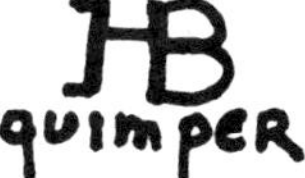

Faïencerie de la Grande Maison HB; 1939

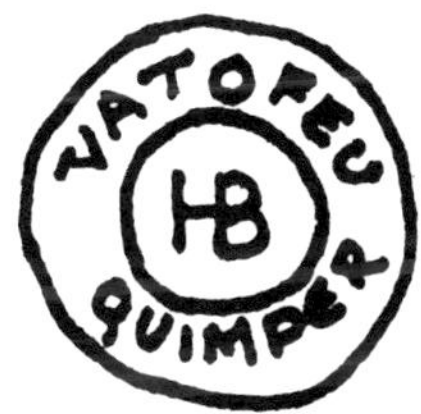

Faïencerie de la Grande Maison HB; 1943

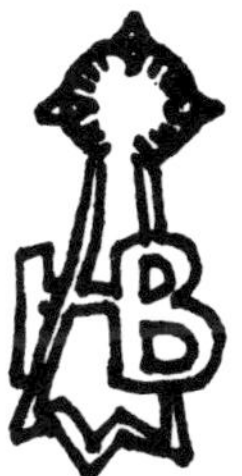

Faïencerie de la Grande Maison; 1943

Faïencerie de la Grande Maison HB; 1954

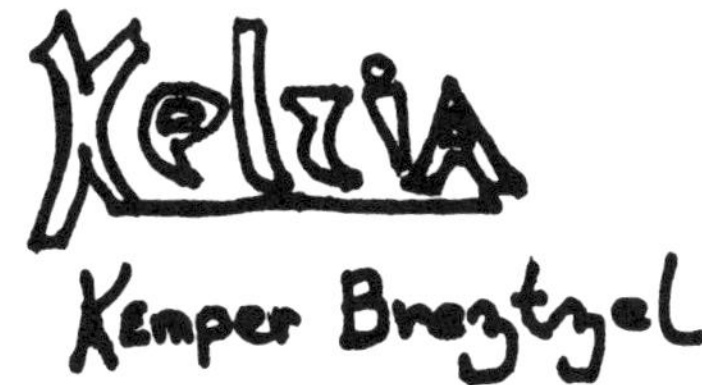

Faïencerie de la Grande Maison HB; 1954

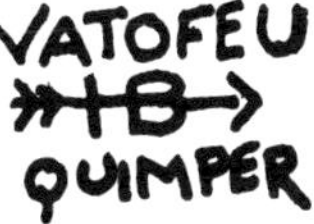

Faïencerie de la Grande Maison HB; 1958

Faïencerie de la Grande Maison HB; 1959

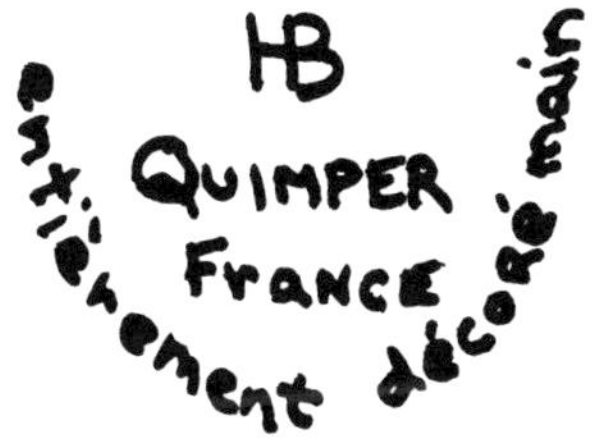

Faïencerie de la Grande Maison HB; stamped in blue and usually having an "f" and "d" mark along with it; 1968 - 1983

Marks of the Eloury-Porquier-Beau Factory

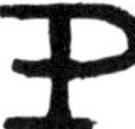

Eloury-Porquier; the earliest mark of this factory dating from about 1845

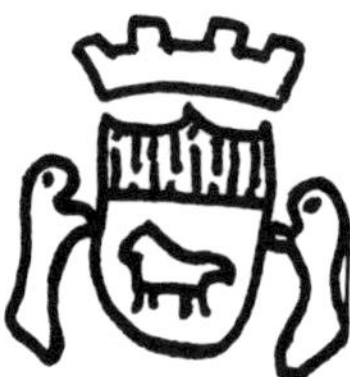

Adolphe Porquier's widow; registered in 1887

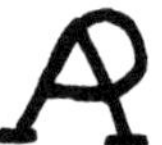

Adolphe Porquier's widow; registered in 1898

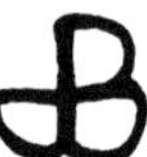

Porquier-Beau mark; formed by the association of Adolphe Porquier's widow, Augustine Caroff, and Alfred Beau; registered in 1898

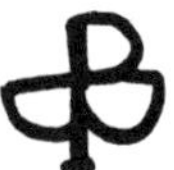

Porquier-Beau mark; registered in 1898

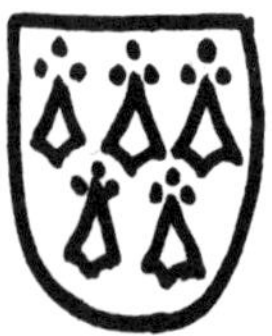

Madame Porquier; registered in 1898

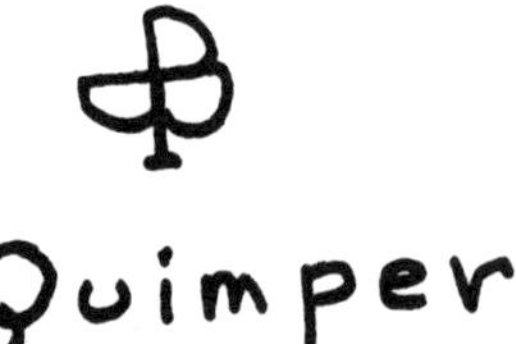

Generally speaking, a re-issue of the original Porquier-Beau molds and patterns under the auspices of the Maison Henriot; 1913

Malicorne Marks

Copies of Quimper Pottery

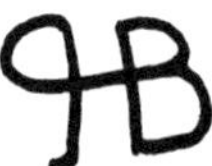

Malicorne factory; Pouplard used this mark to cause confusion between authentic Quimper pottery and his spurious copies; late 19th century

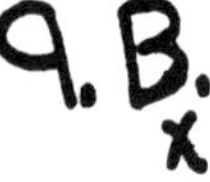

Another Malicorne mark; Pouplard used his initial and the initial of his wife's name, Béatrix, to form a "PB" mark; this mark lead to Porquier-Beau's lawsuit against the Malicorne establishment; late 19th century

Marks of the Dumaine-Tanquerey-Henriot Factory

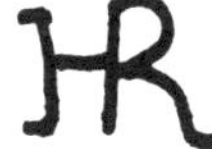

Jules Henriot: registered in 1904, but previously in use

HR
Quimper

Faïencerie Henriot; used up until 1922

HENRIOT
QUIMPER

Faïencerie Henriot; used after 1922

FIRESIDE
HENRIOT
QUIMPER
FRANCE

An example of a mark made on commission by the Faïencerie Henriot; about 1930

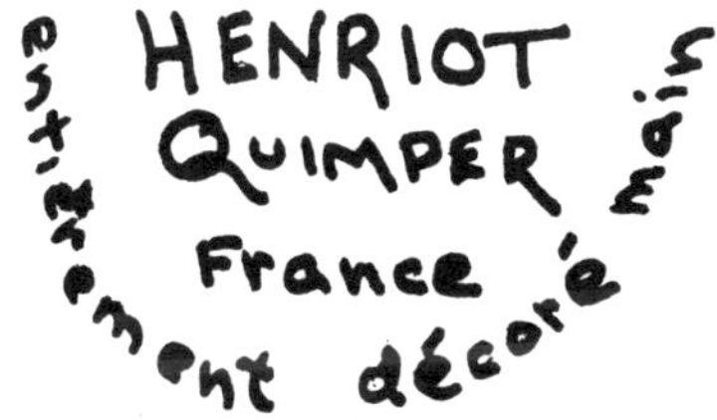

Faïencerie Henriot; stamped in blue and usually having an "f" and "d" mark along with it; 1968 - 1983

Common Decorative Details

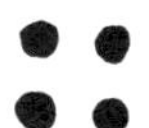

The four dot design: usually in blue, occasionally in red.

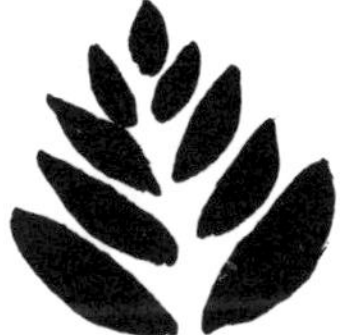

The "à la touche" design: used to make flowers, garland borders, leaves and also to stripe the handles and spouts of holloware.

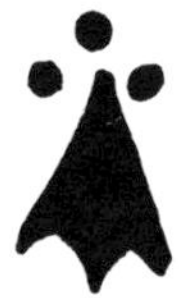

The ermine tail: the symbol of Brittany. (See Page 14)

Border scrolls: occasionally found on late 19th century examples. This motif was borrowed from late 17th century Marseille and early 18th century Strasbourg faïences. It is possible that this simple scroll work influenced the later development of the acanthus border, which is frequently seen on Porquier-Beau examples and "décor riche" pieces.

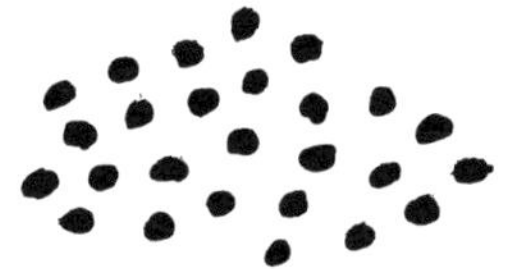

A smattering of tiny blue or red dots: sometimes found on examples dating from the late 19th century. This detail often adorned Rouen faïence borders from the first half of the 18th century. (See the handles on the tray on Page 36)

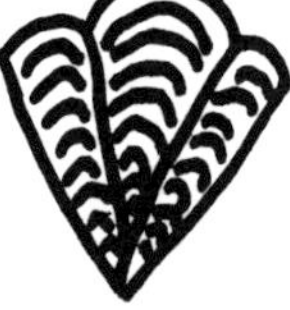

The seashell: an appropriate symbol for a Breton pottery, as the lives of the Breton folk are closely bound to the sea. (See Page 56 Grandfather's clock vase and the finial of the covered butter tub)

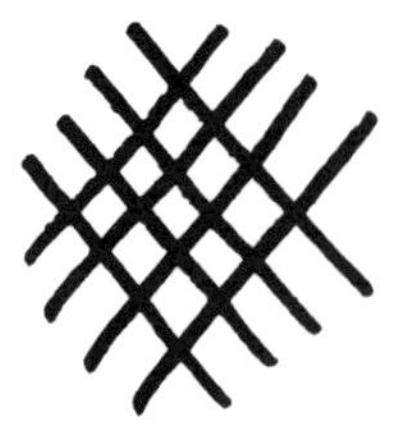

A simple lattice design.

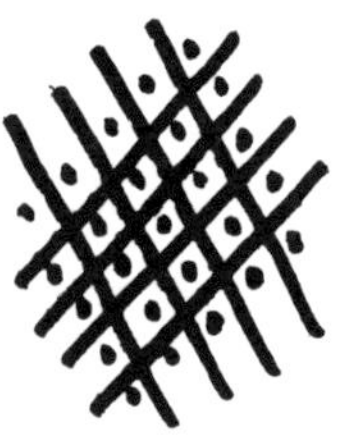

A lattice and dot design: influenced by Rouen and Nevers faïences from the first half of the 18th century.

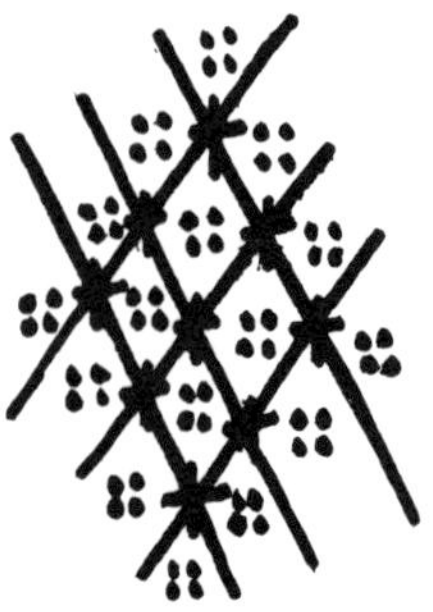

A criss-cross lattice and four dot design: influenced by early 18th century Rouen wares.

Sponging (not illustrated): an internationally acceptable folk art form; used at Quimper to decorate rims, handles, spouts and edges.

Chapter 10

Two Modern Faïenceries in Loc Maria Quimper

Fouillen

Paul Fouillen was born in Pontivy in 1900 and attended the École des Beaux-Arts in Rennes. His travels as a sales representative brought him to Quimper. There he met and married a young woman who worked at the Grande Maison.

In the early 1920's he presented some of his sketches to the factory. He was hired as a contributing artist and in 1925 the P. Fouillen mark began to appear on HB production pieces. He worked both in faïence and in grès. The latter for the Odetta line.

Not content to merely work as an artist, he decided in 1928 to open his own business. Thus, the fourth Quimper factory was born.

Initially he lacked sufficient funds to buy his own kiln. His very first production pieces were taken and fired in the ovens of the Maison Henriot.

In addition to ceramics Fouillen also produced etched and carved wooden pieces, paintings on glass, leather goods and furniture.

His pottery has a strong Celtic flavor. He used Breton embroideries and manuscript borders done by Medieval Irish monks for his inspiration. Some of his examples introduce entirely new techniques in ceramic art i.e. the over dusting of some of his examples with local sand. The medium used was the heavy stoneware, grès. It was fired at 1300°F and glazed with a matte or pebbly finish. The colors are bold; the patterns distinctly Modern Movement.

A word of interest concerning his woodenware, as they are still found somewhat frequently by collectors. He manufactured plates, bowls, covered boxes, trays, etc. in a distictive manner. These examples usually have Breton scenes, incorporating the peasant figure, which are lightly etched into the wooden surface. The figures and backgrounds are vibrantly over-painted in bright, fresh colors. The figures are angular and slightly stylized.

Paul Fouillen died in 1968. His son,Maurice, continues in his father's tradition.

The mark is "P. Fouillen" Quimper.

Keraluc

Victor Lucas, a ceramist from the École de Sèvres, founded the most recent faïence house in Quimper. Keraluc was established in 1946.

Lucas went to the local artists for his designs and thus retained a traditional Breton character for his pottery. However, the style is totally individualistic. A free hand is used for the interpretation of design and a more liberal execution is the result. Colors are vivid and varied. The house still uses the clay from the Anse de Toulven region, but it is now fortified with an additive imported from Lorient. Some pieces are still hand thrown on the potter's wheel. The more demanding method of painting the pattern on top of the glaze is used. The finished product has a heavier look and feel than that of the HB-Henriot Factory.

Since Lucas' death, his son, Pol Lucas and his daughter, Mme. Chauveau have managed the factory.

The mark is: "Keraluc Quimper".

Appendix

MANUFACTURE DE LOCMARIA

FAÏENCES ARTISTIQUES

A. PORQUIER & A. BEAU

QUIMPER (Finistère).

TARIF 1887

FAÏENCES DE FANTAISIE

	FR.	C.
Assiettes		
Assiette dessert, Armes villes, bord Italien.	3	»
— — bord Rouen.	3	»
— — bord Breton.	3	»
— Coupe-Chiffre bord Rouen.	9	»
Baguiers *(voir Cendriers).*		
Baguier cocotte.	6	»
— bateau.	3	»
Banettes		
Banette Deniel. — Figures.	12	50
— — Fleurs.	12	50
— plate. — Armes villes.	18	»
Bénitiers		
Bénitier. — Fleurs.	9	»
— Lambrequins.	12	»
—		
Beurrier rond.	7	50
—		
Bobèche ronde, unie.	1	»
— fest.	1	»
—		
Boite à gants.	12	»
Bonbonnières		
Bonbonnière ronde n° 1.	6	»
— — 2.	8	50
— — 3.	12	»
— — 4.	15	»
— ovale.	6	»

	FR.	C.
Bougeoirs		
Bougeoir ovale, — carré, — triang. } Fleurs.	4	50
— pantoufle.	6	»
— lion, porte-écusson.	8	»
Brûle-Parfums		
Brûle-Parfums, 2 anses.	15	»
— Chinois.	15	»
Cache-Pots		
Cache-pot japonais n° 1.	3	50
— — 2.	4	50
— marmite 1.	5	»
— — 2.	7	50
— tulipe 6 pans.	12	50
— — 6 feuilles.	12	50
— cylindrique 3 pieds.	12	50
— éventail 4 faces.	25	»
Cadres de glace		
Cadre de glace n° 1.	6	»
— 2.	12	50
— 3.	25	»
Carafes		
Carafe couverte.	15	»
— 4 goulots.	12	50
— japonaise (grand modèle).	25	»
— plate japonaise.	12	»
— — anses grecques.	10	»
— pied découpé.	10	»
— italienne.	18	»
Carafon Nancy.	10	»

Cendriers

	FR.	C.
Cendrier carré	3	»
--- carte	2	50
--- éventail	2	50
--- japonais fermé n° 1	2	50
--- — — 2	3	»
--- — poché	2	»
--- oblong	1	75
--- ovale	1	75
--- trèfle	1	75
--- trilobé plat	2	»
--- tube	1	75
--- semelle	1	75

Chandeliers

	FR.	C.
Chandelier Bailly. — Fleurs	5	»
— rocaille. — base triang.	10	»
— — base quad.	10	»
— Rouen. — base 8 pans.	6	»
— grand éventail	18	»

—

	FR.	C.
Clochette	4	»

Compotiers

	FR.	C.
Compotier Deyrolle, oiseaux japonais.	5	»
— moyen	3	50
— — à anses	6	»
— grand —	12	»

Coffrets

	FR.	C.
Coffret carré n° 1	7	50
— — 2	9	»
— oblong	10	»
— rocaille	30	»
— étoile n° 1	18	»
— — 2	25	»

Corbeilles

	FR.	C.
Corbeille allemande	9	»
--- B., anse tordue	6	»
--- carte	7	50
--- carrée à anse	8	»
--- — sans anse	6	»
--- cocotte	10	»
--- croissant	12	50
--- ovale, feuille japonaise	7	50
--- bergère	12	»
--- japonaise n° 3	7	50
--- --- 4	12	»
--- --- creuse 4 anses	10	»
--- hongroise n° 1	8	»
--- --- 2	10	»
--- plate 1 anse	4	50
--- — 4 anses	6	»
--- à revers	10	»
--- saucier	6	»
--- tricorne russe à anse	12	»
--- --- sans anse	12	»
--- trilobée	15	»

—

	FR.	C.
Corne scandinave { jaune ocré	10	»
Corne scandinave { décor à bandes	25	»

Cornets

	FR.	C.
Cornet poche. --- Fleurs	10	»
--- d'angle. } Fleurs et Armoiries.	15	»
--- d'applique.	9	»
--- à torsade.	9	»
--- double.	7	50
--- simple.	5	»

	FR.	C.
Coupe ovale col cygne	12	50

Crêmiers

	FR.	C.
Crêmier n° 1	3	»
--- 2	4	»
--- 3	5	50
--- 4	7	50

Cuirs

	FR.	C.
Cuir carré simple	4	50
— sur pied	7	50
— japonais	7	50
— d'archer	12	»

Drageoirs *(voir Corbeilles)*

	FR.	C.
Drageoir tricorne	7	50
— carré à anse	8	»
— — sans anse	6	»
— paquet à anse	12	»
— — sans anse	10	»
— poche	10	»
— sac	12	»
— coquille Duclos	6	»

—

	FR.	C.
Echarpe d'archer	10	»

Encriers

	FR.	C.
Encrier 2 coquilles	4	50
— 3 —	6	»
— croissant	5	»
— fourneau	12	»
— Gien	15	»
— japonais	4	»
— long 4 pieds	10	»
— rocaille	18	»
— fleur de lys	12	»
— à tiroir et bougeoirs	25	»

Feuilles

	FR.	C.
Feuille figue	4	»
— caoutchouc	6	»
— javanaise	5	»
— Jault simple	3	50
— — double	7	50
Foulard (Drageoir)	12	»

—

	FR.	C.
Génieux. — Fleurs	7	50

Glaces

	FR.	C.
Glace encadrée N° 1	12	50
— 2	20	»
— 3	40	»

—

	FR.	C.
Gobelet d'archer à bandes	9	»
— fleurs	7	50

—

	FR.	C.
Gourde anneau	9	»

Instruments de Musique

	FR.	C.
Clarinette	20	»
Cor de chasse	100	»
Corne de Rolland	60	»
Flûte	15	»
Serpent	60	»
Trompette	50	»
Violon	75	»

FAÏENCES BORD JAUNE

Assiettes

	FR. C.
Assiette dessert	2 »
— plate	2 25
— creuse	2 25
— sur pied haut	5 »

Banettes

	FR. C.
Banette plate	10 »
— creuse	7 50
— Bailly	10 »
Beurrier rond	5 »

Bougeoirs

	FR. C.
Bougeoir ovale	3 50
— triangulaire	3 50
— carré	3 50
Cachepot Bailly	12 »

Compotiers

	FR. C.
Compotier grand	6 »
— moyen	3 »
— étoile	3 50
— sur pied, grand	12 »
— — moyen	7 50
Coquetier	1 50

Coupes

	FR. C.
Coupe à fruits. — Décor simple	6 »
— — Décor double	7 50
Coupe de milieu	12 »
— forme Moustiers	6 »
Corne scandinave	9 »
Cendrier trèfle	1 75

Crêmiers

	FR. C.
Crémier N° 1	2 50
— 2	3 »
— 3	4 50
— 4	6 »
— Sèvres	6 »

Feuilles

	FR. C.
Feuille de figue, grande	3 »
— moyenne	2 50
— Jault	2 50
— de vigne	2 »
— cendrier	1 50
Génieux	6 »

Jardinières

	FR. C.
Jardinière banette	18 »
— — avec plateau	28 »
— Bailly	20 »
— — avec plateau	30 »
— Nancy	15 »
— oblongue	25 »
— — avec plateau	37 »
— Louis XV	9 »
— Jap. oblongue	20 »
— Nevers 3 goulots	6 »

Jattes

	FR. C.
Jatte à fraises	9 »
— à lait	12 »
— — forme Moustiers	12 »

Légumiers

	FR. C.
Légumier ovale	10 »
— — et plateau	15 »
— rond festonné	12 »
— trilobé	25 »
Moutardier rond sur plateau	3 50
— ovale	3 50

Plateaux

	FR. C.
Plateau oblong	10 »
— italien	6 »
— à thé, grand	18 »
— à thé, petit	12 »
— de légumier	5 »

Plats

	FR. C.
Plat à poisson, petit	15 »
— — moyen	20 »
— — grand	27 50
— ovale, de 24 (0,32)	6 »
— — 18 (0,34)	7 50
— — pièce (0,38)	9 »
— — 2 pièces (0,42)	12 50
— rond, de 24 (0,27)	6 »
— — 18 (0,30)	7 50
— — pièce (0,34)	9 »
— — 2 pièces (0,38)	12 50
Pot à crème	2 »
Ravier ovale	2 50

Saladiers

	FR. C.
Saladier rond n° 1 (0,27)	7 50
— — 2 (0,31)	9 »
— — 3 (0,34)	12 50
Salière 2 coquilles	2 50
— 2 sabots	2 »

Sauciers

	FR. C.
Saucier ovale sur plateau sans anse	6 »
— — — à anse	6 »
— moustiers sans plateau	6 »

Services

	FR. C.
Service à thé 12 tasses	73 50
— — 6 tasses	57 »
— fumeur	25 »
— à déjeûner	25 »

Soucoupes

	FR. C.
Soucoupe pochée	1 25
— ronde unie	1 25
— — festonnée	1 25
— chocolat	2 50
— tasse trilobée	1 25
Soupière ronde	18 »

Sucriers

	FR. C.
Sucrier rond grandes dents s' plateau	9 »
— — petites dents —	10 »
— — Ghilino —	10 »
— ovale —	9 »
— — Rossi sans plateau	7 50
— rond Sèvres	10 »
— poché	7 50

Tasses

	FR. C.
Tasse à déjeuner (génieux)	6 »
— à chocolat (avec soucoupe)	6 »
— à thé pochée (avec soucoupe)	2 50
— à café — (avec soucoupe)	2 50
— à thé ronde (avec soucoupe)	2 50
— — trilobée (avec soucoupe)	2 50

Théières

	FR. C.
Théière pochée	12 »
— Japon n° 2	15 »
— — 1	10 »
— lézard	10 »
— Sèvres	12 50
— gourde plate	18 »
— — anneau	18 »
Trifeuille	12 »

Vases

	FR. C.
Vase chinois n° 1	6 »
— — 2	9 »
— pivoine	12 50

DÉCOR FLEURS DE LYS

ET HERMINES

	FR. C.
Assiette à dessert	1 »
Bougeoir ovale	2 50
— triangulaire	2 50
— carré	2 50
Cache-pot Bailly	12 »
Génieux	5 »
Service à déjeûner	15 »
— fumeur	15 »
Soucoupe de tasse	1 »
Tasse et soucoupe	2 »

Jardinières	FR.	C.
Jardinière-aumônière	12	50
— éventail N° 1	12	50
— — 2	15	»
— — 3	60	»
— — 4	60	»
— japonaise longue	25	»
— Louis XV	12	»
— nid de cornets	18	»
— papillon	15	»
— tronc d'arbre	15	»
— vannerie	12	»
— ovale 4 pieds	15	»
—		
Lion porte-écusson	20	»
—		
Mouchoir roulé	10	»
— plié en 4 (Drageoir)	12	»
—		
Mouche (Vase)	12	»
Paniers *(voir Corbeilles)*		
Pendules		
Pendule rocaille ferronnerie	20	»
— riche	25	»
— à corniche	20	»
—		
Pichet plat	9	»
—		
Plaque de porte	4	»
Plateaux		
Plateau éventail	6	»
— oblong. — Feuillages	12	»
— à thé. — Armoiries	25	»
— — Carquois	20	»
— d'archer	12	»
—		
Plumier long	3	50
—		
Porte-menu N° 1	1	50
— 2	2	50
Porte-violettes		
Porte-violettes N° 1	4	»
— 2	5	»
— 3	6	»
— 4 godets	15	»
Porte-bouquets. *(Voir Vases.)*		
Porte-bouquets 4 vases ferr	40	»
— Nevers 3 goulots	7	50
— 4 roseaux	12	»
—		
Porte-pipes à coquille	7	50
—		
Porte-cigares éventail	12	50
—		
Pot à tabac japonais	10	»
—		
Ravier Rossi	3	50
— bateau	4	»
—		
Sabot Noël	7	50

Salières	FR.	C.
Salière 2 coquilles	4	»
— 2 sabots	2	»
— Bailly	3	50
—		
Serviette à assiette	17	50
— pliée (voir Drageoirs)	12	»
Services		
Service d'archer	40	»
— à déjeuner (tête à tête)	30	»
— à bière	50	»
— fumeur	30	»
Soucoupes		
Soucoupe de tasse. — Carquois	1	50
— Armoiries	1	50
— Feuillage japon.	1	50
— Fleur de lys relief.	1	50
— japonaise N° 1	3	»
— — 2	4	50
— — 3	5	»
— — 4. — Fleurs	10	»
— — 4. — Armoiries.	12	»
Sucriers		
Sucrier ovale	12	»
— losange	10	»
— Rossi pied bas	5	»
— — pied haut	7	50
Suspensions		
Suspension N° 1	18	»
— 2	22	50
— 3	25	»
— 4	30	»
— 5	40	»
— Croissant	30	»
Tasses *(avec Soucoupes)*		
Tasse à chocolat	7	50
— à déjeuner (Génieux)	9	»
— thé ou café. — Carquois	3	»
— Feuillage japonais	3	»
— Fleurs de lys relief	3	»
Théières		
Théière japonaise N° 1	12	50
— 2	18	»
— lézard	12	»
— pochée	12	50
Vases		
Vase trompette	30	»
— éventail	30	»
— ruban	12	»
— rond 4 pieds	10	»
— N° 6	7	50
— rocaille anses coquilles	7	50
— anses rocailles	12	»
— pivoine	12	50
— tête de loup	10	»
— à 2 coquilles	12	50

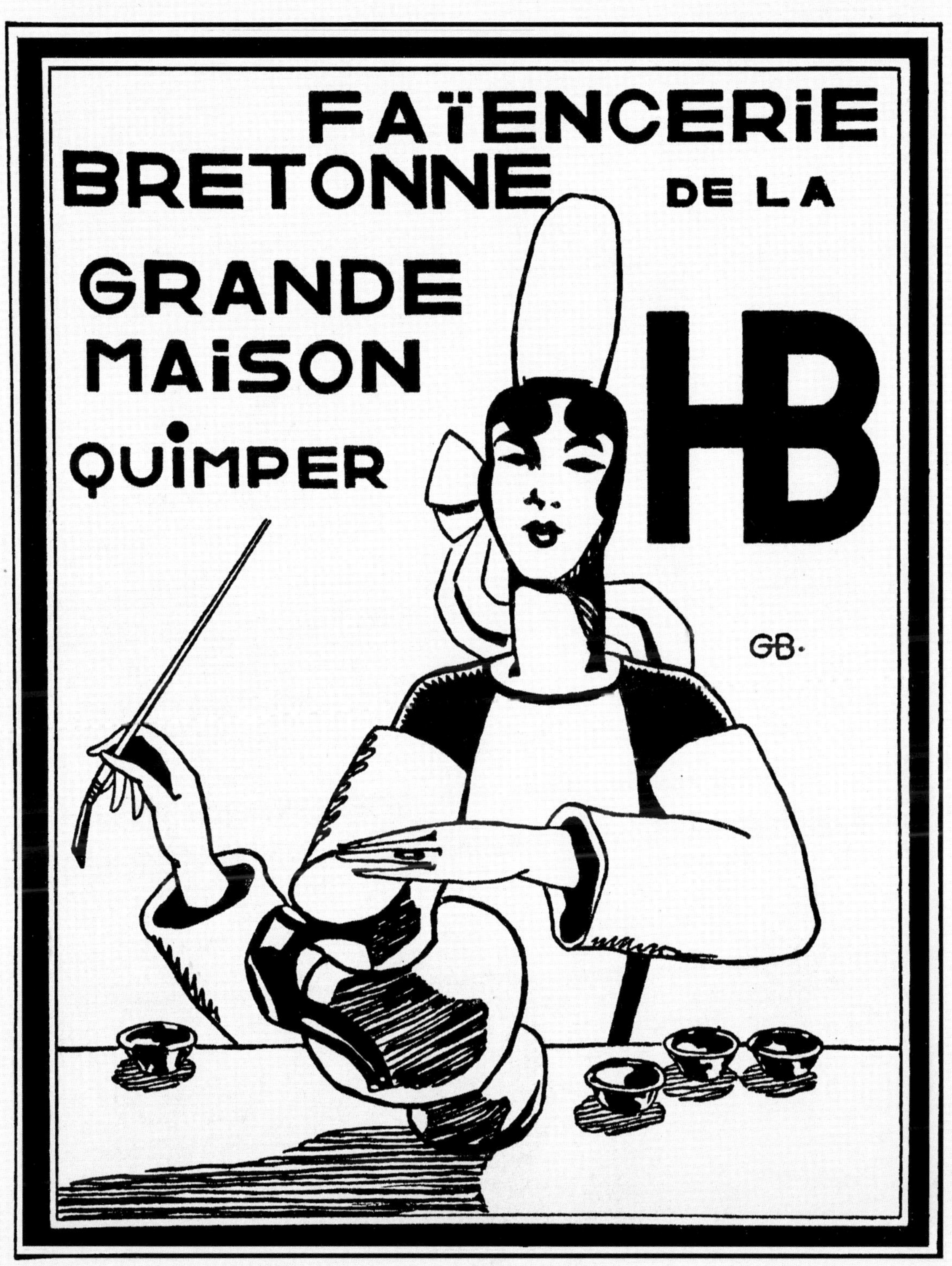
FAÏENCERIE
BRETONNE DE LA
GRANDE
MAISON
QUIMPER
HB
GB·

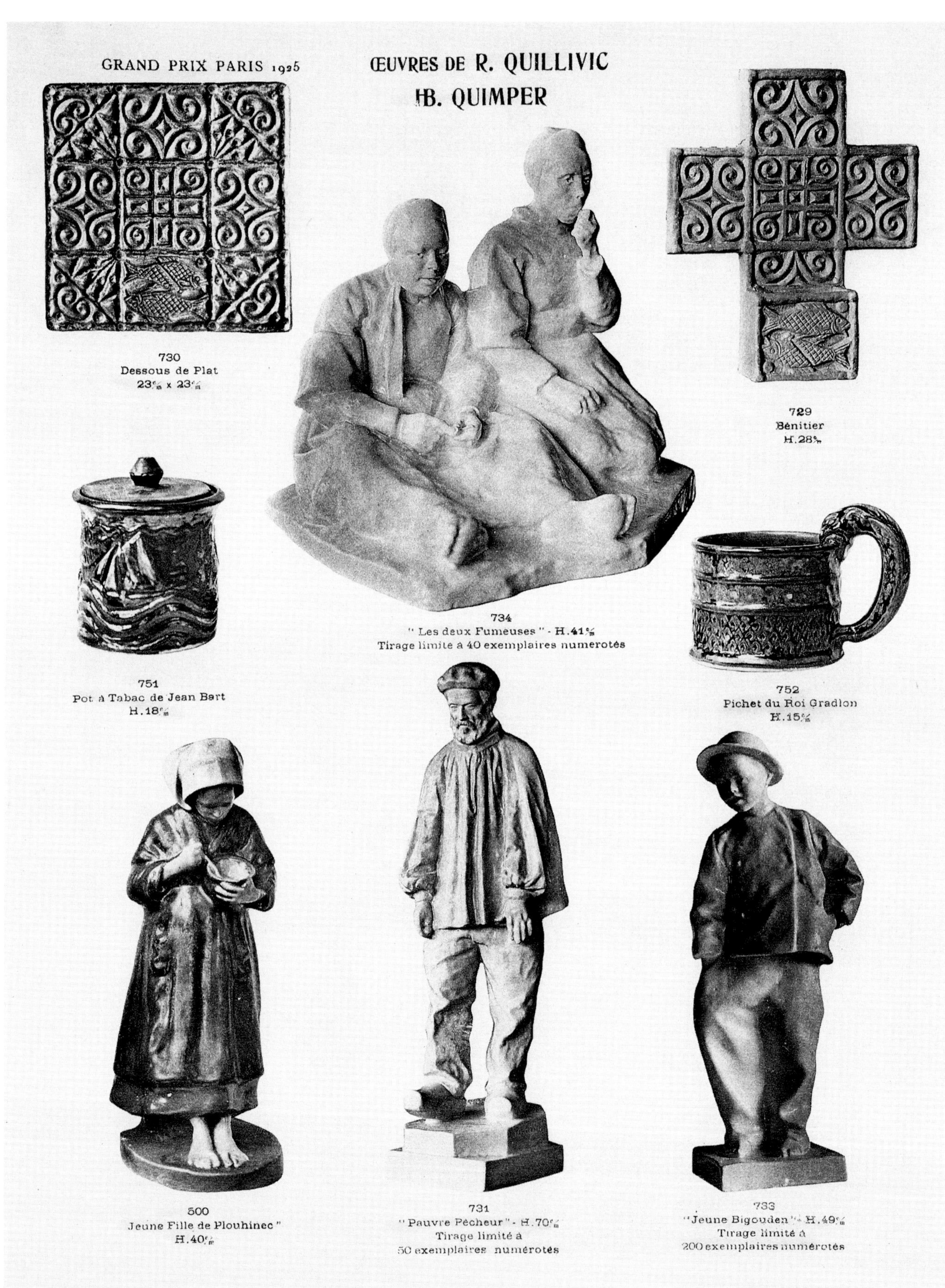
GRAND PRIX PARIS 1925

ŒUVRES DE R. QUILLIVIC

HB. QUIMPER

730
Dessous de Plat
23 c/m x 23 c/m

729
Bénitier
H.28 c/m

734
" Les deux Fumeuses " - H.41 c/m
Tirage limité à 40 exemplaires numerotés

751
Pot à Tabac de Jean Bart
H.18 c/m

752
Pichet du Roi Gradlon
H.15 c/m

500
Jeune Fille de Plouhinec "
H.40 c/m

731
" Pauvre Pêcheur " - H.70 c/m
Tirage limité à
50 exemplaires numérotés

733
"Jeune Bigouden " - H.49 c/m
Tirage limité à
200 exemplaires numérotés

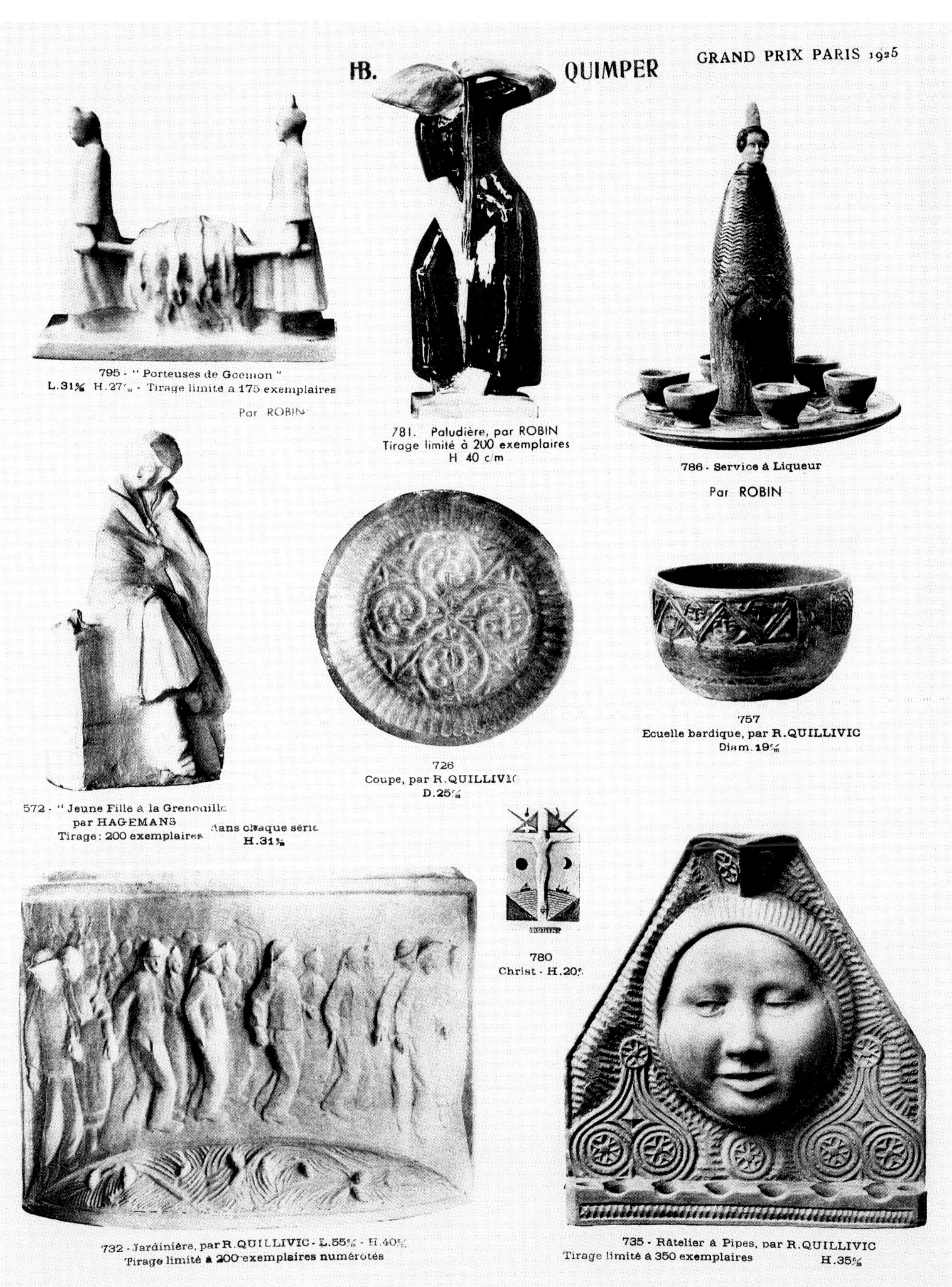

795 - " Porteuses de Goemon "
L.31% H.27% - Tirage limité à 175 exemplaires
Par ROBIN

781. Paludière, par ROBIN
Tirage limité à 200 exemplaires
H 40 c/m

786 - Service à Liqueur
Par ROBIN

757
Ecuelle bardique, par R.QUILLIVIC
Diam.19%

726
Coupe, par R.QUILLIVIC
D.25%

572 - " Jeune Fille à la Grenouille
par HAGEMANS
Tirage: 200 exemplaires dans chaque série
H.31%

780
Christ - H.20%

732 - Jardinière, par R.QUILLIVIC - L.55% - H.40%
Tirage limité à 200 exemplaires numérotés

735 - Râtelier à Pipes, par R.QUILLIVIC
Tirage limité à 350 exemplaires H.35%

HB. QUIMPER

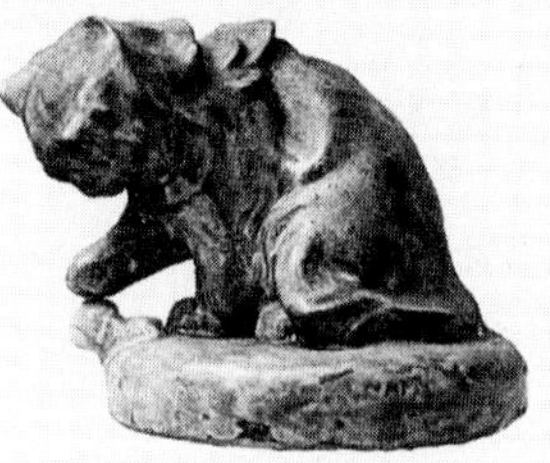

852 - Chat à l'escargot,
par Jacques NAM - H.15%

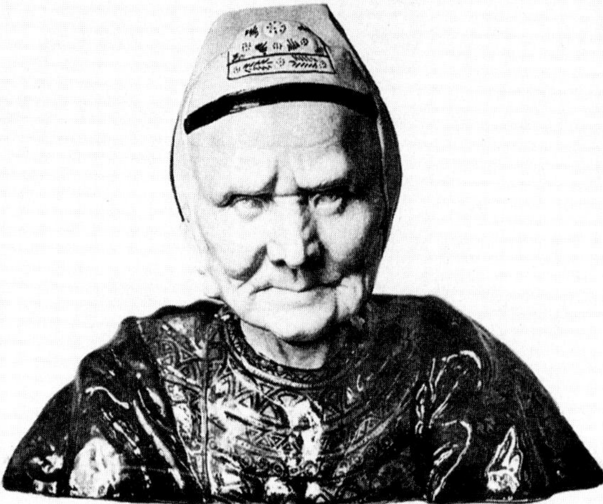

896 - Buste de Bigoudenne, par PORSON
Tirage limité à 200 exemplaires dans chaque série
H' 31 c/m

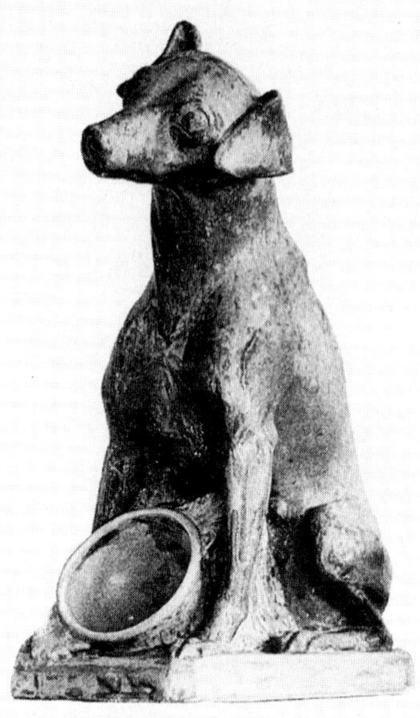

758 - Chien à l'écuelle, par R.QUILLIVIC
H 37% Tirage limité à 100 exemplaires

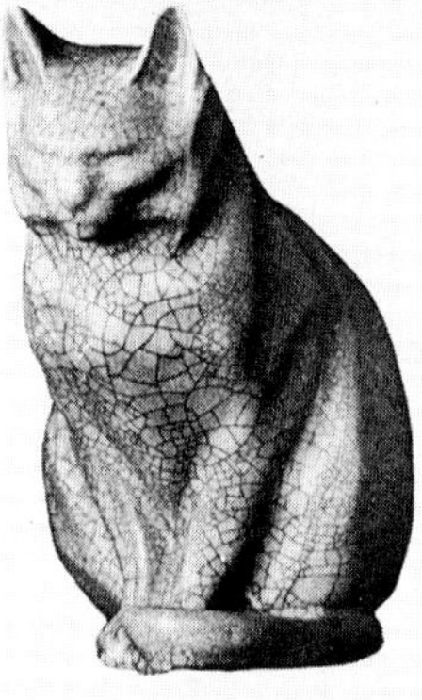

851 - Chat, par J.NAM
H.19%

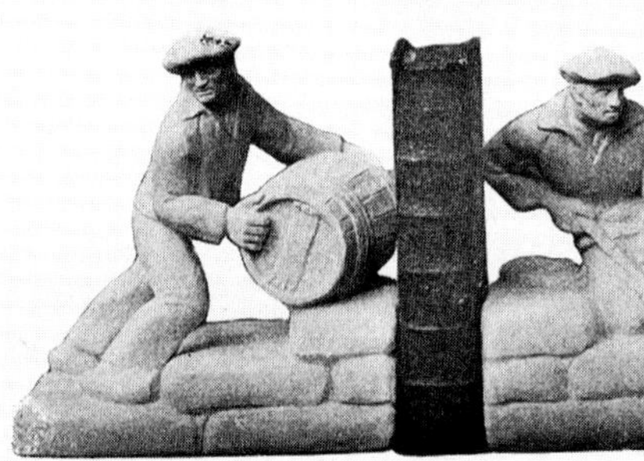

814. Serre-livres
par BOUVIER
L' 35%

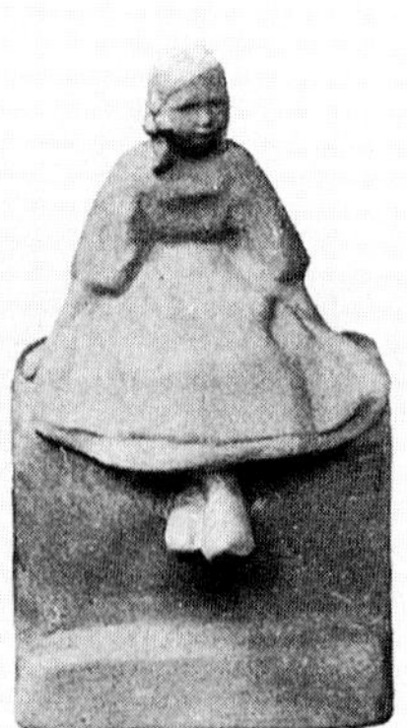

895
Fillette, par PORSON
H.20%

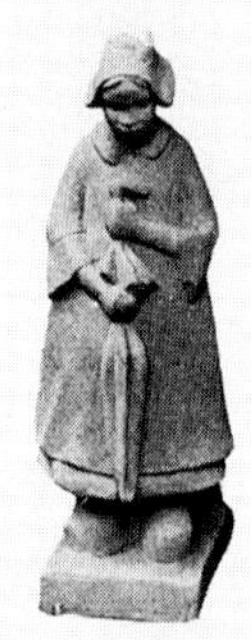

892
Fillette, par PORSON
H.18%

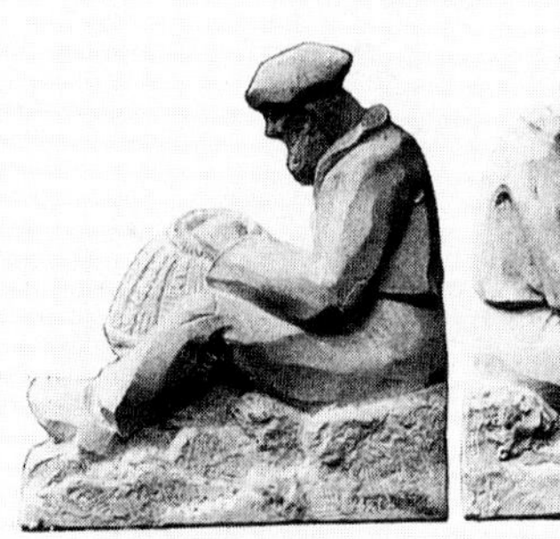

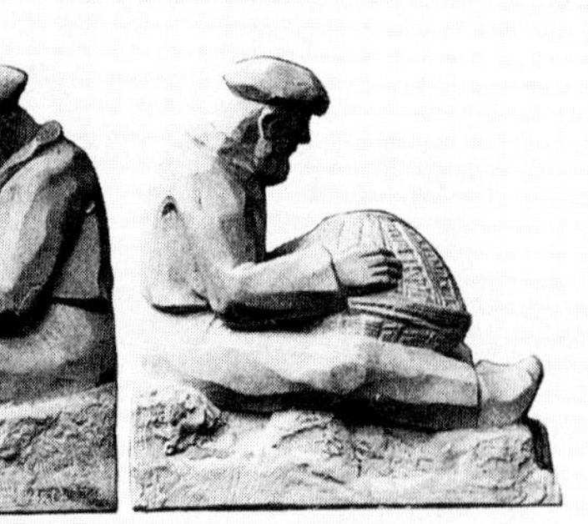

371. Serre-livres, L' 28%

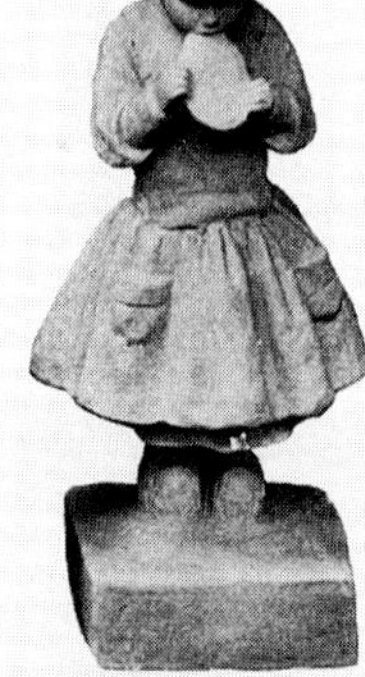

893 - Fillette à la Tartine,
par PORSON - H.23%

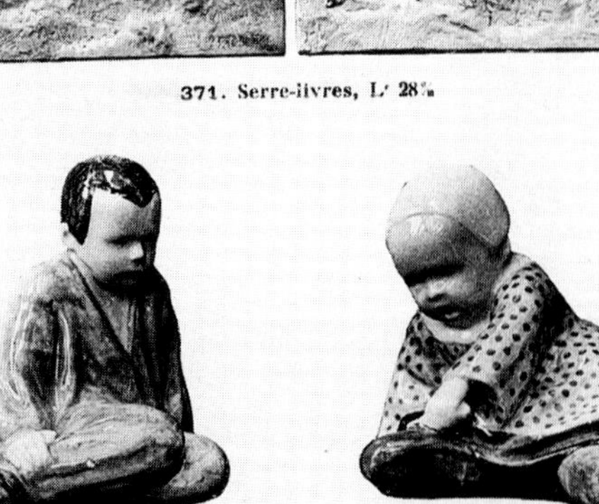

838. Enfant, par SAVIGNY
H' 15%

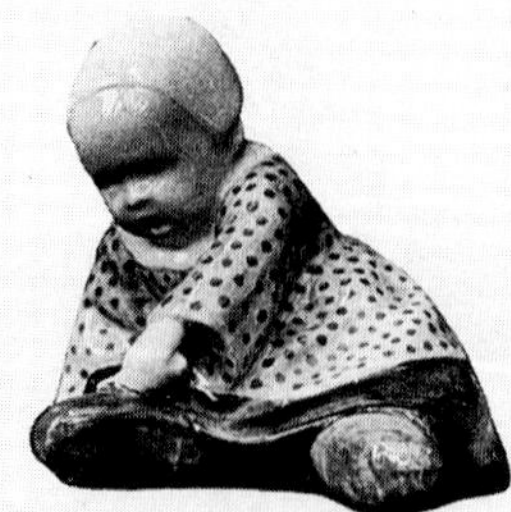

837. Bébé, par SAVIGNY
H' 14%

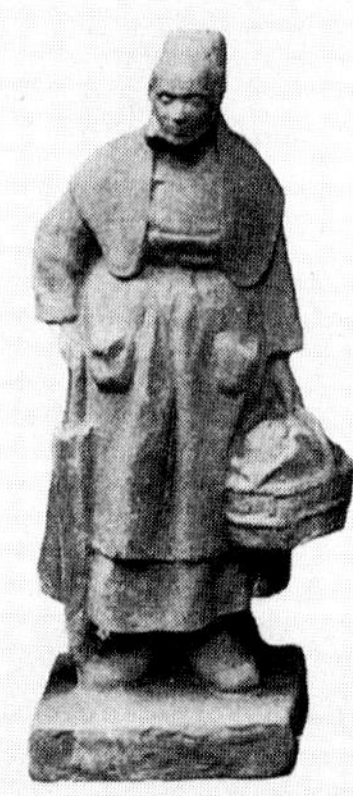

894 - Femme du Faouët
par PORSON - H 22%
Tirage limité a 500 exemplaires
dans chaque série

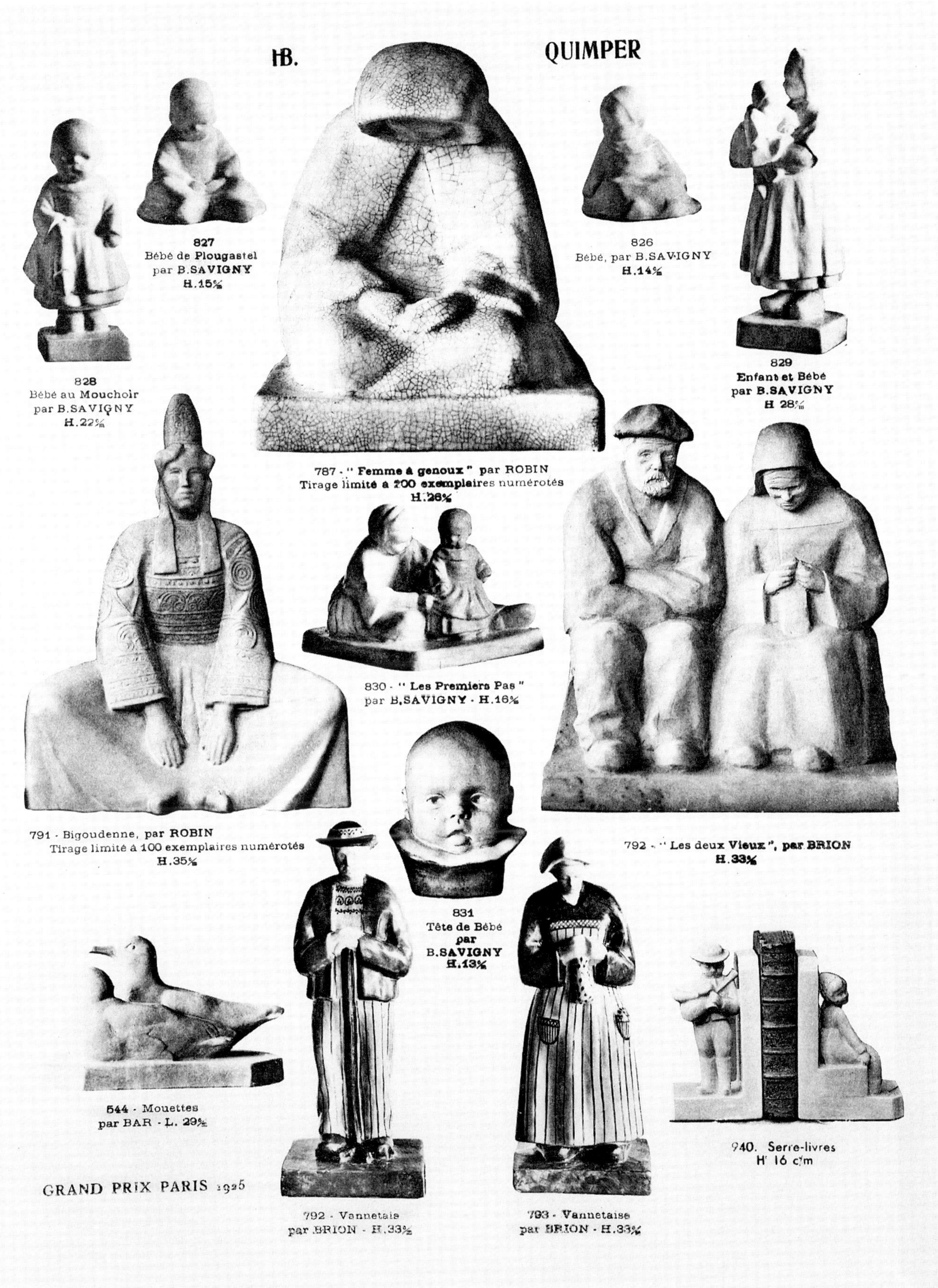
HB. QUIMPER
827
Bébé de Plougastel
par B.SAVIGNY
H.15%
826
Bébé, par B.SAVIGNY
H.14%
828
Bébé au Mouchoir
par B.SAVIGNY
H.22%
829
Enfant et Bébé
par B.SAVIGNY
H 28%
787 - " Femme à genoux " par ROBIN
Tirage limité à 200 exemplaires numérotés
H.26%
830 - " Les Premiers Pas "
par B.SAVIGNY - H.16%
791 - Bigoudenne, par ROBIN
Tirage limité à 100 exemplaires numérotés
H.35%
792 - " Les deux Vieux ", par BRION
H.33%
831
Tête de Bébé
par
B.SAVIGNY
H.13%
544 - Mouettes
par BAR - L. 29%
940. Serre-livres
H' 16 c/m
GRAND PRIX PARIS 1925
792 - Vannetais
par BRION - H.33%
793 - Vannetaise
par BRION - H.33%

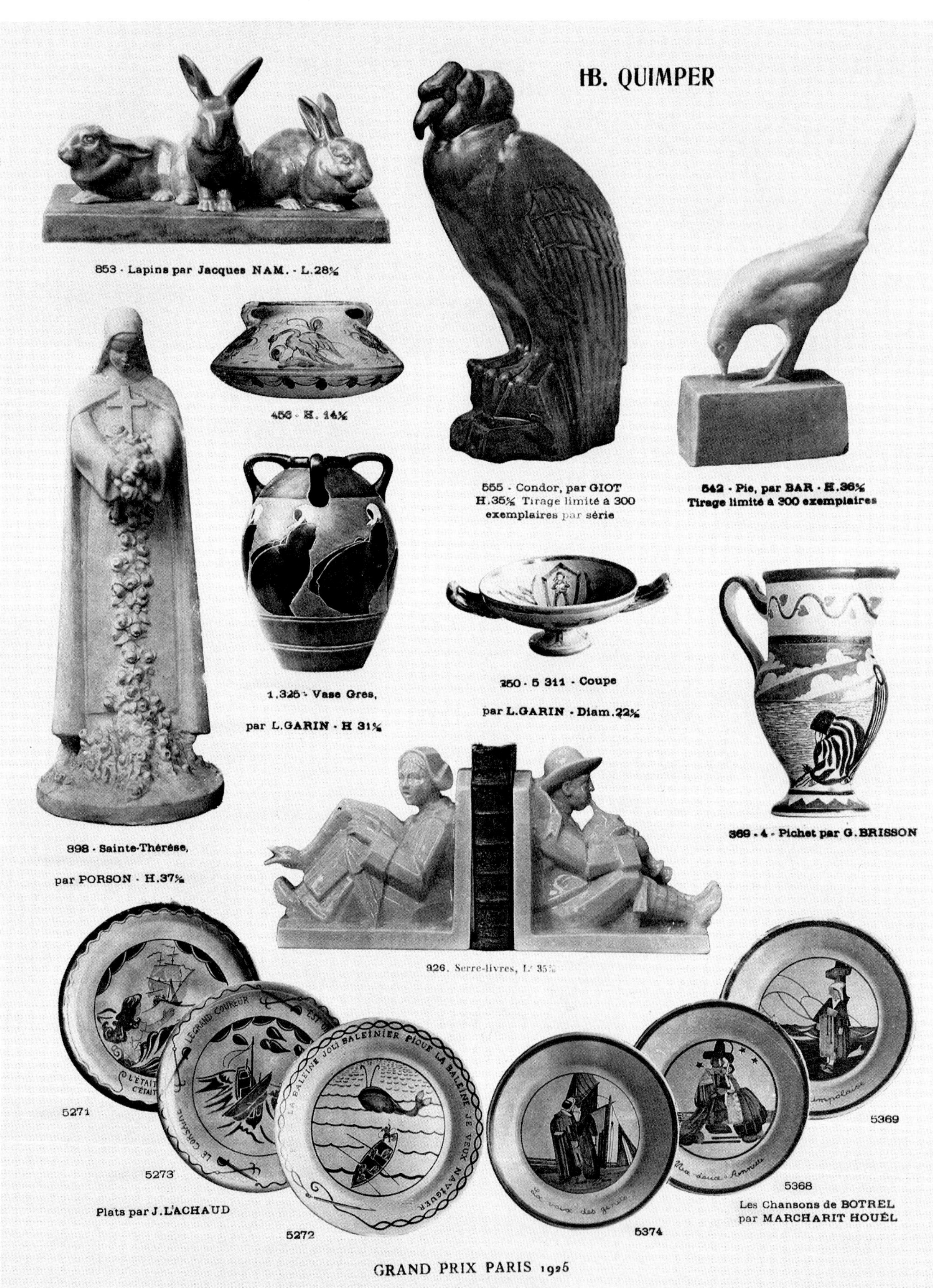

HB. QUIMPER

853 - Lapins par Jacques NAM. - L.28%

456 - H. 14%

555 - Condor, par GIOT H.35% Tirage limité à 300 exemplaires par série

842 - Pie, par BAR - H.36% Tirage limité à 300 exemplaires

898 - Sainte-Thérèse, par PORSON - H.37%

1.325 - Vase Grès, par L.GARIN - H 31%

250 - 5 311 - Coupe par L.GARIN - Diam.22%

369 - 4 - Pichet par G.BRISSON

926. Serre-livres, L. 35%

5271 5273 5272 Plats par J.LACHAUD

5374 5368 5369 Les Chansons de BOTREL par MARCHARIT HOUËL

GRAND PRIX PARIS 1925

HB. QUIMPER

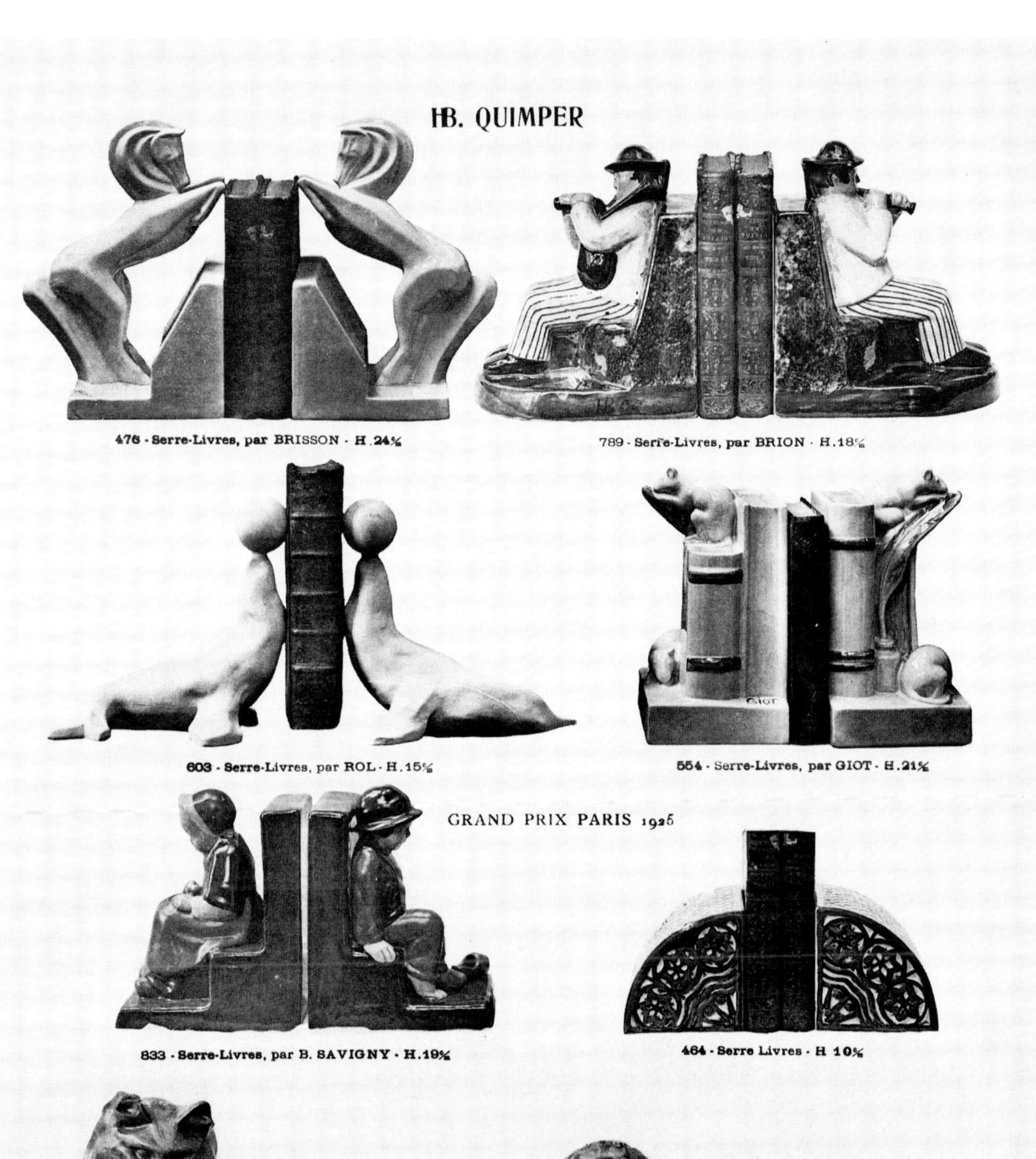

478 - Serre-Livres, par BRISSON - H.24%

789 - Serre-Livres, par BRION - H.18%

603 - Serre-Livres, par ROL - H.15%

554 - Serre-Livres, par GIOT - H.21%

GRAND PRIX PARIS 1925

833 - Serre-Livres, par B. SAVIGNY - H.19%

464 - Serre Livres - H 10%

854 - Basset, par Jacques NAM - L.40%

856 - Chat, par J.NAM - L.34%

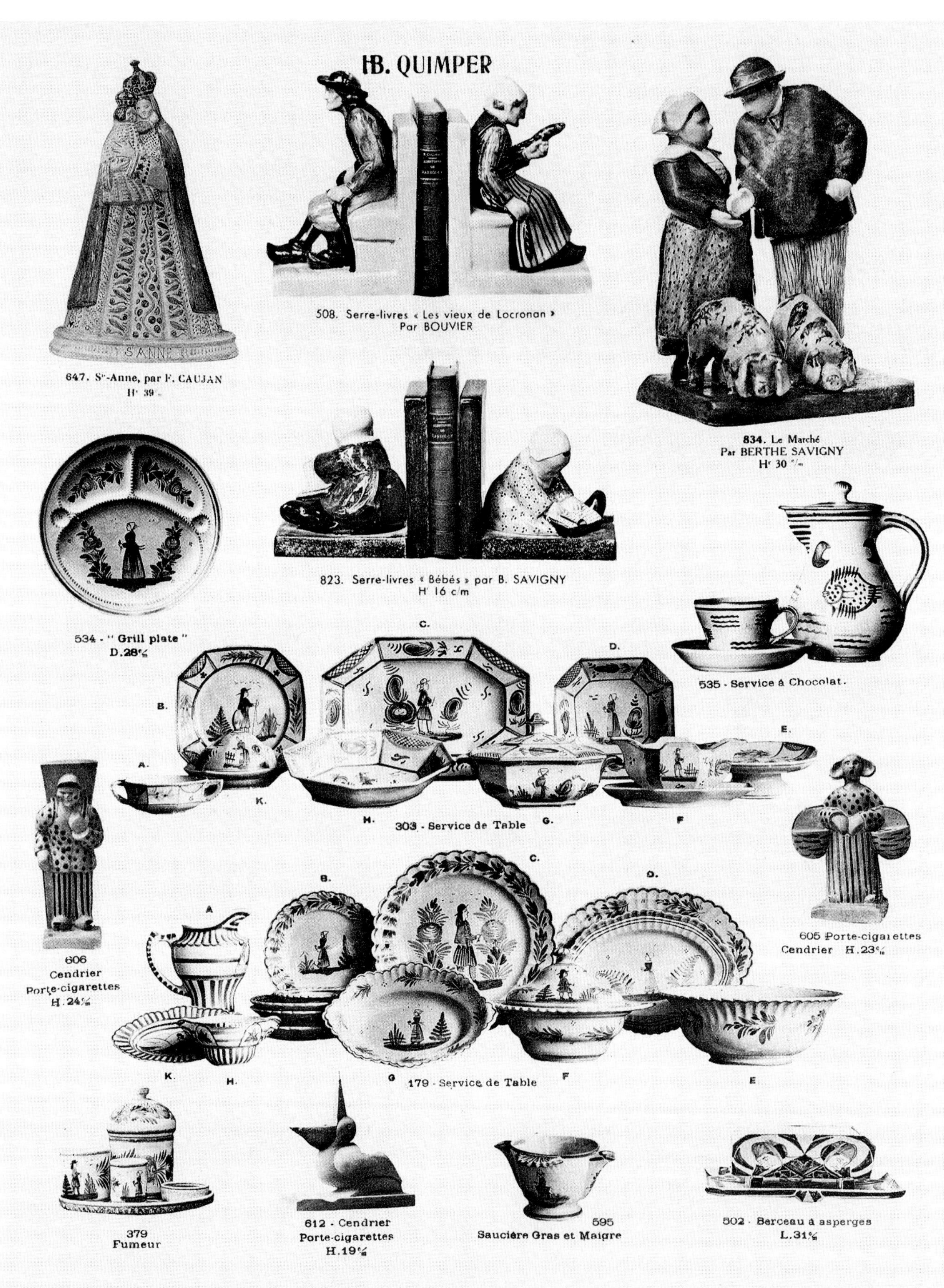

HB. QUIMPER

647. Ste-Anne, par F. CAUJAN
Ht 39 c/m

508. Serre-livres « Les vieux de Locronan »
Par BOUVIER

834. Le Marché
Par BERTHE SAVIGNY
Ht 30 c/m

534 - " Grill plate "
D.28 c/m

823. Serre-livres « Bébés » par B. SAVIGNY
Ht 16 c/m

535 - Service à Chocolat.

303 - Service de Table

606
Cendrier
Porte-cigarettes
H.24 c/m

605 Porte-cigarettes
Cendrier H.23 c/m

179 - Service de Table

379
Fumeur

612 - Cendrier
Porte-cigarettes
H.19 c/m

595
Saucière Gras et Maigre

502 - Berceau à asperges
L.31 c/m

HB. QUIMPER

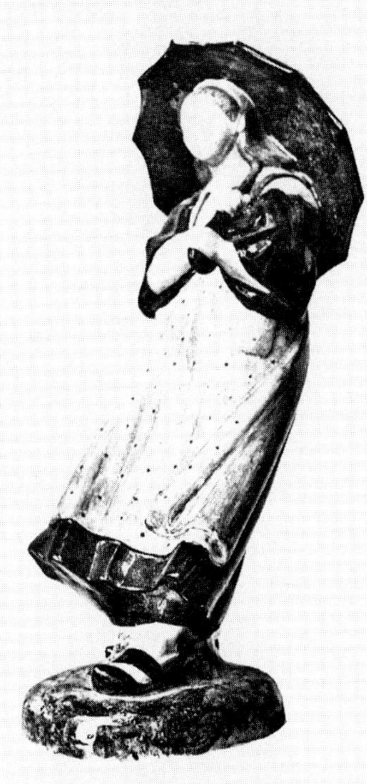

808. Jeune fille sous l'averse
Par LE BOZEC. - H 43 c m
Tirage limité à 200 exemplaires

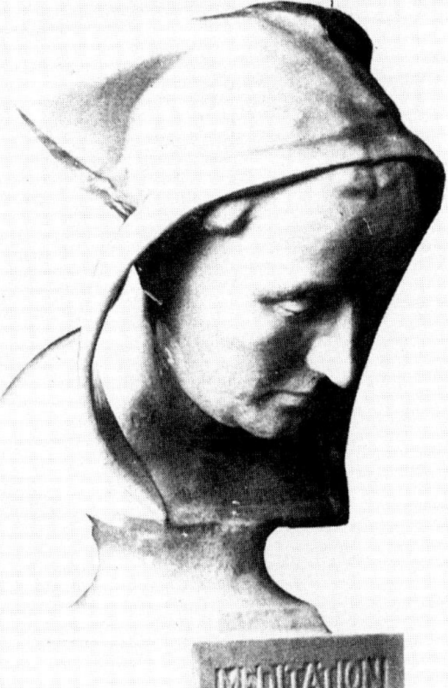

807. « Méditation » par LE BOZEC
Tirage limité à 200 exemplaires
H' 50 c/m

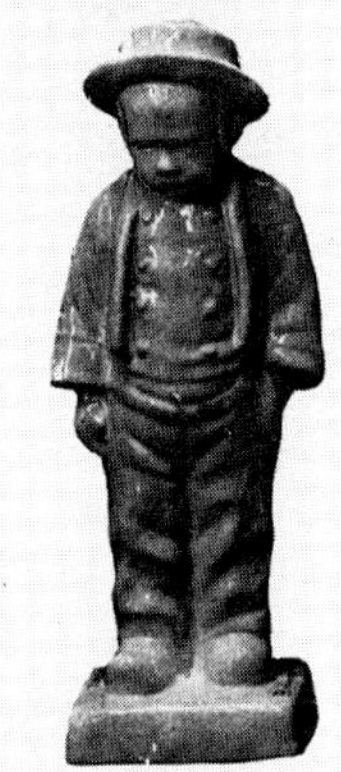

822. Jeune « Pot »
Par B. SAVIGNY. Hr 25 %

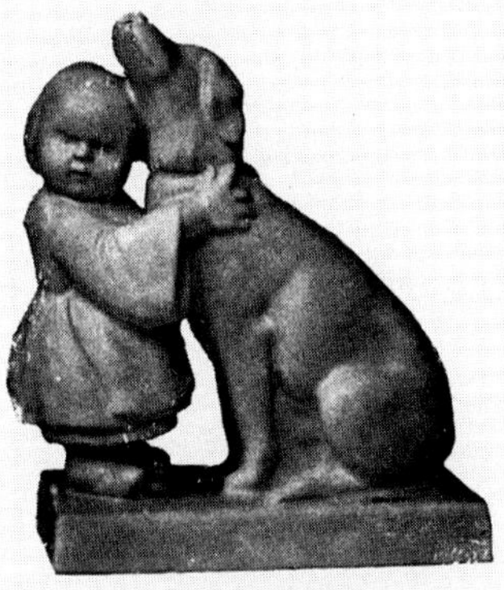

837. Bébé au chien
Par GIOT. Hr 21 %

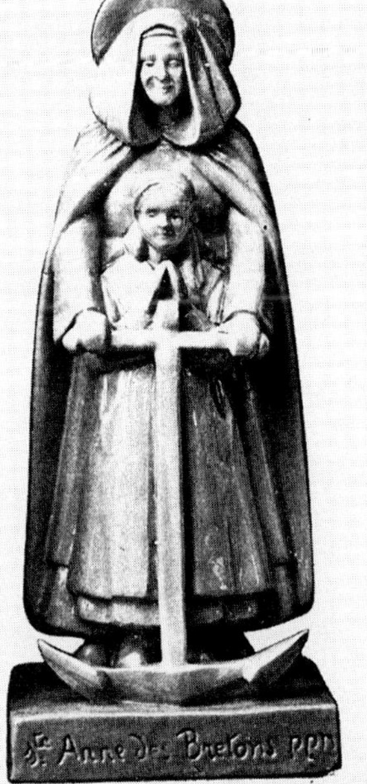

902. par PORSON
Hr 38c

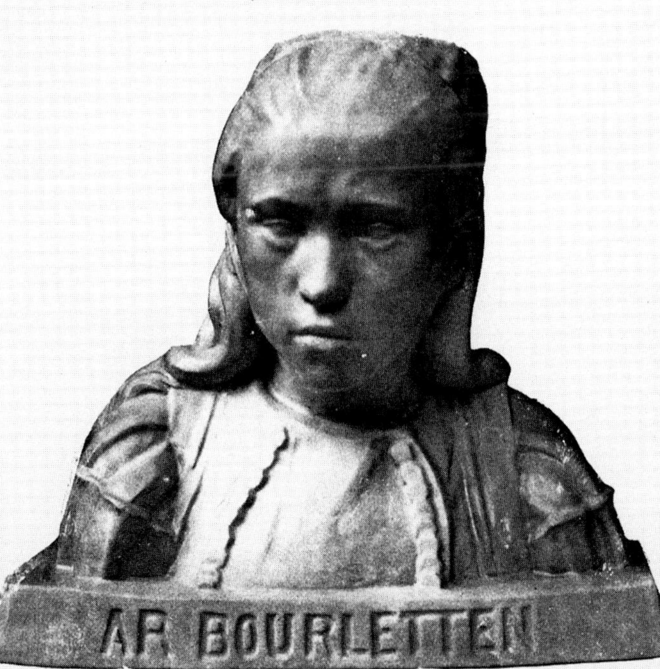

806. « Ar Bourletten » par LE BOZEC
Tirage limité à 200 exemplaires
Hr 37 %

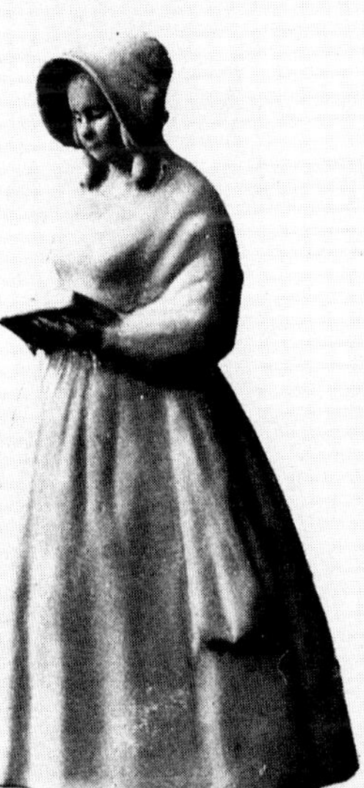

824. Jeune fille 1830
Par B. SAVIGNY
Hr 31 %

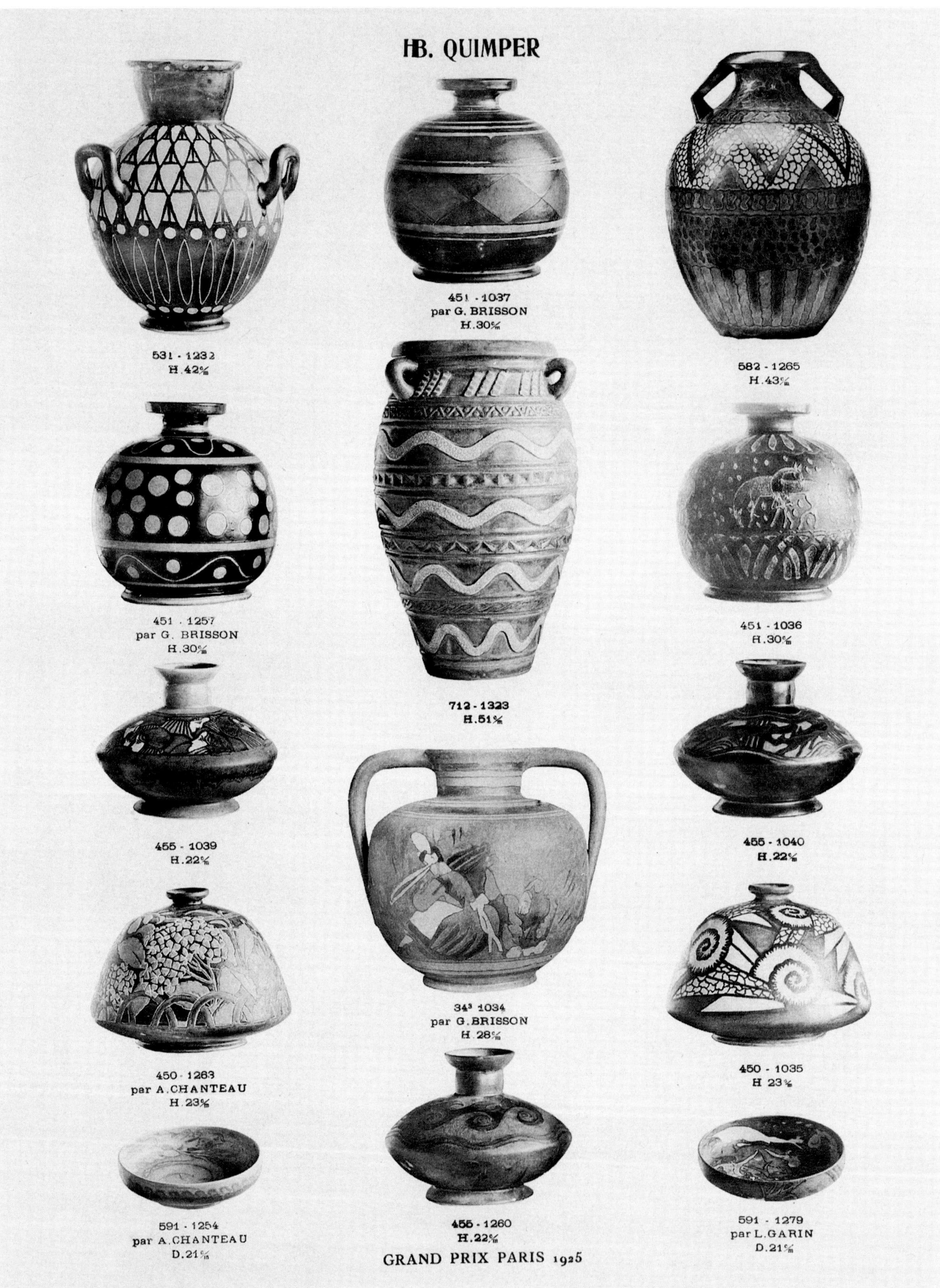

HB. QUIMPER

531 - 1232
H.42 c/m

451 - 1037
par G. BRISSON
H.30 c/m

582 - 1265
H.43 c/m

451 - 1257
par G. BRISSON
H.30 c/m

712 - 1323
H.51 c/m

451 - 1036
H.30 c/m

455 - 1039
H.22 c/m

455 - 1040
H.22 c/m

34³ 1034
par G. BRISSON
H.28 c/m

450 - 1263
par A. CHANTEAU
H.23 c/m

450 - 1035
H 23 c/m

591 - 1254
par A. CHANTEAU
D.21 c/m

455 - 1260
H.22 c/m

591 - 1279
par L. GARIN
D.21 c/m

GRAND PRIX PARIS 1925

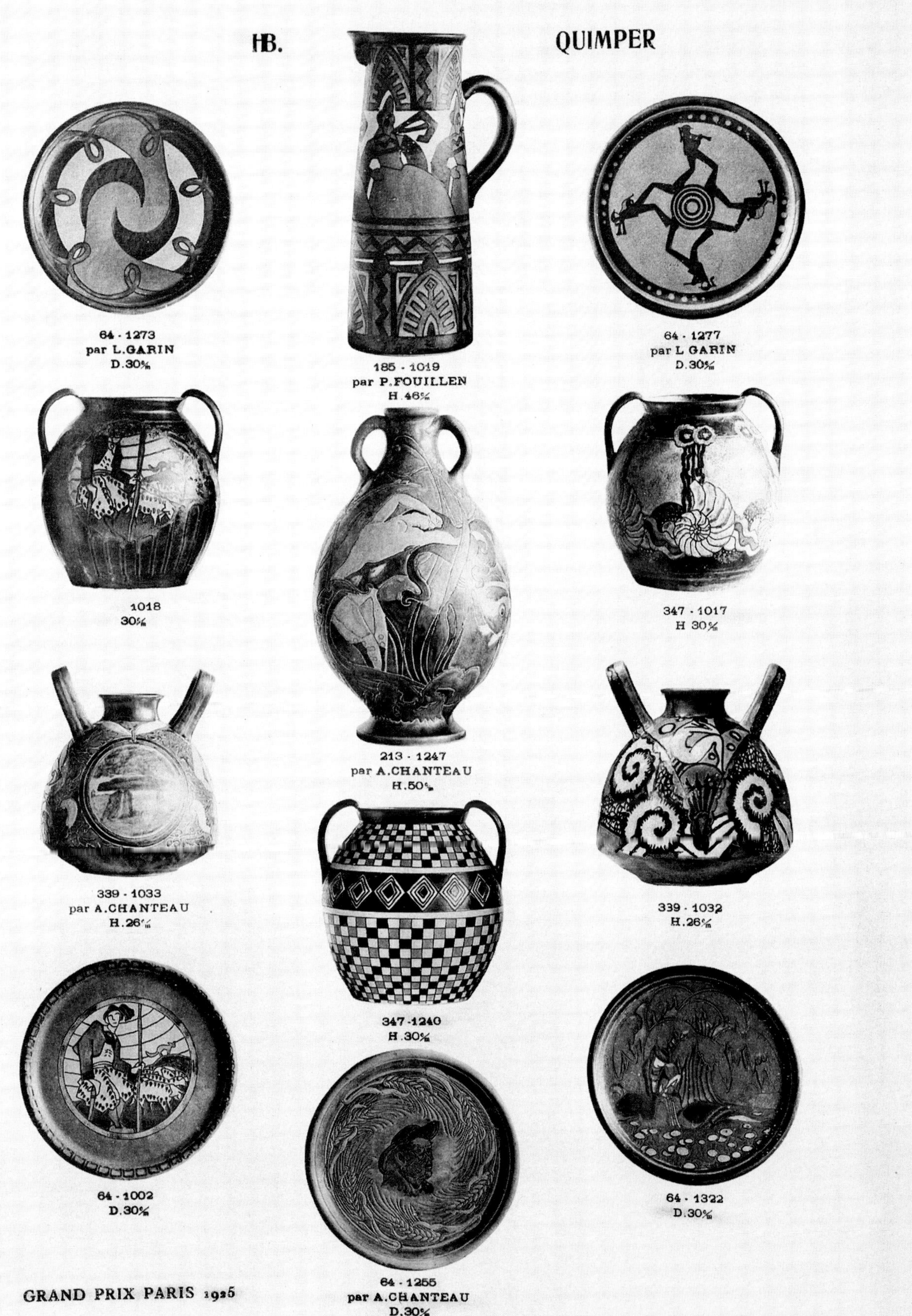
HB.
QUIMPER
64 - 1273
par L.GARIN
D.30%
185 - 1019
par P.FOUILLEN
H.46%
64 - 1277
par L GARIN
D.30%
1018
30%
213 - 1247
par A.CHANTEAU
H.50%
347 - 1017
H 30%
339 - 1033
par A.CHANTEAU
H.26%
347 -1240
H.30%
339 - 1032
H.26%
64 - 1002
D.30%
64 - 1322
D.30%
GRAND PRIX PARIS 1925
64 - 1255
par A.CHANTEAU
D.30%

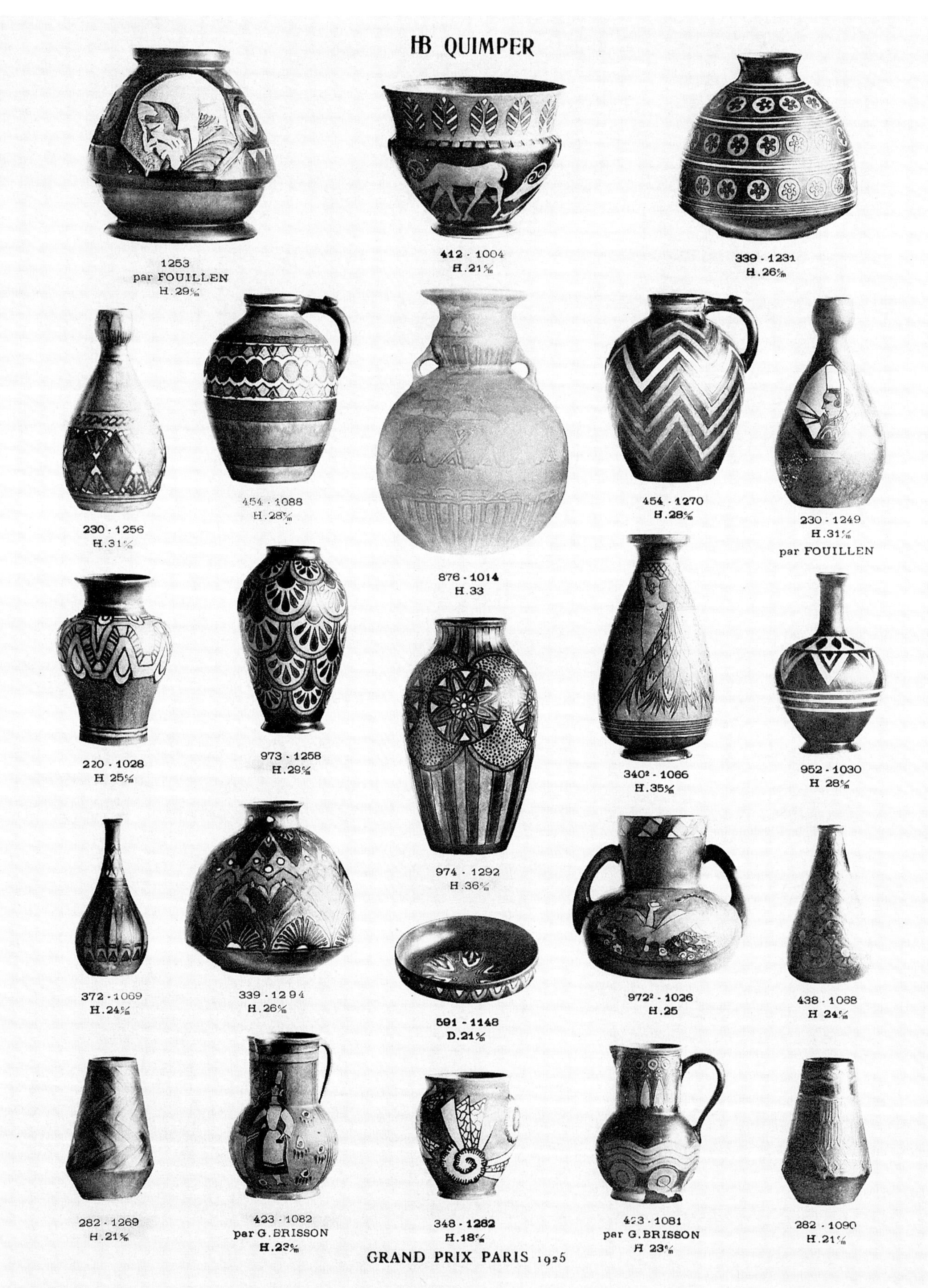
HB QUIMPER
1253
par FOUILLEN
H. 29%
412 - 1004
H. 21%
339 - 1231
H. 26%
230 - 1256
H. 31%
454 - 1088
H. 28%
876 - 1014
H. 33
454 - 1270
H. 28%
230 - 1249
H. 31%
par FOUILLEN
220 - 1028
H 25%
973 - 1258
H. 29%
974 - 1292
H. 36%
340² - 1066
H. 35%
952 - 1030
H 28%
372 - 1069
H. 24%
339 - 1294
H. 26%
591 - 1148
D. 21%
972² - 1026
H. 25
438 - 1068
H 24%
282 - 1269
H. 21%
423 - 1082
par G. BRISSON
H. 23%
348 - 1282
H. 18%
423 - 1081
par G. BRISSON
H 23%
282 - 1090
H. 21%
GRAND PRIX PARIS 1925

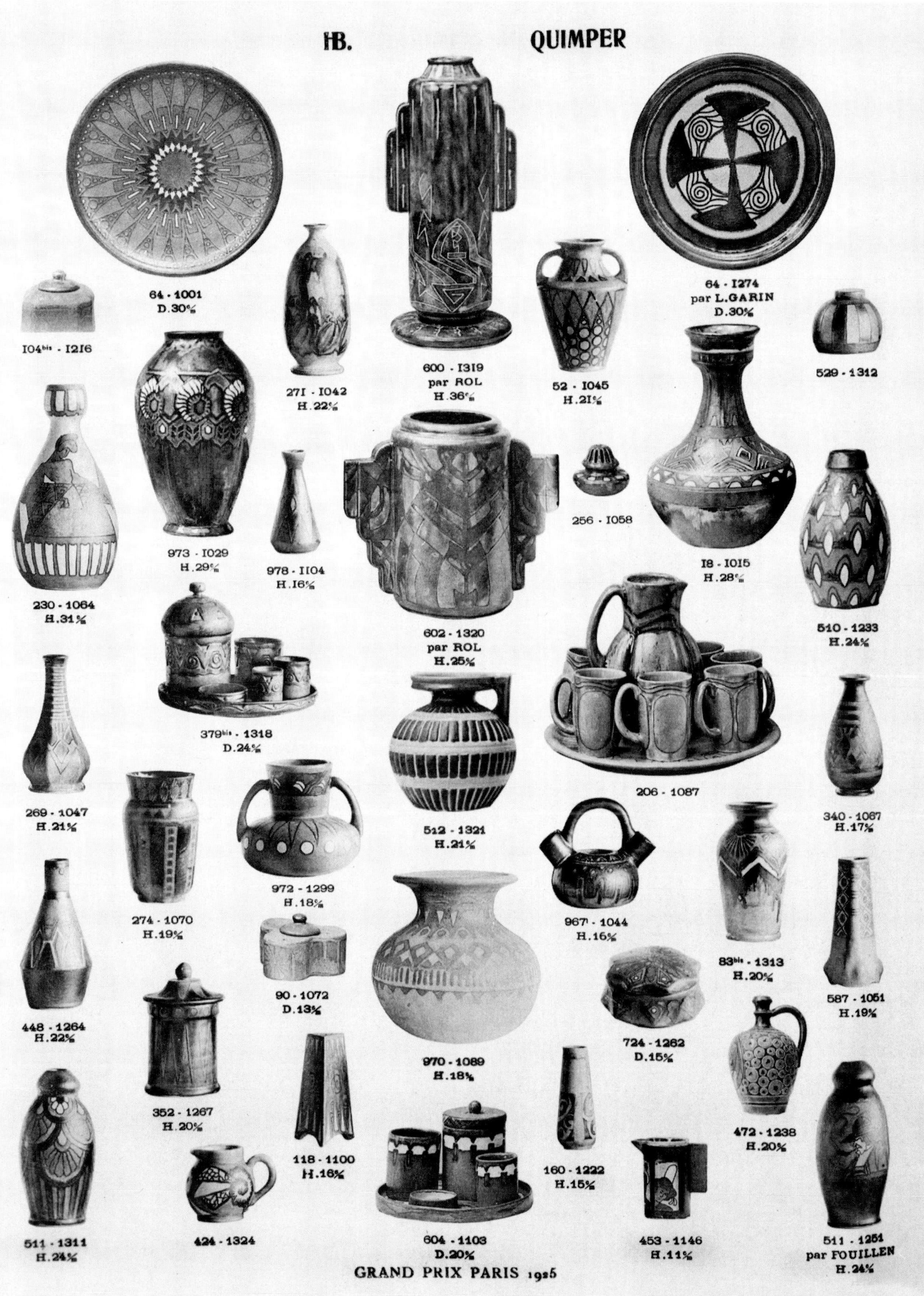
HB. QUIMPER
64 - 1001
D.30%
104bis - 1216
271 - 1042
H. 22%
600 - 1319
par ROL
H. 36%
52 - 1045
H.21%
64 - 1274
par L.GARIN
D.30%
529 - 1312
973 - 1029
H.29%
978 - 1104
H.16%
230 - 1064
H.31%
256 - 1058
18 - 1015
H.28%
602 - 1320
par ROL
H.25%
510 - 1233
H.24%
379bis - 1318
D.24%
206 - 1087
269 - 1047
H.21%
512 - 1321
H.21%
340 - 1067
H.17%
972 - 1299
H.18%
274 - 1070
H.19%
967 - 1044
H.16%
83bis - 1313
H.20%
90 - 1072
D.13%
587 - 1051
H.19%
448 - 1264
H.22%
724 - 1262
D.15%
970 - 1089
H.18%
352 - 1267
H. 20%
472 - 1238
H.20%
118 - 1100
H.16%
160 - 1222
H.15%
511 - 1311
H.24%
424 - 1324
604 - 1103
D.20%
453 - 1146
H.11%
511 - 1251
par FOUILLEN
H.24%
GRAND PRIX PARIS 1925

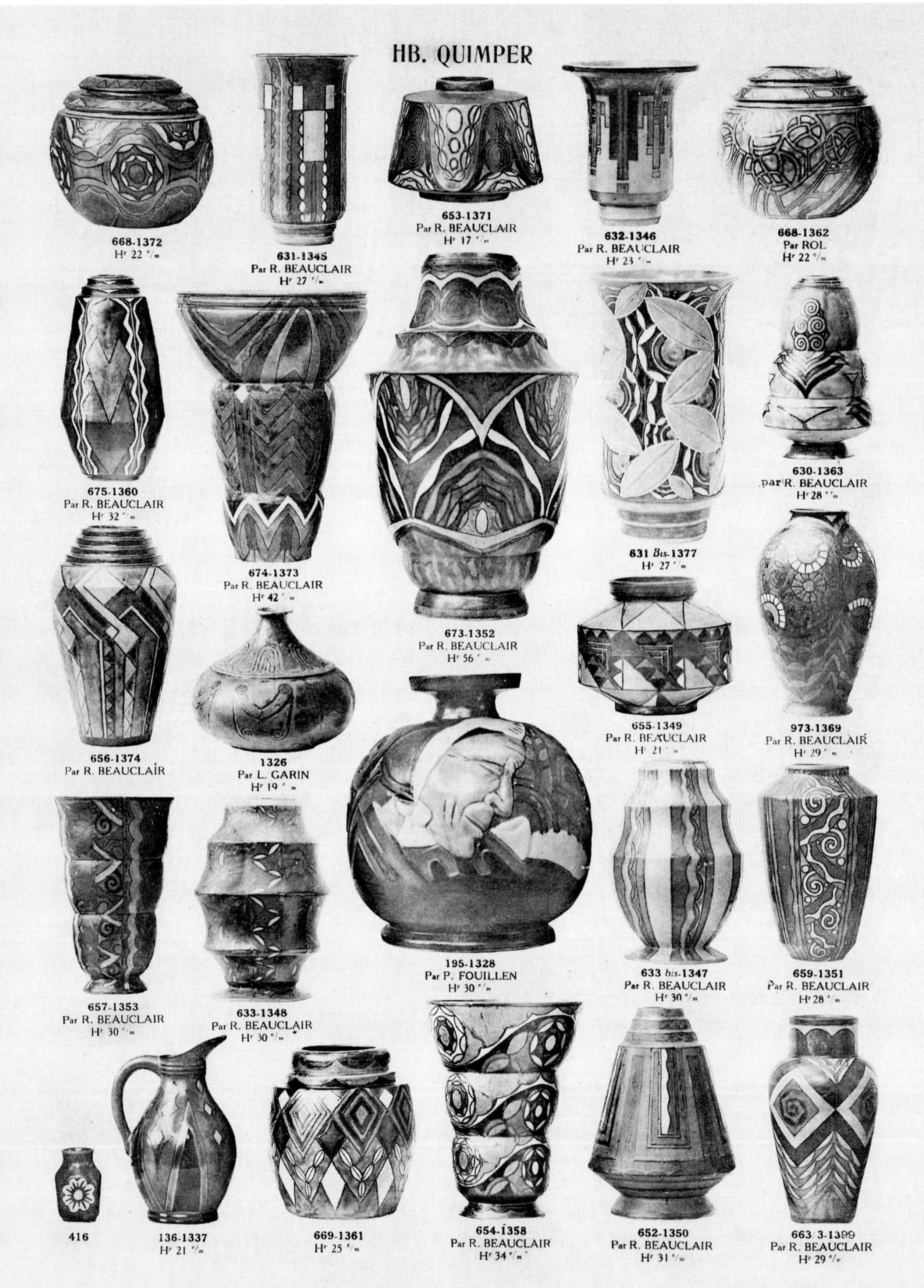
HB. QUIMPER
668-1372
Hr 22 c/m
631-1345
Par R. BEAUCLAIR
Hr 27 c/m
653-1371
Par R. BEAUCLAIR
Hr 17 c/m
632-1346
Par R. BEAUCLAIR
Hr 23 c/m
668-1362
Par ROL
Hr 22 c/m
675-1360
Par R. BEAUCLAIR
Hr 32 c/m
674-1373
Par R. BEAUCLAIR
Hr 42 c/m
673-1352
Par R. BEAUCLAIR
Hr 56 c/m
631 Bis-1377
Hr 27 c/m
630-1363
par R. BEAUCLAIR
Hr 28 c/m
656-1374
Par R. BEAUCLAIR
1326
Par L. GARIN
Hr 19 c/m
655-1349
Par R. BEAUCLAIR
Hr 21 c/m
973-1369
Par R. BEAUCLAIR
Hr 29 c/m
195-1328
Par P. FOUILLEN
Hr 30 c/m
633 bis-1347
Par R. BEAUCLAIR
Hr 30 c/m
659-1351
Par R. BEAUCLAIR
Hr 28 c/m
657-1353
Par R. BEAUCLAIR
Hr 30 c/m
633-1348
Par R. BEAUCLAIR
Hr 30 c/m
416
136-1337
Hr 21 c/m
669-1361
Hr 25 c/m
654-1358
Par R. BEAUCLAIR
Hr 34 c/m
652-1350
Par R. BEAUCLAIR
Hr 31 c/m
663 3-1399
Par R. BEAUCLAIR
Hr 29 c/m

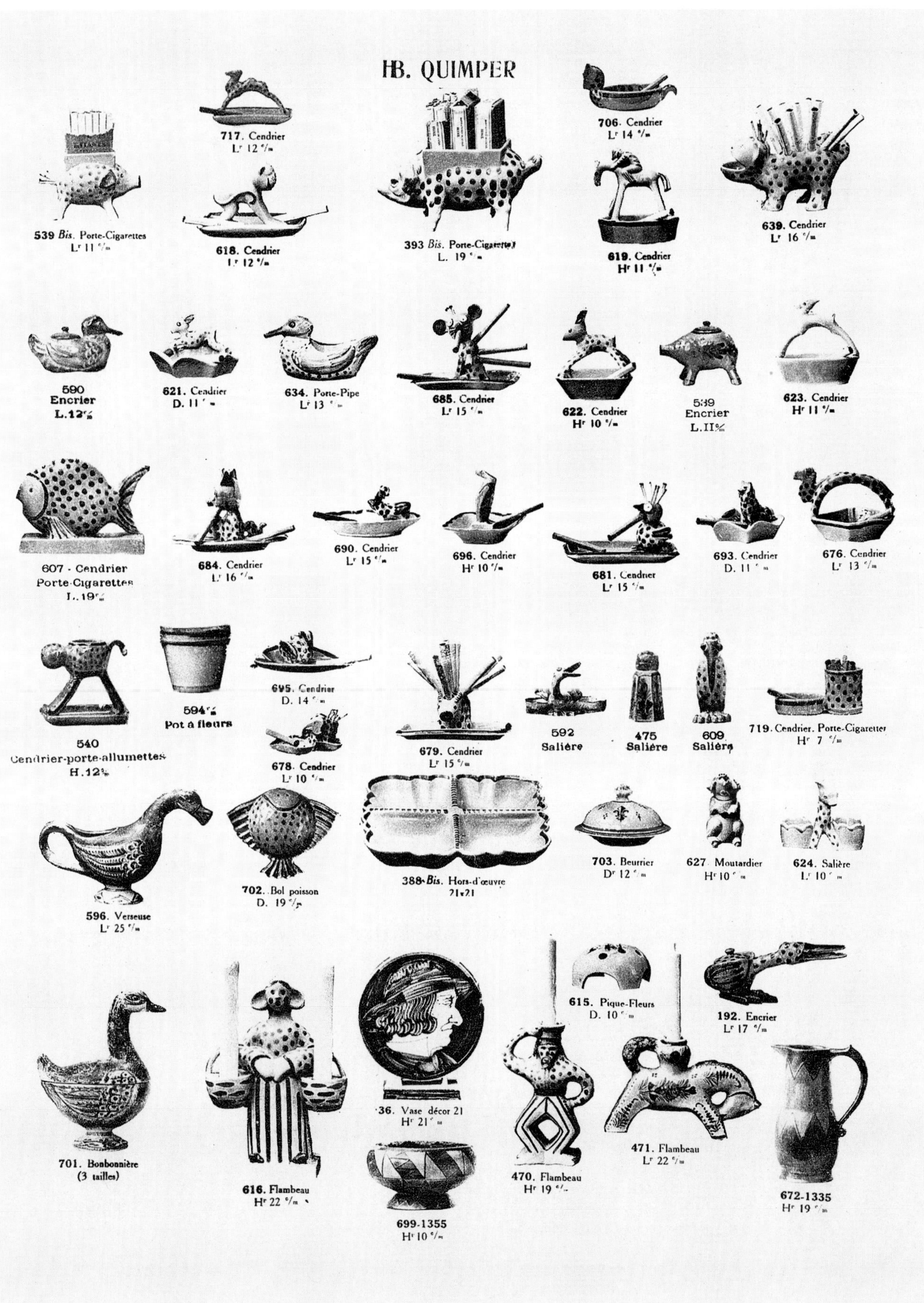
HB. QUIMPER
539 Bis. Porte-Cigarettes
Lr 11 c/m
717. Cendrier
Lr 12 c/m
618. Cendrier
Lr 12 c/m
393 Bis. Porte-Cigarettes
L. 19 c/m
706. Cendrier
Lr 14 c/m
619. Cendrier
Hr 11 c/m
639. Cendrier
Lr 16 c/m
590
Encrier
L. 12c/m
621. Cendrier
D. 11 c/m
634. Porte-Pipe
Lr 13 c/m
685. Cendrier
Lr 15 c/m
622. Cendrier
Hr 10 c/m
589
Encrier
L. 11c/m
623. Cendrier
Hr 11 c/m
607 - Cendrier
Porte-Cigarettes
L. 19c/m
684. Cendrier
Lr 16 c/m
690. Cendrier
Lr 15 c/m
696. Cendrier
Hr 10 c/m
681. Cendrier
Lr 15 c/m
693. Cendrier
D. 11 c/m
676. Cendrier
Lr 13 c/m
540
Cendrier-porte-allumettes
H. 12c/m
594c/m
Pot à fleurs
695. Cendrier
D. 14 c/m
678. Cendrier
Lr 10 c/m
679. Cendrier
Lr 15 c/m
592
Salière
475
Salière
609
Salière
719. Cendrier. Porte-Cigarettes
Hr 7 c/m
596. Verseuse
Lr 25 c/m
702. Bol poisson
D. 19 c/m
388 Bis. Hors-d'œuvre
21x21
703. Beurrier
Dr 12 c/m
627. Moutardier
Hr 10 c/m
624. Salière
Lr 10 c/m
701. Bonbonnière
(3 tailles)
616. Flambeau
Hr 22 c/m
36. Vase décor 21
Hr 21 c/m
699-1355
Hr 10 c/m
615. Pique-Fleurs
D. 10 c/m
470. Flambeau
Hr 19 c/m
192. Encrier
Lr 17 c/m
471. Flambeau
Lr 22 c/m
672-1335
Hr 19 c/m

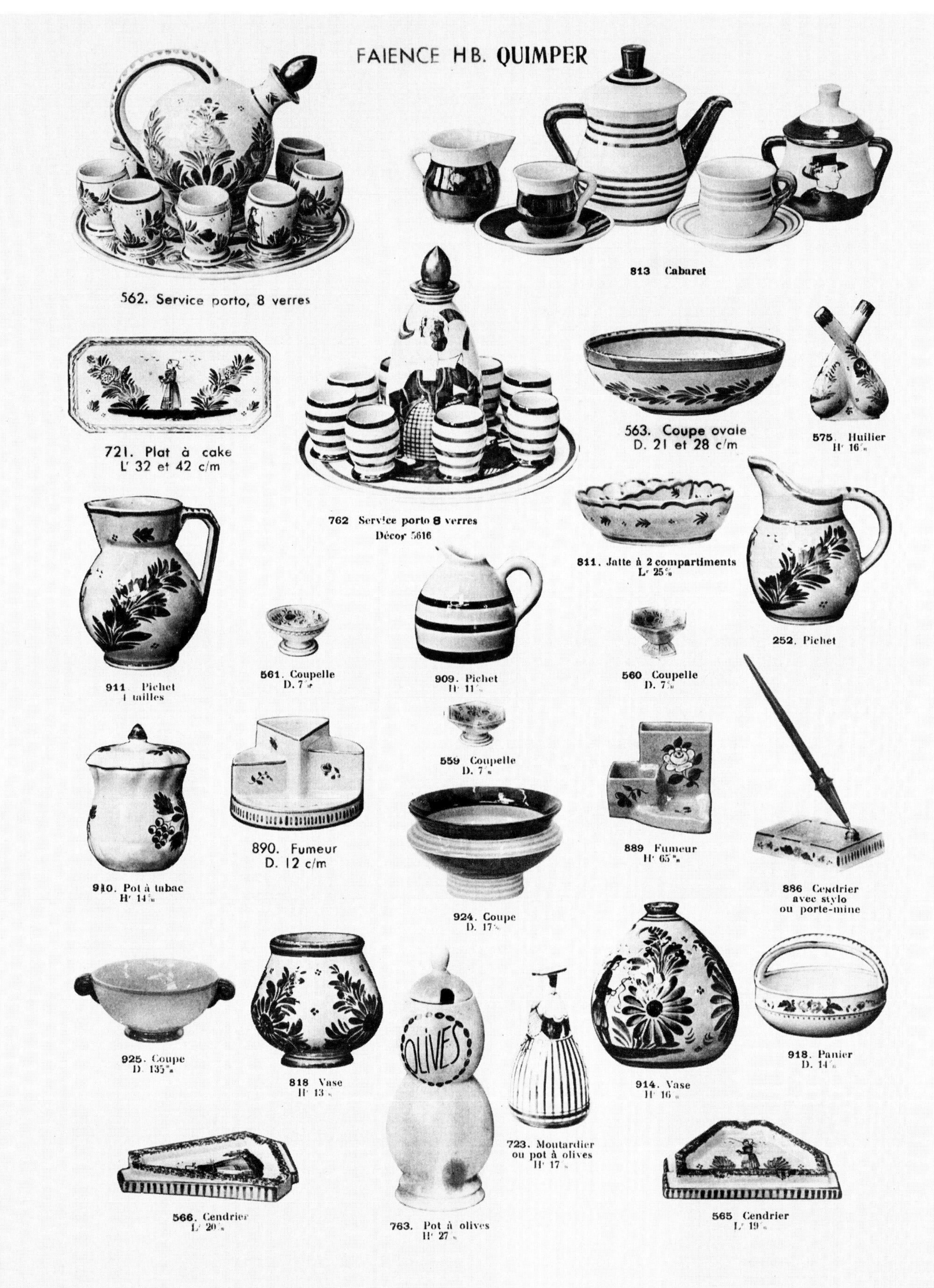

FAIENCE HB. QUIMPER

562. Service porto, 8 verres

813 Cabaret

721. Plat à cake
L' 32 et 42 c/m

762 Service porto 8 verres
Décor 5616

563. Coupe ovale
D. 21 et 28 c/m

575. Huilier
H' 16 c/m

811. Jatte à 2 compartiments
L' 25 c/m

911 Pichet
4 tailles

561. Coupelle
D. 7 c/m

909. Pichet
H' 11 c/m

560 Coupelle
D. 7 c/m

252. Pichet

559 Coupelle
D. 7 c/m

910. Pot à tabac
H' 14 c/m

890. Fumeur
D. 12 c/m

924. Coupe
D. 17 c/m

889 Fumeur
H' 65 m/m

886 Cendrier
avec stylo
ou porte-mine

925. Coupe
D. 135 m/m

818 Vase
H' 13 c/m

723. Moutardier
ou pot à olives
H' 17 c/m

914. Vase
H' 16 c/m

918. Panier
D. 14 c/m

566. Cendrier
L' 20 c/m

763. Pot à olives
H' 27 c/m

565 Cendrier
L' 19 c/m

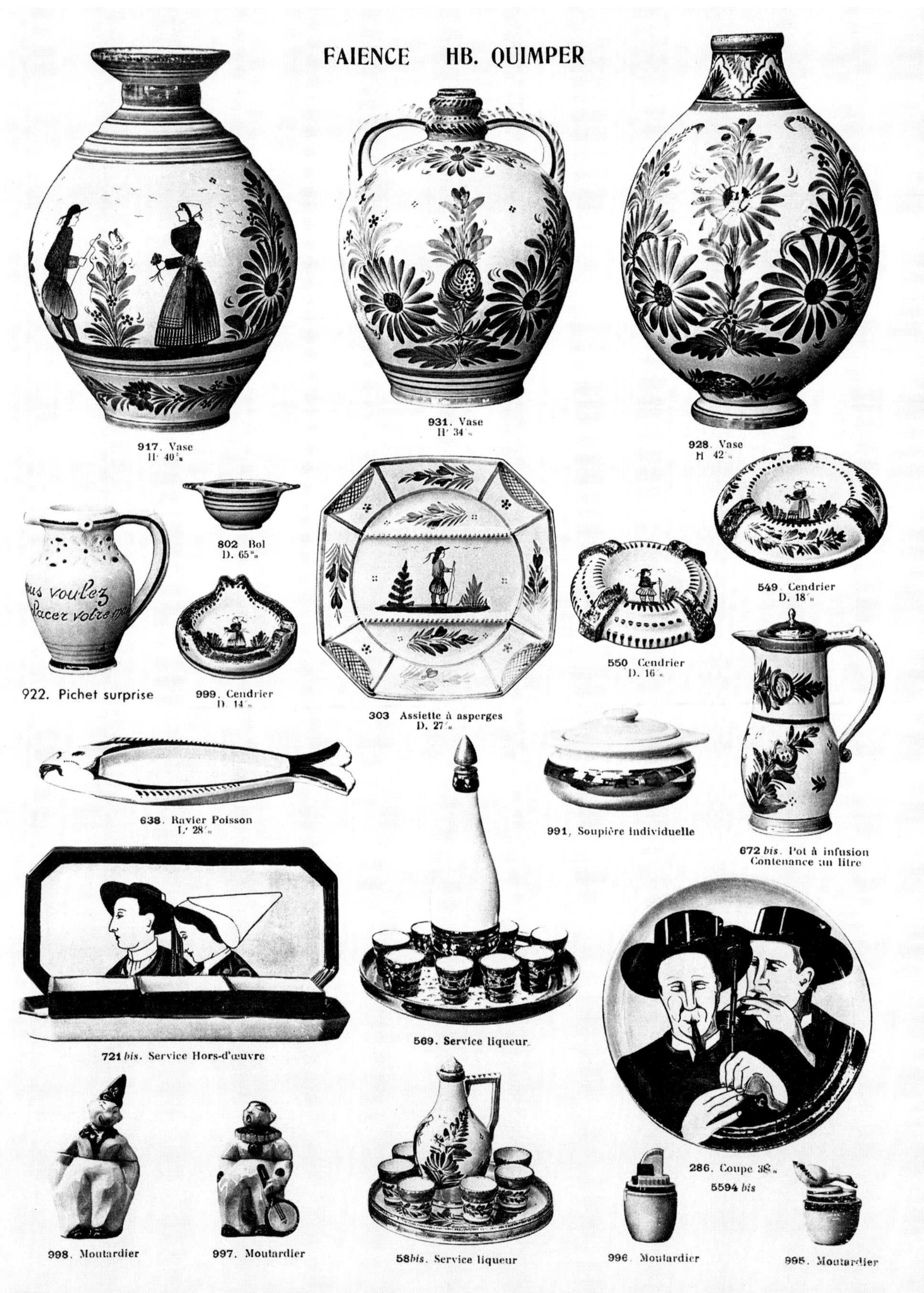

FAIENCE HB. QUIMPER

917. Vase H' 40 c/m

931. Vase H' 34 c/m

928. Vase H' 42 c/m

922. Pichet surprise

802 Bol D. 65 m/m

999. Cendrier D. 14 c/m

303 Assiette à asperges D. 27 c/m

550 Cendrier D. 16 c/m

549. Cendrier D. 18 c/m

638. Ravier Poisson L' 28 c/m

991, Soupière individuelle

672 *bis*. Pot à infusion Contenance un litre

721 *bis*. Service Hors-d'œuvre

569. Service liqueur.

286. Coupe 38 c/m

5594 *bis*

998. Moutardier

997. Moutardier

58*bis*. Service liqueur

996. Moutardier

995. Moutardier

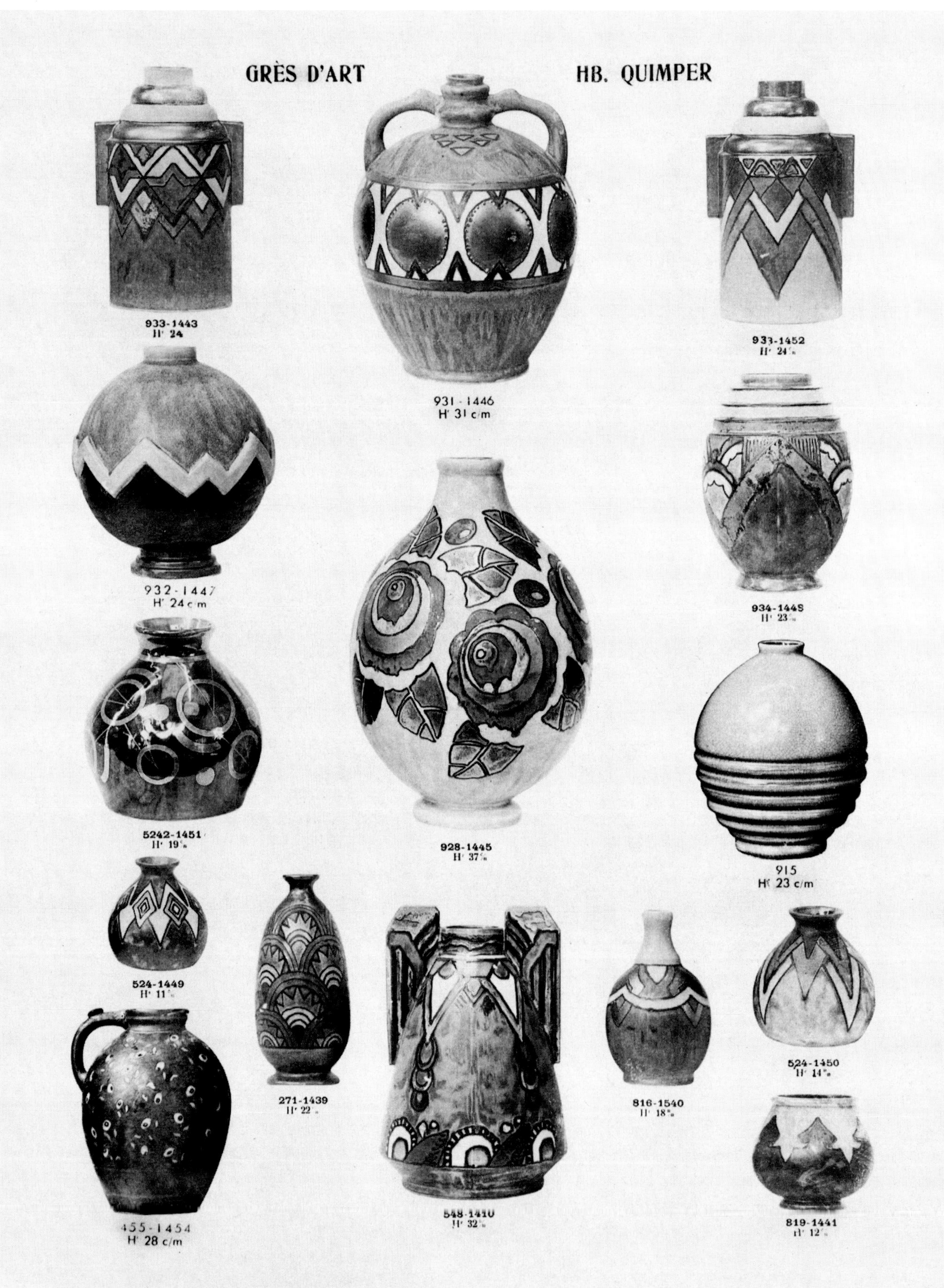
GRÈS D'ART
HB. QUIMPER
933-1443
H' 24
931-1446
H' 31 c/m
933-1452
H' 24 c/m
932-1447
H' 24 c/m
934-1448
H' 23 c/m
5242-1451
H' 19 c/m
928-1445
H' 37 c/m
915
H' 23 c/m
524-1449
H' 11 c/m
271-1439
H' 22 c/m
548-1410
H' 32 c/m
816-1540
H' 18 c/m
524-1450
H' 14 c/m
819-1441
H' 12 c/m
455-1454
H' 28 c/m

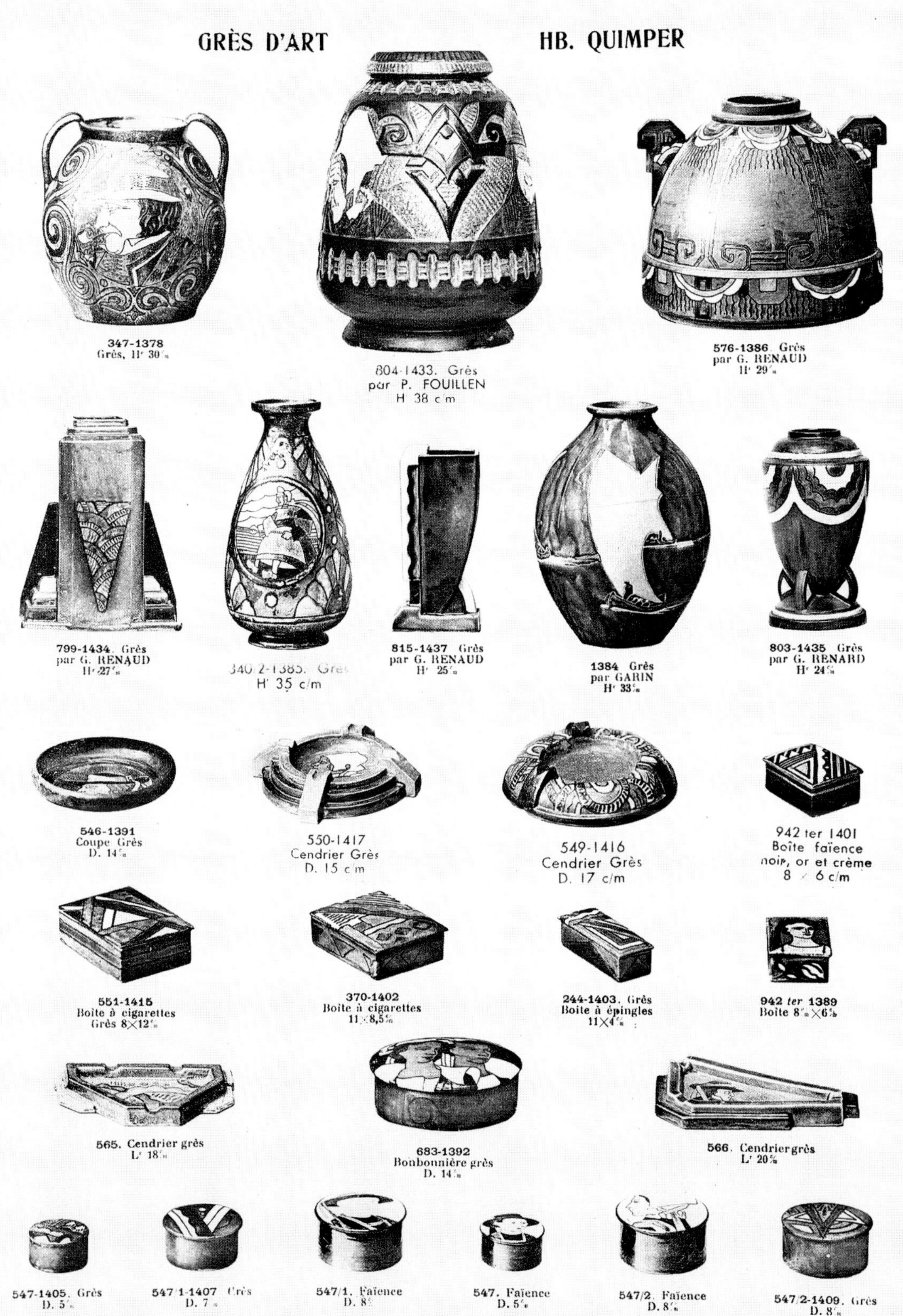

GRÈS D'ART HB. QUIMPER

347-1378
Grès, H' 30 c/m

804-1433. Grès
par P. FOUILLEN
H' 38 c/m

576-1386. Grès
par G. RENAUD
H' 29 c/m

799-1434. Grès
par G. RENAUD
H' 27 c/m

340/2-1385. Grès
H' 35 c/m

815-1437 Grès
par G. RENAUD
H' 25 c/m

1384 Grès
par GARIN
H' 33 c/m

803-1435 Grès
par G. RENARD
H' 24 c/m

546-1391
Coupe Grès
D. 14 c/m

550-1417
Cendrier Grès
D. 15 c/m

549-1416
Cendrier Grès
D. 17 c/m

942 ter 1401
Boîte faïence
noir, or et crème
8 × 6 c/m

551-1415
Boîte à cigarettes
Grès 8×12 c/m

370-1402
Boite à cigarettes
11×8,5 c/m

244-1403. Grès
Boite à épingles
11×4 c/m

942 *ter* 1389
Boite 8 c/m×6 c/m

565. Cendrier grès
L' 18 c/m

683-1392
Bonbonnière grès
D. 14 c/m

566. Cendrier grès
L' 20 c/m

547-1405. Grès
D. 5 c/m

547/1-1407 Grès
D. 7 c/m

547/1. Faïence
D. 8 c/m

547. Faïence
D. 5 c/m

547/2. Faïence
D. 8 c/m

547/2-1409. Grès
D. 8 c/m

GRÈS D'ART HB. QUIMPER

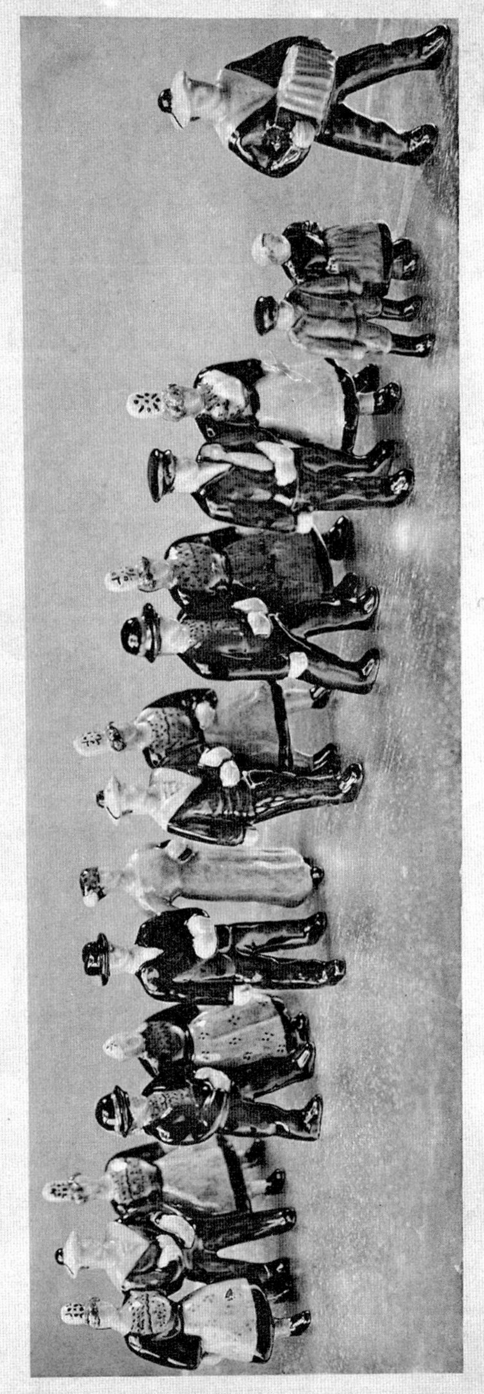

346 Noce Bigoudenne par FANCH

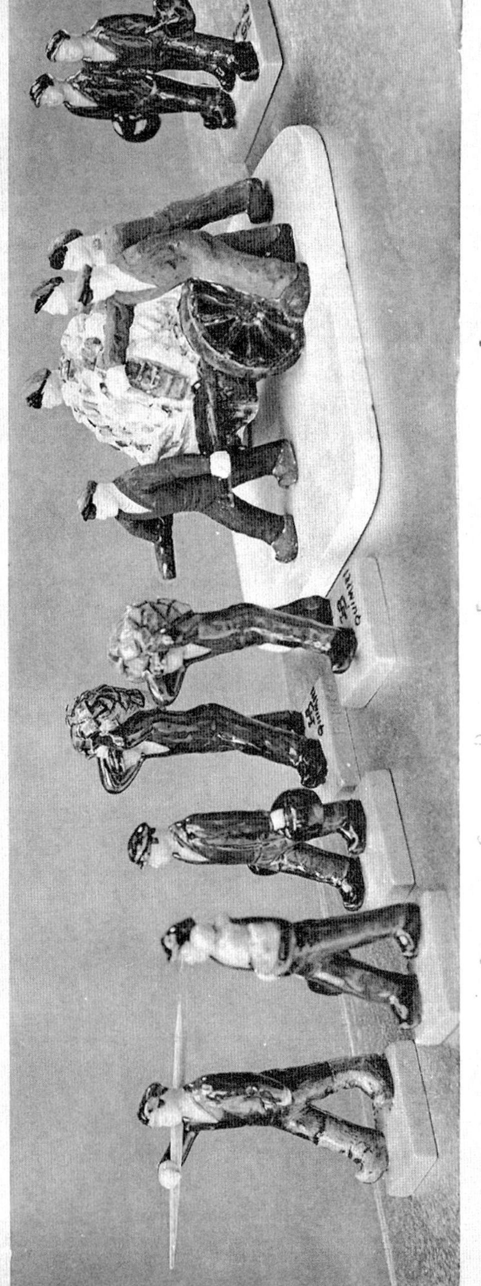

881. Retour de pêche par FANCH

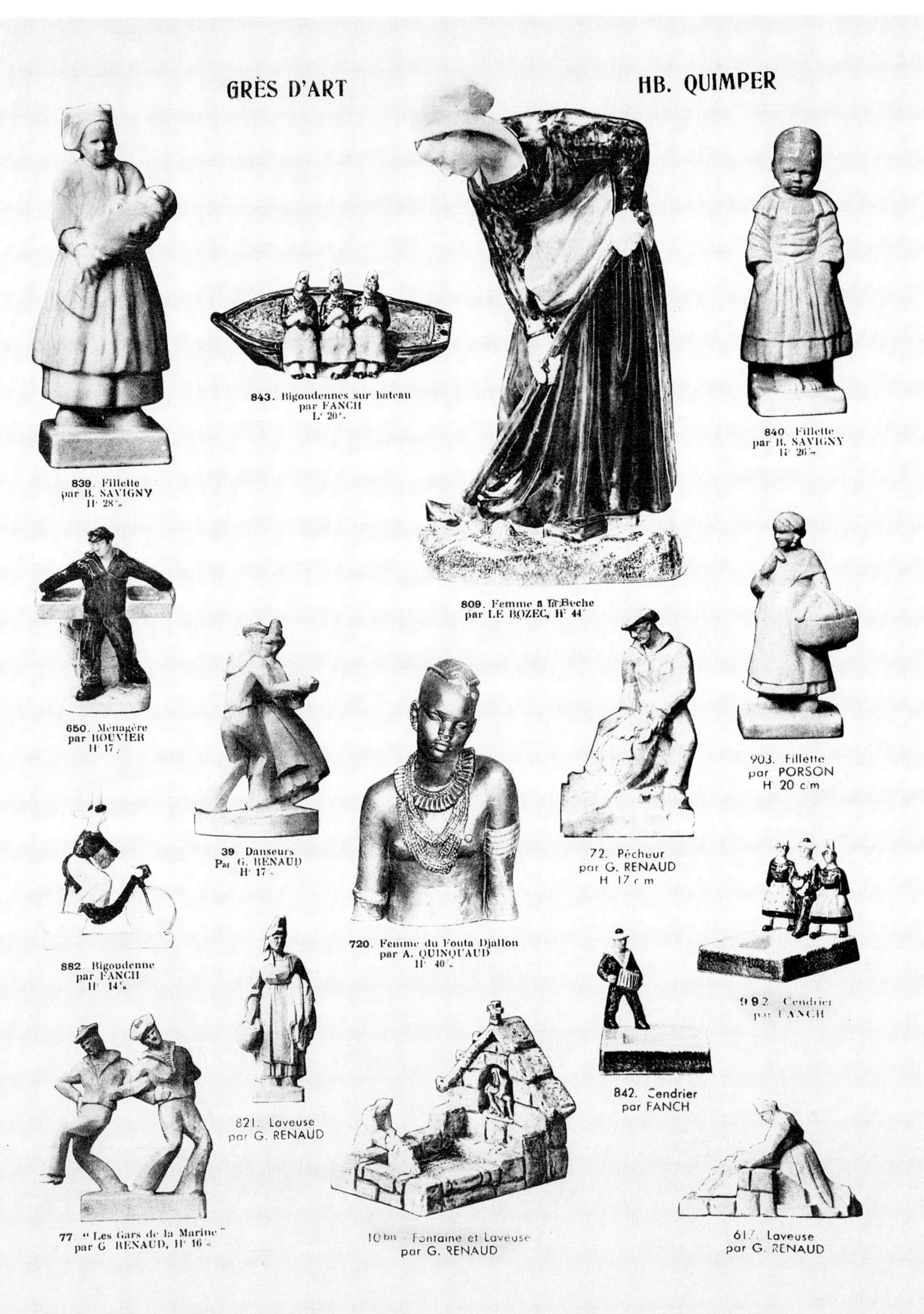

GRÈS D'ART HB. QUIMPER

839. Fillette
par B. SAVIGNY
Ht 28 c/m

843. Bigoudennes sur bateau
par FANCH
Lr 20 c/m

809. Femme à la Bêche
par LE BOZEC, Ht 44 c/m

840. Fillette
par B. SAVIGNY
Ht 26 c/m

650. Ménagère
par BOUVIER
Ht 17 c/m

39 Danseurs
Par G. RENAUD
Ht 17 c/m

720. Femme du Fouta Djallon
par A. QUINQUAUD
Ht 40 c/m

72. Pêcheur
par G. RENAUD
H 17 c m

903. Fillette
par PORSON
H 20 c/m

882. Bigoudenne
par FANCH
Ht 14 c/m

821. Laveuse
par G. RENAUD

842. Cendrier
par FANCH

992. Cendrier
par FANCH

77 "Les Gars de la Marine"
par G RENAUD, Ht 16 c/m

10 bis Fontaine et Laveuse
par G. RENAUD

617. Laveuse
par G. RENAUD

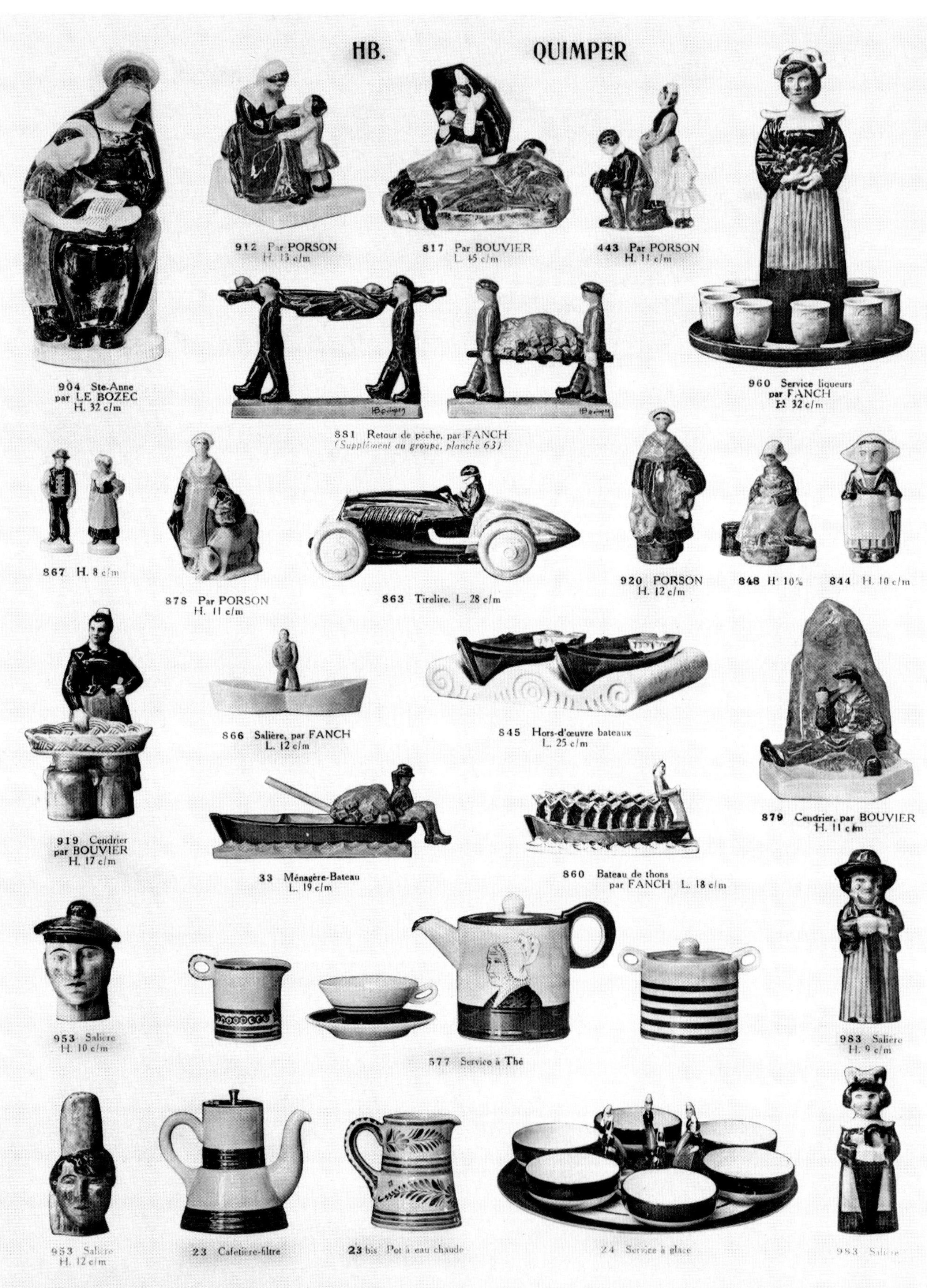
HB. QUIMPER

904 Ste-Anne par LE BOZEC H. 32 c/m

912 Par PORSON H. 13 c/m

817 Par BOUVIER L. 45 c/m

443 Par PORSON H. 11 c/m

960 Service liqueurs par FANCH H. 32 c/m

881 Retour de pêche, par FANCH
(Supplément au groupe, planche 63)

867 H. 8 c/m

878 Par PORSON H. 11 c/m

863 Tirelire. L. 28 c/m

920 PORSON H. 12 c/m

848 H. 10%

844 H. 10 c/m

919 Cendrier par BOUVIER H. 17 c/m

866 Salière, par FANCH L. 12 c/m

845 Hors-d'œuvre bateaux L. 25 c/m

879 Cendrier, par BOUVIER H. 11 c/m

33 Ménagère-Bateau L. 19 c/m

860 Bateau de thons par FANCH L. 18 c/m

953 Salière H. 10 c/m

577 Service à Thé

983 Salière H. 9 c/m

953 Salière H. 12 c/m

23 Cafetière-filtre

23 bis Pot à eau chaude

24 Service à glace

983 Salière

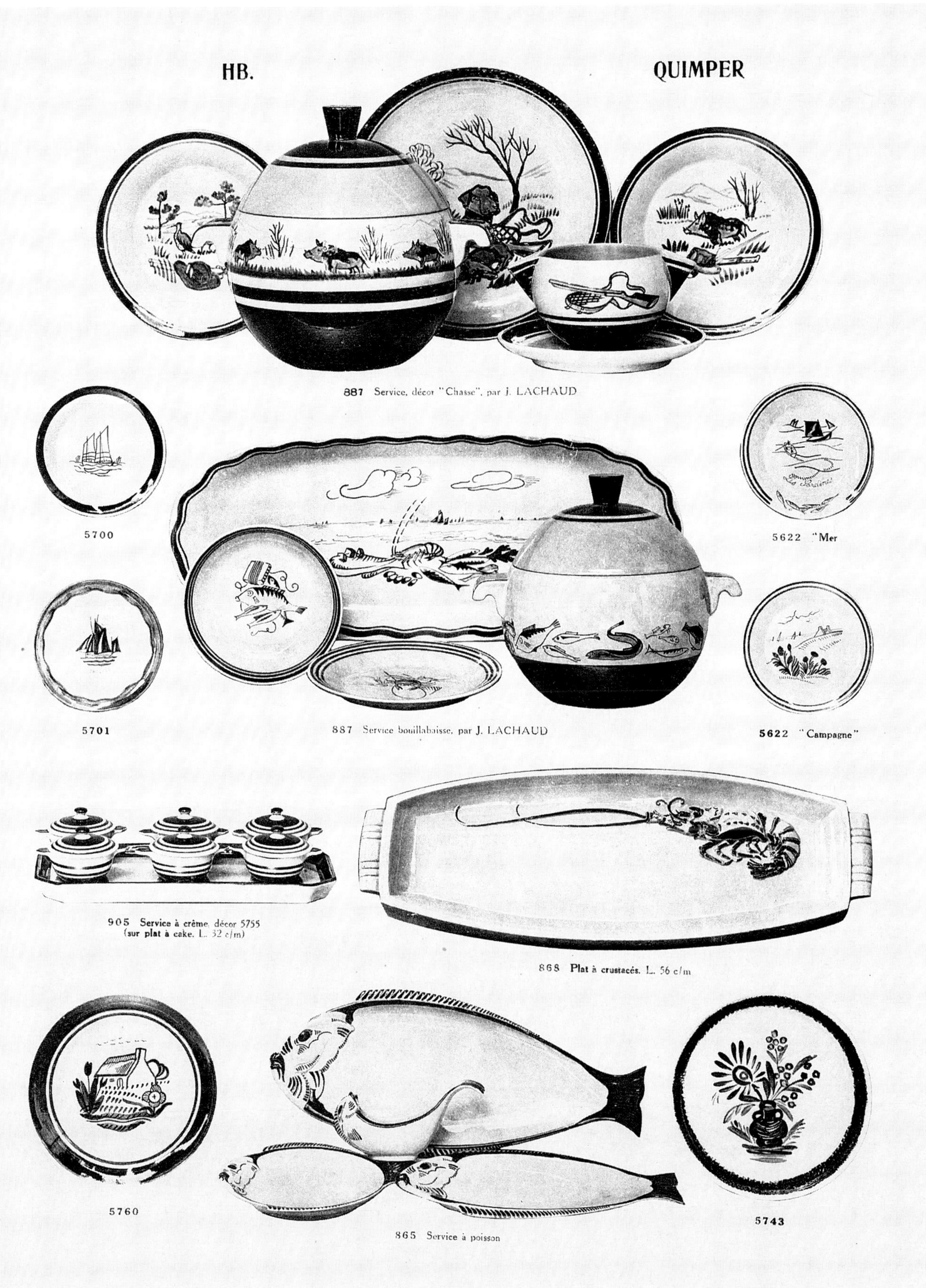
HB.
QUIMPER
887 Service, décor "Chasse", par J. LACHAUD
5700
5622 "Mer"
5701
887 Service bouillabaisse, par J. LACHAUD
5622 "Campagne"
905 Service à crème, décor 5755
(sur plat à cake, L. 32 c/m)
868 Plat à crustacés, L. 56 c/m
5760
5743
865 Service à poisson

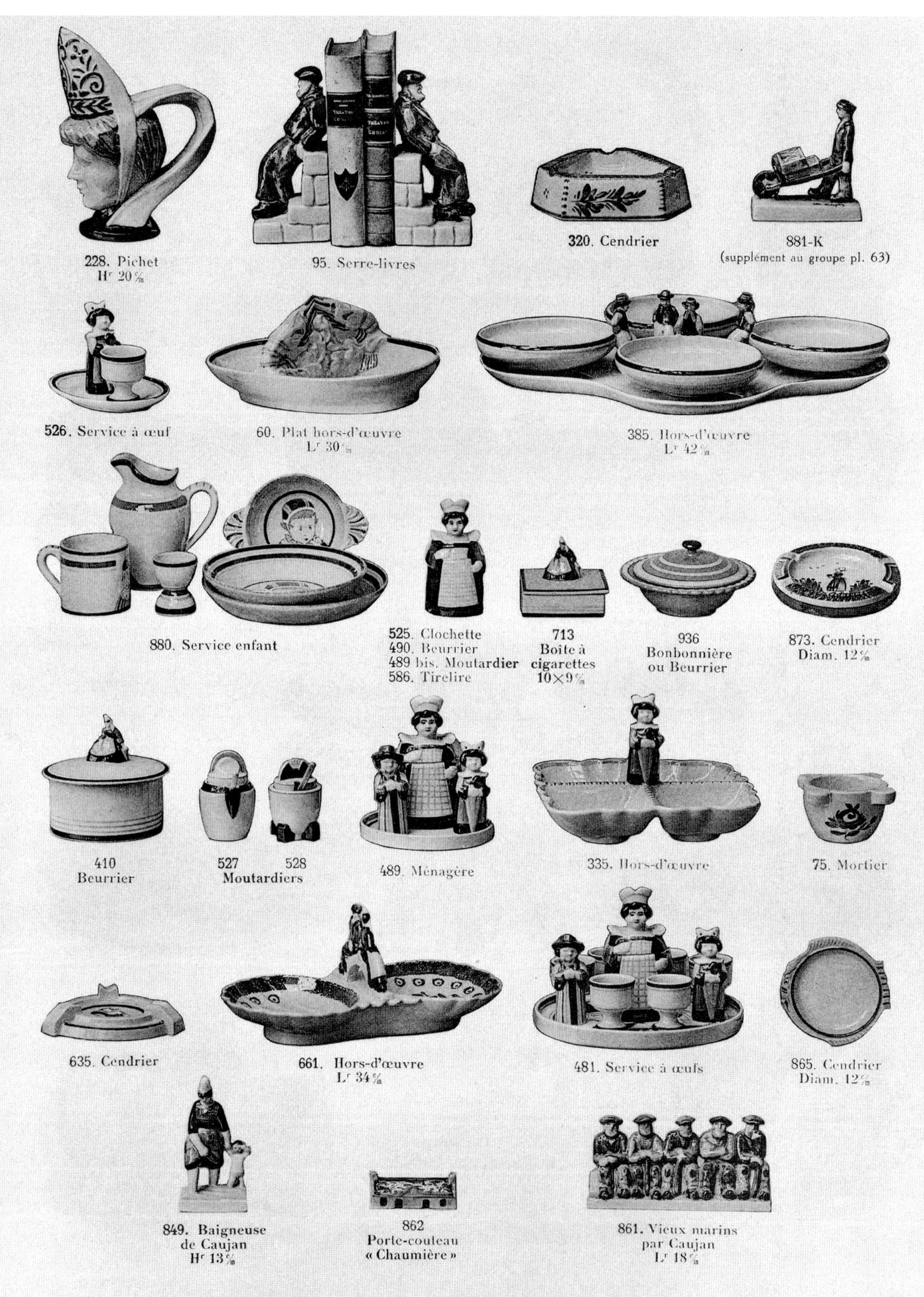

228. Pichet
Hr 20 c/m

95. Serre-livres

320. Cendrier

881-K
(supplément au groupe pl. 63)

526. Service à œuf

60. Plat hors-d'œuvre
Lr 30 c/m

385. Hors-d'œuvre
Lr 42 c/m

880. Service enfant

525. Clochette
490. Beurrier
489 bis. Moutardier
586. Tirelire

713
Boîte à
cigarettes
10×9 c/m

936
Bonbonnière
ou Beurrier

873. Cendrier
Diam. 12 c/m

410
Beurrier

527 528
Moutardiers

489. Ménagère

335. Hors-d'œuvre

75. Mortier

635. Cendrier

661. Hors-d'œuvre
Lr 34 c/m

481. Service à œufs

865. Cendrier
Diam. 12 c/m

849. Baigneuse
de Caujan
Hr 13 c/m

862
Porte-couteau
« Chaumière »

861. Vieux marins
par Caujan
Lr 18 c/m

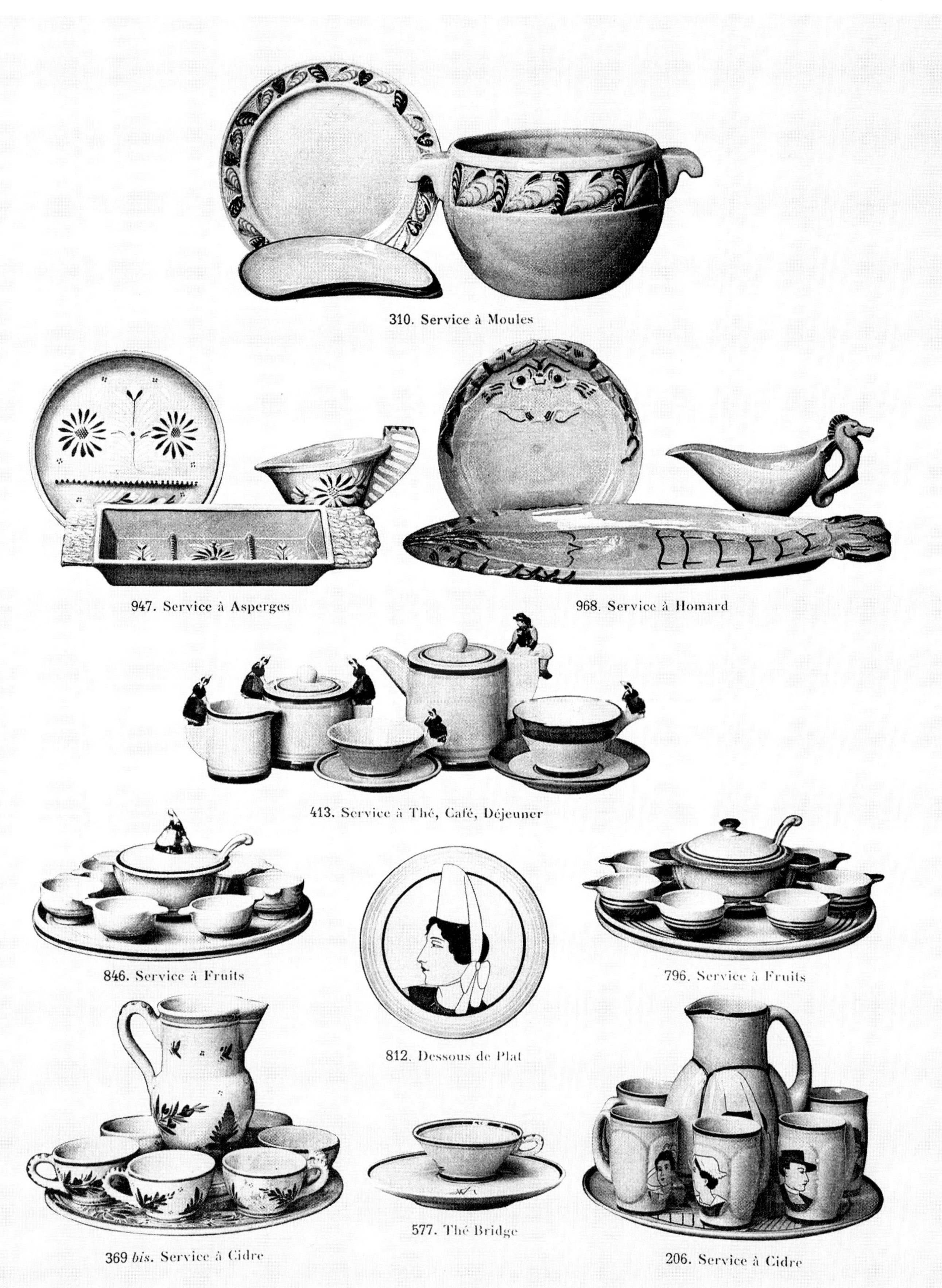

310. Service à Moules

947. Service à Asperges

968. Service à Homard

413. Service à Thé, Café, Déjeuner

846. Service à Fruits

812. Dessous de Plat

796. Service à Fruits

577. Thé Bridge

369 *bis*. Service à Cidre

206. Service à Cidre

HB. QUIMPER

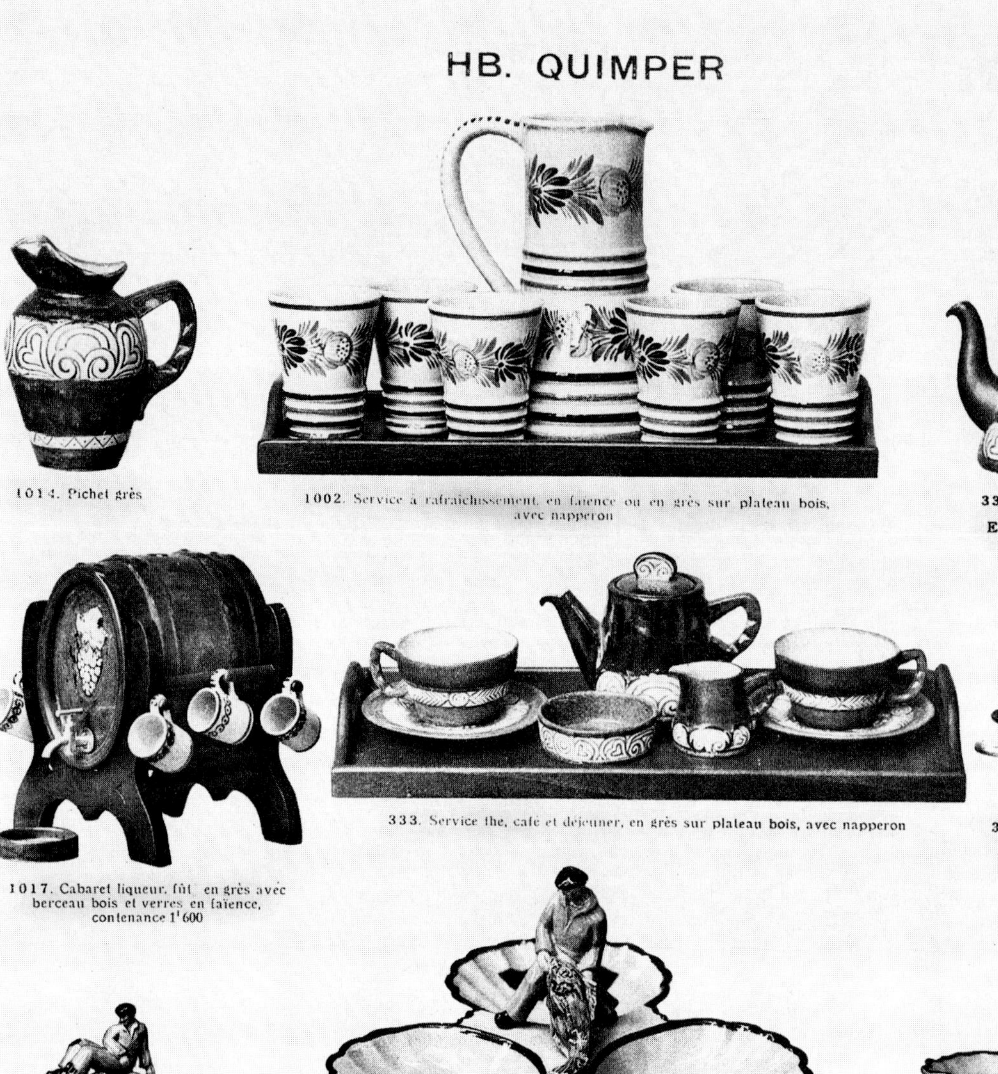

1014. Pichet grès

1002. Service à rafraîchissement, en faïence ou en grès sur plateau bois, avec napperon

333. Cafetière filtre 1er en grès
Existe en 2 tasses et en 6 tasses

1017. Cabaret liqueur, fût en grès avec berceau bois et verres en faïence, contenance 1l 600

333. Service thé, café et déjeuner, en grès sur plateau bois, avec napperon

333. Beurrier couvert 2e en grès
Existe en 2 tailles

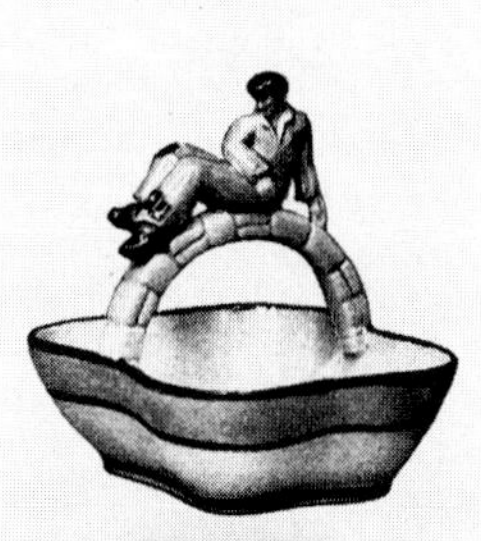

1012. Panier
Long. 18 cm

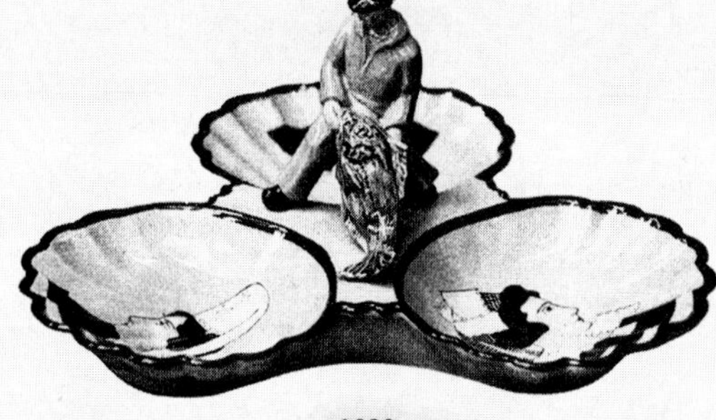

1020
Hors-d'œuvre

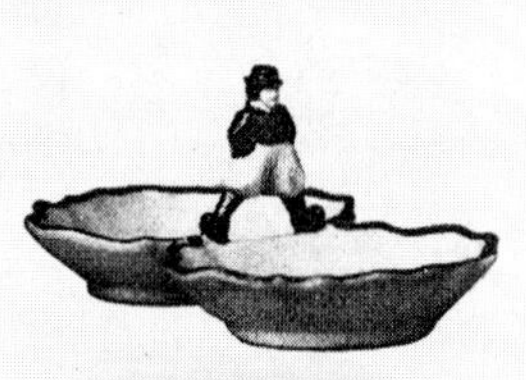

1011. Hors-d'œuvre
Long. 18 cm

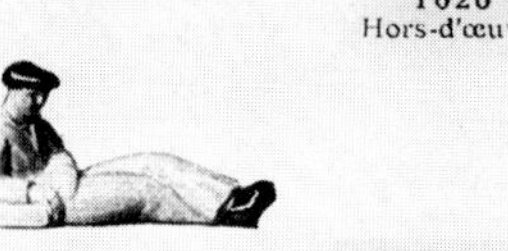

1018 Porte-couteaux 1018

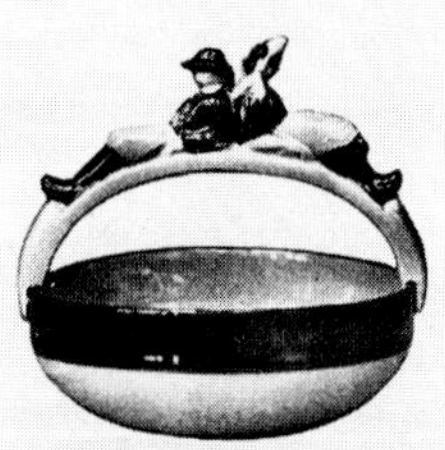

1013. Panier
Diam. 15 cm

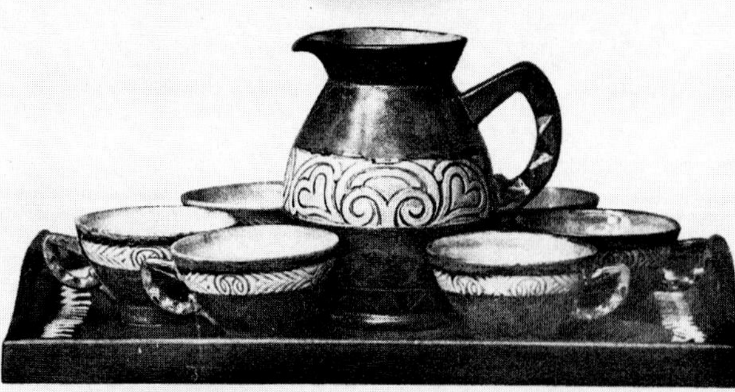

1015. Service à cidre grès, sur plateau bois, avec napperon

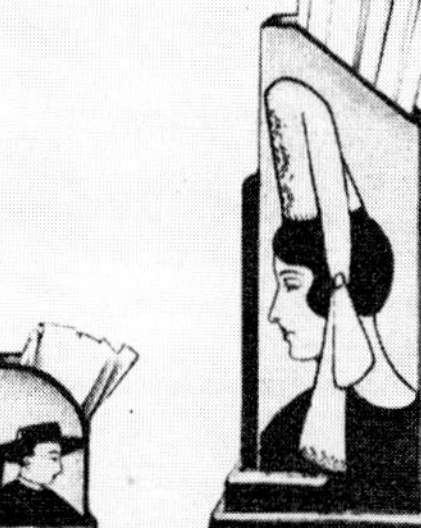

1007
Porte-cure-dents
Haut. 7 cm

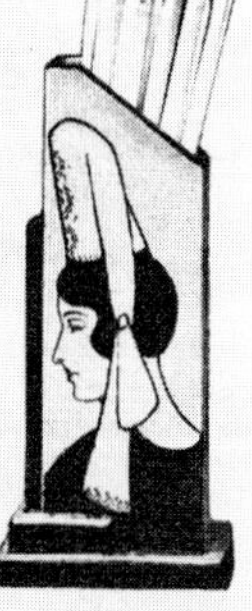

1008
Porte-chalumeaux
Haut. 20 cm

HB. QUIMPER

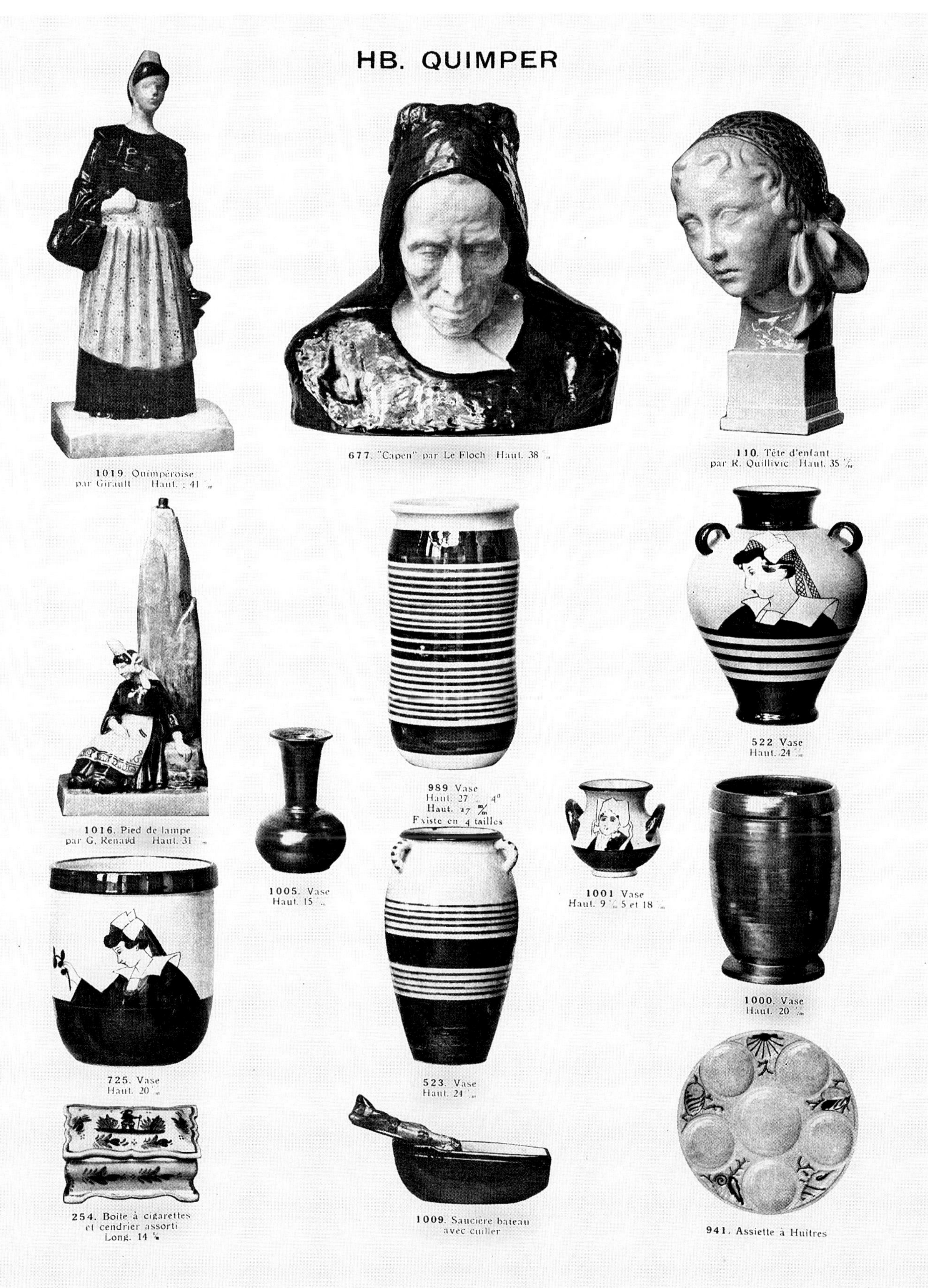

1019. Quimpéroise
par Girault Haut. : 41 c/m

677. "Capen" par Le Floch Haut. 38 c/m

110. Tête d'enfant
par R. Quillivic Haut. 35 c/m

1016. Pied de lampe
par G. Renaud Haut. 31 c/m

989 Vase
Haut. 27 c/m 4°
Haut. 27 m/m
Existe en 4 tailles

522 Vase
Haut. 24 c/m

1005. Vase
Haut. 15 c/m

1001 Vase
Haut. 9 c/m 5 et 18 c/m

725. Vase
Haut. 20 c/m

523. Vase
Haut. 24 c/m

1000. Vase
Haut. 20 c/m

254. Boite à cigarettes
et cendrier assorti
Long. 14 c/m

1009. Saucière bateau
avec cuiller

941. Assiette à Huitres

HB. QUIMPER

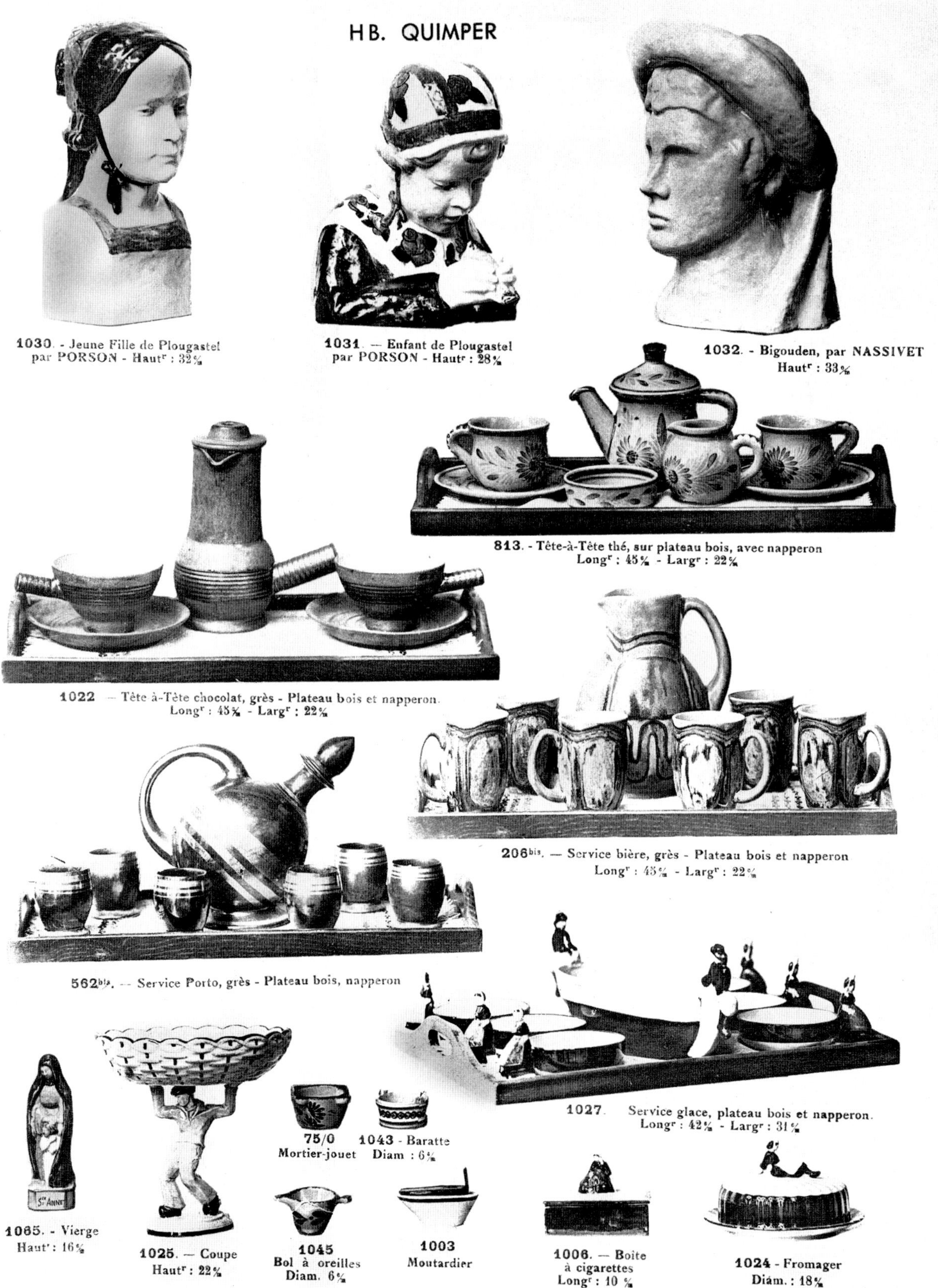

1030. - Jeune Fille de Plougastel par PORSON - Haut^r : 32%

1031. — Enfant de Plougastel par PORSON - Haut^r : 28%

1032. - Bigouden, par NASSIVET Haut^r : 33%

813. - Tête-à-Tête thé, sur plateau bois, avec napperon Long^r : 45% - Larg^r : 22%

1022 — Tête à-Tête chocolat, grès - Plateau bois et napperon. Long^r : 45% - Larg^r : 22%

206bis. — Service bière, grès - Plateau bois et napperon Long^r : 45% - Larg^r : 22%

562bis. — Service Porto, grès - Plateau bois, napperon

1027. Service glace, plateau bois et napperon. Long^r : 42% - Larg^r : 31%

75/0 Mortier-jouet

1043 - Baratte Diam : 6%

1065. - Vierge Haut^r : 16%

1025. — Coupe Haut^r : 22%

1045 Bol à oreilles Diam. 6%

1003 Moutardier

1006. — Boite à cigarettes Long^r : 10 %

1024 - Fromager Diam. : 18%

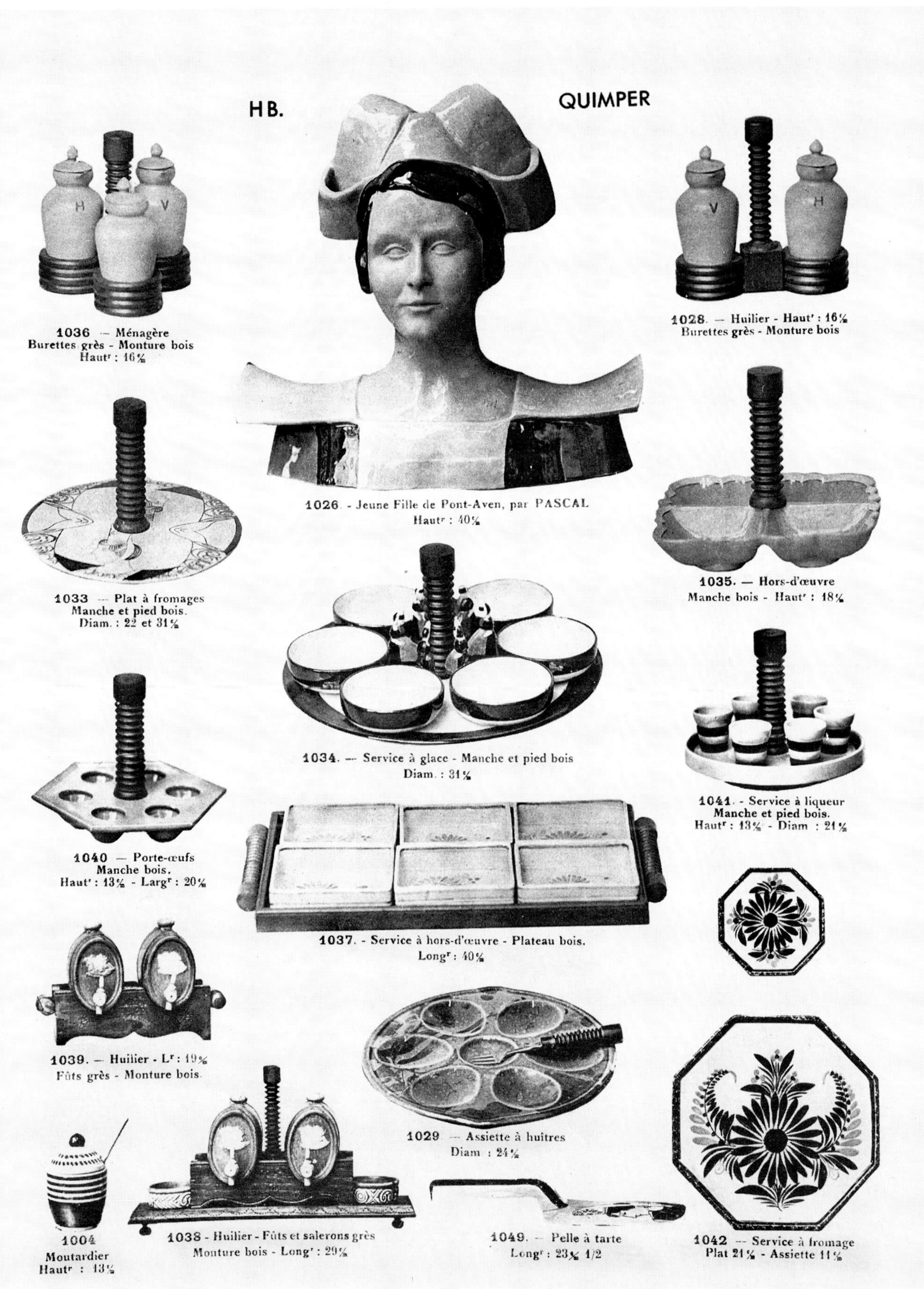

1036 — Ménagère
Burettes grès - Monture bois
Hautr : 16%

1028. — Huilier - Hautr : 16%
Burettes grès - Monture bois

1026. - Jeune Fille de Pont-Aven, par PASCAL
Hautr : 40%

1033 — Plat à fromages
Manche et pied bois.
Diam. : 22 et 31%

1035. — Hors-d'œuvre
Manche bois - Hautr : 18%

1034. — Service à glace - Manche et pied bois
Diam. : 31%

1041. - Service à liqueur
Manche et pied bois.
Hautr : 13% - Diam : 21%

1040 — Porte-œufs
Manche bois.
Hautr : 13% - Largr : 20%

1037. - Service à hors-d'œuvre - Plateau bois.
Longr : 40%

1039. — Huilier - Lr : 19%
Fûts grès - Monture bois.

1029 — Assiette à huitres
Diam : 24%

1004
Moutardier
Hautr : 13%

1038 - Huilier - Fûts et salerons grès
Monture bois - Longr : 29%

1049. — Pelle à tarte
Longr : 23% 1/2

1042 — Service à fromage
Plat 21% - Assiette 11%

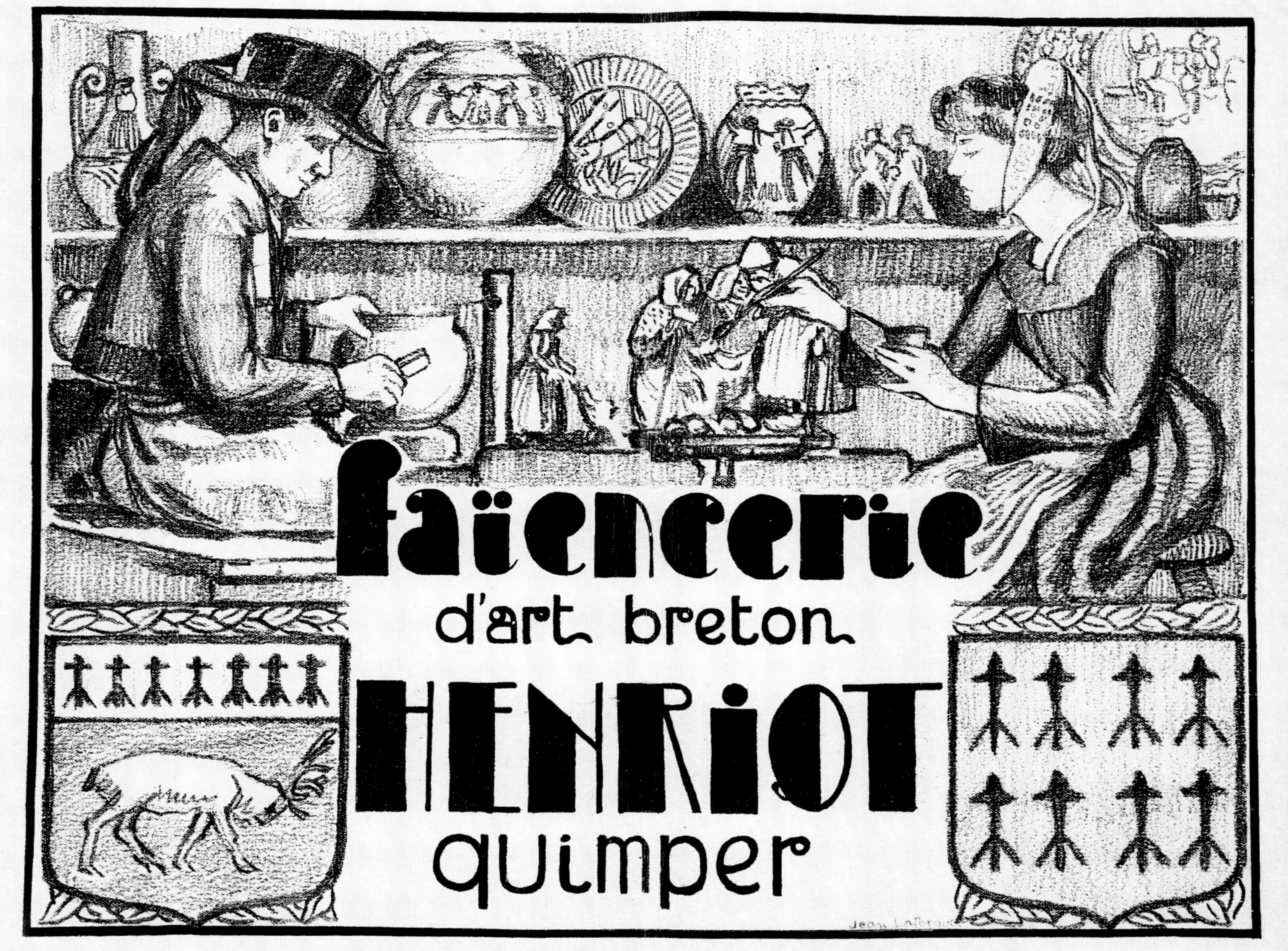
faïencerie
d'art breton
HENRIOT
quimper

HISTORIQUE

C'est en 1778 que GUILLAUME DUMAINE fonda la Maison qui, depuis un siècle et demi, n'a cessé d'être dirigée par ses héritiers directs, les DUMAINE, TANQUEREY, HENRIOT et est devenue la FAÏENCERIE D'ART BRETON HENRIOT.

Sa production consistait, à l'origine, en grès domestiques, en poteries vernissées aux naïfs dessins et en faïences rustiques ou en copies de Moustiers, Nevers, Rouen, puis en souvenirs caractéristiques de la Bretagne.

En 1913, était acquise de la Maison PORQUIER (fondée au 18ème siècle) la propriété de ses modèles et de sa marque P. B. et des dessins artistiques de M. BEAU qui, le premier, adapta aux faïences de Quimper les personnages et scènes pittoresques de la vie bretonne.

En 1919, la Maison obtenait la collaboration du peintre éminent de la Mer, MATHURIN MEHEUT qui sut la placer au premier rang du mouvement moderne ; à ses côtés vinrent se ranger les statuaires BACHELET, LENOIR, NICOT, BEAUFILS, les peintres et décorateurs CRESTON, Géo FOURRIER, POL, SEVELLEC, MICHEAU, LAFORGUE. Mmes Suz. CRESTON, JEAN HAFFEN, ANNIE MOUROUX et L. VINCENT BLANDIN, Les peintres et statuaires coloniaux MONIER, BROQUET et NIVELT.

Ces travaux ont obtenu les plus hautes récompenses aux expositions : PARIS 1878 ; NANTES 1910 ; BREST 1913 ; RENNES 1922 ; ROUEN 1923 ; Arts Décoratifs PARIS 1925 ; Décorateurs PARIS 1928 ; BARCELONE 1929 ; COLONIALE 1931 : Grand Prix, 5 Médailles d'Or, 3 d'Argent, 3 de Bronze, soit 12 récompenses

QUIMPER détient maintenant l'une des premières places dans la céramique. Elle a eu la chance de posséder au moment opportun des industriels intelligents, désireux de réaliser des formules nouvelles, qui se sont attachés à œuvrer de la beauté à côté de la production courante. Ils ont pour cela fait appel à la collaboration de la main d'œuvre éduquée par eux et des artistes les plus renommés parmi les autochtones. Et ceux-ci sont nombreux. Ils forment, selon le mot si juste de notre regretté Anatole Le Braz, la magnifique et pure couronne de notre chère province. La tradition s'allie chez eux à l'originalité. C'est l'explication des succès continus qu'ils obtiennent dans les créations modernes, d'inspiration régionale, qui jaillissent de leur cerveau, de leur cœur et que façonnent avec tant de compréhension les anciens tourneurs d'écuelles cornouaillais, devenus des artistes eux-mêmes.

Ainsi, tout en changeant d'aspect, la céramique bretonne à su conserver les précieuses qualités techniques qui, depuis des siècles, lui ont valu l'estime dans laquelle on l'a toujours tenue.

La Faïencerie d'Art Breton "HENRIOT" a, dans cette voie d'avenir, accompli des prodiges. Des chefs-d'œuvres inimitables, éclatants de lumière et de couleur sont sortis de ses fours. Il suffit de feuilleter ce luxueux catalogue pour le constater. C'est un éblouissement qui laisse dans vos yeux ces ronds dorés de soleil dont parle le poète et qui prouve que la Bretagne n'est pas voilée de gris, ainsi que tant de faux mélancoliques ont essayé de le faire croire en se réclamant de René. Au contraire, les décors sont vibrants et vivants sont les personnages, comme le sont les pardons, les fêtes populaires, la gaieté bretonne qui sait être franche sans jamais sombrer dans la vulgarité.

Chefs-d'œuvres, disions-nous tout à l'heure ! Le terme peut-il paraître exagéré quand on lit sur le socle des pièces présentées les noms de Mathurin Méheut, Armel Beaufils, Pierre Lenoir, Louis Nicot, René Creston et de tant d'autres qui savent délicatement enclore dans un objet de proportions modestes tout l'infini de leur rêve, préciser avec un goût averti et sûr les fins vers lesquelles tend la décoration moderne, traduire dans une matière riche, mais ingrate à travailler, toute la synthèse de de l'Armor: ses paysages pittoresques, ses figures légendaires et ses scènes populaires.

Quand le touriste, sceptique par tempérament, contemple de telles productions, il comprend aussitôt qu'il n'a pas devant lui des bibelots façonnés en séries illimitées pour satisfaire à des nécessités uniquement commerciales, mais des manifestations d'art, comme peut seule en créer une race aux origines millénaires, qui a pieusement veillé "son divin flambeau d'âme" et conservé intact en elle le culte de l'idéal et de la beauté.

Et lorsque ce passant acquiert l'objet qu'il a longuement, amoureusement contemplé, ce n'est pas pour répondre par un réflexe banal à une tentation passagère, mais bien par un besoin impérieux et intime d'emporter chez lui, pour être toujours à même de le pouvoir contempler, l'immortel souvenir d'une expression vraie de la Bretagne.

A. L. Aubert

Directeur de la Bretagne Touristique,
Président de la Chambre de Commerce des Côtes-du-Nord

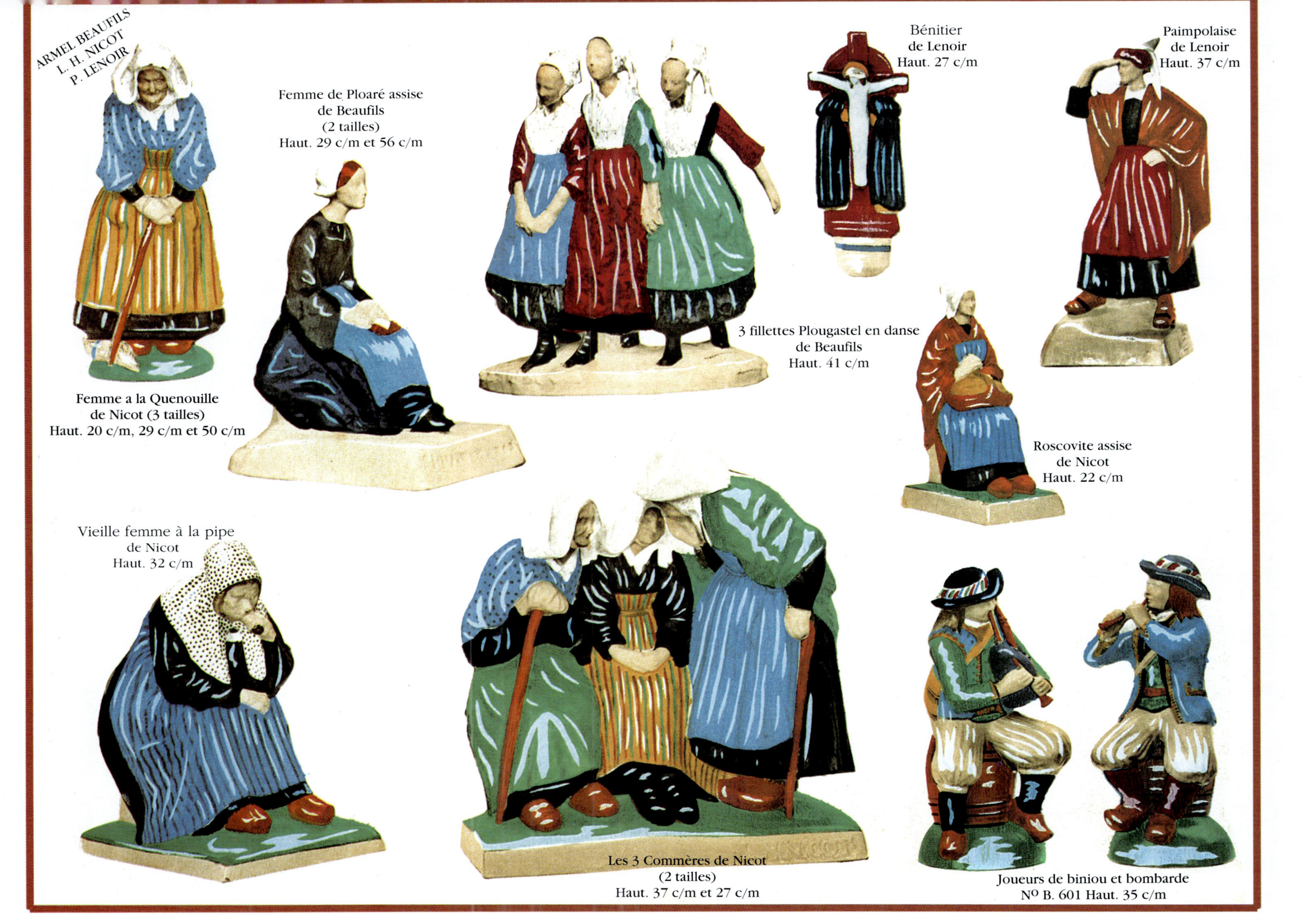

ARMEL BEAUFILS
L. H. NICOT
P. LENOIR

Femme a la Quenouille
de Nicot (3 tailles)
Haut. 20 c/m, 29 c/m et 50 c/m

Femme de Ploaré assise
de Beaufils
(2 tailles)
Haut. 29 c/m et 56 c/m

3 fillettes Plougastel en danse
de Beaufils
Haut. 41 c/m

Bénitier
de Lenoir
Haut. 27 c/m

Paimpolaise
de Lenoir
Haut. 37 c/m

Roscovite assise
de Nicot
Haut. 22 c/m

Vieille femme à la pipe
de Nicot
Haut. 32 c/m

Les 3 Commères de Nicot
(2 tailles)
Haut. 37 c/m et 27 c/m

Joueurs de biniou et bombarde
N° B. 601 Haut. 35 c/m

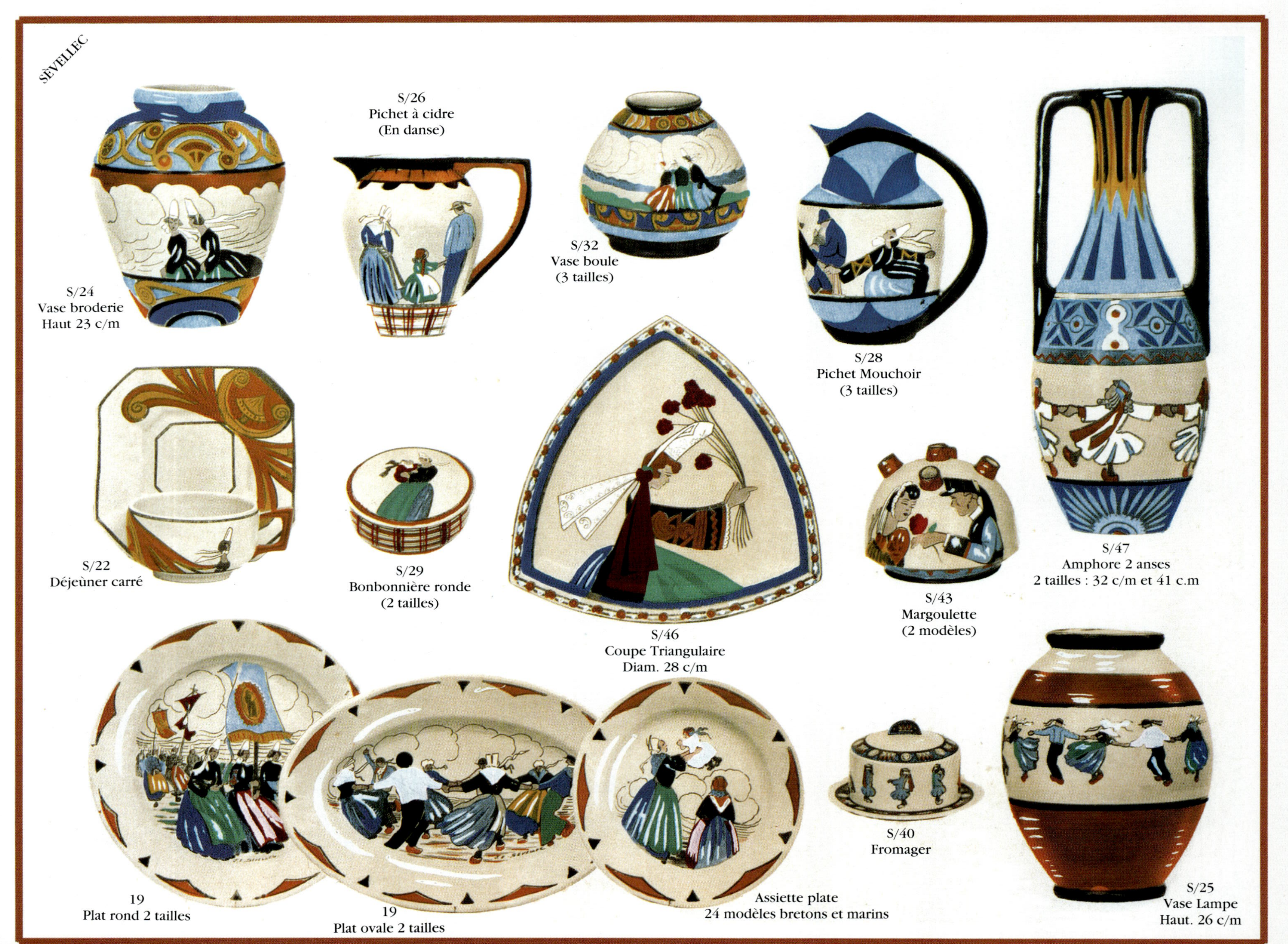

SÈVELLEC

S/24
Vase broderie
Haut 23 c/m

S/26
Pichet à cidre
(En danse)

S/32
Vase boule
(3 tailles)

S/28
Pichet Mouchoir
(3 tailles)

S/47
Amphore 2 anses
2 tailles : 32 c/m et 41 c.m

S/22
Déjeùner carré

S/29
Bonbonnière ronde
(2 tailles)

S/46
Coupe Triangulaire
Diam. 28 c/m

S/43
Margoulette
(2 modèles)

19
Plat rond 2 tailles

19
Plat ovale 2 tailles

Assiette plate
24 modèles bretons et marins

S/40
Fromager

S/25
Vase Lampe
Haut. 26 c/m

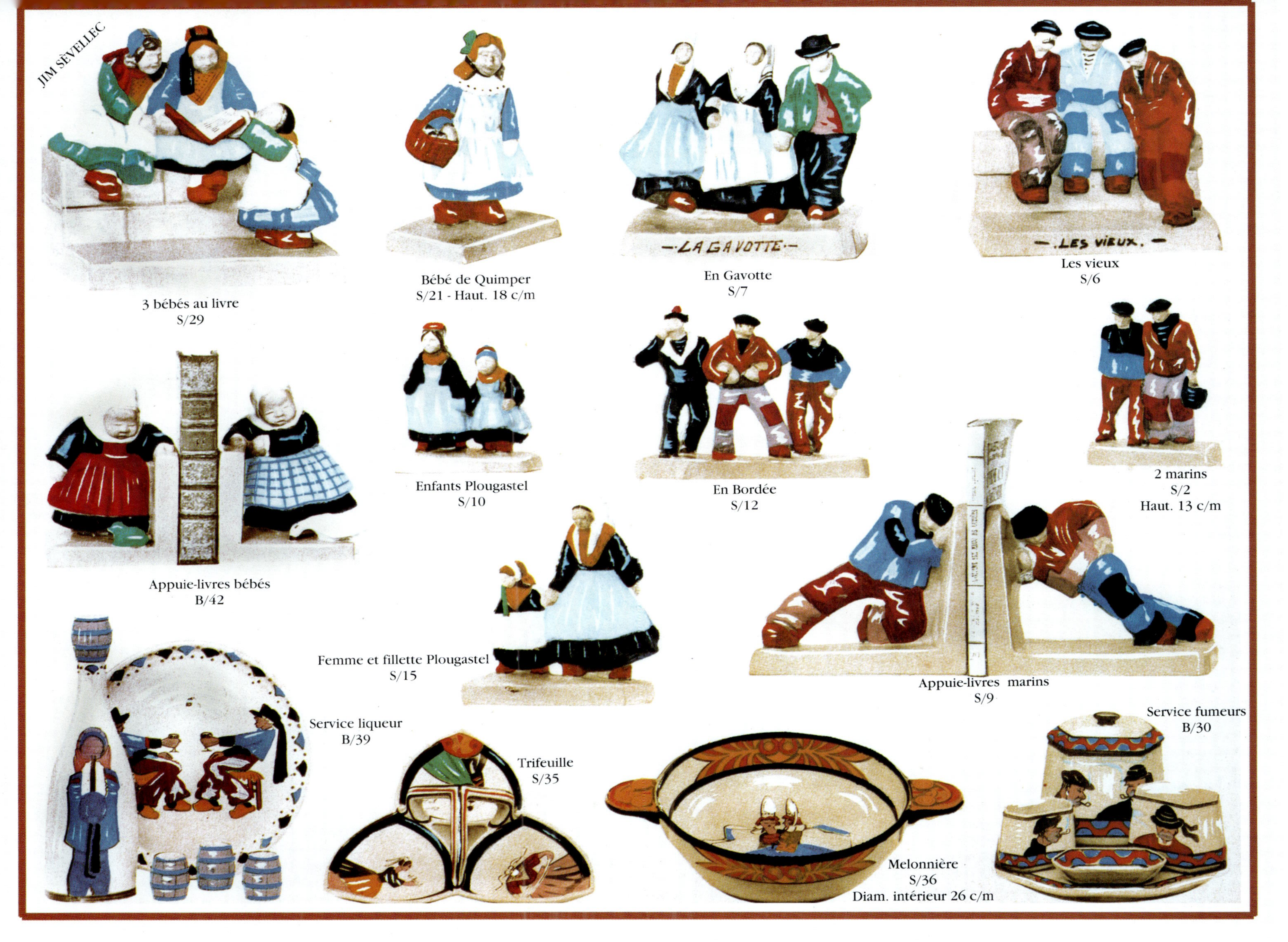

JIM SÈVELLEC

3 bébés au livre
S/29

Bébé de Quimper
S/21 - Haut. 18 c/m

En Gavotte
S/7

Les vieux
S/6

Appuie-livres bébés
B/42

Enfants Plougastel
S/10

En Bordée
S/12

2 marins
S/2
Haut. 13 c/m

Femme et fillette Plougastel
S/15

Appuie-livres marins
S/9

Service liqueur
B/39

Trifeuille
S/35

Melonnière
S/36
Diam. intérieur 26 c/m

Service fumeurs
B/30

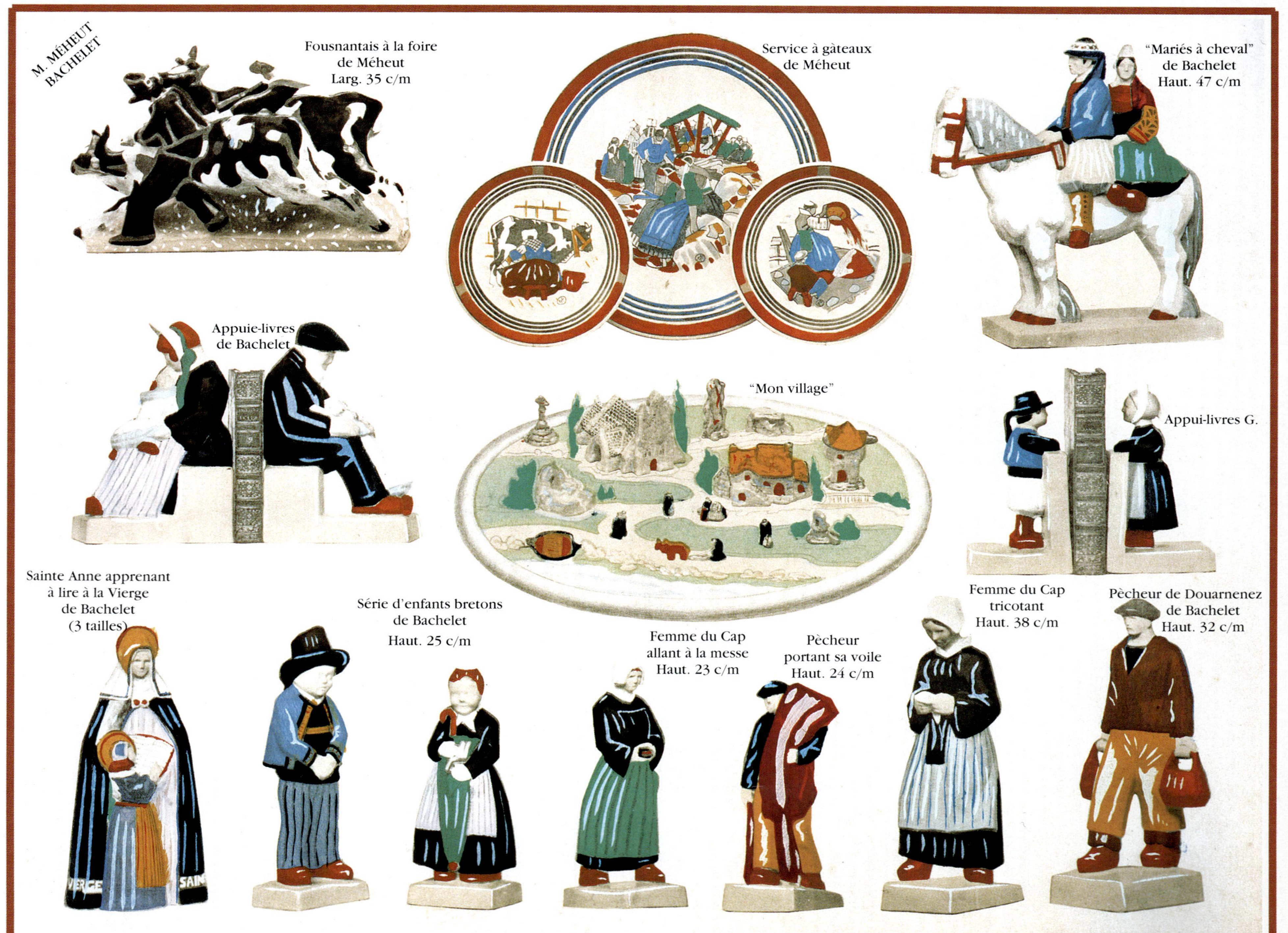

M. MÉHEUT
BACHELET

Fousnantais à la foire
de Méheut
Larg. 35 c/m

Service à gâteaux
de Méheut

"Mariés à cheval"
de Bachelet
Haut. 47 c/m

Appuie-livres
de Bachelet

"Mon village"

Appui-livres G.

Sainte Anne apprenant
à lire à la Vierge
de Bachelet
(3 tailles)

Série d'enfants bretons
de Bachelet
Haut. 25 c/m

Femme du Cap
allant à la messe
Haut. 23 c/m

Pècheur
portant sa voile
Haut. 24 c/m

Femme du Cap
tricotant
Haut. 38 c/m

Pècheur de Douarnenez
de Bachelet
Haut. 32 c/m

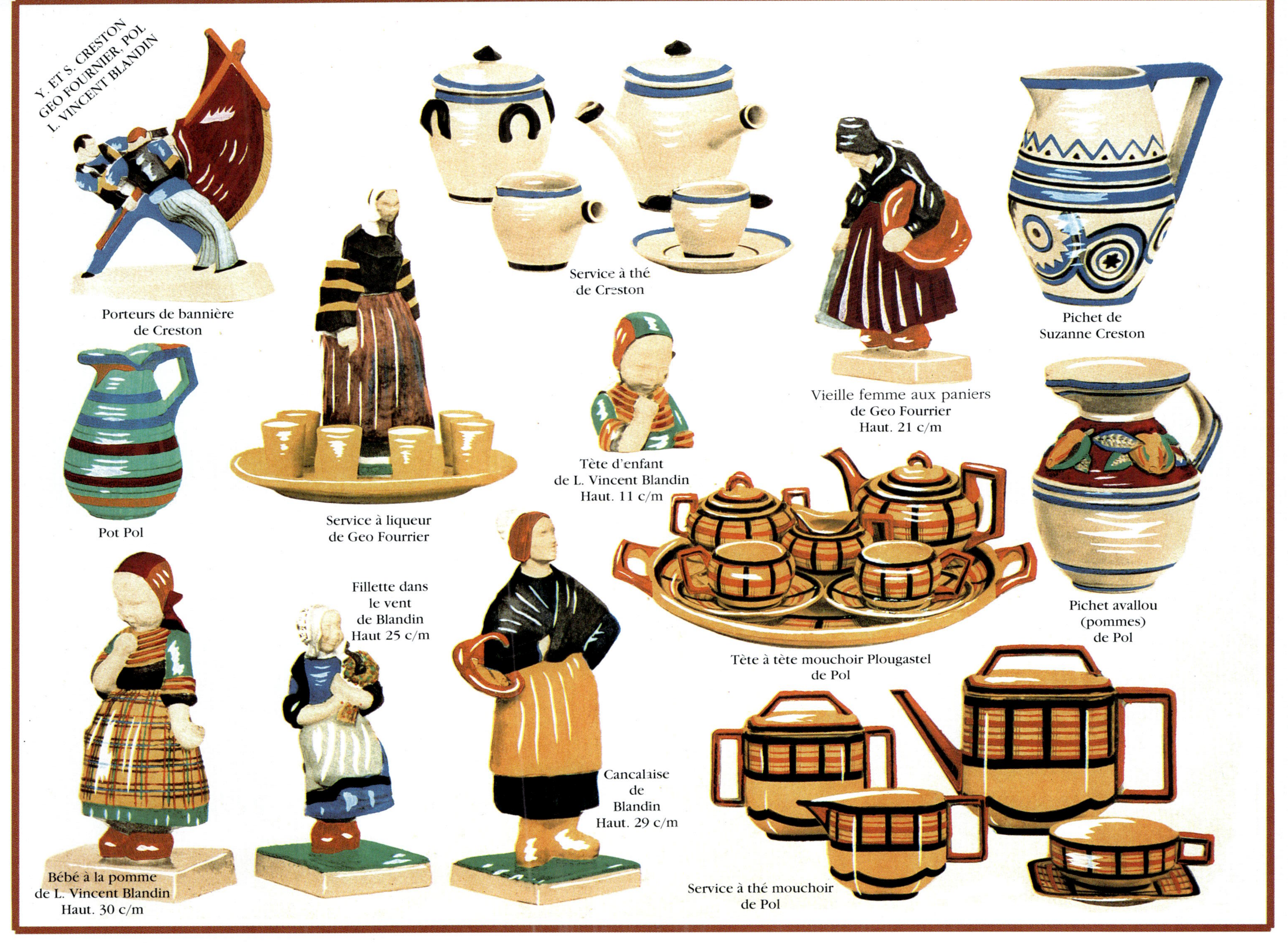

Y. ET S. CRESTON
GEO FOURNIER, POL
L. VINCENT BLANDIN

Porteurs de bannière
de Creston

Service à thé
de Creston

Pichet de
Suzanne Creston

Pot Pol

Service à liqueur
de Geo Fourrier

Tête d'enfant
de L. Vincent Blandin
Haut. 11 c/m

Vieille femme aux paniers
de Geo Fourrier
Haut. 21 c/m

Pichet avallou
(pommes)
de Pol

Tête à tête mouchoir Plougastel
de Pol

Bébé à la pomme
de L. Vincent Blandin
Haut. 30 c/m

Fillette dans
le vent
de Blandin
Haut 25 c/m

Cancalaise
de
Blandin
Haut. 29 c/m

Service à thé mouchoir
de Pol

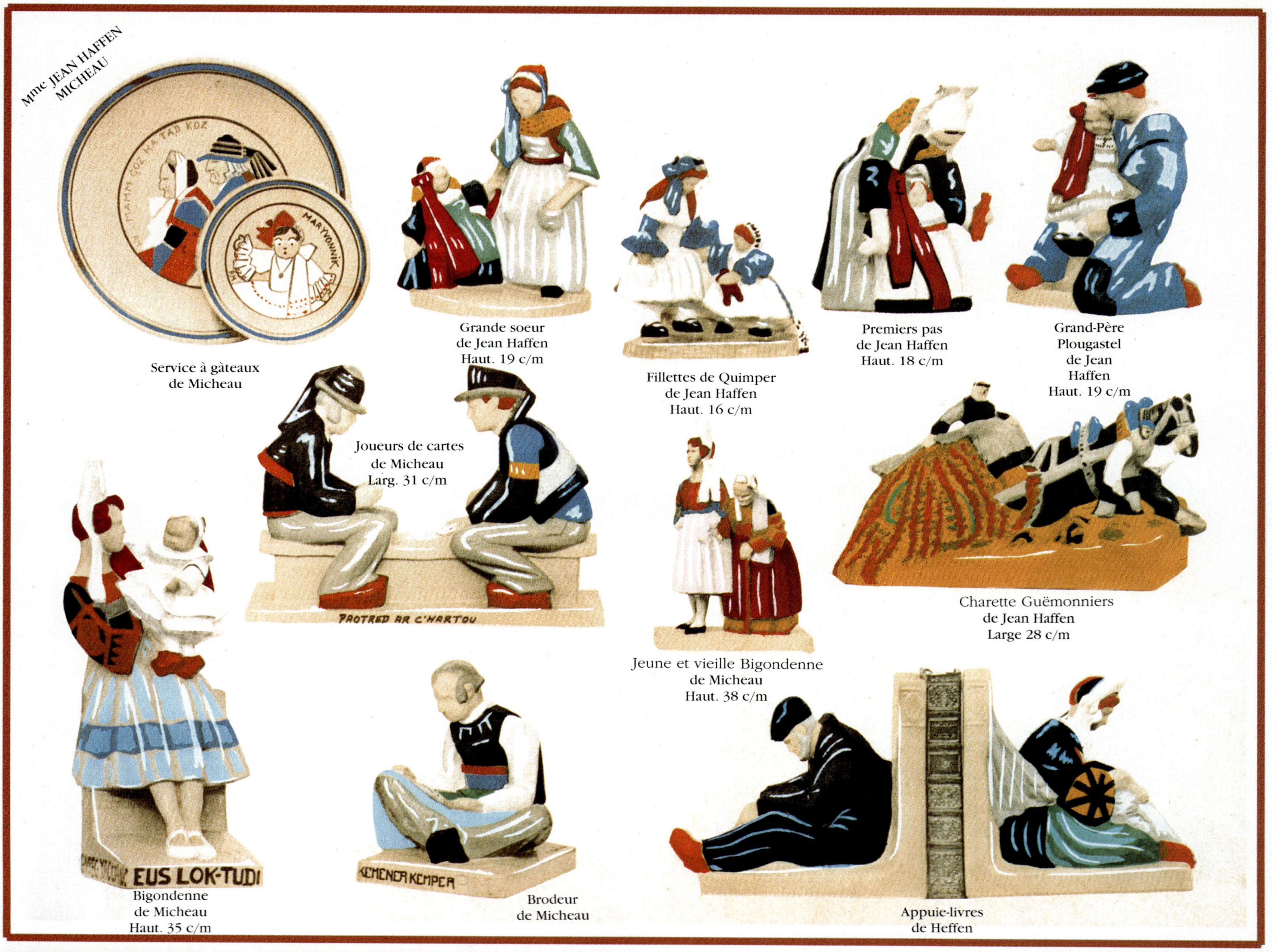

Service à gâteaux de Micheau

Grande soeur de Jean Haffen Haut. 19 c/m

Fillettes de Quimper de Jean Haffen Haut. 16 c/m

Premiers pas de Jean Haffen Haut. 18 c/m

Grand-Père Plougastel de Jean Haffen Haut. 19 c/m

Joueurs de cartes de Micheau Larg. 31 c/m

Jeune et vieille Bigondenne de Micheau Haut. 38 c/m

Charette Guëmonniers de Jean Haffen Large 28 c/m

Bigondenne de Micheau Haut. 35 c/m

Brodeur de Micheau

Appuie-livres de Heffen

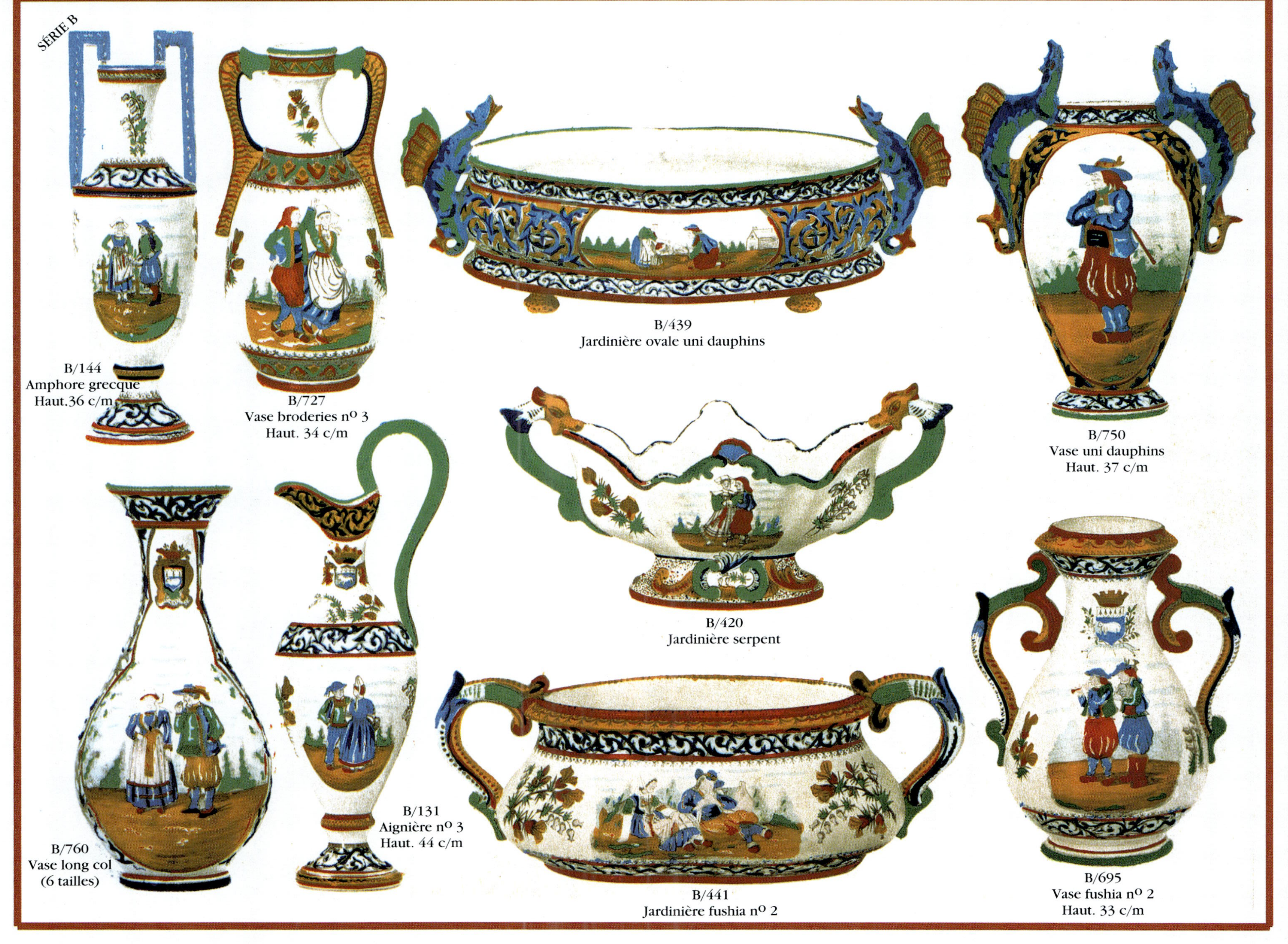

B/144
Amphore grecque
Haut.36 c/m

B/727
Vase broderies n° 3
Haut. 34 c/m

B/439
Jardinière ovale uni dauphins

B/750
Vase uni dauphins
Haut. 37 c/m

B/420
Jardinière serpent

B/760
Vase long col
(6 tailles)

B/131
Aignière n° 3
Haut. 44 c/m

B/441
Jardinière fushia n° 2

B/695
Vase fushia n° 2
Haut. 33 c/m

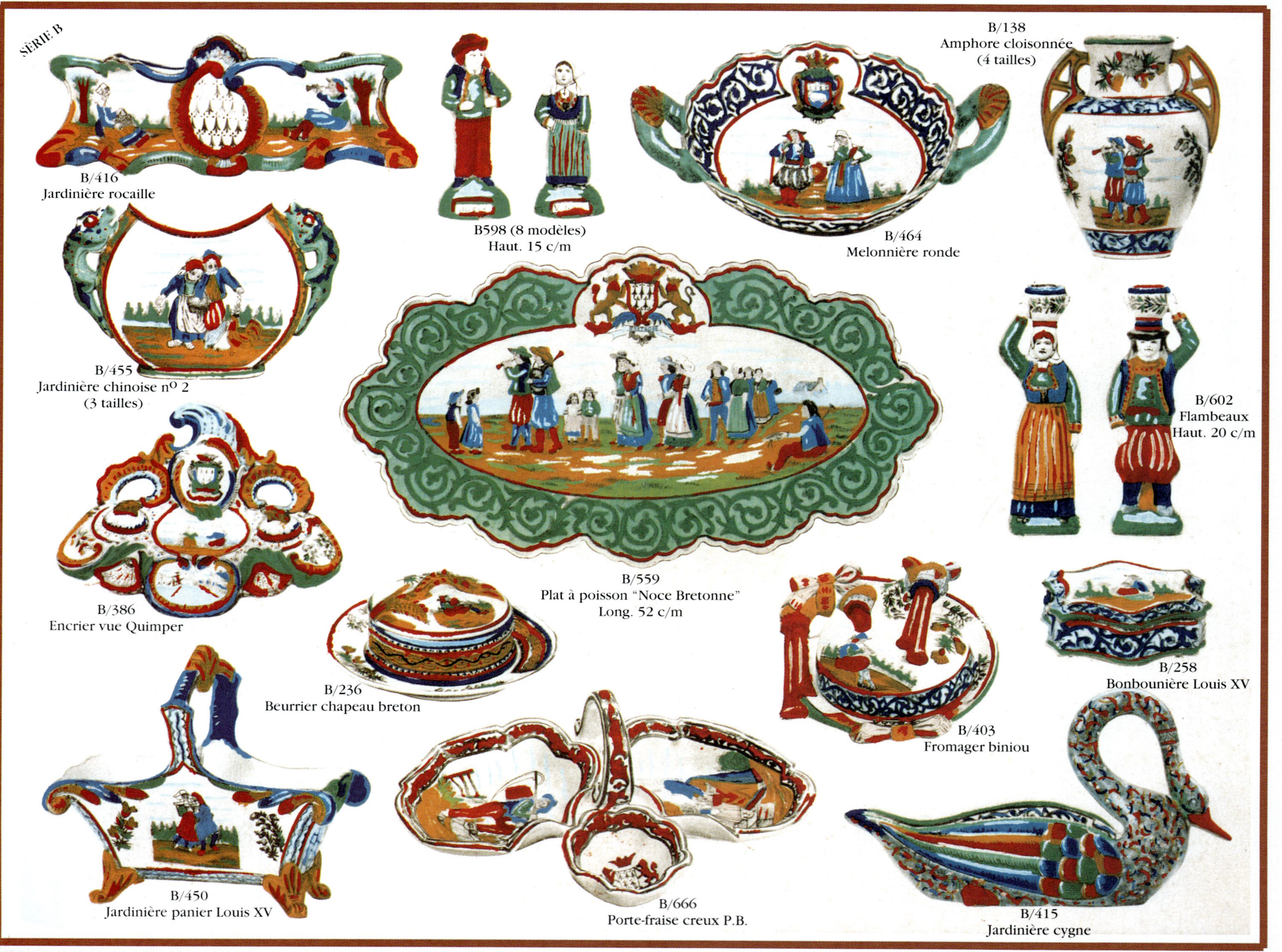

SÉRIE B

B/416
Jardinière rocaille

B598 (8 modèles)
Haut. 15 c/m

B/138
Amphore cloisonnée
(4 tailles)

B/464
Melonnière ronde

B/455
Jardinière chinoise n° 2
(3 tailles)

B/602
Flambeaux
Haut. 20 c/m

B/386
Encrier vue Quimper

B/559
Plat à poisson "Noce Bretonne"
Long. 52 c/m

B/236
Beurrier chapeau breton

B/258
Bonbounière Louis XV

B/403
Fromager biniou

B/450
Jardinière panier Louis XV

B/666
Porte-fraise creux P.B.

B/415
Jardinière cygne

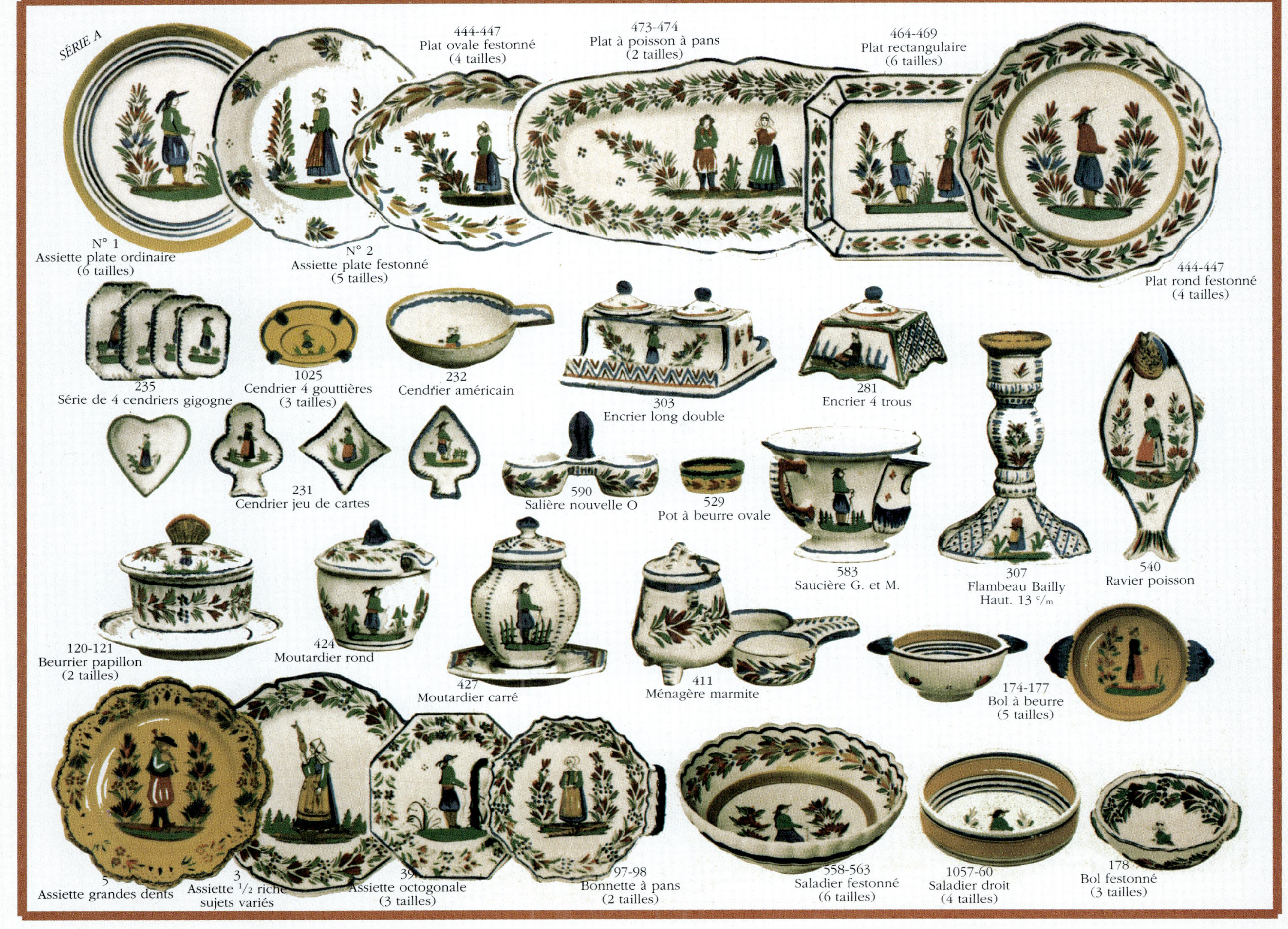
SÉRIE A
N° 1
Assiette plate ordinaire
(6 tailles)
N° 2
Assiette plate festonné
(5 tailles)
444-447
Plat ovale festonné
(4 tailles)
473-474
Plat à poisson à pans
(2 tailles)
464-469
Plat rectangulaire
(6 tailles)
444-447
Plat rond festonné
(4 tailles)
235
Série de 4 cendriers gigogne
1025
Cendrier 4 gouttières
(3 tailles)
232
Cendrier américain
303
Encrier long double
281
Encrier 4 trous
231
Cendrier jeu de cartes
590
Salière nouvelle O
529
Pot à beurre ovale
583
Saucière G. et M.
307
Flambeau Bailly
Haut. 13 c/m
540
Ravier poisson
120-121
Beurrier papillon
(2 tailles)
424
Moutardier rond
427
Moutardier carré
411
Ménagère marmite
174-177
Bol à beurre
(5 tailles)
5
Assiette grandes dents
3
Assiette 1/2 riche
sujets variés
39
Assiette octogonale
(3 tailles)
97-98
Bonnette à pans
(2 tailles)
558-563
Saladier festonné
(6 tailles)
1057-60
Saladier droit
(4 tailles)
178
Bol festonné
(3 tailles)

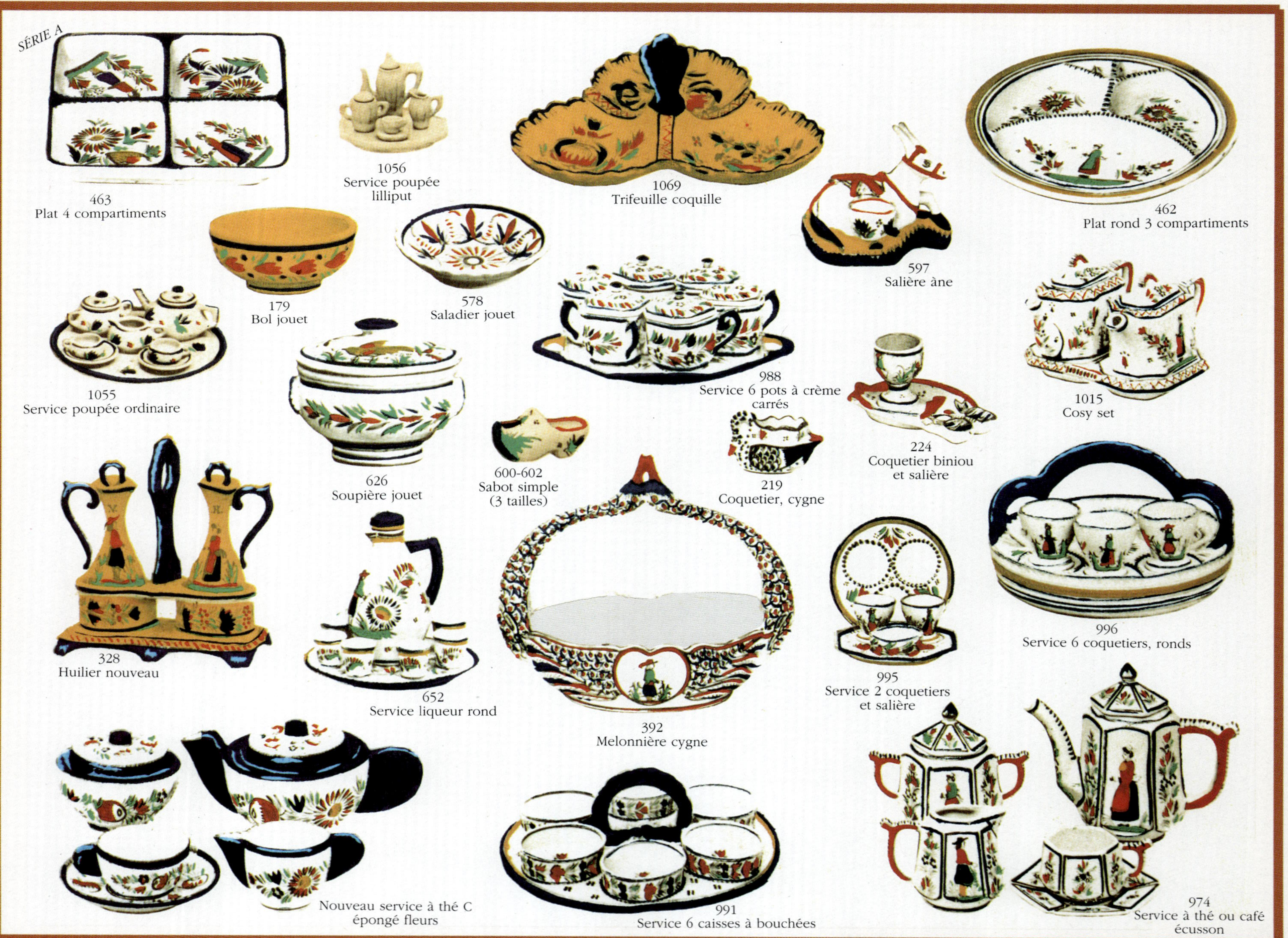

SÉRIE A

463
Plat 4 compartiments

1056
Service poupée
lilliput

1069
Trifeuille coquille

462
Plat rond 3 compartiments

179
Bol jouet

578
Saladier jouet

597
Salière âne

1055
Service poupée ordinaire

988
Service 6 pots à crème
carrés

1015
Cosy set

626
Soupière jouet

600-602
Sabot simple
(3 tailles)

219
Coquetier, cygne

224
Coquetier biniou
et salière

328
Huilier nouveau

652
Service liqueur rond

392
Melonnière cygne

996
Service 6 coquetiers, ronds

995
Service 2 coquetiers
et salière

Nouveau service à thé C
épongé fleurs

991
Service 6 caisses à bouchées

974
Service à thé ou café
écusson

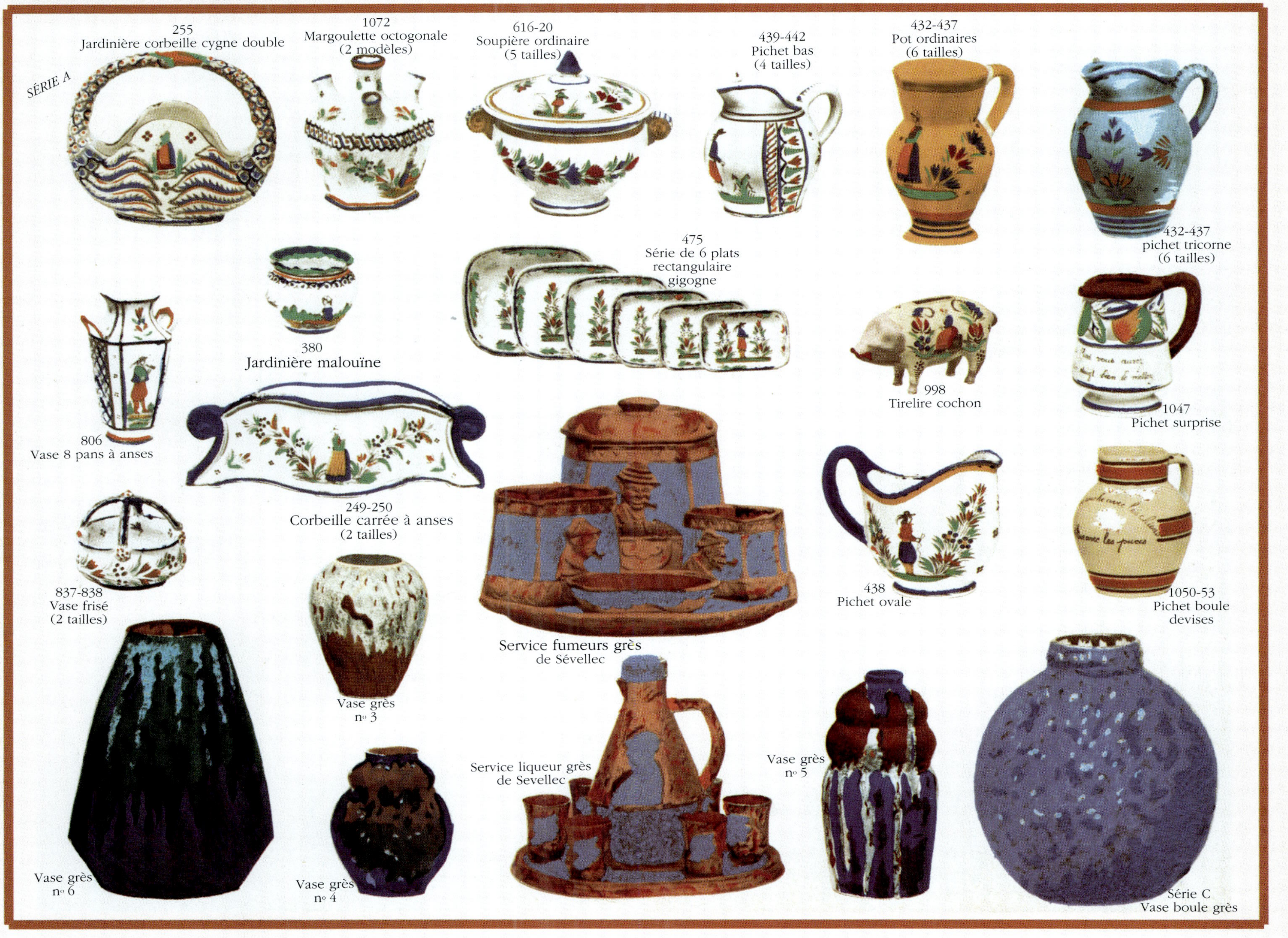
SÉRIE A
255
Jardinière corbeille cygne double
1072
Margoulette octogonale
(2 modèles)
616-20
Soupière ordinaire
(5 tailles)
439-442
Pichet bas
(4 tailles)
432-437
Pot ordinaires
(6 tailles)
432-437
pichet tricorne
(6 tailles)
380
Jardinière malouïne
475
Série de 6 plats
rectangulaire
gigogne
806
Vase 8 pans à anses
998
Tirelire cochon
1047
Pichet surprise
249-250
Corbeille carrée à anses
(2 tailles)
837-838
Vase frisé
(2 tailles)
438
Pichet ovale
1050-53
Pichet boule
devises
Service fumeurs grès
de Sévellec
Vase grès
n° 3
Vase grès
n° 6
Vase grès
n° 4
Service liqueur grès
de Sevellec
Vase grès
n° 5
Série C
Vase boule grès

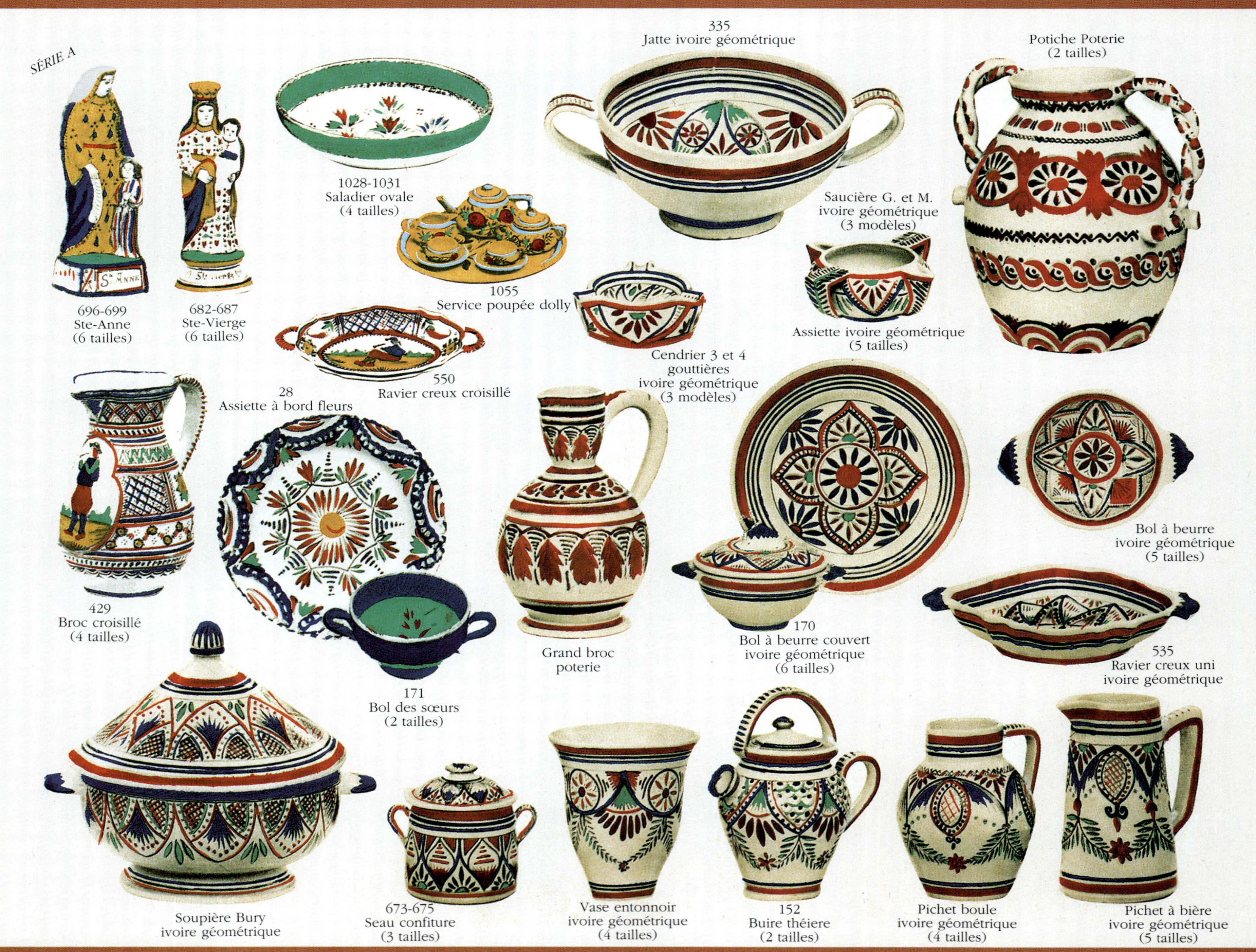

SÉRIE A

696-699
Ste-Anne
(6 tailles)

682-687
Ste-Vierge
(6 tailles)

1028-1031
Saladier ovale
(4 tailles)

1055
Service poupée dolly

335
Jatte ivoire géométrique

Potiche Poterie
(2 tailles)

Saucière G. et M.
ivoire géométrique
(3 modèles)

Assiette ivoire géométrique
(5 tailles)

550
Ravier creux croisillé

Cendrier 3 et 4
gouttières
ivoire géométrique
(3 modèles)

28
Assiette à bord fleurs

429
Broc croisillé
(4 tailles)

171
Bol des sœurs
(2 tailles)

Grand broc
poterie

170
Bol à beurre couvert
ivoire géométrique
(6 tailles)

Bol à beurre
ivoire géométrique
(5 tailles)

535
Ravier creux uni
ivoire géométrique

Soupière Bury
ivoire géométrique

673-675
Seau confiture
(3 tailles)

Vase entonnoir
ivoire géométrique
(4 tailles)

152
Buire théière
(2 tailles)

Pichet boule
ivoire géométrique
(4 tailles)

Pichet à bière
ivoire géométrique
(5 tailles)

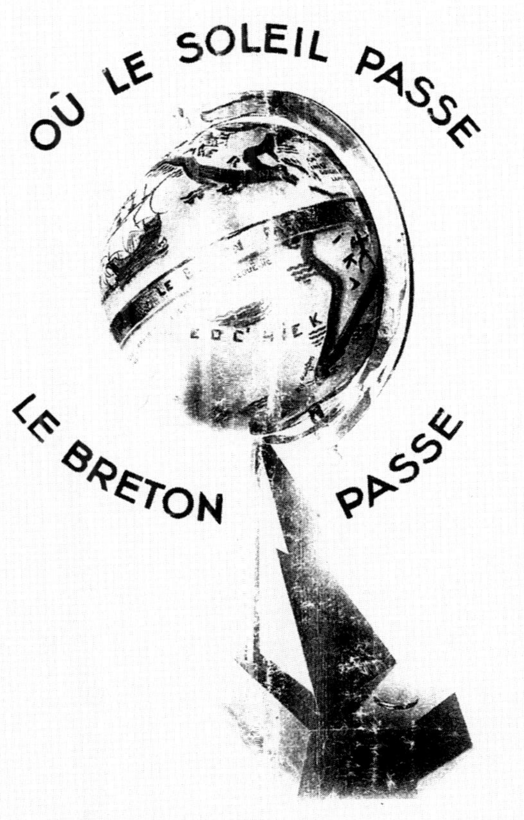
OÙ LE SOLEIL PASSE
LE BRETON PASSE
MAPPEMONDE DE CRESTON
IMPRIMERIE G. BOÜAN
13, Rue des Arquebusiers, Paris

FAÏENCERIE BRETONNE
DE LA GRANDE MAISON
HB QUIMPER HB

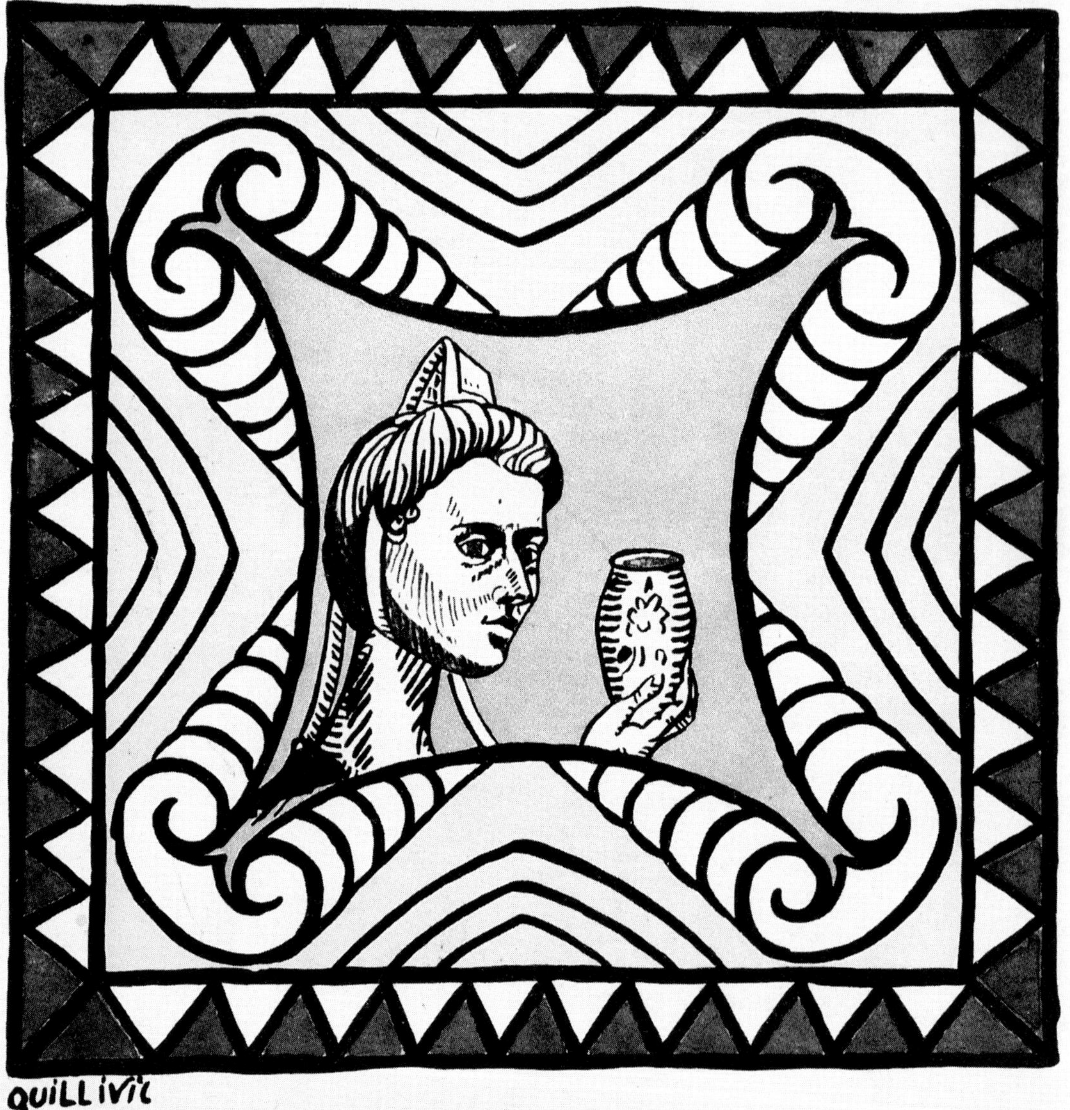

J. VERLINGUE, BOLLORÉ ET CIE

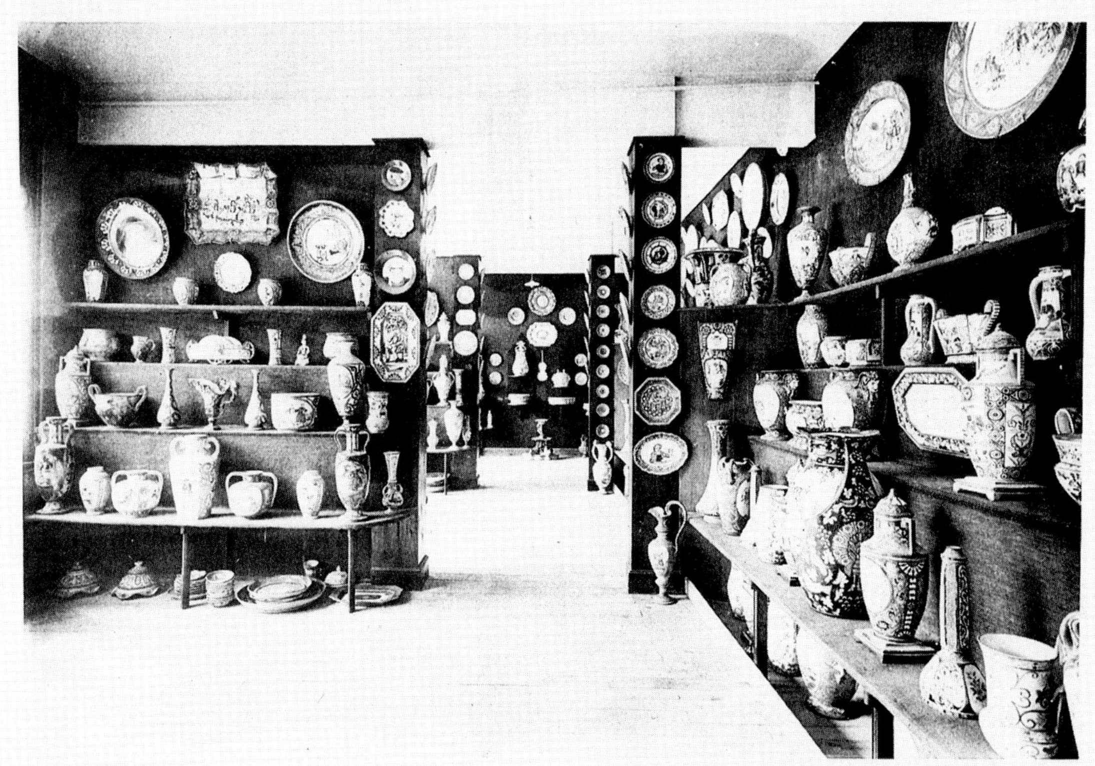

UN COIN DES MUSÉES

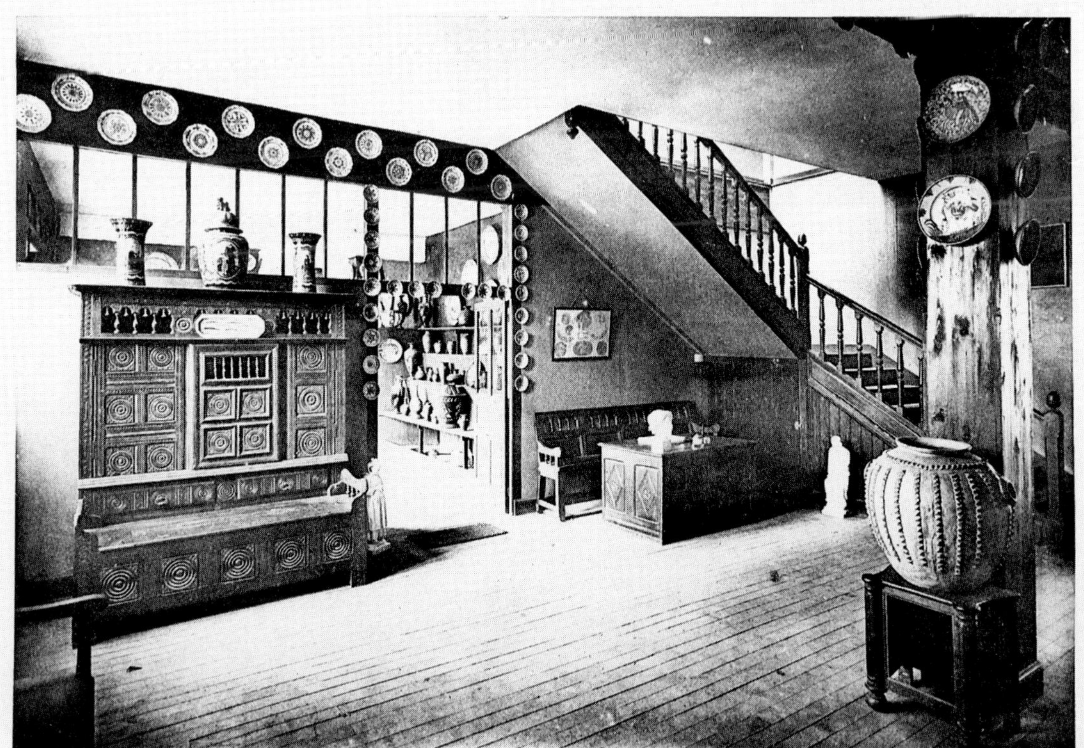

HALL D'ENTRÉE DES BUREAUX ET MUSÉES

FAÏENCERIE BRETONNE

DE LA

GRANDE MAISON HB

QUIMPER

Manufacture fondée en 1420

J. VERLINGUE-BOLLORÉ & CIE

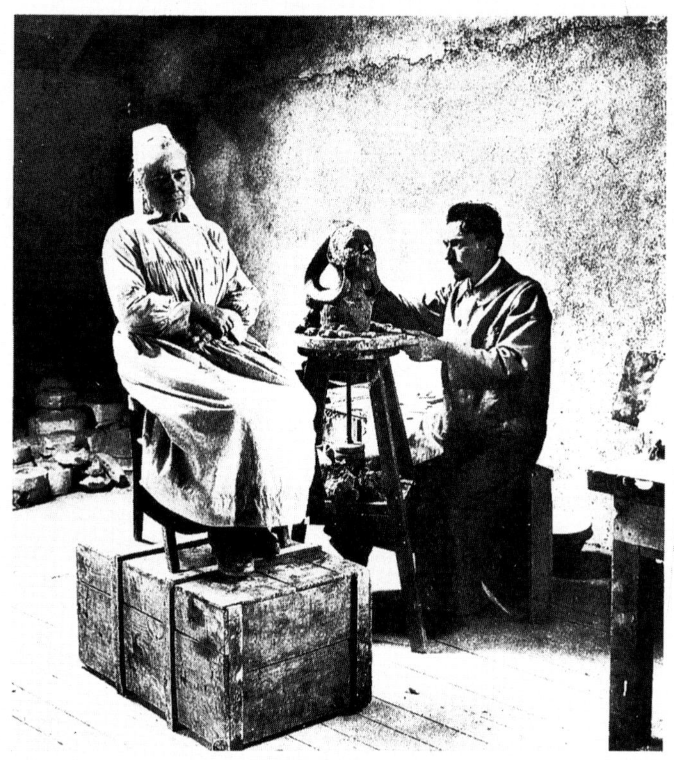

R. Quillivic dans son atelier à la "Grande Maison"

La "Grande Maison" remonte aux temps les plus reculés. En **1420**, en pleine guerre de Cent ans, on y faisait déjà de la Poterie et des Grès vernissés.

C'est en **1652**, avec Jean Bousquet, de Moustiers, que la "Grande Maison" commença la fabrication de la faïence proprement dite. Jean Bousquet mourut en 1708. Son fils Pierre, qui avait déjà pris la direction des affaires en **1685**, donna à la Manufacture une grande extension. En **1708**, il mit à la tête de son usine, son gendre P. Bellevans de Nevers, qui en **1749** maria sa fille Marie-Jeanne à Pierre-Clément Caussy, fils de P.-P. Caussy, directeur de la Manufacture Royale à Saint-Sever-de-Rouen. Caussy introduisit à Quimper tous les décors et secrets de Rouen. Par acte authentique du 9 Novembre 1764, il est dit : « que Noble homme de Caussy ayant donné une très grande extension à sa manufacture, en a été récompensé par l'abandon qui lui a été fait par le Duc de Penthièvre, à titre de péage, de toutes les vases et marais bordant l'Odet à Quimper, jusqu'au niveau du plus grand flot de Mars ».

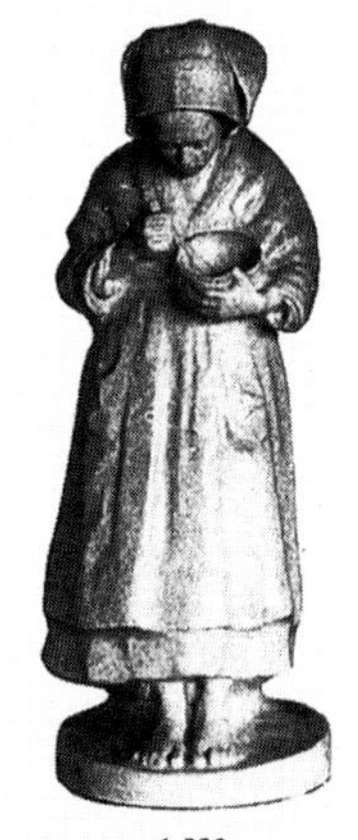

1-500
R. QUILLIVIC

ALBUM N° 1

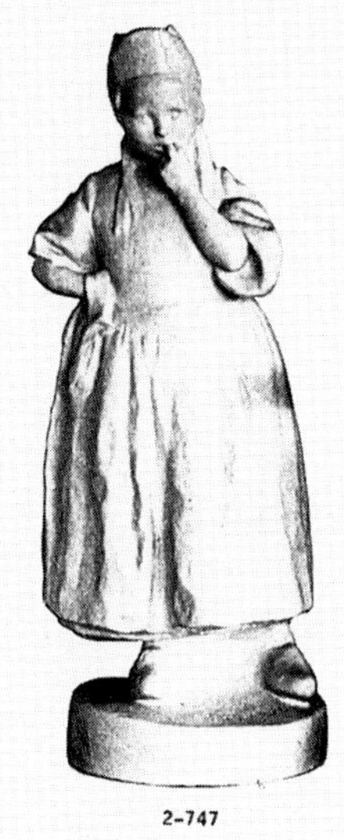

2-747
R. QUILLIVIC

En 1771, il maria sa fille Elisabeth à Antoine de la Hubaudière, " ingénieur du Roy en la province de Bretagne " et l'associa à sa manufacture.

Antoine de la Hubaudière fut massacré à Fougères en 1793. Sa veuve prit la direction de la " Grande Maison ", aidée de son fils Jean-Marie agé de 20 ans.

Ce dernier eut un fils, Félix de la Hubaudière, qui lui succéda en 1853. Il mourut en 1881 laissant sa veuve et son fils Guy. Celui-ci fut tué en 1915 au Champ d'Honneur.

Ses successeurs furent :

J. Verlingue et Cie 1917 ;

J. Verlingue-Bolloré et Cie 1922.

La " Grande Maison " s'est adjoint le concours actif du grand sculpteur et peintre, R. QUILLIVIC (membre du jury au Salon d'Automne, chevalier de la Légion d'honneur), dont les œuvres sont si universellement appréciées.

Elle édite aussi les œuvres modernes de jeunes artistes.

Marque Déposée

HB

QUIMPER

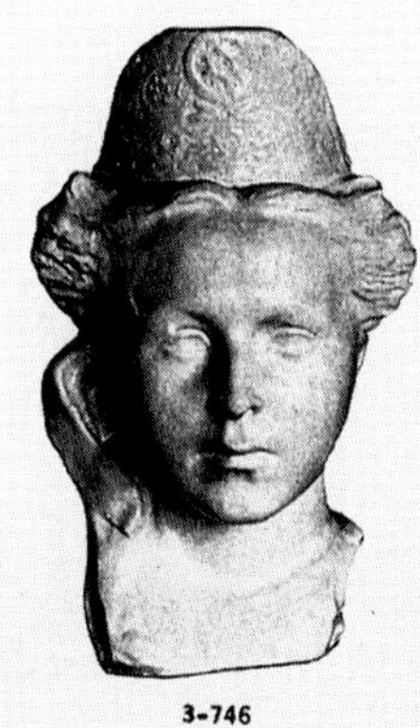

3-746
R. QUILLIVIC

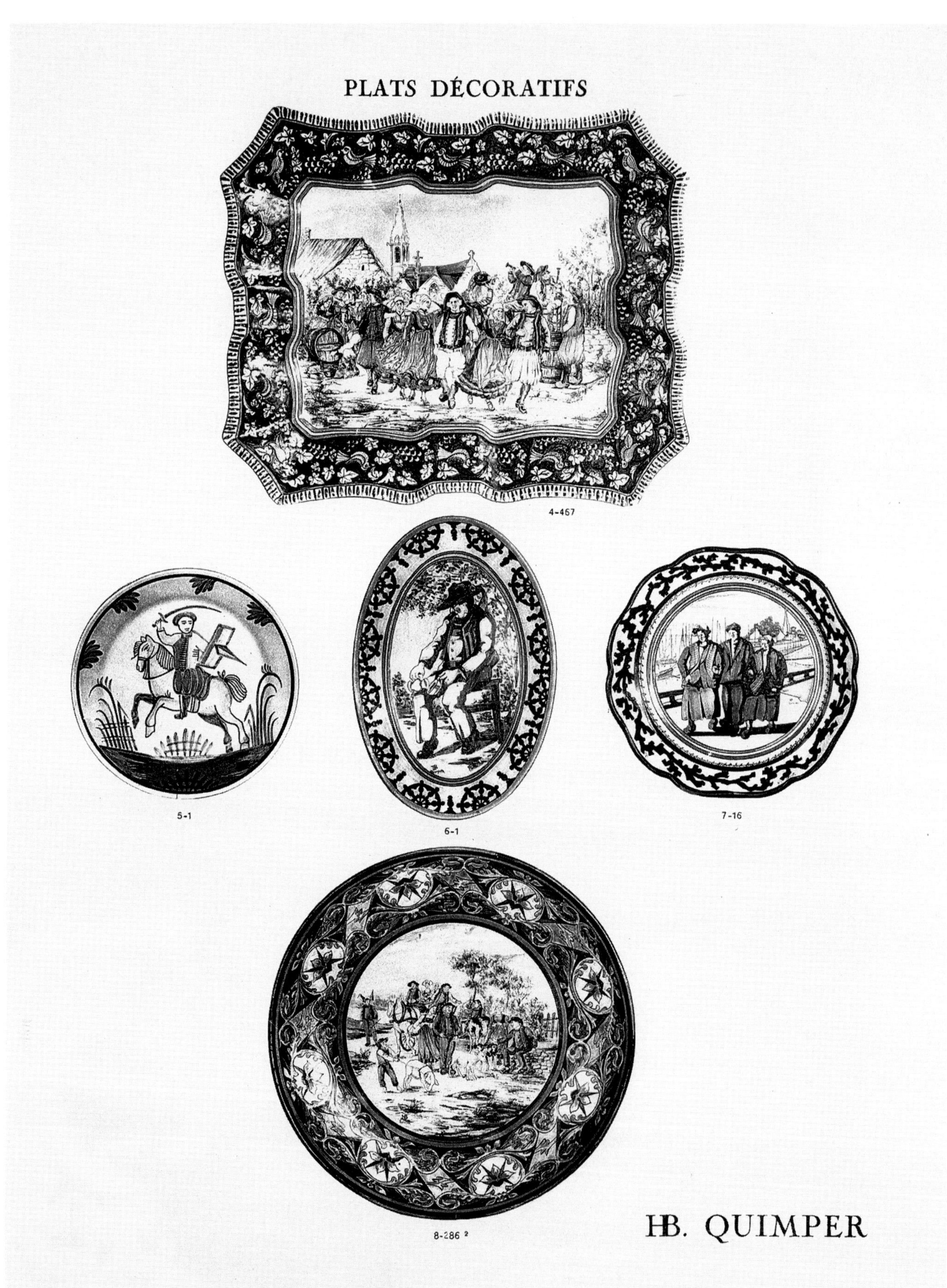
PLATS DÉCORATIFS

4-467

5-1

6-1

7-16

8-286 ²

HB. QUIMPER

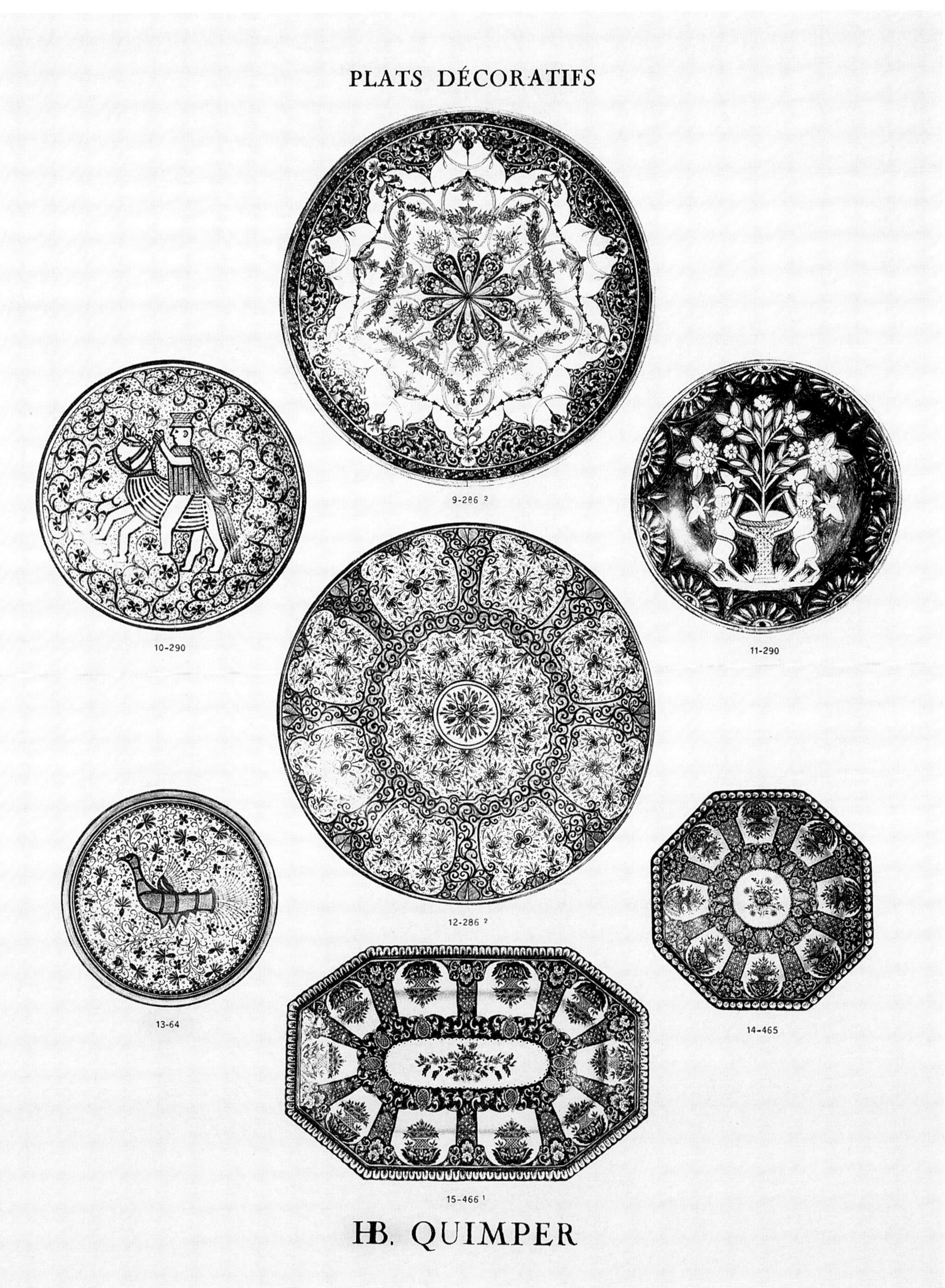

PLATS DÉCORATIFS

9-286 [2]

10-290

11-290

12-286 [2]

13-64

14-465

15-466 [1]

HB. QUIMPER

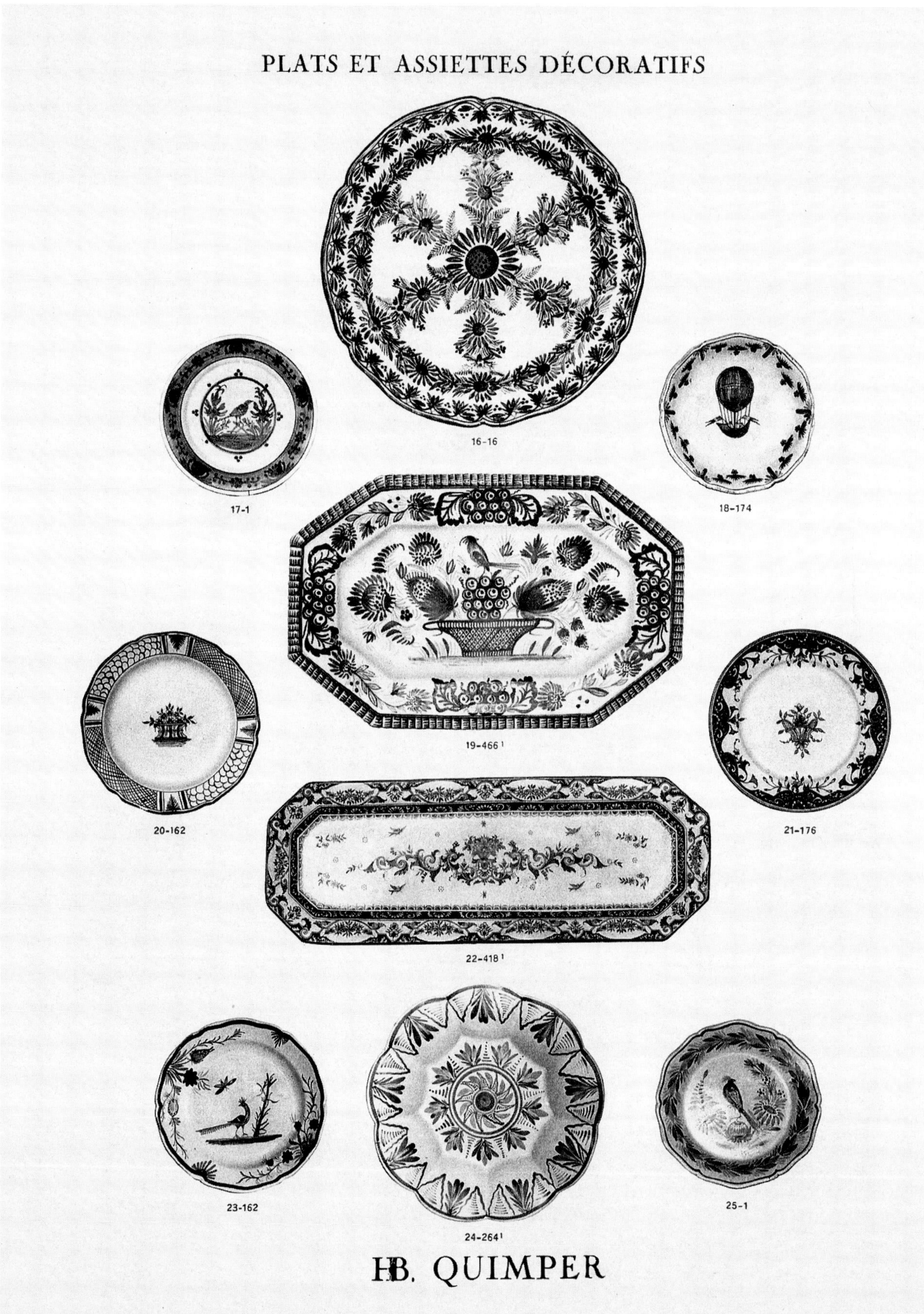
PLATS ET ASSIETTES DÉCORATIFS
16-16
17-1
18-174
19-466 1
20-162
21-176
22-418 1
23-162
25-1
24-264 1
HB. QUIMPER

CACHE-POTS

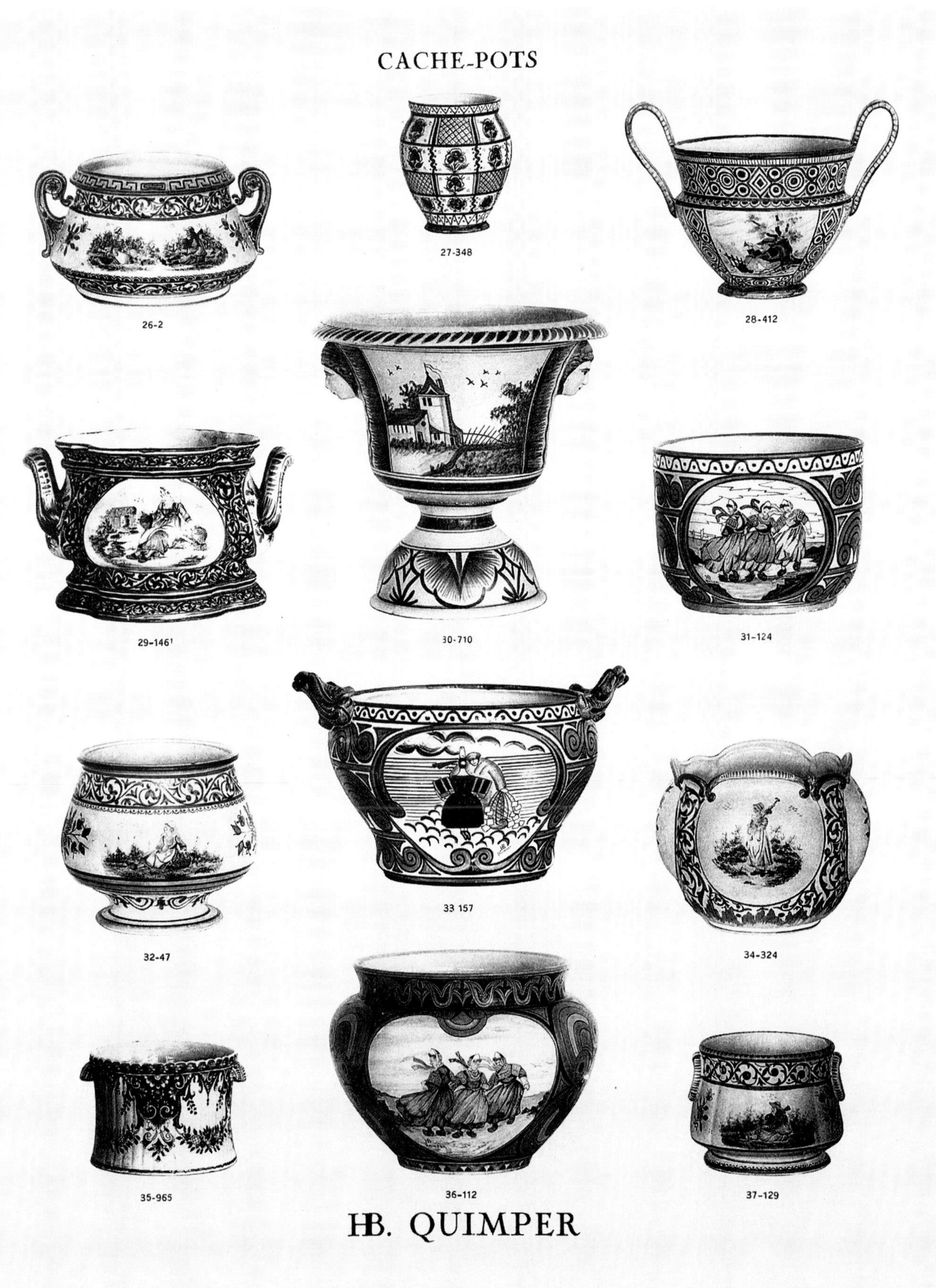

26-2 27-348 28-412 29-146[1] 30-710 31-124 32-47 33 157 34-324 35-965 36-112 37-129

HB. QUIMPER

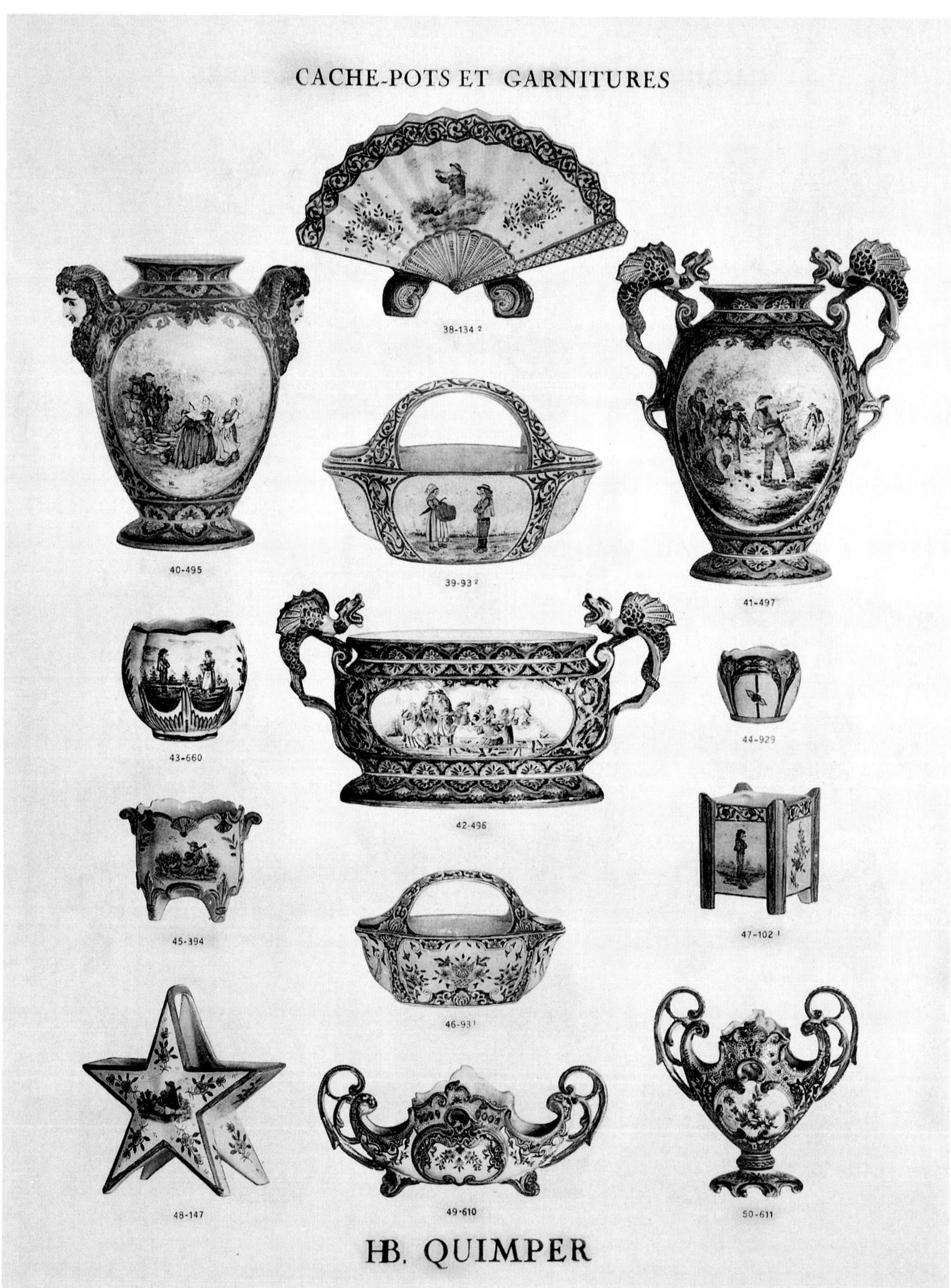
CACHE-POTS ET GARNITURES
38-134 2
40-495
39-93 2
41-497
43-660
42-496
44-929
45-394
47-102 1
46-93 1
48-147
49-610
50-611
HB. QUIMPER

CACHE-POTS -- JARDINIÈRES -- GARNITURES

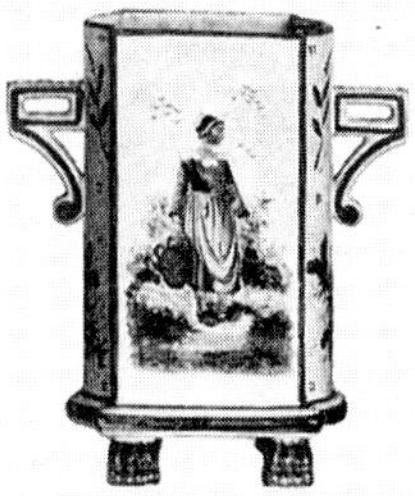

51-202

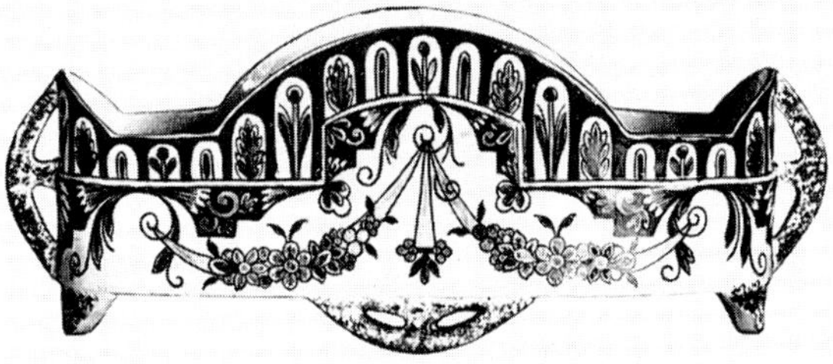

53-365[1]

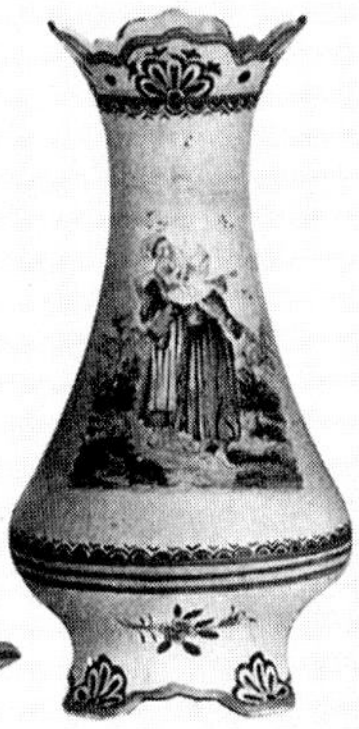

55-169

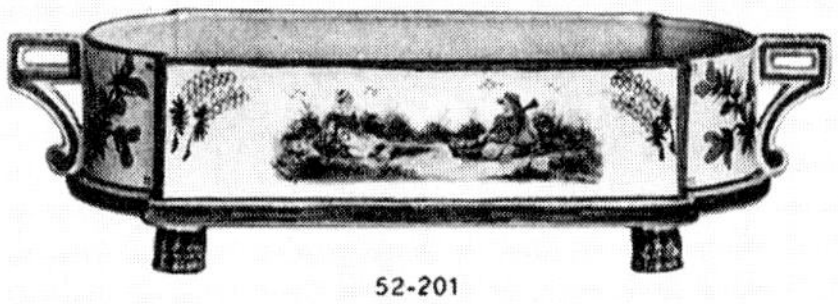

52-201

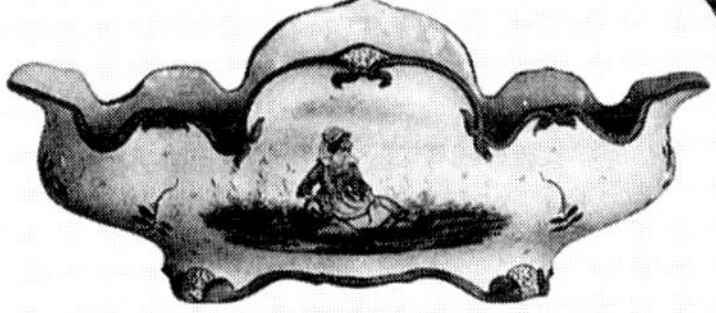

54-168

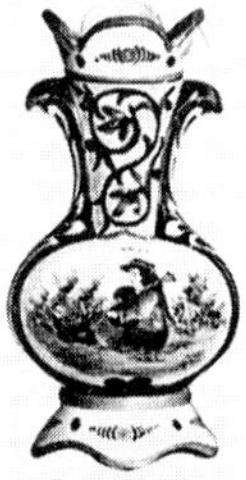

56-305[1]

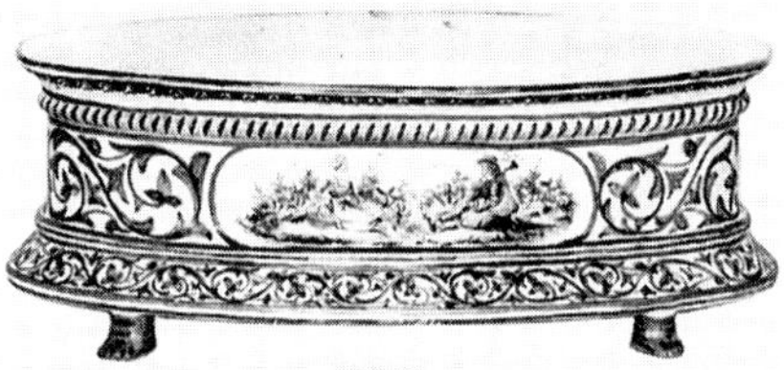

58-68

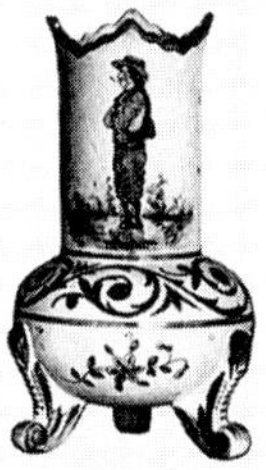

59-116[1]

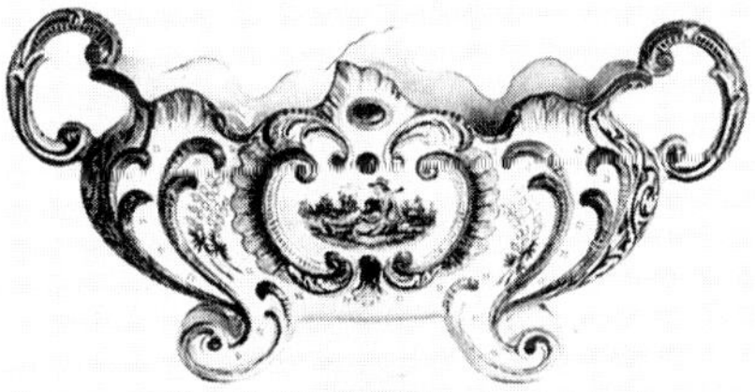

61-509

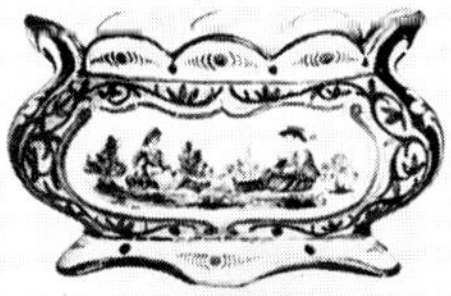

57-304[1]

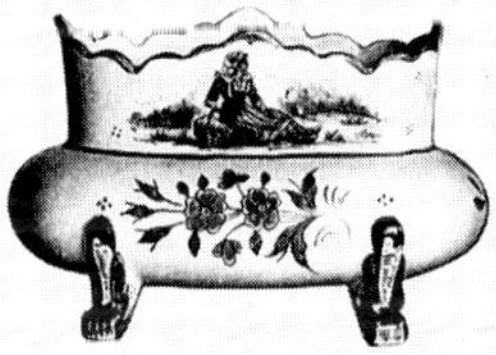

60-115[1]

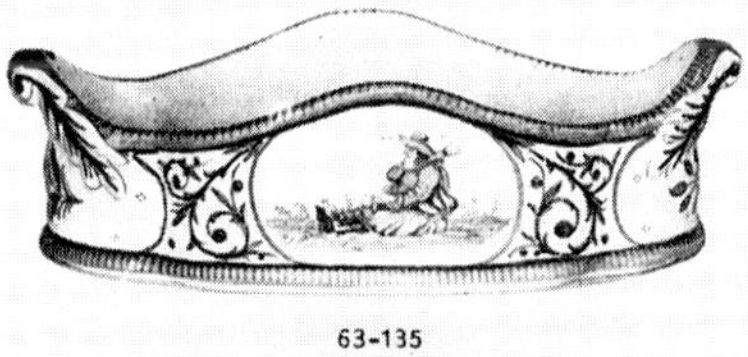

63-135

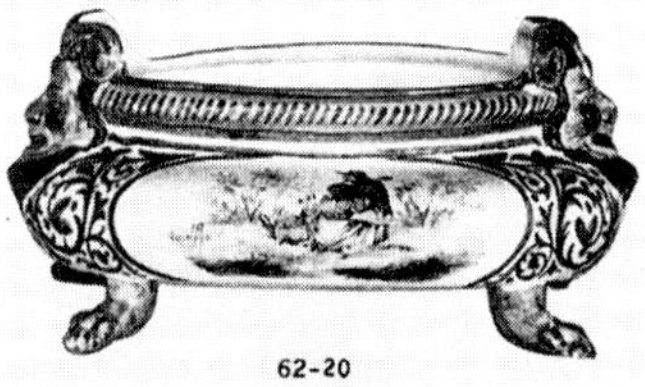

62-20

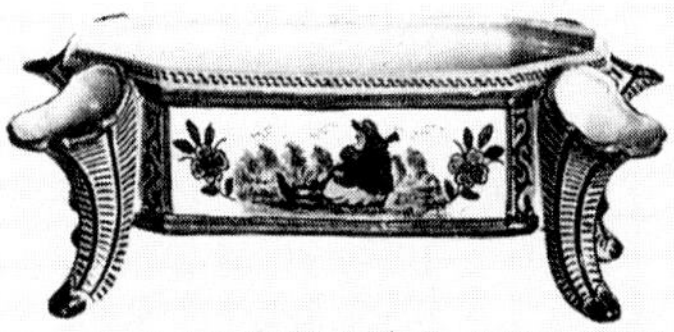

64-964[4]

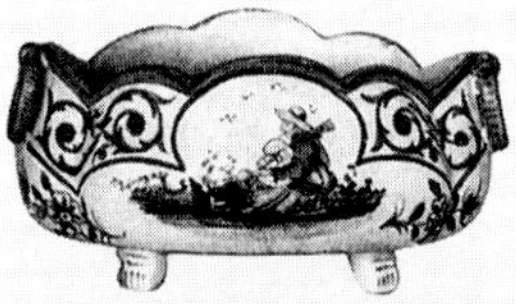

65-128

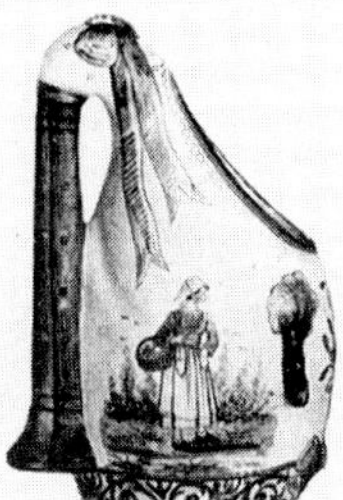

66 204

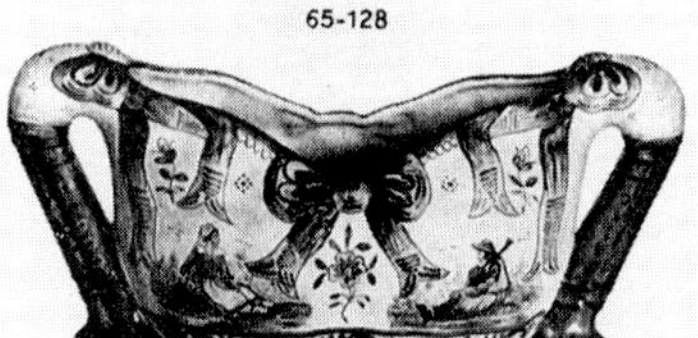

67-203

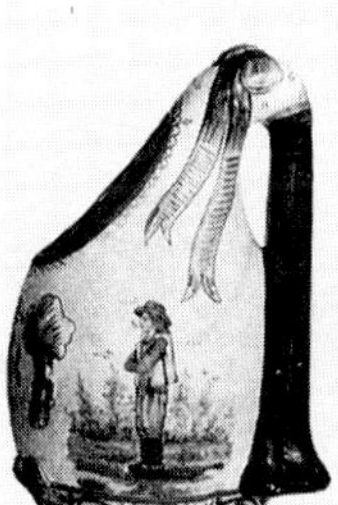

68-204

HB. QUIMPER

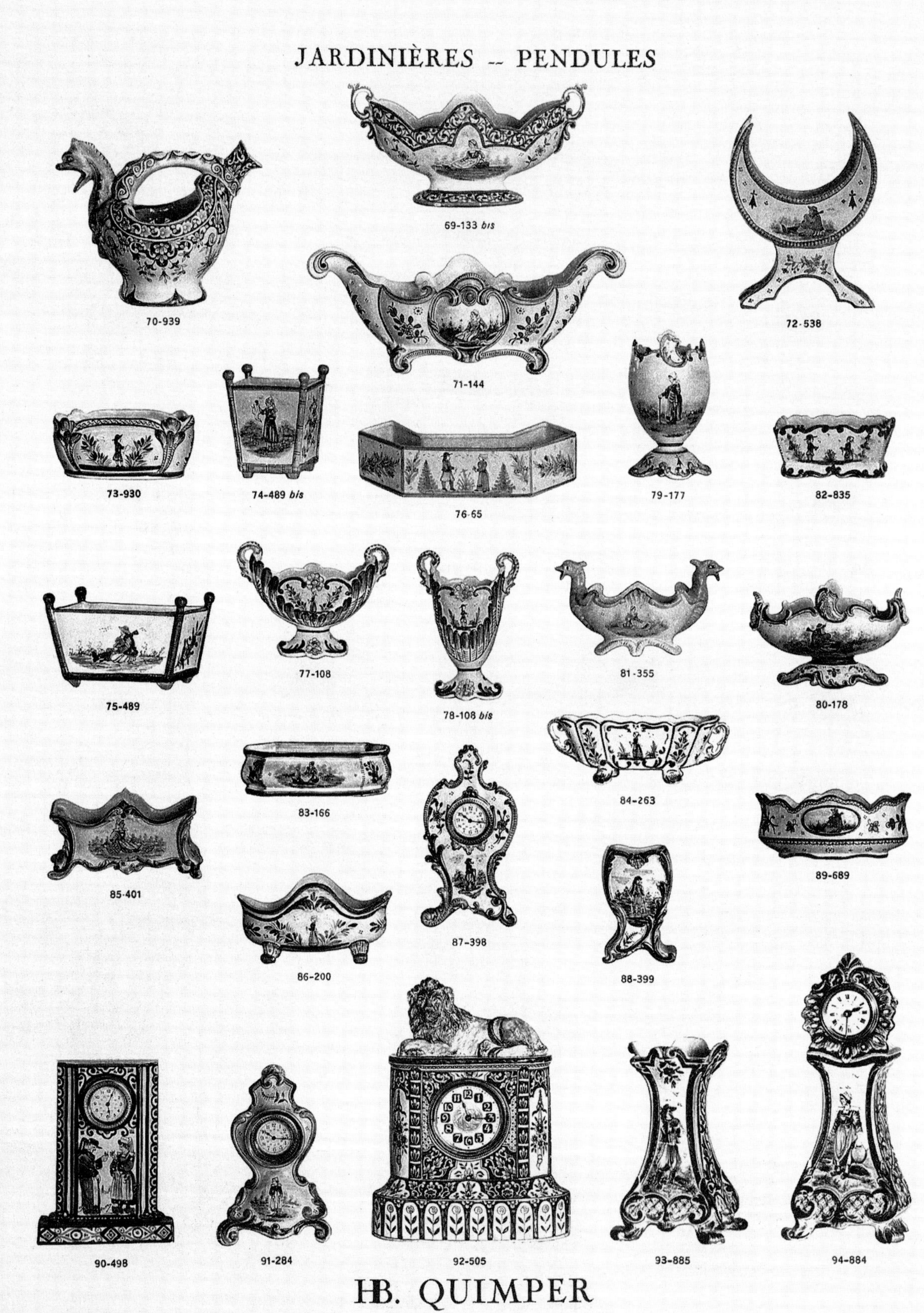
JARDINIÈRES -- PENDULES
69-133 *bis*
70-939
72-538
71-144
73-930
74-489 *bis*
76-65
79-177
82-835
77-108
78-108 *bis*
81-355
80-178
75-489
83-166
84-263
85-401
87-398
89-689
86-200
88-399
90-498
91-284
92-505
93-885
94-884
HB. QUIMPER

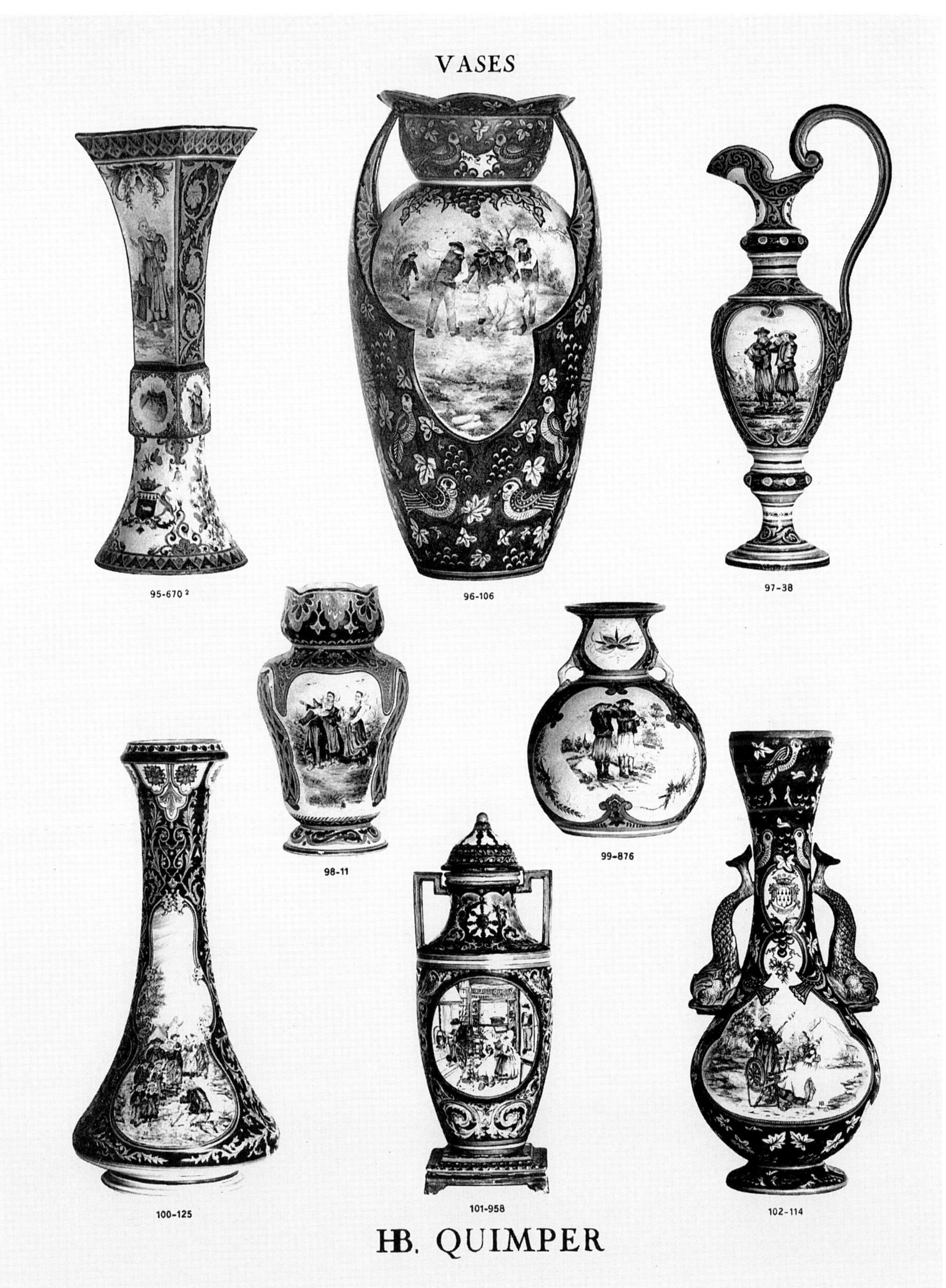
VASES
95-670 2
96-106
97-38
98-11
99-876
100-125
101-958
102-114
HB. QUIMPER

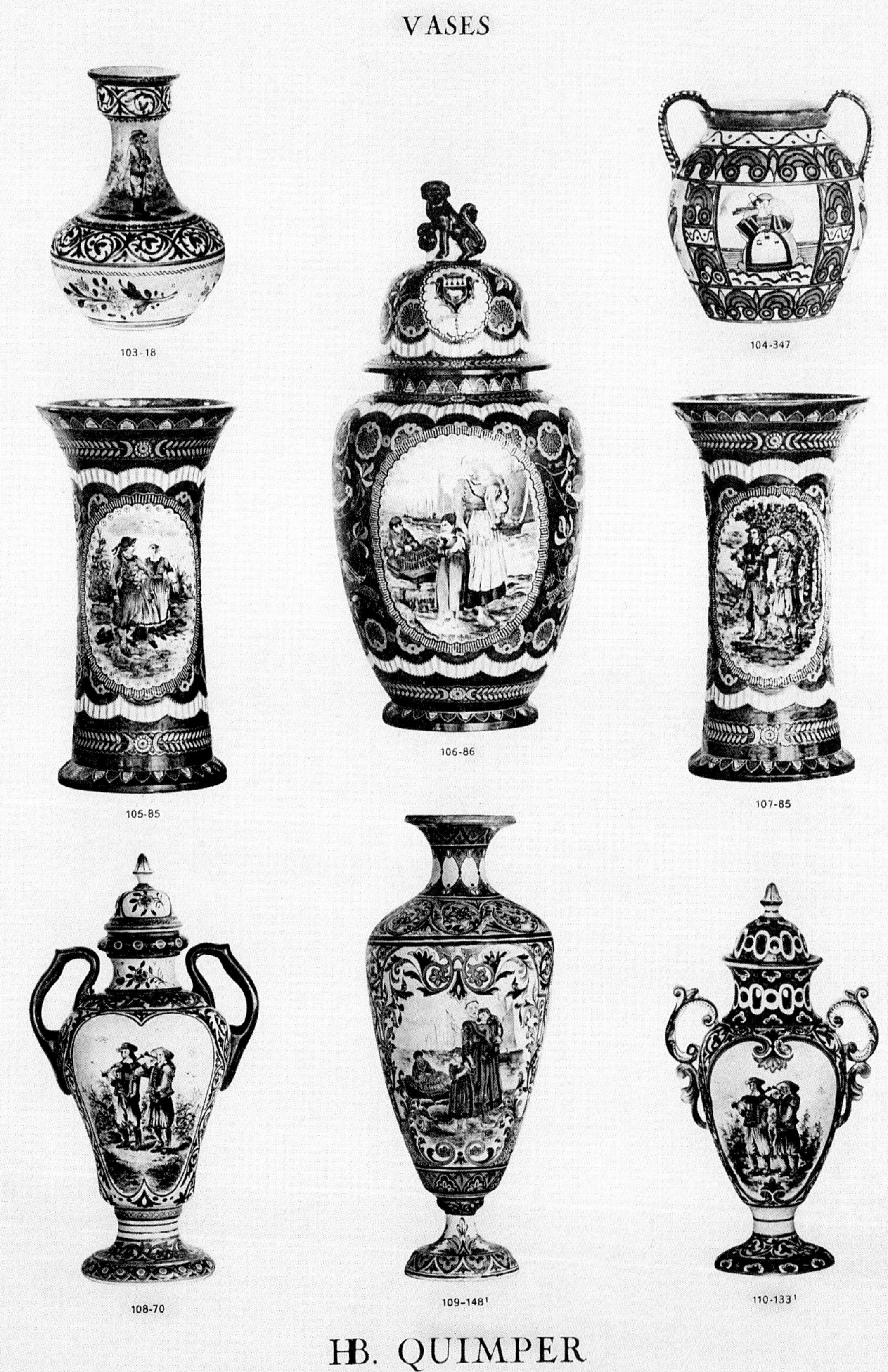
VASES
103-18
104-347
105-85
106-86
107-85
108-70
109-148[1]
110-133[1]
HB. QUIMPER

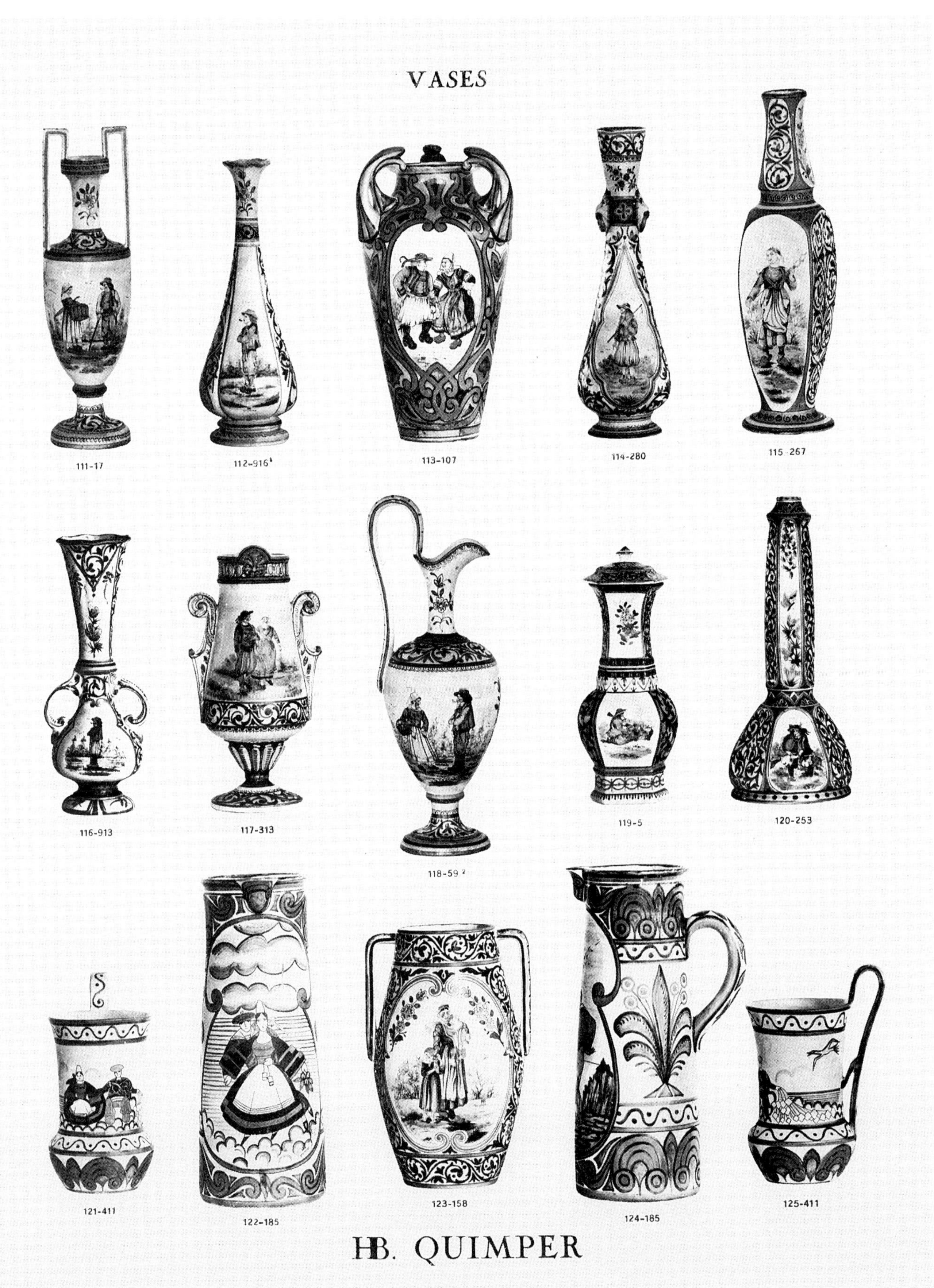
VASES
111-17
112-916
113-107
114-280
115-267
116-913
117-313
118-59
119-5
120-253
121-411
122-185
123-158
124-185
125-411
HB. QUIMPER

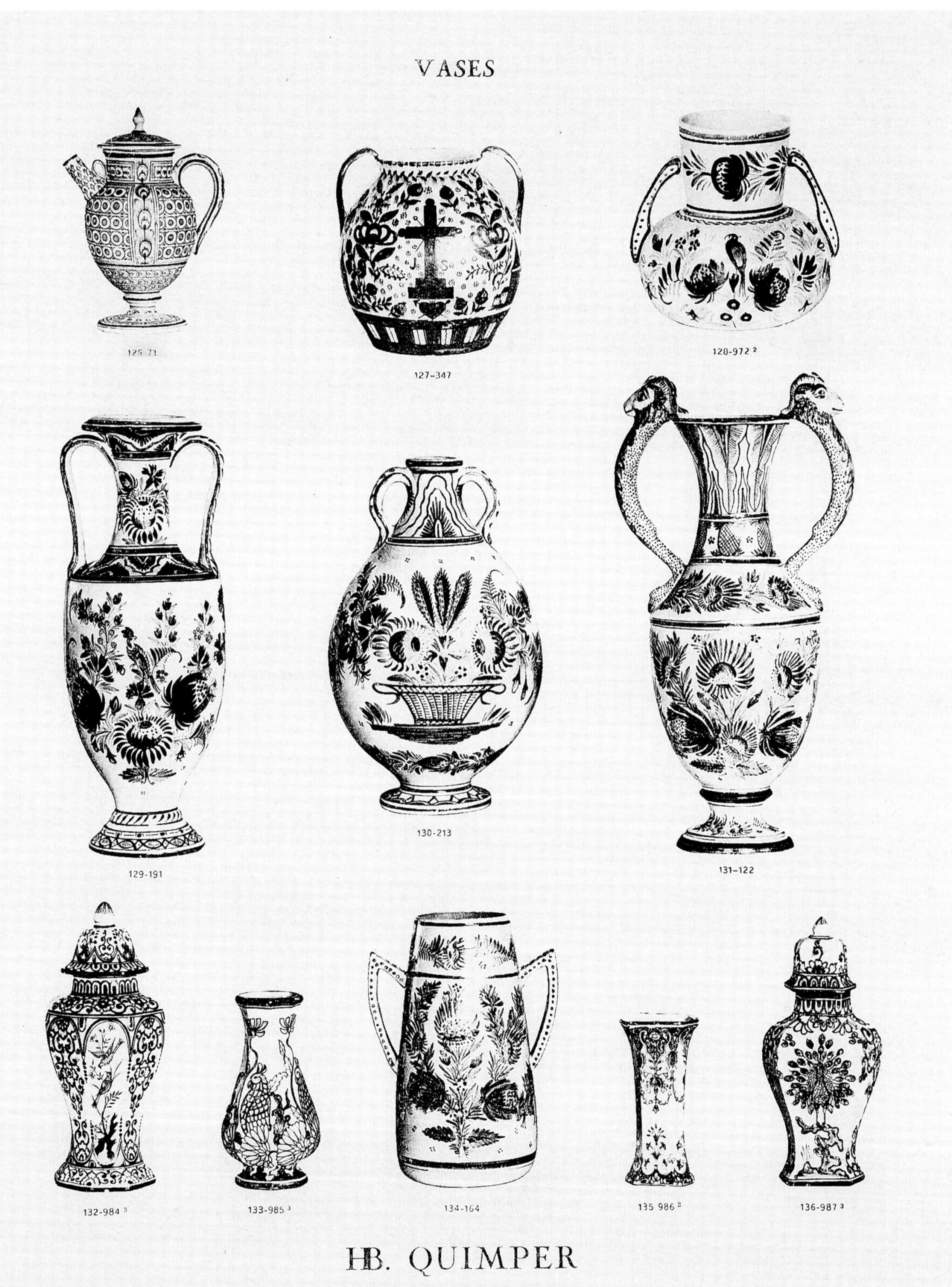
VASES
125-73
127-347
128-972 [2]
129-191
130-213
131-122
132-984 [3]
133-985 [3]
134-164
135 986 [3]
136-987 [3]
HB. QUIMPER

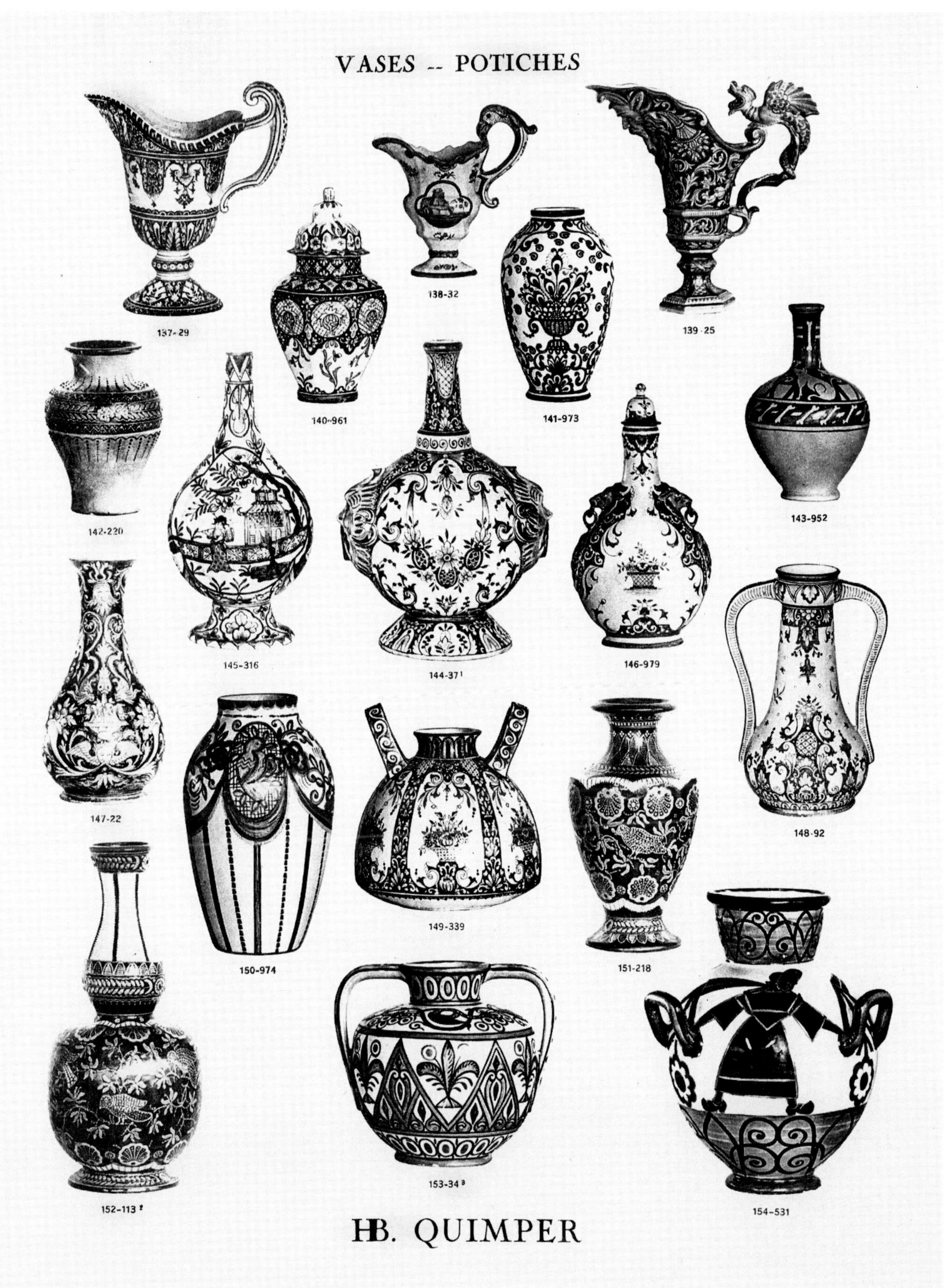
VASES -- POTICHES
137-29
138-32
139-25
140-961
141-973
142-220
143-952
145-316
144-37[1]
146-979
147-22
148-92
149-339
150-974
151-218
153-34[3]
152-113[2]
154-531
HB. QUIMPER

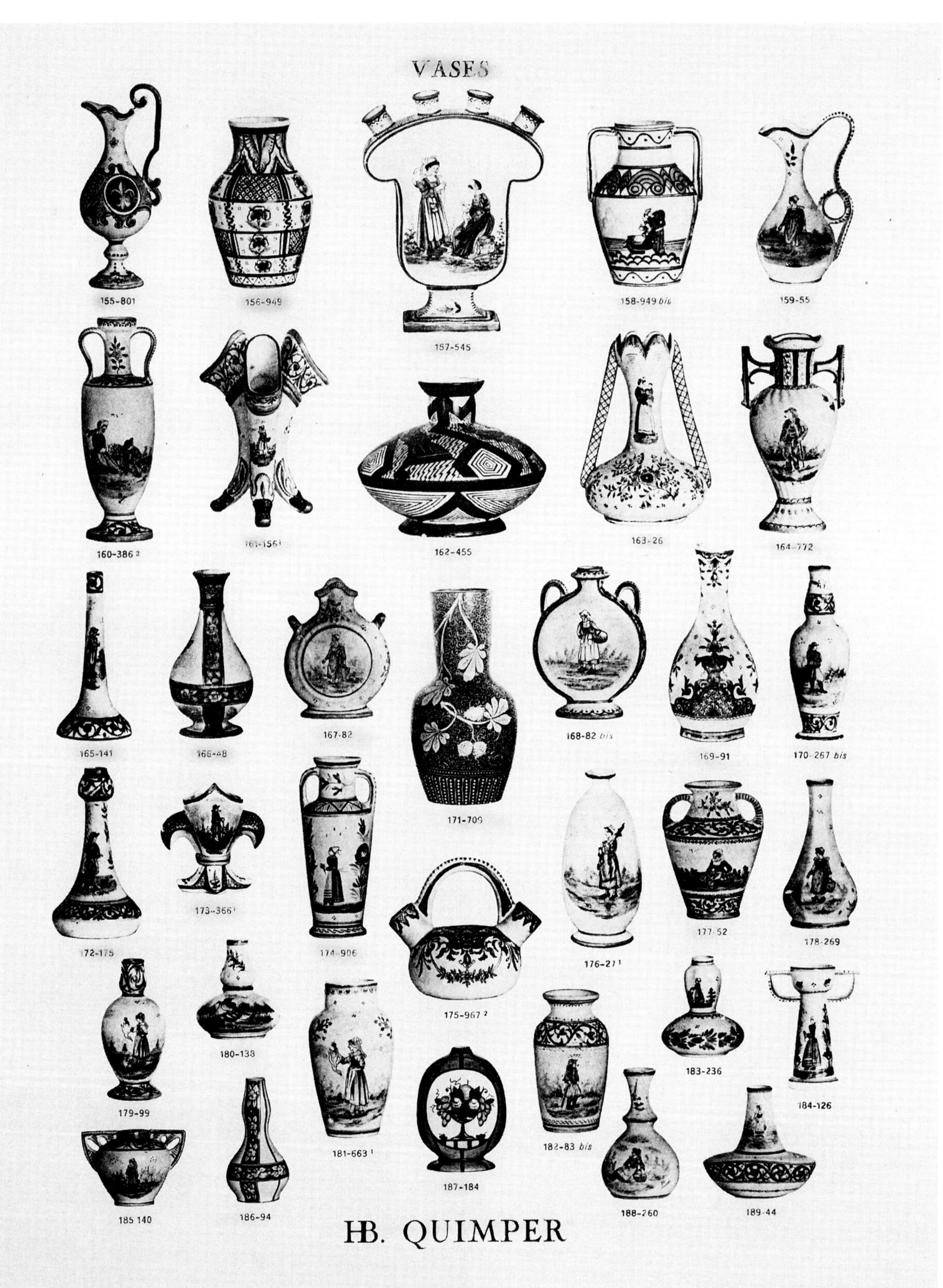
VASES
155-801
156-949
157-545
158-949 bis
159-55
160-386 [2]
161-156 [1]
162-455
163-26
164-772
165-141
166-48
167-82
168-82 bis
169-91
170-267 bis
171-709
172-175
173-366 [1]
174-906
175-967 [2]
176-27 [1]
177-52
178-269
179-99
180-138
181-663 [1]
182-83 bis
183-236
184-126
185 140
186-94
187-184
188-260
189-44
HB. QUIMPER

VASES -- BOUQUETIÈRES -- APPLIQUES

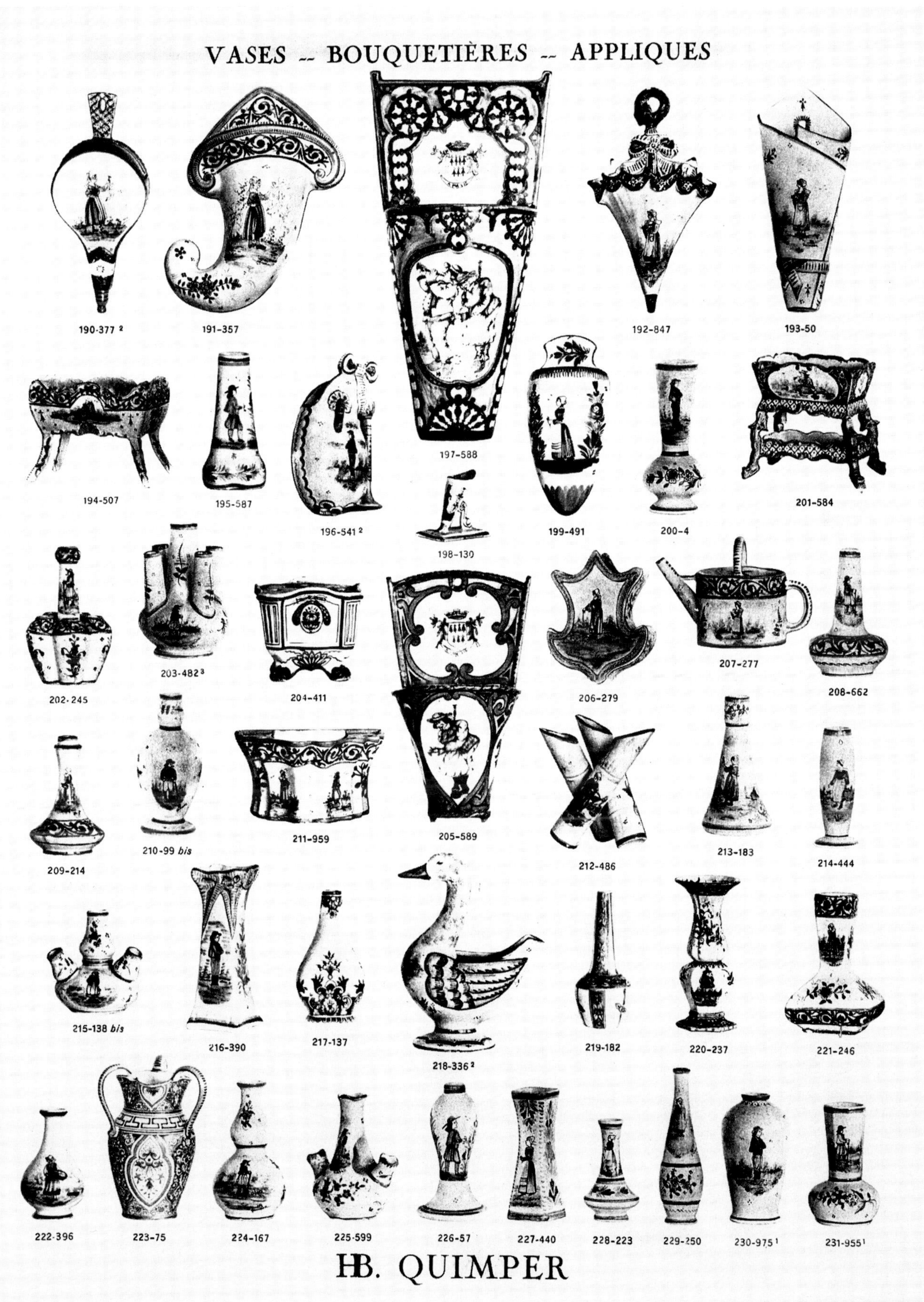

HB. QUIMPER

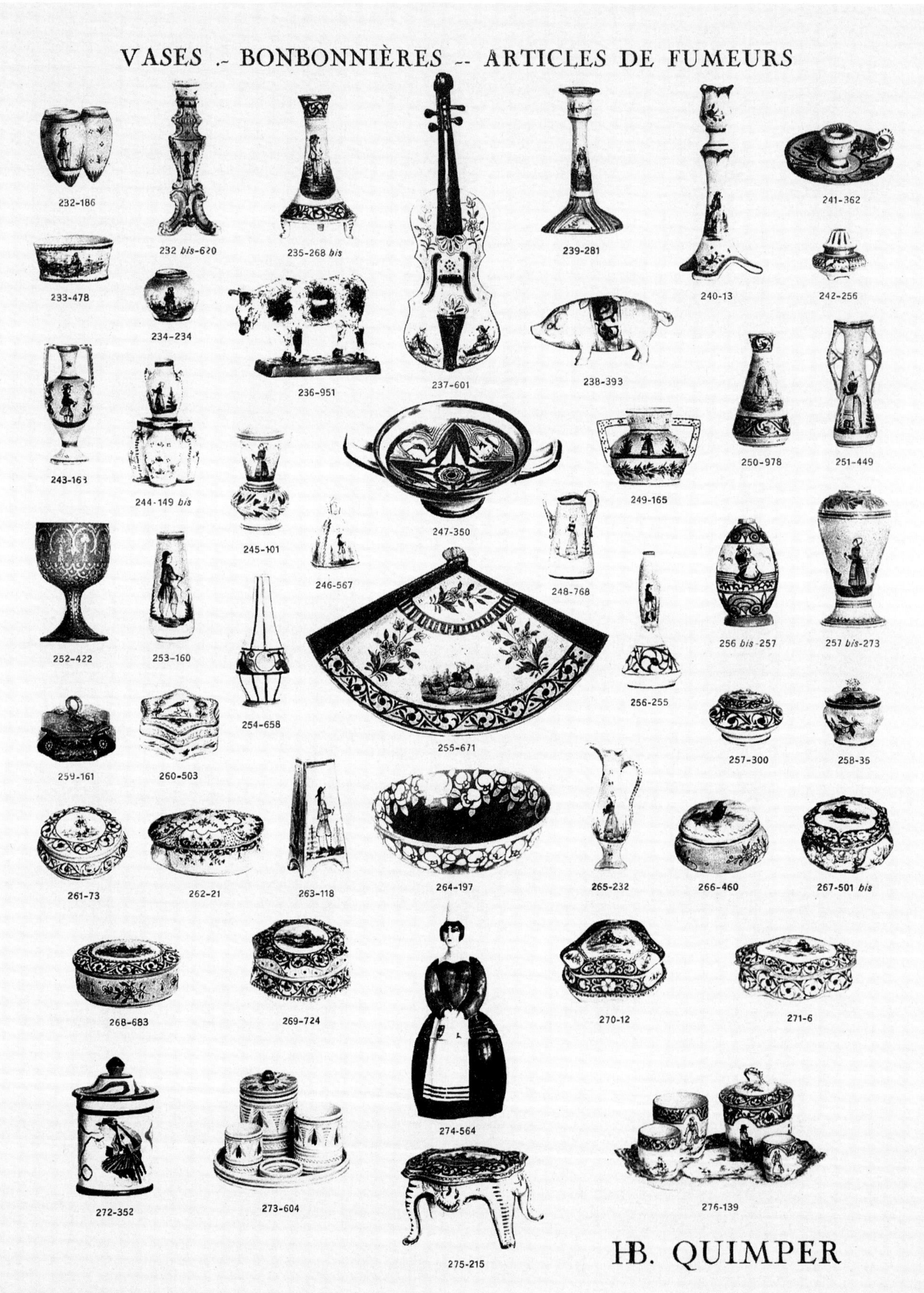
VASES .- BONBONNIÈRES -- ARTICLES DE FUMEURS
232-186
232 bis-620
235-268 bis
237-601
239-281
240-13
241-362
242-256
233-478
234-234
236-951
238-393
243-163
244-149 bis
245-101
247-350
249-165
250-978
251-449
246-567
248-768
252-422
253-160
254-658
255-671
256-255
256 bis-257
257 bis-273
259-161
260-503
257-300
258-35
261-73
262-21
263-118
264-197
265-232
266-460
267-501 bis
268-683
269-724
270-12
271-6
274-564
272-352
273-604
275-215
276-139
HB. QUIMPER

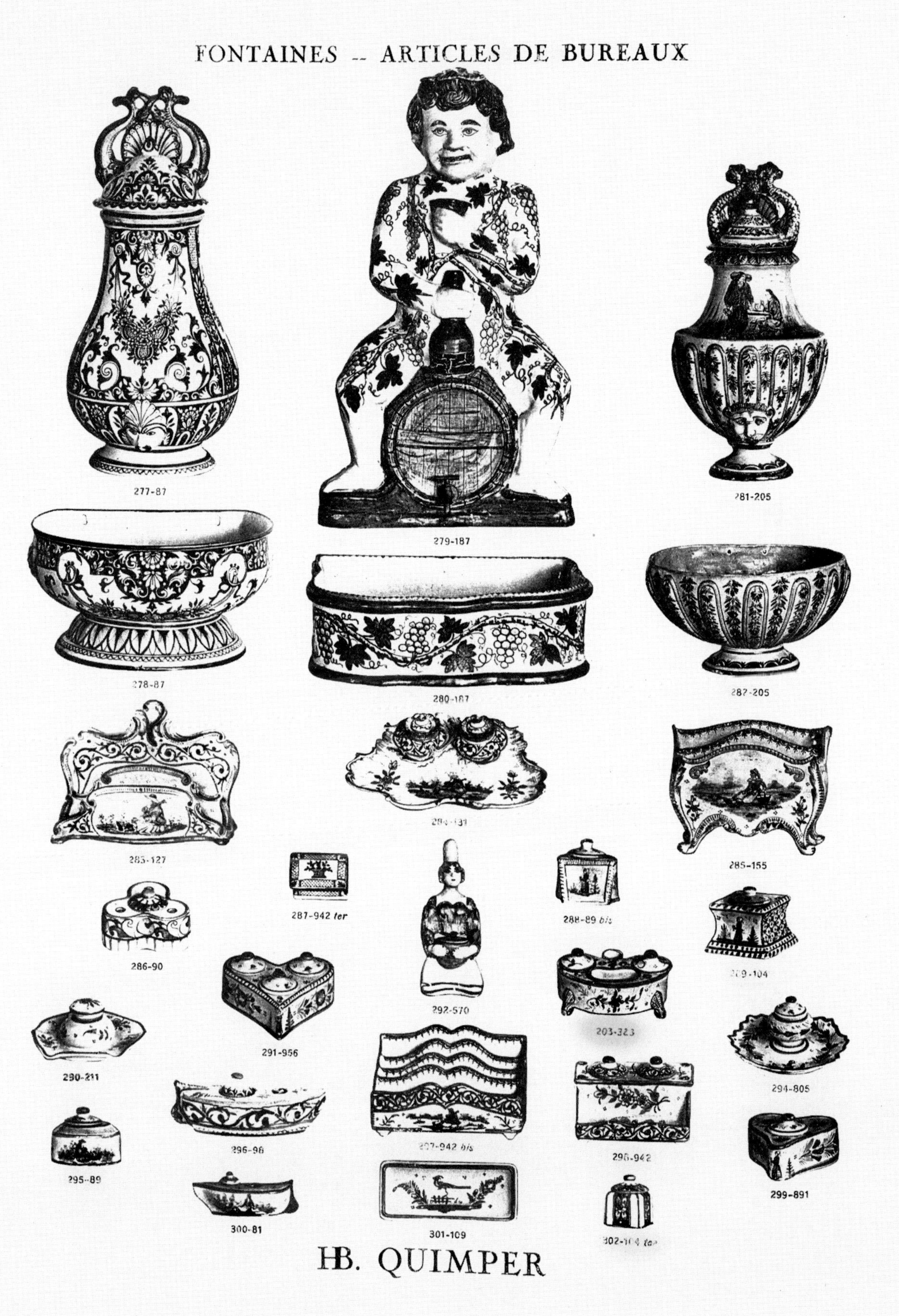
FONTAINES -- ARTICLES DE BUREAUX
277-87
279-187
281-205
278-87
280-187
282-205
285-155
287-942 ter
286-90
292-570
291-956
290-211
294-805
296-96
295-89
299-891
300-81
301-109
HB. QUIMPER

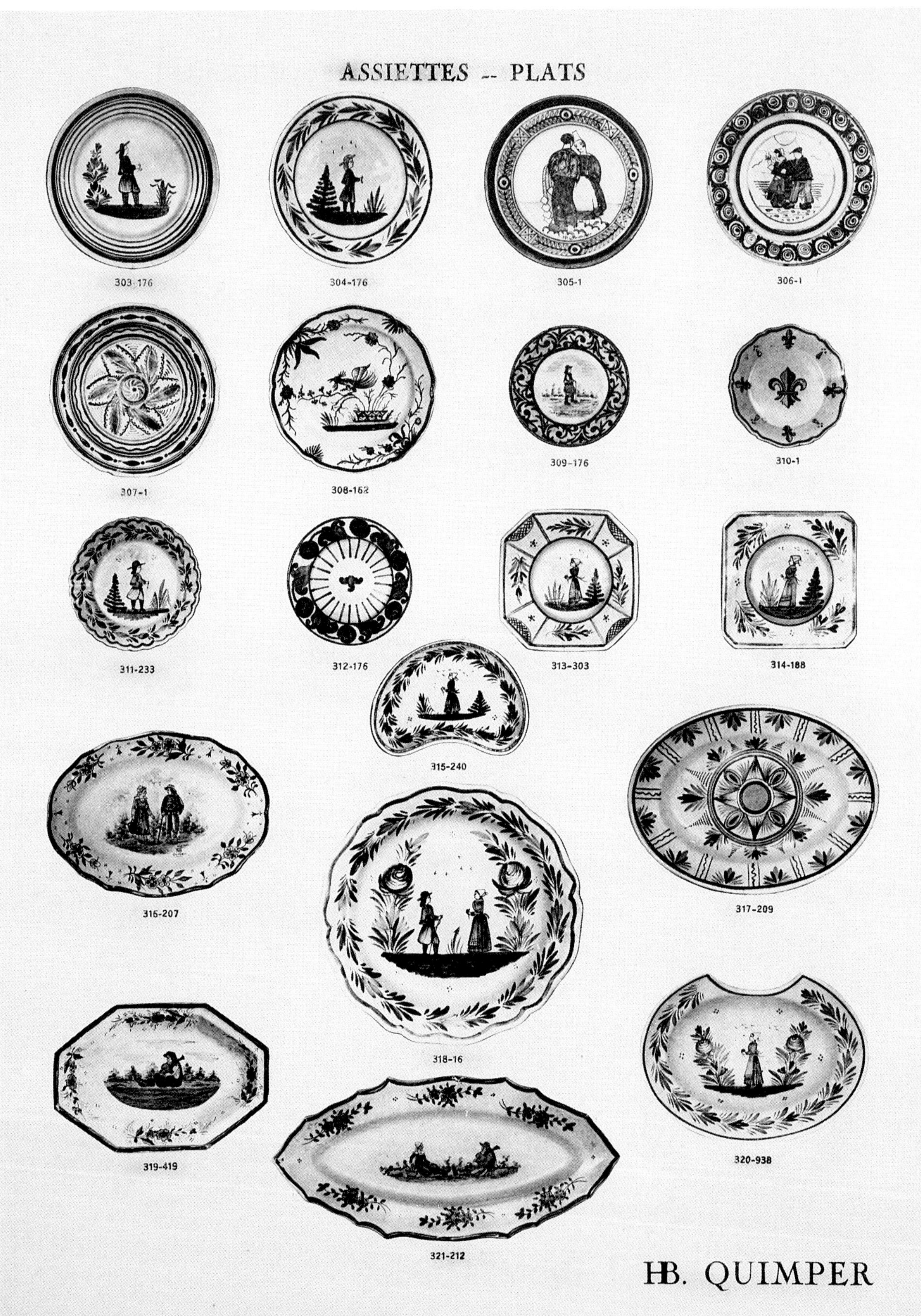
ASSIETTES -- PLATS
303-176
304-176
305-1
306-1
307-1
308-162
309-176
310-1
311-233
312-176
313-303
314-188
315-240
316-207
317-209
318-16
319-419
320-938
321-212
HB. QUIMPER

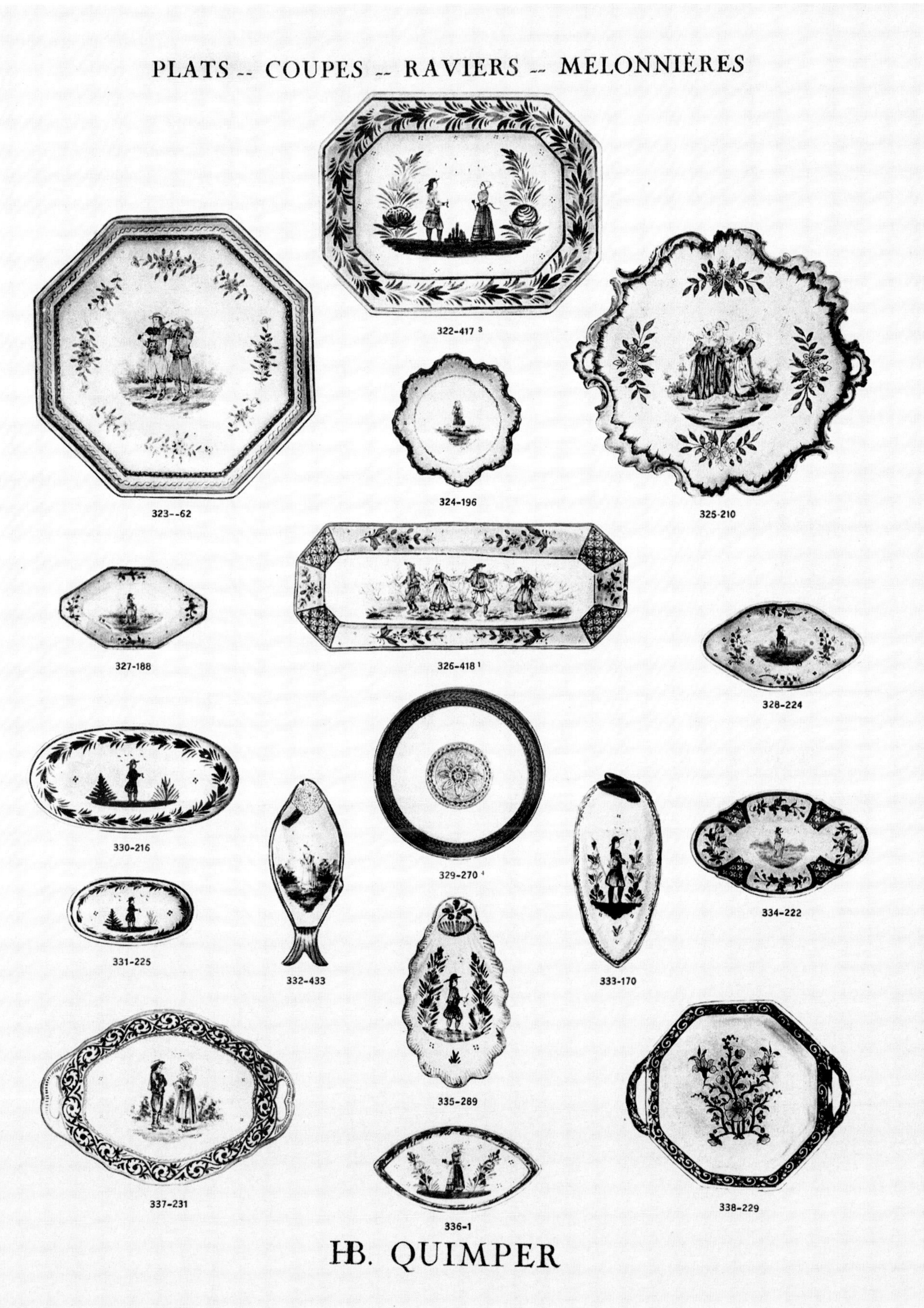
PLATS -- COUPES -- RAVIERS -- MELONNIÈRES
322-417 3
323--62
324-196
325-210
327-188
326-418 1
328-224
330-216
329-270 4
334-222
331-225
332-433
333-170
335-289
337-231
338-229
336-1
HB. QUIMPER

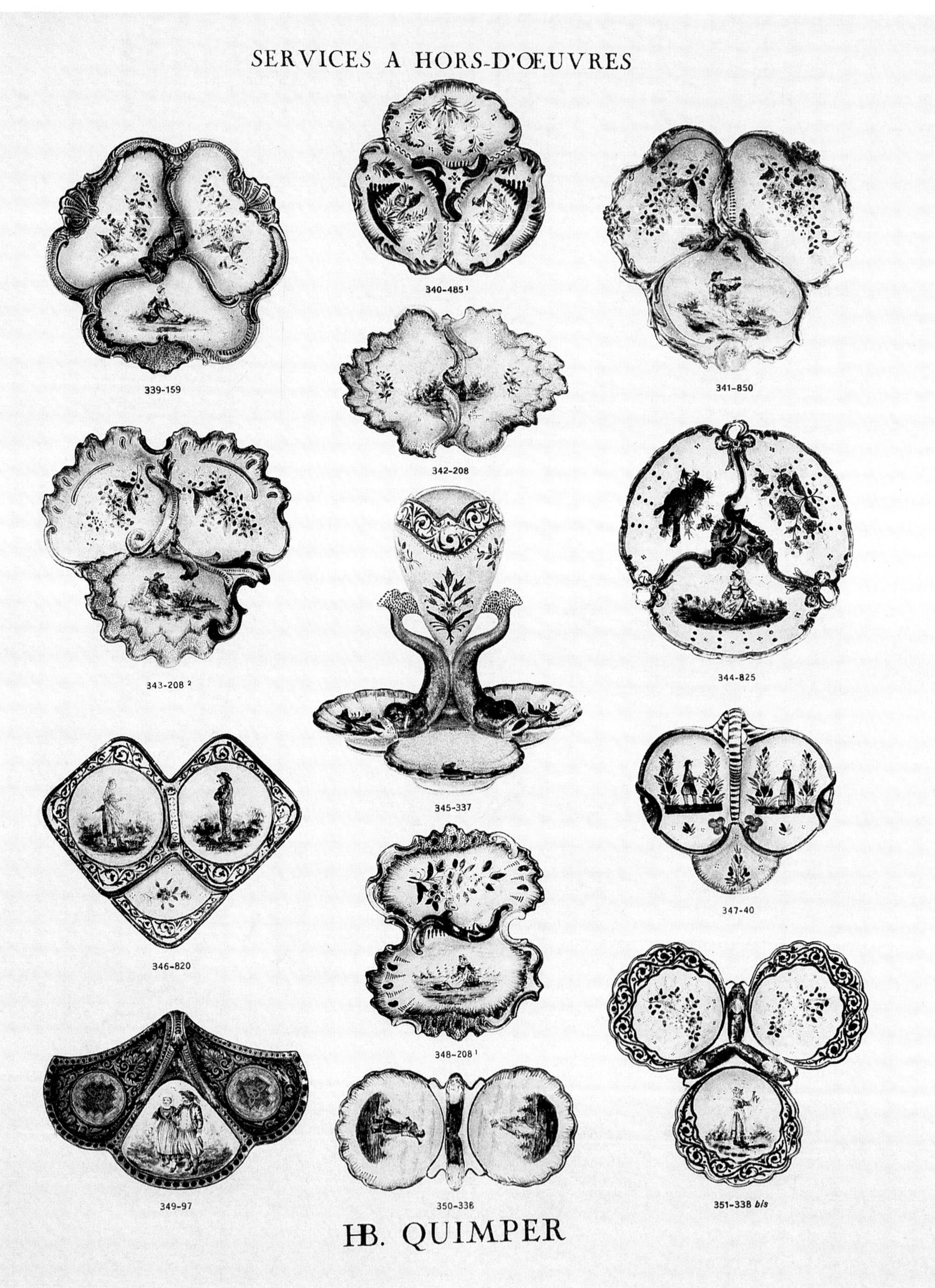
SERVICES A HORS-D'ŒUVRES
339-159
340-485 1
341-850
342-208
343-208 2
344-825
345-337
346-820
347-40
348-208 1
349-97
350-338
351-338 bis
HB. QUIMPER

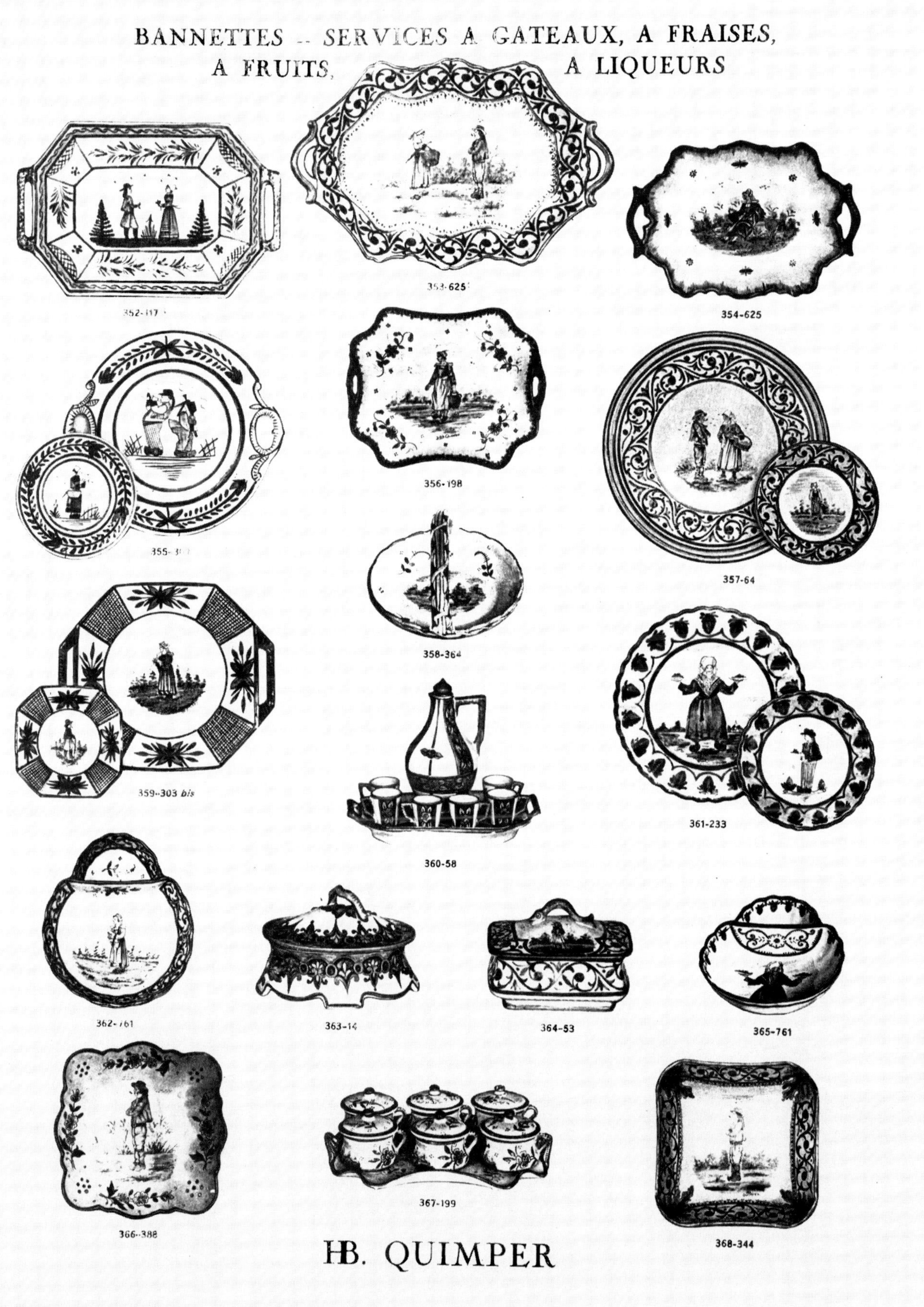
BANNETTES -- SERVICES A GATEAUX, A FRAISES,
A FRUITS, A LIQUEURS
352-117
353-625
354-625
355-3
356-198
357-64
358-364
359-303 bis
360-58
361-233
362-761
363-14
364-53
365-761
366-388
367-199
368-344
HB. QUIMPER

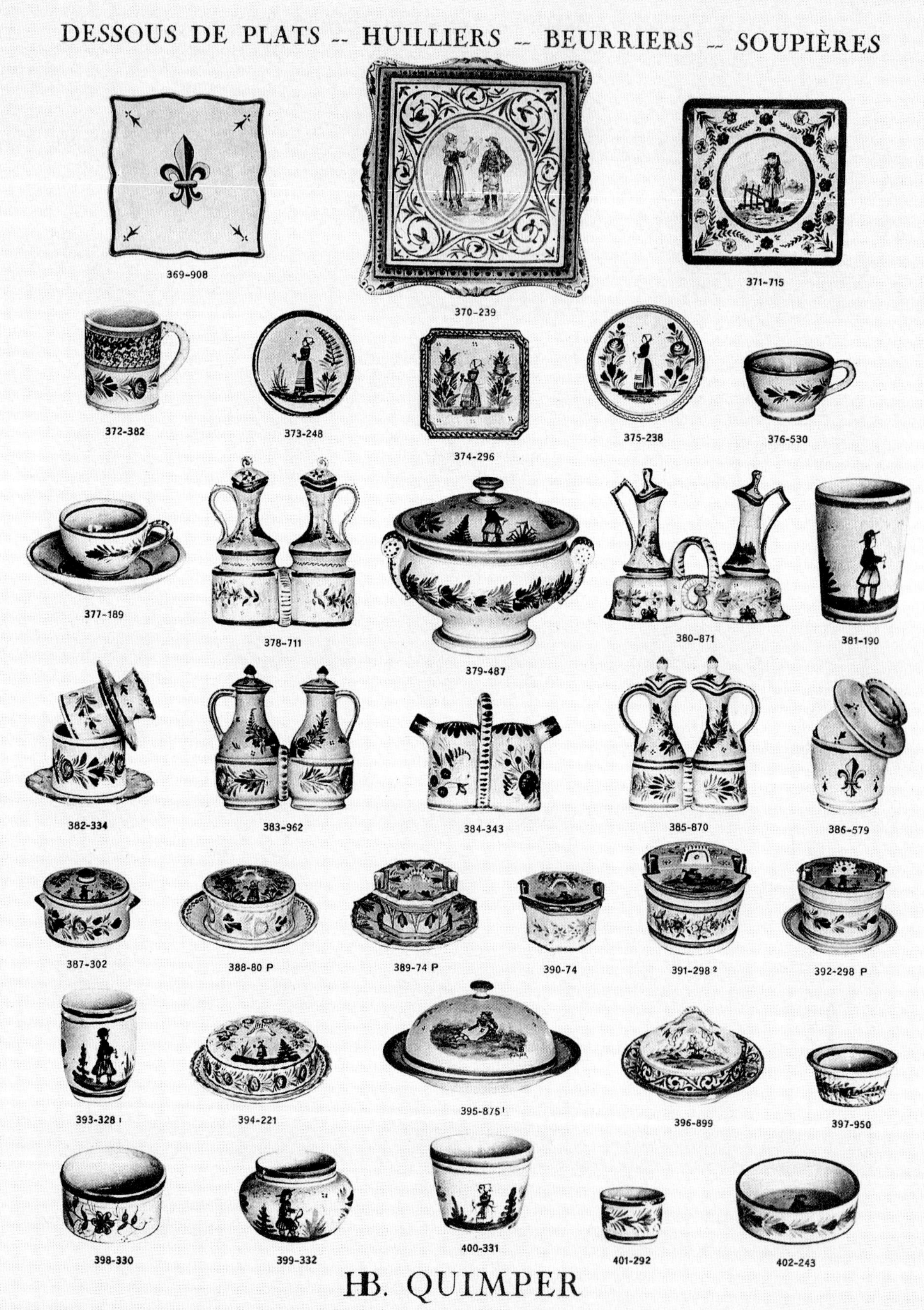
DESSOUS DE PLATS -- HUILLIERS -- BEURRIERS -- SOUPIÈRES

369-908 370-239 371-715

372-382 373-248 374-296 375-238 376-530

377-189 378-711 379-487 380-871 381-190

382-334 383-962 384-343 385-870 386-579

387-302 388-80 P 389-74 P 390-74 391-298 2 392-298 P

393-328 1 394-221 395-875 1 396-899 397-950

398-330 399-332 400-331 401-292 402-243

HB. QUIMPER

PICHETS -- BOLS A OREILLES -- MARMITES

403-249 404-249 405-428 406-369 407-369

408-295 409-295 [1] 410-275 411-391 412-391

413-288 414-295 415-369 416-172 [2] 417-259

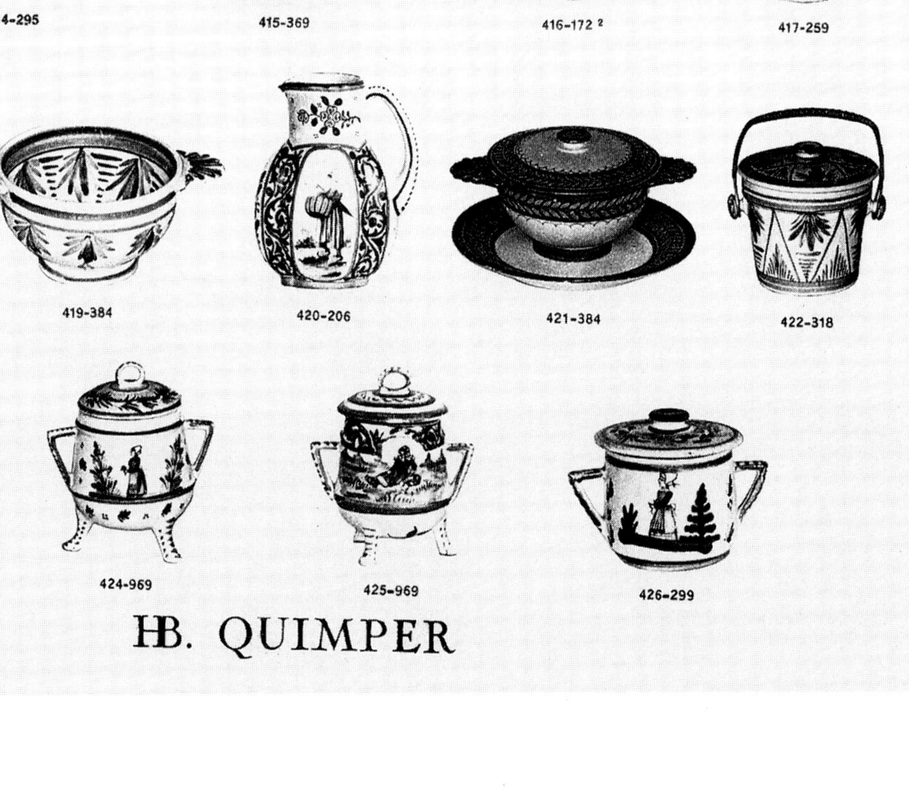

418-384 419-384 420-206 421-384 422-318

423-103 424-969 425-969 426-299

HB. QUIMPER

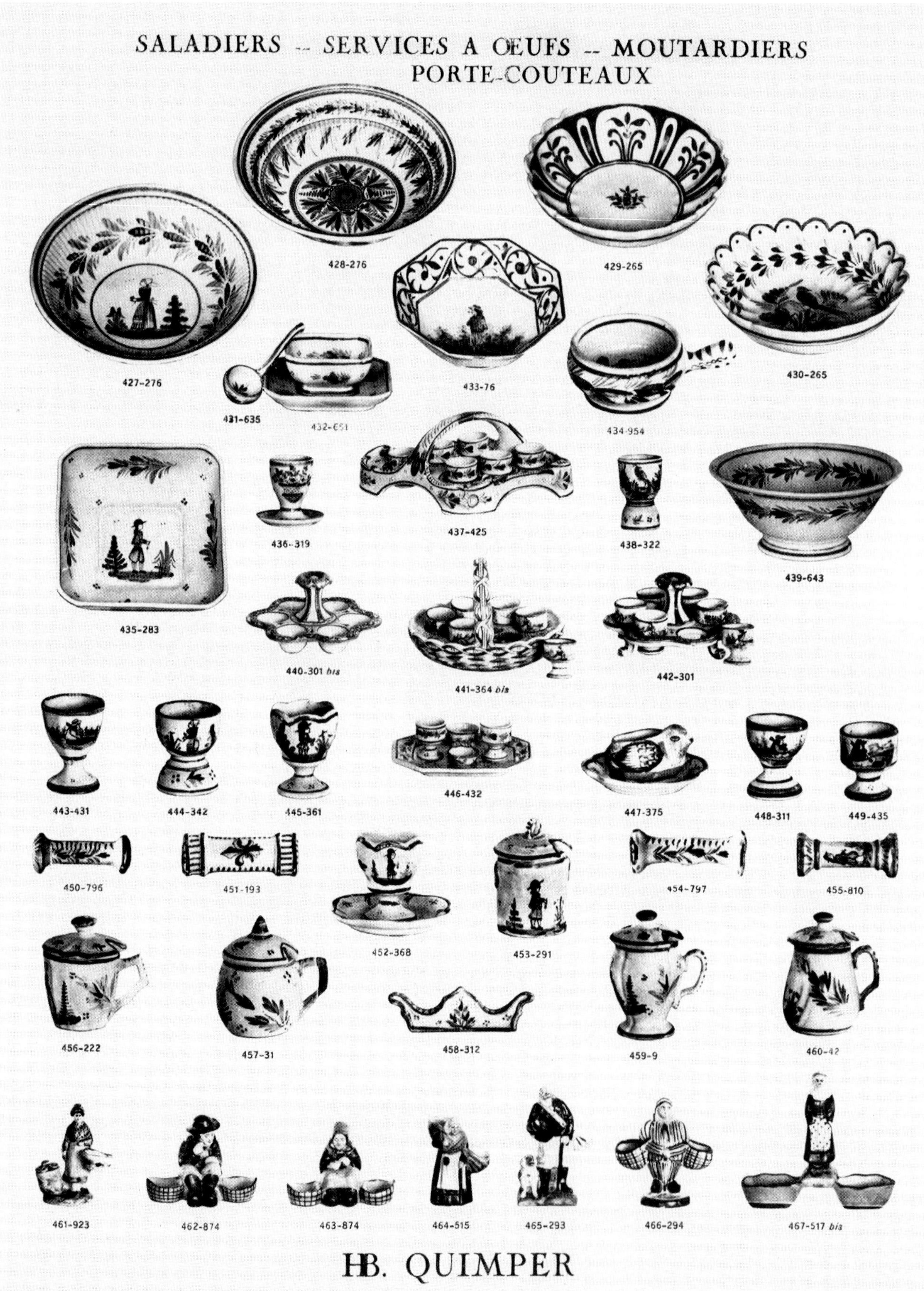
SALADIERS -- SERVICES A ŒUFS -- MOUTARDIERS
PORTE-COUTEAUX
428-276
429-265
427-276
433-76
430-265
431-635
432-651
434-954
437-425
436-319
438-322
439-643
435-283
440-301 bis
441-364 bis
442-301
446-432
443-431
444-342
445-361
447-375
448-311
449-435
450-796
451-193
454-797
455-810
452-368
453-291
456-222
457-31
458-312
459-9
460-42
461-923
462-874
463-874
464-515
465-293
466-294
467-517 bis
HB. QUIMPER

MÉNAGÈRES -- SALIÈRES -- CENDRIERS

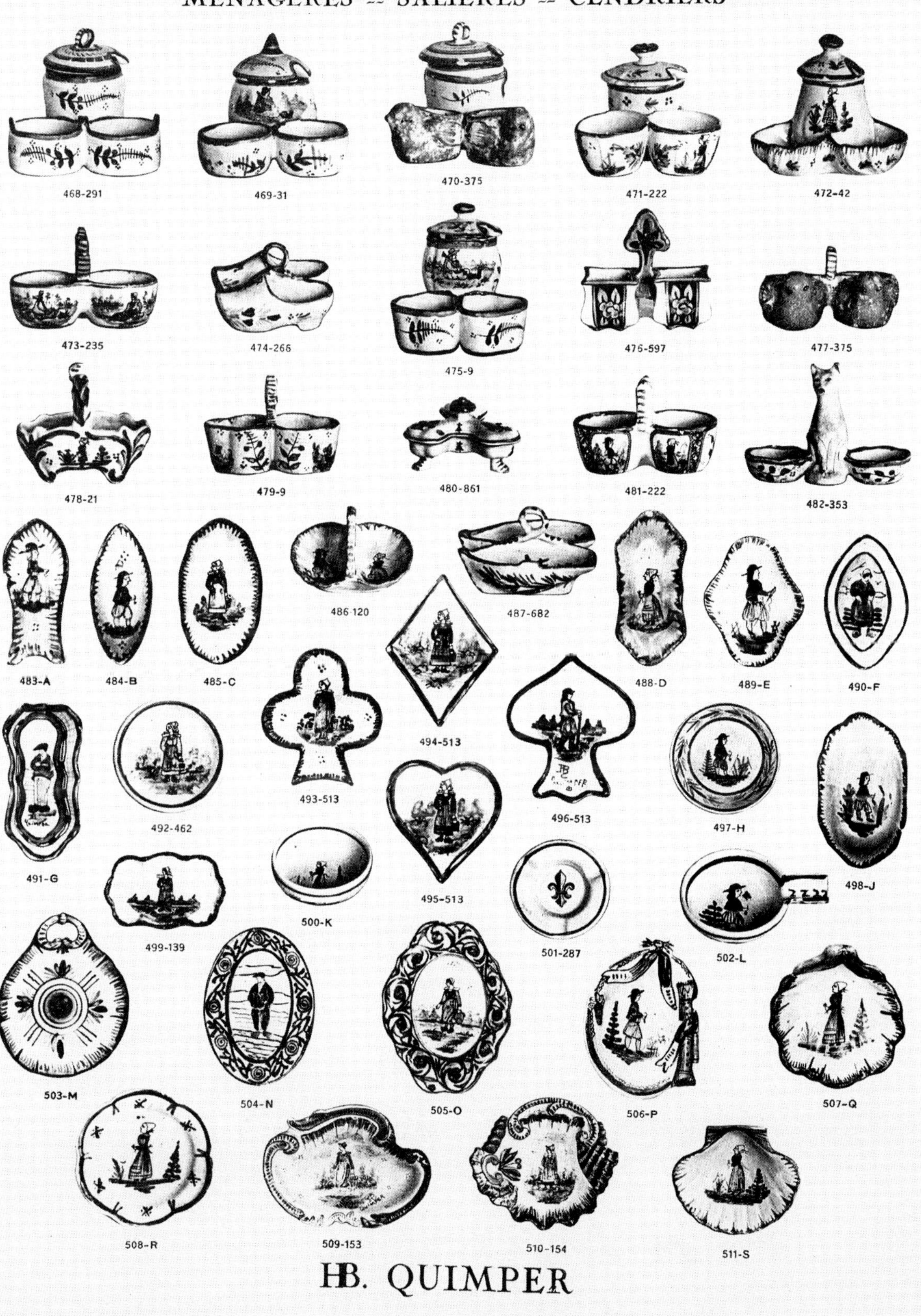

HB. QUIMPER

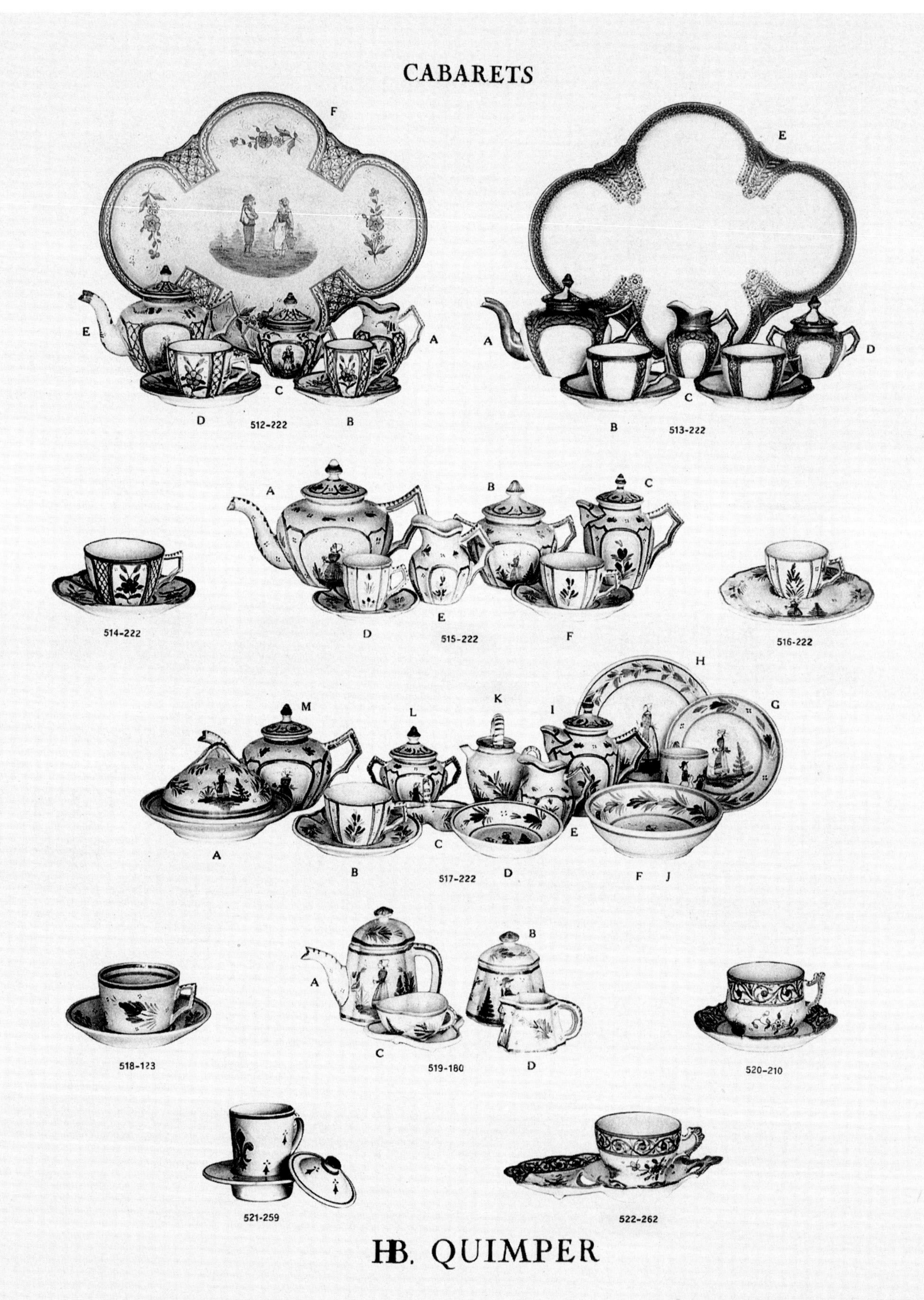
CABARETS
F
E
A
D
512-222
C
B
E
A
D
B
513-222
C
A
B
C
514-222
D
515-222
E
F
516-222
H
M
L
K
I
G
A
B
C
517-222
D
E
F
J
B
A
518-123
C
519-180
D
520-210
521-259
522-262
HB. QUIMPER

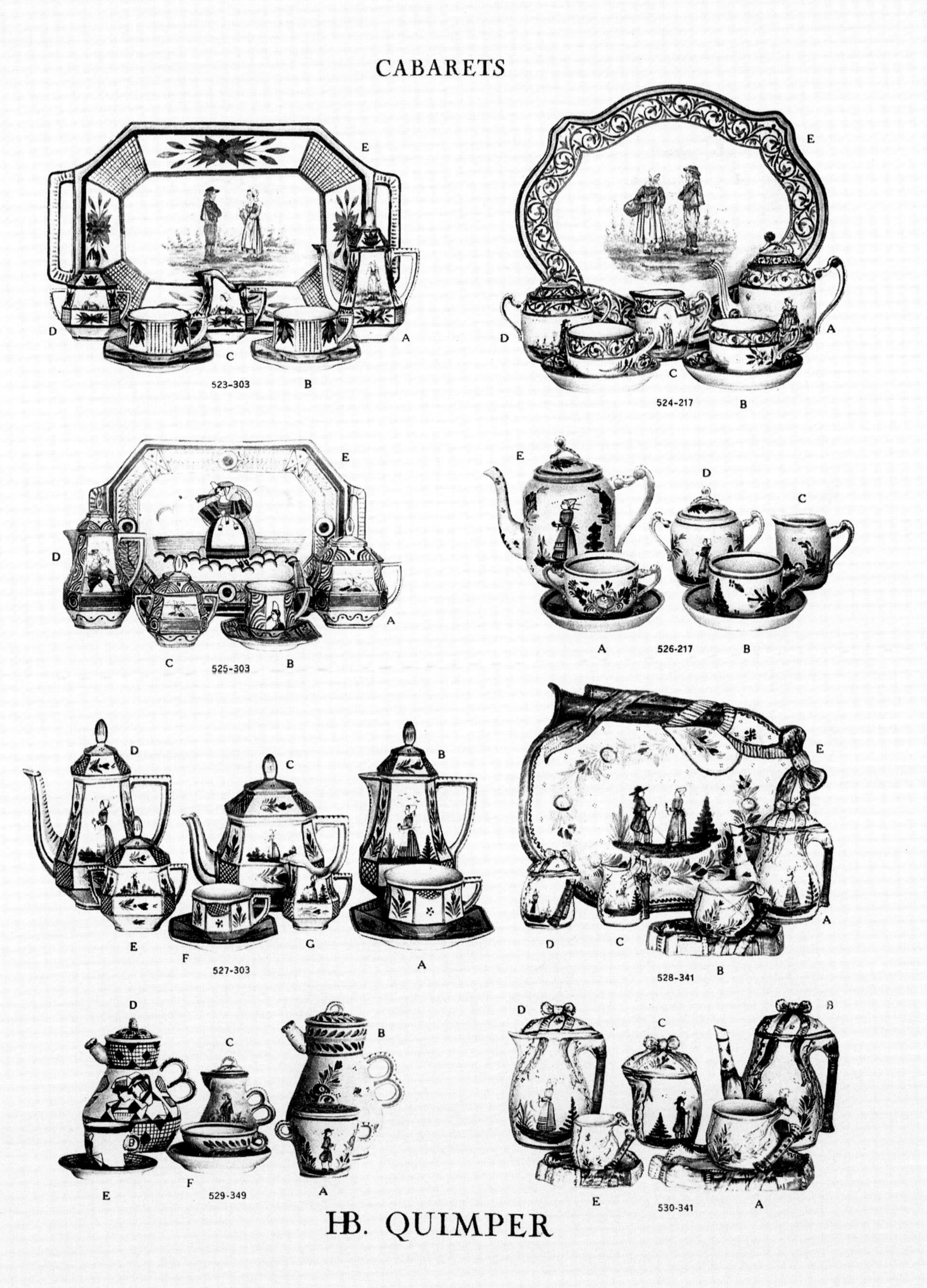
CABARETS
E
D
C
A
523-303
B
E
D
C
A
524-217
B
E
D
C
B
A
525-303
E
D
C
A
526-217
B
D
C
B
E
F
G
A
527-303
E
D
C
A
528-341
B
D
C
B
E
F
529-349
A
D
C
B
E
530-341
A
HB. QUIMPER

CABARETS -- SERVICES DE TABLE

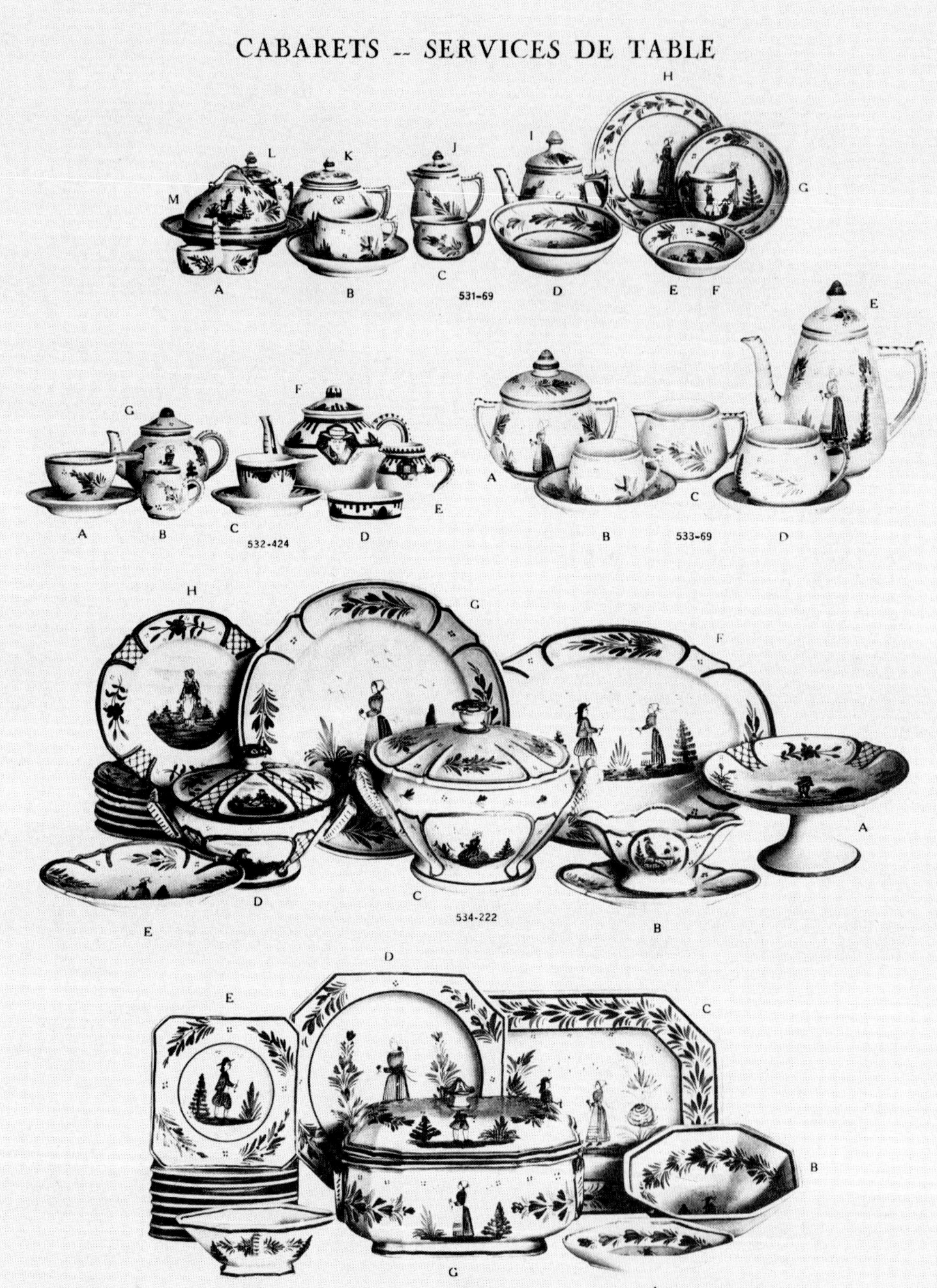

HB. QUIMPER

SERVICES DE TABLE -- ASSIETTES SPÉCIALES

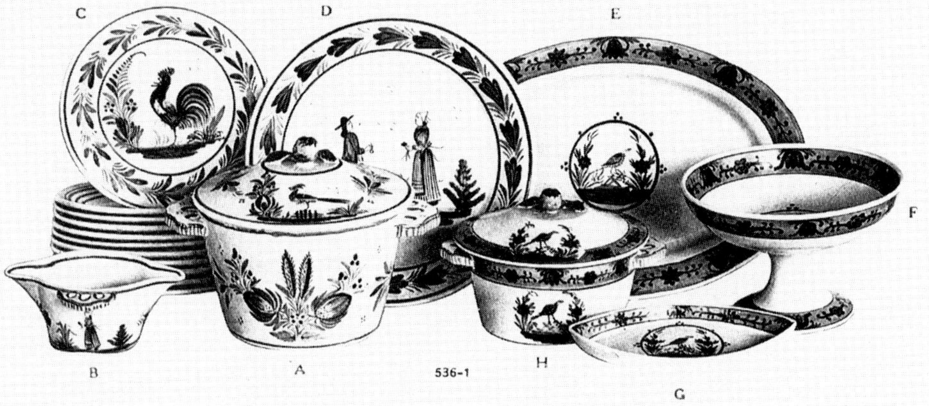

C D E F B A H G

536-1

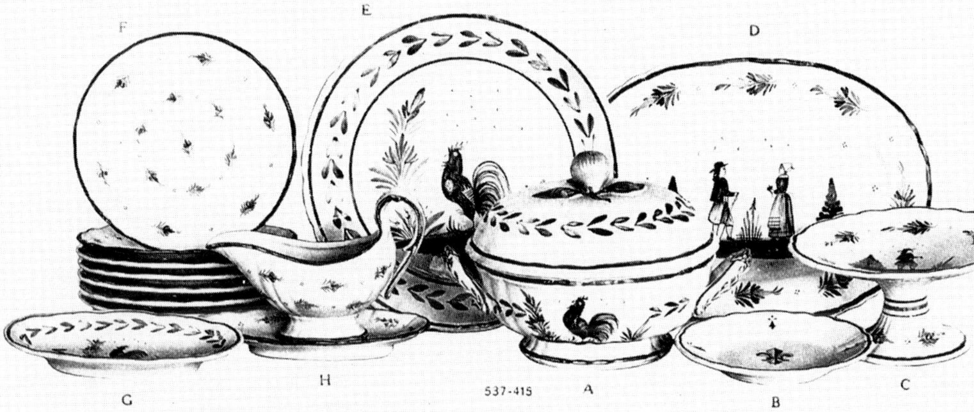

F E D G H A B C

537-415

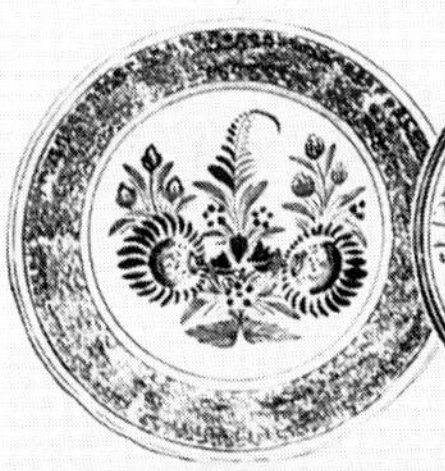

538-415 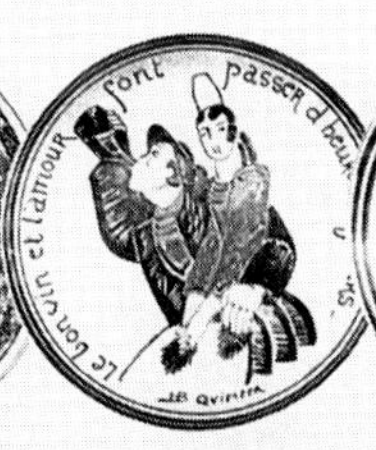 539-1 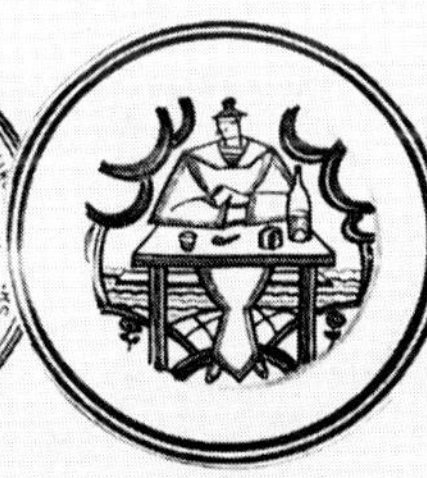 540-176 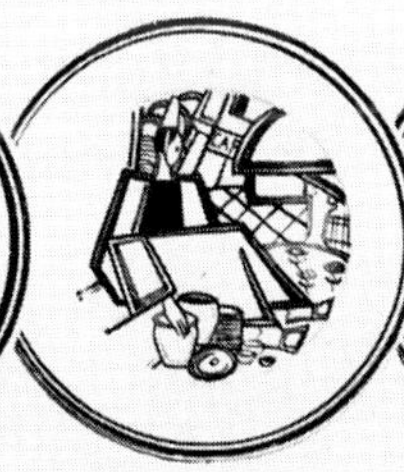 541-176 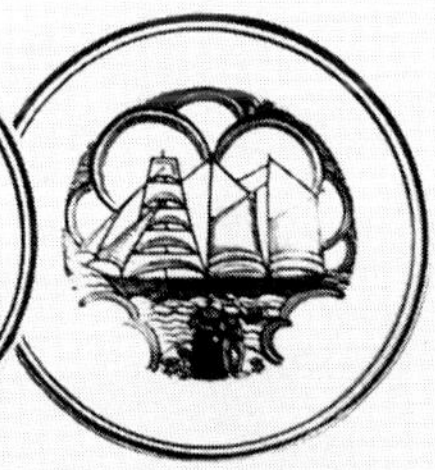 542-176

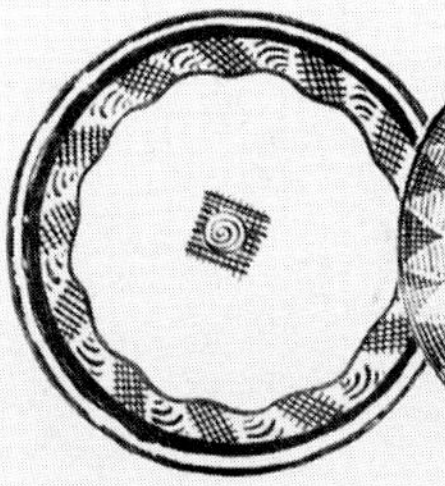

543-415 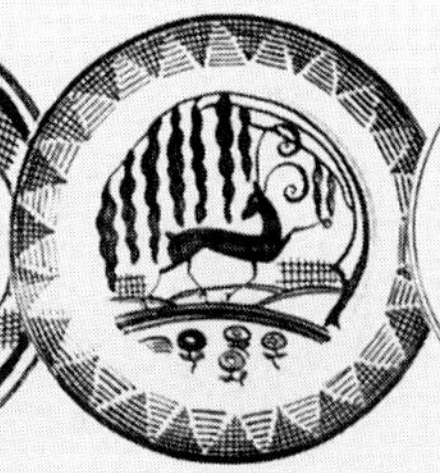 544-176 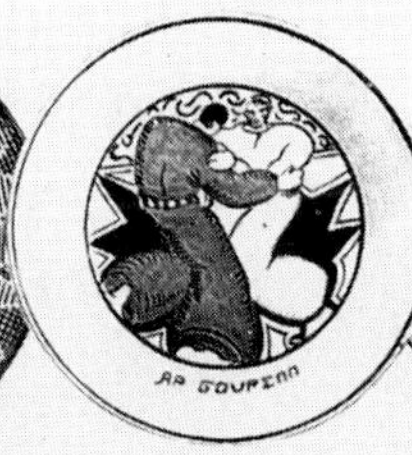 545-1 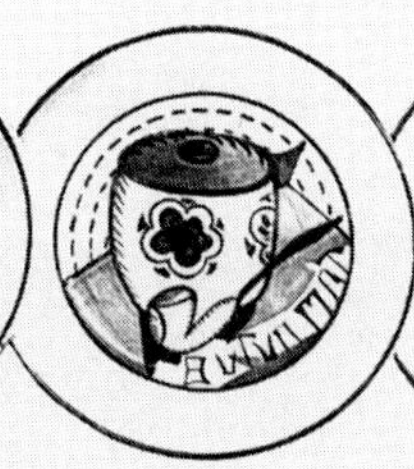 546-1 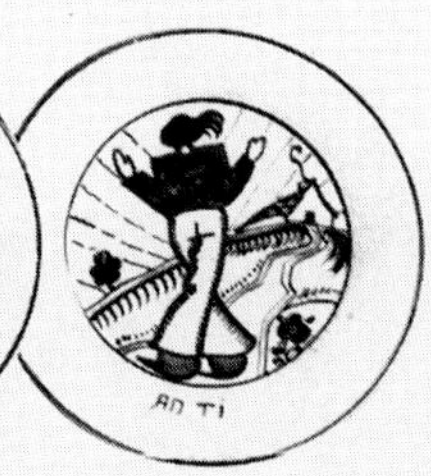 547-1

HB. QUIMPER

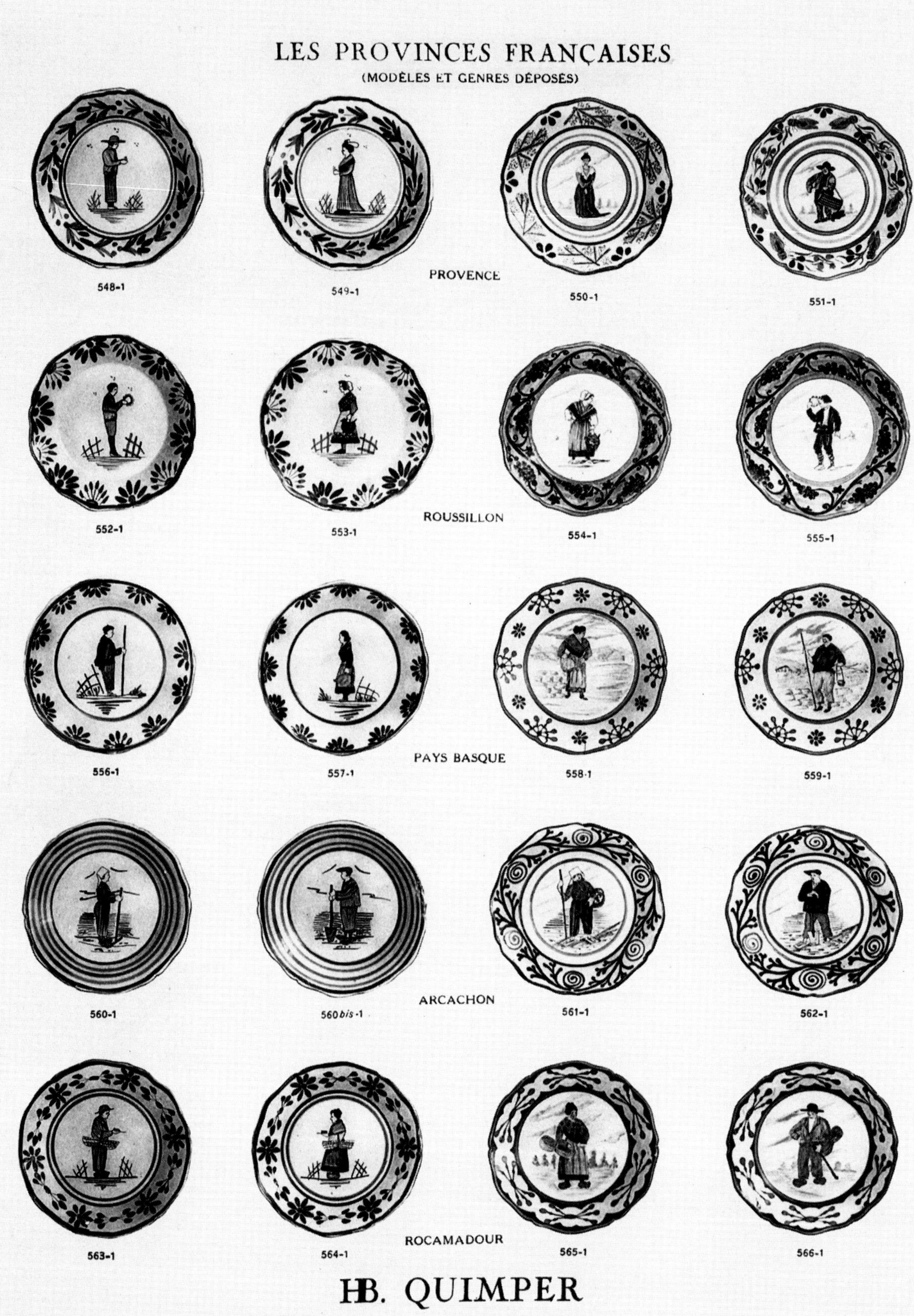
LES PROVINCES FRANÇAISES

(MODÈLES ET GENRES DÉPOSÉS)

PROVENCE

548-1 549-1 550-1 551-1

ROUSSILLON

552-1 553-1 554-1 555-1

PAYS BASQUE

556-1 557-1 558-1 559-1

ARCACHON

560-1 560*bis*-1 561-1 562-1

ROCAMADOUR

563-1 564-1 565-1 566-1

HB. QUIMPER

LES PROVINCES FRANÇAISES

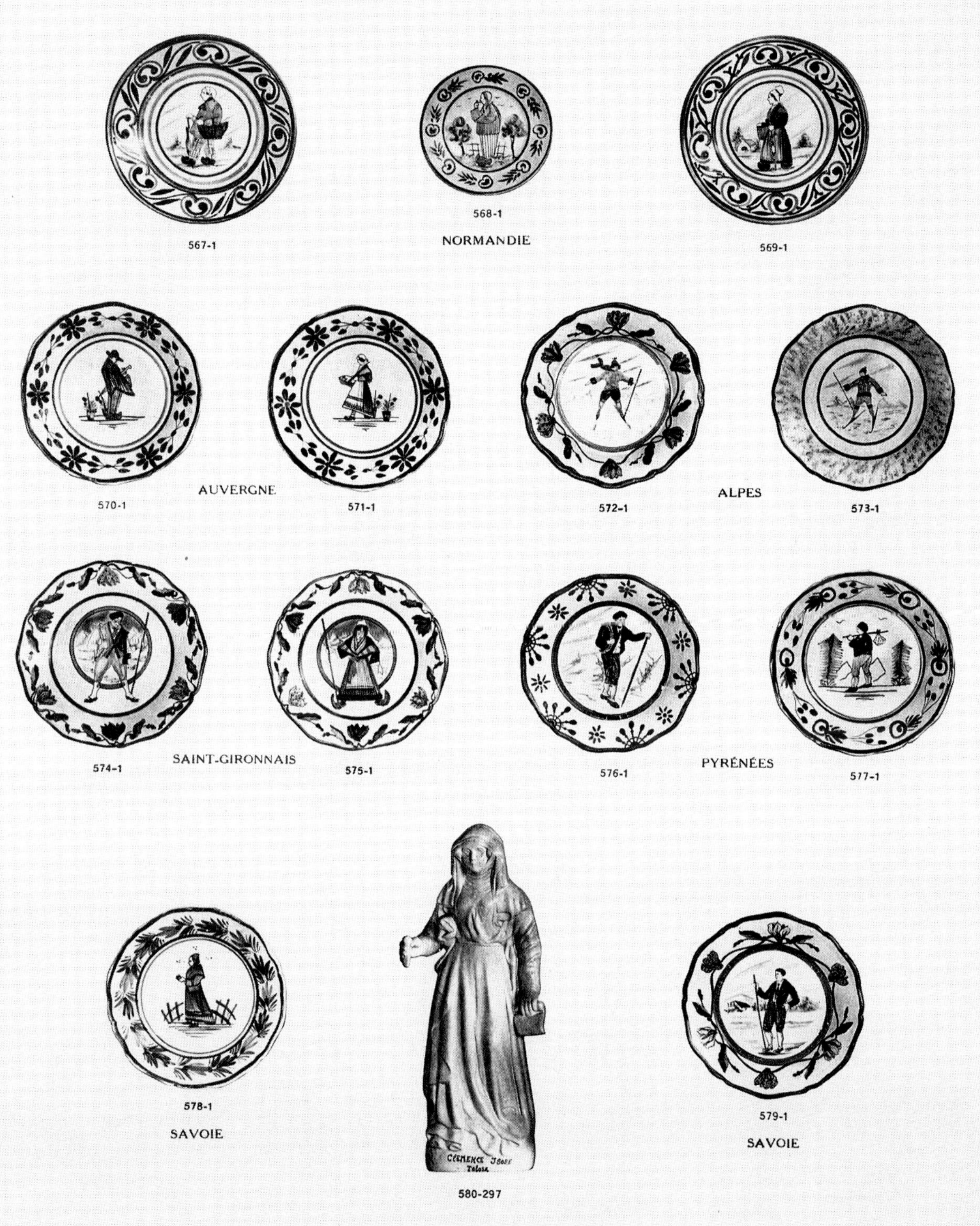

567-1 568-1 NORMANDIE 569-1

570-1 AUVERGNE 571-1 572-1 ALPES 573-1

574-1 SAINT-GIRONNAIS 575-1 576-1 PYRÉNÉES 577-1

578-1 SAVOIE

580-297

579-1 SAVOIE

HB. QUIMPER

STATUES DE SAINTS

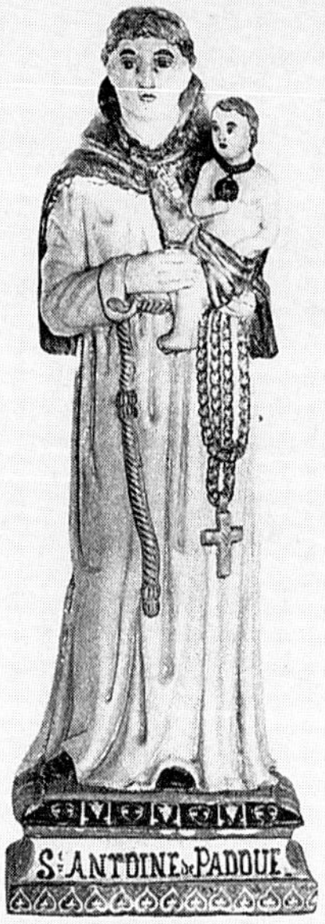

St ANTOINE DE PADOUE

581-323

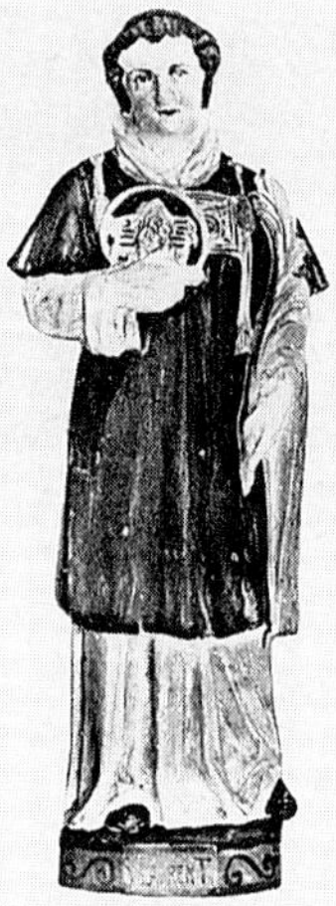

582-315

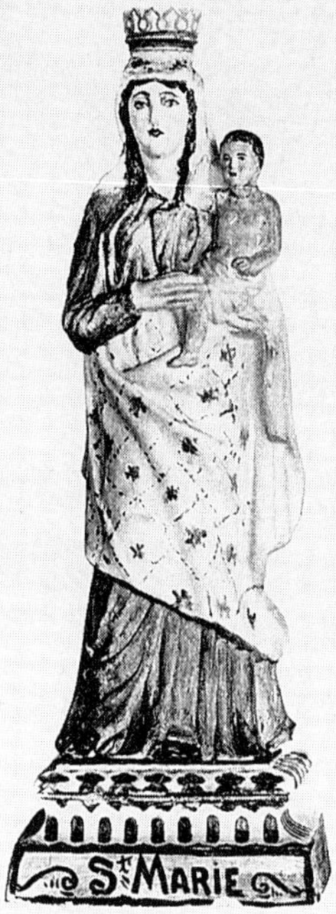

St MARIE

583-317

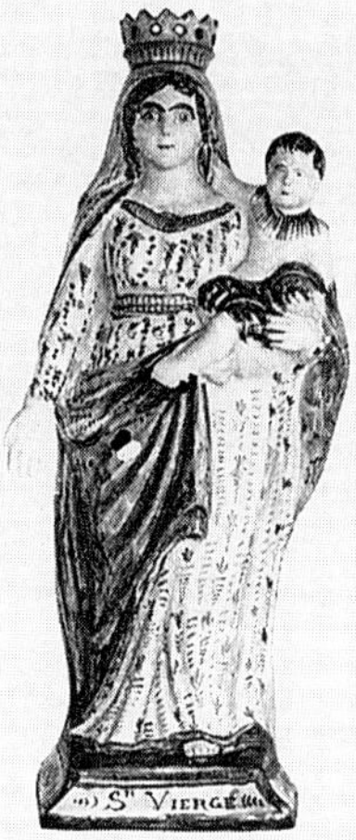

St VIERGE

584-308

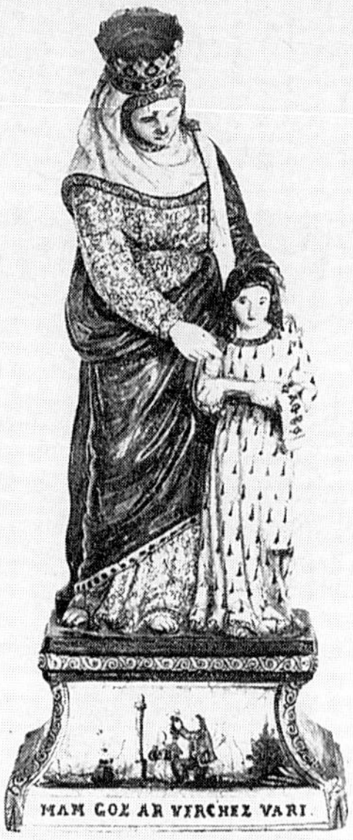

MAM GOZ AR VERCHEZ VARI

585-327

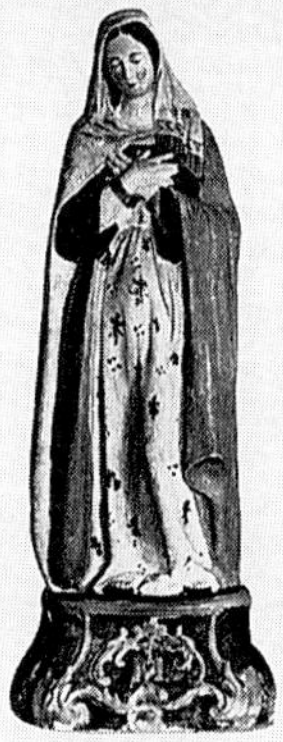

586-345

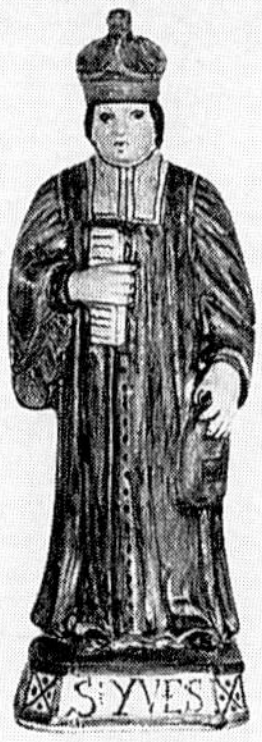

St YVES

587-360[1]

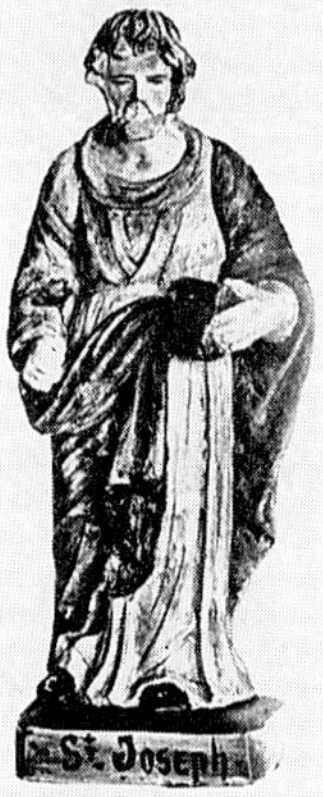

St Joseph

588-373

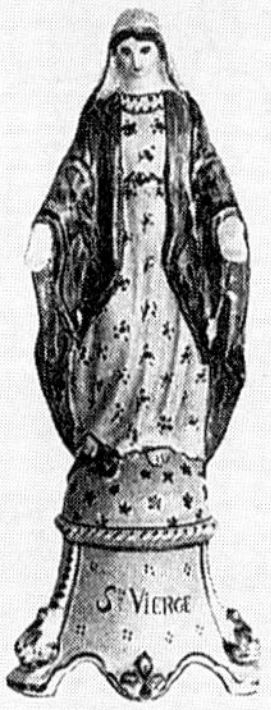

St VIERGE

589-363

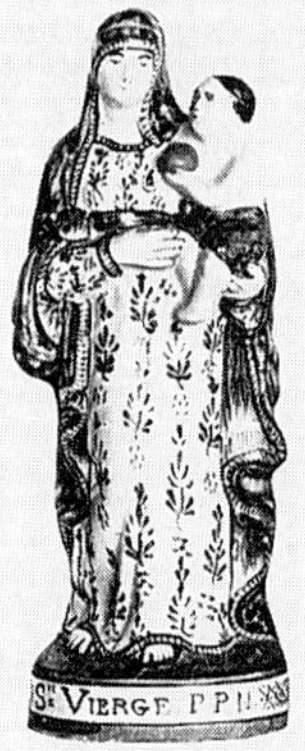

St VIERGE P.P.N.

590-367

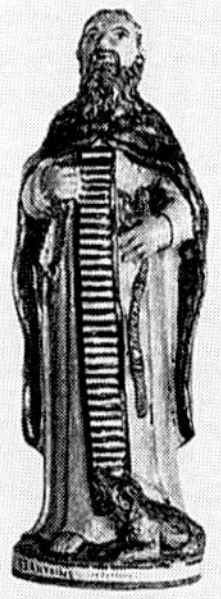

591-374

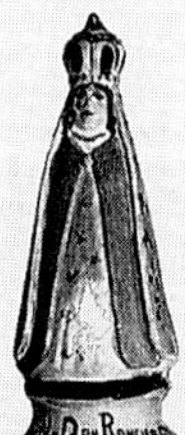

592-376

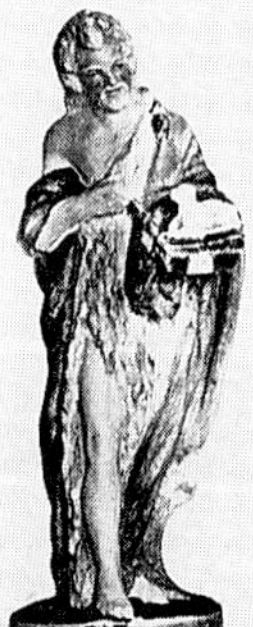

St JEAN

593-309

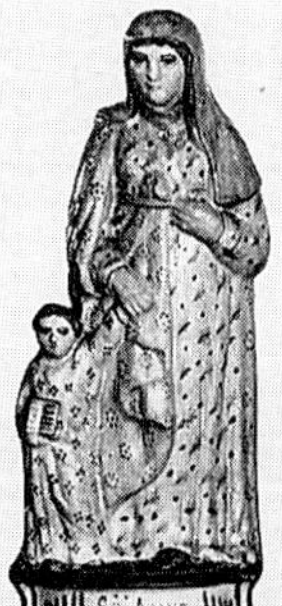

St ANNE

594-378

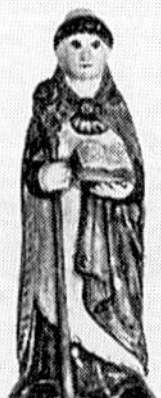

595-227

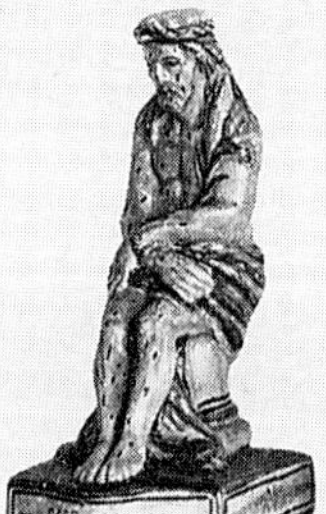

ECCE HOMO

596-380

HB. QUIMPER

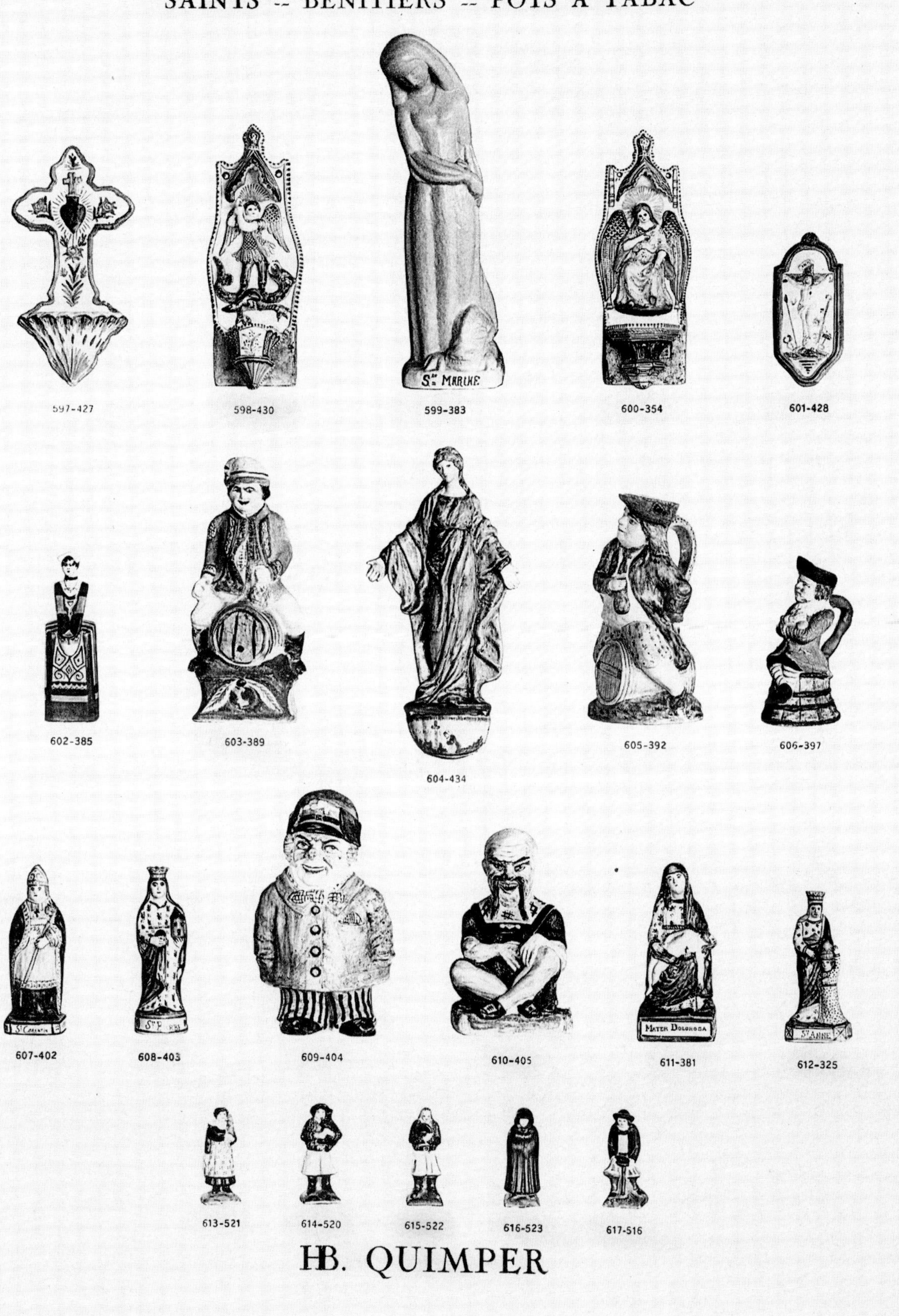
SAINTS -- BÉNITIERS -- POTS A TABAC
597-427
598-430
Ste MARTHE
599-383
600-354
601-428
602-385
603-389
604-434
605-392
606-397
607-402
608-403
609-404
610-405
MATER DOLOROSA
611-381
Ste ANNE
612-325
613-521
614-520
615-522
616-523
617-516
HB. QUIMPER

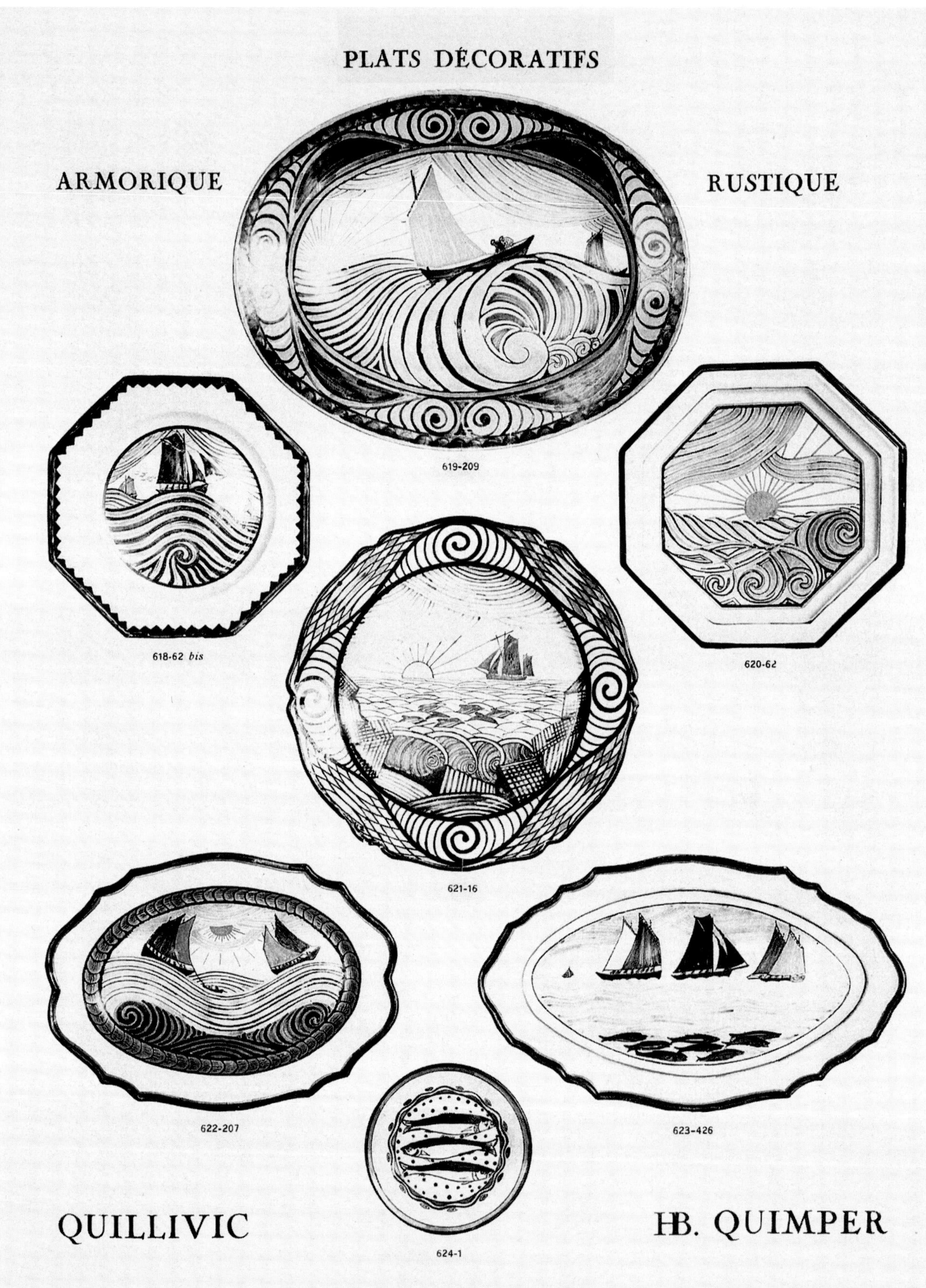
PLATS DÉCORATIFS
ARMORIQUE
RUSTIQUE
619-209
618-62 *bis*
620-62
621-16
622-207
623-426
624-1
QUILLIVIC
HB. QUIMPER

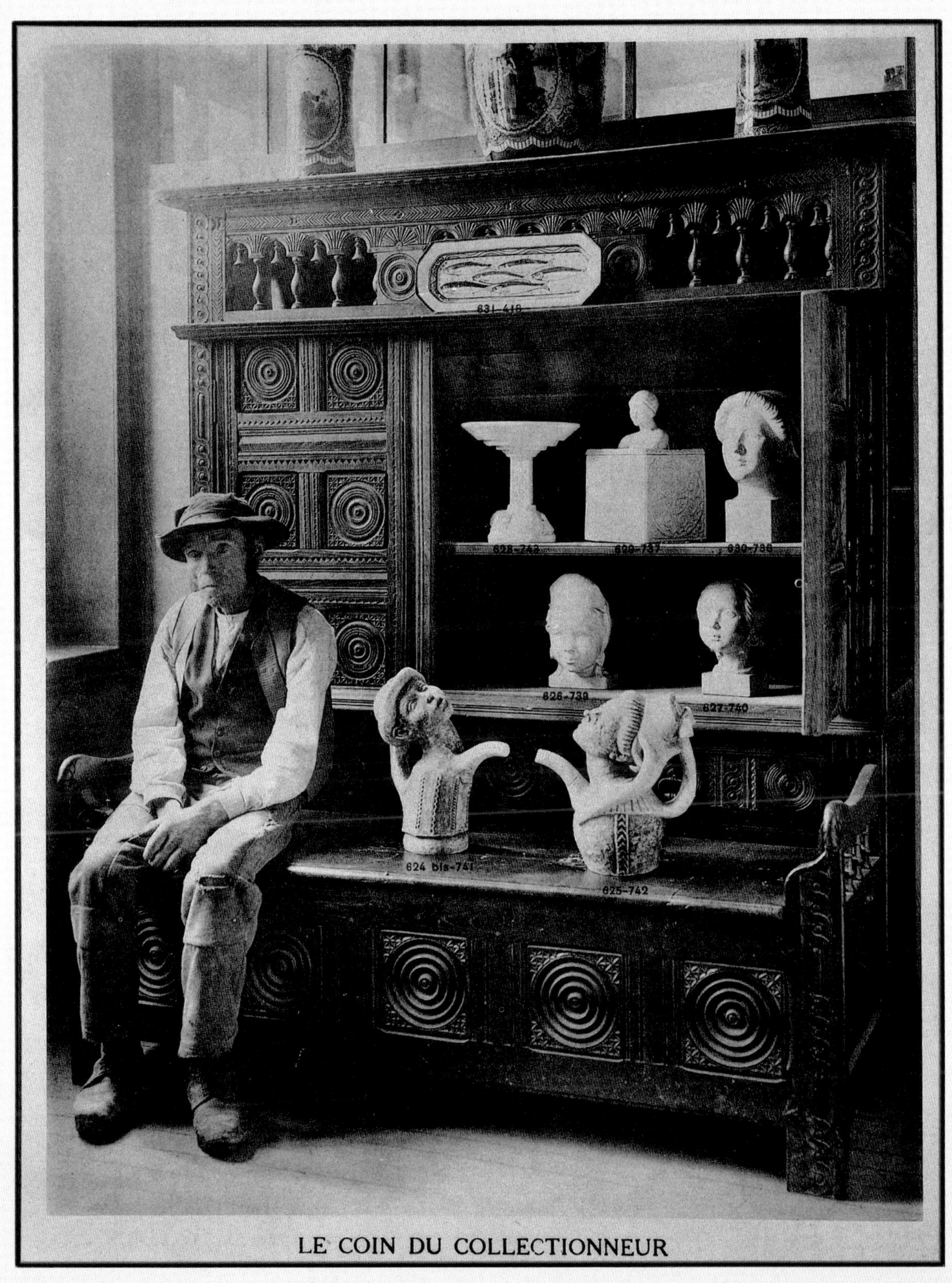

LE COIN DU COLLECTIONNEUR

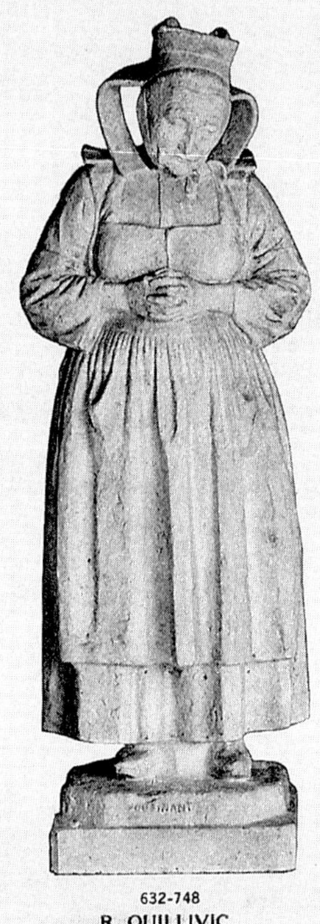
632-748
R. QUILLIVIC

Tous les plats et assiettes décoratifs, les vases, etc... de Quillivic, sont tous marqués :

ARMORIQUE
RUSTIQUE
QUILLIVIC
HB
QUIMPER

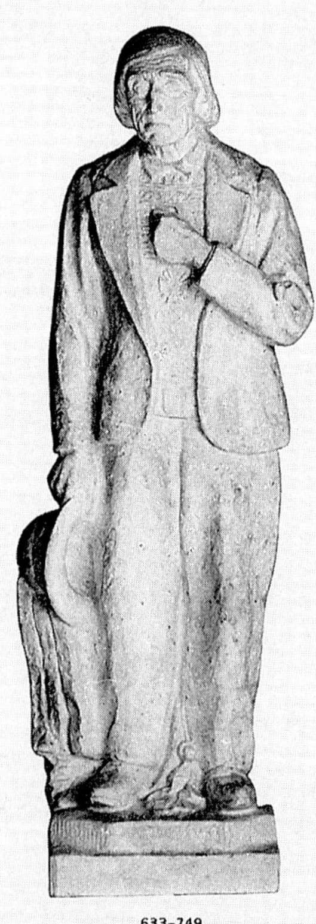
633-749
R. QUILLIVIC

Les bustes, les statues, et en général tous les articles de sculpture pure sont seulement marqués :

R. Quillivic
HB
QUIMPER

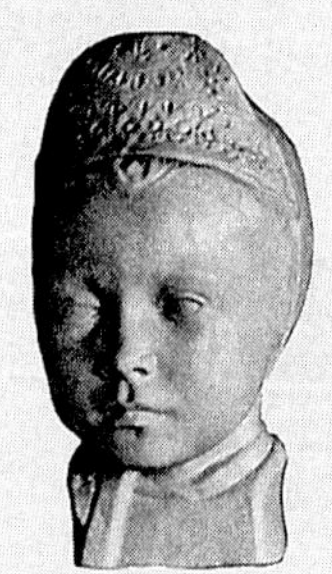
634-750
R. QUILLIVIC

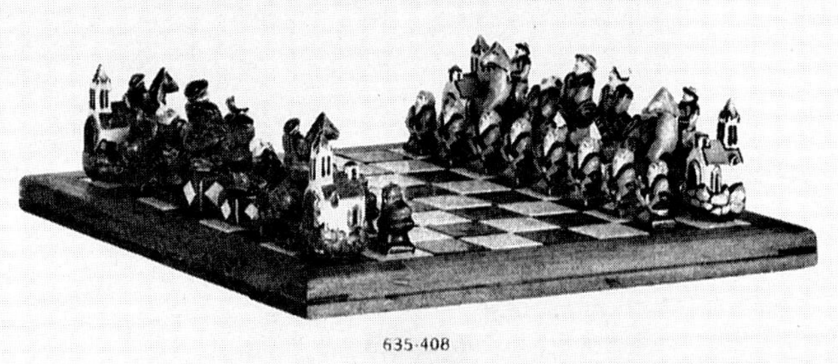

635-408

Les photographies du présent catalogue ne sont données qu'à titre d'indication et ne peuvent engager la "Grande Maison", qui se réserve le droit d'apporter dans le décor ou dans la forme, toute modification qu'elle jugerait utile.

La reproduction sans autorisation, par écrit, des figures du présent album, sera poursuivie selon la loi.

Un exemplaire de cet album a été déposé au Greffe du Tribunal de Commerce de Quimper pour garantir l'ensemble de sa disposition et les détails des figures contre toute initation.

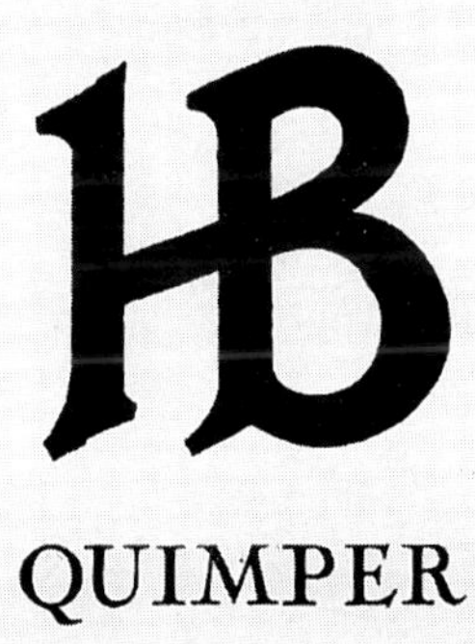

QUIMPER

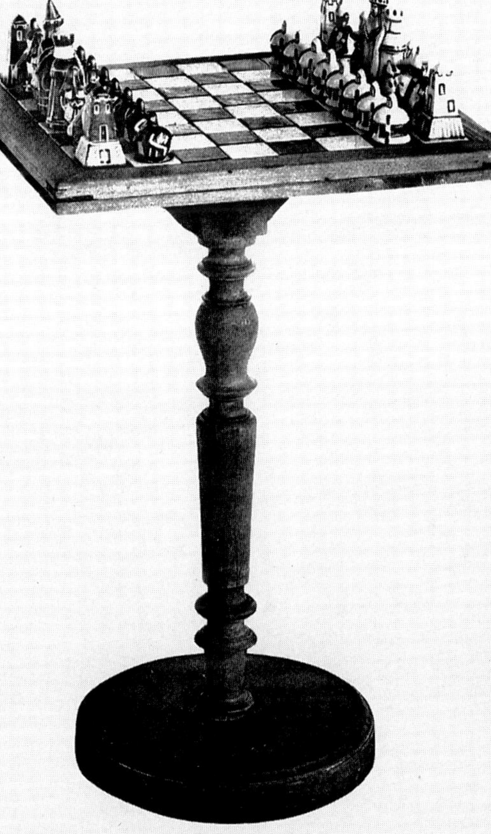

Voir nos Conditions de Vente

sur notre Tarif.

639-409

Phototypie A. Dantan
Paris.

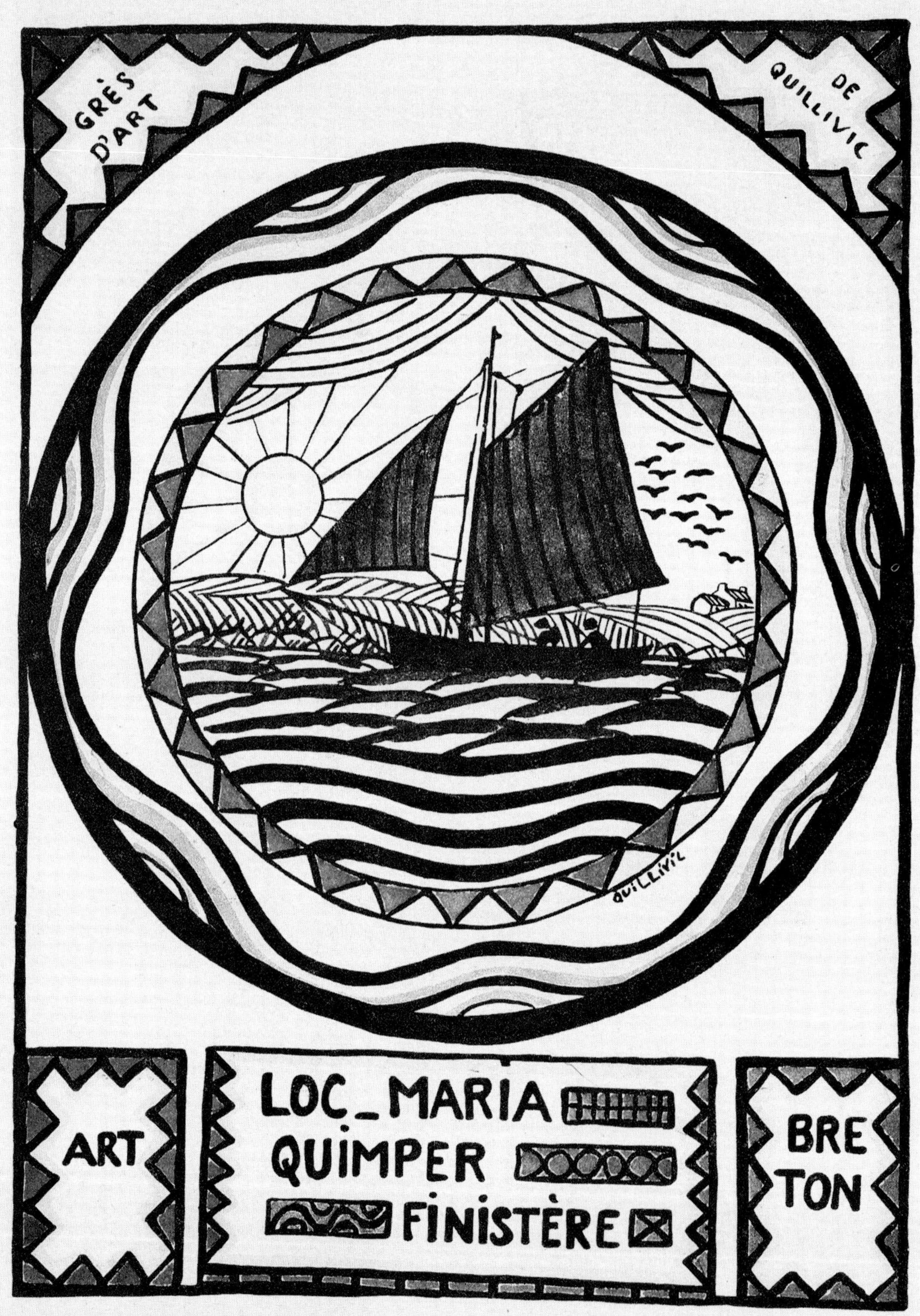

ALBUM No 1

Imprimerie de la Faïencerie Bretonne de la Grande Maison

FAÏENCERIE D'ART BRETON
HENRIOT - QUIMPER

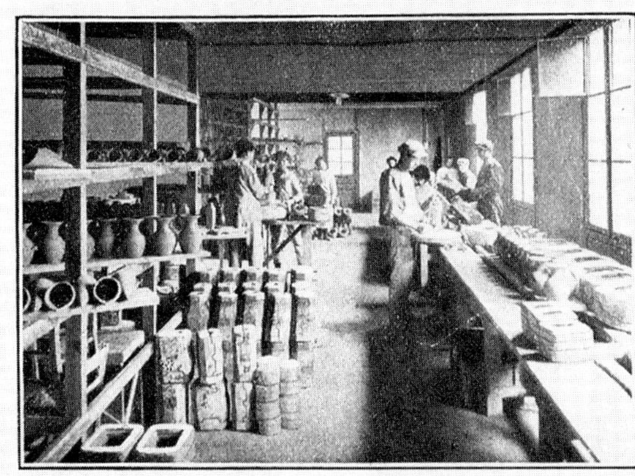

Un atelier de coulage

C'est en 1778 que GUILLAUME DUMAINE quittait sa propriété de la Josserie, aux abords de Ger, où, de temps immémorial, sa famille exploitait une fabrique de grès, et venait fonder à Loc Maria, Quimper, la Maison qui est devenue la *Faïencerie d'Art breton Henriot.*

Cette Maison s'est toujours transmise par voie d'héritage, et, depuis un siècle et demi à Quimper, n'a cessé d'être dirigée par les héritiers directs de son fondateur, les DUMAINE, TANQUEREY, HENRIOT.

Sa production consistait à l'origine, en grès servant aux usages domestiques de la région, bouteilles, cruches, saloirs; en poteries vernissées aux naïfs dessins hispano-mauresques, rouges, noirs, blancs, décorant les écuelles et les plats utilisés dans les noces et les fermes bretonnes; en faïences rustiques aux grosses fleurs, coqs, ornements linéaires, ou en copies des anciennes fabrications de Moustiers, Nevers,

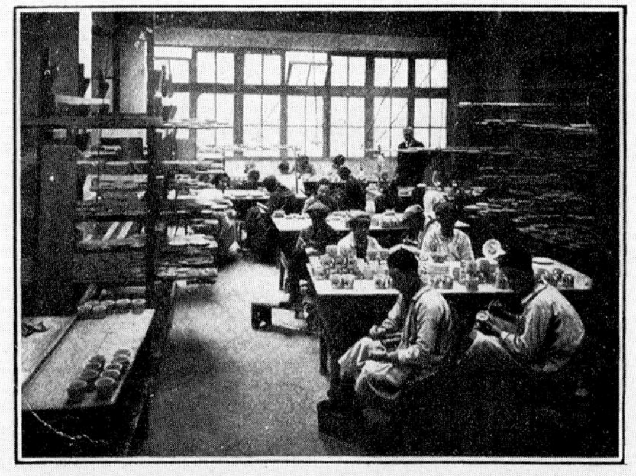

Un atelier de peinture

HENRIOT - QUIMPER

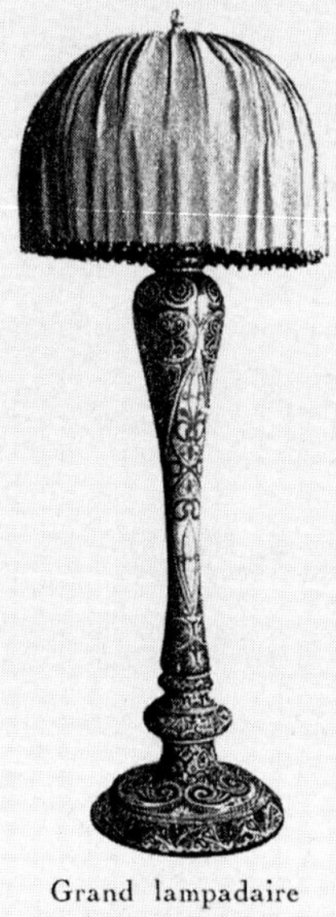
Grand lampadaire
décors celtiques

Rouen ; puis en assiettes et plats décoratifs, vases et bibelots divers, souvenirs caractéristiques de la Bretagne.

En 1913, était acquise de la Maison Porquier, fondée à Quimper à la fin du XVIIIe siècle, et qui depuis 1904 avait cessé de fabriquer, la propriété de ses modèles, de sa marque ꝎB (Porquier-Beau) et des dessins artistiques créés pour elle, en 1872, par M. Alfred BEAU, Conservateur du Musée de Quimper.

C'est à ce dernier qu'est due la reproduction sur les faïences stannifères de Quimper, de ces personnages et scènes pittoresques de la vie bretonne qui ont fait la réputation mondiale des faïences de Quimper.

Aux nombreux modèles qui constituaient le fond de sa fabrication, la Maison a ajouté récemment l'édition des gravures anciennes de " la Galerie Armoricaine " et d'œuvres modernes dues au grand talent du peintre éminent de la Mer, Mathurin MEHEUT, et des peintres et décorateurs CRESTON, BURIE, des statuaires BACHELET, LENOIR, NICOT.

Ces travaux ont obtenu les plus hautes récompenses aux expositions de céramique bretonne, notamment : Paris 1878 ; Nantes 1910 ; Brest 1913 ; Huelgoat, Morlaix 1921 ; Rennes 1922 ; Rouen 1923.

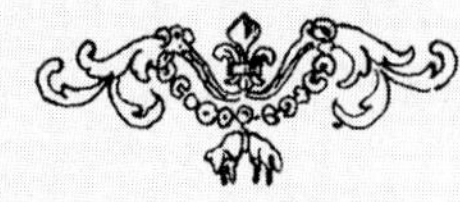

Décor riche - Série B - ASSIETTES & PLATS DÉCORATIFS

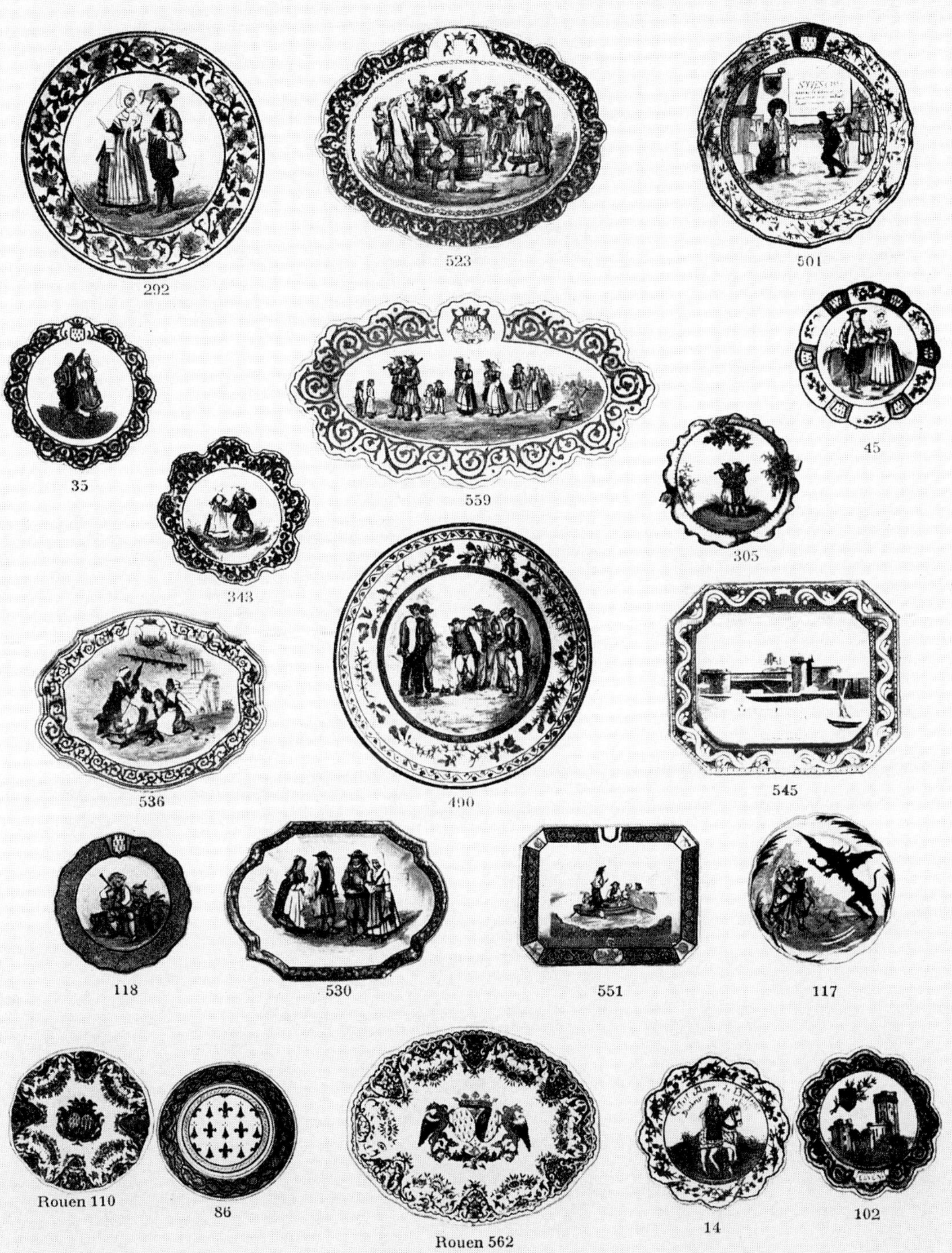

HENRIOT - QUIMPER

Décor riche - Série B

APPLIQUES - BANNETTES - BÉNITIERS

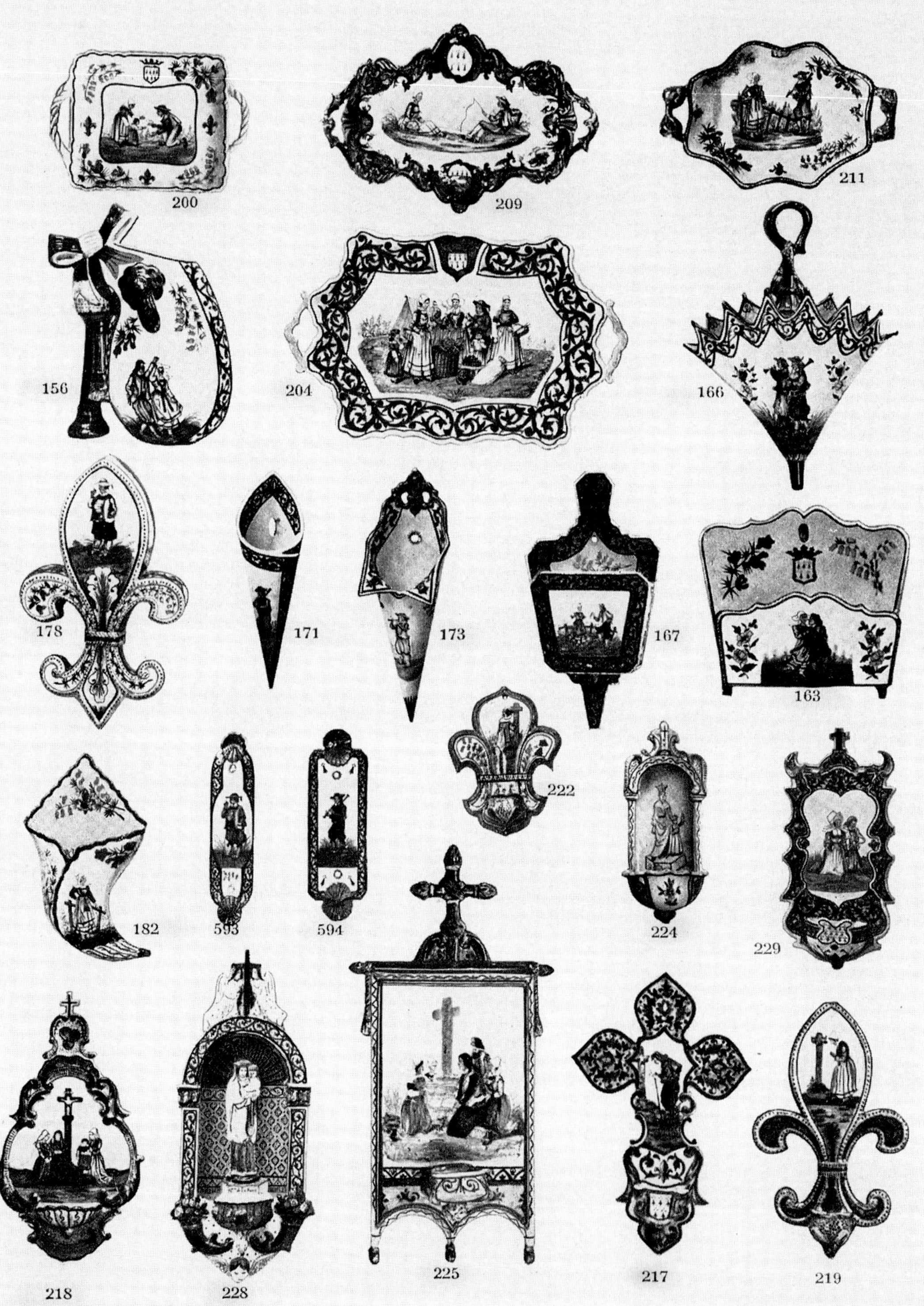

HENRIOT - QUIMPER

Décor riche - Série B

BEURRIERS - BONBONNIÈRES - BOUGEOIRS
CENDRIERS - CLOCHETTES - CADRE PHOTO - MENUS

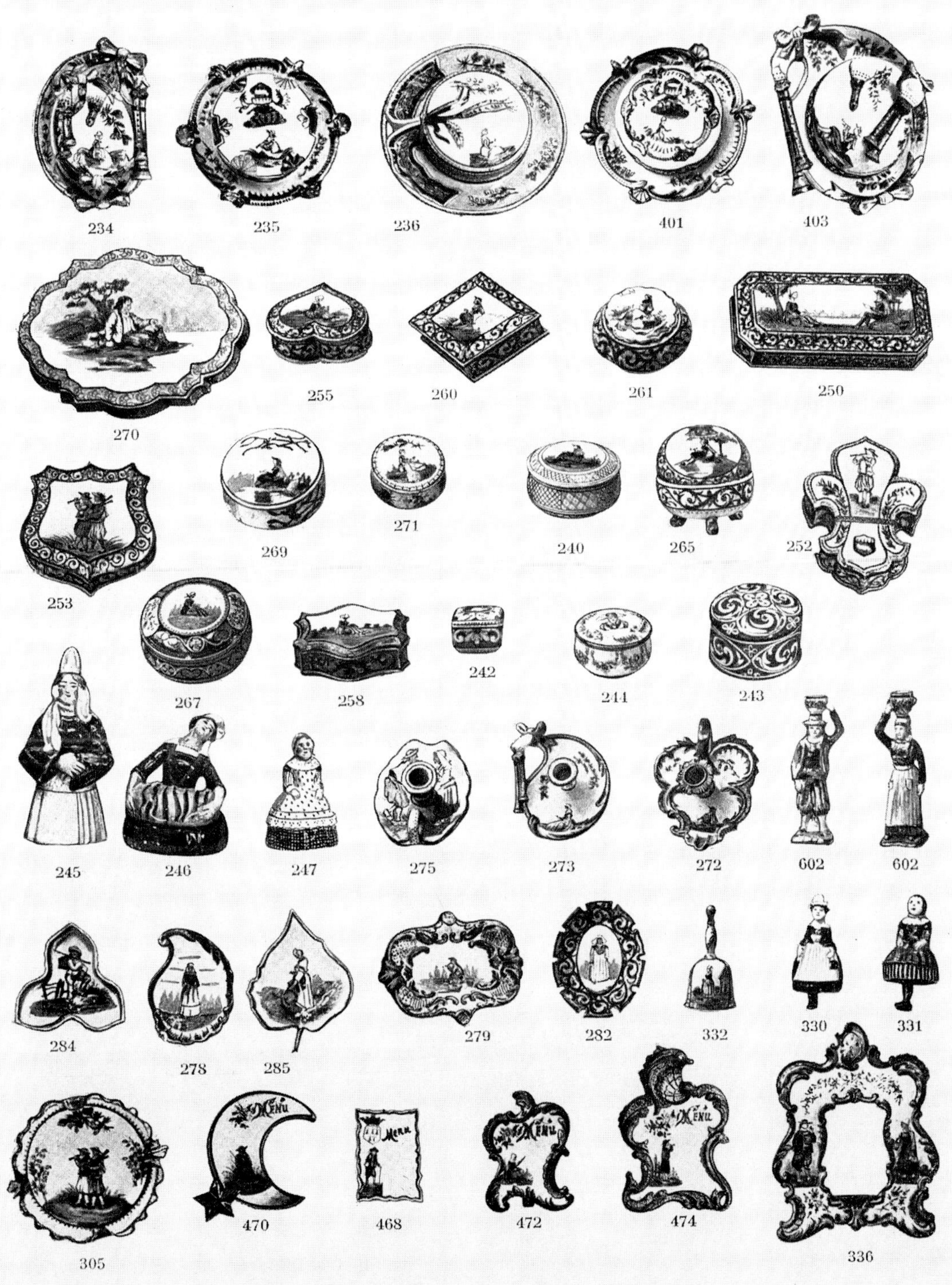

HENRIOT - QUIMPER

Décor riche - SÉRIE B - ENCRIERS

DESSOUS DE PLAT - HORS-D'ŒUVRE - FONTAINE

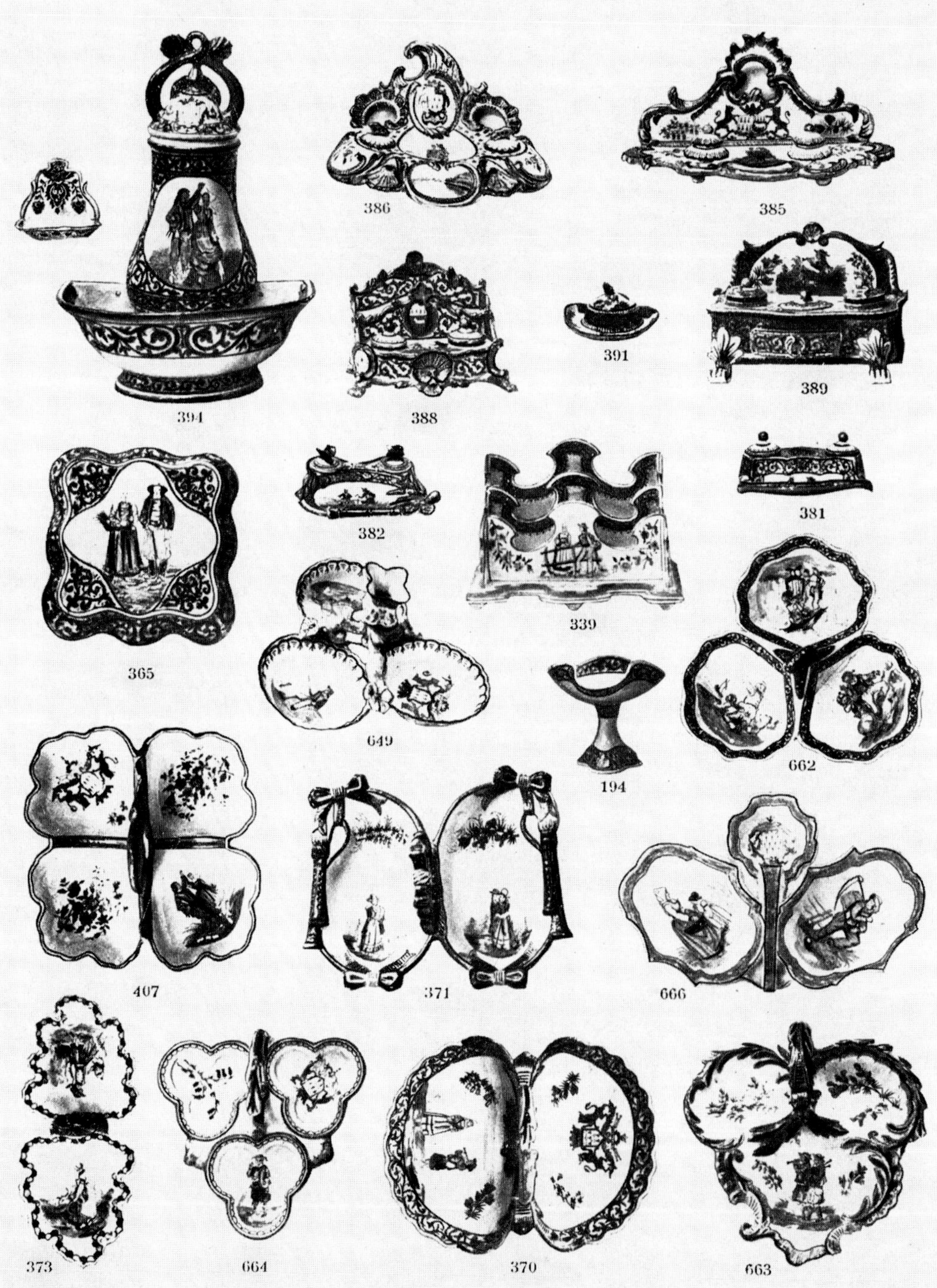

HENRIOT - QUIMPER

Décor riche - Série B - SERVICE THÉ ET FUMEURS
TÊTE-A-TÊTE - PORTE-CARTES

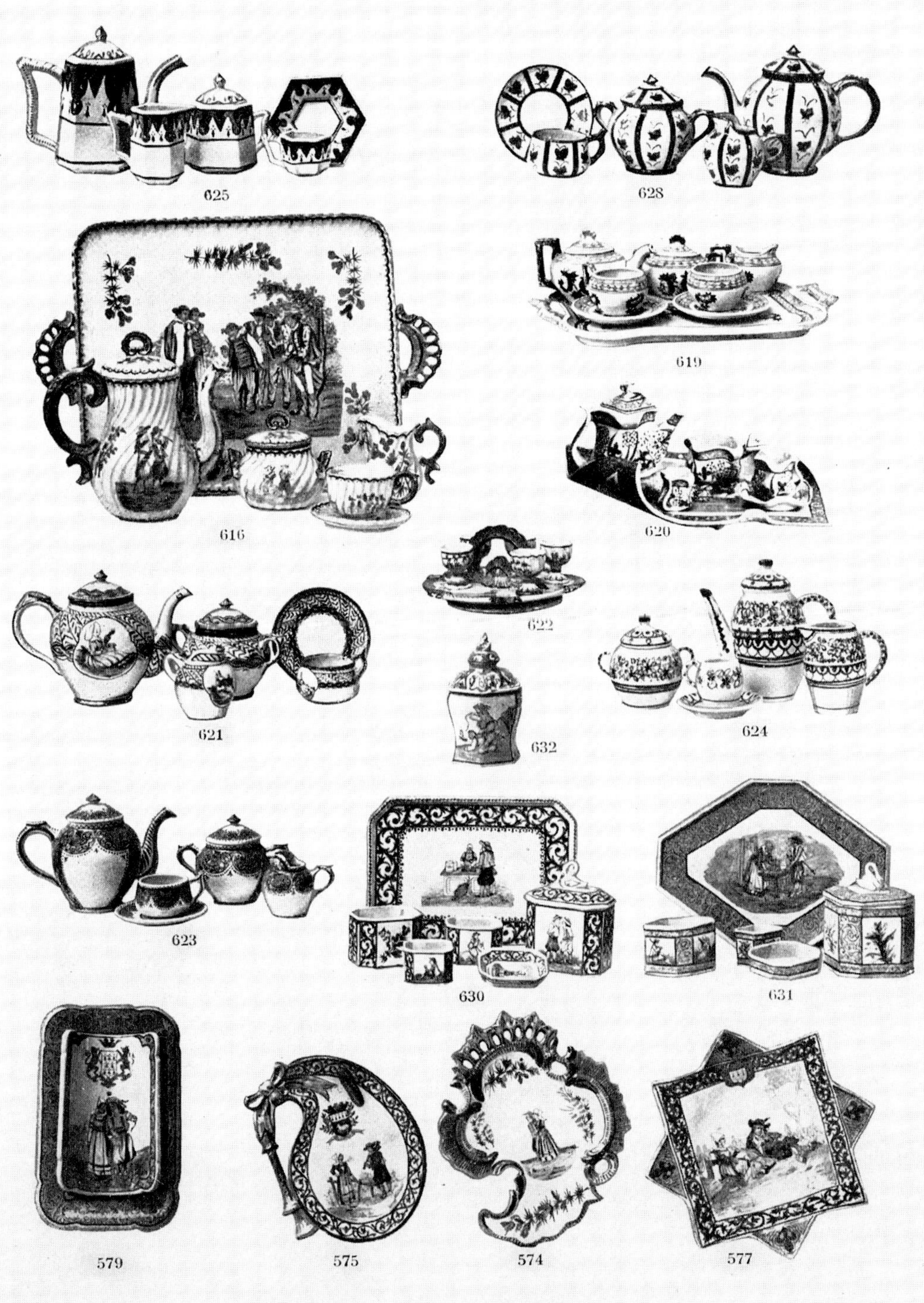

625 628 616 619 620 622 621 632 624 623 630 631 579 575 574 577

HENRIOT - QUIMPER

Décor riche. - SÉRIE B

MELONNIÈRES - SURTOUT - DÉJEUNERS
PORTE-PIPES - PERSONNAGES - PORTE-PARAPLUIE

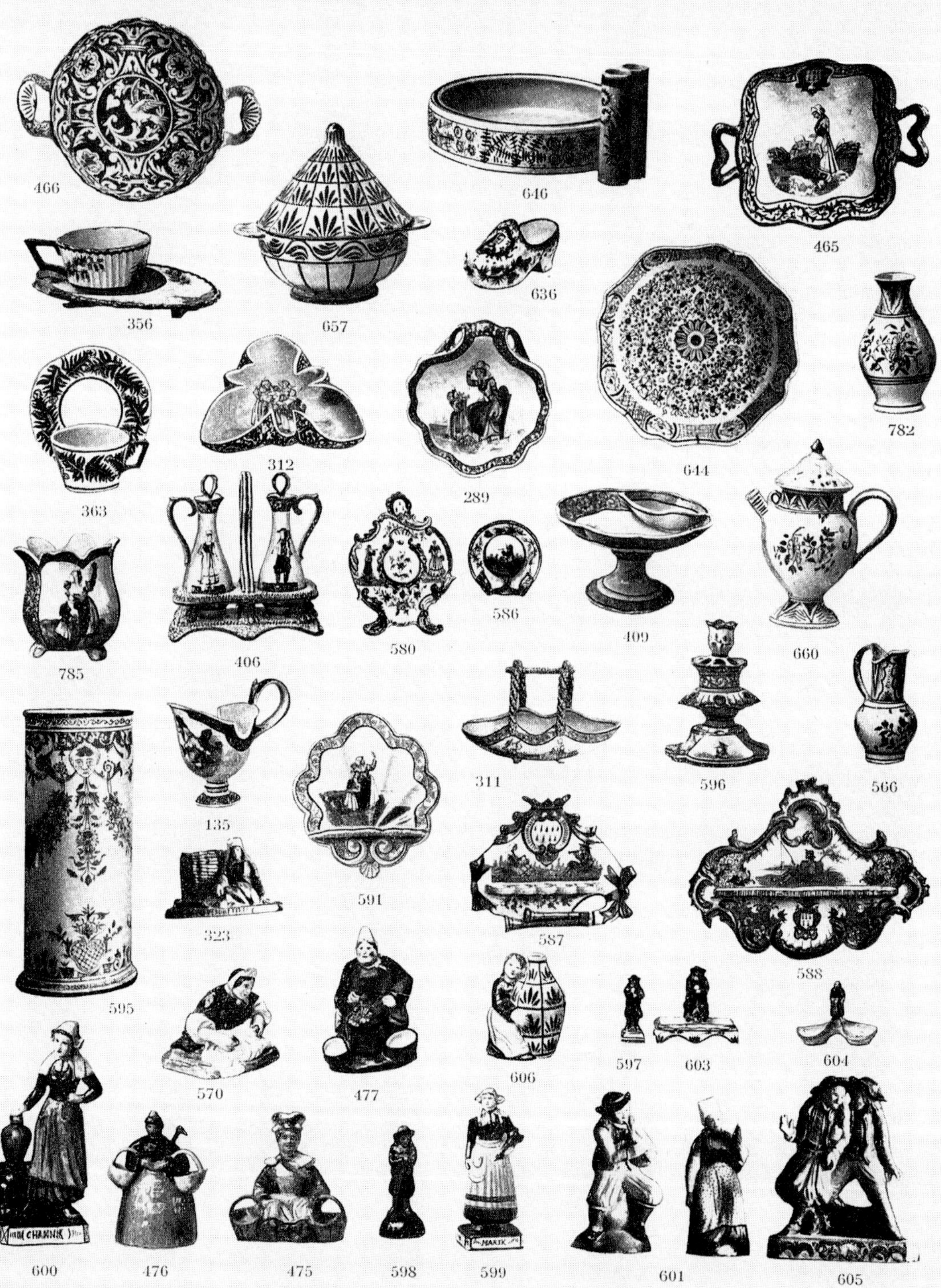

HENRIOT - QUIMPER

Décor riche - SÉRIE B - VASES - JARDINIÈRES

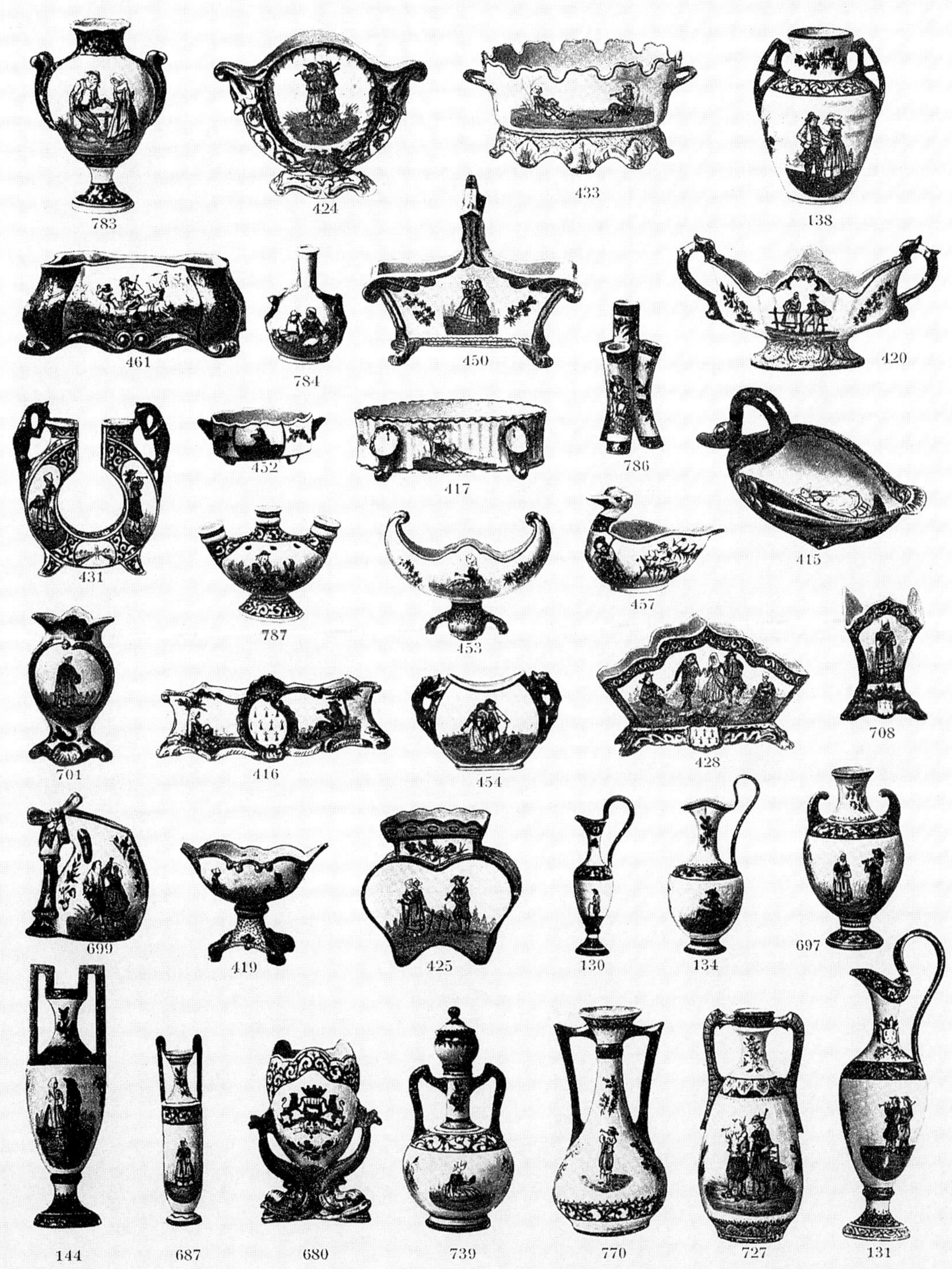

HENRIOT - QUIMPER

Décor riche - Série B - VASES - JARDINIERES

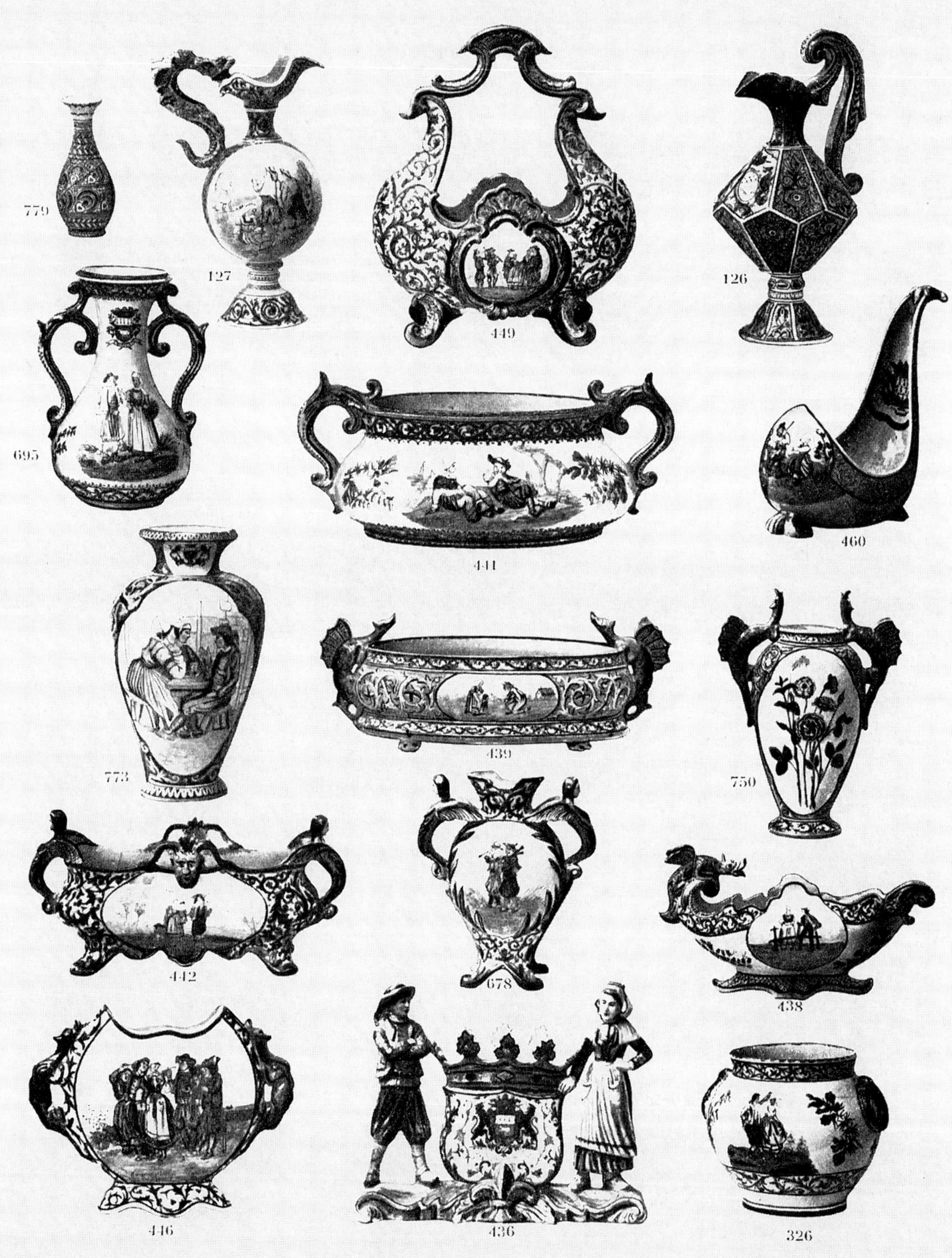

HENRIOT - QUIMPER

Décor riche - Série B - VASES - JARDINIÈRES - PENDULES

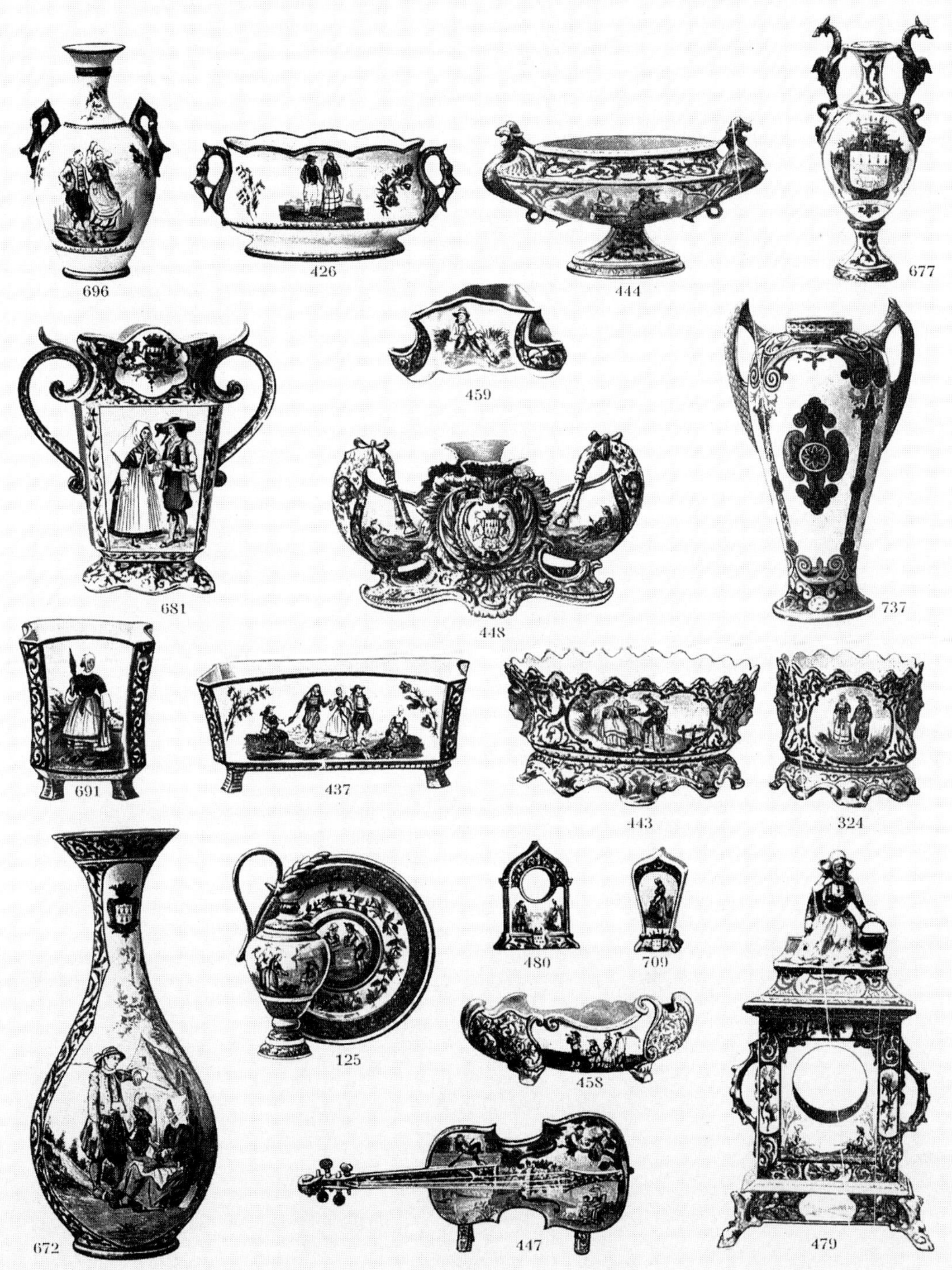

HENRIOT - QUIMPER

Décor ordinaire et demi-riche - SÉRIE A - ASSIETTES - PLATS

SERVICES DESSERT - SAUCIÈRES

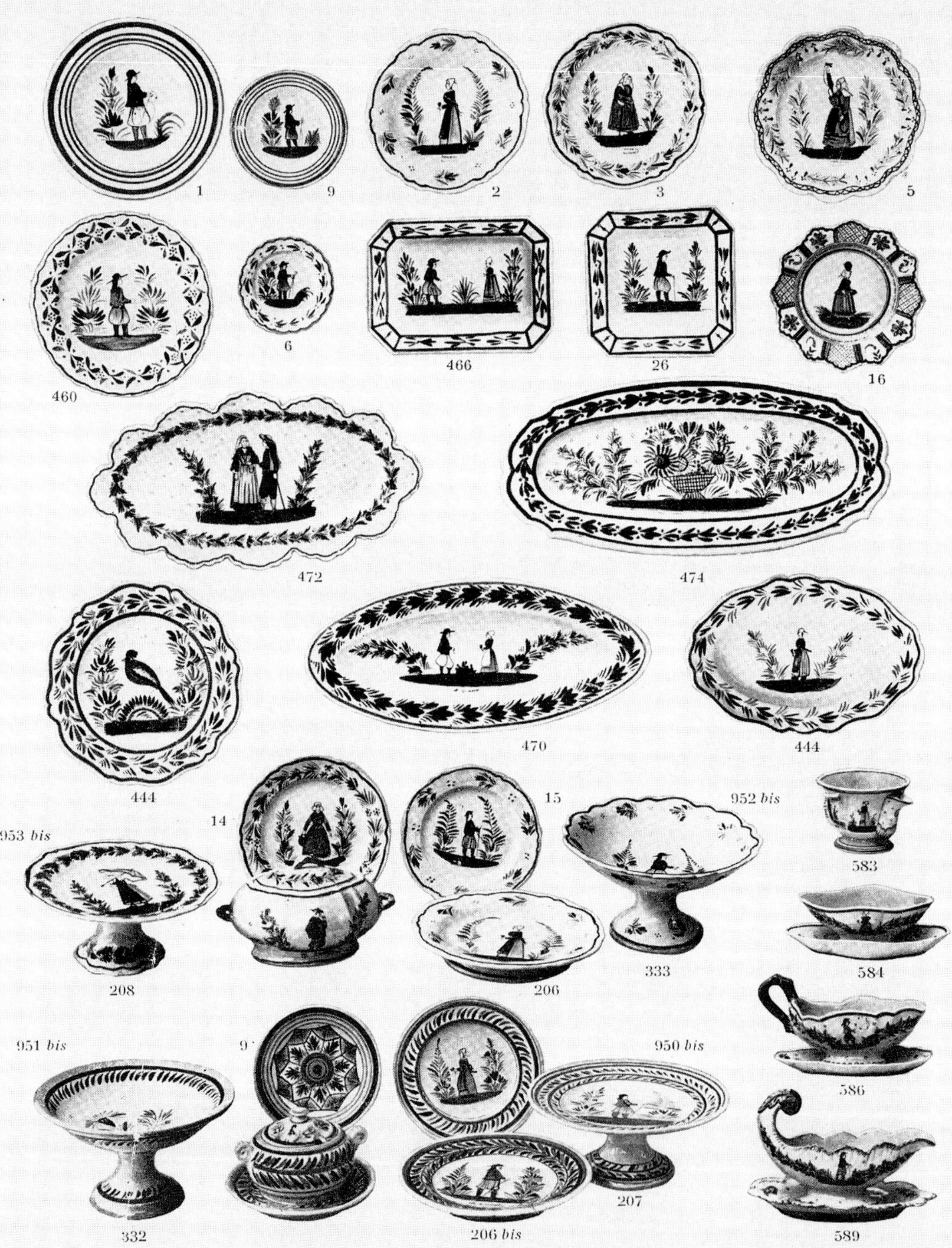

HENRIOT - QUIMPER

SERVICES DE TABLE ORDINAIRES ET DEMI-RICHES

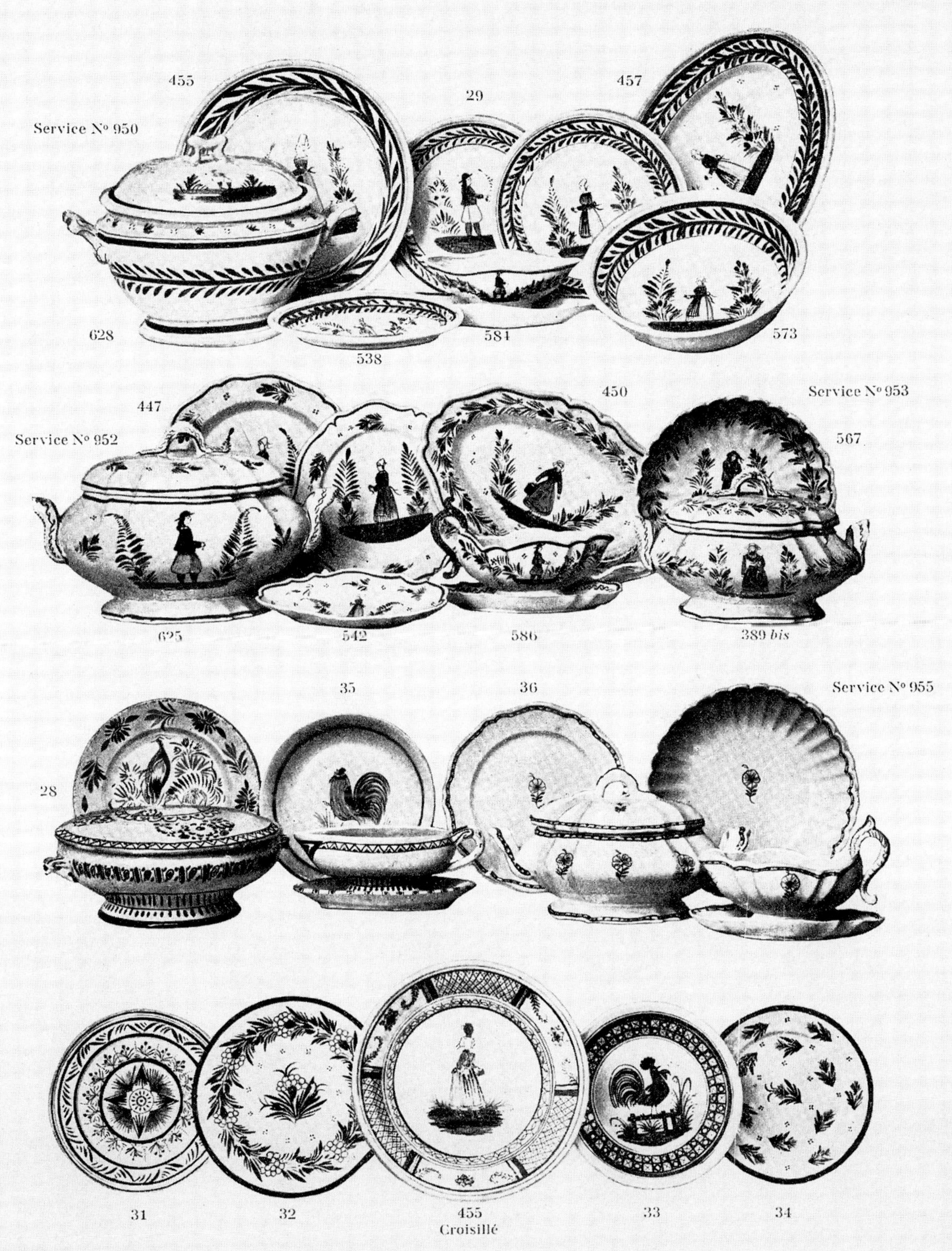

HENRIOT - QUIMPER

SÉRIE A *ordinaire et demi-riche* — APPLIQUES - BÉNITIERS

BANNETTES - BOUGEOIRS - FLAMBEAUX - BUIRES

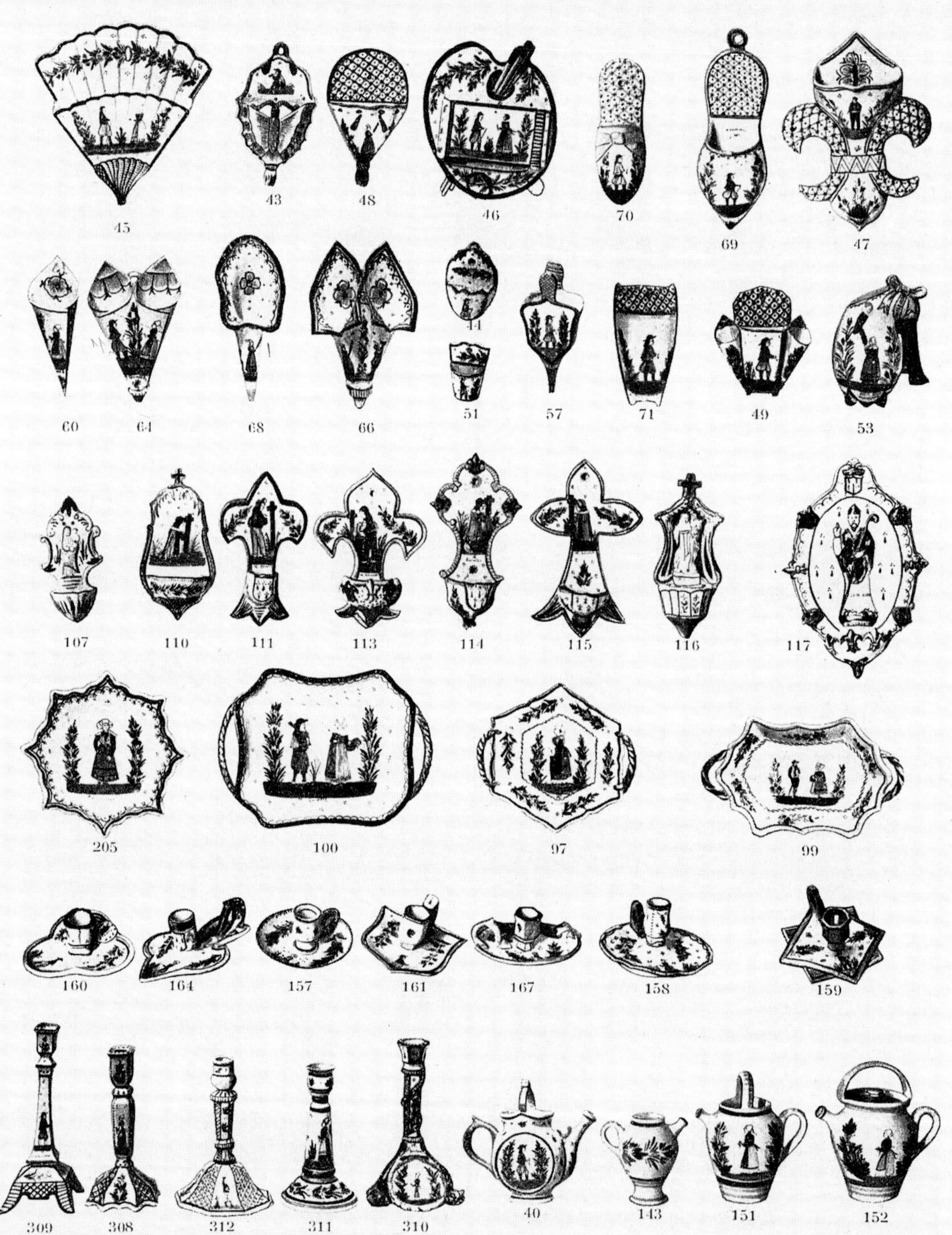

HENRIOT - QUIMPER

SÉRIE A *ordinaire et demi-riche* - BEURRIERS - BOLS - CENDRIERS COQUETIERS - CLOCHETTES - FROMAGERS

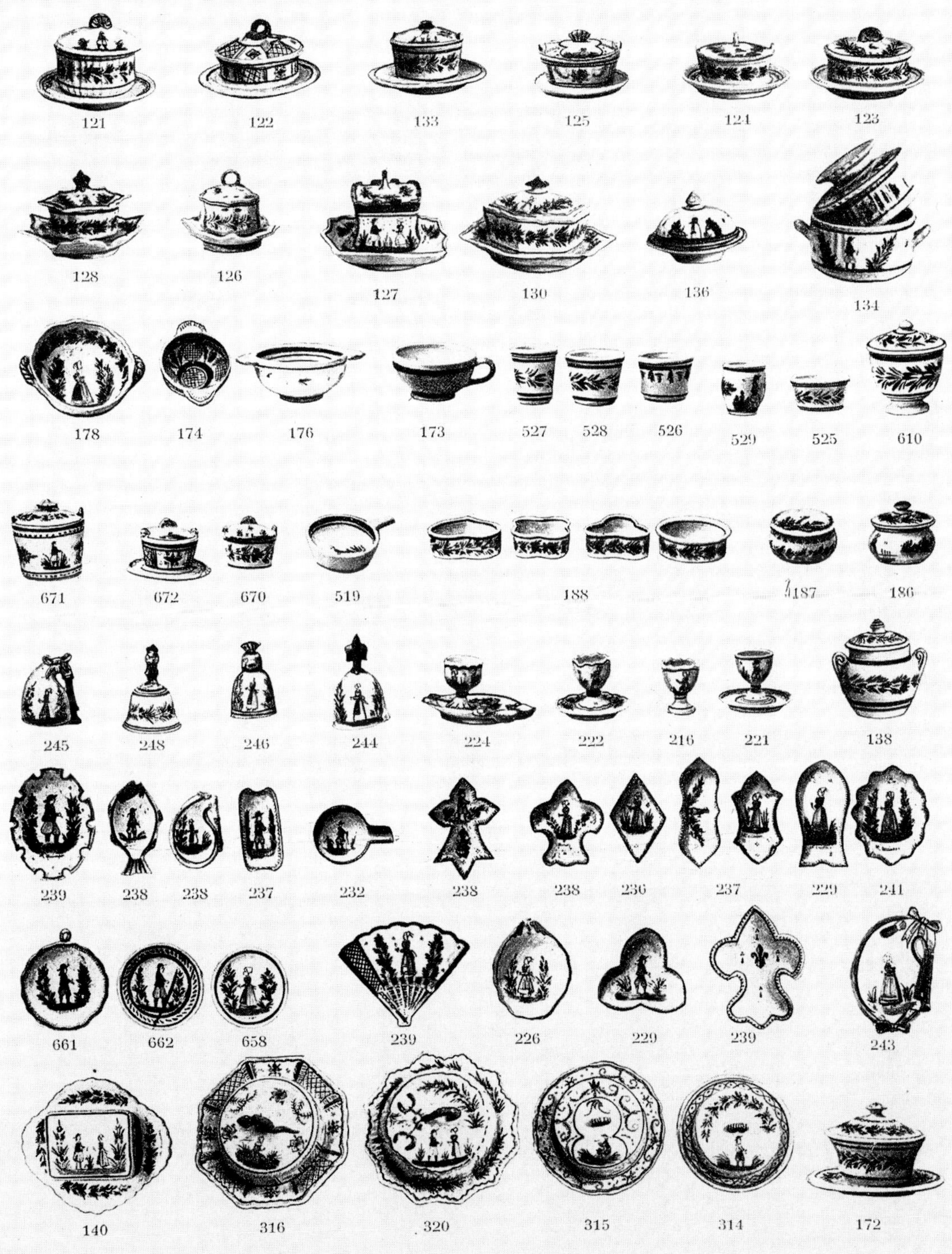

HENRIOT - QUIMPER

SÉRIE A *ordinaire et demi-riche* - PORTE-PHOTOS ET MONTRES MENUS - ENCRIERS - DESSOUS DE PLAT - HUILIERS MÉNAGÈRES - HORS-D'ŒUVRE

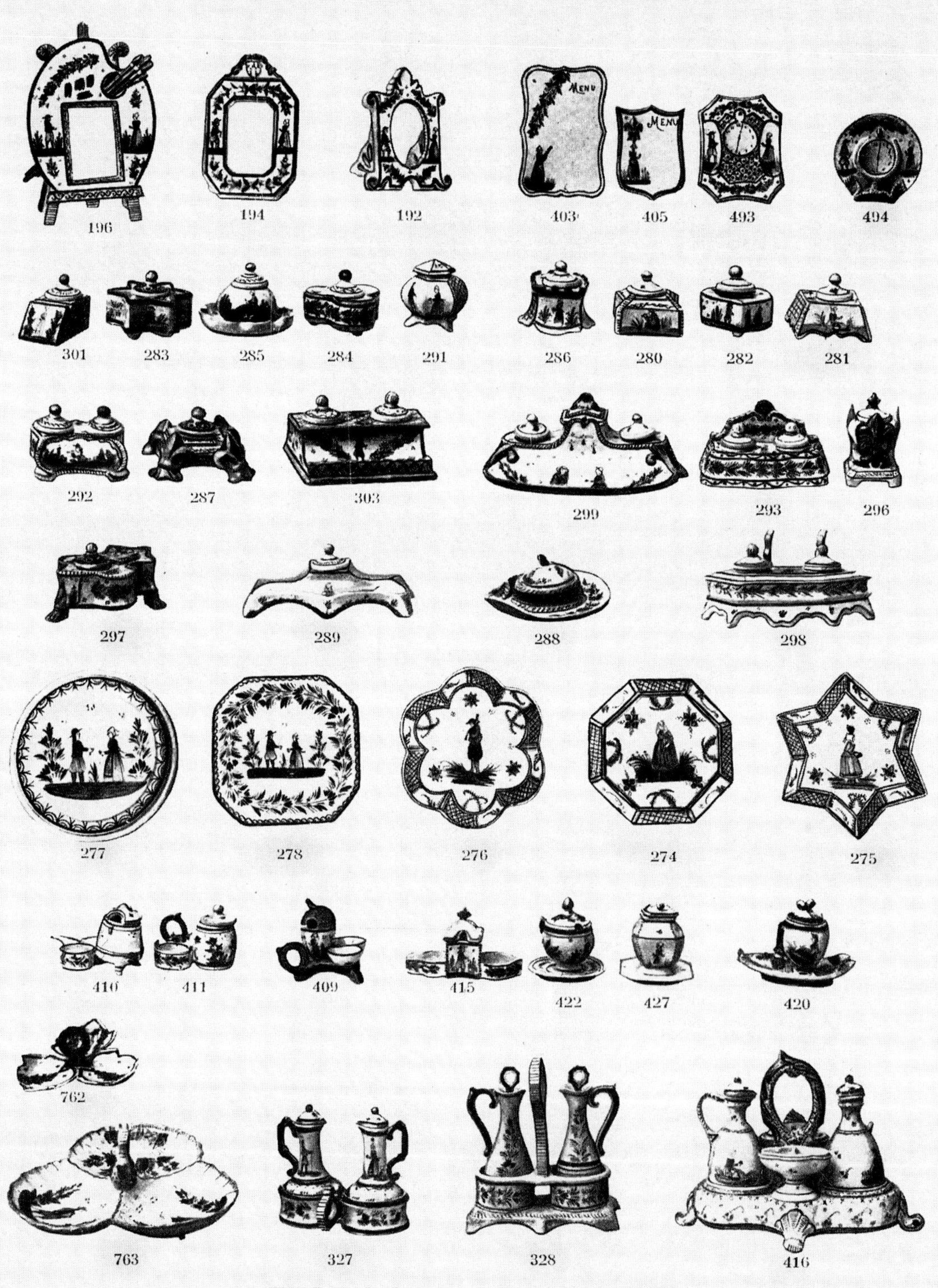

HENRIOT - QUIMPER

SÉRIE A *ordinaire et demi-riche* — PICHETS - PORTE-PIPES

SALIÈRES - RAVIERS - DÉJEUNERS

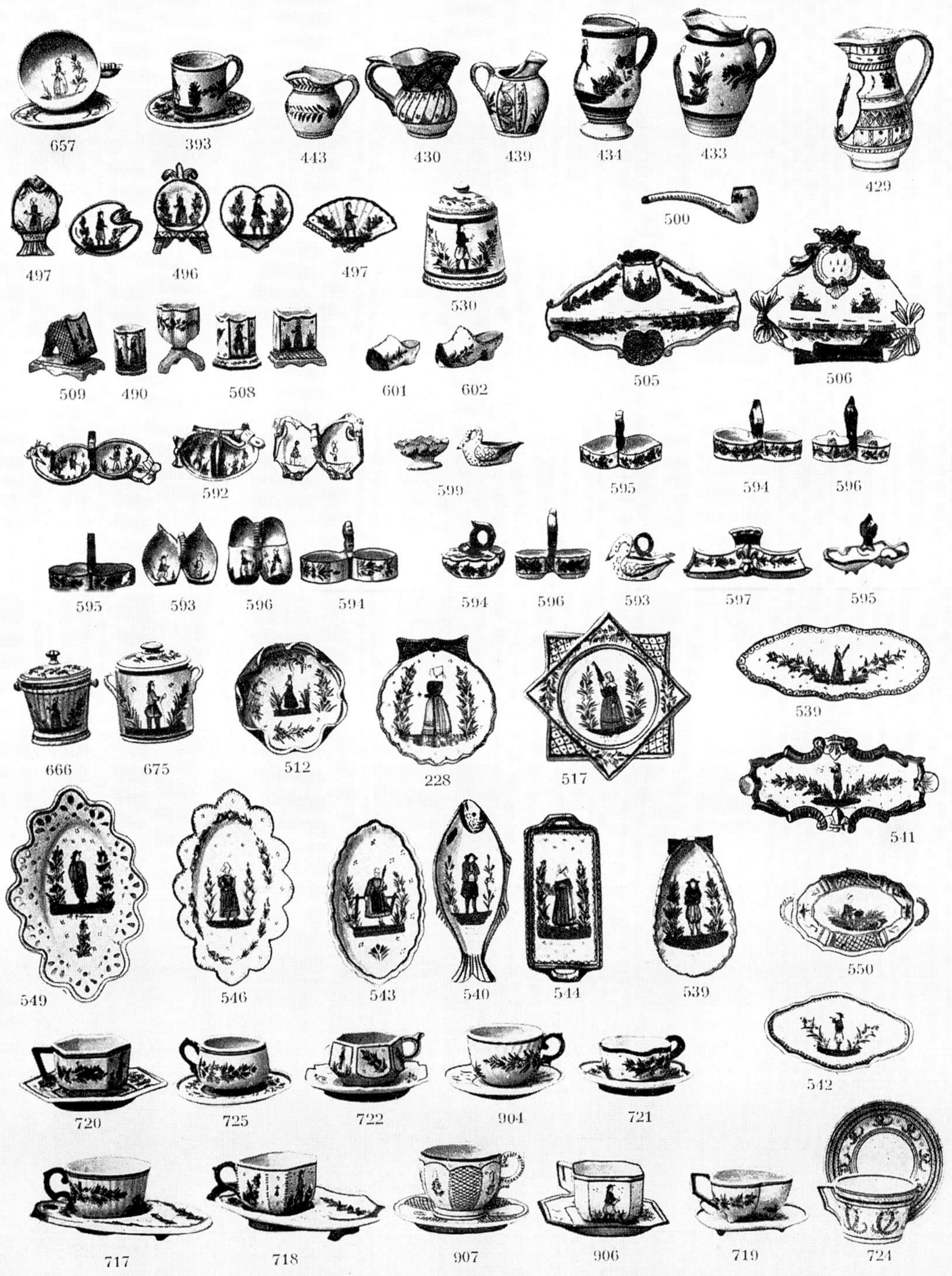

HENRIOT - QUIMPER

Décor ordinaire et demi-riche - Série A - TÊTE-A-TÊTE
SERVICES COQUETIERS - SERVICES A GATEAUX ET A CREME
SERVICES FUMEURS ET A HUITRES

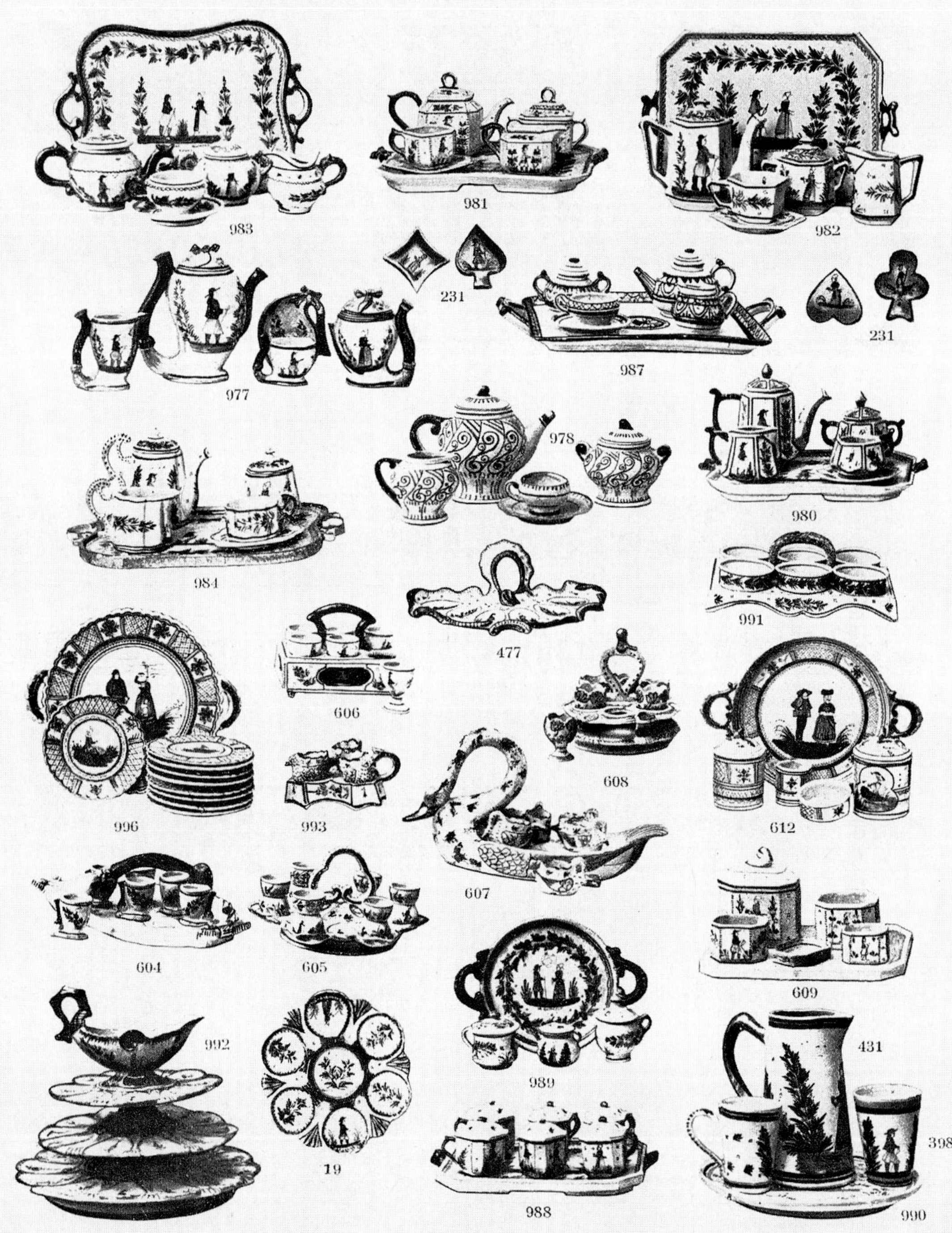

HENRIOT - QUIMPER

Décor ordinaire et demi-riche - Série A - SERVICES THÉ ET CAFÉ

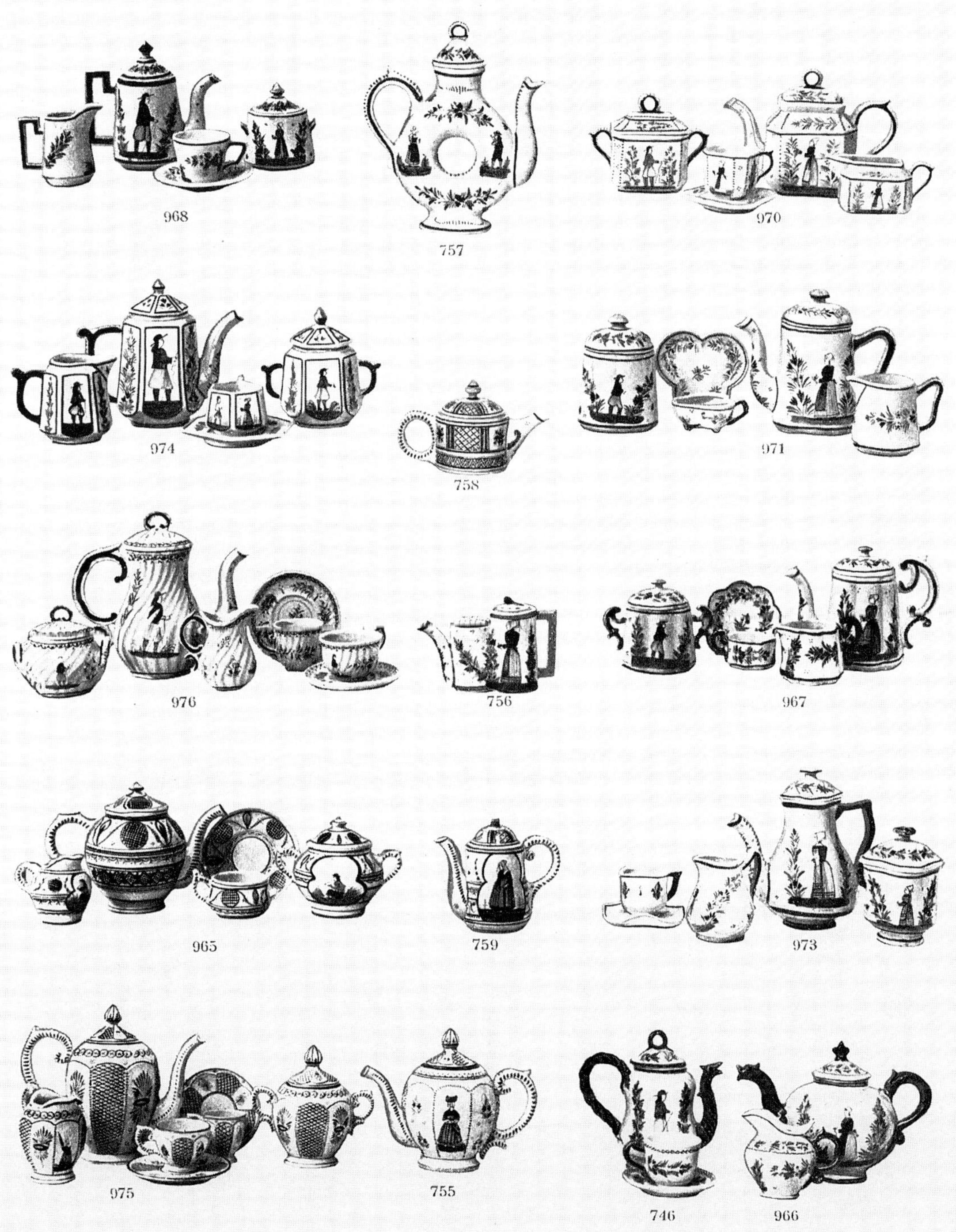

HENRIOT - QUIMPER

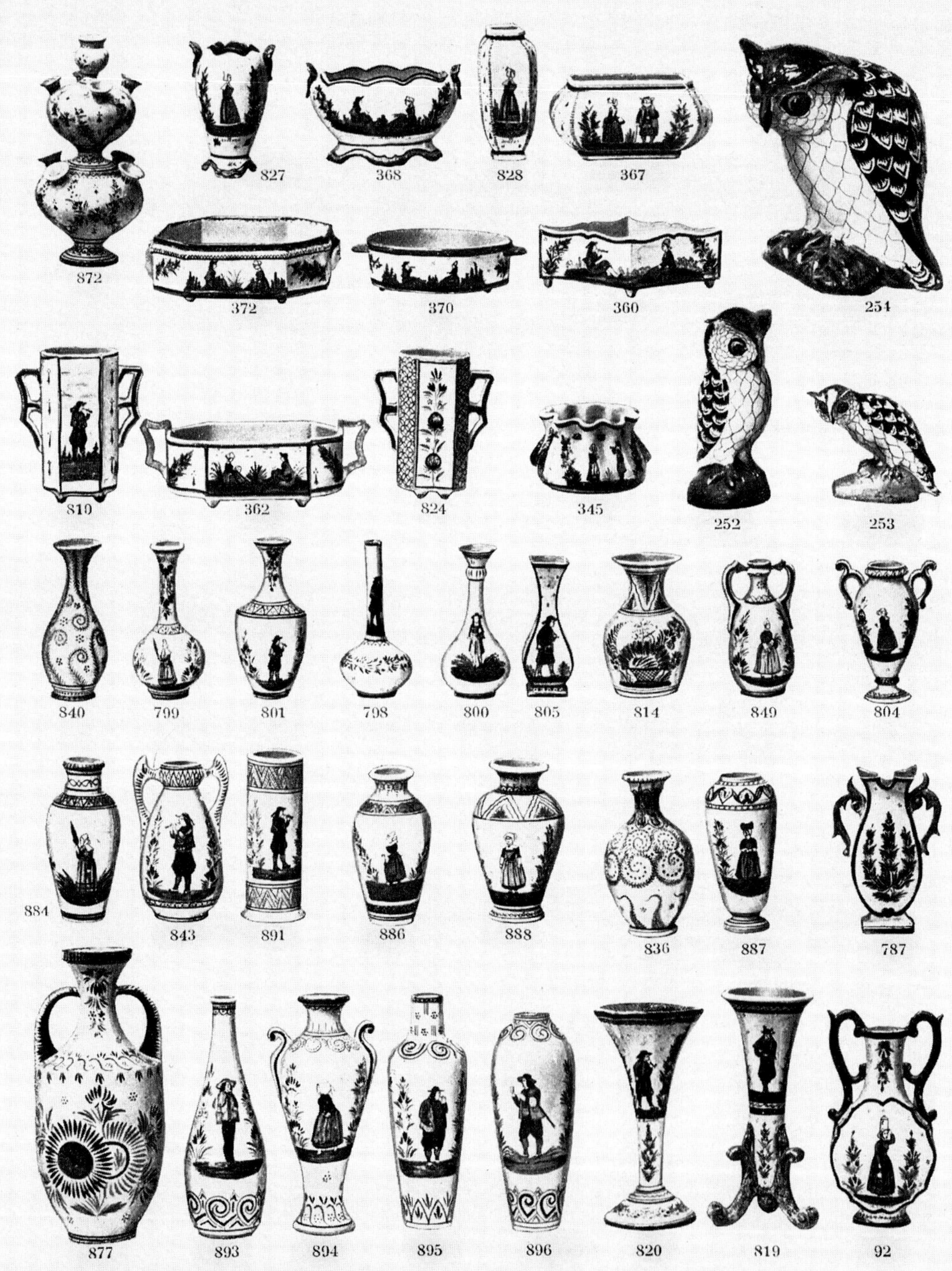

HENRIOT - QUIMPER

Décor ordinaire et demi-riche - SÉRIE A - VASES ET JARDINIÈRES

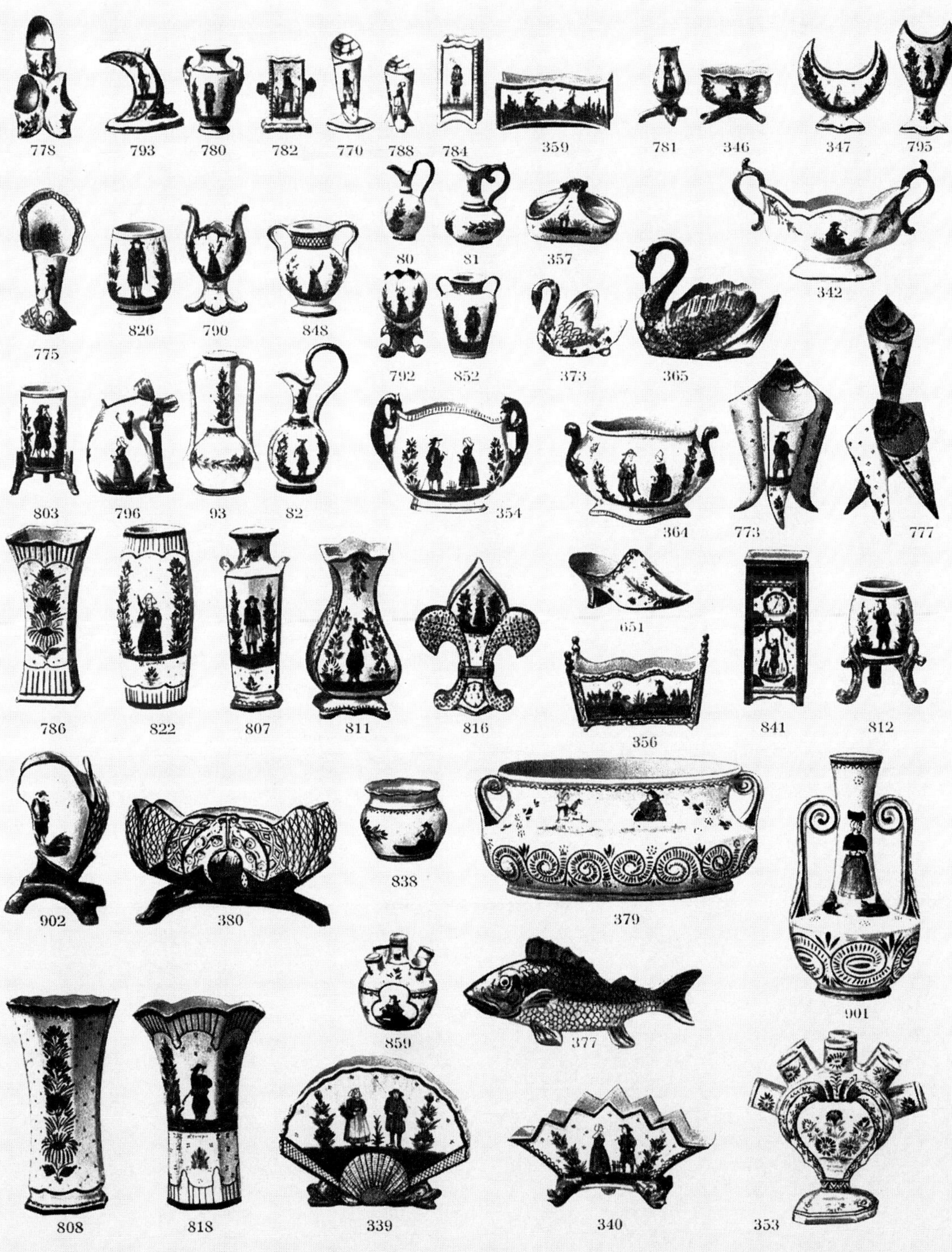

HENRIOT - QUIMPER

Décor ordinaire - SÉRIE A - SOUPIÈRES - SALADIERS

VAPORISATEURS - JOUETS - CORBEILLES - STATUES

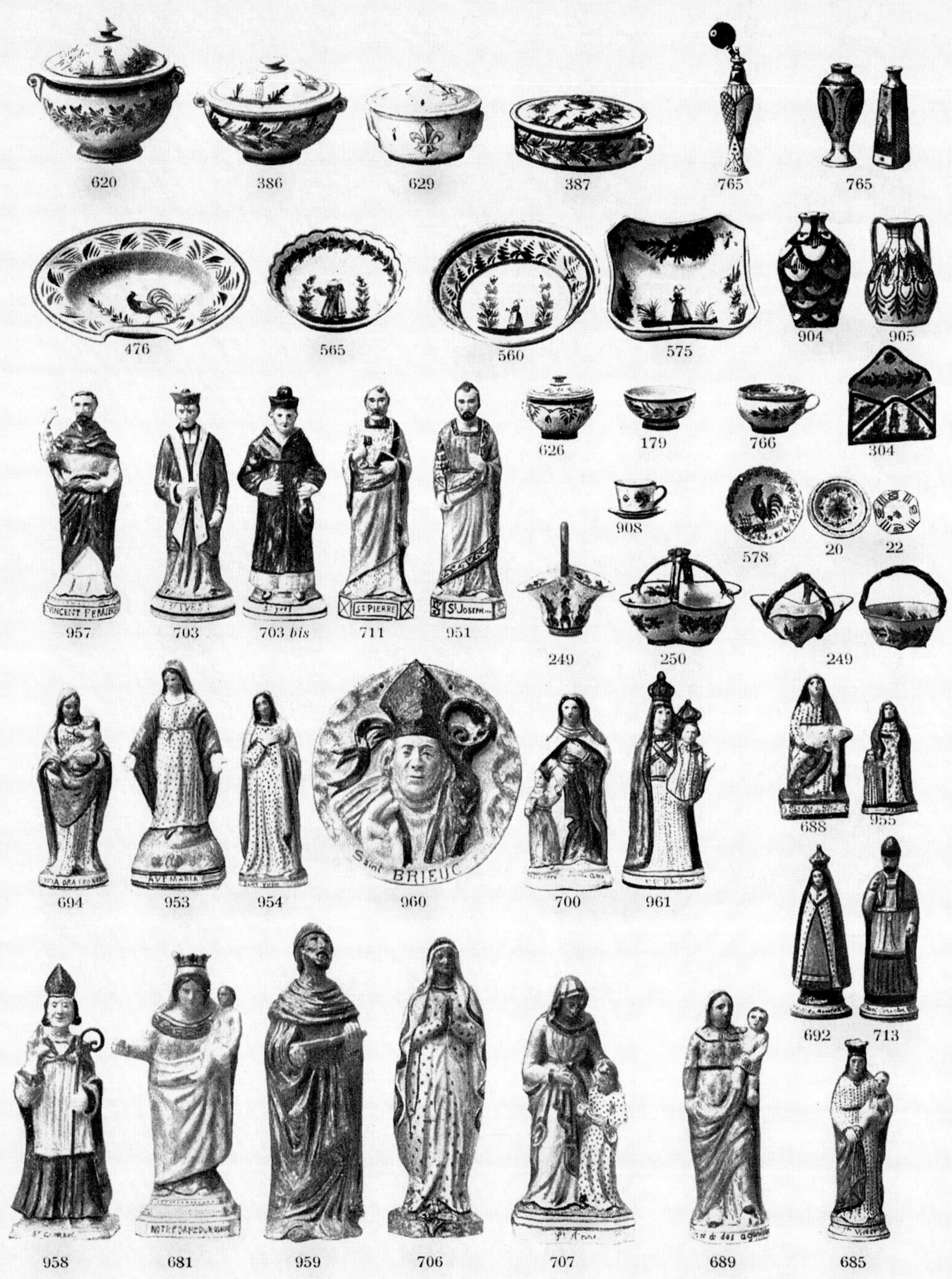

HENRIOT - QUIMPER

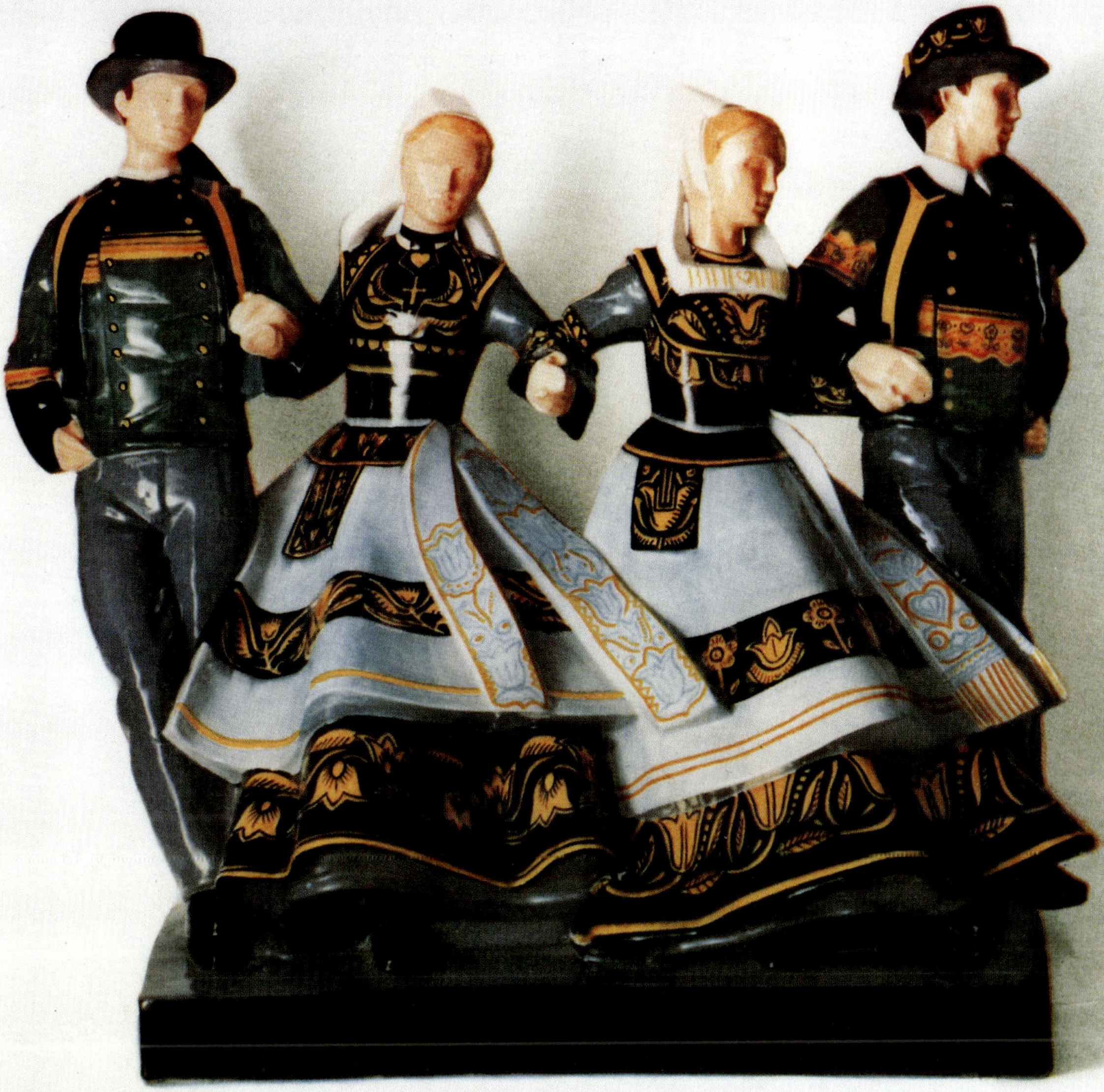

FAÏENCERIE

HENRIOT

QUIMPER

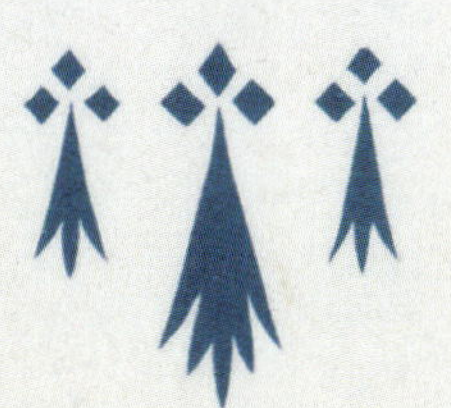

HENRIOT - QUIMPER

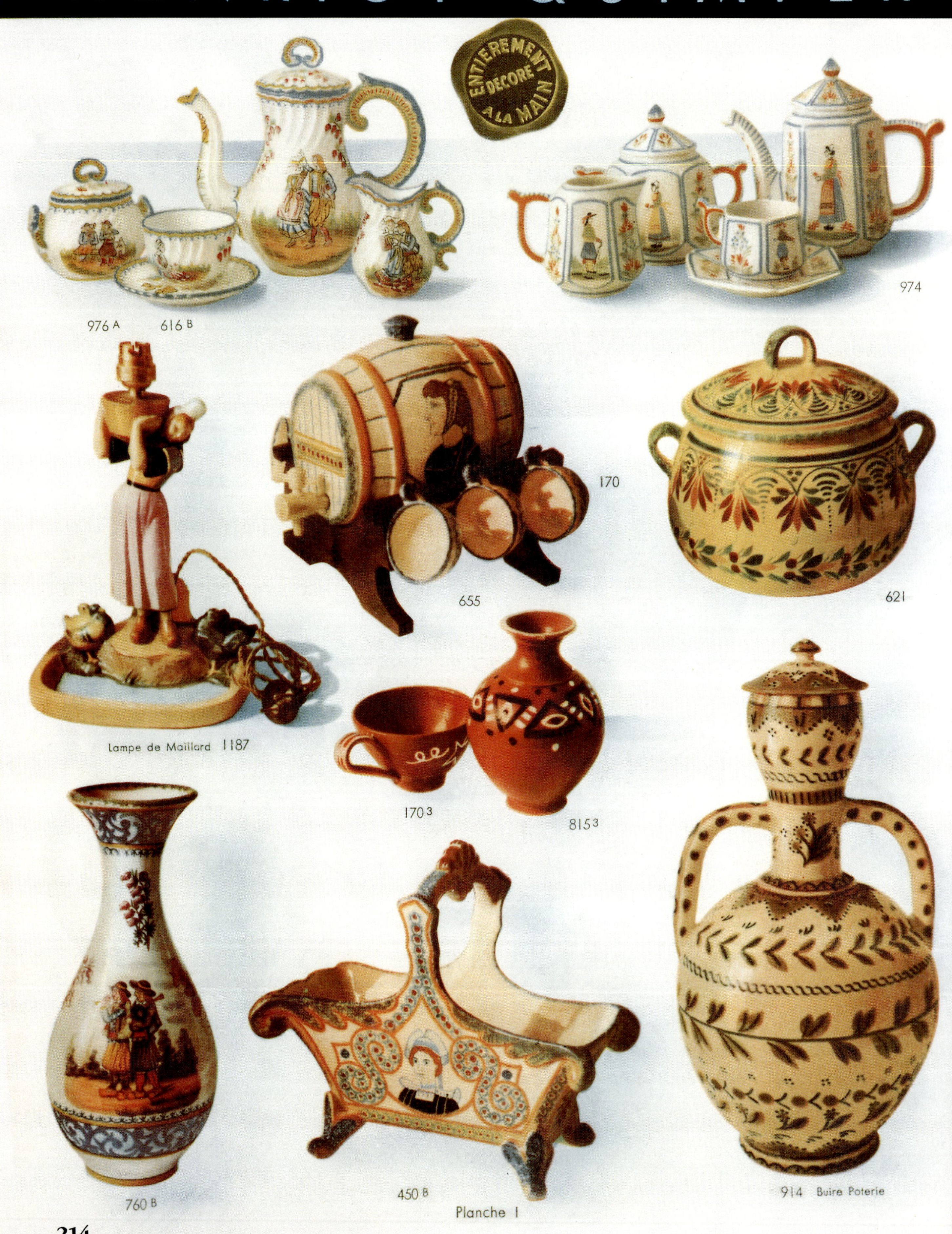

976 A 616 B

974

170

655

621

Lampe de Maillard 1187

170 3

815 3

760 B

450 B

Planche I

914 Buire Poterie

HENRIOT-QUIMPER

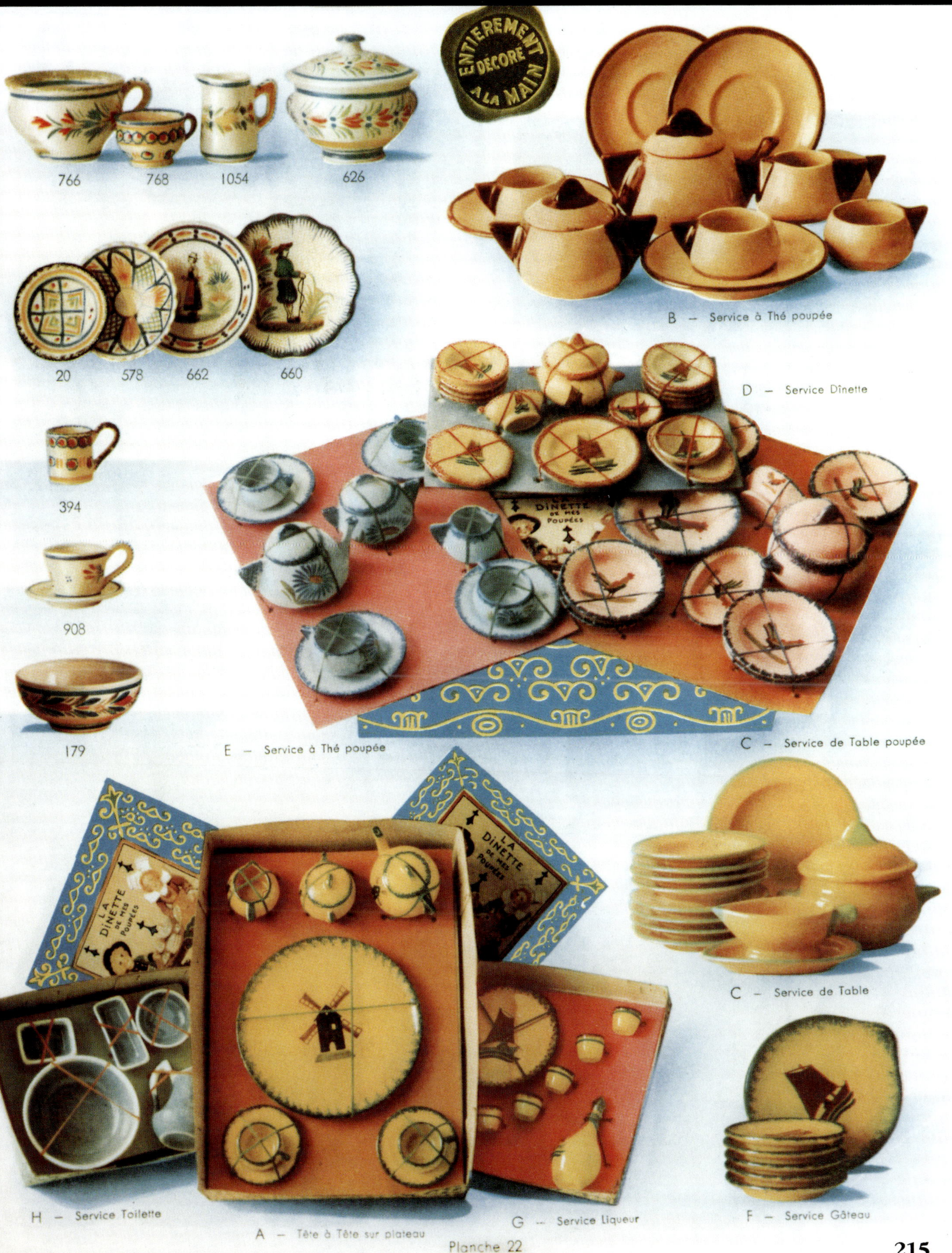

B – Service à Thé poupée

D – Service Dînette

E – Service à Thé poupée

C – Service de Table poupée

C – Service de Table

H – Service Toilette

A – Tête à Tête sur plateau

G – Service Liqueur

F – Service Gâteau

Planche 22

HENRIOT · QUIMPER

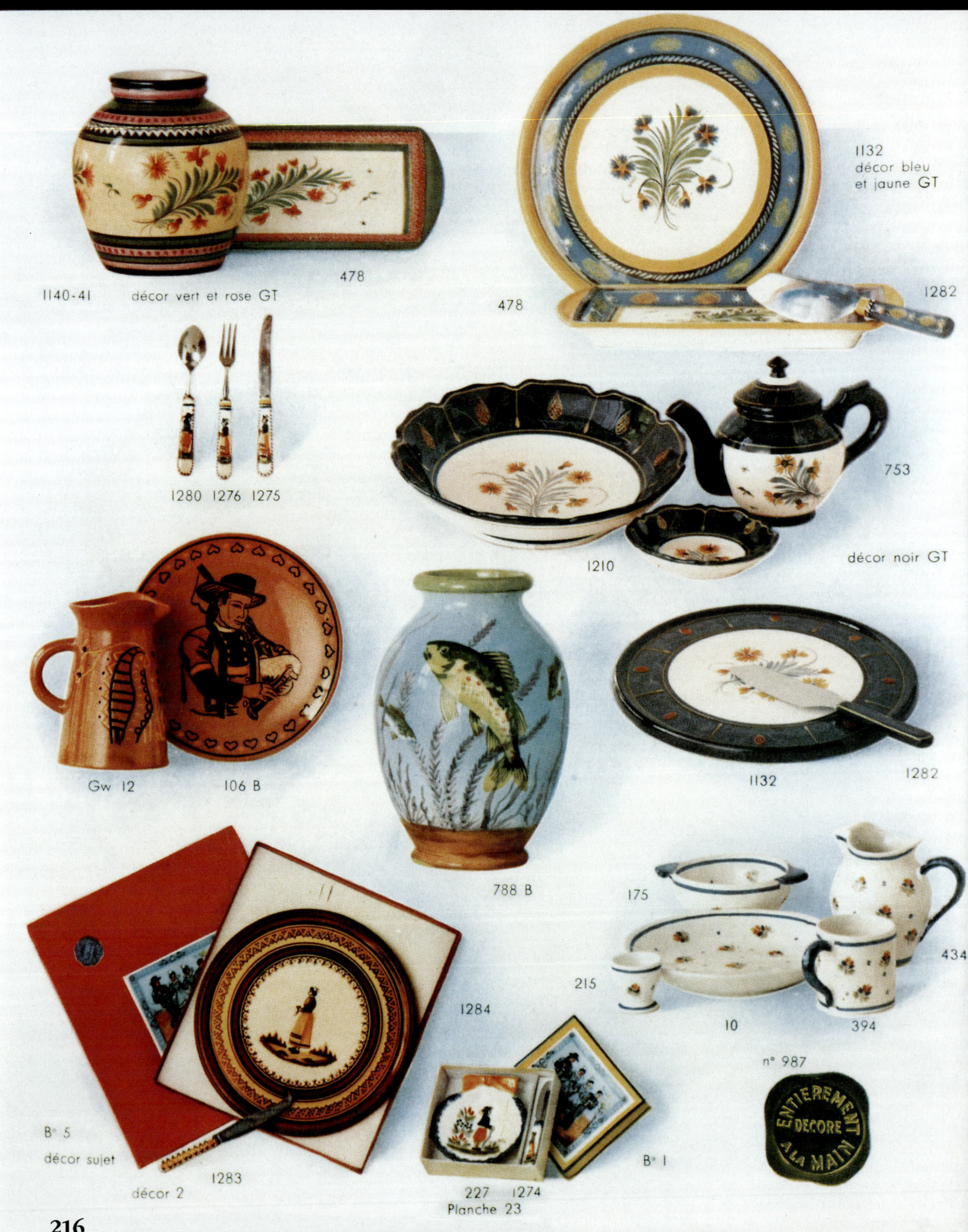

HENRIOT - QUIMPER

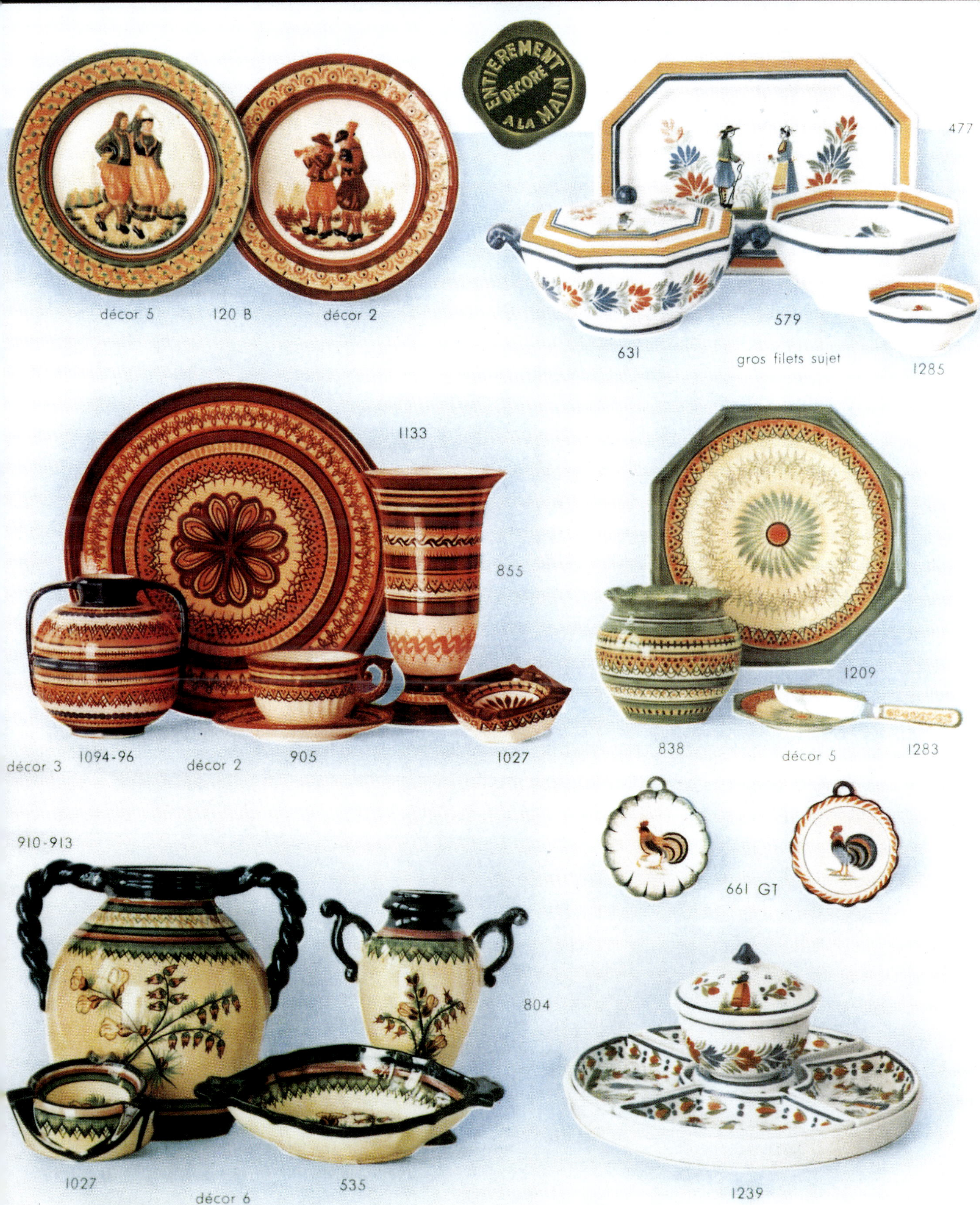

Planche 24

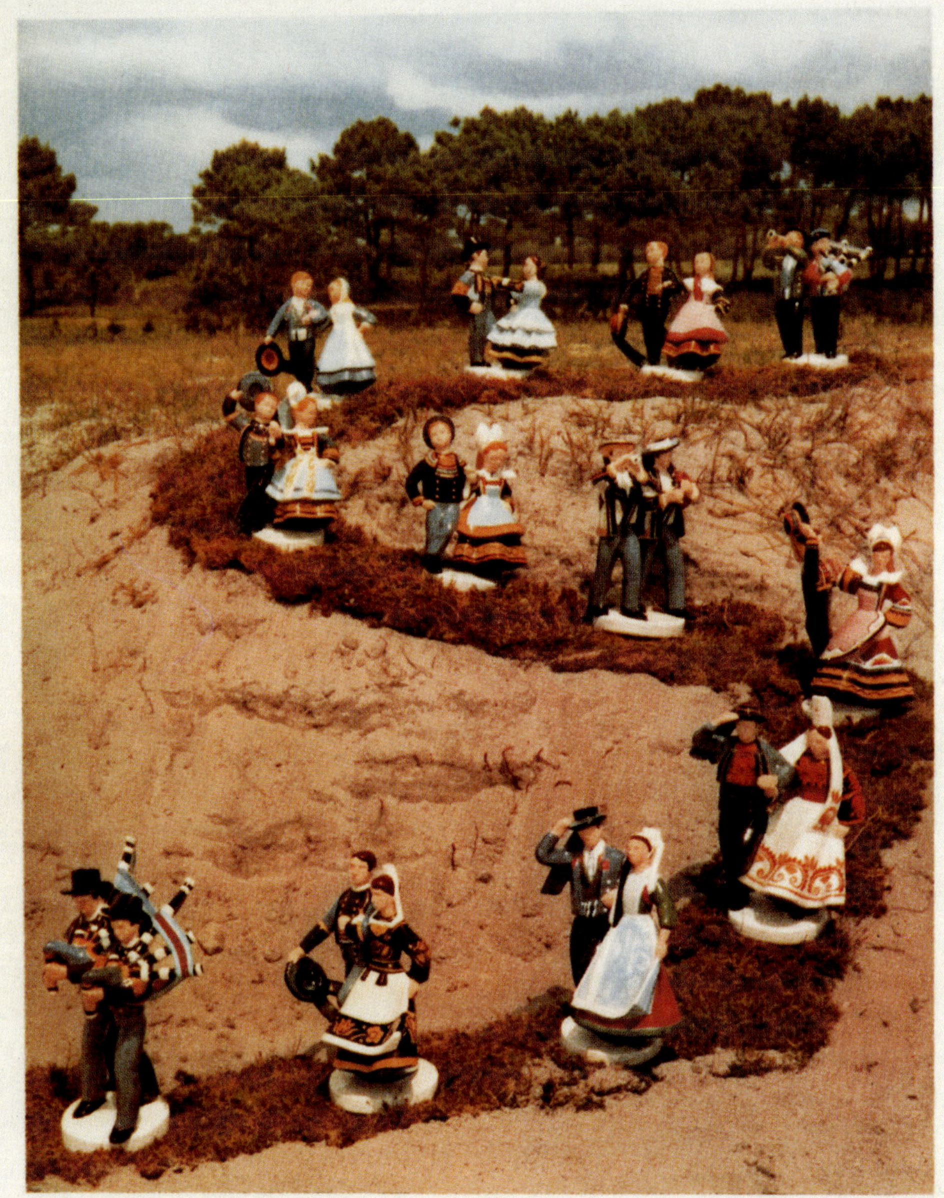

cliché Kerisit, Quimper

MICHEAU-VERNEZ

HENRIOT QUIMPER

IMP. BEUCHET & VANDEN BRUGGE — NANTES-PARIS

HENRIOT-QUIMPER

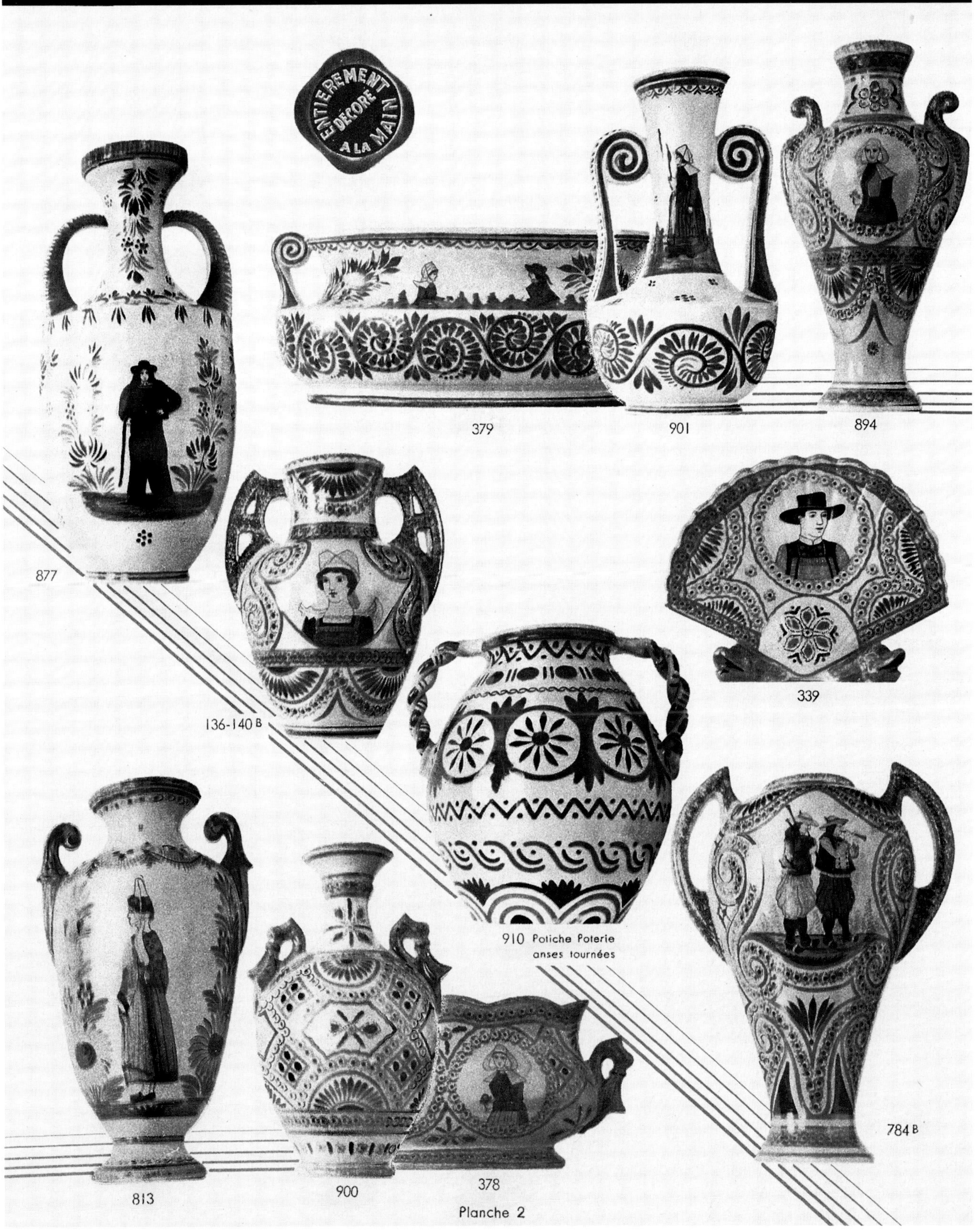

Planche 2

HENRIOT - QUIMPER

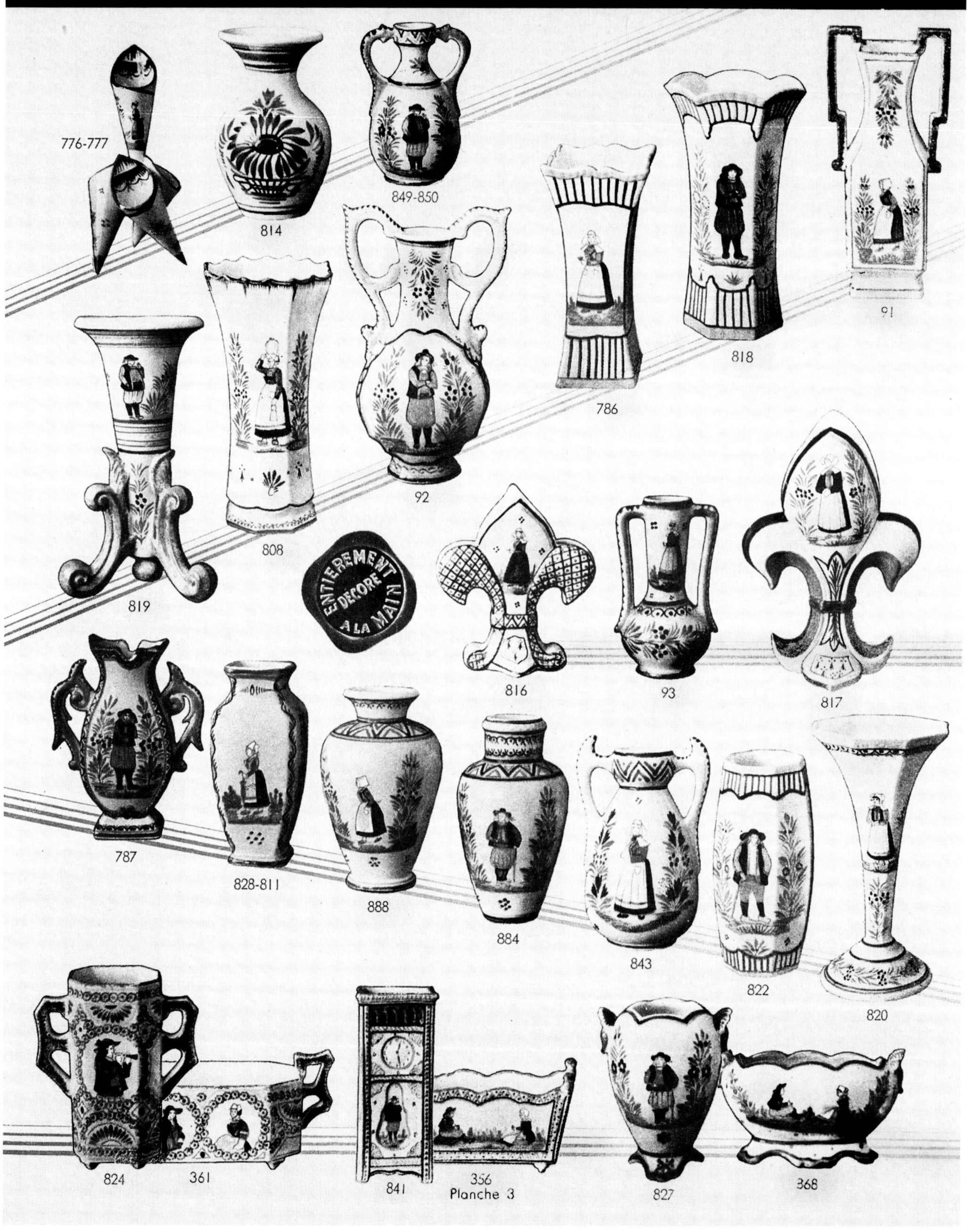

Planche 3

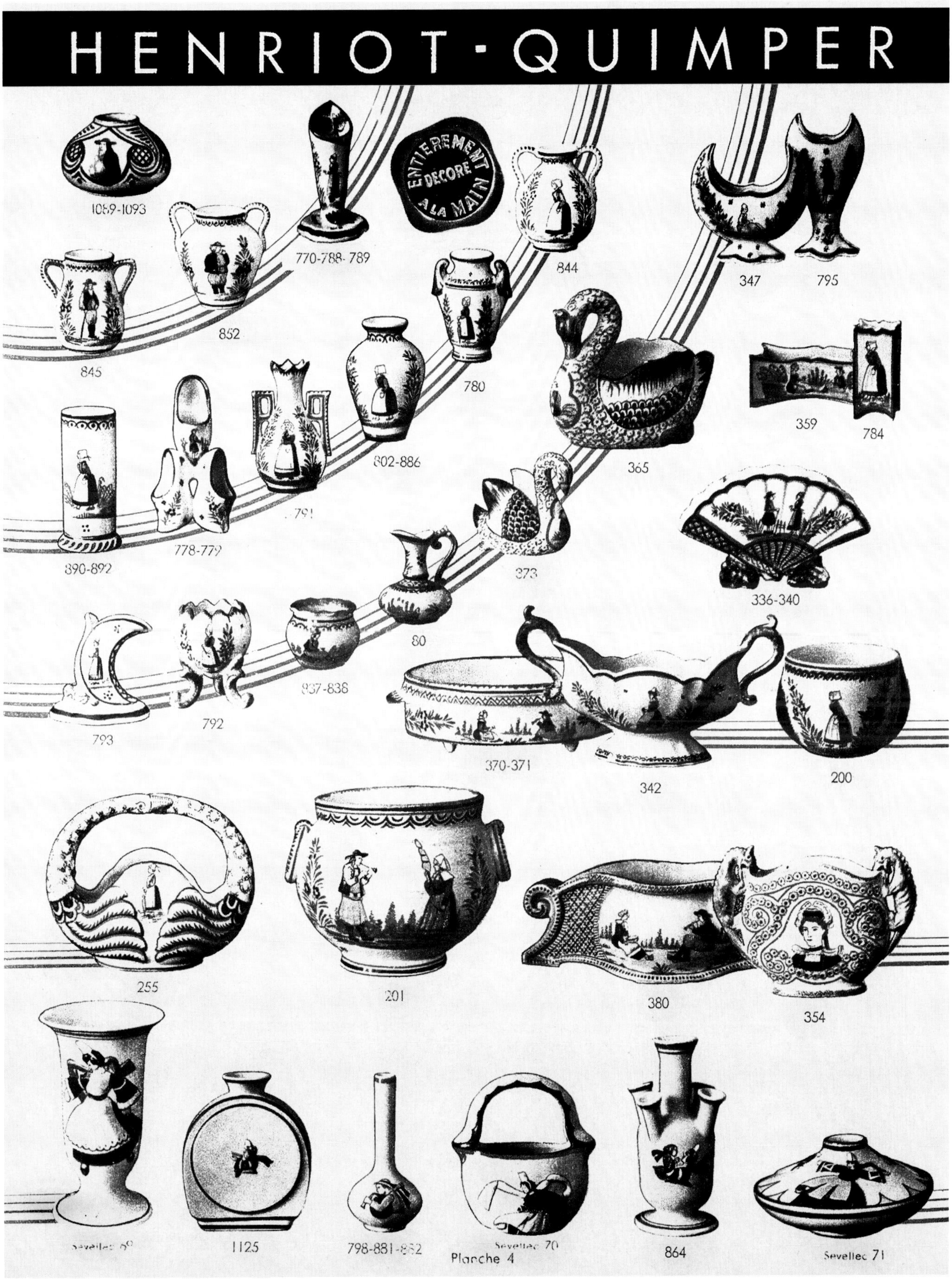

HENRIOT · QUIMPER

ENTIEREMENT DECORE A LA MAIN

1089-1093

770-788-789

844

347 795

852

845

780

359 784

802-886

365

890-892

778-779

791

873

336-340

80

793

792

837-838

370-371

342

200

255

201

380

354

Sevellec 69

1125

798-881-852

Sevellec 70

864

Sevellec 71

Planche 4

HENRIOT - QUIMPER
88
799-897
800-879
839-840
801-875
806
86
803
1094-1096
848
82
85
85
85
55-57
775
796-797
771-773
861
1072-1073
872
352-353
862
858-860
865-867
1120
1125-27
ENTIÈREMENT DÉCORÉ A LA MAIN
790
1128-1129
868-869

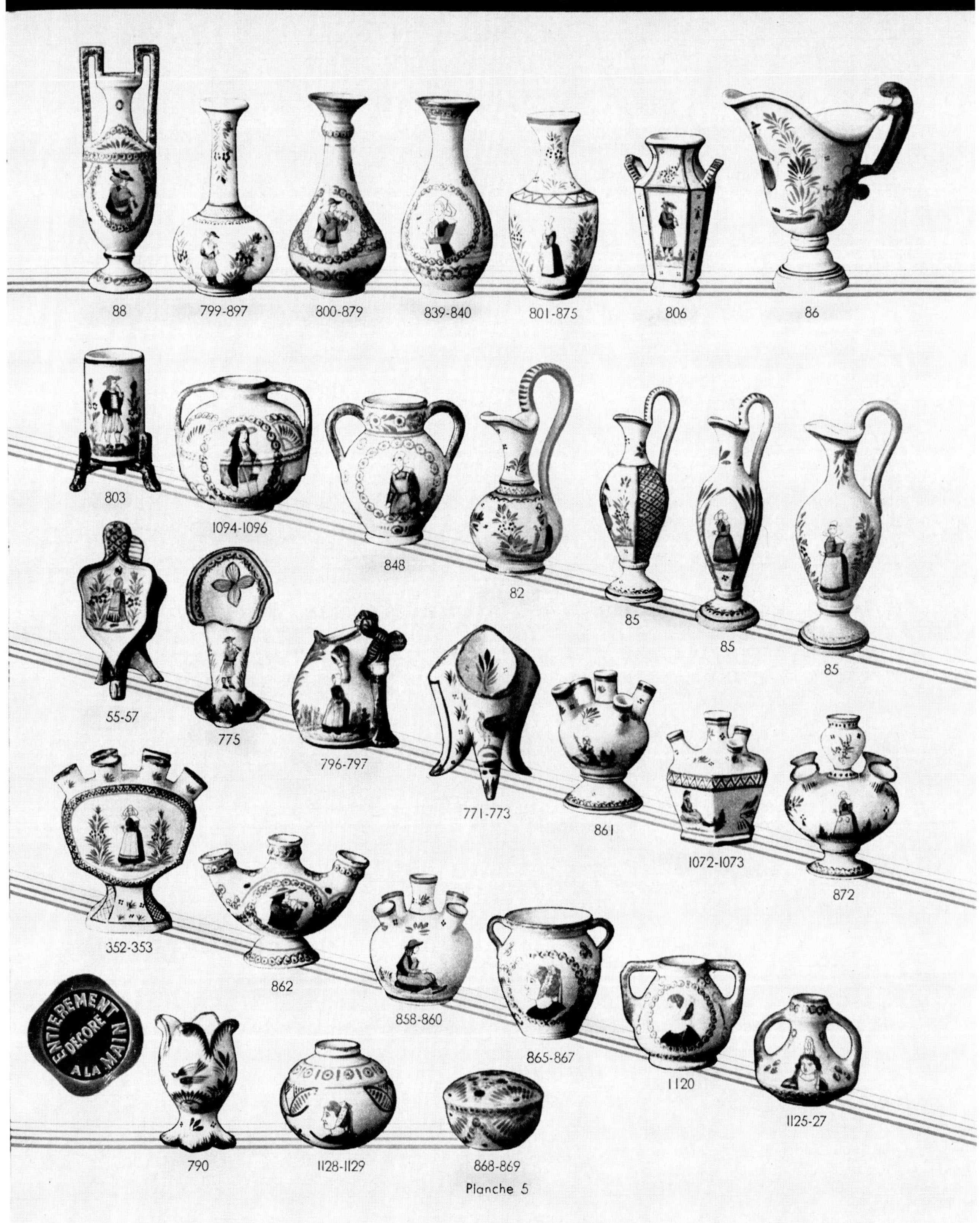

Planche 5

HENRIOT-QUIMPER

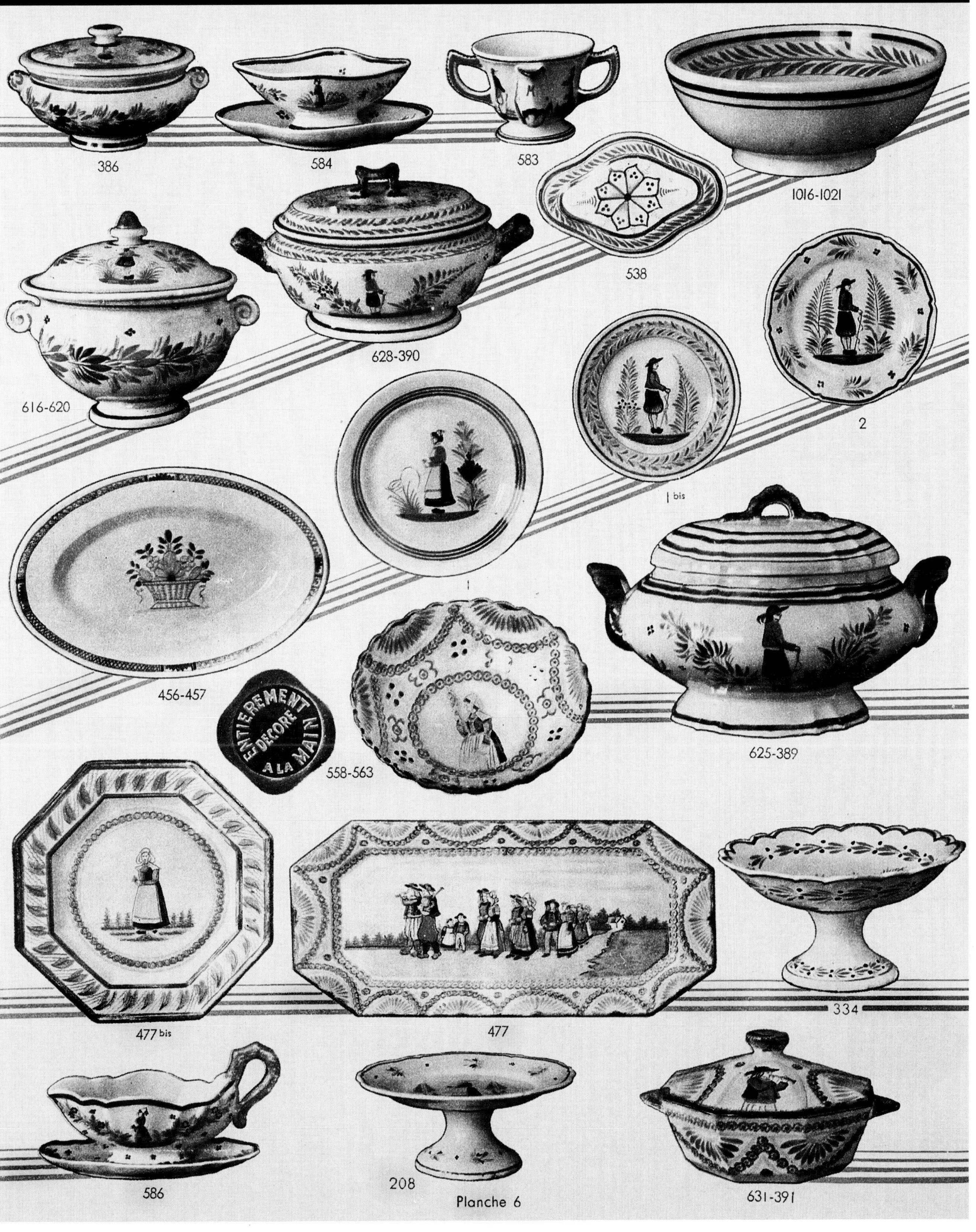

Planche 6

HENRIOT · QUIMPER
481
1100
39
465-469
1101
462
558-563
ENTIEREMENT DECORE A LA MAIN
26
459
475
18
471-559 B
470
473-474
Planche 7

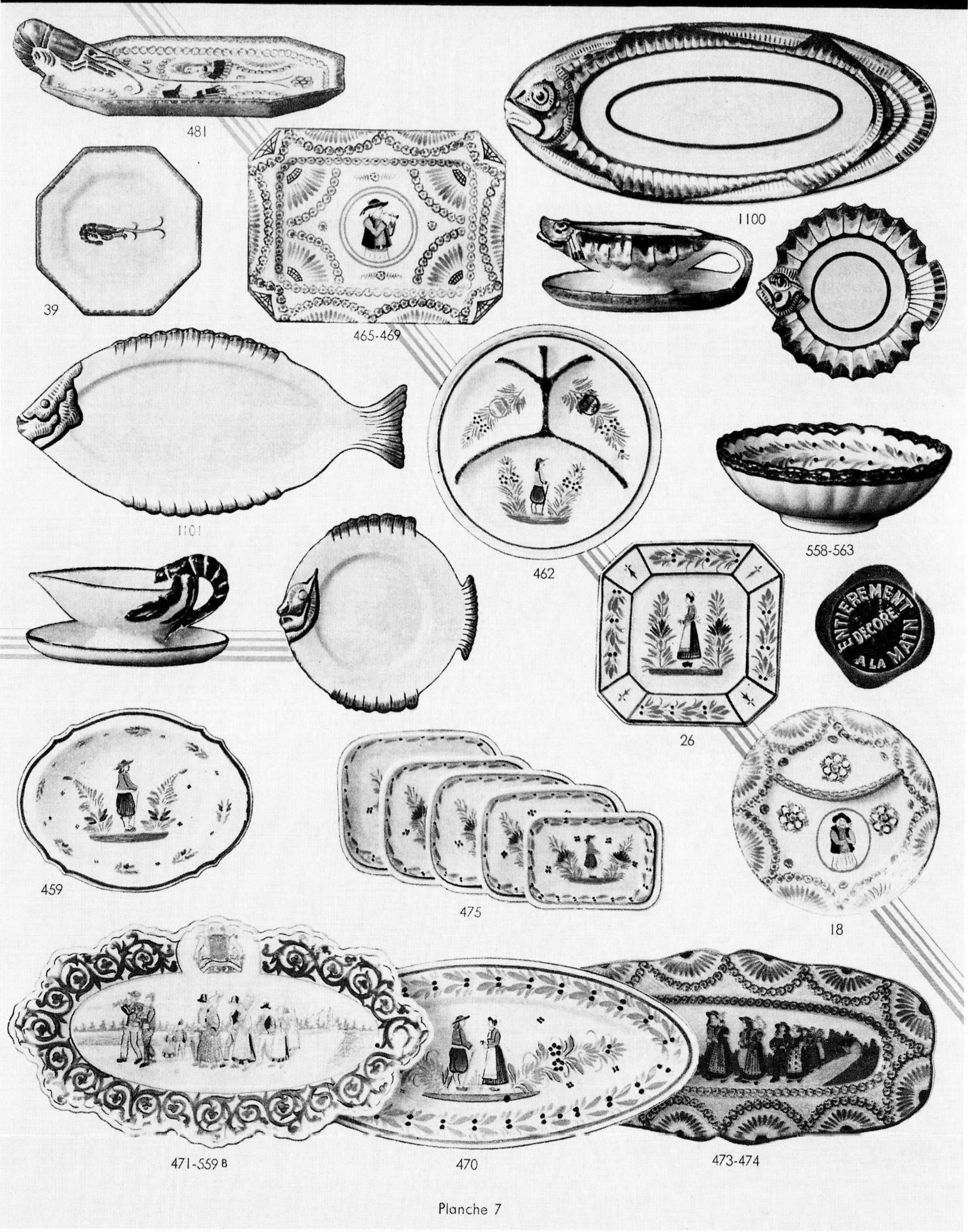

HENRIOT - QUIMPER
125
120-121
1086
318
136-137
134-135
1085
122
130
140
1007-1010
670
673 675
527
530
528
527
527
529
525
526
671
124
320
316
666-667
133
185-255 B
314-315
142-234 B
672
316 bis
185-255 B
131-132
266
185-255 B
1085 bis
317-403 B
265
185-255 B
B 29
180
L 140
185-255 B
185-255 B
186-269 B
185-255 B
148
251 B
L 141
627
185-255 B
252 B
Planche 8

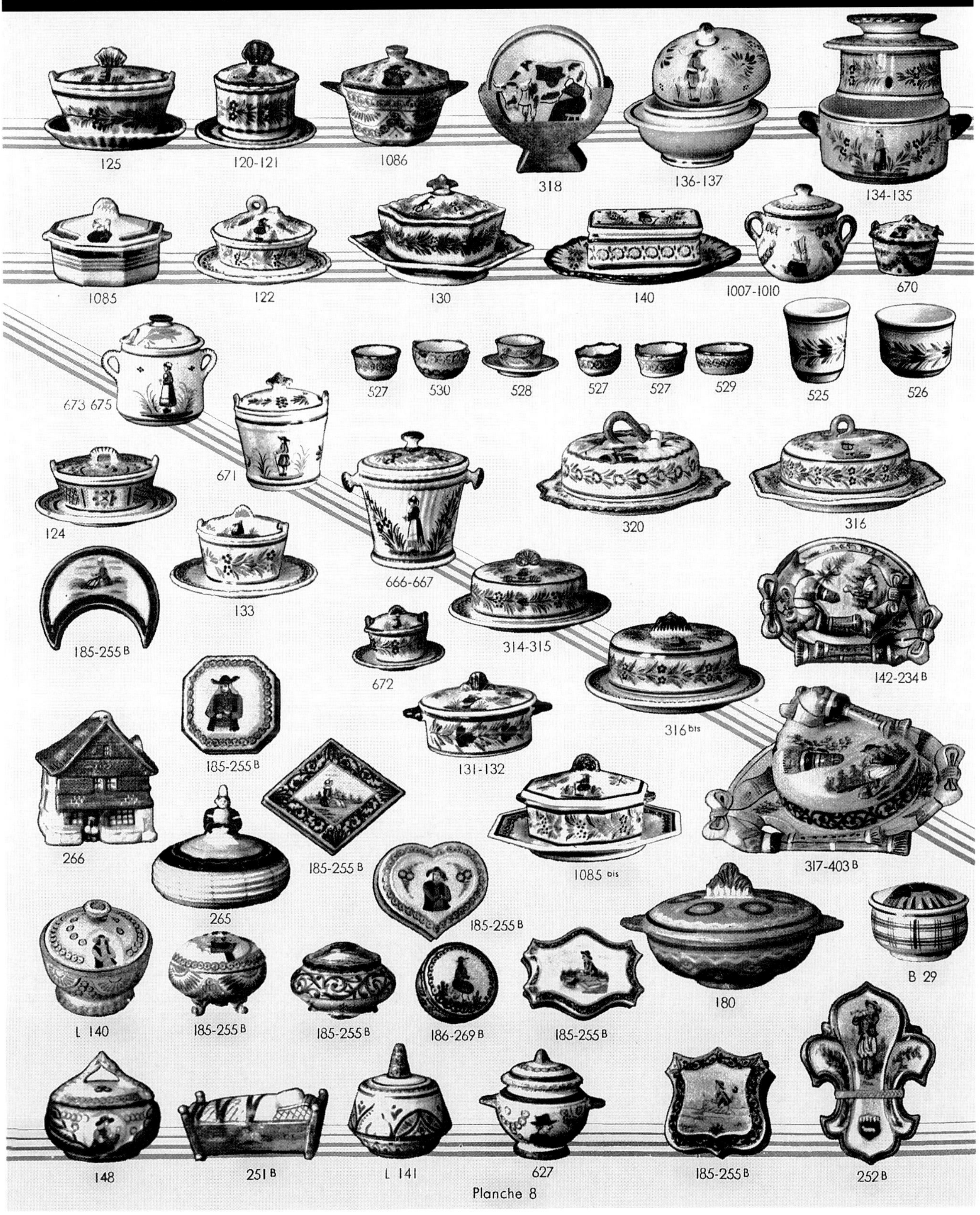

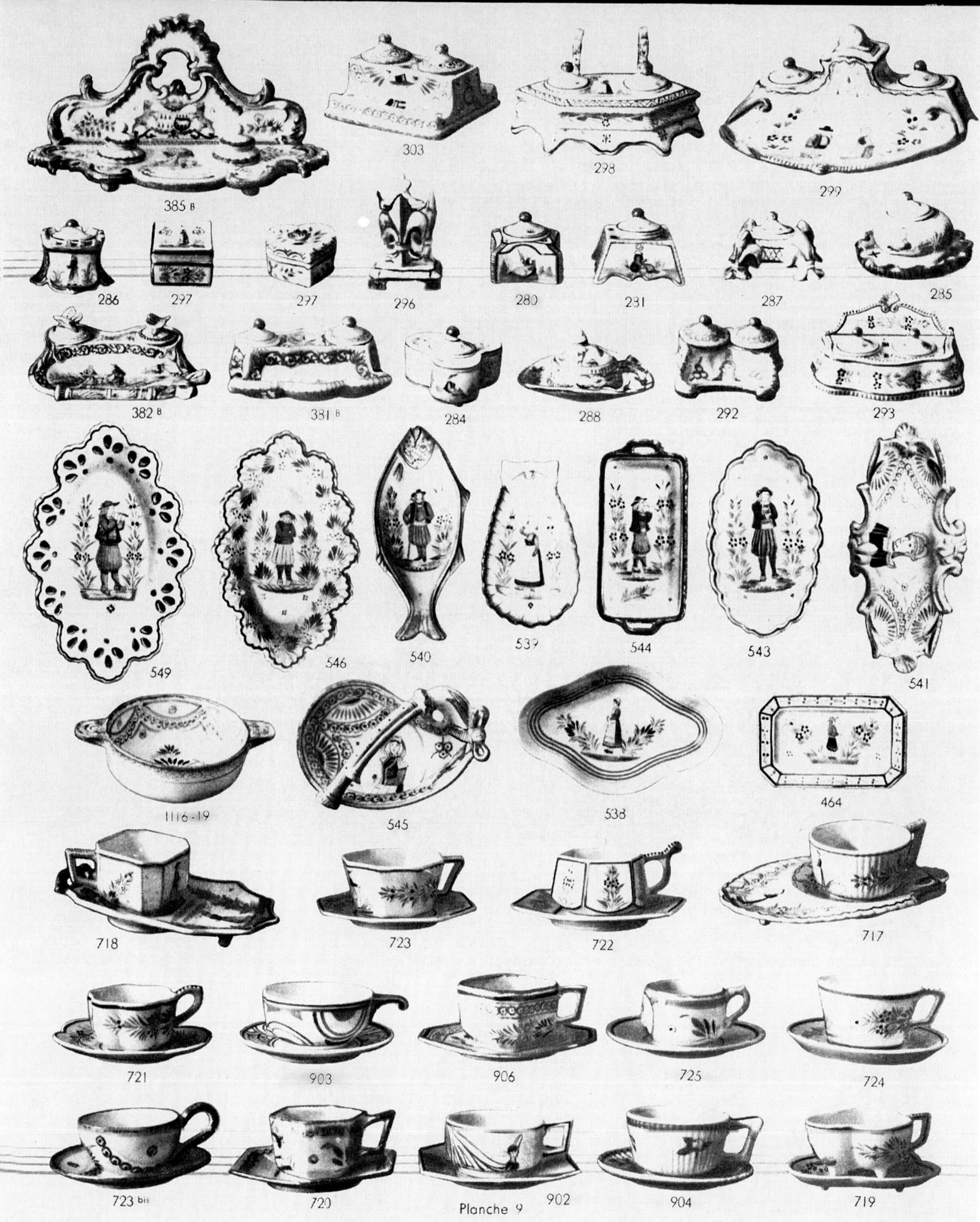
HENRIOT · QUIMPER
385 B
303
298
299
286
297
297
296
280
231
287
285
382 B
381 B
284
288
292
293
549
546
540
539
544
543
541
1116-19
545
538
464
718
723
722
717
721
903
906
725
724
723 bis
720
Planche 9
902
904
719

HENRIOT-QUIMPER

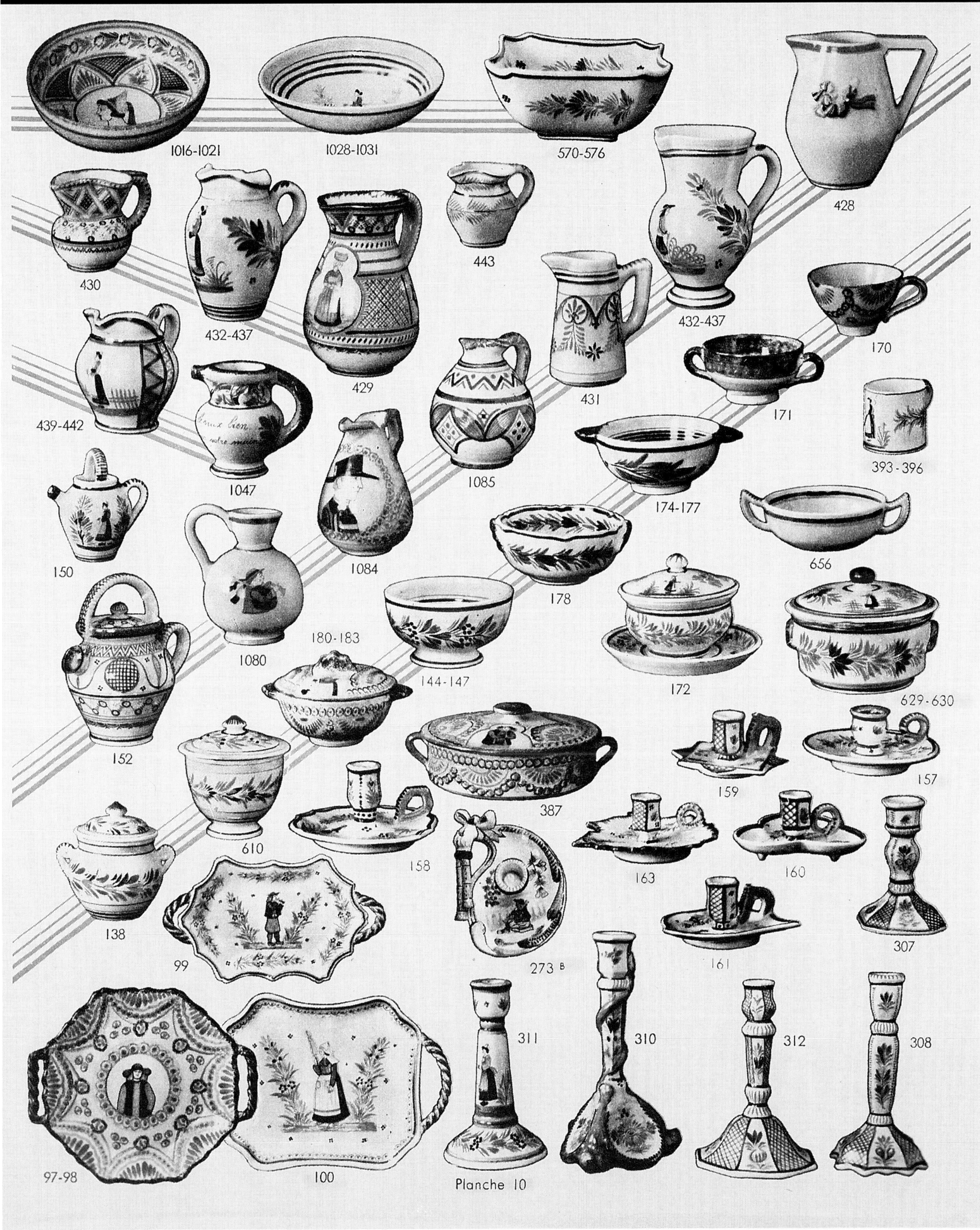

HENRIOT · QUIMPER

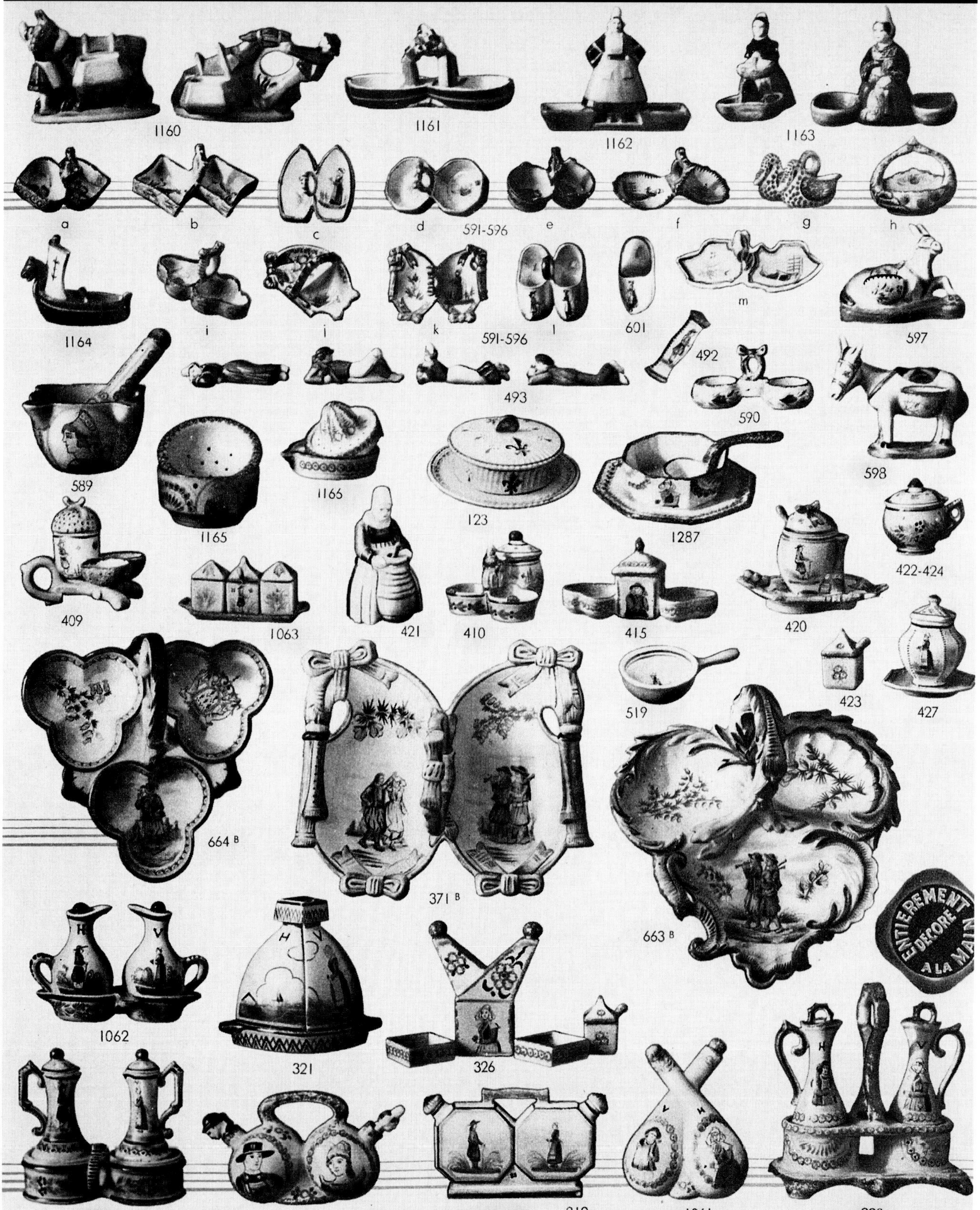

1160 1161 1162 1163

a b c d 591-596 e f g h

1164 i j k 591-596 l 601 m 597

492 493 590

589 1166 123 1287 598

1165

422-424

409 1063 421 410 415 420

519 423 427

664 B

371 B

663 B

ENTIÈREMENT DÉCORÉ A LA MAIN

1062

321 326

327 322 Planche 11 319 1061 328

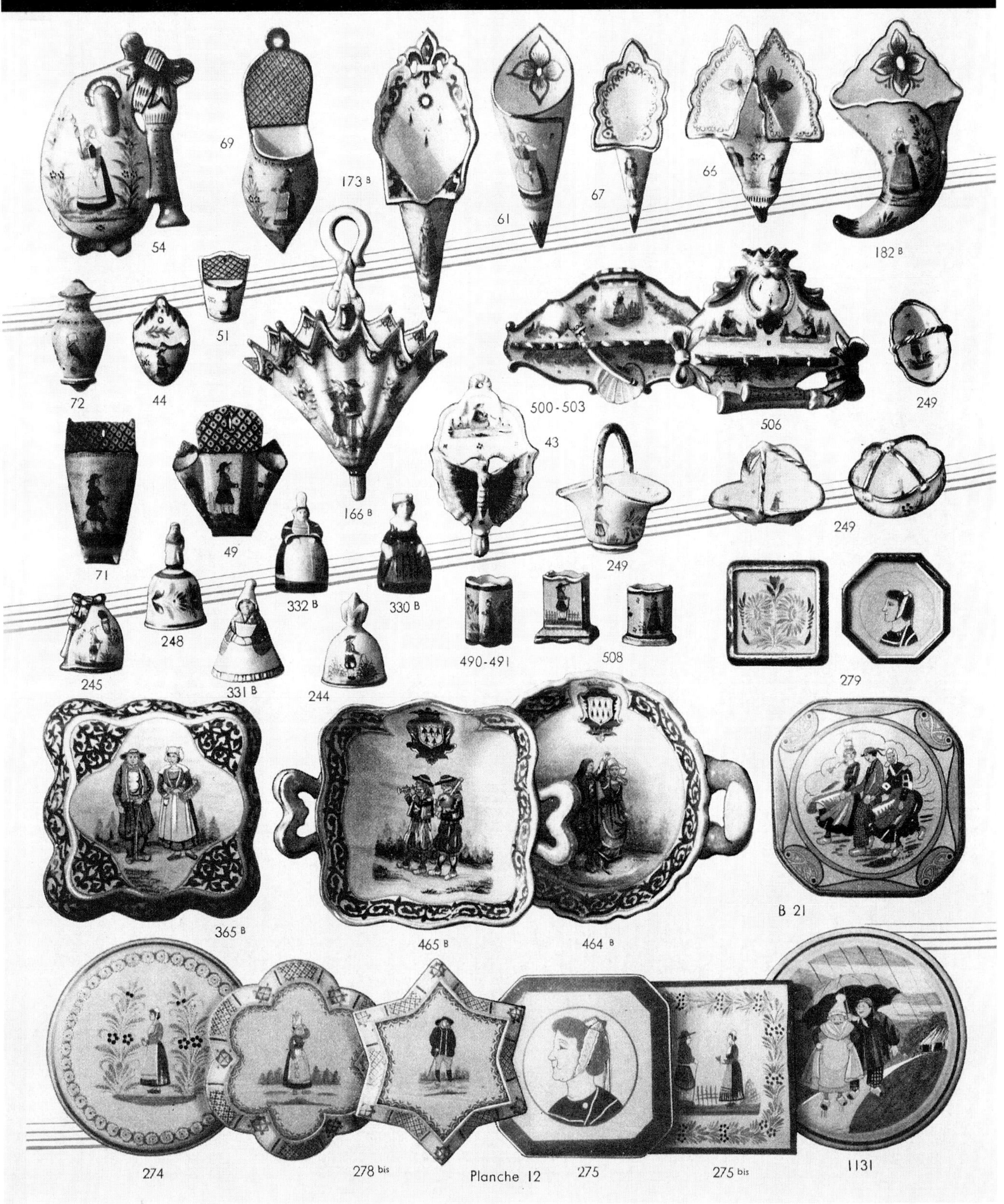
HENRIOT-QUIMPER
69
173 B
61
67
66
182 B
54
51
72
44
500-503
506
249
43
166 B
249
249
71
49
332 B
330 B
248
490-491
508
279
245
331 B
244
365 B
465 B
464 B
B 21
274
278 bis
Planche 12
275
275 bis
1131

HENRIOT - QUIMPER

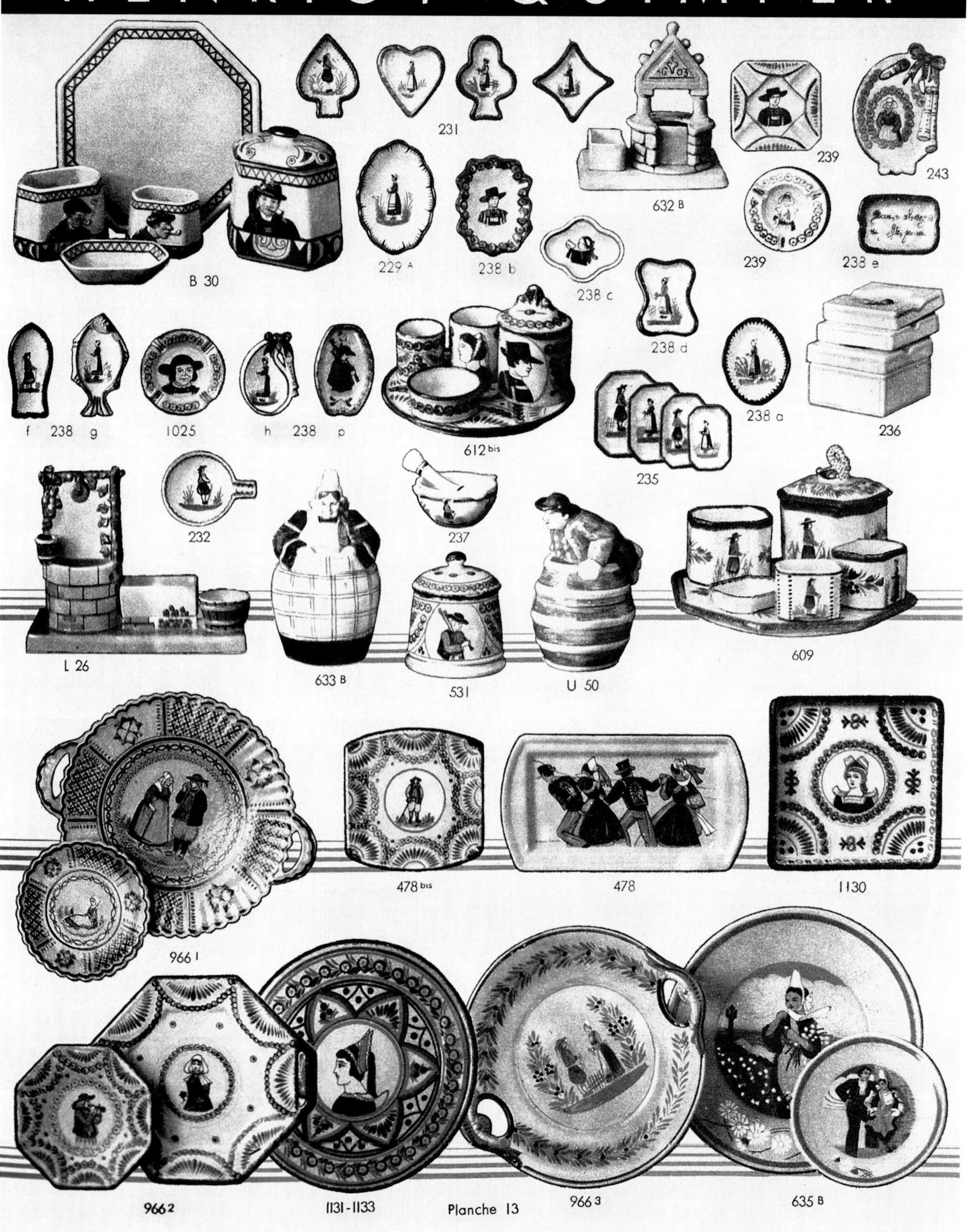

Planche 13

HENRIOT-QUIMPER

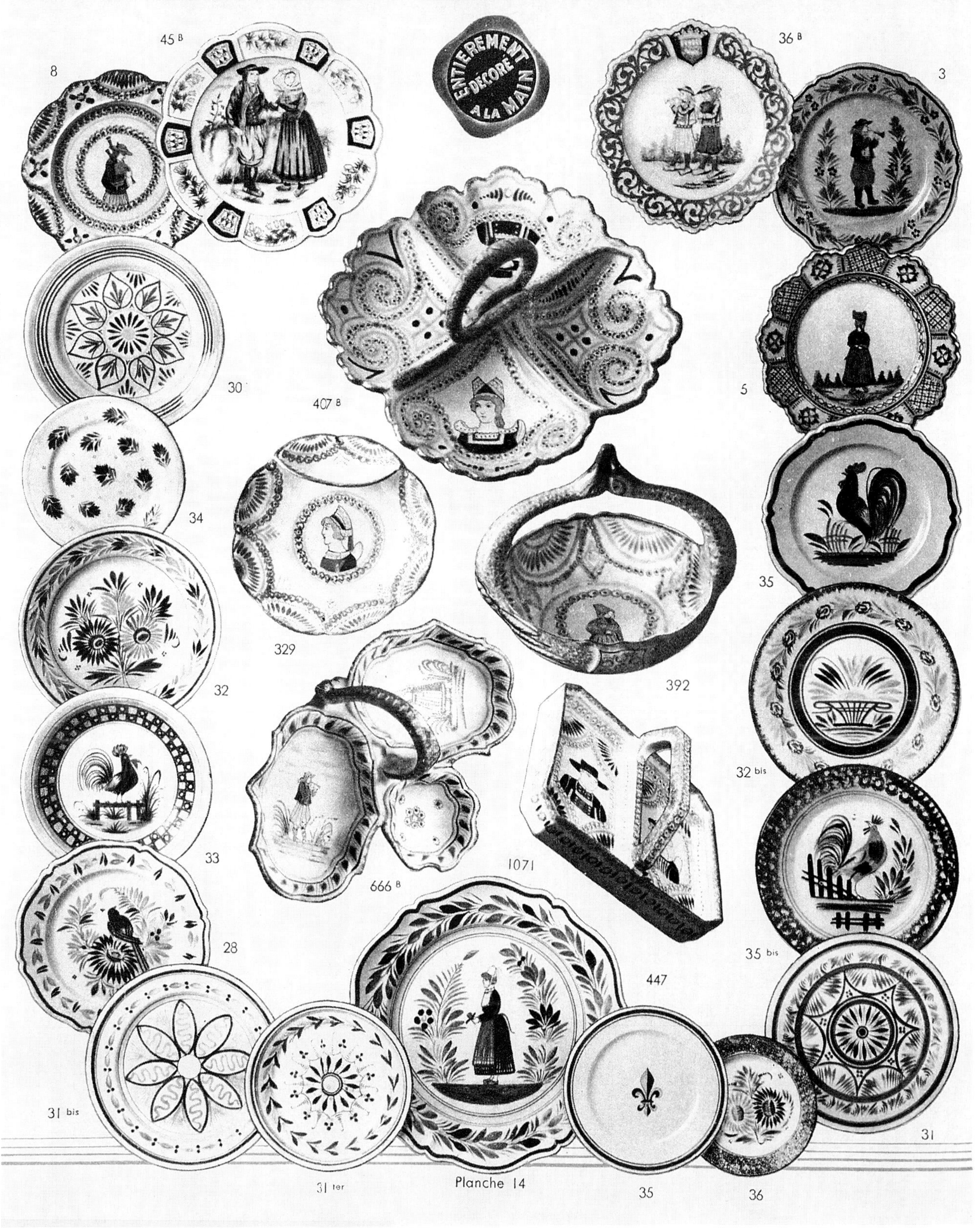

Planche 14

HENRIOT · QUIMPER
968
969
967
972
971
ENTIEREMENT DÉCORÉ A LA MAIN
978
970
966
977
964
975
Planche 17

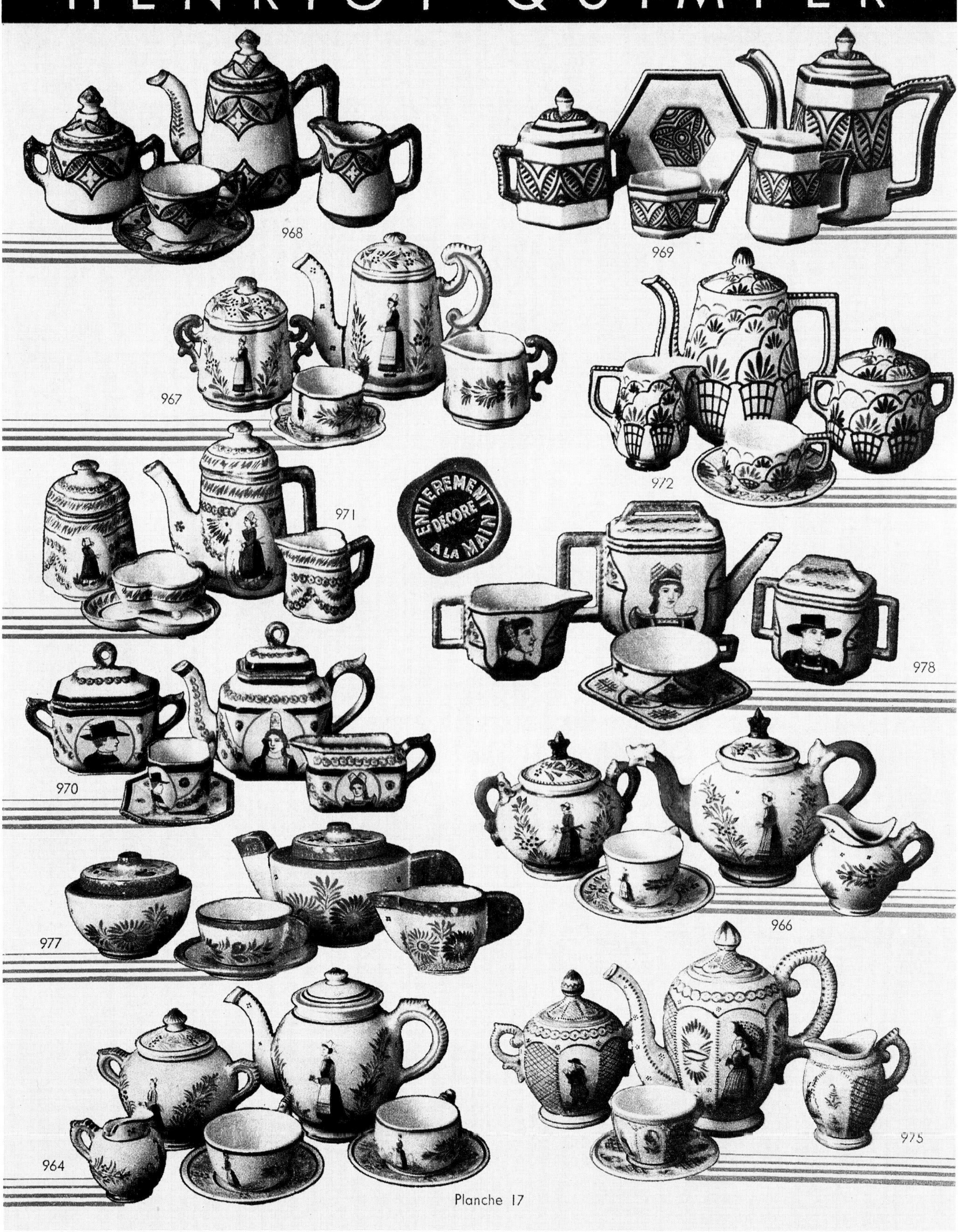

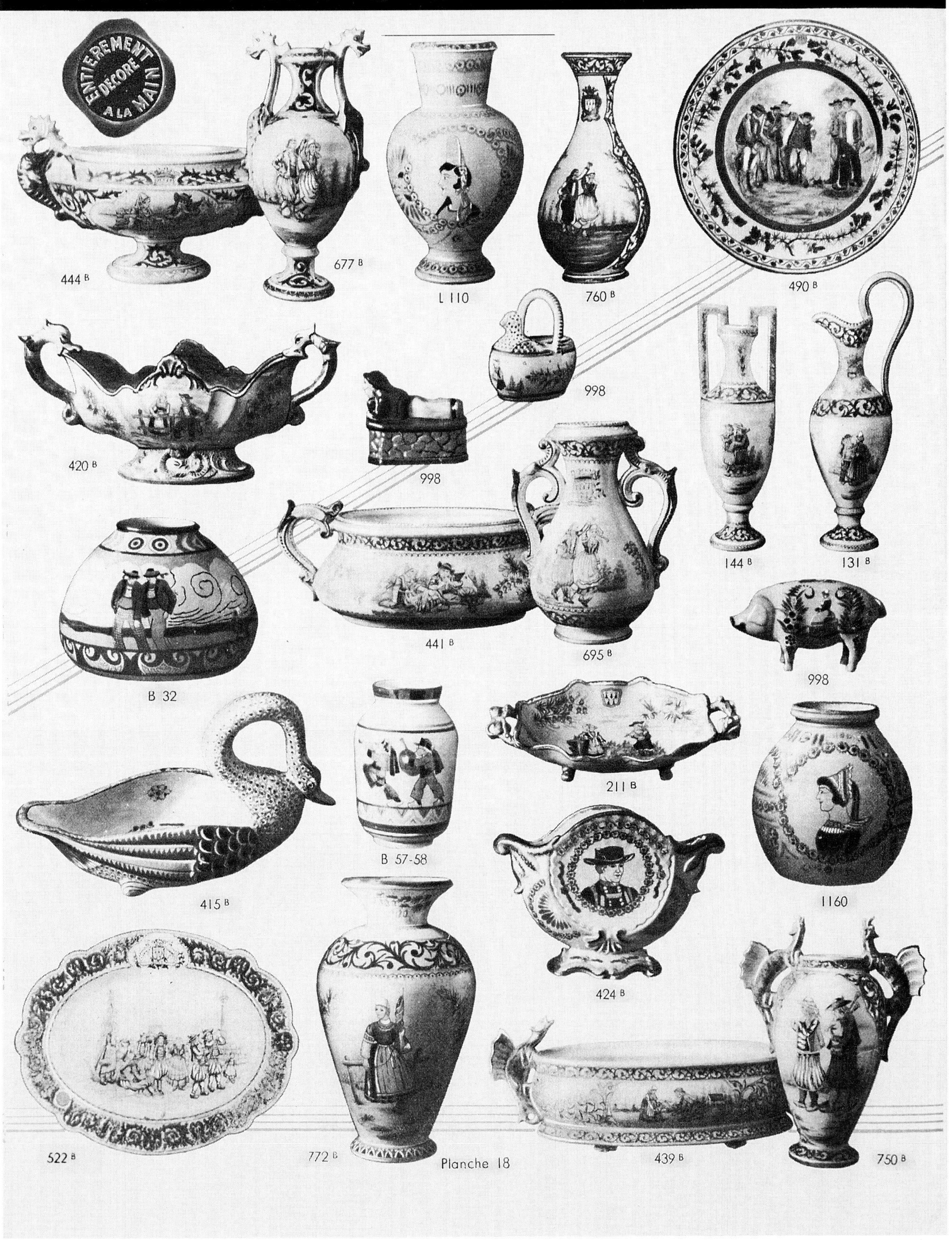
HENRIOT-QUIMPER
ENTIEREMENT DECORE A LA MAIN
444 B
677 B
L 110
760 B
490 B
420 B
998
998
998
144 B
131 B
441 B
695 B
B 32
211 B
B 57-58
415 B
1160
424 B
522 B
772 B
Planche 18
439 B
750 B

HENRIOT - QUIMPER
ENTIÈREMENT DÉCORÉ A LA MAIN
1178
602
1176
B 42
1170
1177
S - 9
B 53
1171
1179
1172
U 53-54
1174
CORN'AN
1175
1173
1181
YANN
CATEL
PONT. AVEN
601
U 42-43
599-600
1180
Planche 19

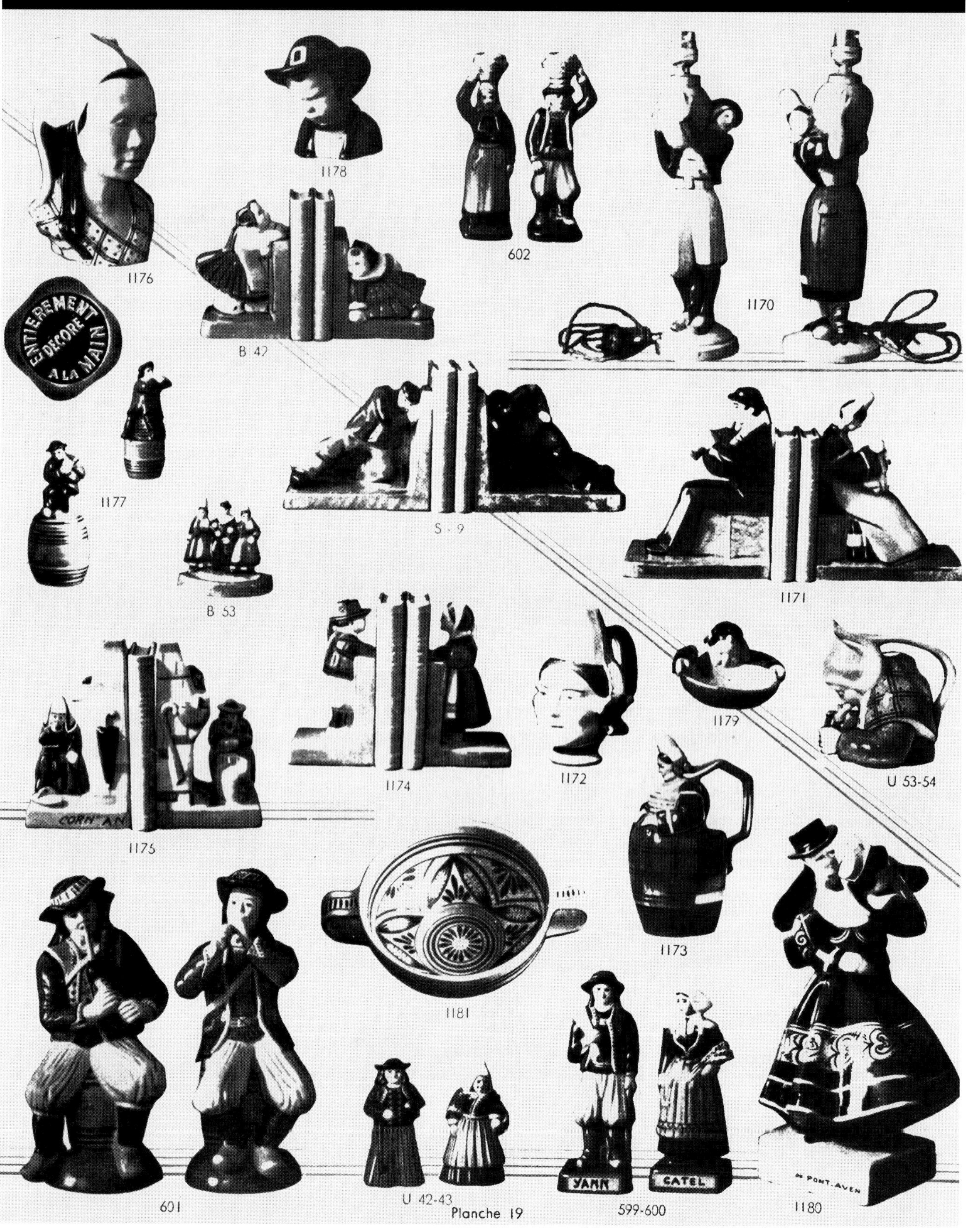

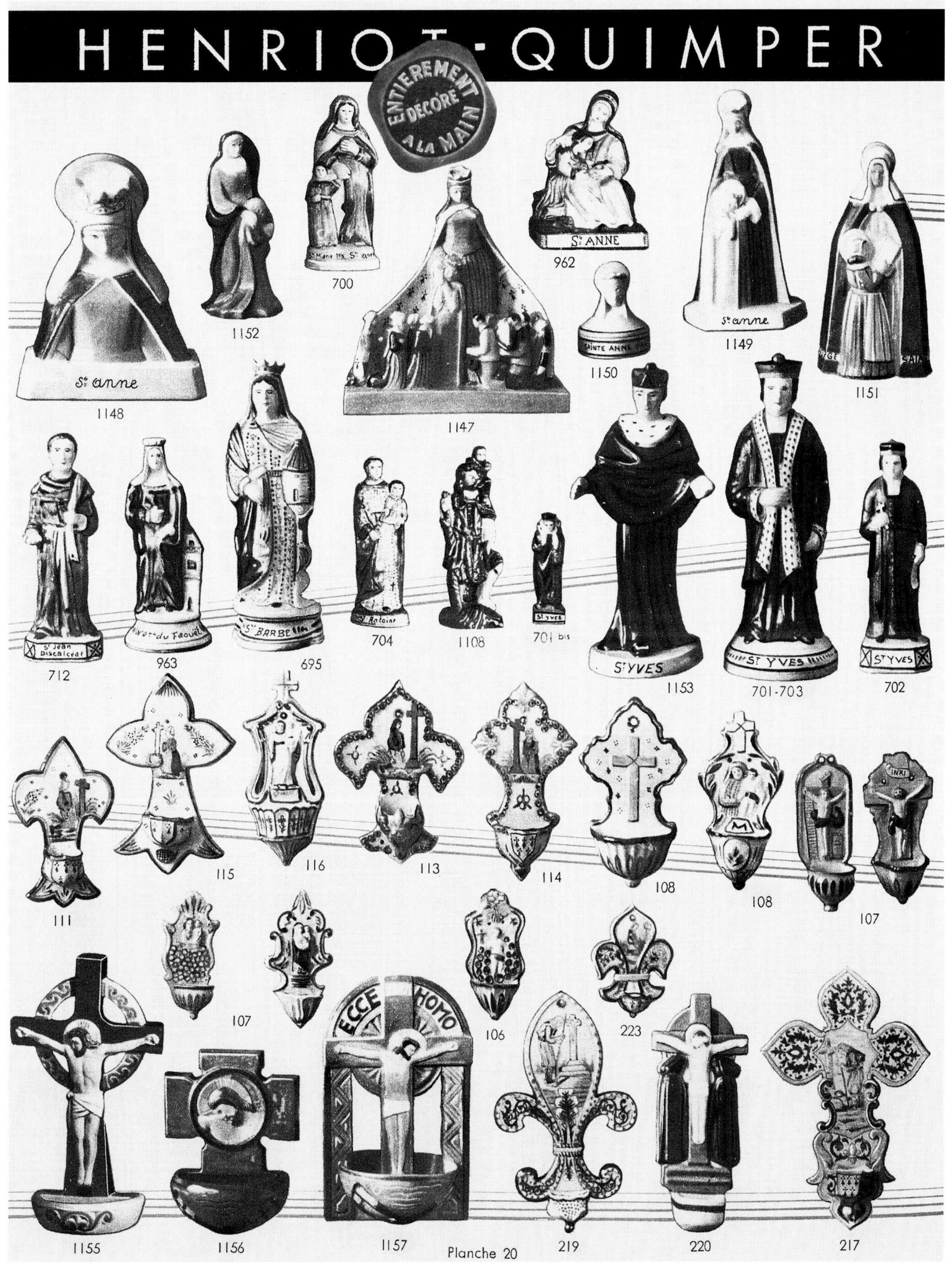

1148 1152 700 1147 962 1150 1149 1151
712 963 695 704 1108 701 bis 1153 701-703 702
111 115 116 113 114 108 108 107
107 106 223
1155 1156 1157 219 220 217

Planche 20

HENRIOT - QUIMPER

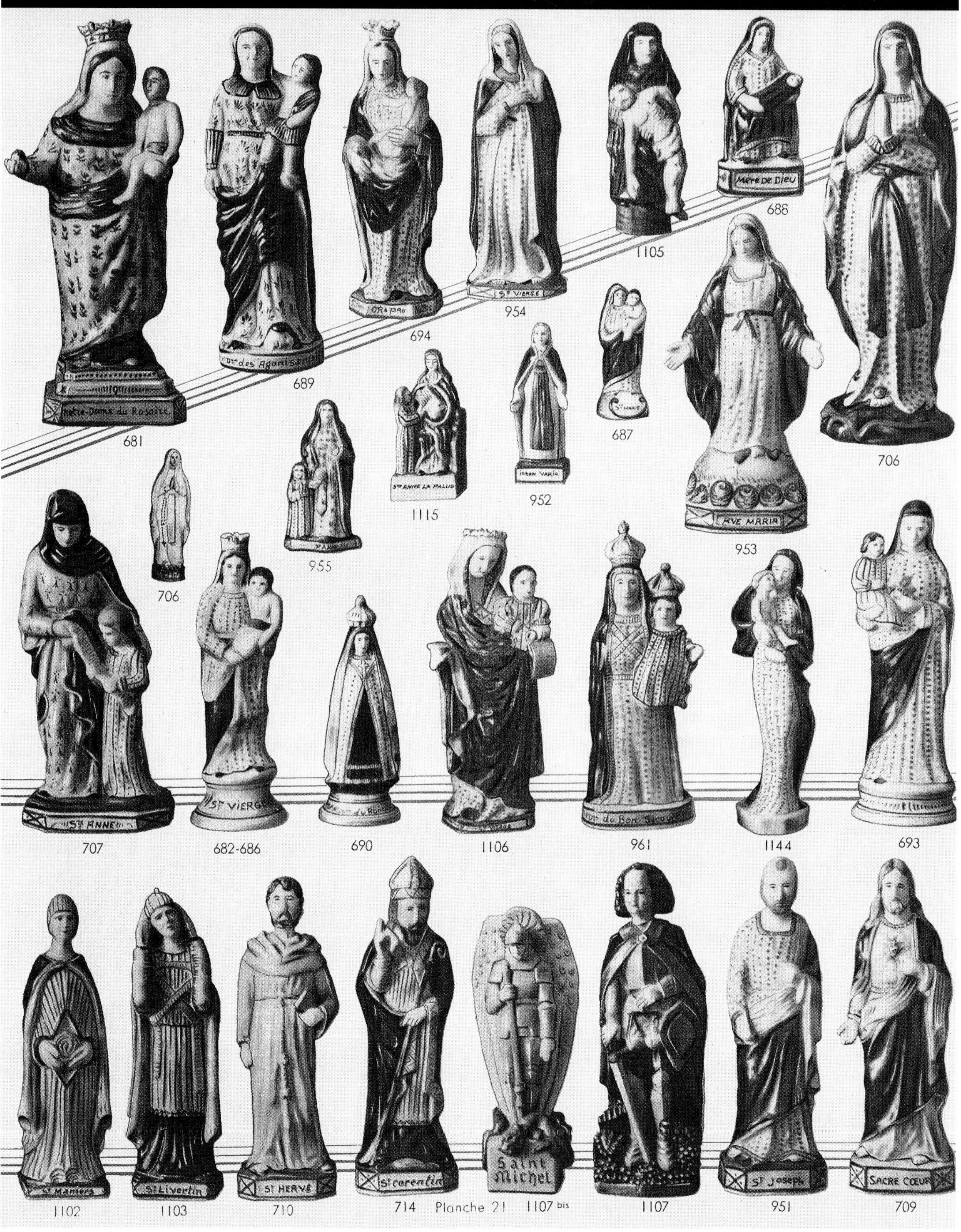

Les années 1973 et 1974 seront, pour l'industrie de la Faïence, très favorables. On remarque sur le marché français, et même extérieur, une tendance à la simplification de l'art de la table, ce qui revient à dire qu'on abandonne les services à compositions riches et que l'on fait valoir les services les plus simples.

C'est ainsi que le grand public donne depuis ces dernières années, de plus en plus la préférence au service de table en faïence.

Pour les décors, on apprécie de plus en plus nettement ceux de tons pastels, genre « Quimper », etc..

L'attention se concentre sur la question des décors car ils jouent toujours un grand rôle lors de la vente de la faïence.

Tandis que le grand feu permet des couleurs à grands éclats : bleu de cobalt, le jaune de l'antimoine, le vert de cuivre, le rouge de fer et le pourpre de manganèse, le petit feu permet une gamme beaucoup plus variée de couleurs avec des effets plus tendres et délicats.

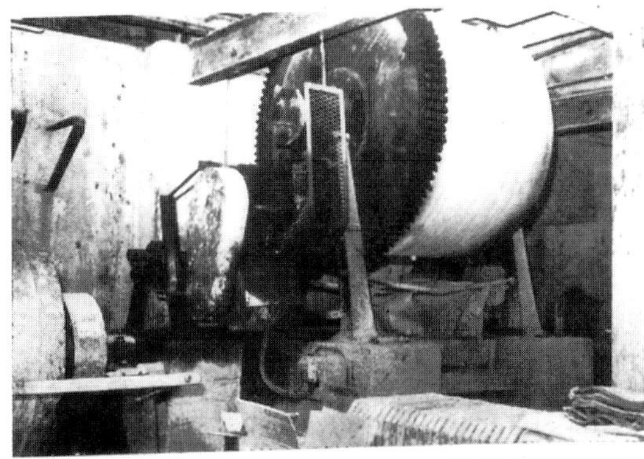

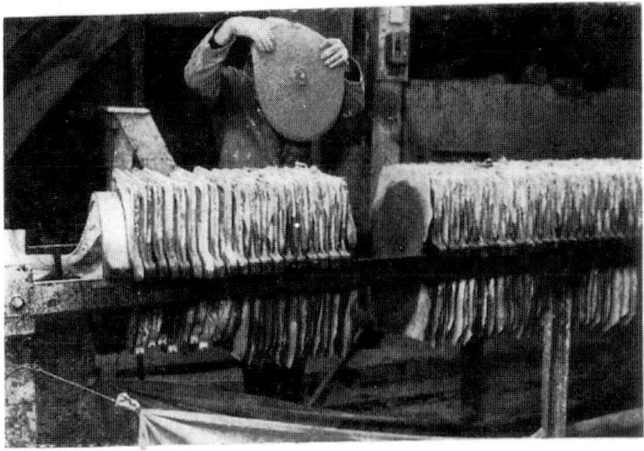

LA PRÉPARATION :

Les matières premières argileuses : kaolins et argiles, sont concassés, puis délayés en une barbotine, suspension aqueuse de fines particules, à la consistance d'une bouillie fluide, les autres matières premières, silice et dolorin, matériaux durs, sont également mis en suspension aqueuse après un énergique broyage effectué dans les BROYEURS.

Les barbotines argileuses et de matières dures sont ensuite réunies suivant un dosage déterminé, épurées par tamisage, puis raffermies dans des FILTRES-PRESSES qui expriment l'eau et donnent des galettes de pâte d'une consistance voisine de celle de la pâte à modeler.

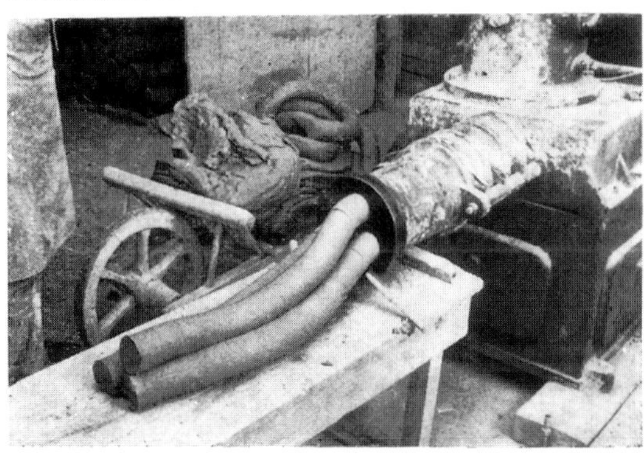

MALAXAGE ET DESAREAGE sous vide :

Homogénéise et rend la pâte plus plastique en boudin.

LE FAÇONNAGE

Comment sont façonnées les pièces à partir de cette pâte ?

Deux procédés sont utilisés à cette fin :

le calibrage et le coulage.

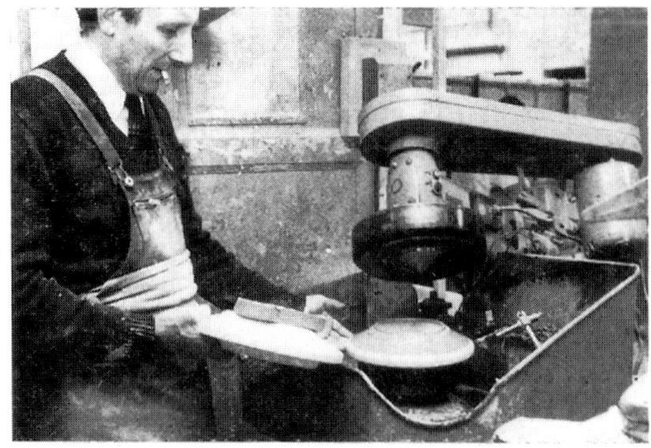

Calibrage automatique des assiettes par machines type ROLLER.

L'innovation la plus importante réside dans le remplacement pour des productions de grandes séries, de la calibreuse à main complétée par une machine automatique ainsi que des accessoires automatisés en amont et une chaine automatique de séchage en aval.

Son principe est le suivant : la pâte plastique (dont la fermeté est supérieure à celle des pâtes destinées à être façonnées suivant le procédé traditionnel) est étalée contre la surface d'un moule en plâtre en rotation autour d'un axe vertical.

Un calibre, plaque généralement métallique reproduisant le profil de l'une des faces de l'assiette à former, enlève l'excédent de pâte et ne laisse à la surface du moule qu'une couche constituant l'assiette.

La seconde face de celle-ci est directement formée au cours du processus par moulage de la pâte contre le moule de plâtre à qui l'on a préalablement donné le profil approprié.

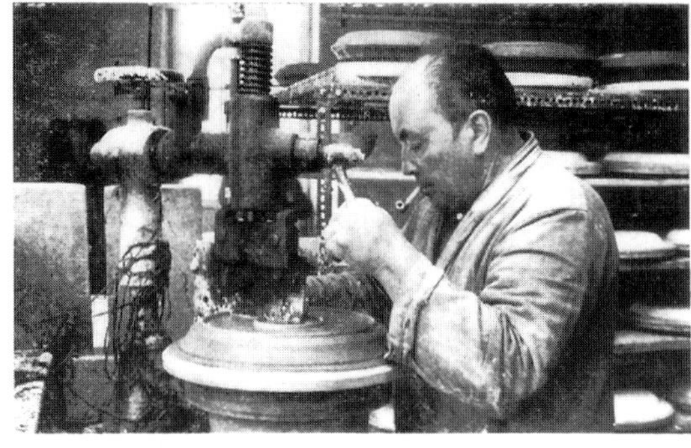

Calibrage à main des plats. Vous concevez aisément, néanmoins, qu'un tel procédé soit difficilement applicable à la réalisation de certaines pièces.

Il suppose toujours une forme de révolution ; aussi, certaines pièces se prêtent-elles mal à une telle mise en forme.

On substitue alors au calibrage plusieurs procédés, le PRESSAGE pour les plats et le coulage pour d'autres pièces que nous verrons plus loin.

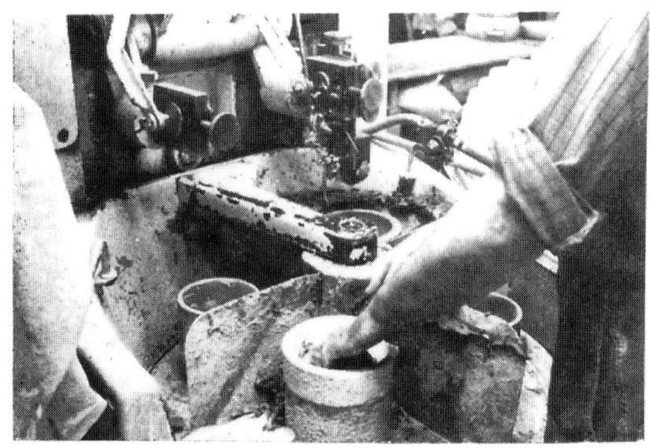

Calibrage des bols.

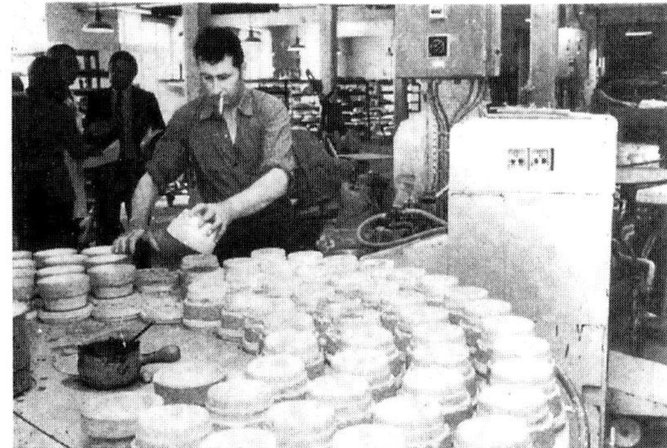

Le séchage des bols ainsi formés entraine un retrait, les bols se détachant des moules qui sont remis en service.

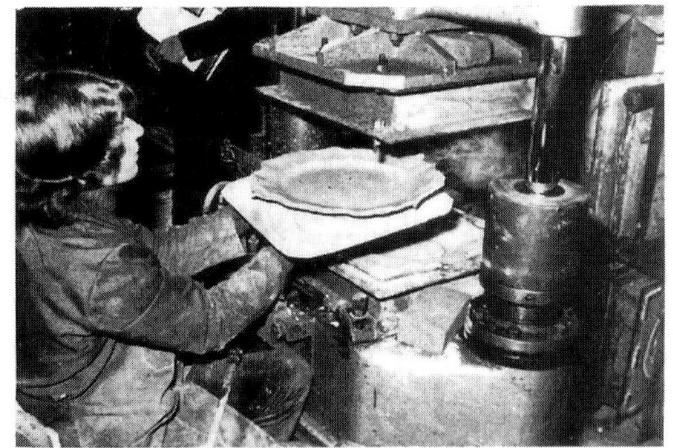

Moulage en pâte plastique d'un plat par pressage avec des moules en plâtre par presse hydraulique.

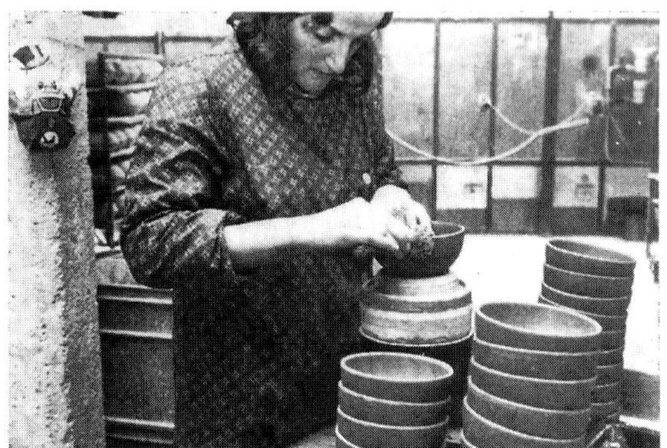

Finissage des bols.

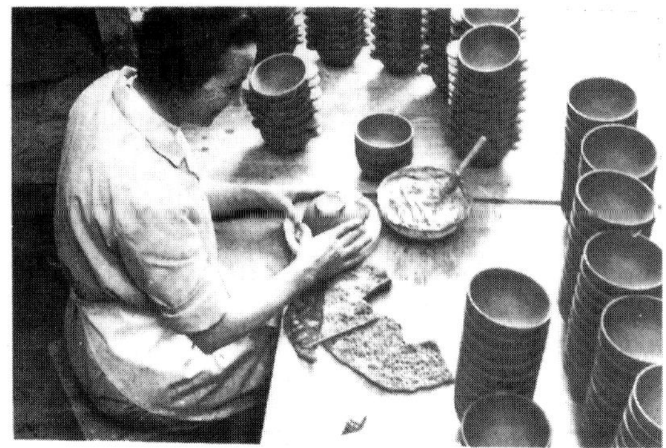

Garnissage des bols.

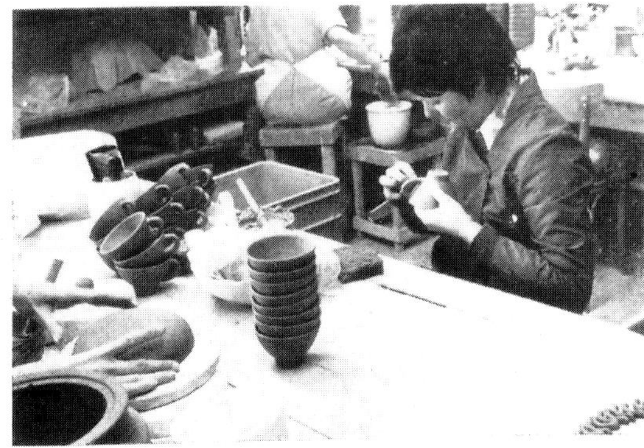

Pour la realisation de certaines pièces, on est conduit a mettre en jeu les deux procedés, ainsi le corps des tasses et des bols est calibré (photo plus haut), les anses ou les oreilles sont coulées après raffermissement, les deux parties sont assemblées avec une barbotine de même composition, qui, apres cuisson, fera corps avec les deux parties.

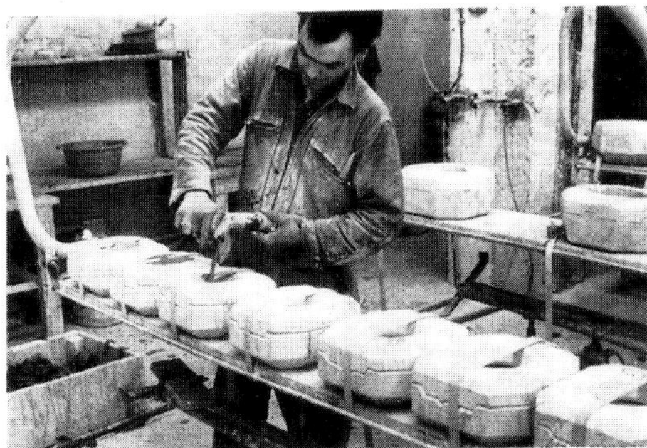

LE COULAGE

Poste de coulage fixe avec chaine continue de déplacement des moules. Le coulage utilise la propriété du plâtre d'absorber facilement l'eau d'une suspension, sans laisser entrer les particules de cette suspension dans ses pores. A partir de la pâte préparée comme nous l'avons vu plus haut, il faut donc constituer une barbotine par délayage ; que l'on verse par procédé semi-automatique.

Cette barbotine est dans un moule reproduisant généralement l'extérieur de la pièce à réaliser, l'eau est absorbée par capillarité, tandis que les particules de pâte se déposent sur la paroi absorbante, puis on laisse l'objet prendre de la cohésion par séchage, et on démoule la pièce lorsqu'elle est suffisamment ferme.

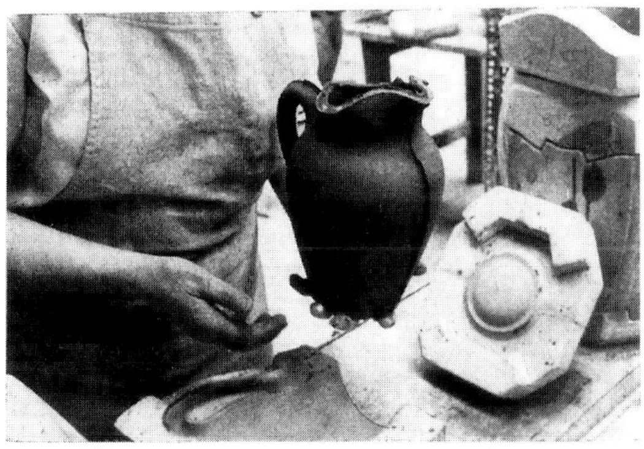

Démoulage d'une pièce.

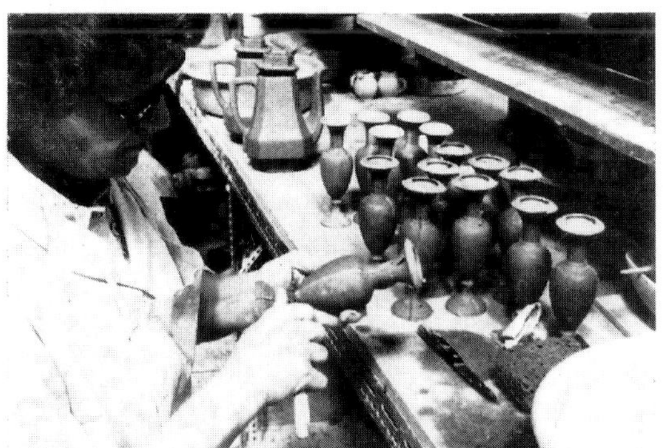

Les pièces sont maintenant formées. Elles vont y être RACHEVEES, c'est-à-dire reprises et débarrassées des imperfections dues au façonnage proprement dit et aux ceintures du moule.

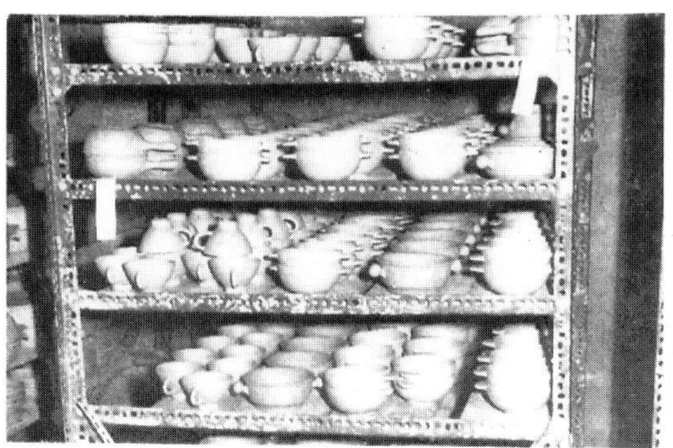

Puis, ensuite séchées avec beaucoup de precautions dans un sechoir à 60 %, car le fort retrait des substances argileuses les rend tres sujettes aux fentes.
LA CUISSON

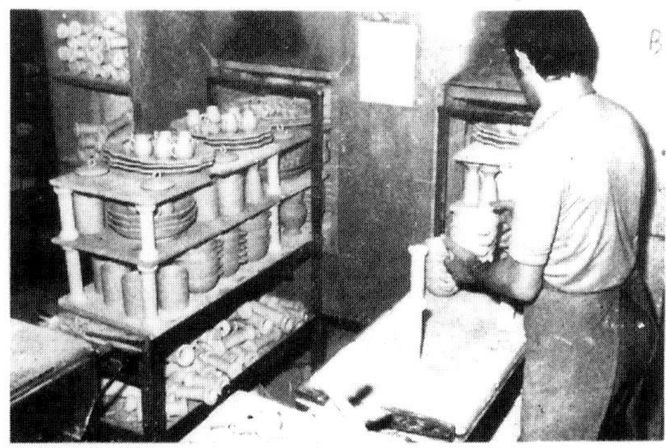

LA CUISSON

Après séchage, les pièces sont soumises à une cuisson voisine de 1 040°. C'est la **CUISSON DITE DU BISCUIT** dans les fours continus du type Fours passages chauffés au fuel. Ce sont des appareils importants, ils permettent des cuissons d'une grande précision.

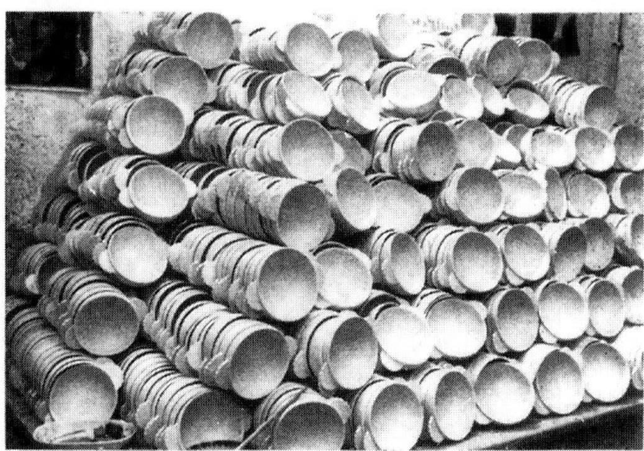

Stock des « biscuits ».

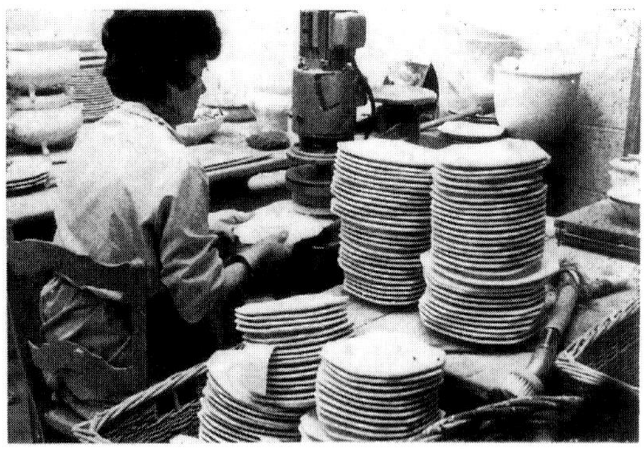

Après le triage, brossage mécanique de certaines pièces en « biscuit »,

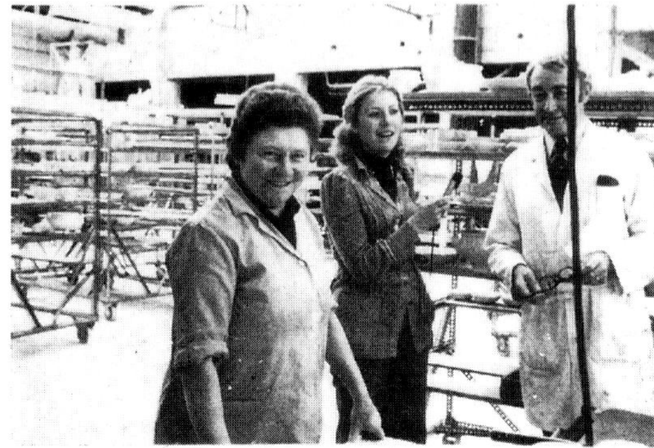

Brossage et retouchage à la main du « biscuit » avant la décoration.

LA DECORATION

DES POSSIBILITES DE DECORS ET DE COULEURS IMMENSES

Le grand charme de la faïence par opposition à la poterie vernissée, consiste dans la variété et les possibilités de décors et de couleurs, qui peuvent être apposés, soit sur l'émail cru, procédé appelé « au grand feu » soir sur l'émail déjà cuit et devenu lisse et recuit au feu « doux de mouffle », procédé aussi nommé « au petit feu ».

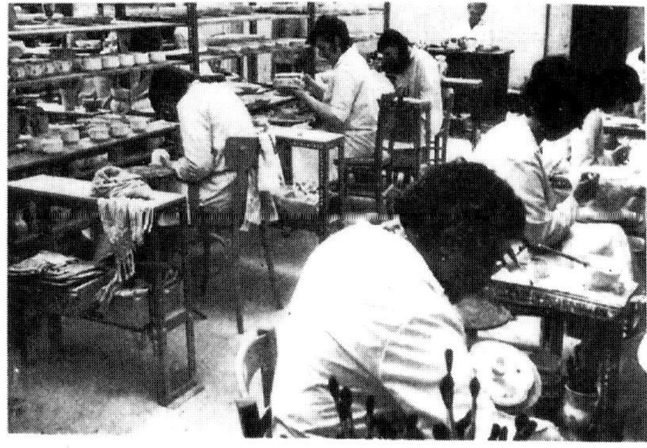

Le decor au pinceau, consiste essentiellement a peindre un décor a l'aide de couleurs ceramiques composees d'oxydes métalliques et d'ajouts vitrifiables.

Le décorateur peut s'aider d'un poncif, surtout lorsqu'il doit répéter plusieurs fois un même motif sur une même pièce.

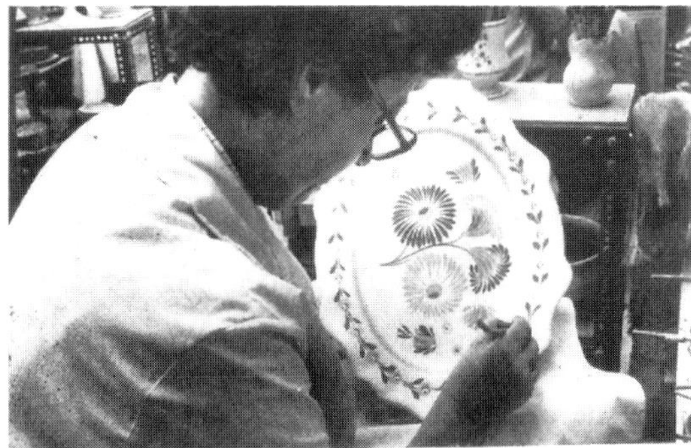

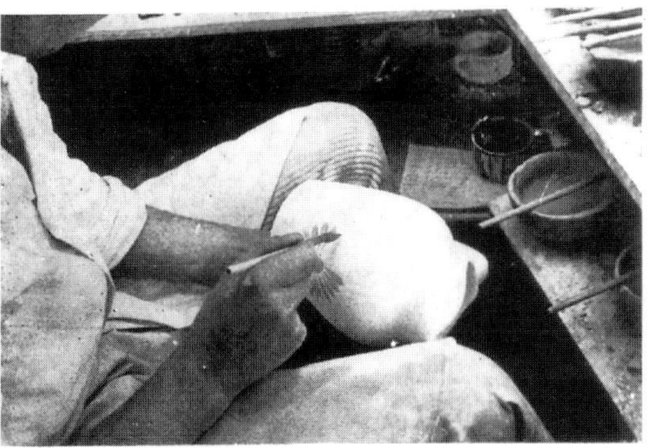

Le décor peint à la main d'une manière générale est un décor noble et coûteux, nécessitant des décorateurs ou décoratrices très habiles et très soigneux.

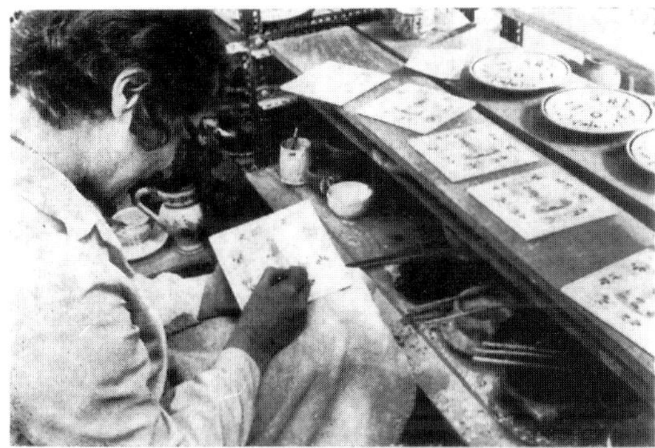

Cette faïencerie emploie, malgré un équipement assez mécanisé, plus de 250 personnes, dont la moitié est employée dans les Ateliers de décor.

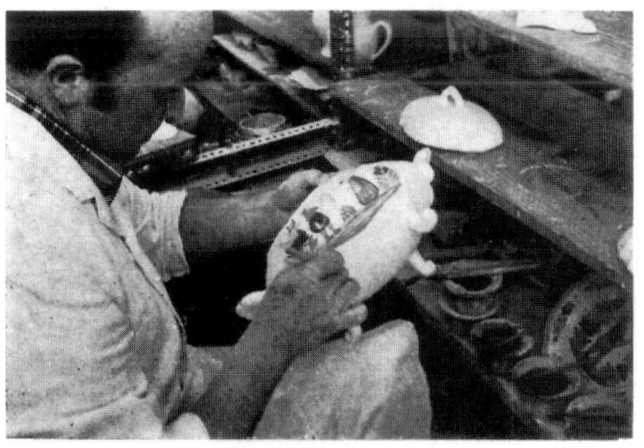

EMAILLAGE AU TREMPE

Une fois la pièce décorée, intervient l'émaillage, qui est pratiqué par la méthode dite « au trempé », qui consiste essentiellement en une courte immersion de la pièce dans une suspension aqueuse d'émail, qui, par un mécanisme de succion du tesson, se dépose en une mince couche sur le biscuit poreux.

Pour émailler l'intérieur des pièces creuses, on met en jeu une très simple variante du trempage qui consiste à verser un certain volume d'émail dans la pièce et à renverser immédiatement celle-ci en lui imprimant un mouvement spirale, pour uniformiser le dépôt.

Il faut garder en mémoire que l'émaillage est une opération délicate.

Sachez simplement que la seule présence de grains de poussières ou de marques de doigts sur le biscuit peut conduire à des défauts d'émaillage qui déclasseraient la pièce.

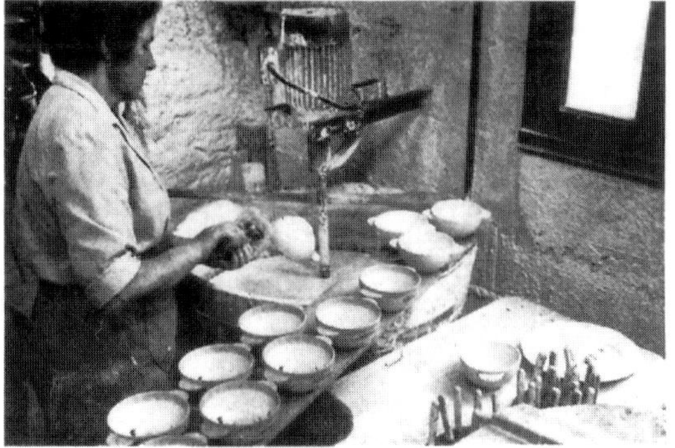

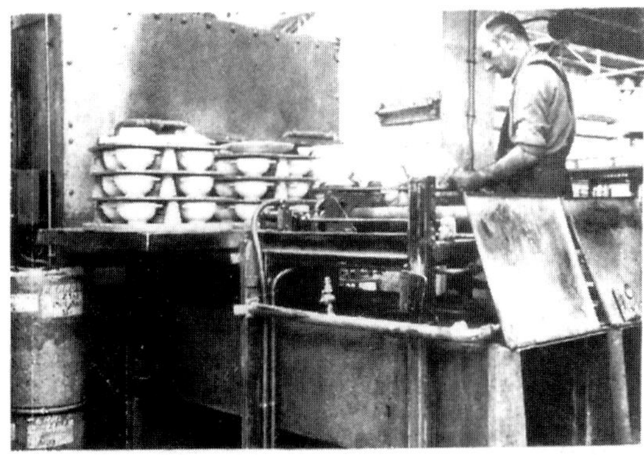

La pièce après avoir reçu son email est soumise à une seconde cuisson, à une température variant de 920 à 950° et destinée à la seule vitrification de son email.

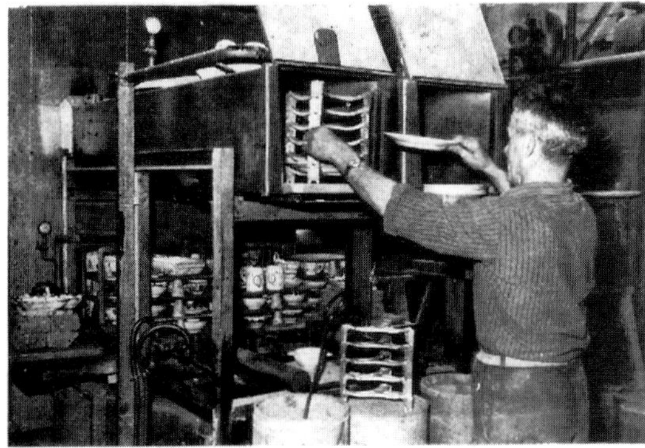

Cette cuisson est réalisée dans un four à passage électrique donnant une atmosphère neutre pour les cuissons d'émaux.

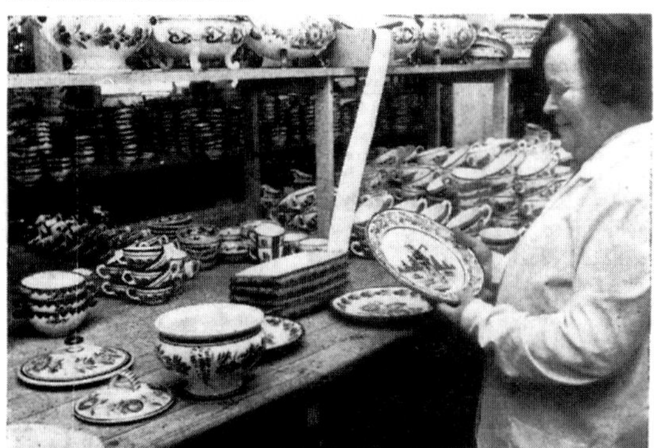

Nous avons considéré préparation, fabrication et décoration dans leurs grandes lignes, la réalisation des faïences fait intéresser de nombreuses opérations annexes : l'enfournement et le défournement, les triages répétés, choix, réassortiment, stockage, des pièces émaillées et décorées.

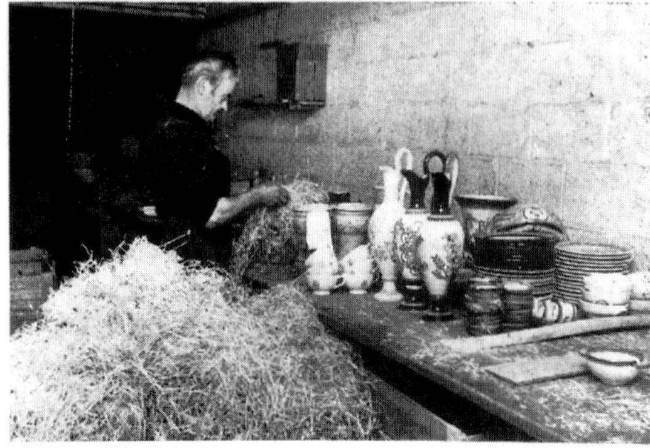

EMBALLAGE - CONDITIONNEMENT

De gros progrès ont été réalisés dans ce domaine. Beaucoup de faïences sont acheminées et vendues maintenant conditionnées, l'emballage carton s'est maintenant généralisé pour la vaisselle de table.

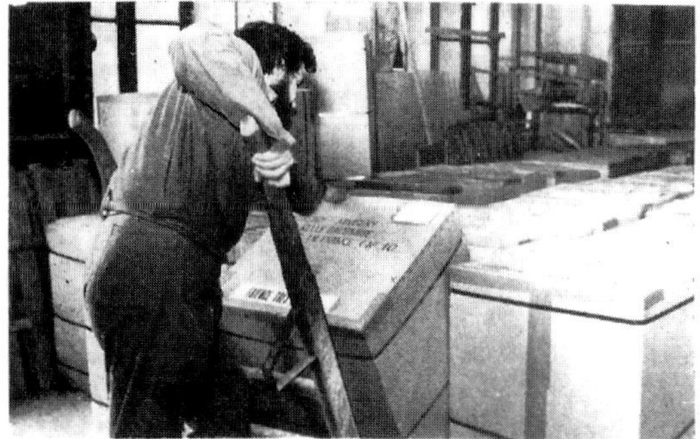

L'expédition des caisses sur tous les continents du monde.

Bibliography

Archives of the Faïencerie HB-Henriot, Quimper.

"Bulletin d'information de l'Association' Faïences de Quimper 1690-1990'"
Bulletin numbers 1 through 8.

Bulletin de la Société Archeologique du Finistère, Tome ler, 1873–1874.

"De la Protection des Faïences Bretonnes ou Faïences de Quimper", Jules Henriot, Kerangel, Quimper 1908.

French Faïence, Jeanne Giacomotti, Universe Books, New York 1963.

French Faïence, Arthur Lane, Praeger Publishers, New York 1970.

"Gazette des Beaux Arts", Number 14 1876.

Histoire de la Céramique, Alfred Mame, Tours, Second Edition 1882.

A History and Description of the Old French Faïence, M.L. Solon, Cassell, London 1903.

"La Céramique en France au XIX Siècle", Ernould Marelle, Grund, Paris 1969.

"La Faïence de Quimper", Marjatta Taburet, Imprimerie Cornouaille, Quimper 1975.

La Faïence de Quimper, Marjatta Taburet, Éditions Sous le Vent, Paris 1979.

"La Faïence de Quimper Le Guide de Collectionneur, Marjatta Taburet, Éditions Sous le Vent, Paris 1990

"La Faïencerie D'Art Breton 'Henriot' à Quimper", Factory Pamphlet 1930's.

"Les Faïences artistiques de Quimper aux XVIIe et XIXe siècles," Michel Roullot, Art-Media Edition, Lorient 1980.

"Les Faïences de Quimper", Factory Pamphlet, edited by "Offrir", Paris.

"Les Faïences de Quimper et Les Faïences de Rouen", Gaston Le Breton, 1876.

Les Poteries et Les Faïences Françaises, Adrian Lesur and Tardy, Tardy, Paris.

"Locmaria Quimper", J. Charpy, Hélio-Lorraine, Nancy 1966.

"L'Oeuvre des Faïences Françaises du XVI à la fin du XVIII Siècle", Henry-Pierre Fouresh, Hachette, Paris 1966.

Marques et Signatures de la Faïence Française, Henri Curtil, Éditions Charles Marsin, Paris 1969.

Modern Porcelain, Alberta C. Trimble, Harper and Brothers, New York 1962.

Notre Vieux Quimper, Locmaria au XVIII Siècle, Jean Savina, Quimper 1950.

Quimper, Quimperlé, Locronan, Penmarch, Alexandre Masseron, Librairie Renauard, Paris 1928.

"Operation Portes Ouvertes dans Une Faïencerie", Jean Rouillard and Louis Leonus, Samie S.A. Bordeau 1973.

"The Old Quimper Review", Millicent S. Mali, East Greenwich, R.I.

Vierges et Saints Les Statuettes en Faïence de Quimper, Laurent Cahn, Quimper, 1990

Victoria and Albert Museum, French Ceramic Department, London.

Index

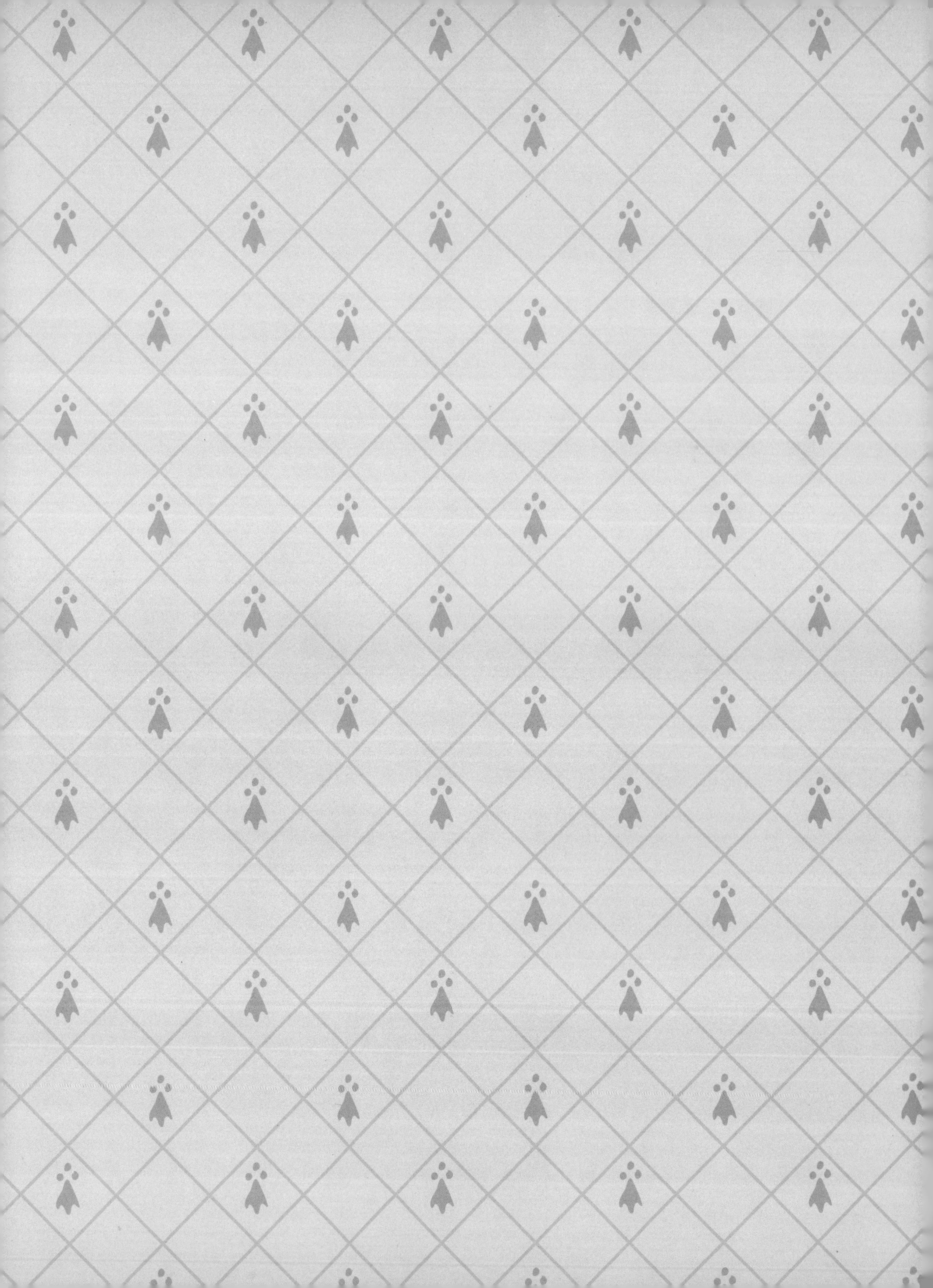